THE GILDED AGE AND PROGRESSIVE ERA

A Student Companion

OXFORD

Student Companions to American History
WILLIAM H. CHAFE, GENERAL EDITOR

THE GILDED AGE AND PROGRESSIVE ERA

A Student Companion

*Elisabeth Israels Perry and
Karen Manners Smith*

OXFORD
UNIVERSITY PRESS

OXFORD
UNIVERSITY PRESS

To our grandchildren, present and future

Oxford University Press, Inc., publishes works that further
Oxford University's objective of excellence
in research, scholarship, and education.

Oxford New York
Auckland Cape Town Dar es Salaam Hong Kong Karachi
Kuala Lumpur Madrid Melbourne Mexico City Nairobi
New Delhi Shanghai Taipei Toronto

With offices in
Argentina Austria Brazil Chile Czech Republic France Greece
Guatemala Hungary Italy Japan Poland Portugal Singapore
South Korea Switzerland Thailand Turkey Ukraine Vietnam

Published by Oxford University Press, Inc.
198 Madison Avenue, New York, New York 10016
www.oup.com

Library of Congress Cataloging-in-Publication Data

Perry, Elisabeth Israels.
  The Gilded Age and Progressive Era : a student companion / Elisabeth Israels Perry and Karen Manners Smith.
    p. cm. — (Oxford student companions to American history)
  ISBN-13: 978-0-19-515670-6 (alk. paper)
  ISBN-10: 0-19-515670-6 (alk. paper)
  1. United States—History—1865-1921—Encyclopedias. I. Smith, Karen Manners. II. Title. III. Series.
  E661.P44 2006
  973.803—dc22
                            2006000927

Printing number: 9 8 7 6 5 4 3 2 1

Printed in the United States of America
on acid-free paper

Design: Sandy Kaufman
Layout: Alexis Siroc

On the cover: The World's Columbian Exposition in Chicago, 1893; Piute mother and children (top left);
Progressive party campaign poster, 1912

Frontispiece: A 12-year-old spinner in a cotton mill in North Pownal, Vermont, 1910.

CONTENTS

INTRODUCTION

Historians use the terms Gilded Age and Progressive Era to designate the two periods in American history that straddle the turn of the 20th century. Some historians begin the Gilded Age in 1865, the year that marked the end of the Civil War. Others start the period in 1873, the year Mark Twain and Charles Dudley Warner published a satirical novel called *The Gilded Age.* Still others begin in 1877, the end of the post–Civil War era known as Reconstruction, or the period of rebuilding after the war. We have selected 1877 as the beginning date for this *Companion,* but in some of our articles we mention earlier events so as to make later events clear.

There is even less agreement among historians on how to date the start of the Progressive Era. Some historians end the Gilded Age around 1900 and begin the Progressive Era at that point. Others see the two periods as more interconnected, with "progressive" ideas developing much earlier out of Gilded Age economic, political, and social conditions. This is the approach we have taken here. In addition, even though some historians would end the Progressive Era as early as 1912, when the Progressive party met defeat in the Presidential election, or in 1914, which marked the start of World War I, we carry the era up through the end of President Woodrow Wilson's term of office in 1921.

What were the major trends in the period? The most far-reaching economic development was the expansion of American industry. Between the 1870s and the early 1900s, the number and variety of manufactured goods available for purchase increased beyond imagination. In the last decades of the 19th century, mass production techniques increased the number of available manufactured goods. Between

1872 and 1880, for example, the Singer Sewing Machine Company increased production from 220,000 to 500,000 units annually. In 1914, Ford Motor Company produced 300,000 Model T automobiles; in 1923, 2,000,000 Model T's rolled off its assembly lines. The increased efficiency gained by mass production also lowered the price of manufactured goods. As a result, between 1877 and 1900, the buying power of wage earners rose by nearly 50 percent. In addition, technology changed rapidly, creating new industries and expanding old ones. To exploit new fields on a scale large enough to make them profitable, businessmen pooled funds and resources. Soon they were creating ever larger corporations and combining them into trusts and monopolies. The vast financial and political influence of these businesses over American life gave rise to the predominant issue in the politics of the era: should the government impose regulations to curb the power of these vast financial interests, or should it maintain the policy of laissez-faire, or minimal government interference, and allow business free rein?

Related to this issue was the extent to which government should protect the interests of the working people who kept big businesses going. The industrial workforce swelled in this period, fed by streams of immigrants from abroad and the movement of native-born Americans away from farms and into cities, where they could find factory work. These laborers worked long hours for low wages, in conditions that were often dangerous and unhealthy. They also endured pay cuts and layoffs during bad times and long periods of unemployment during depressions. By the late 1800s, strikes protesting such conditions had become almost constant. Costly to both employers and workers, this labor unrest convinced many Americans that government should more actively regulate the relations of industry and labor.

Technological advances brought about rapid changes in this period, altering the ways Americans constructed buildings and bridges, traveled from place to place, and communicated with one another. Westward expansion accelerated. Americans had already settled west of the Mississippi River and along parts of the Pacific coast. Now, they filled in the areas in between—the Great Plains, the Northwest, and the Southwest. Using new industrial technologies, they turned the Great Plains into a granary and extracted increasing amounts of the land's natural resources of ores and precious metals from the mountains and deserts. This process nearly exterminated Native Americans and destroyed their culture. It also led to white, or "Anglo," domination of the Spanish-speaking peoples of the Southwest.

Meanwhile, immigration to the United States was on the rise, increasing annually by hundreds of thousands and peaking at over a million new arrivals in 1907. For the most part, the new immigrants settled in cities, where they were joined by growing numbers of rural, native-born citizens. Many of these newcomers were African Americans seeking work and better living conditions far from their traditional rural southern homes. These expanding urban working classes not only changed the nation's ethnic and racial makeup, but soon were an important factor in determining the country's future political course.

The rapid changes of the Gilded Age created a host of social, economic, and political problems. In times of economic downturn, which were frequent in the latter decades of the 19th century, unemployment caused massive misery and led to almost continual labor unrest. Ethnic and racial tensions often erupted into violent outbreaks and race riots, and living conditions in the nation's industrial cities became increasingly congested and unhealthy. The influence of the nation's wealthiest industrialists and financiers over the nation's politics grew so powerful that many Americans worried about the future of their nation's democratic institutions. Various individuals and groups proposed reforms to solve these and other problems. Some argued that restricting immigration and controlling social behavior were the answers. Nativism, temperance and prohibition, and movements to end prostitution grew out of this approach. Other reformers argued that contemporary problems were not the fault of immigrants and poor people and that society had to take greater responsibility for human welfare. Charity organizations and the settlement-house movement were a part of this more positive approach, as were more political movements such as the one for government reform.

The Progressive movement drew together these various reform strands into a concerted effort to bring about constructive change. People who identified themselves as progressives were primarily from the business and professional worlds and included many college-educated women. In general they supported a larger role for government in assuring human welfare, but otherwise rejected revolutionary or radical solutions, such as the wholesale restructuring that socialist or communist systems would bring about. During the early 1900s, progressives won enough political support to redefine government's role and enact some lasting reforms, including government regulation of industry, support for labor unions, and electoral reforms.

The final major trend of the era was the emergence of the United States as a world power. In keeping with its pursuit of economic and strategic interests abroad, the U.S. government soon found itself "protecting" smaller countries and even annexing some of them. By 1900, critics of this development were saying that the United States was behaving in international affairs like any other imperialist nation. In the end, most Americans reconciled themselves to imperialism, as they did to U.S. participation in World War I. Although the United States was actively engaged in the war for only 18 months, American financiers had been loaning money to the European belligerents since the war began in 1914. Later, the U.S. government loaned more money to its allies. By war's end, these financial transactions had made the United States the world's strongest economic power.

In the pages of this *Companion* you will find many references to President Theodore Roosevelt. Born in 1858 and coming to maturity in the Gilded Age, TR, as he was called, represented, in many of his ideas and achievements, the transition from Gilded Age to Progressive Era politics. A military hero in the Spanish-American War, he won election to the Vice Presidency as a Republican in 1900 and came to the Presidency after the 1901 assassination of William McKinley. TR was a skilled diplomat and a brash imperialist, as

well as a champion of fair business practices and conservation. He became immensely popular, winning a second term in 1904. After retiring in 1908, he returned to bid again for the Presidency in 1912. In this race, he campaigned under the new Progressive party banner, running against his successor, Republican William Howard Taft, Democrat Woodrow Wilson, and Socialist Eugene V. Debs. Although he lost, TR remained a popular and important political figure until his death in 1919. If one person could be said to sum up the entire era covered by this *Companion,* it would be TR.

President Theodore Roosevelt speaking in Wyoming on a western tour in 1903. On this trip Roosevelt laid a cornerstone at the gates of Yellowstone National Park, camped with naturalist John Muir at Yosemite, and received three honorary degrees.

HOW TO USE THIS BOOK

The articles in this *Companion* are arranged alphabetically, so you can look up words, concepts, or names as you come across them in other readings. You can also use the SEE ALSO listings at the end of each article to find entries about related subjects. Sometimes, you may find that the *Companion* deals with information under a different article name than what you looked up. The book will then refer you to the proper articles. For example, if you look up Mexicans, you will find the notation "SEE Hispanic Americans." If you cannot find an article on a particular subject, look in the index to guide you to the relevant articles. All people are listed alphabetically by last name. In the case of individuals who are known by more than one name, the entry will be found under the legal name rather than the one assumed later in life. So if you look up Mark Twain, you will find "SEE Clemens, Samuel Langhorne."

The Introduction will familiarize you with many of the major concepts, terms, events, and people that are covered more fully throughout the *Companion,* and it should provide you with a general understanding of the Gilded Age and Progressive Era before you begin your research.

In addition to looking up specific articles, you can also use this *Companion* topically, by reading all the articles about a particular aspect of the history. Below are several groupings of topics around common themes.

Notable individuals: Short biographies cover a wide range of historical figures: Presidents, reformers, leaders of social movements, journalists, composers, and inventors, among others. But many more people appear in this book than those who have entire articles devoted to them. For example, we discuss author Frank Norris and his novel *The Octopus*—about the brutal struggle between wheat farmers and greedy railroad owners—in the article on literature. Consult the index for proper names to discover where information about a particular figure is located.

Concepts: We discuss political concepts—such as anarchism and communism, as well as broader topics, such as government reform—within individual articles as well as throughout the *Companion*. For example, when we look at social movements, as in the article on the woman suffrage movement, we also, naturally, discuss the politics of the period and how American society at the time promoted—or hindered—change.

We also look at cultural and economic concepts and trace their development through articles on topics such as conservation, medicine, divorce, and monetary policies. In all of these articles, in addition to emphasizing causes and consequences, we identify trends—that is, customs, attitudes, or behaviors that changed significantly during the period.

Historic events: Important events that occurred during the Gilded Age and Progressive Era, such as the Spanish-American War or the influenza epidemic of 1918, are discussed for their relevance to both American and world history. Information on events that do not have a separate entry, such as the Armory Show of modern art in New York City in 1913, can often be found in other entries, such as the one on fine arts, in this case. Again, use the index to look up specific events.

Landmark Supreme Court decisions as well as specific laws, such as the Sherman Antitrust Act, are discussed at length in their own articles, and the SEE ALSO listings will tell you which broader articles are also relevant.

Groups and organizations: Many articles are devoted to the groups that reformers, women, labor organizers, and others formed during the Progressive Era to advance their work for social or political change. You can look up the National American Woman Suffrage Association, for example, to read about how women organized to secure the right to vote. But you will also find information about this group in articles on suffrage or women's voluntary associations. Consult the index and the SEE ALSO listings to find all the articles that are relevant. In addition to focusing on particular groups, articles also cover entire social movements, such as the peace movement or the temperance and prohibition movements.

Other kinds of groups to which people belonged are also included. You can look up religious denominations—Protestantism, Judaism, Catholicism—as well as individual ethnic groups—Native Americans or Asian Americans, for example.

Technology and inventions: The Gilded Age and Progressive Era were rich with discoveries and inventions that shaped American life into the following

century. You will find separate articles on many of these inventions—telephone and telegraph, airplane, and motion pictures—as well as biographies of the inventors, such as Thomas Edison and Wilbur and Orville Wright. To read about how technological changes shaped different aspects of American life, look up overview articles on such topics as work, agriculture, or railroads.

Further reading: To help you find out more about a specific topic or subject, important recent books are listed at the end of most entries. General sources and broad overviews appear in the FURTHER READING guide at the back of the book.

Websites: Many of the topics discussed in this *Companion* can be explored in depth through Internet sites. The list at the back of the book gives you a range of general sites that cover the history of the period as well as specific ones for detailed information about particular people, groups, or events.

THE GILDED AGE AND PROGRESSIVE ERA
A Student Companion

Addams, Jane

- *Born: Sept. 6, 1860, Cedarville, Ill.*
- *Education: Rockford Female Seminary, Rockford, Ill., graduated 1881, awarded B.A., 1882*
- *Accomplishments: founder, Hull House settlement (1889); first woman president, National Conference of Charities and Corrections (1909–10); founder, International Congress of Women, The Hague, and first president of the Women's International League for Peace and Freedom (1919); Nobel Peace Prize (1931)*
- *Died: May 21, 1935, Chicago, Ill.*

JANE ADDAMS, the founder of Hull House settlement, a neighborhood center that served immigrant urban residents of Chicago, led many Progressive-Era social reform movements. She grew up in the care of her widowed father, a businessman and local political leader, who encouraged her education. She wanted to study medicine, but problems with her spine caused her to abandon this plan. After graduating from college, she toured Europe, where English efforts to alleviate the misery of the poor in London impressed her. On her return in 1889, she and her friend Ellen Gates Starr settled into the former suburban home of Charles J. Hull on Chicago's Near West Side, a district that had become filled with thousands of immigrant families.

The young women's goal was to learn the needs of the poor from the poor themselves. Slowly, they developed innovative activities and programs to serve them, such as day nurseries, clubs, and lectures. The admiration these programs won from social commentators and philanthropists enabled Addams to expand them over the following years. Helen Culver, Charles Hull's heir, ultimately bequeathed the mansion to Addams and donated

Settlement-house leader Jane Addams holds a peace banner during a 1917 demonstration. As founder and first president of the Women's International League for Peace and Freedom, Addams tried in vain to avert World War I.

$50,000 for a boys' building. Mary Rozet Smith, Addams' close friend, was the settlement's largest financial contributor, but local professionals, such as University of Chicago philosophy professor John Dewey and reform lawyer Clarence Darrow, also contributed. Other help for salaries, buildings, and programs came from the wealthy members of the Chicago Woman's Club and Chicago's Kindergarten Association. In his 1902 book, *The Battle with the Slum,* Jacob Riis, an investigative reporter and photographer based in New York City, said of Addams, "They have good sense in Chicago. Jane Addams is there."

As Hull House's chief resident, Addams eventually administered a complex of 13 structures that included a playground, art gallery, gymnasium, swimming pool, library, employment bureau, labor museum, handicraft shops, and an apartment house for working girls. Hull House's facilities and programs became models for other settlements across the country.

Addams's accomplishments at Hull House earned her worldwide fame. The professional field of social work credits her as one of its founders. She inspired efforts to pass progressive labor laws in the United States, including those for workmen's compensation, improved hours and wages for working women, and an end to child labor. She also become involved in politics, formulating much of the Progressive party's social justice platform on equal suffrage and working conditions, and campaigning for the election of Theodore Roosevelt as President in 1912. She campaigned for woman suffrage and, when World War I loomed, for world peace. She helped found the Woman's Peace Party. She also published many articles and books, which included her autobiography, interpretations of immigrant life, and philosophical works on the nature of democracy.

In the 1910s and 1920s, many Americans criticized Addams's pacifism as unpatriotic. When she won the first Nobel Peace Prize given to an American woman, she found her reputation was restored. The Nobel committee praised her for "trying to raise the ideal of peace in [the American] people and in the whole world" for 25 years. They continued, "we also pay homage to the work which women can do for the cause of peace and fraternity among nations."

SEE ALSO

Child labor; Hull House; Peace movement; Progressive party; Riis, Jacob; Settlement-house movement; Woman's Peace Party

FURTHER READING

Addams, Jane. *Twenty Years at Hull House.* 1910. Reprint, edited by Victoria Bissel Brown. Boston: Bedford/St. Martin's, 1999.
Davis, Allen F. *American Heroine: The Life and Legend of Jane Addams.* New York: Oxford University Press, 1973.
Elshtain, Jean Bethke, ed. *The Jane Addams Reader.* New York: Basic Books, 2002.
Kittredge, Mary. *Jane Addams.* New York: Chelsea House, 1988.
Knight, Louise W. *Citizen: Jane Addams and the Struggle for Democracy.* Chicago: University of Chicago Press, 2005.

African Americans

THREE CONSTITUTIONAL amendments had a profound effect on African Americans after the Civil War. The 13th Amendment (1865) freed the slaves, the 14th (1868) granted them and their descendents full civil rights and protections as U.S. citizens, and the 15th (1870) guaranteed black men the right to vote. These new rights met bitter resentment among white southerners who hated losing the superiority they had held in the pre-war South. Northern troops occupying southern states had done much to protect the rights of the newly freed African Americans, but, as the last of these occupation troops pulled out in 1877, white supremacists intensified their efforts to defeat the purposes of the three "Reconstruction Amendments." Stepping up their use of intimidation and terror, including lynching, they kept African Americans from voting and holding elected offices. The few black men who managed to hold public office did so only at the lowest levels, and only at the pleasure of powerful white Democratic party leaders.

In addition to their tacit acceptance of racist violence, white lawmakers in most southern states exerted further control over African Americans by passing "Black Codes." These codes restricted African Americans' mobility and property ownership, curtailed their civil and political rights, and required the segregation of public facilities, such as schools and transportation systems. The federal government later declared that the harshest

A photomontage depicts prominent African American leaders of the late 19th century (clockwise, from top left): T. Thomas Fortune, editor of the New York Age newspaper; Booker T. Washington, founder and president of Tuskegee Institute; Ida B. Wells, journalist and antilynching crusader; and author Irvine Garland Penn. In the center is Frederick Douglass, former slave and prominent abolitionist.

aspects of these codes were illegal. They provided a basis, however, for the so-called "Jim Crow" laws that relegated southern black Americans to a second-class citizenship status long into the 20th century. Increasingly, most prisoners in the South were black men. To keep them under control, prison officials developed a convict lease system, which allowed prisons to rent out their convicts to work on farms and road gangs. Chained to each other and worked to exhaustion, the convicts received minimal shelter and food. Many succumbed to injuries or illnesses. Convict leasing became part of the racial system of the late 19th-century South.

Most former slaves knew nothing but farming. Reconstruction had not brought them property or land. Instead, many fell into the practice of sharecropping, that is, leasing acres from white landowners and paying the rent with a share of the crop. While sharecropping was initially beneficial, putting land back into production and giving former slaves control over their own farming practices and family lives, it gave sharecroppers little eco-

nomic advantage. Because they borrowed seed and farming implements from their landlords, and bought necessities on credit from local suppliers, a disappointing crop yield left them owing more than they could pay. Their debts might then compound year after year, leaving them no way out of the system.

Despite the hardships under which they labored, black Americans built communities throughout the rural South, and black neighborhoods developed in southern cities. Within these communities, African Americans established businesses and services and began fostering the education of the professionals that the community needed, such as teachers, lawyers, and doctors. Black communities founded their own churches and hired their own ministers. The most popular denominations were African Methodist Episcopal and Baptist. Above all else, former slaves wanted their children to have an education, and parents often made sacrifices to make sure their children completed elementary school and at least some high school. Unlike the practices that were developing in immigrant communities in major U.S. cities, where teenaged children worked full-time in factories and sweatshops, and mothers took care of the house, African American parents both worked at farm labor or for wages so that children could stay in school. African American women often worked as poorly paid domestic servants and laundresses, or as field hands, the same sorts of jobs they had had as slaves. In a country that enshrined an exclusively domestic role for women, the privilege of being "just a housewife" was not available to most black women.

As the racial divide and white hostility intensified in the southern states, alongside deepening rural poverty, many African Americans moved into cities in search of work. Others went farther, traveling in mule trains or on foot to Kansas, Oklahoma, and Nebraska. There they hoped to take advantage of homesteading, the process by which individuals or families could claim free ownership of 160 acres of federal land once they had built a home and grown crops on it for five years. These African American pioneers were known as the Exodusters, a reference to the story of "Exodus" in the Bible, when the prophet Moses led the Jews out of bondage in Egypt. A number of their small farming communities still remain in the Plains states.

In 1875, Congress had passed a Civil Rights Act, which had guaranteed all people, regardless of race, color, or previous condition of servitude, access to public accommodations, facilities, transportation systems, and juries. In 1883, however, the Supreme Court ruled this act unconstitutional, thereby opening the door to legalized segregation. Voicing the majority opinion, Chief Justice Joseph Bradley held that the 14th Amendment did not protect black people from discrimination by private businesses and individuals but only from discrimination by states. Almost immediately

southern states—following a segregation pattern originally established on northern rail cars, but since abandoned—enacted laws keeping blacks and whites separate in all public accommodations—trains, restrooms, theaters, restaurants, and, most significantly, public schools. In the 1896 Supreme Court case *Plessy* v. *Ferguson*, the court ruled against an African American plaintiff, Homer Plessy, who had sued the Louisiana Railroad for discriminating against him. The decision gave legal permission for separate facilities provided they were equal. "Whites Only" and "Colored" signs appeared throughout the South, even over public drinking fountains. In 1899, a Supreme Court decision paved the way for localities to maintain separate schools even if the schools for black children were inferior to those for whites, and even to shut down the black schools in cases of financial hardship. All southern states, and some northern ones, had antimiscegenation laws, forbidding marriages between white and black people. Some antimiscegenation laws stayed on the books until the mid-20th century.

Increasingly, black men could not exercise their right to vote in the southern states. By 1900 most states had legalized poll taxes of one to two

These black migrants were among the more than 900 African American families who made the trek westward in 1880 to take advantage of federal farmland grants.

dollars a year per voter, payable in advance, and literacy tests, with white registrars interpreting a black voter's ability to read. Other techniques restricting black voters included grandfather clauses, which exempted anyone whose ancestors had voted before the Civil War from having to pay the poll tax or take a literacy test. Of course, before the Civil War, only whites had voted. Within one decade in the 1880s, half the black electorate, intimidated by both legal means and acts of terrorism, had ceased trying to vote.

African Americans responded to segregation and disfranchisement in a variety of ways, in some cases challenging the system and in others trying to find ways to live with dignity and self-respect despite the system. Among those who challenged the violence that accompanied segregation was journalist Ida B. Wells, whose 1890s anti-lynching campaign exposed the practice as an act of white supremacist terror against African Americans and not a "defense" of law and order as its perpetrators claimed. W. E. B. DuBois, an African American sociology professor born in the North, spoke out for civil rights and full equality, urging black Americans to stop appeasing whites, to resist segregation and disfranchisement, and to claim their "manhood" and the rights granted them in the Constitution. DuBois would help to found two influential black advocacy groups, the National Association for the Advancement of Colored People (NAACP) in 1909, and the National Urban League in 1910. Opposed to the confrontational style of DuBois, Booker T. Washington, the president of Tuskegee Institute in Alabama, a college for black students, urged African Americans to establish an economic base in American life before pushing for equal rights with whites.

African American communities and workplaces responded to segregation with the creation of mutual benefit societies and self-help organizations, ranging from fraternal societies and social clubs to life-insurance programs and volunteer fire departments. Members of the African American women's club movement, federated in 1895 as the National Association of Colored Women's Clubs, embraced education, civic improvement, and women's issues. Middle-class black club women were especially concerned about helping working-class black women achieve respectability and escape the stigmas inherited from slavery days. Their motto was "Lifting as We Climb."

Black colleges and universities—Morehouse, Fisk, Howard, Tougaloo, and others—began to appear on the American scene during Reconstruction and steadily gained ground during the next decades. Spelman College in Atlanta, founded in the basement of a Baptist church in 1881, became an elite African American women's college. A hundred years after its founding in Nashville, Tennessee, Fisk would become the first of the historically black colleges to achieve university status.

African Americans had drifted away from the South ever since the end of the Civil War. During World War I, the drift became a migration stream, as African American men joined the army and thousands of other black men and women left their home counties for jobs in industrial cities in the North. With white men being drafted for the war, and the need for wartime industrial production increasing, jobs opened up that had never previously been available to black men. After the men were hired, their family members followed. Women found jobs in factories and in domestic service, where they could earn three or four times what they made doing similar work in the South. The "Great Migration," as this population shift of a million came to be called, created African American communities in northern cities when black-owned businesses, churches, and community organizations brought together the industrial migrants and created a new urban black culture. In the decade that followed the war, a million more African Americans migrated to northern cities. Their presence exacerbated white racism that had simmered in the North, while being blatantly expressed in the South, and led to race riots in cities as far apart as Chicago and Tulsa, Oklahoma. The Ku Klux Klan reorganized in 1915. A white supremacist organization founded in the South in 1866, the Klan used intimidation and terror to prevent African Americans from achieving equality. It spread into the North and the Midwest after World War I, enrolled several million new members, and expanded its hate campaigns to include Jews, Roman Catholics, and political radicals.

Among the many positive imports southern blacks brought to northern cities were jazz and blues music and other African American art forms in the fields of dance, theater, literature, and graphic arts. Among the African American musicians winning worldwide fame in this era were Scott Joplin, whose ragtime compositions stimulated the emergence of jazz, and the Jubilee Singers of Fisk University, who popularized the "Negro Spiritual" as an art form. Although most African Americans despised the stereotypes of black life contained in minstrel shows, there is no doubt that forms of humor, dance, and music associated with these shows had a huge impact on American popular culture.

Though segregation and disfranchisement were not legal in states outside the South, prejudice, negative stereotyping, and discrimination remained major facts of life for black Americans in every part of the United States. African Americans continued to build lives and communities, however, and to emphasize education and professional advancement for their children, but not until the 1960s would they win full civil rights throughout the country.

SEE ALSO

Civil rights; Colleges and universities; Dance; Democratic party; DuBois, William Edward Burghardt (W. E. B.); Education; Jim Crow; Joplin, Scott; Jubilee Singers; Ku Klux Klan; Law; Music; National Association for the Advancement of Colored People; National Urban League; *Plessy* v. *Ferguson* (1896); Race relations; Race riots; Reform movements; Religion; Segregation; Suffrage; Supreme Court, U.S.; Wells-Barnett, Ida B.; Washington, Booker T.; World War I

FURTHER READING

Franklin, John Hope, and Alfred A. Moss, Jr. *From Slavery to Freedom: A History of African Americans.* 8th ed. New York: Knopf, 2000.
Kelley, Robin D. G., and Earl Lewis, eds. *To Make Our World Anew: A History of African Americans.* New York: Oxford University Press, 2000.
Painter, Nell Irvin. *Creating Black Americans: African American History and its Meanings, 1619 to the Present.* New York: Oxford University Press, 2005.
Patton, Sharon. *African American Art.* New York: Oxford University Press, 1998.
Stewart, Jeffrey C. *1001 Things Everyone Should Know About African American History.* New York: Gramercy Books, 2006.

Agriculture

AMERICAN AGRICULTURE both expanded and modernized during the latter decades of the 19th century.

Between 1870 and 1900, more land came under cultivation than the total acreage occupied since the first colonial settlement of 1607. To optimize their use of this land, farmers took advantage of new technologies to mechanize their operations and ship perishable products over longer distances, thus expanding their output and their markets.

Americans had already settled west of the Mississippi River and along parts of the Pacific coast before the Civil War. Afterward, they filled in the areas in between, the Great Plains, the Northwest, and the Southwest. Federal legislation helped make this possible. The Morrill Land-Grant Act of 1862 granted 140 million acres of western lands to state governments in order to fund agricultural colleges. To raise cash to build the colleges, the states sold their grants to speculators, who resold them to settlers at a profit. The government also gave land directly to settlers through the 1862 Homestead Act, which offered settlers 160 acres of public land for a $10 registration fee. After five years of continuous residence and property improvement, a settler could claim full ownership. Finally, the government granted huge tracts of land to railroads to encourage the building of tracks into the West. In turn, the railroads also sold plots to settlers.

Homesteaders' lives were hard. Many lived first in crude houses formed from three-foot strips of sod mounted atop one another, with openings left for windows and doors. Sod houses were cool in summer and warm in winter, but also dank and filthy. Farm women, who arrived after their husbands had staked a claim, reported that they wept when they saw where they had to live. "When our covered wagon drew up beside the door of the one-roomed sod house that father had provided," Carrie Lassell Detrick recalled in a narrative written for the *Kansas Woman's Journal* in the 1920s, "he helped mother down and I remember how her face looked as she gazed about that barren farm, then threw her arms about his neck and gave way to the only fit of weeping I ever remember seeing her indulge in." As soon as they could, farmers built houses of wood. Rainfall was sparse and unpredictable on the Plains. Settlers collected rainwater in buckets or cisterns until they could dig wells. Before the railroads brought in coal, fuel consisted of wood, if available, or dried buffalo or cow dung ("chips"). There was little lumber for building homes or fences. Plowing and planting the new land—sodbusting—was exhausting work because the roots of the native prairie grasses bore down so deeply. Poor rainfall in the 1870s, coupled with waves of grasshoppers and locusts—which ate everything from crops to clothing to wooden plow handles—caused great hardship.

According to a report written by Grand Canyon explorer and conservationist John Wesley Powell in 1879, "All the...agriculture of more than four-tenths of the area of the United States is dependent upon irrigation." Still, the federal government did not fund expensive irrigation projects and develop federal water policies for the arid Southwest until the end of the century. In the meantime, until well-drilling machinery became available in the 1880s, farmers dug wells by hand. Many farmers used "dry farming" techniques, digging deep furrows so that subsurface water could reach plant roots. They also cultivated fields after every rainfall, covering plants with a dust mulch to prevent water evaporation.

African American farmers in the South haul their crops to market. By the 1890s farmers like these had formed collectives to share the costs of purchasing equipment and storing and marketing crops.

In the East, 80 acres of farmland could provide a living. In the West, because of the dry climate, which made the land less fertile, farmers needed 360 acres to survive. Thus farmers welcomed any mechanical means to reduce their time and effort. During the 1870s, improvements in farm implements multiplied. Soon farmers were riding behind plows or plowing several furrows at once. Other inventions followed: harrows equipped with spring teeth that dislodged debris, automatic drills to spread grain, a "checkrower" that spaced corn rows evenly, and a "lister" that planted corn deeply in semiarid regions. By 1880, farmers were using automatic grain binders and later "headers" drawn by six horses to cut off the heads of standing grain. Steam-powered threshers had appeared by 1875 and cornhuskers and corn binders by the 1890s.

Small-scale farmers often went heavily into debt to buy such machines. Entrepreneurs with large landholdings invested in them more easily, hoping to reap a bonanza from supplying foodstuffs to the increasing populations of the East. Companies formed partnerships to establish huge farms. The owners rarely saw their land, instead allowing it to be managed by professionals. "Bonanza"

farms specialized in single cash crops. But when the market for a particular crop became glutted, and prices fell, even corporate giants felt the blow.

The U.S. Department of Agriculture (USDA), founded in 1862, helped farmers modernize. It distributed experimental seeds, published pamphlets to advise farmers on agricultural techniques, and studied livestock diseases and pest control. It gathered statistics on markets, crops, and diseases that affected agriculture and set up sections to study forestry, trends in animal and dairy industries, and the cultivation of fruits and vegetables. In 1887 the USDA established state experimental stations that performed research in agriculture-related fields. In cooperation with agricultural colleges, these stations held farmers' institutes to advise and inspire farm families. The USDA became a cabinet-level department in 1889.

Despite this help, farmers often suffered. Drought and harsh winters in the late 1880s and a drop in wheat and cotton prices in the late 1890s sent many into debt. Sharecropping, already widespread in the South, was a farm labor system that allowed people to work on land they did not own. In exchange for the loan of the land, they had to give the landowner a large share of the crops they produced. A bad crop yield could start the laborer on a downward spiral of debt. Farmers elsewhere also faced problems. Unable to pay mortgages, taxes, machinery costs, and high railroad rates for shipping, many became tenants on their own land, beholden to corporate owners far away. To fight high costs, farmers had been organizing into cooperatives since the 1870s. By 1892, these had evolved into the People's, or Populist party, which in addition to fighting high costs also called for government ownership of railroads and communication systems, a graduated income tax, direct election of U.S. senators, and a shorter work-week for industrial laborers. The 1890s marked the highpoint of farmer agitation. Frank Norris depicted some of this agitation in his novel *The Octopus* (1901), which describes the struggles of California wheat farmers against the railroads.

Economic matters improved for farmers after the turn of the 20th century, and angry political confrontations subsided. As the cities filled with immigrants, demand for agricultural products rose, along with their prices. California's Central Valley, developed by native-born and immigrant Asian farmers, was becoming an all-season resource for fruits and vegetables. The South was still hard-pressed, however, primarily because planters refused to diversify, instead sticking to cotton as a cash crop. When cotton prices fell, many sharecroppers and southern tenant farmers moved north to take up industrial and service jobs.

Concerned about the decline of farm life, especially in the South, urban progressives developed a "Country Life" movement. In 1908 President Theodore Roosevelt appointed a Country Life Commission to suggest how to improve rural life. It proposed better schools, roads, health services, and communication systems. Farmers improved their own lives by using their renewed buying power to obtain more manufactured goods and mechanize their farms. In 1900, farm families produced 60 percent of what they consumed; by 1920, they were producing only 40 percent, purchasing the rest through mail-order catalogs.

World War I brought new government interest in American agriculture. Convinced that the nation with the best control over food production would win the war, President Woodrow Wilson spearheaded the passage of the 1917 Food Production Act and Food Control Act. He appointed Herbert Hoover, who would become President in 1928, as food administrator to distribute seed, machinery, and fertilizer to American farmers. When the war ended, these supports vanished. As soon as Europe reestablished its farms and could feed itself, overseas markets declined. Facing falling prices, American farmers could not pay off their loans on the machinery they had bought when the market was expanding. The 1920s, as a result, was an era of depression on American farms.

SEE ALSO

Consumer culture; Environment; Family life; Populism; Powell, John Wesley; Pure Food and Drugs Act (1906); Science and technology; South, the; West, the; Wilson, Woodrow T.; World War I

FURTHER READING

Danbom, David B. *Born in the Country: A History of Rural America.* Baltimore: Johns Hopkins University Press, 1995.
Fite, Gilbert Courtland. *The Farmers' Frontier, 1865–1900.* Albuquerque: University of New Mexico Press, 1977.
Hurt, R. Douglas. *American Agriculture: A Brief History.* Ames: Iowa State University Press, 1994.
Starr, Kevin. *Americans and the California Dream, 1850-1915.* New York: Oxford University Press, 1973.

Airplane

ALTHOUGH INVENTORS in several countries had been experimenting with flight since the mid-19th century, American bicycle mechanics and self-taught engineers Wilbur and Orville Wright can certainly be credited with the invention

of the airplane. Familiar with the technology of gliders, which only flew short distances and had no pilots, they felt it should be possible to design a machine capable of sustained flight. They adapted gliders' wing shape, added propellers and an engine, and altered the overall design so that their aircraft could be piloted by a human being rather than a built-in engineering device.

By late 1903 the Wright brothers had tested six experimental aircraft. On December 17, on the beach at Kitty Hawk, North Carolina, Orville won a coin toss to see who would pilot the seventh. He flew a 605-pound biplane with a 12-horsepower motor 120 feet. The flight lasted only 12 seconds but it was the first powered, piloted flight in history.

The Wright brothers quickly adapted their invention for sustained flight. They made public demonstration flights starting in 1908, took out patents, and opened the American Wright Company in 1909. There they built planes and developed new designs. They sold plans for aircraft to the U.S. military, and the airplane became an important tool for aerial combat and observation during World War I.

Until the late 1920s, the only people who flew airplanes, aside from military pilots, were hobbyists and daredevil entertainers at air shows. The use of flight for commerce and passenger travel would develop throughout the decades that followed.

SEE ALSO

Inventions; Science and technology; World War I; Wright, Wilbur and Orville

FURTHER READING

Crouch, Tom D. *Wings: A History of Aviation from Kites to the Space Age.* New York: Norton, 2003.

———. *A Dream of Wings: Americans and the Airplane, 1875–1905.* Washington, D.C.: Smithsonian Institution Press, 2002.

Dunmore, Spencer, and Fred E. C. Culik. *On Great White Wings: The Wright Brothers and the Race for Flight.* New York: Hyperion, 2001.

Freedman, Russell. *The Wright Brothers: How They Invented the Airplane.* New York: Holiday House, 1991.

Hallion, Richard. *Taking Flight: Inventing the Aerial Age from Antiquity through the First World War.* New York: Oxford University Press, 2003.

Jakab, Peter L. *Visions of a Flying Machine: The Wright Brothers and the Process of Invention.* Washington D.C.: Smithsonian Institution Press, 1997.

Alger, Horatio, Jr.

- *Born: Jan. 13, 1832, Chelsea, Mass.*
- *Education: Harvard College, A.B., 1852; Harvard Divinity School, B.Div., 1857*
- *Accomplishments: author,* Frank's Campaign *(1864),* Ragged Dick; or, Street Life in New York with the Boot-Blacks *(1868), and more than 100 similar books and biographies*
- *Died: July 18, 1899, Natick, Mass.*

THE SON OF A UNITARIAN minister and farmer, young Horatio Alger, Jr., grew up wanting to be a writer. Although his early short stories and poems received good reviews, he needed a reliable income and so decided to study for the ministry. He continued to write for magazines and newspapers, publishing sensational pieces on moral themes, travel literature, and patriotic fiction and verse. In 1863, he turned to juvenile fiction, publishing his first book in this genre, *Frank's Campaign,* which depicted home life during the Civil War.

Ordained a Unitarian minister in 1864, Alger took a post in Brewster, Massachusetts, but had to resign after 15 months when accused of having molested boys. He then moved to New York where he spent most of his time at various charitable institutions for boys. He befriended boys easily, and

On the cover of Luck and Pluck *by Horatio Alger Jr., a boy heads off to make his way in the world. The heroes of Alger's novels often ended up in big cities where, with a combination of luck, brains, and honesty, they achieved success.*

saw them as his prime readership, but he was never again accused of sexual misconduct.

With *Ragged Dick,* Alger established what became known as his "rags-to-riches" formula, a highly successful pattern of plot and character that he could repeat, with variations, in future books. The formula was simple: a young male hero, often a street urchin, is tempted by vice in the city. Through strong character, hard work, and the intercession of a kind adult, the boy defeats evil and becomes "respectable." Alger heroes do not become wealthy; in general, they aspire to middle-class comfort rather than vast riches. Still, Alger himself admired people who had risen from lowly beginnings to great heights, and thought that their lives were more inspiring than his books. As he wrote in 1879 to one of his publishers, Francis Street, who went to work at age twelve and eventually became a wealthy newspaper owner, "In all my stories and books I have labored to induce boys to rise in the world by precisely the same means which have

helped you to rise. The example of individuals is of more value than the appeals of writers, and you may unconsciously by your success have led to the success of many others."

Much of Alger's fiction sold as "dime novels," that is, cheap paperbacks directed toward a mass audience. Not everyone approved of them. Ministers of religion, especially, took Alger to task for writing overly sensational stories. Despite such criticism, Alger's books became increasingly popular, especially after his death. His readers were mostly middle-class and working-class boys, but the books also held strong appeal for the sons of immigrants, who were looking for ideas about how to assimilate and succeed in American life. During the 1910s and 1920s, the term "Horatio Alger hero" came to describe almost any young man who rose up from poverty, temptation, or other adversity and was able to build a successful middle-class life.

SEE ALSO
Literature

FURTHER READING
Alger, Horatio Jr. *Ragged Dick and Struggling Upwards.* Edited by Carl Bode. New York: Penguin, 1985.
Scharnhorst, Gary, with Jack Bales. *The Lost Life of Horatio Alger, Jr.* Bloomington: Indiana University Press, 1985.

American Expeditionary Force

THE AMERICAN Expeditionary Force (AEF) was the name given to the combined forces of the army, navy, and marines who fought alongside European allies in France and other theaters of World War I.

In peacetime, the U.S. military had amounted to fewer than one million servicemen. But in May 1917, six weeks after declaring war on Germany and its allies, Congress passed the Selective Service Act to draft men into a national army of 4 million. Despite concerns that the new recruits would need months of training, support for U.S. allies required the prompt dispatch of a number of combat-ready soldiers. The first regiments embarked for France in June 1917, following General John J. Pershing, commander in chief of the AEF, and his staff. Regular convoys of recruits sailed to Europe monthly throughout the rest of the war.

Of the 4.7 million Americans mobilized during the war, most served in the army, 600,000 served in the navy, and 79,000 were marines. Fewer than 130,000 professional soldiers made up the core of the force. The rest consisted of hundreds of thousands of volunteers and draftees never before in uniform. In part because the arrival of the forces helped to bring the war to such a swift conclusion, only half of the expected AEF reached France before the armistice in November 1918.

Nicknamed "doughboys," a term dating back to the 1848 Mexican War but otherwise of uncertain origin and meaning, more than one million American soldiers saw combat in France, Belgium, Italy, and Russia; 650,000 others worked in supplies and services, operating transportation and communication systems, driving ambulances, and running hospitals, military police, and gas warfare units. About 180,000 African American soldiers served in segregated regiments. Some of them fought with the French army, earning great distinction. Members of the black 369th Regiment won the French Croix de Guerre, a high honor for

bravery, and spent more days in combat than any other units of the AEF.

By the end of the war, the AEF in France and Flanders commanded 83 miles of the 392-mile-long Western Front. More than 116,700 American servicemen died, less than half killed outright, many from disease; 204,000 suffered non-fatal wounds. Of the 71,000 gassed during enemy attacks, about 1,500 died. Others, lungs weakened by gassing, succumbed to the Spanish flu epidemic of 1918. Their deaths, too, are included in World War I casualty lists.

SEE ALSO

African Americans; International relations; Military; Navy, U.S.; Pershing, John Joseph; World War I

FURTHER READING

Hallas, James H. *Doughboy War: The American Expeditionary Force in World War I*. Boulder, Colo.: Lynne Rienner, 2000.
Mead, Gary. *The Doughboys: America and the First World War*. Woodstock, N.Y.: Overlook Press, 2000.
Stallings, Lawrence. *The Doughboys: The Story of the AEF, 1917–1918*. New York: Harper & Row, 1963.

American Federation of Labor

IN THE LAST DECADES of the 19th century, skilled workers, such as carpenters, plumbers, and typesetters, became dissatisfied with the Knights of Labor, the chief labor organization of that time. Founded in 1869, the Knights were open to all men and women workers, regardless of level of skill. The Knights embraced ideas that seemed radical for their time, such as equal pay for equal work, and pushed for political reforms, including the graduated income tax. The Knights' association with boycotts and strikes made them unpopular with many Americans.

Skilled workers thought a different type of organization would better protect their interests, which primarily concerned higher pay. In 1886, they formed a federation, an "umbrella" organization that allowed its members to remain in their separate craft unions while working together for common goals. They called this new organization the American Federation of Labor (AFL).

Samuel Gompers, a master cigar maker, was the federation's president for nearly 40 years. Gompers believed that because skilled workers were harder to replace than unskilled workers, AFL members would have greater bargaining power with bosses. Therefore, unskilled industrial workers were not invited to AFL membership, and the AFL made no demands on their behalf. Instead, the individual craft unions that made up the membership of the AFL focused on higher wages and shorter hours for themselves only. At the same time, however, they also worked hard to gain such political goals as workers' compensation and child labor laws, and they encouraged sympathy strikes across craft union lines. Thus, for example, members of the painters' union could help the carpenters' union win their demands by joining them in labor protests.

The AFL systematically excluded women, African Americans, and Asians from its ranks, assuming that these groups would compete too heavily with white male workers. The AFL fought for men to be able to support their families. The federation felt little obligation to fight for better wages for minorities or unmarried women workers, who might be supporting families on pay that was half of what skilled white men earned.

AFL membership ebbed and flowed with the country's economic cycles, but it was by far the largest labor federation in the United States up to 1955, when it merged with the Congress of Industrial Organizations (CIO), a federation of unions formed in 1935. The AFL-CIO today includes unions of both skilled and unskilled workers.

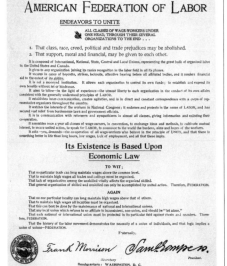

SEE ALSO

Gompers, Samuel; Knights of Labor; Labor; Labor unions; Socialism; Strikes

FURTHER READING

Foner, Philip S. *The AFL in the Progressive Era, 1910–1915.* New York: International-al Publishers, 1980.
Greene, Julie. *Pure and Simple Politics: The American Federation of Labor and Political Activism, 1881–1917.* New York: Cambridge University Press, 1998.
Simonds, Patricia. *The Founding of the AFL and the Rise of Organized Labor.* New York: Silver Burdett, 1991.

Anarchism

ANARCHISM IS a political philosophy that holds that government is an abusive device used by the rich to oppress the poor. Anarchists believe that human society can be perfected with either the gradual or abrupt disappearance of government. They are not, however, opposed to all social organization. Optimistic about the capacity of human beings for cooperation, anarchists believe that, after government disappears,

This 1881 broadside features the American Federation of Labor manifesto, which explains its reason for being. Although it claimed to be open to all workers, the AFL included only members of skilled trades and was closed to African Americans and women.

communities can perform all previous governmental functions cooperatively at a local level. Such a system, they argue, maximizes individual liberty and social equality.

Anarchist theory derived from several European sources. Its chief exponents were 19th-century French philosopher Pierre-Joseph Proudhon, who coined the phrase "property is theft," and the Russian political activists Mikhail Bakunin and Pyotr Kropotkin. The philosophy traveled across the Atlantic with radical immigrants from Germany and eastern Europe. Its best known American exponents were the "Haymarket Martyrs," German-American labor leaders hanged for their role in an 1886 protest in Chicago's Haymarket Square, which resulted in the deaths of eight policemen. Feminist Emma Goldman, an immigrant lecturer and champion of workers' and women's rights, also advocated anarchism. The Industrial Workers of the World and other radical labor organizations of the late 19th century also attracted anarchists. Most anarchists were also socialists, in that they stressed cooperation and the welfare of the larger society over that of only a few, but not all socialists took the extreme anti-government position of anarchism.

Some anarchists believed that violence would inevitably accompany such sweeping social change as they proposed. A small minority actually planned and carried out assassinations, believing that violent deeds would demonstrate the seriousness of their cause. During a major strike in the steel industry that took place in Homestead, Pennsylvania, in 1892, anarchist Alexander Berkman tried to assassinate Henry Clay Frick, the steel plant's manager. This attempt was definitely part of an anarchist plot. Leon Czolgosz, the disturbed young man who assassi-

nated President William McKinley in 1901, claimed that anarchists had influenced him, but anarchists denied any relationship to him at all. The majority of anarchists neither planned nor committed violent acts, even if they believed that violence would someday become a tragic necessity.

Most American citizens and all government officials feared anarchism and its implied threat of social revolution. In times of heightened national tension, such as a massive strike or the hysteria of the Red Scare—a wave of anticommunism that followed World War I—social or labor activists found themselves jailed as suspected anarchists. Immigration officials at Ellis Island turned away potential immigrants suspected of anarchistic leanings. In the notorious Sacco and Vanzetti robbery and murder case of the 1920s, two immigrant Italians were executed on scant evidence after being tried by a judge who referred to them as "anarchist bastards."

Anarchism never took hold as a viable means of social organization, but it exists today as a political philosophy with a small number of adherents around the world.

This 1886 handbill in English and German announces a meeting in Chicago to protest a police attack on workers who were striking for an eight-hour day. Violence erupted at this meeting, resulting in the "Haymarket Square riot."

SEE ALSO

Communism; Goldman, Emma; Haymarket Square riot (1886); Homestead strike (1892); Industrial Workers of the World; Labor; McKinley, William; Red Scare (1919–20); Socialism; World War I

FURTHER READING

Gay, Kathlyn, ed. *Encyclopedia of Political Anarchy.* Santa Barbara, Calif.: ABC-CLIO, 1999.
Goldman, Emma. *Anarchism and Other Essays.* 1910. Reprint, Mineola, N.Y.: Dover, 1969.

Guérin, Daniel. *Anarchism: From Theory to Practice.* Translated by Mary Klopper. New York: Monthly Review Press, 1970.
Sonn, Richard D. *Anarchism.* Boston: Twayne, 1992.

Angel Island

THE IMMIGRATION STATION at Angel Island, in San Francisco Bay, first opened in 1910. The facility controlled the entry of Asians into the United States and enforced the race-based legislation of the Chinese Exclusion Act, which attempted to end further Chinese immigration into the United States, and the Gentlemen's Agreement (1907–8), which regulated Japanese immigration. The majority of Asian immigrants coming through Angel Island were Chinese, Japanese, and Korean. South Asians (from India) and Southeast Asians came to the United States only in very small numbers during this period. Since their homelands were part of the British or French empires, they tended to migrate to countries in other parts of those empires. If they came to the West Coast of the United States, however, they would enter through Angel Island.

For immigrants whose papers were incomplete or irregular, the station at Angel Island functioned as a detention center. Immigrants could spend anywhere from two weeks to two years at Angel Island. If they could not get permission to enter, they were sent back to their country of origin.

Immigration officials subjected detainees to rigorous questioning about their home villages and families, and they carefully scrutinized all claims of an American connection that would make their applications for permission to immigrate acceptable.

Sometimes detainees underwent callous physical examinations. Surrounded by barbed wire and armed guards, and separated from family members, they lived in prison-like conditions. Depressed, lonely, or rejected, some committed suicide. Others occupied the waiting period by penciling, carving, or brush-painting poetry on the walls of the dormitories. Despair and frustration were common themes.

Whereas New York's Ellis Island supported European immigrants and helped them enter the country, Angel Island made Asian applicants feel unwelcome. Between 1910 and 1940, immigration authorities detained 175,000 Chinese at Angel Island, as well as thousands of people from other Pacific Rim countries. Nearly 20,000 Japanese "picture brides" endured varying periods of detention. Picture brides were young women who had agreed to marry, sight unseen, Japanese men resident in the United States with whom they had exchanged only a few pictures and letters. If the prospective husband, who paid for his bride's passage, did not show up to claim her in a short amount of time, Angel Island authorities sent her back to Japan.

Angel Island remained open until 1940, when it ceased to be an immigrant processing station. It functioned

Chinese women sit with a missionary in the waiting room of the Angel Island immigration station. Asian immigrant women often had to wait for months for permission to enter the United States and join their husbands.

briefly as a prison for captured enemy soldiers during World War II, and today it is an immigration museum.

SEE ALSO
Asian Americans; Chinese Exclusion Act (1882); Ellis Island; Gentlemen's Agreement; Immigration

FURTHER READING
Hoobler, Dorothy, and Thomas Hoobler. *The Chinese American Family Album.* New York: Oxford University Press, 1994.
Lai, Him Mark, Genny Lim, and Judy Yung. *Island: Poetry and History of Chinese Immigrants on Angel Island, 1910–1940.* Seattle: University of Washington Press, 1991.
Wong, Kevin Scott, and Sucheng Chan, eds. *Claiming America: Constructing Chinese American Identities During the Exclusion Era.* Philadelphia: Temple University Press, 1998.

Anthony, Susan Brownell

- *Born: Feb. 15, 1820, Adams, Mass.*
- *Education: district schools, home school, and the Friends' Seminary (1837–38), a private Quaker boarding school near Philadelphia*
- *Accomplishments: cofounder, Woman's New York State Temperance Society (1853); agent, American Anti-Slavery Society (1856–61); co-organizer, Women's National Loyal League (1863); cofounder, American Equal Rights Association (1866); publisher, The Revolution (1868–70); cofounder, National Woman Suffrage Association (1869); cofounder, International Council of Women (1888); president, National American Woman Suffrage Association (1892–1900)*
- *Died: Mar. 13, 1906, Rochester, N.Y.*

SUSAN B. ANTHONY was active in many 19th-century reform movements, including antislavery and temperance. But her name is most closely associated with the woman suffrage movement, to which she devoted the greater part of her life from the early 1850s onward.

She became an advocate of securing the vote for women after meeting Elizabeth Cady Stanton, who in 1848 had organized the first woman's rights convention at Seneca Falls, N.Y. Stanton persuaded Anthony that without the vote, women would remain powerless to convince legislators to end slavery and the liquor trade.

Years of organizational work followed. In close partnership with Stanton, Anthony spoke out and wrote on both temperance and the "woman question," traveling widely and organizing state and national conventions. At these conventions, hundreds of women and some sympathetic men debated resolutions in favor of the vote and other women's rights. Anthony and Stanton campaigned successfully for New York State laws that granted married women the right to control their own property. In 1868 the two women launched *The Revolution,* a radical newspaper promoting a broad range of civil rights for women. They convinced two legislators to introduce the first woman suffrage amendment into the U.S. Congress. They then founded the National Woman Suffrage Association to win the amendment's passage.

Anthony spent much of the next 30 years on the road, gathering support for the federal suffrage amendment and assisting in state suffrage campaigns. In the early 1870s, she argued, along with other suffragists, that women as U.S. citizens already had the right to vote. To test this idea she attempted to vote in the 1872 Presidential election. For this she was arrested, tried, and fined $100. On refusing to pay, she accused the judge of having "trampled under foot every vital principle of our government" and degrading her sex "from the status of a citizen to that of a subject."

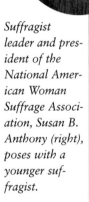

Suffragist leader and president of the National American Woman Suffrage Association, Susan B. Anthony (right), poses with a younger suffragist.

In 1869 the woman suffrage movement had split into two branches. Anthony and Stanton's organization, the National Woman Suffrage Association, worked principally for the federal constitutional amendment. The American Woman Suffrage Association, led by Lucy Stone and her husband, Henry Blackwell, focused on state campaigns for woman suffrage. In 1890, the two organizations united, forming the National American Woman Suffrage Association. Anthony became its president in 1892. Now age 70, she tried to curtail her travels but continued, from her sister's home in Rochester, to lead the woman suffrage movement. In 1899, acknowledging Anthony's longtime support of the right of labor to organize into unions, the American Federation of Labor endorsed her call for woman suffrage. During the period of Reconstruction after the Civil War, Anthony had opposed the 14th and 15th Amendments because they gave political rights only to black men instead of to both sexes. In later years she spoke out vehemently against racial discrimination of any kind. Anthony attended her last woman suffrage convention in February 1906. There she announced that "failure is impossible," a motto that inspired the movement to the end. With the ratification of the 19th Amendment in 1920, women finally won the right to vote.

SEE ALSO

National American Woman Suffrage Association; Stanton, Elizabeth Cady; Woman suffrage movement; Women's rights movement

FURTHER READING

Barry, Kathleen. *Susan B. Anthony: A Biography of a Singular Feminist.* New York: New York University Press, 1988.
Lutz, Alma. *Susan B. Anthony: Rebel, Crusader, Humanitarian.* Boston: Beacon Press, 1959.
Sherr, Lynn. *Failure Is Impossible: Susan B. Anthony in Her Own Words.* New York: Times Books, 1995.
Ward, Geoffrey C. *Not for Ourselves Alone: The Story of Elizabeth Cady Stanton and Susan B. Anthony.* New York: Knopf, 1999.
Weisberg, Barbara. *Susan B. Anthony.* New York: Chelsea House, 1988.

Anthropology

MODERN ANTHROPOLOGY, the study of human beings and their cultures, began in the 19th century at the same time that the theory of evolution was finding acceptance among scientific thinkers. Scientists, explorers, missionaries, doctors, and biologists began to create anthropological associations to encourage research on the peoples of colonized and unfamiliar lands. In addition to studying human physiology and varieties of human societies around the globe, they amassed worldwide collections of everything from pots and baskets to bones and skulls. These artifacts formed the basis of many natural history museums still operating today.

In the early 20th century, anthropology became a professional academic discipline in American colleges and universities. Franz Boas, a professor at Columbia University, was considered the father of the field. Boas questioned the idea, then popular among other anthropological thinkers, that one race or culture was superior to any other. In a speech called "Human Faculty as Determined By Race," delivered to the American Association for the Advancement of Science in 1894, Boas said "...historical events appear to have been much more potent in leading races to civilization" than their natural abilities, or "faculties," and that therefore "it follows that achievements of races do not warrant us to assume that one race is more highly gifted than the other." Boas and his followers, Ruth Benedict, Alfred Kroeber, and Margaret Mead, encouraged anthropologists to live with their subjects, immerse themselves in the study of other cultures, and write scientifically scrupulous studies, known as "ethnographies," of individual societies.

Anthropological studies include the subfields of physical anthropology, cultural anthropology, archaeology, and linguistics. Anthropology continues to evolve, periodically reexamining its theories and embracing new subjects and research techniques.

SEE ALSO

Colleges and universities; Race relations; Social sciences

FURTHER READING

Benedict, Ruth. *Patterns of Culture.* 1934. Reprint, Boston: Houghton Mifflin, 1989.
Boas, Franz. *A Franz Boas Reader: The Shaping of American Anthropology, 1883–1911.* Edited by George W. Stocking, Jr. Chicago: University of Chicago Press, 1974.
Cole, Douglas. *Franz Boas: The Early Years, 1858–1906.* Seattle: University of Washington Press, 1999.
Monaghan, John, and Peter Just. *Social and Cultural Anthropology: A Very Short Introduction.* New York: Oxford University Press, 2000.

Anti-Saloon League

FOUNDED IN 1893, the Anti-Saloon League (ASL) had a single purpose: to win the passage of laws that would prohibit the manufacture, sale, and consumption of intoxicating beverages. The league argued that saloons, the establishments that sold beer and distilled liquors, encouraged working men to spend their earnings on drink instead of supporting their families. The ASL worked closely with Protestant churches to convince voters to approve "local option laws," which allowed towns, cities, counties, and eventually entire states to vote themselves "dry."

On its 20th anniversary in 1913, the ASL launched a campaign to achieve national prohibition through a constitutional amendment. To accomplish this goal, it raised money, which it received mostly in small donations, to help elect congressmen who favored prohibition. By 1916 the ASL had achieved the election of the two-thirds majorities necessary in both houses of Congress to begin the process of passing the 18th Amendment to the Constitution of the United States, which occurred in 1917. The 21st Amendment, adopted on December 21, 1933, repealed the 18th Amendment.

Daddy's in There---

And Our Shoes and Stockings and Clothes and Food Are in There, Too, and They'll Never Come Out.
—*Chicago American.*

An Anti-Saloon League broadside shows two ragged children outside a saloon where their father is spending the family's money. Pro-family, anti-liquor propaganda was central to the League's crusade to ban alcohol.

SEE ALSO

18th Amendment; Temperance and prohibition movements

FURTHER READING

Kerr, K. Austin. *Organized for Prohibition: A New History of the Anti-Saloon League.* New Haven, Conn.: Yale University Press, 1985.
Odegard, Peter H. *Pressure Politics: The Story of the Anti-Saloon League.* New York: Octagon Books, 1966.

Antitrust laws

STATE AND FEDERAL governments began to pass antitrust laws beginning in the late 1880s in order to regulate large corporate combinations called "trusts." A trust is a legal device for managing property in the interest of someone else. In the early 1880s, Standard Oil of Ohio used the trust to bring about a corporate merger, convincing 40 competitors to turn over their own companies' assets to a board of nine trustees. The board then managed all of the companies as a single unit and delivered shares (called "dividends") of the trust's profits to all participants. In this way, Standard Oil controlled 90 percent of the oil-refining capacity of the country.

Since U.S. law regarded other types of corporate mergers, such as "pools" and "cartels," as "conspiracies" that undercut free trade and competition, the trust appealed to companies looking for legal ways to protect profits against competition. Soon, the railroads and many other important industries formed trusts similar to Standard Oil's. Farm and small-business groups became alarmed. How could they possibly compete against such powerful corporate giants?

Legal action against trusts began at state levels. Between 1888 and 1890, some 15 states passed laws allowing officials to break up "combinations in restraint of trade." Congress also took action and in 1890 almost unanimously passed the Sherman Antitrust Act. This act declared illegal "every contract, combination in the form of trust or otherwise, or conspiracy, in restraint of trade or commerce among the several states, or with foreign nations."

The Sherman Act proved hard to enforce, however. Not only was its language vague ("restraint" was only one of the terms that the act did not define), but it did not set up an administrative body to enforce its provisions. Corporate mergers simply continued under new forms, such as the "holding company," which was a company that "held" the stock of other companies in order to act in their behalf.

President Theodore Roosevelt used the Sherman Act to prosecute several important antitrust cases. Most notably, in 1904 he used it to break up Northern Securities, a railroad "holding company" formed to eliminate competition among northern and northwestern railroads. An Antitrust Division in the Justice Department and a Bureau of Corporations that investigated and prosecuted antitrust cases assisted Roosevelt in his prosecutions, as they did his successor, William Howard Taft.

By the 1910s, many economists were arguing that large corporations helped the nation maintain its competitive edge. Antitrust "fever" subsided but remained a major topic of debate. During the election campaign of 1912, candidates from each of the political parties offered competing versions of how much government should regulate trusts. In 1914 Congress passed the

The fat king in this 1902 cartoon represents trusts, enormous business combinations that made their owners and shareholders rich while making it almost impossible for smaller business owners to compete. Uncle Sam and his searchlight stand for Congressional action to curb the power of trusts.

Clayton Antitrust and Federal Trade Commission acts. The first exempted labor and farm organizations from prosecution under antitrust laws and the second strengthened the government's role in antitrust actions. As President Woodrow Wilson's administration developed partnerships with big business during the period of preparation for entering World War I, however, the number of antitrust prosecutions declined. By war's end, government had relied so heavily on corporate giants to contribute to the nation's war effort and economy that few theorists continued to support vigorous antitrust enforcement. Antitrust debates revived during the Great Depression of the 1930s.

SEE ALSO

Industry; Regulation; Roosevelt, Theodore; Taft, William Howard; Wilson, Woodrow T.

FURTHER READING

Dewey, Donald J. *The Antitrust Experiment in America.* New York: Columbia University Press, 1990.
Fligstein, Neil. *The Transformation of Corporate Control.* Cambridge, Mass.: Harvard University Press, 1990.
Himmelberg, Robert F., ed. *The Monopoly Issue and Antitrust, 1900–1917.* New York: Garland, 1994.

Architecture

IN THE GILDED AGE, the expansion of city populations created a need for large public buildings. Municipalities, corporations, and even individuals therefore began to commission educational institutions, churches, railroad stations, libraries, museums, concert halls, office buildings, and department stores, among other structures. In designing these buildings, American architects drew inspiration primarily from selectively chosen historical sources. In the 1870s and 1880s, they looked to medieval times for ideas, incorporating Gothic towers and massive stonework and arches inspired by late Roman times. In the 1890s they favored more "classical" forms, such as the columns and domes of ancient Greece and Rome. By that time, the British Arts and Crafts Movement had begun to influence architects who specialized in smaller structures, such as private homes. The movement promoted greater simplicity of design and the employment of skilled craftsmen who worked in natural materials. By the early 1900s, "modern" architects were developing even more innovative styles, incorporating sleeker, more geometric lines in their designs.

Henry Hobson Richardson was the chief proponent of medieval and Romanesque architectural forms in public buildings. "Richardsonian Romanesque," as his style came to be called, combined textured stone, broad arches, and dramatic towers, all brought together into an organic whole. Trinity Church in Boston and New York State's capitol building in Albany are among the most famous of Richardson's buildings still standing. Critics believed that Richardson's combination of medieval and Romanesque architectural forms created a distinctive "American" style in public architecture.

Richardson inspired many other Gilded Age architects, especially Louis Sullivan and Frank Lloyd Wright. Sullivan, an architect based in Chicago, was best known for his work on skyscrapers, a new phenomenon on the American urban landscape. Architects had been designing towers for centuries, but to support the towers' weight they had to build thick foundations and restrict the number of

31

windows in the walls or risk making the walls weak. In the 1880s, civil engineer William LeBaron Jenney employed iron, and later steel, vertical columns and horizontal beams to support higher walls. These supports permitted thinner walls and multiple windows. Thanks to Jenney's innovations, the nation's first 10-story office building, the Home Insurance Building (now demolished), went up in Chicago in 1885.

Louis Sullivan worked in Jenney's office. His first and best-known work was Chicago's Auditorium Building (1886–89), a complex structure that combined a theater, hotel, and office building (now part of Roosevelt University). Sullivan envisioned tall structures that would be "proud" and "soaring." He ornamented St. Louis's Wainwright Building (1891) and Buffalo's Guaranty Building (1896) with terra-cotta facades embellished with organic or geometric designs. Inside he featured marble mosaics, a stained-glass lobby skylight, and intricate cast-iron stairways. Frank Lloyd Wright began his career in Sullivan's office.

Boston's Trinity Church is one of the architectural masterpieces of the Gilded Age. Designed by Henry Hobson Richardson, it is in the Romanesque style, characterized by rounded arches, cupolas, and the combined use of stone, brick, and terra cotta.

Even though he eventually broke with Sullivan, Wright called him "lieber meister," or "dear master," thus acknowledging Sullivan as his most important mentor.

Because most late-19th-century Americans interested in architecture studied at the Ecole des Beaux-Arts (School of Fine Arts) in Paris, where classical forms found favor, "neoclassical" (or "new" classical) ideas dominated public building styles around the turn of the 20th century. The style of buildings constructed for the 1893 Chicago World's Columbian Exposition overwhelmingly favored classical forms, and had a tremendous impact upon popular taste. Some critics blame the exposition, which attracted 28 million visitors, for making many American architects reluctant to experiment with more imaginative forms in the decades that followed.

Two of H. H. Richardson's assistants, Charles Follen McKim and Stanford White, along with their colleague William Rutherford Mead, furthered neoclassicism. In 1879, the three formed one of the most successful architectural firms in the country, McKim, Mead, and White. Among their more important constructions were Columbia University's Low Library (1898), inspired by the Pantheon in Rome, and New York City's Pennsylvania Railroad Station (1910, now demolished), modeled partly on the Roman Baths of Caracalla. Among their other large buildings are the Boston Public Library, the Rhode Island Statehouse, and the Brooklyn Museum of Art. McKim and White also specialized in designing many country mansions for Gilded Age elites.

Beginning in the 1880s, designers of American homes looked to the British Arts and Crafts Movement for new ideas. Promoted by British writers and art critics, including William Morris, John Ruskin, and Oscar Wilde, the movement rejected the cluttered and ornate style of Victorian homes and the mass-produced goods of the industrial age. These critics argued for greater simplicity in overall design, organic decorations, and the employment of skilled craftsmen who worked in wood, clay, and fieldstone. Oscar Wilde's lecture, "The House Beautiful," delivered to American audiences in 1882, sums up this advice. "Have nothing in your houses that is not useful or beautiful," he commanded. "Let there be no sham imitations of one material in another, such as paper representing marble, or wood painted to resemble stone, and have no machine-made ornaments." American architects designed homes in this spirit, offering houses modeled after Swiss chalets or English cottages for the more well-to-do and bungalows for the middle classes. The bungalow design came from India, where Europeans adapted local styles to create homes for themselves. Appearing in the United States first in California in the early 1900s, bungalows spread rapidly throughout the South and Midwest. They were usually one to one and a half stories, with fieldstone foundations and chimneys, wide front porches, and gabled roofs. Bungalows became so popular that in 1908 the Sears Roebuck Company began to sell bungalow building plans through its mail-order catalog.

Inspired in part by the Arts and Crafts Movement, Frank Lloyd Wright set American domestic architecture upon a new course. He approached each project with an eye to harmonizing a home's interior, its external setting, and its owners' lifestyle. Rather than imitating classical or medieval forms, he looked to the American landscape, especially the Midwestern prairie. His "prairie" houses featured horizontal lines, geometric shapes, and natural materials, such as wood and stone.

Because American architects of this period drew from many different sources, art historians often call them "eclectic," which means that they incorporated many different styles into their final structures. Eventually, modernism replaced eclecticism. Still, the remaining great structures of the Gilded Age and Progressive Era continue to impress us with their massive solidity and ornate designs.

SEE ALSO

Cities; Decorative arts; Fine arts; Wright, Frank Lloyd

FURTHER READING

Duchscherer, Paul. *The Bungalow: America's Arts and Crafts Home.* New York: Penguin Studio, 1995.
Kidney, Walter C. *The Architecture of Choice: Eclecticism in America, 1880–1930.* New York: G. Braziller, 1974.
O'Gorman, James F. *Three American Architects: Richardson, Sullivan, and Wright, 1865–1915.* Chicago: University of Chicago Press, 1991.
Platt, Frederick. *America's Gilded Age: Its Architecture and Decoration.* South Brunswick, N.J.: A. S. Barnes, 1976.
White, Samuel G. *The Houses of McKim, Mead & White.* New York: Rizzoli, 1998.

Arthur, Chester A.

- *Born: Oct. 5, 1829, Fairfield, Vt.*
- *Education: Union College, B.A., 1848*
- *Accomplishments: New York State quartermaster general (1861–65); collector, port of New York (1871–78); Vice President of the United States (1881); President of the United States (1881–85)*
- *Died: Nov. 18, 1886, New York, N. Y.*

CHESTER ALAN ARTHUR, 21st President of the United States, took office in 1881 upon the death of President James Garfield, who was assassinated just a few months into his term. In his pre-Presidential career, Arthur had been a state official who owed his appointments to a notoriously corrupt New York political machine. Many people therefore expected that his administration would be riddled with graft, but he won the respect of his detractors and angered his old cronies by using his new authority to champion civil service reform.

Arthur was the son of an Irish immigrant Baptist minister and a New England schoolteacher. After graduating from college he worked as a teacher and school principal before passing the bar and establishing a law practice in New York City. An opponent of slavery, he worked on Fugitive Slave Law cases and helped desegregate New York streetcars.

As a reward for helping to elect a Republican to the New York governorship in 1860, Arthur received appointment as state engineer-in-chief. During the Civil War, he served as New York's quartermaster general, running the office that supplied the state's troops. After the war, Senator Roscoe Conkling, a powerful New York political boss, arranged for President Ulysses Grant to appoint Arthur as collector of the Port of New York, a key patronage position in the "spoils system" under which government jobs were handed out as political favors. As collector, Arthur had nearly 1,000 jobs to distribute and controlled the highest volume of U.S. customs income in the country.

Arthur came to national attention in 1877 and 1878 when reform-minded President Rutherford B. Hayes fought a drawn-out political battle with Conkling over the patronage issue. The President fired Arthur from his government job, and the affair ended with a residue of hostility between factions within the Republican party. At

the party's 1880 convention, Arthur started out in Conkling's camp as a supporter of Grant. But after more than 30 ballots and six days of wrangling, he agreed to join a compromise ticket as Vice Presidential running mate to Ohio Congressman James A. Garfield.

The Garfield-Arthur ticket won the election, but Garfield was assassinated soon after taking office. Arthur, sworn in as President, continued Garfield's push to eliminate civil service corruption, thereby turning his back on the patronage system on which he had built his own political career. He continued to prosecute officials receiving kickbacks from private contractors who did business with the government and sided with reformers pressing for a merit system in the civil service. In 1883, he signed the Pendleton Act, which instituted a non-partisan, merit-based federal civil service system.

Like President Hayes before him, Arthur disagreed with Congress over a bill to exclude Chinese immigrant laborers. Arthur argued that the bill violated U.S. treaties with China, but Congress passed it over his veto in 1882. When Arthur attempted to cut tariffs, arguing that the surplus in the U.S. treasury was keeping money out of circulation and causing prices to fall, he failed to overcome Congressional resistance.

Arthur was a widower when elected to office, and his sister served as his White House hostess. Charming and handsome, Arthur loved good company, lengthy dinner parties, and elegant surroundings. He had the White House redecorated and installed its first elevator.

In 1884 Arthur lost the Republican Presidential nomination to former Congressman James Blaine. Blaine

Chester A. Arthur succeeded to the presidency in 1881 after the assassination of James A. Garfield. Arthur served honorably and fulfilled Garfield's promise to initiate civil service reform for government jobs.

then lost the general election to Democrat Grover Cleveland, putting an end to 24 years of a Republican White House. Already suffering from kidney disease, Chester Arthur retired to New York and died two years later. Looking back on Arthur's career in the early 20th century, one journalist noted: "No man ever entered the Presidency so profoundly and widely distrusted, and no one ever retired…more generally respected."

SEE ALSO

Chinese Exclusion Act (1882); Garfield, James A.; Hayes, Rutherford B.; Presidency

FURTHER READING

Karabell, Zachary. *Chester Alan Arthur.* New York: Times Books, 2004.
Reeves, Thomas C. *Gentleman Boss: The Life of Chester Alan Arthur.* New York: Knopf, 1975.

Asian Americans

AMERICANS OF ASIAN origin who came to the United States during the Gilded Age and Progressive Era were primarily Chinese, Japanese, Korean, and Filipino. South Asians (from India) and Southeast Asians came to the United States in very small numbers during this period. Because their homelands were at that time part of the British or French empires, they tended to migrate to countries in other parts of those empires.

For the most part, the new Asian immigrants to the United States performed manual labor or became involved in the service economy, working in restaurants or laundries, or in merchandising and trade in the western states. Despite their many contributions to the U.S. economy, they all encountered immigration restrictions,

legal roadblocks, and racial prejudice. These conditions prevented their social acceptance and integration until the mid-20th century.

The first Asians to arrive in any great numbers in North America were the Chinese, who began coming to the United States during the California gold rush in 1849. These immigrants were "sojourners" who planned to make enough money to return to China and live comfortably in their native provinces. Chinese men came alone, or with fathers, sons, brothers, cousins, and other males from their villages. They left wives, mothers, and daughters behind. For half a century, Chinese American society remained a bachelor society, seriously undermining the tradition of the strong Chinese family and leading to the importation and exploitation of Chinese prostitutes.

Many Chinese ended up staying in the United States for years, and some remained permanently, working first in mining, fishing, and agriculture and, after the Civil War, building the country's transcontinental railroads. Their labor laid the foundation for the growth of the West. Hundreds of Chinese entrepreneurs operated farms in California, where they made important contributions to the development of agriculture. Chinese immigrants also found a niche providing goods and services in the rapidly growing cities of the far West, performing domestic service and running laundries, dry goods shops, restaurants, and grocery stores. Initially welcomed as workers, by the 1870s and 1880s Chinese men were encountering vicious bigotry and physical attack from white laborers who feared losing jobs to lower-paid Chinese workers. They also met with hostility from nativists, Americans of European ancestry who felt that the

A Chinese woman and her children pose for this formal photograph in Hawaii in 1913. Hawaii, a U.S. possession, was a destination for some Asians or a stopover for others headed to the continental United States.

Chinese were so different from them in looks, customs, religion, and behavior that they could never be assimilated into American life. Forced into enclaves apart from white society, the Chinese developed Chinatowns in San Francisco, Los Angeles, Seattle, and other large cities. The "Six Companies," a powerful mercantile elite officially called the Chinese Consolidated Benevolent Association, emerged to run the Chinatowns. This organization functioned as social arbiter and welfare agent for the Chinese community and also acted as a liaison with the white establishment.

Laws passed as early as the 1850s determined that nonwhite immigrants could not become naturalized U.S. citizens. A series of Chinese Exclusion Acts (passed in 1882, 1892, 1902, and later), followed by quota acts in the 1920s, ended almost all Chinese immigration, essentially isolating a remnant Chinese community with very few women and families. The Chinese population in the United States did not begin to recover from decline and gender imbalance until the late 1920s.

The Japanese population in the United States was minute until after 1884, when the Japanese government finally allowed a certain number of skilled male agricultural laborers to leave Japan for work on Hawaiian sugar plantations. From Hawaii, some Japanese immigrants continued on to the United States mainland. Their numbers reached about 2,000 by 1890, almost all concentrated on the West Coast.

Partly because Japanese workers were supplying labor that had become scarce when the Chinese were excluded, the Japanese maintained a steady rate of immigration until 1907–8, when agitation from nativist organizations, labor unions, and politicians resulted in the "Gentlemen's Agreement" between the United States and Japan. The agreement effectively stopped further immigration of laborers, but it permitted wives and children of laborers to continue to enter the country. This practice helped to end the gender imbalance in Japanese America. Up until 1924, when a new Immigration Act excluded almost all Asians, a large number of Japanese women immigrated as "picture brides," agreeing to marry Japanese men already in the United States after an exchange of photographs. Picture bride marriages were a variation of the arranged marriages common throughout Japanese society.

Some Japanese of the immigrant generation—the *Issei*—lived in large West Coast cities and towns, where they ran businesses such as boardinghouses, barbershops, restaurants, and gambling establishments, mostly catering to Japanese itinerant laborers. Agriculture, however, was the main attraction that drew Japanese immigrants to rural areas on the West Coast. Japanese laborers became an indispensable part of the region's agriculture and fishing industries, and, early in the 20th century, they began to own and operate their own farms, vineyards, and orchards. In order to own real estate, they had to circumvent California's 1913 Alien Land Law, which barred all Asian immigrants from owning land. Their strategies included registering their property in the names of friendly European Americans, or in the names of their own U.S.-born children. Japanese producers organized agricultural enterprises and their offshoots—packing, shipping, and retailing—vertically along ethnic lines, thereby controlling all operations from seed to sales. Japanese agricultural organizations and cooperatives had a significant share of the West Coast agricultural market up to the start of World War II in 1939.

A number of rural towns witnessed the development of *nihonmachi,* Japanese sections of town, with small businesses and Buddhist and Japanese Christian churches serving the needs of immigrants and their families in the surrounding area. In time, these communities founded Japanese newspapers and Japanese-language schools for their American-born children, the *Nisei* generation. Central California eventually had a few all-Japanese communities.

Koreans began coming to the United States, especially to Hawaiian plantations and California farms, around the turn of the century. Even though many Koreans were Christian, they met with the same hostility as Chinese and Japanese immigrants. Their numerical presence in the United States was small, as was that of Asian Indians, until after World War II.

The only other large group of immigrant Asians during this era came from the Philippines, which the United States annexed after the Spanish-American War in 1898. Annexation meant that Filipinos were U.S. nationals and could enter the country as they pleased. Like members of all the other Asian groups, however, they could not become citizens and were subject to antimiscegenation laws, which meant that they were not allowed to intermarry with European Americans.

Because the Philippines had been under Spanish control for 300 years, Filipino immigrants to the United States were Catholic and spoke Spanish in addition to indigenous languages such as Tagalog. The first arrivals were students. Starting in 1906, Hawaiian plantations began recruiting Filipino farm workers between the ages of 15 and 30, paying them very low wages for hard labor in relentless heat, and using them to undercut the higher wages of Japanese workers. Unless they were farm workers, Filipino immigrants to the U.S. mainland tended to perform service work in urban locations. *Pinoys,* as they were called, became busboys, waiters, janitors, and kitchen staff.

Everywhere Filipinos went they met racial hostility and threats of violence from whites. Writing an essay for an Americanization class, one Filipino worker said, "I have been four years in America..., and I am still a stranger. It is not because I want to be. I have tried to be as 'American' as possible. I live like an American, eat like American, and dress the same, and yet everywhere I find Americans who remind me of the fact that I am a stranger."

Some Filipino men built successful lives in the United States and even married white women, despite the antimiscegenation laws. However, like Japanese and Chinese immigrants they were not permitted to purchase American land or real estate. It was not until the 1940s, with Philippine independence at the end of World War II, that Filipinos, no longer mere "nationals," were allowed to immigrate and apply for U.S. citizenship.

37

By the late 20th century, Chinese, Japanese, Korean, and Filipino immigrants and their families had been in the United States for generations, making homes and pursuing occupations in all parts of the country. After new immigration laws were passed in 1965, the United States opened its doors to immigrants from Vietnam and other parts of Southeast Asia, initiating a second wave of Asian immigration about a century after the first.

SEE ALSO

Agriculture; Chinese Exclusion Act (1882); Civil rights; Gentlemen's Agreement; Immigration; International relations; Labor; Mining; Nativism; Race relations; Railroads; Spanish-American War; West, the

FURTHER READING

Chan, Sucheng. *Asian Americans: An Interpretive History.* Boston: Twayne, 1991.
Daniels, Roger. *Asian America: Chinese and Japanese in the United States since 1850.* Seattle: University of Washington Press, 1988.
Franks, Joel. *Asian Pacific Americans and the U.S.* New York: McGraw-Hill, 1996.
Takaki, Ronald: *Strangers from a Different Shore: A History of Asian Americans.* Boston: Little, Brown, 1989.
Zia, Helen: *Asian American Dreams: The Emergence of an American People.* New York: Farrar, Straus & Giroux, 2000.

Automobile

NO SINGLE PERSON invented the automobile. It evolved from the work of many individuals who, for decades, had tried to create fuel-driven vehicles. They wanted a vehicle that did not have to rely on either rails, which limited where they could go, or on steam engines, which were too heavy and took up too much space.

The earliest advances in automobile production occurred in Europe. These included the development, pri-

In 1907, *when this picture appeared on the cover of* Collier's *magazine, the automobile was a novelty. Automobiles were still the toys of the rich, and not the preferred mode of transportation they quickly became.*

marily by German engineers, of a successful internal combustion engine (mid-1870s), a carburetor (mid-1880s), and lightweight chassis designs (1890s). These advances inspired American inventors, including Charles and Frank Duryea. Bicycle mechanics from Springfield, Massachusetts, the Duryeas built their first working automobile in 1893 out of a carriage driven by a one-cylinder gasoline engine. Mechanic Henry Ford built his first car in 1896.

The only people who owned these early cars were wealthy men who regarded them as amusing toys rather than as serious transportation. By the 1910s, Ford was working to reduce his manufacturing costs by developing more efficient mass-production methods. Having reached this goal in 1914, he cut the price of his automobiles by half, thereby making them much more affordable.

Even though mass ownership of automobiles did not arrive until the 1920s, by the late 1910s cars had already changed many aspects of American life. They helped reduce rural isolation and gave adolescents more privacy for courting. They stimulated the economy by encouraging the consumption of rubber, gasoline, and petroleum and by spurring the advertising and tourist industries. As an increasing number of Americans used cars to take vacations and run errands, government at all levels began to funnel taxes into new road systems, parks, and beaches. Cars also had some distinctly negative effects. They introduced traffic jams, smog, and rising rates of road fatalities. They also led to the decline in public transit systems and to the increase in the use of fossil fuels.

SEE ALSO

Ford, Henry; Inventions; Science and technology

FURTHER READING

Ling, Peter J. *America and the Automobile: Technology, Reform and Social Change, 1893–1923.* New York: Manchester University Press, 1990.
May, George S., ed. *The Automobile Industry, 1896–1920.* New York: Facts on File, 1990.
Rae, John Bell. *The American Automobile: A Brief History.* Boston: Twayne, 1984.

Bell, Alexander Graham

- *Born: Mar. 3, 1847, Edinburgh, Scotland*
- *Education: studied vocal anatomy at University College (London), 1868–70*
- *Accomplishments: inventor of the telephone; founder, Bell Telephone Company (1877); cofounder (1888) and president (1898), National Geographic Society; elected regent of the Smithsonian Institution, 1898*
- *Died: Aug. 2, 1922, Baddeck, Nova Scotia, Canada*

ALEXANDER GRAHAM BELL, inventor of the telephone, was the son of a hearing-impaired mother and a father who developed a widely used

Alexander Graham Bell listens through headphones to a radiophone, a device that transmits speech via radio waves.

system for teaching deaf people to speak. Inheriting a family interest in the scientific study of speech, Bell grew up to achieve one of the most momentous technological breakthroughs of the Gilded Age, an invention that enabled people to transmit their voices by wire across long distances.

Bell moved from Scotland to Canada in 1870, and a year later to the United States, where he soon became a citizen. He taught at a Boston school for the deaf and took a position as a professor at Boston University.

His invention of the telephone grew out of his research on improved telegraph communication. The original telegraph, invented by Samuel F. B. Morse, could transmit only one message at a time. Bell and his assistant, Thomas Watson, developed an upgraded version that could send multiple messages simultaneously over one wire. The success of this device convinced Bell that he could find a way to convert the vibrations of the human voice into electrical signals that would travel along a wire and emerge as recognizable speech sounds at the other end.

Legend has it that the first telephone connection was established between rooms in Bell's laboratory when he and Watson were testing their device. According to the story, Bell spilled battery acid on himself and exclaimed,

"Mr. Watson, come here, I want you," a sentence that his assistant heard clearly through the wire. Whether or not the incident actually occurred, millions of other words were soon coursing through telephone wires in the United States and around the world. Bell received a patent for the telephone in 1876 and founded the Bell Telephone Company (later AT&T) the following year.

Bell continued experimenting and inventing throughout his life. He made advances in aviation technology and high-speed water transportation, created a precursor to the iron lung, and invented a method of transmitting speech on a beam of light. He also invented a prototype wax recording cylinder and the metal detector. Bell made contributions in phonetics, acoustics, the education of the deaf, architectural engineering, and genetics. But of all his accomplishments, the telephone remained most closely associated with his name. When he died in 1922, phones all over North America observed a minute of silence in honor of his revolutionary contribution to human communication.

SEE ALSO
Inventions; Science and technology

FURTHER READING
Grosvener, Edwin S., and Morgan Wesson. *Alexander Graham Bell: The Life and Times of the Man Who Invented the Telephone.* New York: Abrams, 1997.
MacKay, James A. *Alexander Graham Bell: A Life.* New York: John Wiley & Sons, 1998.
Pasachoff, Naomi. *Alexander Graham Bell: Making Connections.* New York: Oxford University Press, 1996.

Bellamy, Edward

- *Born: Mar. 26, 1850, Chicopee Falls, Mass.*
- *Education: some study at Union College (Schenectady, N.Y.), some study of law*
- *Accomplishments: founder, Springfield (Mass.) Daily News (1880); author, Looking Backward, 2000–1887 (1888)*
- *Died: May 22, 1898, Chicopee Falls, Mass.*

EDWARD BELLAMY trained as a lawyer but chose a writing career instead. In response to the economic troubles and labor violence of the 1870s and 1880s, he wrote a wildly popular "science fiction" novel called *Looking Backward, 2000–1887*. It told the story of a man who fell asleep in 1887 and awoke in the year 2000 to a completely different world. This was a world free of war, class distinctions, and other negative consequences of capitalist competition. A democratically elected government operated all industries and provided all citizens with equal incomes. A universal credit/debit card system replaced cash transactions. Closely allied with Christian Socialism, a political philosophy that emphasized profit sharing and communal cooperation over individual competition, Nationalism, as Bellamy's ideas came to be called, preached that a socialist economy could thrive and its citizens become prosperous without a totalitarian government or hostility to religion.

In response to the novel's ideas, Nationalist Clubs, sometimes called Bellamy Clubs, flourished all across the country in the late 1880s and early 1890s. Their members advocated a gradual transition, without violent revolution, from capitalism to socialism. They campaigned for federal takeover of the railroad, telegraph, and telephone industries and for the establishment of utility companies run by municipal governments. They also favored such reforms as the eight-hour workday, votes for women, racial equality, and the abolition of child

Edward Bellamy, a lawyer and author from Massachusetts, became a nationwide celebrity in 1888 with his novel Looking Backward, 2000–1887, *which depicted a utopian future free of war and economic inequality.*

labor. The movement lasted only a few years, but other reform groups continued to push for some of these policies. Baptist minister Francis Bellamy, the novelist's cousin and author of the Pledge of Allegiance, was a prominent Nationalist leader. Feminist author Charlotte Perkins Gilman lectured often at Nationalist Clubs.

Bellamy's movement faded by the mid-1890s. In 1897 he published *Equality,* a sequel to *Looking Backward,* in which he developed his ideas further, but the book had only limited success.

SEE ALSO

Gilman, Charlotte Perkins; Literature; Reform movements; Socialism

FURTHER READING

Bellamy, Edward. *Looking Backward, 2000–1887.* Edited by Daniel H. Borus. Boston: Bedford/St. Martin's, 1995.

Bowman, Sylvia. *Edward Bellamy.* Boston: Twayne, 1986.

Lipow, Arthur. *Authoritarian Socialism in the United States: Edward Bellamy and the Nationalist Movement.* Berkeley: University of California Press, 1982.

Bicycle

THE BICYCLE FIRST appeared in Europe in the 1860s. By the 1870s, a bicycle with a small back wheel and with pedals attached to a large front wheel had become popular in the United States. Nicknamed the "penny-farthing" because the wheels reminded people of the size of two British coins, the large penny and the small farthing, this bicycle offered little stability and was hard to ride.

The introduction in the 1880s of the "safety" bicycle launched the

beginning of a bicycle craze for Americans. The "safety" had two wheels of equal dimension, a seat mounted in the center, and a chain driving the rear wheel. This structure gave the bicycle more stability. A later addition of pneumatic rubber tires made the ride more comfortable. In 1885, Lucius D. Copeland mounted a steam engine to a "reversed ordinary" or "farthing-penny" bicycle. This first attempt at a "motorcycle," which achieved a speed of 12 miles per hour, was not very practical, as one had to keep a fire lit behind the engine.

By the 1890s, mass production had reduced the price of a safety bicycle from $150 to about $85, about a month's wages for a middle-class American and still beyond the reach of workers. Historians estimate that in 1896, even in the midst of a great economic depression, more than 300 companies were producing bicycles and Americans were riding 3 million of them. Cyclists formed bicycle clubs, pressing local governments to pave and map more roads. Orville and Wilbur Wright, inventors of the airplane, got their start as bicycle mechanics.

Women found cycling liberating, as it provided them with both physical exercise and greater mobility. Because cycling required practical clothing, it changed women's fashions. To ride comfortably, women had to abandon corsets, which constricted their breathing, and bustles, which were too bulky. Women who cycled wore "shirtwaists" (ready-made blouses) tucked into "bloomers," or loose-fitting trousers gathered in at the knee. Although cycling made bloomers more socially acceptable, the sight of women riding bicycles remained controversial, as did bicycle riding in general. People on horseback complained about having to share the road with

A cyclist perches atop an 1891 penny-farthing, the first bicycle popular in the United States. The pedals turn the large front wheel, while the rear wheel provides stability.

"wheels," and pedestrians feared being run down. The bicycle craze persisted until an automobile craze replaced it in the early 1900s, but until then cycling gave Americans of modest means considerable mobility.

SEE ALSO
Fashions; Sports; Wright, Wilbur and Orville

FURTHER READING

Dodge, Pryor. *The Bicycle*. New York: Flammarion, 1996.
The Noblest Invention: An Illustrated History of the Bicycle. Emmaus, Pa.: Rodale, 2003.
Smith, Robert. *A Social History of the Bicycle.* New York: American Heritage Press, 1972.

Birth control movement

THE BIRTH CONTROL movement began in the early 20th century. Its purpose was to give women the possibility of controlling the spacing and number of their children. Before 1900, women had few reliable birth control methods available to them. Reliability increased when condoms made of vulcanized rubber became more widely available after 1843, and after diaphragms were introduced in 1860. Only the well-to-do could afford such devices, however. Nineteenth-century advocates for women's rights favored the idea that motherhood should be voluntary, but the only counsel they could offer most women anxious to avoid pregnancy was to deny sex to their husbands.

Around 1900, psychologists such as Sigmund Freud and Havelock Ellis began to argue that women's psychological lives would be improved if they enjoyed their sexuality. Influenced by their writings, early 20th-century feminists began to proclaim that women should not have to deny their sexuality in order to avoid pregnancy. In this period, however, contraceptive information was hard to come by. In 1873, the federal government had passed the Comstock Law, named after Anthony Comstock, a special agent for the U.S. post office, who had persuaded Congress to declare the sending of contraceptive information obscene and to outlaw its transmission through the mails. A birth control movement arose when feminists challenged this law.

Early leaders of the movement included the anarchist Emma Goldman, a trained nurse and midwife, who in fiery speeches and writings contended that women should have as much sexual freedom as men. Margaret Sanger, also a trained nurse, coined the term *birth control*. She publicized contraceptive information in her periodical *The Woman Rebel* (1914), founded the National Birth Control League (1915), and opened the first birth control advice center in Brooklyn, New York (1916). After the police raided her center and charged her with having dispensed illegal information, Sanger endured a 30-day jail sentence.

Mary Ware Dennett, a suffragist, pacifist, and socialist, became interested in birth control when she could not find sex education materials for her sons. She reorganized Sanger's league to focus it on educating the public about contraception and lobbying for the repeal of the Comstock Law. In 1918 Dennett became director of the Voluntary Parenthood League, a post she held until 1925, when the group voted to adopt Sanger's strategy of using the medical community to help legalize access to birth control.

Sanger's strategy came out of a loophole in the Comstock Law that allowed physicians to prescribe contraception to women for medical reasons. In 1921, Sanger established the American Birth Control League to publicize the need for birth control and to win the support of physicians and social workers. This approach worked well for Sanger. Not only physicians but also middle- and upper-class women flocked to her cause. In 1923, now the undisputed leader of the birth control campaign, Sanger founded the Birth Control Clinical Research Bureau, a doctor-run clinic that collected data on the effectiveness of contraceptives.

The obscenity classification of birth control information ended in 1936. At that point, birth controllers across the country founded hundreds of clinics modeled on Sanger's Research Bureau. The American Birth Control League and the Birth Control Clinical Research Bureau merged in

MOTHERS!
Can you afford to have a large family?
Do you want any more children?
If not, why do you have them?
DO NOT KILL, DO NOT TAKE LIFE, BUT PREVENT
Safe, Harmless Information can be obtained of trained Nurses at
46 AMBOY STREET
NEAR PITKIN AVE. — BROOKLYN.
Tell Your Friends and Neighbors. All Mothers Welcome
A registration fee of 10 cents entitles any mother to this information.

A 1916 circular in English, Yiddish, and Italian invites New York City women to the nation's first birth control clinic. When the clinic opened in a neighborhood housing immigrants and poor working families, women lined up around the block to learn how to limit the size of their families.

1939 into the Birth Control Federation of America, which was later renamed the Planned Parenthood Federation of America. Major religious groups, especially Roman Catholics, continued to oppose birth control, arguing that God's chief purpose for sexual intercourse was to create children. In addition, many states restricted access to birth control information, even for husbands and wives. Finally, as a result of the Supreme Court case of *Griswold* v. *Connecticut* in 1965, contraception for married couples was made legal.

SEE ALSO

Comstock Law (1873); Goldman, Emma; Reform movements; Sanger, Margaret Higgins; Sex education movement; Sexuality; Women's rights movement

FURTHER READING

Gordon, Linda. *Woman's Body, Woman's Right: A Social History of Birth Control in America.* Rev. ed. New York: Penguin, 1990.
Reed, James. *From Private Vice to Public Virtue: The Birth Control Movement and American Society since 1830.* New York: Basic Books, 1978.

Blaine, James Gillespie

- *Born: Jan. 31, 1830, West Brownsville, Pa.*
- *Education: Washington and Jefferson College, B.A., 1847*
- *Accomplishments: Maine House of Representatives (1859–62); U.S. House of Representatives (Republican–Maine, 1863–76; Speaker, 1869–75); U.S. Senate (Republican–Maine, 1876–81); U.S. secretary of state (1881; 1889–92); Republican nominee for President, 1884; author, Twenty Years of Congress (1884–86)*
- *Died: Jan. 27, 1893, Washington, D.C.*

ONE OF THE GILDED AGE'S most charismatic and powerful politicians, Republican party leader James G.

Blaine studied law while working as a teacher in Kentucky. In 1850, after marrying Harriet Stanwood, he moved to her home state of Maine, where through her connections he landed a job as editor of a weekly newspaper. Later, as manager of the *Portland Advertiser,* he turned that newspaper into an organ of the young Republican party and entered politics himself.

Blaine won a seat in the state legislature, where his skill in debate and oratory led to his becoming Speaker of the Maine House of Representatives. He also became chair of the Republican State Committee, a post he held until 1881. Election to Congress came during the Civil War. As Speaker of the U.S. House of Representatives during his last three terms, Blaine worked to convince his political colleagues to cease dwelling on Civil War legacies and instead to consider the economic and organizational changes necessary for advancing the nation's interests. He helped formulate the 14th Amendment to the U.S. Constitution, opposed military governments for the rebellious southern states, and argued against the payment of the public debt in "greenbacks," or paper money. A staunch advocate of the separation of church and state, he proposed a constitutional amendment prohibiting the use of public funds for any religious purpose. Although the amendment failed, a majority of states adopted laws nicknamed "Blaine amendments," which mirrored its intent.

By any measure a successful Gilded Age politician, Blaine never achieved the political goal he desired most, the Presidency. He sought the nomination first in 1876, but fell victim to allegations of shady financial dealings. His opponents charged that he had helped the Little Rock and Fort Smith Railroad secure a land grant and then profited

from the later sale of the railroad's land. Blaine pleaded innocent, dramatically reading incriminating letters on the House floor and claiming he had actually lost money in the affair. Even so, the reform wing of his party refused him their support.

Blaine received an appointment to fill out the unexpired term of Maine's U.S. Senator Lot M. Merrill and then ran successfully for the seat in his own right. He later left the Senate to serve as secretary of state for three presidents (James Garfield, Chester Arthur, and Benjamin Harrison). In this role, Blaine pursued reciprocal trade agreements with Korea and Latin America. His championing of international economic cooperation among the states of the Western Hemisphere laid the groundwork for the later founding of the Pan American Union (1910). Blaine also fostered American imperialist ambitions by supporting the annexation of Hawaii, an event that took place after his death.

A man of great charm, wit, and dynamism, Blaine had few friends but many admirers. In speeches they called him colorful names, such as the "Plumed Knight" and the "Magnetic Man." He finally won his party's Presidential nomination in 1884, but his followers, whom some called "Blainiacs," could never repair the damage of his earlier

An 1884 poster promotes Maine Senator James Blaine and Illinois Senator John Logan, Republican candidates for President and Vice President. During the campaign, Blaine's arrogant attacks on Catholics and former Confederates lost him many supporters.

financial scandals. He lost the election narrowly to Grover Cleveland.

SEE ALSO

Cleveland, Grover; Garfield, James A.; Harrison, Benjamin; Imperialism; International relations; Monetary policies; Presidency; Taxes and tariffs

FURTHER READING

Crapol, Edward P. *James G. Blaine: Architect of Empire.* Wilmington, Del.: SR Books, 2000.
Muzzey, David Saville. *James G. Blaine, A Political Idol of Other Days.* New York: Dodd, Mead, 1934.

Boston police strike (1919)

ON SEPTEMBER 9, 1919, more than 1,100 Boston police officers walked off the job, striking against city officials who had refused to allow them to form a union affiliated with the American Federation of Labor. The police had substantial grievances about pay and working conditions. To them, a labor action seemed inevitable, despite the antiunion clause in their contracts. One of many strikes in the volatile years after World War I, the police walkout was the country's first major strike of public sector employees.

The immediate effect of the strike was social disorder. Boston underwent 48 hours of looting and rioting, followed by several days of violence, fatalities, injuries, and extensive property damage. The nation watched these events with horror. They feared that the strike was the beginning of a "Bolshevist" takeover of the government, as had recently happened in the Russian revolution of 1917. The Massachusetts governor, Calvin Coolidge, restored order by calling in the state guard and later replaced the striking policemen with young World War I veterans. Coolidge declared, "There is no right to strike against the public safety by anybody, anywhere, any time."

Breaking the strike gave Coolidge a national reputation and earned him the Vice Presidency in an era marked by a fear of radicalism.

SEE ALSO

American Federation of Labor; Labor unions; Strikes

FURTHER READING

Murray, Robert K. *Red Scare: A Study in National Hysteria, 1919–1920.* New York: McGraw-Hill, 1955.
Russell, Francis. *A City in Terror: Calvin Coolidge and the 1919 Boston Police Strike.* Boston: Beacon, 2005.

Boy and Girl Scouts

AMERICAN SCOUTING had its origins in a British program founded by Sir Robert Baden-Powell. While serving as an army officer in South Africa in the late 1890s, Baden-Powell became concerned about the inability of the young, over-civilized soldiers under his command to survive in the wild. After returning to England as a war hero, he discovered that leaders of boys' groups were using the wilderness survival manual, *Aids to Scouting,* which he had written for his soldiers. Asked to rewrite the manual for a nonmilitary audience, Baden-Powell gathered ideas from naturalists and then tested them out on a camping trip with a group of 22 boys. In 1908, his new manual, *Scouting for Boys,* became the basis for the first official boy scout organization.

The scouting movement spread around the world. In 1910 Chicago publisher William D. Boyce, impressed

Boy Scouts carrying an injured comrade on a stretcher display their knowledge of first aid and wilderness survival in this cover illustration for a 1915 piano piece.

by Baden-Powell's ideas, founded the Boy Scouts of America. Other American boys' groups, such as the Woodcraft Indians and the Sons of Daniel Boone, merged with Boyce's organization. Scout troops began meeting regularly all over the country, soon adding summer scout camps to their nationwide program. Using an incentive system of badges, pins, and ranks, they encouraged boys to learn survival skills, develop knowledge about the world, and become good citizens. Scouting's two mottoes—"Do a good turn daily" and "Be prepared"—reflect the basic ideas behind this character-building program.

Scouting appealed as much to girls as it did to boys. Baden-Powell had allowed girls to participate only in a separate movement called Girl Guides. This program emphasized wilderness survival as well as skills associated with keeping house. When Juliette Gordon Low, a wealthy widow from Savannah, Georgia, met Baden-Powell in 1911, she became convinced that scouting would be superb training for American girls. After experimenting with girls' troops, first on her estate in Scotland and then in Savannah, she founded the Girl Scouts of America in 1913. Her

program remains as popular today as that of the boys.

SEE ALSO

Childhood; Low, Juliette ("Daisy") Magill Kinzie Gordon

FURTHER READING

Baden-Powell, Robert. *Scouting for Boys: A Handbook for Instruction in Good Citizenship*. Edited by Elleke Boehmer. New York: Oxford University Press, 2004.

Low, Juliette Gordon. *How Girls Can Help Their Country, adapted from Agnes Baden-Powell and Sir Robert Baden-Powell's Handbook*. Savannah, Ga.: Press of M. S. & D. A. Byck Co., 1916.

Rosenthal, Michael. *The Character Factory: Baden-Powell and the Origins of the Boy Scout Movement*. New York: Pantheon, 1986.

Shultz, Gladys Denny, and Daisy Gordon Lawrence. *Lady From Savannah: The Life of Juliette Low*. New York: Girl Scouts of the U.S.A., 1988.

Seton, Ernest Thompson. *Boy Scouts of America; a Handbook of Woodcraft, Scouting, and Life-craft*. New York: Doubleday, Page, 1910.

Brandeis, Louis Dembitz

- *Nov. 13, 1856, Louisville, Ky.*
- *Education: Annen-Realschule, Dresden, Germany, 1873–75 (no degree); Harvard Law School, LL.B., 1877*
- *Accomplishments: author,* Other People's Money, and How the Bankers Use It *(1914); appointed Associate Justice, U.S. Supreme Court (1916–39)*
- *Died: Oct. 5, 1941, Washington, D.C.*

IN 1916, LOUIS BRANDEIS became the first Jewish justice on the U.S. Supreme Court. He began his distinguished career as a young lawyer in Boston. While he was the attorney for many small businessmen there, he also accepted nonpaying clients when he thought that representing them would serve the public. Working *pro bono publico* (for the public good), Brandeis helped to create inexpensive Savings

Louis Brandeis, appointed to the Supreme Court in 1916, was a champion of individual liberty. He described "the right to be let alone," that is, freedom from government harassment, as "the most comprehensive of rights and the right most valued by civilized men."

Bank Life Insurance for workers. These and other generous accomplishments earned him the name the "People's Attorney." Brandeis also served as a mediator in labor disputes, especially in the garment industry. Recognizing that unions were not strong enough to prevail over powerful industries, he favored limited government action to improve industrial working conditions.

An article Brandeis published with his law partner Samuel D. Warren in 1890 played an important role in establishing the idea that the law protects privacy. Courts later applied this concept to cases concerning individual civil liberties and freedom from government interference in one's private life. Brandeis was especially innovative in labor cases. In the Supreme Court case of *Muller* v. *Oregon,* which involved a state government's right to limit working hours for women, he developed a unique way of arguing in court. Rather than focus on legal precedents (earlier court decisions), he used social science researchers to collect economic and social facts to support his arguments. His brief in the case cited dozens of British and American medical reports proving that "there is material danger to the public health (or safety) or to the health (or safety) of the employees…if the hours of labor are not curtailed." The "Brandeis brief," as this method of case presentation came to be called, established the principle that social realities and expert opinion should guide legal decisions.

In 1912, presidential candidate Woodrow Wilson asked Brandeis to help formulate the economic policies he would propose to the American people. The result of their discussions was Wilson's "New Freedom," a progressive program that emphasized controlling big business not through more government regulation but by better enforcement of the rules of competition. This program included eliminating monopolies and trusts, which restricted business competition, and the creation of the Federal Reserve Act, which would regulate the supply of money, the operation of commercial banks, and the federal government's international finances. As a Progressive, Brandeis believed that these ideas were vital to achieving the nation's economic and social well-being.

In 1916, President Wilson nominated Brandeis to the Supreme Court. During his confirmation hearings in the Senate, Brandeis successfully overcame attacks against his social and economic policies. Those policies angered industrialists who wanted an even freer hand in running their businesses than he would allow.

Brandeis was a nonpracticing Jew, but his belief that the world's Jews needed a homeland in Palestine led him to play leadership roles in the American Zionist movement. On the court he continued to promote the idea of using sociological and statistical information in cases and to guard the rights of free speech and privacy. In a famous 1927 case about whether the law can prevent speech that incites people to violence (*Whitney* v. *People of State of California*), he agreed that it can but also defended free speech, saying, "Fear of serious injury alone cannot justify oppression of free speech and assembly. Men feared witches and burnt women. It is the function of speech to free men from the bondage of irrational fears."

After his death, educators named two important institutions for him: Brandeis University in Waltham, Massachusetts, and the Louis D. Brandeis School of Law at the University of Louisville in Kentucky.

SEE ALSO

Federal Reserve Act (1913); Labor; Progressivism; Regulation; Social sciences; Supreme Court, U.S.; Wilson, Woodrow T.

FURTHER READING

Baker, Leonard. *Brandeis and Frankfurter: A Dual Biography.* New York: Harper & Row, 1984.

Paper, Lewis. *Brandeis.* Englewood Cliffs, N.J.: Prentice-Hall, 1983.

Strum, Philippa. *Louis D. Brandeis: Justice for the People.* Cambridge, Mass.: Harvard University Press, 1984.

Urofsky, Melvin. *Louis D. Brandeis and the Progressive Tradition.* Boston: Little, Brown, 1981.

Brooklyn Bridge

THE BROOKLYN BRIDGE, which joins New York's Manhattan Island to the borough of Brooklyn, was 16 years in the making. After the Civil War, Brooklyn's population was on the rise, but the only way for its residents to reach Manhattan was by ferry across the East River. In winter, ice or gales often made the river impassable. A bridge was clearly needed, but building one high enough for river traffic to pass underneath or long enough to span such a large distance would challenge engineers' ingenuity.

John A. Roebling, a German engineer, took on the task. He designed a suspension bridge, one that holds a span in place with opposing forces. One force goes down through huge piers or towers sunk into bedrock, while the other goes across thick cables made out of spun steel wires strung between the towers and anchored into the ground. Roebling's building of successful bridges at Niagara Falls (1855) and the Ohio River at Cincinnati (1867) qualified him for the Brooklyn Bridge assignment. At 1,600 feet long, it would be the longest bridge in the world, with massive stone piers and Gothic towers at either end, connected by a lacework of graceful steel cables.

Work began on the bridge in 1867. Roebling did not live to see it completed. After injuring his foot in an accident, he died horribly of lockjaw. His son Washington took over the project, but he, too, became ill. Sinking towers deep into bedrock required men to labor long hours under high atmospheric pressure in underwater chambers called caissons. Many, including Washington Roebling, developed the bends, an illness that occurs when one returns to the surface too rapidly; it could end in paralysis and death. As the project neared completion, Washington Roebling could watch only

New York's Brooklyn Bridge, connecting Manhattan and Brooklyn, opened in 1883. Hailed as a great engineering achievement and an artistic masterpiece, it was at the time the world's longest suspension bridge and the first to be built with steel cables.

through binoculars from his sick room window, sending his wife Emily to deliver messages to his staff.

The bridge, which carried pedestrians, carts, and electric-powered cable cars, opened on May 24, 1883. President Chester A. Arthur came for the ceremony. Crowds thrilled when a switch lit up electric bulbs strung along the cables, and again when the lights went out to herald a magnificent fireworks display. Connecting Brooklyn to Manhattan made commuting convenient and hastened the day when Brooklyn, which had been an independent city, became a borough of New York City. Subway trains and additional bridges have crossed the East River since the Brooklyn Bridge was built, but no other structure compares to the elegance of its design.

SEE ALSO

Cities; Industry; Science and technology

FURTHER READING

Mann, Elizabeth. *The Brooklyn Bridge.* New York: Miyaka, 1995.
McCullough, David. *The Great Bridge: The Epic Story of the Building of the Brooklyn Bridge.* New York: Simon & Schuster, 1972.

Bryan, William Jennings

- *Mar. 19, 1860, Salem, Ill.*
- *Education: Illinois College (Jacksonville), A.B., 1881; Union College of Law, Chicago, LL.B., 1883*
- *Accomplishments: U.S. House of Representatives (Democrat–Nebr., 1890, 1892); Democratic party Presidential nominee (1896, 1900, 1908); U.S. secretary of state (1913–15); prosecutor, Scopes trial (1925)*
- *Died: July 26, 1925, Dayton, Tenn.*

WILLIAM JENNINGS BRYAN, known as the "Great Commoner," was a major force in American politics for three

decades. Trained in the law in Illinois, Bryan moved to Nebraska, where he was elected to Congress at the age of 30 and served two terms. He became involved in the Free Silver campaign, a movement spearheaded by populist farmers and labor leaders for basing the value of paper money on silver as well as on gold. Their argument was that, as silver was more easily mined than gold and thus cheaper, using silver as a standard would increase the money supply and make it easier for working people to pay off their debts. He also favored an income tax and opposed high tariffs, which raised the price of foreign goods and depressed the prices farmers could get abroad for their produce. After twice losing bids for the U.S. Senate, Bryan became the editor of the *Omaha World-Herald.* Bryan used his newspaper and a series of lectures to attack monopolies, trusts, and corruption and to promote a number of specific issues, among them woman suffrage, direct election of U.S. senators, civil rights, workers' rights, and America's role in world peacekeeping.

Arriving at the Democratic National Convention in Chicago in 1896, Bryan found his party divided over monetary policies. Grover Cleveland led those who supported gold as the basis for paper money. Using a gold standard would tighten the supply of money and make it worth more. Bryan made an impassioned speech in favor of Free Silver that ended with the stirring phrase, "You shall not press down upon the brow of labor this crown of thorns! You shall not crucify mankind upon a cross of gold!" The convention erupted, and Bryan became a hero. He received the Democratic nomination for the presidency and the endorsement of three other parties, all supporters (including the populists) of basing the value of money on both silver and gold. In the election, he lost to Republican William McKinley, who supported both a gold standard and high tariffs.

Assuming a role as America's conscience, Bryan ran twice more for President, promoting his causes and increasingly turning to anti-imperialism and the advocacy of world peace. He led the opposition to Republican administrations and conservative Democrats alike. After Bryan's third defeat as a Presidential candidate, some of the reforms to which he had dedicated his career, such as the income tax, became law under Presidents William Howard Taft and Woodrow Wilson.

In return for supporting Wilson's nomination in 1912, Bryan was rewarded with the post of secretary of state. Instinctively an isolationist, Bryan was also a fervent nationalist. His concerns about protecting Latin America against European encroachment led him to accede to Wilson's plans for expanding U.S. control over the Caribbean. Initially he opposed the use of force in Mexico, but eventually had to give in on that score as well. As an anti-imperialist he tried to get Congress to commit to a date for the independence of the Philippines, but failed. He was, however, able to get 30 nations to sign treaties calling for arbitration before resorting to war.

Bryan resigned from Wilson's cabinet in 1915, after World War I had begun in Europe, when he feared that U.S. pressure on Germany for engaging in submarine warfare might lead his country into war. Although he sacrificed his political career through his resignation, Bryan remained an advocate of world peace and disarmament. He led prohibitionists in gaining passage of the 18th Amendment, which banned the manufacture and sale of alcoholic beverages, and also helped suffragists to win the vote for women. Ironically, even though many of the basic ideas for the League of Nations, an organization to resolve international disputes, had originated with Bryan himself, political pragmatism led him to oppose Wilson's league on the grounds that it could not win Senate approval.

In the last years of his life, Bryan embraced fundamentalist Christianity and attacked the teaching of evolution in schools. His last public appearance came in the 1925 Scopes "monkey trial," in which he prosecuted a Tennessee schoolteacher named John Scopes who was accused of breaking the law by teaching evolution in his classroom. Bryan won the case but was humiliated by the brilliant defense attorney, Clarence Darrow, who demonstrated Bryan's ignorance of science. He died a few days after the end of the trial.

SEE ALSO

Democratic party; 18th Amendment; Imperialism; International relations; League of Nations; McKinley, William; Monetary policies; Populism; Taft, William Howard; Taxes and tariffs; Wilson, Woodrow T.; Woman suffrage movement; World War I

FURTHER READING

Ashby, LeRoy. *William Jennings Bryan: Champion of Democracy.* Boston: Twayne, 1987.

Noted for his skill as an orator, populist William Jennings Bryan won the Democratic Party's Presidential nomination three times, but lost to William McKinley in 1896 and 1900 and to William Howard Taft in 1908.

Cherny, Robert. *A Righteous Cause: The Life of William Jennings Bryan.* Norman: University of Oklahoma Press, 1994.

Koenig, Louis W. *Bryan: A Political Biography of William Jennings Bryan.* New York: Putnam, 1971.

Levine, Lawrence W. *Defender of the Faith: William Jennings Bryan, the Last Decade, 1915–1925.* Cambridge, Mass.: Harvard University Press, 1987.

Buffalo

THE BUFFALO, called bison by scientists, is the largest land animal native to North America. The adult male of the species can weigh more than 2,000 pounds and stand six feet from hoof to shoulder. Buffalo once roamed in enormous herds across most of the continent, particularly the Great Plains region between the Mississippi River and the Rocky Mountains.

Despite thousands of years of hunting by Indians, the buffalo population had reached approximately 60 million before the expansion of American settlers into the West. This expansion, which included railroad construction and frontier settlement, exposed the animal to new dangers. Although Native Americans had used every part of the buffalo for food, clothing, shelter, and making tools, white hunters killed buffalo only for sport or for

hides. In the 1870s buffalo hides usually sold for less than $3 apiece, but the slaughter was profitable. Gangs of hunters and skinners could kill hundreds of peacefully grazing creatures in a day, leaving behind the piled-up carcasses of whole herds. "Sportsmen" sometimes shot buffalo from passing trains. In a memoir that recollected a hunt in which he had participated in 1875, former buffalo hunter W. S. Glenn wrote, "I have seen their bodies so thick after being skinned that they would look like logs where a hurricane had passed through a forest."

By the 1880s, only a few hundred bison remained on the Great Plains. Historians believe that the federal government permitted the near extermination of the buffalo as part of a strategy to destroy the food supply of the Plains Indians, thereby forcing them onto reservations. Protests against the slaughter, however, led the government to pass a buffalo protection law in 1894. In 1905, preservationists founded the private American Bison Society to promote the revival of the species. In 1913, the U.S. Treasury began minting nickels with a portrait of an Indian man on one side and the image of a buffalo on the other. Living today in small, protected herds, buffalo populations continue to recover.

SEE ALSO

Native Americans; Conservation; Railroads; West, the

FURTHER READING

Dary, David. *The Buffalo Book: The Full Saga of the American Animal.* Rev. ed. Athens, Ohio: Swallow Press/Ohio University Press, 1974.

Geist, Valerius. *Buffalo Nation: History and Legend of the North American Bison.* Stillwater, Minn.: Voyageur Press, 1998.

Sandoz, Mari. *The Buffalo Hunters: The Story of the Hide Men.* 1954. Reprint, Lincoln: University of Nebraska Press, 1978.

Shooting buffalo from trains was a popular sport during the 1860s and 70s. It was encouraged by the western railroads as a way to eliminate the enormous herds that blocked their routes.

Buffalo Soldiers

IN 1866 CONGRESS authorized the creation of two cavalry and four infantry regiments of African American troops. Most of them Civil War veterans, the men who enlisted in these regiments saw military service as a way to improve their lot in life. The pay was low, about $13 a month, but African Americans could find few better jobs in that era.

During the Gilded Age, black regiments played a major role in the expansion of the West and the final subjugation of Native Americans. The Plains Indians are said to have nicknamed the mounted men "Buffalo Soldiers," thinking their black curly hair resembled that of buffalos. Because the buffalo was a powerful spiritual symbol to the Indians, the soldiers adopted the nickname proudly.

Buffalo Soldier units served separately from white units. All their officers were white until the 1877 appointment of Second Lieutenant Henry O. Flipper, the first black graduate of West Point, to the 10th Cavalry at Fort Sill, Oklahoma. Serving on the frontier, Buffalo Soldiers built forts and telegraph lines and escorted railroad crews, settlers, and cattle drovers.

Buffalo Soldiers often found themselves building or defending military facilities they were not permitted to use. Their own living quarters were poor, and they frequently encountered racist attitudes from their officers or from white settlers. Nevertheless, Buffalo Soldiers had the lowest desertion rate in the army.

Although some black leaders protested that the government was using one oppressed group (African Americans) to destroy another (Native

Americans), the U.S. Army regularly employed the Buffalo Soldiers in fighting Cheyenne, Arapahoe, Kiowa, Comanche, and Apache warriors. Their most famous campaigns included the hunt for the Apache leader, Geronimo, and the pursuit of Victorio, an Apache warrior who eluded them several times, eventually slipping over the border into Mexico, where Mexican soldiers killed him and members of his band.

Units of the 9th and 10th cavalry went on to fight in Cuba during the Spanish-American War and took part in General John J. Pershing's unsuccessful 1916 expedition against the Mexican revolutionary Pancho Villa. A number of Buffalo Soldiers received the Congressional Medal of Honor for bravery. The army finally disbanded the cavalry units in 1944.

SEE ALSO

African Americans; Geronimo; Military; Native Americans; Pershing, John Joseph; Race relations; Spanish-American War; West, the

FURTHER READING

Cox, Clinton. *The Forgotten Heroes: The Story of the Buffalo Soldiers.* New York: Scholastic, 1993.
Hooker, Forrestine C. *Child of the Fighting Tenth: On the Frontier with the Buffalo Soldiers.* New York: Oxford University Press, 2003.
Kenner, Charles L. *Buffalo Soldiers and Officers of the Ninth Cavalry, 1867–1898: Black & White Together.* Norman: University of Oklahoma Press, 1999.

Troops of the 25th Infantry, nicknamed Buffalo Soldiers by Indians, pose with tools and weapons at Fort Keogh, Montana, in 1890. The 25th was one of four all-black regiments formed after the abolition of slavery.

Leckie, William H., and Shirley A. Leckie. *Buffalo Soldiers: A Narrative of the Black Cavalry in the West.* Rev. ed. Norman: University of Oklahoma Press, 2003.

Schubert, Frank N. *Voices of the Buffalo Soldier: Records, Reports, and Recollections of Military Life and Service in the West.* Albuquerque: University of New Mexico Press, 2003.

Bull Moose party

SEE Progressive party

Carnegie, Andrew

- *Born: Nov. 25, 1835, Dunfermline, Scotland*
- *Education: elementary school*
- *Accomplishments: industrialist; philanthropist; author,* The Gospel of Wealth *(1889) and* The Autobiography of Andrew Carnegie *(1920)*
- *Died: Aug. 11, 1919, Lenox, Mass.*

ANDREW CARNEGIE was an immigrant who rose from poverty to make himself one of the wealthiest American industrialists of the Gilded Age and one of the richest people in the world. He then turned his attention to philanthropy and became as famous for giving away his immense fortune as he had been for acquiring it.

Carnegie grew up on the east coast of Scotland. His father was a weaver, one of the countless skilled artisans whose livelihoods suffered as the Industrial Revolution introduced machines to replace human workers. Many members of Carnegie's extended family were involved in radical reform movements to improve the lives of the working class.

Economic hardship in Scotland drove Carnegie's parents to move the family to the United States, where they settled in western Pennsylvania. Young Andrew, 13 years old, found work first in a cotton mill, then in a telegraph office, then with a railroad company where he climbed the ranks to divisional superintendent by the age of 24. He began investing in iron mills and other profitable enterprises and by his 30s had amassed enough wealth to quit his railroad job and concentrate on building his own industrial empire in the iron and steel business.

The manufacture of steel involves purging the impurities from iron ore and alloying the purified iron with carbon and other strengthening agents. Paying close attention to breakthroughs in British steelmaking technology, Carnegie introduced efficient, economical new processes in his American manufacturing plants. In addition, he pioneered the practice of "vertical" business integration, acquiring mines, railroad lines, and factories, so that Carnegie Steel controlled every step in the process of steel manufacture, from the mining of iron ore to the sales and distribution of the finished product. Andrew Carnegie built his company into an industrial giant responsible by 1900 for one-quarter of all the iron and steel produced in the United States.

Andrew Carnegie relaxes in front of a fireplace in 1911. An immigrant from Scotland who rose from poverty to become a titan of the U.S. steel industry, Carnegie devoted his final years to philanthropic work.

Despite his family's tradition of working-class radicalism, Carnegie gained notoriety as an enemy of organized labor. In 1892, a strike by workers at his Homestead, Pennsylvania, steel plant escalated into a bloody, armed conflict between unionized plant employees and guards brought in to protect nonunion strikebreakers. Although Carnegie was out of the country during the strike, as the corporation's primary owner, he suffered significant damage to his reputation.

In 1901, Carnegie sold his company to J. P. Morgan and Elbert Gary, founders of the United States Steel Corporation, and retired from the business world to devote the rest of his life to philanthropy. Convinced that the accumulation of riches was honorable, he also believed that to die rich would be a disgrace. "Surplus wealth is a sacred trust which its possessor is bound to administer in his lifetime for the good of the community," he wrote. Acting on that philosophy, before his death he gave away more than $350 million.

In order to do the maximum amount of good, Carnegie said, philanthropists had a moral obligation to manage their charitable giving as carefully as they managed the businesses that made them rich. Providing educational opportunities for the poor was one cause that he considered especially important, so he devoted many millions of dollars to establishing free public libraries in towns and cities across the nation. He also contributed heavily to schools, the arts, and international peace efforts. The Carnegie Corporation of New York, a charitable foundation he established in 1911, continues his work today by providing millions of dollars in grants each year to programs that further "the advancement and diffusion of knowledge and understanding."

SEE ALSO
Homestead strike (1892); Industry; Labor union movement; Morgan, John Pierpont; Science and technology; Strikes

FURTHER READING
Carnegie, Andrew. *The Autobiography of Andrew Carnegie*. 1920. Reprint, Boston: Northeastern University Press, 1986.
———. *The Gospel of Wealth and Other Timely Essays*. Edited by Edward C. Kirkland. Cambridge, Mass.: Harvard University Press, Belknap Press, 1962.
Krass, Peter. *Carnegie*. New York: John Wiley & Sons, 2002.
Livesay, Harold C. *Andrew Carnegie and the Rise of Big Business*. 2nd ed. New York: Longman, 2000.
Meltzer, Milton. *The Many Lives of Andrew Carnegie*. New York: Franklin Watts, 1997.

Carver, George Washington

- *Born: 1864 or 1865, Diamond Grove (now called Diamond), Newton County, Mo.*
- *Education: Iowa Agricultural College, B.S., 1894, M.S., 1896; Simpson College, honorary doctorate, 1928*
- *Accomplishments: educator, chemist, plant and soil scientist; elected to the British Royal Society of Arts (1916); awarded Spingarn Medal by the National Association for the Advancement of Colored People (1923); awarded Theodore Roosevelt medal (1939)*
- *Died: Jan. 5, 1943, Tuskegee, Ala.*

GEORGE WASHINGTON CARVER was a world-renowned scientist who specialized in agricultural research. His studies of peanuts, soybeans, sweet potatoes, and other crops helped to diversify the economy of the rural South and rescue farmers from over-reliance on cotton.

Born into slavery on a Missouri farm near the end of the Civil War, Carver grew up in the first generation of African American freedom. He barely

George Washington Carver examines a plant specimen at Tuskegee Institute in Alabama, where he worked for nearly half a century. Born in slavery, Carver achieved an education at a time when many schools would not admit black students.

knew his mother, who was kidnapped by slave stealers when he was an infant, and never knew his father, who apparently died in a work accident shortly after Carver was born. Until he was 10 or 11, Carver lived with the white couple who had been his mother's owners, then moved away to support himself with odd jobs while attending various Missouri and Kansas schools that were open to black students.

After graduating from high school, Carver applied to a Kansas college that accepted him but later refused to admit him when college officials learned that he was black. He recovered from that setback to study music and art at Simpson College in Iowa, later transferring as a science student to Iowa Agricultural College (later, Iowa State University). Carver earned both bachelor's and master's degrees in agricultural science and taught classes at Iowa Agricultural, becoming the first black faculty member in the college's history. In 1896 Carver accepted an invitation from Booker T. Washington to head the agricultural teaching and research program at Tuskegee Institute in Alabama.

Carver taught that farmers could protect the health of their land by using the science of crop rotation, planting different crops from one year to the next. Cotton's long domination of southern agriculture had taken the nutrients out of the soil, but there were other crops, such as peanuts, which actually enriched and revitalized agricultural land. In order to encourage farmers to plant soil-strengthening crops, Carver realized he would have to build a market for them. His research led to the discovery of more than 300 peanut-

derived products, including soap, dye, candy, glue, coffee substitute, paper, and ink. He went on to devise dozens of uses for the soybean, the sweet potato, and other plants that could help restore the health of southern farmland.

Carver received international recognition and a number of medals and honors during his lifetime. His work in crop diversification and soil conservation, initially begun to help black sharecroppers improve their land, encouraged the transformation of agriculture throughout the South and advanced agricultural studies nationally. In 1943, the year of his death, Carver's Missouri birthplace became a National Monument, the first to honor an African American.

SEE ALSO

African Americans; Agriculture; Colleges and universities; Race relations; Science and technology; Washington, Booker T.

FURTHER READING

Adair, Gene. *George Washington Carver.* New York: Chelsea House, 1989.

Carver, George Washington. *George Washington Carver: In His Own Words.* Edited by Gary R. Kremer. Reprint, Columbia: University of Missouri Press, 1987.

McMurray, Linda. *George Washington Carver: Scientist and Symbol.* New York: Oxford University Press, 1981.

Cather, Willa Sibert

- *Born: Dec. 7, 1873, Back Creek Valley (now Gore), Va.*
- *Education: University of Nebraska, B.A., 1895*
- *Accomplishments: managing editor, McClure's Magazine (1906–12); Pulitzer Prize for* One of Ours *(1922); author of 12 novels and more than 60 stories*
- *Died: Apr. 24, 1947, New York, N.Y.*

CONSIDERED ONE of the nation's major writers of fiction, Willa Cather was born on a farm in Virginia and moved with her family to Nebraska at age nine. She began her writing career as a journalist, working first in Pittsburgh and, after 1906, in New York City, where she became the managing editor of *McClure's*, an important "muckraking" magazine, that is, a magazine dedicated to investigative reporting of corruption or mismanagement. Her first collection of verse came out in 1903, her first collection of stories, in 1905.

Cather later said that "Most of the basic material a writer works with is acquired before the age of fifteen." And indeed, she peopled her fiction with the immigrant families she had known on the Nebraska plains. Her strongest characters were women, such as Alexandra Bergson in *O Pioneers!* (1913). Because Alexandra is the most capable of her family's offspring, her father bids her secure the future of her three brothers and then passes the family farm on to her. After turning down marriage to a childhood friend, she survives drought, economic depression, and the tragic death of her youngest brother, but eventually finds happiness with her lover. *The Song of the Lark* (1915) presents the story of a singer who outgrew her small-town Midwestern upbringing to emerge as a major opera star. *My Ántonia* (1918), written as the memories of a city lawyer of his prairie boyhood and love for Antonia Shimerda, evokes the pioneering spirit of Nebraska's Czech immigrants.

One of Ours (1922), a novel about a man who went to war to escape his Midwestern upbringing, won a Pulitzer Prize, the nation's most prestigious literary award. Later novels also set their characters in opposition to their roots. *A Lost Lady* (1923) was based on the wife of the governor of Nebraska; *The Professor's House* (1925) concerned a historian strug-

gling to retain spiritual meaning in his life; and *My Mortal Enemy* (1926) was a story of failed love and religious bigotry. Critics generally consider *Death Comes for the Archbishop* (1927) to be Cather's best work. An experimental work in historical fiction, it was inspired by a trip Cather took to the Southwest in 1912 and by a biography she read about Roman Catholic priests who had served as missionaries in the area. It consists of a series of tales based on the experiences of the priests as they interacted with the native populations of early 19th-century New Mexico.

In all of her writing, Cather combined a keen sense of "place" with a profound sympathy for the struggles of humankind to prevail over bigotry, ignorance, and harsh environments. As she wrote in *O Pioneers!*, "there are only two or three human stories, and they go on repeating themselves as fiercely as if they had never happened before; like the larks in this country that have been singing the same five notes over for thousands of years."

SEE ALSO

Journalism; Literature; Muckraking

FURTHER READING

Cather, Willa. *Stories, Poems, and Other Writings.* Edited by Sharon O'Brien. New York: Library of America 1992.

Keene, Ann T. *Willa Cather.* New York: Julian Messner, 1994.

Lee, Hermione. *Willa Cather: Double Lives.* New York: Pantheon, 1989.

O'Brien, Sharon. *Willa Cather: The Emerging Voice.* New York: Oxford University Press, 1987.

Woodress, James. *Willa Cather: A Literary Life.* Lincoln: University of Nebraska Press, 1987.

Willa Cather works on an article at the Nebraska State Journal, *where she wrote theater reviews and other pieces in the 1890s. She won the Pulitzer Prize for fiction in 1922 and earned praise for her depictions of strong female characters.*

Catholicism

ROMAN CATHOLICISM was the prevailing religious affiliation of many of America's earliest settlers, especially among those from Spain, France, Mexico, Germany, and Ireland. Before the Civil War, however, the United States was home to only about 3 million Catholics. In the late 1800s, this population began to swell. By 1920, the arrival of Catholics from French Canada, Mexico, Ireland, Belgium, Germany, Italy, central European countries such as Slovakia, Croatia, and Hungary, and Spanish-speaking countries such as Cuba, the Philippines, and the Caribbean islands had brought Catholic numbers to almost 18 million, or about a sixth of the entire population. Thus Catholics made up the largest single denomination in the entire country.

Certain features of Catholicism contributed to cohesiveness in the American Catholic community. All masses were in Latin, and all Catholics participated in regular confessions, revered the sacraments, and honored days of fasting and other holy obligations. The hierarchical structure of Roman Catholicism—starting at the top with the pope in Rome and descending through cardinals, archbishops, and bishops down to parish priests—maintained cohesion, as did the strategic construction of cathedrals in locations throughout the country.

The denomination was far from united, however. Hoping to preserve their old languages, customs, and rituals, Catholic ethnic groups set up their own churches with priests who spoke their native languages or honored the patron saints of their original hometowns. Poles eventually established 61 parishes in and around Chicago. By 1916, Germans had 1,890 parishes around the country. For all ethnic enclaves, Catholic churches served as focal points essential to the survival of their communities.

Many Protestants regarded Catholics as not truly "American" because they submitted to a foreign authority, the pope, which, the Protestants claimed, undermined American democracy. Resentment against Catholics surged when groups such as the Irish began to establish parochial schools and gain predominance in certain locales over political offices and labor unions. In response to Catholics' growing influence, nativist groups, such as the Ku Klux Klan and the American Protective Association, intensified their anti-Catholic campaigns, which included campaigning against Catholic political candidates and opposing further immigration from predominately Catholic countries.

In an effort to disarm their enemies, some American Catholic leaders, such as Archbishop John Ireland of St. Paul, Minnesota, and James Cardinal Gibbons of Baltimore, Maryland, argued that American Roman Catholic churches should adopt more "American" positions on key principles. These Americanists, as they were called, advocated the separation of church and state and supported democratic institutions and religious toleration. Pope Leo XIII opposed independence for American Catholics, however, in 1899 issuing an encyclical (a formal letter written to the faithful) rebuking the Americanists and reasserting Rome's authority in all matters.

Modernism—or the contemporary trend to accept nonliteral interpretations of the Bible as well as modern scientific ideas about the origins of human life—led to other problems with the papacy. In 1870 a church council declared the pope's authority infallible and final for all Catholics. Catholics attracted to modernism resisted this declaration, provoking a variety of papal responses. In 1891 Leo XIII made an important concession to modern social ideas in the encyclical entitled *Rerum Novarum*. Written out of concern that working-class people were drifting away from the church, the encyclical accepted labor unions and minimum wage laws as legitimate social reforms, and urged Roman Catholic churches to become more involved with social issues. In 1898, however, Leo condemned a professor at the University of Notre Dame in Indiana for teaching that God could have used evolution as a method of creation. In 1907, Pope Pius X condemned all theological modernism.

By 1900, American Catholics were fully committed to separate educational facilities. To them, the public schools were, at best, too secular and, at worst, a threat to Catholic values and religious beliefs. American Catholic nuns played a vital role in American life. They sustained Catholic culture by staffing parochial schools, in addition to performing essential welfare work among all immigrant groups and founding hospitals and orphanages. In 1892, Mary Katharine Drexel founded the Sisters of the Blessed Sacrament for Indians and Colored People, an order that established missions and schools throughout the Indian territories, the South, and the urban North. Her work led eventually to the founding in 1925 of Xavier University in New Orleans, the nation's only Catholic college for African Americans.

Despite the many contributions of all Catholics, anti-Catholicism remained a striking feature of American politics until the election of John F. Kennedy, the first Catholic President, in 1960.

SEE ALSO

Immigration; Ku Klux Klan; Nativism; Religion

FURTHER READING

Dolan, Jay P. *The American Catholic Experience: A History from Colonial Times to the Present.* Notre Dame: University of Notre Dame Press, 1992.
Fisher, James T. *Catholics in America.* New York: Oxford University Press, 2000.
Gillis, Chester. *Roman Catholicism in America.* New York: Columbia University Press, 1999.
Hennessy, James. *American Catholics: A History of the Roman Catholic Community in the United States.* New York: Oxford University Press, 1981.
McGreevy, John T. *Catholicism and American Freedom: A History.* New York: Norton, 2003.

Catholic bishops gather for a meeting in Baltimore. In the late 1800s and early 1900s, immigrants from Ireland, Italy, and other countries transformed Catholicism into the largest single denomination in the United States.

Catt, Carrie Chapman

- *Jan. 9, 1859, Ripon, Wis.*
- *Education: Iowa State College, B.S., 1880*
- *Accomplishments: first woman superintendent of schools, Mason City, Ia. (1883); president, National American Woman Suffrage Association (1900–4, 1915–20); president, International Woman Suffrage Alliance (1904–23); founder, National League of Women Voters (1921); founder (1925) and chair (1925–32), National Committee on the Cause and Cure of War*
- *Died: Mar. 9, 1947, New Rochelle, N.Y.*

CARRIE CHAPMAN CATT directed the movement for women's right to vote during its final triumphant stages. A highly independent woman, she grew up on the Wisconsin frontier, defying her father to attend college and supporting herself as a teacher, dishwasher, and library assistant. She planned to go on to law school but instead became a high school administrator. Her first husband was Leo Chapman, a California newspaper publisher who died of typhoid a year after the wedding. Carrie Chapman worked for a San Francisco newspaper, and then returned to Iowa as a lecturer and state woman suffrage advocate. In 1890 she married civil engineer George Catt, an old college friend. Before marrying, they formally agreed that she could spend two months every spring and fall on suffrage work. George's death in 1905 would leave her financially independent for the rest of her life.

In 1895, Catt joined the administrative staff of the National American Woman Suffrage Association (NAWSA). Her first task was to systematize the association's work. She insisted that local branches develop "plans of work," organization manu-

Mrs. Park, President

Mrs. Catt, Honorary President

als, and courses in political science and government. She persuaded NAWSA to set up state headquarters, a consistent membership system, and a plan for sound national finances. When in 1900 Susan B. Anthony stepped down as NAWSA's president, she chose Catt as her successor. Catt held this job only four years before leaving to care for her dying husband.

Between 1905 and 1915, Catt concentrated on the New York State suffrage campaign. In 1915 she returned to the NAWSA presidency, determined to bring its cause to victory. Because she feared that militant tactics would alienate potential supporters, she opposed the actions of the National Woman's Party (NWP). The NWP worked for the electoral defeat of politicians who refused to endorse votes for women; later they organized demonstrations in front of the White House in Washington, D.C. Deploring such tactics, Catt instead pursued a three-pronged political strategy designed to increase the numbers of states with women voters: winning suffrage amendments in state constitutions; convincing state legislatures to pass laws allowing women to vote in Presidential elections; and securing women's right to vote in party primaries. Catt's "Winning Plan," as it

Members of the board of directors of the National League of Women Voters in Chicago in 1920, the year that the 19th Amendment extended voting rights to women.

was called, worked. A string of state suffrage victories compelled legislators to support the resolution that led to the 19th Amendment to the U.S. Constitution, which guaranteed women the right to vote.

While overseeing the American movement, Catt also headed international suffrage movements. After the ratification of the 19th Amendment in August 1920, she spearheaded the founding of the National League of Women Voters, a voter education group still in existence today. Much honored and admired for her political work in the winning of votes for women, she spent her final years working for international peace and endeavoring to preserve a "true" history of the woman suffrage movement. Above all, according to a 1925 letter, she was anxious to establish NAWSA's "long devotion to the Federal Amendment" and prove that "the [National] Woman's Party did not win suffrage single handed and alone."

SEE ALSO

National American Woman Suffrage Association; National Woman's Party; 19th Amendment

FURTHER READING

Fowler, Robert Booth. *Carrie Catt: Feminist Politician.* Boston: Northeastern University Press, 1986.
Van Voris, Jacqueline. *Carrie Chapman Catt: A Public Life.* New York: Feminist Press, 1987.

Charity organization movement

GOVERNMENT-SPONSORED, or public, assistance to the poor is largely a 20th-century innovation. In the 19th century, only private or religious chari-

ties provided welfare to the needy. As the numbers of the poor increased late in the century, American charities not only expanded their work but became more organized. They drew inspiration from Great Britain's charity organization movement, launched in 1869 to prevent duplication in the work of charitable agencies and to make this work more efficient. British charity workers had become disenchanted with giving relief to just anyone who asked for it. They began to keep better records, coordinate their work with other agencies, and send out "friendly visitors" (usually women) to applicants' homes to assess whether they were "worthy" of receiving aid.

The following decade, American charity workers adopted the British example. They founded a Charity Organization Society (COS) in Boston (1877), Baltimore (1881), and New York (1882). The journal of the New York COS, *Charities* (later, *The Survey*), became America's leading forum for the discussion of issues related to charitable giving, social investigation, and reform. Its landmark 1907–8 study of working-class life in Pittsburgh ("The Pittsburgh Survey") looked at such topics as women's work, child labor, work accidents, the steel industry, local housing and factory inspection laws, the impact of poor sanitation and diseases, such as typhoid, on working-class neighborhoods, and the court system. These studies provided a firm statistical basis for industrial and social reform and inspired reformers in other cities to engage in similar surveys. The COS professionalized the field of charity work, transforming it into what is now known as social work. They organized conferences to exchange views on contemporary social problems, such as congested, sub-standard housing and the prevalence of crime in the slums, and discussed how to solve them with preventive work and more government involvement. In 1898 the COS established the nation's first professional training school for social work, the New York School of Philanthropy.

Women found leadership roles in the charity organization movement. Josephine Shaw Lowell, appointed in 1876 as the first female commissioner on the New York State Board of Charities, was one of the founders of the New York COS. Lowell pioneered reforms not only in charity work but also in the treatment of women prisoners and of those suffering from mental disorders. At first Lowell, like many early charity workers, blamed poverty on immorality, such as indulgence in alcohol and sexual vice. After coming to understand that a greater cause of poverty derived from inequities in the industrial system, she became active in pro-labor organizations, including the National Consumers' League, which investigated unsafe and unfair working conditions.

The goal of charity organization was not just to give money but to transform the poor into productive citizens. To achieve this goal, COS workers investigated the personal lives of the poor, a process that could humiliate and alienate its targets. For this reason, critics called the movement heartless. Nonetheless, it played vital roles in convincing local governments to make important reforms, such as passing laws to regulate the construction of tenement houses so that they would be safer, more healthful places to live. The professionalization of social work set the stage for modern approaches to the problems caused by poverty, approaches that emphasize prevention and remedial work rather than punishment.

SEE ALSO

Cities; National Consumers' League; Poverty; Social work

FURTHER READING

Katz, Michael B. *In the Shadow of the Poorhouse: A Social History of Welfare in America.* New York: Basic Books, 1996.
Waugh, Joan. *Unsentimental Reformer: The Life of Josephine Shaw Lowell.* Cambridge, Mass.: Harvard University Press, 1997.

Chicago fire (1871)

ON THE NIGHT of October 8, 1871, a fire started at 137 De Koven Street in a barn belonging to Patrick and Catherine O'Leary. Historical legend blames Mrs. O'Leary's cow for kicking over an oil lantern and starting the blaze, but her guilt has never been proved. The fire raged for two days and nights, covering more than 2,100 acres, about 3.3 square miles. Residents fled before the flames, many rushing westward over the city's few bridges, some plunging into the cold waters of Lake Michigan. Rain on October 10 helped firefighters extinguish the blaze in two days, but by then the fire had caused more than 250 deaths, destroyed 17,450 buildings, and left more than 80,000 homeless out of a population of 324,000.

Many Chicagoans, as well as investors nationwide, saw the fire as a chance for the city to rebuild and expand. Within six weeks, the city had

The January 2, 1909, edition of Charities and the Commons *magazine features the landmark Pittsburgh Survey. The survey was a yearlong study of on-the-job accidents, child labor, and other issues affecting the lives of the working poor.*

A lone figure surveys a devastated LaSalle Street in the wake of the 1871 Chicago fire. Burning for two days and nights, the blaze reduced more than three square miles of the city to rubble.

reestablished basic services and started construction on hundreds of "fireproof" stone and brick buildings in the business district. The poor and immigrant families who had lost homes were less lucky; the new building codes forbade wooden structures, all that they could afford.

In Chicago's "Great Rebuilding," the city's downtown doubled in size and business and residential areas became separate, the sign of a modern city. The fire had set the stage for the Gilded Age flowering of Chicago, giving civic leaders and architects a chance to replace an unplanned frontier city with a well-designed business and commercial center from the ground up. Within 20 years, Chicago would win the bid to host the World's Columbian Exposition of 1893, a world's fair commemorating the 400th anniversary of Christopher Columbus's voyage of discovery and a showcase for American prosperity and power at the height of the Gilded Age.

SEE ALSO
Cities; World's fairs and exhibitions

FURTHER READING
Miller, Ross. *The Great Chicago Fire.* Champaign: University of Illinois Press, 2000.
Murphy, Jim. *The Great Fire.* New York: Scholastic, 1995.
Sawislak, Karen. *Smoldering City: Chicagoans and the Great Fire, 1871–1874.* Chicago: University of Chicago Press, 1995.

Chicago race riot (1919)

THE YEAR 1919 brought postwar economic depression and nationwide civil unrest. In addition to the resurgence of lynching and Ku Klux Klan violence against African Americans in the South, more than 20 race riots occurred that year. A number of these riots took place in northern cities, where the presence of newly arrived African Americans exacerbated preexisting racial tensions. Thousands of black Americans had left the South during the war years, migrating to northern industrial cities to look for work in factories. After the war was over, many stayed in the North, where pay scales and living conditions were better than in the South, although they still faced discrimination. For the most part, they lived in urban neighborhoods separate from but next door to white neighborhoods.

The worst northern riot took place in Chicago in late July, following the stoning death of a black youth at a lakeshore beach informally limited to whites. The refusal of the police to make an arrest led to protests, rumors, and then violence between mobs of black and white men on the city's South Side. Some of the African Americans drawn into the violence, especially army veterans, felt they were finally fighting back against their second-class

White National Guard troops armed with rifles and bayonets confront a black Chicago resident in the summer of 1919. Race riots spread throughout the country that year, fueled in part by economic hard times after World War I.

citizenship. The former soldiers had served their government, risking their lives for world democracy, and they had received a certain amount of respect for that, even though the armed services remained segregated after the war. They were determined to hold onto their hard-won self-esteem. Others were determined to protect their homes and retain the economic progress they had made doing industrial work.

For 13 days, the city was in chaos; police and state militia were powerless to quell the violence. In the end, 38 people died, 23 black and 15 white. There were more than 500 reported injuries, and hundreds of families lost homes and possessions to arson and looting. Race relations dominated newspaper reporting and editorials on the riot. An August editorial in the *Chicago Defender,* an African American newspaper, claimed the paper had "little sympathy with lawlessness," but then located the source of black anger in America's history of lynching and mob action. Referring to the distinguished service of black Americans in World War I, the paper warned, "A Race that has furnished hundreds of thousands of the best soldiers that the world has ever seen is no longer content to turn the left cheek when smitten upon the right."

The *Chicago Daily Tribune*, which represented the city's white residents, took a different tack, suggesting that the answer lay in segregation. "If you are looking for a solution of the race problem," the paper advised, "you need consider nothing more complex than simple zoning and the establishment of race equalities for both Negroes and whites—making it as incumbent upon one as the other to stay in their place." Many whites pressured city officials to impose formal segregation ordinances, decreeing separation of blacks and whites in all public places. The city's Commission on Race Relations, however, rejected segregation. Its investigation of the causes of the rioting led it to recommend improving the urban environment—rehabilitating housing, fixing streets, installing street lighting, establishing parks—to make better lives for both black and white Chicagoans.

SEE ALSO

African Americans; Cities; Ku Klux Klan; Lynching; Race relations; Segregation; World War I

FURTHER READING

Chicago Commission on Race Relations. *The Negro in Chicago: A Study of Race Relations and a Race Riot.* Chicago: University of Chicago Press, 1922.
Spear, Allan H. *Black Chicago: The Making of a Negro Ghetto, 1890–1920.* Chicago: University of Chicago Press, 1969.
Tuttle, William M., Jr. *Race Riot: Chicago in the Red Summer of 1919.* New York: Atheneum, 1970.

Childhood

BEFORE THE MID-1800s, most people thought of children as little adults. Thus, as soon as children were able to contribute to a family's income, parents

put them to work, even as young as five or six years of age. Children worked in homes, gardens, or fields at whatever tasks they could perform, such as stitching, weeding, or tending livestock. Industrialization, which raised the standard of living for many people, tended to change this custom, especially for the middle classes. Middle-class urban mothers kept their small children at home, providing them with both more educational opportunities and more time to play. For middle-class urban children of the Gilded Age and Progressive Era, childhood could last deep into the teenage years.

Depending on a child's social class, ethnicity, race, sex, or place of residence, quality of life could vary widely in this era. Many poor families depended on children's wages. In large cities and towns, children worked as newsboys or ran errands; other children helped their parents in sweatshops, pulling out basting stitches or delivering goods. Those children who could stay at home were rarely idle: older children cared for younger ones, or they scavenged for wood, coal, or even food. Textile mills and coal mines relied heavily on child labor: mill girls repaired broken threads and changed

bobbins, "breaker boys" separated coal from slate and rock. At age 5 or 6, rural children hoed weeds or guarded crops against birds or livestock; at age 10, they performed a range of chores, such as milking, churning, feeding livestock, doing laundry, and planting and harvesting. Farm children attended one-room schoolhouses maintained by the community, but because of their need to help out with harvests and planting, they went to school only a few months a year. Sharecropper children rarely went to school beyond the first few grades, if they attended at all.

Urban children's educational opportunities improved during the era. School attendance rose from 7 million in 1870 to 20 million in 1915. Increasing numbers of urban youth went to high school, the highest level of education that most children reached in this period. In wealthy families, governesses or tutors educated the children during their youngest years. Teenage boys might attend a college-preparatory boarding school, and teenage girls, a young ladies' academy, which was usually little more than a finishing school. Only a privileged few of either sex went to college,

Boys play stickball in the alley in a poor Boston neighborhood. Until the advent of playgrounds and ball fields in the Progressive Era, the streets were the only outdoor play space for city children.

although their numbers rose steadily in the early 20th century.

Public involvement in children's welfare grew in the Progressive Era. Urban social settlements established nurseries, kindergartens, and playgrounds so that children could play in safe environments while their parents worked. Pressure from settlement workers led to the 1912 founding of the first federal agency concerned with children, the U.S. Children's Bureau. One of this agency's first goals was to reduce childhood mortality and win legislation to curb child labor. Its birth registration system helped government track infant survival and keep children in school instead of being sent out to work at a young age.

Immigrant children played an important role as translators and interpreters of American culture for their parents. Adapting more quickly than their elders to the language and customs of their adopted land, they helped parents negotiate with landlords and local officials. Over time, however, the cultural gap between second-generation immigrant children and their parents widened. Americanized by their schools and friends, second-generation children wore American fashions and sought out secular "American" activities. They were more eager to attend commercial dance halls and movie theaters than take part in their parents' cultural and religious traditions.

In the early 20th century, psychologists began to regard the onset of puberty as a critical stage in a child's development. Experts began to use the term *adolescence* to demarcate this stressful time in a child's life, and suggested that teenagers needed to receive special attention to their mental, emotional, and physical needs. Youth programs such as the Boy Scouts and Girl Scouts originated in the early 1910s and proved increasingly popular.

Regardless of a particular child's ethnic origin or economic status, all children in this era faced the possibility of an early death. In 1895, one in every sixth child could expect to die, usually of disease, before reaching his or her fifth birthday. Although child mortality rates declined in the early 20th century, poor children still died at a higher rate than more wealthy children, but even wealthy families rarely escaped the death of at least one child. The experience of being an orphan touched poor children more harshly than it did wealthy children. In this era the authorities could ship off poor urban orphans to be adopted, sight unseen, by western farm families, who then used them as labor.

SEE ALSO

Child labor; Children's Bureau, U.S.; Education; Family life; Psychology; Settlement-house movement

FURTHER READING

Gordon, Linda. *The Great Arizona Orphan Abduction.* Cambridge, Mass.: Harvard University Press, 1999.
Macleod, David. *The Age of the Child: Children in America, 1890–1920.* New York: Twayne, 1998.
Mintz, Steven. *Huck's Raft: A History of American Childhood.* Cambridge, Mass.: Harvard University Press, 2004.

Child labor

THROUGHOUT HISTORY children have worked to help support their families. In late 19th-century America, families clung to the old farming custom of family labor, where parents and all the children work to make the farm succeed. They brought this custom into the industrial workplace, which meant that

With a pickaxe slung over his shoulder, a pipe clenched in his mouth, and a lamp fixed to his hat, this eight-year-old boy is ready for work in a West Virginia coal mine.

children worked for wages, sometimes in the same mills or factories as their parents.

About one in six children between the ages of 10 and 15 supplemented meager family incomes with paying jobs in textile mills, coal mines, canning factories, and tobacco-processing plants. Children of immigrants worked in sweatshops or assembled pieces of garments or hats alongside their parents in the kitchens of city tenements. In the South, both white and African American children picked cotton all day in the hot sun.

Child laborers earned from a few pennies to 75 cents a day, a fraction of what adult workers earned. They worked long shifts, often 10 or 12 hours a day. Sometimes they worked in dangerous conditions, handling toxic substances, exposed to dangerous machinery, or threatened by coal-mine cave-ins or gas leaks. Usually they lost out on education, so desperate was their need to earn money.

Many Americans believed that children of the working classes or immigrants ought to work long hours in order to stay out of trouble. In the early 1900s, 28 states passed laws to restrict child labor, but employers routinely ignored or evaded them. They lied to authorities about their employees and instructed children to hide when factory inspectors came around. The Supreme Court repeatedly blocked attempts at national regulation, arguing that employers and employees in the United States should be "free" to buy or sell labor in any way they chose.

After 1900, progressive reformers began to agitate for an end to the abuses of child labor. In 1904, a coalition of concerned citizens, politicians, and investigators organized the National Child Labor Committee. The committee sent photographer Lewis Hine to document violations of the law in mines and mills that employed young children. Hine's powerful photographs and the Child Labor Committee's mass public relations campaign helped turn public opinion against child labor.

In 1912, the National Consumers' League, inspired by veterans of the settlement-house movement, succeeded in creating a Children's Bureau within the Department of Labor. By 1916, Congress had started to pass laws to regulate child labor, and by 1920 most states had outlawed the employment of children under 14 and mandated compulsory education up to that age. It was not until the late 1930s, however, that the Fair Labor Standards Act banned the full-time employment of children under 16. A campaign to outlaw child labor by a constitutional amendment never succeeded.

SEE ALSO

Childhood; Children's Bureau, U.S.; Family life; Labor; National Consumers' League; Photography; Progressive movement; Reform movements; Settlement-house movement

FURTHER READING

Bartoletti, Susan Campbell. *Growing up in Coal Country.* Boston: Houghton Mifflin, 1996.
Freedman, Russell. *Kids at Work: Lewis Hine and the Crusade Against Child Labor.* New York: Clarion, 1994.
Hindman, Hugh D. *Child Labor: An*

Children's Bureau, U.S.

LEGEND HAS IT that the idea for a federal Children's Bureau came up over breakfast at the Henry Street Settlement House in New York. In 1903, social reformers Lillian Wald and Florence Kelley were reading their mail and newspapers when Kelley opened a letter asking why nothing was being done about the high rate of child mortality during summertime. After Wald wondered where to find information on variable death rates for children, Kelley read aloud a newspaper article announcing a federal investigation of boll weevil damage in the South. Wald asked why the government could investigate the cotton crop and not its "child crop." This question led to a nine-year campaign to win approval for a federal agency that could conduct such investigations.

President Theodore Roosevelt supported the idea for such an agency, and President William Howard Taft signed it into law in 1912. The Children's Bureau, a subdivision of the Department of Labor, was the first federal agency in the world that concerned itself solely with children. Charged by Congress to report "on all matters pertaining to the welfare of children and child life among all classes of our people," the agency received only a small initial appropriation of $25,640. Julia Lathrop, the nation's first female head of a federal department and a former social worker at the Hull House settlement in Chicago, served as its first chief from 1912 to 1921.

The agency's first task was to start a birth registration system that could help the government track infant survival and enforce school attendance.

Its efforts to abolish child labor were not immediately successful. The Supreme Court declared unconstitutional two of the child-labor bills the bureau had sponsored in conjunction with the National Child Labor Committee. The Children's Bureau staff also mobilized national campaigns for unemployment and health insurance, minimum-wage and maximum-hour statutes, mothers' pensions, and juvenile justice codes.

One major success involved attempts to lower the mortality rate for infants and child-bearing mothers. In 1921 the bureau achieved passage of the Sheppard-Towner Maternity and Infancy Act, the first federal legislation to concern itself with maternal and child health. The Act helped states improve midwife training and disseminate information on nutrition and hygiene through prenatal and child health clinics. It provided funds to send visiting nurses to assist pregnant women and nursing mothers. Some legislators and medical personnel criticized the Act as a new form of government intrusion into private affairs. Even though Sheppard-Towner was funded only until 1929, some historians see it and the work of the Children's Bureau as having set precedents for the child and family welfare aspects of the 1935 Social Security Act.

Happy and healthy children carry picnic baskets up a hill on this poster proclaiming 1918 Children's Year. The U.S. Children's Bureau promoted fresh air and exercise for the well-being of children.

SEE ALSO

Child labor; Hull House; Kelley, Florence; Settlement-house movement; Wald, Lillian

FURTHER READING

Ladd-Taylor, Molly, ed. *Raising a Baby the Government Way: Mothers' Letters To the Children's Bureau, 1915–1932.* New Brunswick, N.J.: Rutgers University Press, 1986.

Lindenmeyer, Kriste. *"A Right to Childhood": The U.S. Children's Bureau and Child Welfare, 1912–46.* Urbana: University of Illinois Press, 1997.

Chinese Americans

SEE Asian Americans

Chinese Exclusion Act (1882)

WITH THE CHINESE Exclusion Act of 1882, the United States attempted to put an end to Chinese immigration, although certain classes of visitors—teachers, students, merchants, tourists, and officials—could still gain entrance to the United States. The Act also declared that no Chinese resident could become a citizen. (People of Chinese descent born in the United States were automatically citizens.) Congress renewed the Exclusion Act every ten years, making it permanent in 1904. The courts extended it in subsequent years to apply to Asians generally.

The nation's first ethnically based anti-immigration law, the Exclusion Act emerged from growing labor tensions and cultural prejudices, particularly on the West Coast. During the depression of the 1870s, labor unions blamed the Chinese for causing unemployment and driving down wages.

Antagonism flared when several companies imported Chinese strikebreakers. In addition, "old stock" Americans everywhere responded to the Chinese presence with deep suspicion and outright hostility. By the election campaign of 1880, all political parties supported an exclusion act.

A number of very determined Chinese found ways to circumvent the Exclusion Act. Many newly arrived male immigrants claimed they were the sons of American-born Chinese. A so-called "paper son" produced papers explaining to immigration officers that his American-born father had returned to China on a visit and married a Chinese woman, whose son he was. Since record keeping was irregular, and many birth records had been lost in fires following the 1906 San Francisco earthquake, there was no way for immigration authorities to discover if he was a real son of an American citizen. Some American-born Chinese men provided documentation for numerous "paper sons" unrelated to themselves, who then entered the country legally. Nevertheless, the number of Chinese and their descendants residing in the United States declined steadily until the 1920s. Congress did not lift race-based restrictions against Chinese immigrants until 1943.

A stereotyped Chinese man flees the booted foot of a member of the Workingman's Party of California, who kicks him back to China. Those who feared competition from Chinese labor convinced Congress to pass a Chinese Exclusion Act prohibiting Chinese immigration.

SEE ALSO
Asian Americans; Civil rights; Immigration; Labor; Race relations

FURTHER READING
Chang, Gordon H. *Asian Americans and Politics: Perspectives, Experiences, Prospects.* Palo Alto, Calif.: Stanford University Press, 2001.
Gyory, Andrew. *Closing the Gate: Race, Politics, and the Chinese Exclusion Act.* Chapel Hill: University of North Carolina Press, 1998.
Hoobler, Dorothy, and Thomas Hoobler. *The Chinese American Family Album.* New York: Oxford University Press, 1994.
Lee, Erika. *At America's Gates: Chinese Immigration During the Exclusion Era, 1882–1943.* Chapel Hill: University of North Carolina Press, 2003.

Cities

BETWEEN 1880 AND 1920, millions of people from rural areas and from abroad moved into American cities. By 1900 the population of New York City alone—almost 3.5 million—equaled the nation's total urban population of 50 years earlier. By 1920, New York had 5 million residents; Chicago, 3 million. Between 1880 and 1920, the populations of Boston, St. Louis, and San Francisco doubled.

This growth transformed American urban life. Before the Civil War, cities were rarely more than three or four miles across. Most people lived at or near their workplaces. Horse-drawn streetcars, introduced in the 1850s, and later electric trolleys (Richmond, Virginia, had the first one in 1888), speeded up the separation of work from home. Those who could afford the fares moved into suburbs. Cable cars and elevated trains, automobiles—which first appeared in 1893—and subways—Boston's was first in 1897—made commuting easier.

To accommodate larger populations, city buildings grew higher. Before the war, none was higher than four or five stories. Elevators, developed in 1861 and run by electricity beginning in the 1890s, and steel girders made skyscrapers possible. The first appeared in Chicago. By 1900, buildings reached 30 stories. Cities also developed specialized business areas. Banks, financial offices, lawyers, and government offices congregated in one neighborhood, retail shops and department stores in another. Industrial, wholesale, and warehouse districts formed in a ring around the center.

Most newcomers to the city had few choices about housing. Some moved into houses built for them by mill and factory owners. The rest found rooms or apartments in buildings abandoned by middle-class residents and converted into multifamily units. Speculators also built cheap tenements in vacant lots or backyards. As trees and shrubs disappeared, killed off by the soot and grime from coal-fired steam engines and boilers, many old urban residential neighborhoods turned into slums.

Slum life was miserable. Hundreds of families crammed into spaces meant for a few. The air stank from open sewers, horse droppings, and backyard privies. Basements were damp or flooded, making homes for rats, vermin, and disease. There were few toilets and almost no bathtubs. Highly contagious diseases raged. In his novel *Yekl: A Tale of the New York Ghetto* (1896), recent immigrant Abraham Cahan described a character on New York's Lower East Side having to "pick and nudge his way through dense swarms of bedraggled half-naked humanity; past garbage barrels rearing their overflowing contents in sickening piles, and lining the streets in malicious suggestion of rows of trees; underneath tiers and tiers of fire escapes, barricaded and festooned with mattresses, pillows, and featherbeds not yet gathered in for the night. The pent-in sultry atmosphere was laden with nausea. . . . " In this kind of atmosphere, fires, such as those that struck Chicago in 1871 and Boston in 1872, were devastating. Crime and vice also flourished in the slums. Some slums became ghettos, sections of cities identified with certain ethnic or racial groups.

While some ghettos were voluntary, forming when immigrants chose to live where others of their ethnic group had settled, others were involuntary, taking shape when real estate restrictions, known as covenants, forced certain groups into segregated neighborhoods or confined them to certain areas. African Americans, Mexicans, and Asian Americans often lived in such ghettos, which tended to be in the worst sections of town.

As industrial wage earners moved into the cities, many native-born, white, professional, and wealthier urban dwellers built homes in the suburbs. A few cities preserved wealthy areas near the city center, such as Boston's Beacon Hill, Chicago's Gold Coast, or San Francisco's Nob Hill. But those who lived there also had country estates and were quite insulated from poverty. For them, city life was new and exciting. They enjoyed commercial and personal services unimaginable to earlier generations and could take advantage of cities' cultural and entertainment resources—museums and libraries, sporting events, theatrical and operatic spectaculars, luxurious restaurants and ballrooms, and eventually grand motion picture houses. Even though the working classes were less able to enjoy such pleasures, they also delighted in the many cheap recreational venues that cities now offered, such as saloons, dance halls, nickelodeons, excursion boats, and amusement parks.

As cities expanded in this period, pressures increased on officials to provide improved police and fire protection, sewage disposal, electricity and water, transportation systems, and health care. To deliver these services, cities had to raise taxes and set up offices. Whoever dominated these offices could make a great deal of

This bird's-eye view of Oklahoma City in 1890 depicts an established community laid out in a neat grid. The city, in the former Indian territory of Oklahoma, was less than a year old at the time.

money through graft, a bribe in exchange for the award of a city job or contract.

Various groups vied for control. Often, one group would represent the middle and upper classes, which tended to be of native-born, white, and Protestant or German Jewish backgrounds. Opposing this group might be another made up primarily of immigrant and working-class residents representing Irish or Italian Catholics or eastern European and Russian Jews. State legislatures and city governments also vied for power. Because states levied taxes that provided services to cities, state and city governments fought over which had priority in jurisdiction. In addition, rural interests resisted having to pay higher taxes or sacrifice natural resources, such as water or acreage, to meet city needs.

Out of these clashing political and economic interests, city "machines" often arose. These were unofficial organizations designed to keep a particular party or group in power. "Bosses" usually ran them, sometimes holding political office themselves, but more usually picking others to run for office and then helping them win. The bosses also appointed leaders, usually saloon or hotel keepers, for each of a city's political districts, or wards. These men handed out city jobs and contracts and did favors for residents. In return, residents supported the machine ticket on election day.

Machines held sway in dozens of Gilded Age cities, controlling jobs in police and fire departments, public works, and even education. Sometimes they encouraged fraudulent voting. When investigations exposed their corruption, some bosses landed in jail. But their organizations usually survived, primarily because working people relied on them for jobs and favors.

SEE ALSO

Health, public; Immigration; Machine politics; Parks and playgrounds; Progressive movement; Reform movements; Transportation, public

FURTHER READING

Barth, Gunther. *City People: The Rise of Modern City Culture in Nineteenth-Century America.* New York: Oxford University Press, 1978.
Monkkonen, Eric H. *America Becomes Urban: The Development of U.S. Cities and Towns, 1780–1980.* Berkeley: University of California Press, 1988.
Riis, Jacob. *How the Other Half Lives: Studies Among the Tenements of New York.* Edited by David Leviatin. Boston: Bedford/St. Martin's, 1996.
Shumsky, Neil Larry, ed. *Encyclopedia of Urban America: The Cities and Suburbs.* 2 vols. Santa Barbara, Calif.: ABC-CLIO, 1998.
Steffens, Lincoln. *The Shame of the Cities. 1904.* Reprint, Mineola, N.Y.: Dover, 2004.

Civil rights

CIVIL RIGHTS are the government-protected legal rights that citizens hold in a free society. In the United States, the Constitution guarantees citizens the rights of free speech, freedom of religion, and freedom from persecution at the hands of the government, among other rights. In the years following the Civil War, the U.S. government passed a series of constitutional amendments and Civil Rights Acts to guarantee these rights and to extend others. The 14th and 15th amendments to the Constitution (passed in 1868 and 1870) and a Civil Rights Act of 1866 required that individual states extend civil rights to all citizens and guaranteed full citizenship, including voting rights, to freed slaves. In 1871 Congress passed another Civil Rights Act outlawing terrorist activities designed to deprive

African American demonstrators carry a banner with a passage from the Declaration of Independence as they parade in silence along New York City's Fifth Avenue.

minorities of their civil rights. An 1875 Civil Rights Act prohibited racial discrimination in hotels, theaters, and other places of public accommodation.

Over the next 30 years, more than a dozen states in the North and West passed civil rights statutes establishing their own antidiscrimination policies. In those same 30 years, however, an increasingly conservative Supreme Court invalidated both the 1871 and 1875 acts. The Court held that Congress had no power under the 14th Amendment to regulate "private" (nongovernmental) discrimination. African Americans in southern states lost both civil rights and voting rights as white supremacy and segregation became entrenched in the late 1800s.

The country's civil rights laws contained some important inconsistencies. For example, women citizens in most states could not vote. Their voices went unheard in political issues that affected them, and they were taxed without representation in government. Native Americans did not have U.S. citizenship or voting rights until the late 1880s, when the Dawes Severalty Act granted citizenship to a few Indian property owners. The majority of Native Americans, however, remained noncitizens, lacking both voting rights and civil rights protections. Moreover, police and soldiers were free to invade

their homes, drive them off their lands, and put them in jail. Finally, the government retained the right to strip citizens of their civil rights in the case of felony conviction or in times of national crisis or states of war. During the Red Scare, a period following World War I that was characterized by mass hysteria over the presence of communists ("Reds") on American soil, the government reserved the right to revoke some civil rights and protections guaranteed in the Constitution.

Not even free speech was a certainty in the Gilded Age and Progressive Era. In 1873, Congress passed an act to suppress the circulation of "Obscene Literature and Articles of Immoral Use." Nicknamed the Comstock Law after Anthony Comstock, the moral crusader who had persuaded Congress to take this step, the law classed erotic art and literature, as well as information about women's reproductive health and contraception, as obscene. It forbade distribution of any such material through the mails. The law violated the right to free speech guaranteed by the Constitution, but its concern for sexual morality appealed to Victorian-era Americans. In his 40 years as a special agent of the U.S. Postal Service, Anthony Comstock prosecuted 3,500 individuals and destroyed 120 tons of "obscene" literature.

Many Americans supported limitations on freedom of expression in the name of morality. Many also supported increasingly restrictive naturalization laws, which determine how a resident alien becomes a U.S. citizen, entitled to full civil rights and protections. To gain citizenship, an immigrant first declared his or her intention to become a citizen and then waited five years for naturalization. Until 1906, even a county court could grant citizenship. After that date, however, naturalization became a matter for state supreme courts and federal courts, which worked in conjunction with the U.S. Bureau of Immigration and Naturalization. Until 1922, an alien woman became a citizen immediately if she married a citizen; after that date, she had to undergo her own naturalization process. Children born abroad became citizens when their parents were naturalized. Children born in the United States were automatically citizens, regardless of their parents' status. After 1918, army veterans, navy veterans, and wartime enlistees could gain citizenship through an accelerated naturalization process. In 1924, with the passage of the Indian Citizenship Act, all Native Americans finally gained full citizenship.

Chinese and Japanese immigrants, Koreans, and other Asians, however, constituted a whole class of aliens that was simply barred from citizenship. Adhering to a law passed in 1790, which stipulated that "whites only" could be naturalized as citizens, Congress could enact laws barring Asians from immigration as well as citizenship and eventually exclude them altogether. Starting in 1882, a series of Chinese Exclusion Acts suspended any further immigration of Chinese laborers and denied naturalization to those who were already in the United States. Immigrants from China remained aliens, lacking a right to vote or buy property and suffering discrimination at the hands of whites. Japanese immigration came to a complete halt with the total exclusion of Asians under the 1924 Immigration Quota Laws. Indians from South Asia found themselves ineligible for citizenship because, although Caucasian in anthropological terms, they did not look "white." Americans eager to exclude them argued that they would not assimilate well into the dominant culture.

Women, Asians, Native Americans, and African Americans resisted discrimination that deprived them of citizenship and civil rights. In 1912, American-born Chinese in California, faced with mistreatment by both the general public and the authorities even though they were citizens, founded the Chinese American Citizens Alliance to defend their civil rights. In the courts, Chinese, Japanese, and Asian Indians tested the laws that discriminated against them because of race, though fair treatment eluded them until after World War II.

Starting in 1909, the National Association for the Advancement of Colored People (NAACP) began a long struggle to win civil rights for African Americans. With the aid of highly skilled lawyers, they challenged racial discrimination in the courts. They sometimes won legal victories. For example, their lawyers won court victories over voter disfranchisement in 1915 and residential segregation in 1917, but failed to have lynching made a federal crime. In 1917, the Supreme Court conceded that the states could not officially segregate African Americans into residential districts (*Buchanan v. Warley*) and NAACP lawyers won the right for African Americans to be commissioned as military officers. Full civil rights for African Americans would not come until the 1960s, however. American women won the vote in 1920, 72 years after they had begun their struggle for that basic civil right of American citizenship.

SEE ALSO

African Americans; Asian Americans; Chinese Exclusion Act (1882); Comstock Law (1873); Dawes Severalty Act; Immigration; Law; National Association for the Advancement of Colored People; Native Americans; Race relations; Red Scare (1919–20); Reform movements; Segregation; Suffrage; Woman suffrage movement

FURTHER READING

Deloria, Vine, and David E. Wilkins. *Tribes, Treaties, and Constitutional Tribulations.* Austin: University of Texas Press, 2000.

DuBois, Ellen Carol. *Woman Suffrage and Women's Rights.* New York: New York University Press, 1998.

Klarman, Michael J. *From Jim Crow to Civil Rights: The Supreme Court and the Struggle for Racial Equality.* New York: Oxford University Press, 2004.

Park, John S. W. *Elusive Citizenship: Immigration, Asian Americans, and the Paradox of Civil Rights.* New York: New York University Press, 2004.

Pohlmann, Marcus D., and Linda Vallar Whisenhunt. *Student's Guide to Landmark Congressional Laws on Civil Rights.* Westport, Conn.: Greenwood, 2002.

Clemens, Samuel Langhorne

- *Born: Nov. 30, 1835, Florida, Mo.*
- *Accomplishments: author,* The Innocents Abroad *(1869),* The Gilded Age *(1873),* The Adventures of Tom Sawyer *(1876),* The Prince and the Pauper *(1882),* Life on the Mississippi *(1883),* The Adventures of Huckleberry Finn *(1884),* A Connecticut Yankee in King Arthur's Court *(1889),* Puddn'head Wilson *(1894),* The Man That Corrupted Hadleyburg and Other Stories *(1900),* King Leopold's Soliloquy *(1905),* Letters from the Earth *(1909), and many other novels, stories, and works of non-fiction.*
- *Died: Apr. 21, 1910, on his estate, Stormfield, near Redding, Conn.*

KNOWN PRIMARILY by his pen name, Mark Twain, Samuel Langhorne Clemens was one of the most beloved writers and lecturers of the Gilded Age. He grew up in Hannibal, Missouri, a thriving town north of St. Louis that later served as the setting for several of his novels. When his father died in 1847, Samuel, aged 12, had to go to work. He set type for a printer until his older brother bought a newspaper and

took him on as typesetter and editorial assistant. This paper published Samuel's first humorous sketches, which were mostly about local life. In 1853, Clemens began to wander, working as a typesetter in St. Louis, New York City, Philadelphia, and Cincinnati. In 1857, he learned how to be a river pilot on the Mississippi River and continued to educate himself with studies in French and serious reading.

When the Civil War closed down traffic on the river and put him out of work, Clemens joined the Confederate Army. At heart an abolitionist, he deserted within a few weeks and headed west. First he worked as an assistant to his brother, recently appointed secretary of the Nevada Territory. He then tried mining, lumbering, and newspaper reporting. In 1863 he began to use as a pen name the words *Mark Twain*, the Mississippi boatmen's call for a depth sounding of 12 feet. Some of his humorous yarns found wide readership, especially "Jim Smiley and His Jumping Frog." One newspaper sent him to Hawaii (then, the Sandwich Islands) to write travel letters. Upon his return, he achieved such success lecturing about his travels that newspapers hired him to write about other exotic locales. His pieces led eventually to contracts for topical columns and books, such as *The Innocents Abroad* (1869), his best-selling book about his travels in Europe.

By the early years of the 20th century, Mark Twain's writing and popular lecture tours had made him the most acclaimed literary figure in the United States.

Huck Finn, a character created by Mark Twain, in an illustration from the 1884 first edition of The Adventures of Huckleberry Finn.

In 1870, Clemens married Olivia Langdon. The couple settled in Hartford, Connecticut, where Clemens experienced a long period of creativity and profitability from his writings. *Roughing It* (1872), about his travels into the West, was followed by the political satire *The Gilded Age* (1873), written with Charles Dudley Warner, the editor of the Hartford *Courant*. Historians later took the title Gilded Age as their name for post-Reconstruction America. Clemens's classic story of the adventures of a mischievous boy named Tom Sawyer came out in 1876, followed by *A Tramp Abroad* in 1880, *The Prince and the Pauper* in 1882, *Life on the Mississippi* in 1883, and his sequel to Tom Sawyer, *The Adventures of Huckleberry Finn,* in 1884. The story of the adventures of a wily youngster and an escaped slave and their travels down the Mississippi River, it is widely regarded as an American masterpiece for its vivid language and frank depictions of race, social class, and cultural conflicts in American society.

Many of Clemens's writings commented critically on American life. *The Tragedy of Pudd'head Wilson* (1884), a murder mystery, condemned slavery. His fantasy about sixth-century England, *A Connecticut Yankee in King Arthur's Court* (1889), satirized American society and politics. Not all of his books were equally successful. Reviewers criticized *Huckleberry Finn*'s vulgar language, seeming approval of "primitive" over "civilized" lifestyles, and the positive characterization of the runaway slave, Jim. The book did well enough, however, to win Clemens more lucrative contracts.

As Clemens basked in the renown and income his writings brought him, he continued to write stories, biographies, commentaries, and satires. He traveled throughout the world with his family, lecturing to enthusiastic audiences and receiving honors from royalty and cultural institutions. In his last years he took part in some political movements, including those to improve the operations of government and anti-imperialist causes. His writings remain popular to this day.

SEE ALSO
Gilded Age; Literature

FURTHER READING
Budd, Louis J. *Our Mark Twain: The Making of His Public Personality.* Philadelphia: University of Pennsylvania Press, 1983.
Camfield, Gregg. *The Oxford Companion to Mark Twain.* New York: Oxford University Press, 2003.
Kaplan, Justin. *Mr. Clemens and Mark Twain, a Biography.* New York: Simon & Schuster, 1966.
Ward, Geoffrey C. *Mark Twain.* New York: Knopf, 2001.

Cleveland, Grover

- *Born: Mar. 18, 1837, Caldwell, N.J.*
- *Education: secondary schools until 1853*
- *Accomplishments: mayor of Buffalo, N.Y. (1881–82); governor of New York (1882–84), President of the United States (1885–89, 1893–97)*
- *Died: June 24, 1908, Princeton, N.J.*

GROVER CLEVELAND, 22nd and 24th President of the United States, served two nonconsecutive terms in the White House. Elected in 1884, defeated in 1888, then returned to office in 1892, he was the only Democrat elected to the Presidency in an era dominated by Republicans, from Abraham Lincoln in 1861 through William Howard Taft in 1913.

He was born Stephen Grover Cleveland, son of a Presbyterian minister. After working as a store clerk and teaching in a school for the blind, he became a law clerk, passed the bar exam, and practiced law in Buffalo, New York, without ever attending college or law school. He avoided serving in the Civil War by paying $300 to hire a substitute, an advantage of the era's draft law. Cleveland was active in Democratic party politics and law enforcement, holding office as an assistant district attorney, sheriff, and hangman. After winning a race for mayor of Buffalo, he gained statewide attention for cleaning up a corrupt city government. In 1882, he won New York's governorship, becoming nationally known as an opponent of the dishonest use of public money. In 1884, he won his party's nomination for President.

That year's Presidential campaign featured fierce personal attacks on both sides. Democrats charged the Republican nominee, former Speaker of the House James Blaine, with corruption in his public career, while Republicans accused Cleveland of immorality in his private life. Cleveland acknowledged that he might be the father of a child out of wedlock. Republicans accused Democrats of being the party of "Rum, Romanism, and Rebellion," that is, the party associated with legalized drinking, Catholicism, and the secession of the South in the Civil War. Benefiting from public anger over this label, and aided by the defection of many reform-minded Republicans who voted for the Democratic candidate, Cleveland defeated Blaine by a small margin.

As President, Cleveland opposed public spending that he considered irresponsible, such as pensions for individual Civil War veterans or other federal aid legislation, including a modest $10,000 to buy seed for farmers stricken by drought. Cleveland felt that government should not do the work of private charity and that federal assistance to the poor "weakens the sturdiness of our national character." He fought unsuccessfully to reduce protective tariffs, which he saw as favoring certain manufacturers over others and raising the cost of living. In 1887, however, he approved the Interstate Commerce Commission, a federal regulatory agency designed to ensure that the railroads charged fair rates to all of their customers.

One of Cleveland's most popular acts, his marriage while in office, took place in 1886. His bride, Frances Folsom, the daughter of a former law partner, was more than 25 years his junior. Despite his wife's success as a Washington hostess, Cleveland's unpopularity on other issues, such as his opposition to high tarriffs, led to his loss to Republican Benjamin Harrison in 1888. In a rematch four years later, however, Cleveland made an unprecedented comeback, defeating Harrison and reclaiming the White House.

An 1884 campaign poster advertises the Democratic candidates for President and Vice President, New York governor Grover Cleveland and former Indiana governor and senator Thomas Hendricks.

FOR PRESIDENT
GROVER CLEVELAND
of NEW YORK.

for VICE PRESIDENT
THOS. A. HENDRICKS
OF INDIANA.

The Panic of 1893, which touched off the most serious economic depression in U.S. history, dominated Cleveland's second term. Prices rose, the Treasury's gold supply ran dangerously low, and unemployment soared. Cleveland blamed the crisis on an inflated money supply caused by increased minting of silver currency during the Harrison administration. He persuaded Congress to repeal the Bland-Allison Act, which had required the government to purchase and coin large quantities of silver. Cleveland remained adamantly opposed to government welfare spending, refusing to relax his principles even when Ohio businessman Jacob Coxey marched on Washington, D.C., with 500 desperate protestors to demand veterans' benefits and unemployment relief. The economy did not begin to recover until 1896–97, when new gold production raised public confidence and stabilized the markets.

Cleveland also reversed another Harrison administration policy, withdrawing politcal support from the sugar planters who wanted the U.S. government to annex Hawaii. He further resisted imperial expansion by refusing to send troops to Cuba to support a revolution against Spain. When Pullman company railroad workers went on strike in Illinois in 1894, Cleveland dispatched thousands of federal troops to break it up. The union defeat that followed weakened organized labor for decades to come. Cleveland's second term ended in 1897 when Republican William McKinley defeated former Nebraska congressman William Jennings Bryan, who ran on both the Democratic and Populist tickets.

Among the most memorable accomplishments of Grover Cleveland's eight years in office was his success in repealing the Tenure of Office Act and thus restoring the President's authority to fire his own cabinet officials without Senate approval. Cleveland vetoed more legislation than all previous U.S. Presidents combined, thereby preparing the way for the stronger executive office of the 20th century.

SEE ALSO

Blaine, James G.; Bryan, William Jennings; Coxey's Army; Harrison, Benjamin; Imperialism; McKinley, William; Monetary policies; Native Americans; Presidency; Pullman strike (1894); Populist party; Tariffs and taxes

FURTHER READING

Brodsky, Alyn. *Grover Cleveland: A Study in Character.* New York: St. Martin's, 2000.
Graff, Henry F. *Grover Cleveland.* New York: Times Books, 2002.
Jeffers, Paul H. *An Honest President: The Life and Presidencies of Grover Cleveland.* New York: Morrow, 2000.
Summers, Mark Wahlgren. *Rum, Romanism, & Rebellion: The Making of a President, 1884.* Chapel Hill: University of North Carolina Press, 2000.

Colleges and universities

IN 1860, THE COUNTRY'S college students, like their professors, were almost exclusively white and male. The numbers of this elite group amounted to only 1 percent of all white college-age men. By 1920, a larger and more diverse group—almost 6 percent of the entire college-age population—was attending institutions of higher learning. Because the country's population had skyrocketed, however, the absolute number of college students had actually shot up even more dramatically.

American colleges and universities began to expand during the Civil War with the passage of the Morrill Land-Grant Act of 1862. By this act, the

U.S. government gave each state massive tracts of federally owned land. The states sold the land and used the proceeds to finance state colleges. The Morrill Act required land-grant schools to offer vocational education in "agriculture and mechanic arts" and to provide students with military training. Many of these land-grant colleges had teacher-training branches known as "normal schools."

A provision in the Morrill Act allowing state colleges to teach "scientific and classical studies" enabled many land-grant colleges to become major universities over time. As universities, they offered graduate as well as undergraduate programs and other advanced degrees in specialized areas, such as law and medicine.

A follow-up to the Morrill Act in 1890 extended the public education program to the southern states that had been excluded when the original act passed during the Civil War. The 1890 law also brought segregation to higher education campuses, by authorizing the establishment of separate land-grant colleges for black students. These colleges were supposed to be equal to white colleges. In practice, however, they suffered from inferior funding and substandard facilities.

Religious and philanthropic groups responded by establishing private colleges and universities exclusively for black students. Support came from white northern groups and individuals as well as from black religious organizations. Fisk University, founded in Nashville, Tennessee, in 1865; Howard University, founded in Washington, D.C., in 1867; and Morehouse and Spelman colleges, founded in Atlanta, Georgia, in 1867 and 1881, became respected centers of African American scholarship.

Initially, white administrators ran many black colleges and universities. But in 1881, black educator Booker T. Washington became president of the new Tuskegee Normal and Industrial Institute (later Tuskegee University) in Alabama. Dedicated to training black students in such practical skills as farming, mechanical trades, and teaching, Tuskegee reflected Washington's belief that African Americans had to establish a solid middle-class presence in the U.S. economy before they could aspire to full social and political equality.

Other black leaders, notably activist professor W. E. B. DuBois, favored giving black students a complete liberal arts education. In 1904, Mary McLeod Bethune, the daughter of freed slaves,

Wellesley College students pose for a group portrait in 1903. Founded in 1875, Wellesley was one of the earliest private colleges to offer women higher education at a level equivalent to that available for men.

founded Daytona Normal and Industrial Institute for Training Negro Girls. She started with $1.50 and a patch of donated Florida land that had once been a garbage dump. By 1929, the school had become Bethune-Cookman College.

Many land-grant and all-black colleges started out as, or became, coeducational. When he took over as president of the University of Michigan in 1871, James Burrill Angell not only oversaw the introduction of coeducation, but afterward took many opportunities to point to the "brilliant successes" of Michigan's women students. In 1893, African American educator Anna Julia Cooper explained in a speech that colleges for blacks "were almost without exception co-educational" because funds were "too limited to be divided on sex lines, even had it been ideally desirable...." Most of the nation's elite private universities, such as Harvard, Yale, and Princeton, admitted only men.

Despite resistance from traditionalists, who claimed that higher education might overtax a woman's brain, harm her reproductive system, or make her unmarriageable, advocates of higher education for women were determined to give female students their own elite colleges. Vassar, founded in New York State in 1865; Smith and Wellesley, both founded in Massachusetts in 1875; and Bryn Mawr, founded in Pennsylvania in 1884, all offered women access to the same rigorous academic and scientific disciplines taught at men's colleges. Some male institutions eventually agreed to establish affiliated women's schools, or "annexes." Barnard College, affiliated with Columbia University in New York City, opened in 1889 as an annex, as did Radcliffe College, affiliated with Harvard, in 1894.

By 1920, the rise of public colleges run by cities and states, and of private colleges, many run by religious institutions, had made higher education much more accessible to American youth. The sons and daughters of farmers, factory workers, immigrants, and minorities, all of whom in earlier years would never have dreamed of going to college, could now earn advanced degrees, even in courses they attended at night while holding down jobs during the day. While the most dramatic growth in colleges and universities would not occur until after World War II, the expansion of American higher education in the Gilded Age and Progressive Era was unique among democratic Western nations.

SEE ALSO

African Americans; DuBois, William Edward Burghardt (W. E. B.); Education; Segregation; Washington, Booker T.

FURTHER READING

Drewry, Henry N., and Humphrey Doermann. *Stand and Prosper: Private Black Colleges and Their Students.* Princeton, N.J.: Princeton University Press, 2003.
Solomon, Barbara Miller. *In the Company of Educated Women: A History of Women and Higher Education in America.* New Haven, Conn.: Yale University Press, 1985.
Thelin, John R. *A History of American Higher Education.* Baltimore, Md.: Johns Hopkins University Press, 2004.

Commerce

EVERY NATION'S commerce, or the buying and selling of goods, takes place at two levels: domestic (within its own borders) and foreign (with other nations). American commerce at both of these levels changed significantly during the Gilded Age and Progressive Era. Through the expansion of the railroads, domestic trade operated increasingly through nationwide rather than just regional networks. Domestic trade also came under increased government oversight through federal regulation of the railroads. Foreign trade expanded so much that by 1920 American manufactured goods dominated world markets.

In the past, producers of salable goods had to rely on wagons, canal barges, and steamships to reach their markets. These means of transport were not only slow but often unreliable. By the end of the 1800s, however, some 190,000 miles of railroad tracks linked businesses and customers across every state and territory in the nation. American domestic commerce now existed on a national basis. Businesses could market manufactured goods and producers could ship raw materials and agricultural products anywhere, including to the nation's seaports for shipping abroad.

During this era, as the urban population increased, more Americans consumed rather than grew their own food. This development led to the emergence of a national market in foodstuffs. City dwellers bought ever-growing quantities of beef, pork, bread, and milk to feed their families. Americans imported more sugar and coffee in this era, in turn affecting the commercial and political relationships of the United States with the countries that produced these commodities, especially Hawaii and Cuba. Americans also demanded more fruits and vegetables from farmers. These demands influenced the emergence of new types of farming and spurred legislation to improve irrigation in the Southwest. Farmers planted citrus groves in Florida in order to supply northern cities with lemons and oranges. The availability of refrigerated railroad cars after 1874 facilitated the shipping of all perishable foodstuffs across long distances.

Some discriminatory and anticompetitive practices by the railroads led to dissatisfaction among the shippers. The practices at issue included charging customers more for short- than long-haul transport, giving rebates to corporations, and forming "pools" with competing railroads to keep shipping costs high. Pressure from merchants, farm organizations, and independent businessmen led first to state railroad regulatory commissions and finally to federal action. The Interstate Commerce Act of 1890 prohibited pools and rebates and some differential rates for short and long hauls. Although the act created the Interstate Commerce Commission (ICC) to administer the law, it gave the commission no power to enforce the law's provisions or set railroad shipping rates. Federal acts passed in subsequent years corrected this deficiency.

Two trends marked U.S. foreign trade during the Gilded Age and Progressive Era. First, the United States moved steadily toward the center of international trade relations. Between 1890 and 1920, its exports rose from $910 million to $8.6 billion a year, and its investments abroad went from less than half a billion to more than 7 billion dollars. World War I stimulated

Ohio farmers deliver wagonloads of produce to a train that will carry the crops to markets in the East. The growth of the railroad after the Civil War stimulated commerce by connecting producers with customers hundreds of miles away.

this extraordinary expansion. After the war, Americans sent more manufactured goods to Latin American markets than did Britain and Germany, and because of its large loans to the Allies, the United States was by the 1920s the world's largest creditor.

The second major trend was that an increasing amount of the nation's exports consisted of manufactured goods rather than raw materials. In the past, the United States had shipped abroad large amounts of food (primarily wheat and corn), tobacco, and cotton. By the early 1900s, U.S. industrialists were sending abroad more machines and machine-made goods, such as sewing machines and farm tools.

As foreign trade expanded, American industries also expanded overseas, first establishing sales outlets for their goods and then manufacturing plants abroad. The first super-corporation to do this was Singer Sewing Machine, which established plants in Scotland in 1867 and Russia in 1905. American Smelting and Refining established factories in Mexico by 1901. The American Tobacco Company expanded globally in the 1890s, employing local agents in Shanghai, India, and Kyoto, and in 1901 resolving its growing rivalry with the British Tobacco Company by agreeing to share its global markets. In 1905 Ford Motorcar expanded first into Canada, and eventually created a global network of plants, sales operations, and dealers.

Tariffs were an almost constant source of political controversy in this period. Tariffs are special duties, or taxes, imposed by the government on imports. They not only bring in income to the federal government but also protect domestic industries from foreign competition by making imports more expensive than goods produced at home. Before the Progressive Era,

politicians set tariff rates. Progressives, who wanted to "take the tariff out of politics," campaigned for a greater reliance on scientific expertise to regularize rates. To this end, in 1911 President William Howard Taft appointed a temporary tariff commission. President Woodrow Wilson made it permanent in 1916. Authorized only to give advice, the commission provided Congress with technical information useful in its later tariff revisions.

SEE ALSO
Railroads; Taft, William Howard; Taxes and tariffs; Wilson, Woodrow T.

FURTHER READING
Eysenbach, Mary Locke. *American Manufactured Exports, 1879–1914: A Study of Growth and Comparative Advantage.* New York: Arno Press, 1976.
Hamilton, Neil. *American Business Leaders: From Colonial Times to the Present.* Santa Barbara, Calif.: ABC-CLIO, 1999.
Kroos, Herman. *American Business History.* Englewood Cliffs, N.J.: Prentice Hall, 1972.
McCraw, Thomas K. *American Business, 1920–2000: How it Worked.* Wheeling, IL: Harlan Davidson, 2000.
Wilkins, Mira. *Ford on Six Continents.* Detroit, Mich.: Wayne State University Press, 1964.

Committee on Public Information, U.S.

IN APRIL 1917, one week after the United States entered World War I, President Woodrow Wilson created the Committee on Public Information (CPI). The committee was soon nicknamed the Creel Committee after its leader, Colorado newspaperman George Creel. The committee's aims were to enlist public support for the war through propagandizing America's war aims at home and abroad and to stifle dissent.

With images of warplanes and a fierce American eagle, a Committee on Public Information poster encourages citizens to lend money to the war effort during World War I.

Although it avoided direct censorship, the CPI branded antiwar sentiment as unpatriotic. This tactic silenced the radical and socialist press, which never recovered after the war. Even more successful, the CPI's pro-war propaganda effort was the largest government undertaking of its kind in history, costing in all more than $2 million. With 19 domestic departments and several foreign "missions," the CPI recruited experts from business, media, academia, and the art world who demonstrated a skillful use of advertising techniques and recruited expertise from business, media, academia, and the art world. Employing the talents of translators and prominent novelists and essayists, including Walter Lippmann and John Dewey, the agency published 30 booklets in several languages, circulating 75 million copies in America, and many more abroad. A daily newspaper reached 100,000 readers. Creel's goal for the CPI, articulated in his 1920 memoir, was to create "a passionate belief in the justice of America's cause that would weld the American people into one white hot mass instinct with fraternity, devotion, courage and deathless determination."

The CPI also enlisted the work of cartoonists and artists for posters and advertisements, including army recruiting posters featuring a character known as Uncle Sam, and other posters urging people to conserve scarce resources and cooperate fully with the country's war aims. One such poster depicted the Statue of Liberty surrounded by immigrants. The text read: "Food Will Win the War. You

came here seeking freedom. You must now help to preserve it. WHEAT is needed for the Allies. Waste nothing." Samples of this artwork remain as icons of World War I to this day.

Hollywood filmmakers eagerly cooperated with the Creel Committee, producing such popular propaganda films as *The Kaiser: The Beast of Berlin* and *Pershing's Crusaders*. The CPI also planned war exhibits for state fairs and Allied war expositions, defraying some of their costs by securing millions of dollars' worth of free advertising. Historians credit the Creel Committee with having invented modern advertising. After the war, Edward Bernays, who worked for Creel, went on to develop the field of public relations into a profession.

Creel and his committee are best remembered for the creation of "Four-Minute Men," volunteer speakers who gave short, rousing pro-war speeches everywhere in the country, from church suppers to factory floors, selling war bonds, generating enlistments, and promoting volunteer efforts. Creel claimed that 75,000 speakers, including Yiddish-speaking rabbis and at least one Sioux Indian, operated in 5,200 communities. By war's end, they had made more than 750,000 speeches.

A political thinker as well as an advertising man, George Creel remained closely connected to President Wilson throughout the war. His successful promotion of Wilson's two post-war visits to Europe ensured that Wilson and his peace program, the Fourteen Points, received an enthusiastic popular response prior to the Paris peace talks at Versailles. At home, Creel's brash, aggressive campaigning on behalf of Wilson's program alienated many members of Congress and may have contributed to Congress' ultimate rejection of the Versailles Treaty.

SEE ALSO
Dewey, John; Motion pictures; Versailles Treaty; Wilson, Woodrow T.; World War I

FURTHER READING
Cornebise, Alfred. *War as Advertised: The Four Minute Men and America's Crusade, 1917–1918*. Philadelphia: American Philosophical Society, 1984.
Creel, George. *How We Advertised America.* 1920. Reprint, New York: Arno, 1972.
Mock, James Robert. *Words That Won the War: The Story of the Committee on Public Information, 1917–1919*. New York: Russell & Russell, 1968.

Communism

COMMUNISM IS the ideal of a perfected society in which all property and land are collectively owned. Because there would be no social classes in such a society, and therefore no superiors and inferiors and no cause for envy, the people would need neither government nor money to maintain order. Philosophers have imagined such societies for centuries, but only small religious or utopian communities have created purely communist societies.

Communism became a political ideology in the 19th century. In *The Communist Manifesto* (1848) and other writings, two German theorists, Karl Marx and Friedrich Engels, gave the ideology its fullest explanation. They began by saying that "The history of all hitherto existing society is the history of class struggles." By this they meant that the economic competition between social classes determines the course of history. Observing in their own time that industrialization had caused the gap between the rich and the poor to widen, they predicted that the working classes (which they called the "proletariat") would eventually overthrow the wealthy classes (the "bourgeoisie," or capitalists) and then redistribute property equally across all of society.

Marx and Engels foresaw a world in which the workers, not the bosses, would control all natural resources and means of production, such as farms, factories, mines, and transportation systems. In this perfected world, Marx and Engels believed, everybody would contribute to society and to the production of goods and services according to their abilities. In return, they would receive, from communal sources, what they needed in order to survive. Marx and Engels felt that this peaceful, egalitarian, communist society would be achieved only through revolutionary upheaval, however. They ended their manifesto by calling for proletarians everywhere to unite and forcibly "overthrow"... "all existing social conditions." "Let the ruling classes tremble at a communist revolution," they warned. "The proletarians have nothing to lose but their chains. They have a world to win."

The prospect of violent revolution turned Americans against communism and those who tried to promote it as a social ideal. By the beginning of the 20th century, the word *Communist* had become an epithet hurled at radicals, socialists, strikers, and left-wing politicians. During the Progressive Era, American fear of communism peaked after the violent birth of the Soviet Union in 1917 under the red flag of revolutionaries in Russia. The resultant Red Scare in the United States, which took place in 1919 amid an unprecedented number of strikes, led to a widespread antiradical campaign, arrests, deportations, and the persecution of outspoken socialists and other reformers, often in defiance of democratic processes and the civil liberties guaranteed in the Constitution.

Communism survived the Red Scare and became somewhat more popular during the 1930s, when many Americans were suffering economically because of the Great Depression. It came under attack again during the Cold War from the 1950s to the 1980s. Since the dissolution of the Soviet Union in 1989, fear of communism in the United States has lessened. An American Communist party still exists and regularly runs candidates for political offices, without arousing public anxiety or achieving much success.

SEE ALSO

Red Scare (1919–20); Socialism

FURTHER READING

Marx, Karl, and Friedrich Engels. *The Communist Manifesto.* Reprint, New York: Signet Classic, 1998.
Singer, Peter. *Marx: A Very Short Introduction.* New York: Oxford University Press, 2000.
Marx, Karl, and Friedrich Engels. *The Communist Manifesto and Other Writings.* Edited by George Stade. New York: Barnes & Noble Classics, 2005.

Company towns

A COMPANY TOWN was an extension of the corporation that owned it. Company employees and their families made up the town's residents. They lived in company-built or company-owned housing, shopped at company-owned stores, and sent their children to company-run schools. Company employees even entrusted their spiritual and physical care to company-operated churches and hospitals. Employees often paid their bills with scrip, vouchers that the workers could spend only in the town's company-run businesses. In some cases, workers paid their rent, grocery bills, and other expenses by means of automatic deductions from their paychecks, a system that kept some employees permanently in debt to their companies.

In the decades around the turn of the 20th century, well-known communities of this type included the chocolate company town of Hershey, Pennsylvania, the steel company town of Homestead, Pennsylvania, and the railroad car company town of Pullman, Illinois. Some industries built company towns of sturdy materials. Many, like Pullman, were attractive. In this town, the company kept the streets clean, built shopping malls, provided parks and promenades, and designed, equipped, and maintained all the homes. In company towns carved out of existing towns or neighborhoods adjacent to factories, however, the housing was often substandard and minimally maintained by the industrial landlord.

The establishment of company towns allowed industrialists to feel that they were providing decent homes and communities for their workers while also giving themselves a way to control their employees. By keeping close watch over the town's residents, owners could more easily limit habits that might undermine efficient production, such as drinking and other vices. Arranging for employees to be dependent on the company for housing and community services also kept the workers tied to the industry.

Company towns often figured prominently in labor disputes. The

Pullman, Illinois, was founded by industrialist George Pullman as a hometown for railroad workers. George Pullman touched off a strike in 1894 when he cut employees' wages without cutting rents and other expenses.

Pullman strike of 1894 started when railroad car manufacturer George Pullman cut wages for his workers but refused to lower rents and other prices in his company town. The Ludlow Massacre of 1914 occurred at a tent encampment that Colorado coal miners set up after their employer evicted them from company-owned homes when they went on strike. In order to remove the encampment, Colorado state troopers set fire to the tents and machine-gunned people trying to escape. Twenty-one people died, including eleven children.

As automobiles and highways became more common and workers no longer needed to live near their places of employment, company towns declined. Many former company towns died out when mines or industries shut down; others became independent communities; still others were absorbed into growing metropolitan areas.

SEE ALSO:

Homestead strike (1892); Industry; Labor; Mining; Pullman strike (1894); Strikes

FURTHER READING

Carlson, Linda. *Company Towns of the Pacific Northwest.* Seattle: University of Washington Press, 2003.

Crawford, Margaret. *Building the Workingman's Paradise: The Design of American Company Towns.* New York: Verso, 1996.

Shifflett, Crandall A. *Coal Towns: Life, Work, and Culture in Company Towns of Southern Appalachia, 1880–1960.* Knoxville: University of Tennessee Press, 1991.

Compromise of 1877

A SECRET POLITICAL agreement, the Compromise of 1877 resolved the disputed national election of 1876. Republican Presidential candidate Rutherford B. Hayes and the Democratic candidate Samuel J. Tilden, then governor of New York, each claimed that they had won a majority of electoral votes. Tilden, in fact, had won more popular votes than Hayes, but accusations of voting fraud left some 20 electoral votes in dispute. Congress created a 15-member Electoral Commission to determine who had won. This body consisted of 10 congressmen and 5 Supreme Court justices, evenly divided by party, with 1 independent. When the independent declined to serve and was replaced by a Republican, the Commission gave Hayes the election.

Angered by this result, Democrats began a filibuster, making endless speeches on the floor of Congress to block the commission's report. Republicans worked to win the support of southern Democrats to resolve the crisis. In a series of secret meetings, Hayes's supporters agreed to withdraw the rest of the federal troops still remaining in the South, where they had been stationed since the end of the Civil War. They also agreed to approve funding for a southern transcontinental railroad and to help the South industrialize. Appeased, southern Democrats then split off from their northern party colleagues, who were supporting Tilden, and accepted Hayes as President.

The compromise signaled the end of Reconstruction, or the period of rebuilding the Union after the Civil War. It also marked the end of Republican efforts to protect the civil and political rights of ex-slaves in the South. Historians generally use the date 1877 to mark the beginning of the Gilded Age.

Democratic Presidential candidate Samuel Tilden (left) and his running mate, Thomas Hendricks, illustrate the cover of an 1876 campaign song, "Tilden and Reform."

SEE ALSO
Hayes, Rutherford B.; Politics

FURTHER READING

Polakoff, Keith Ian. *The Politics of Inertia: The Election of 1876 and the End of Reconstruction.* Baton Rouge: Louisiana State University Press, 1973.
Woodward, C. Vann. *Reunion and Reaction: The Compromise of 1877 and the End of Reconstruction.* 1951. Reprint, New York: Oxford University Press, 1991.

Comstock Law (1873)

THE COMSTOCK LAW banned the circulation of materials considered "obscene." The official name of this law was Act for the Suppression of Trade in and Circulation of Obscene Literature and Articles of Immoral Use. Most people refer to it, however, by the name of the man who first proposed it, Anthony Comstock.

Comstock was born in New Canaan, Connecticut, served as an infantryman in the Civil War, and then moved to New York City, where he worked as a sales clerk. Inspired by the Young Men's Christian Association to combat sexual immorality, he organized a committee to suppress the city's sex trade. Defining the trade broadly, the committee targeted even printed material concerning sex, such as advertisements for abortion and birth control devices. In 1873, Comstock persuaded Congress to make it a crime to send these materials, as well as pornography and all information concerning contraception, through the U.S. mail or across state lines. He also founded the New York Society for the Suppression of Vice and won appointment as a volunteer postal inspector

In this 1887 letter, New York Society for the Suppression of Vice founder Anthony Comstock congratulates a fellow crusader for engineering the destruction of obscene materials.

with the charge of executing the law that bore his name.

Most Americans ignored the Comstock Law and the police were lax in enforcing it. Still, in 1914 Comstock boasted of having prosecuted 3,697 individuals. His influence persisted after his death in 1915. Birth control pioneer Margaret Sanger was prosecuted under the Comstock Law in 1916, as was sex educator Mary Ware Dennett in 1929 for disseminating her pamphlet "The Sex Side of Life." Dennett appealed her conviction and saw it overturned in 1930. In 1936, the U.S. Circuit Court of Appeals ruled in *United States* v. *One Package* that doctors could distribute contraceptives across state lines. These decisions marked the decline of "Comstockery," the term coined by British playwright George Bernard Shaw that came to mean any attempt to censor speech about sex on the grounds of obscenity.

SEE ALSO

Birth control movement; Civil rights; Sanger, Margaret Higgins; Sex education movement; Sexuality

FURTHER READING

Bates, Anna Louise. *Weeder in the Garden of the Lord: Anthony Comstock's Life and Career.* Lanham, Md.: University Press of America, 1995.

Beisel, Nicola Kay. *Imperiled Innocents: Anthony Comstock and Family Reproduction in Victorian America.* Princeton, N.J.: Princeton University Press, 1997.

Conservation

CONSERVATION IS a philosophy of natural resource management. It allows use of resources while protecting their quality and quantity so that both humans and the environment may benefit. In addition to mineral deposits and arable soil, a nation's natural resources consist of its coastal areas, lakes, rivers, streams, forests, grasslands, deserts, mountain ranges, and other places that are scenically appealing or unique. A nation's wild animals, birds, fish, and plants are also among its natural resources, as are the habitats of wild species.

Toward the end of the 19th century, organizational support for conservation began to grow with the founding of the Appalachian Mountain Club in 1876, the Audubon Society in 1886, and the Sierra Club in 1892. Members of these societies dedicated their work and funds to the study of wildlife, the preservation of habitat, and the protection of remote wilderness areas such as the Sierra Nevada and Appalachian mountain ranges. They also became adept at pressuring the government to preserve these areas from exploitation and harmful development.

Throughout the country, members of the General Federation of Women's Clubs, increasingly concerned about the quality of life for their families, became active preservationists, pressuring and petitioning states and the federal gov-ernment to set aside and preserve areas of natural wonder and to clean up the country's water systems, which had become polluted by industrial waste. Perhaps the most effective of all conservationists was John Muir, the California naturalist and first president of the Sierra Club, whose writings inspired Theodore Roosevelt and many others to support wilderness preservation. "So far our government has done nothing effective with its forests," he wrote in his 1901 book, *Our National Parks,* "...but is like a rich and foolish spendthrift who has inherited a magnificent estate in perfect order, and then has left his fields and meadows, forests and parks, to be sold and plundered and wasted at will...." "In their natural condition, or under wise management... these forests would be a never failing fountain of wealth and beauty."

Over several decades Congress and the President responded to citizens' growing perception of the need to preserve and protect wilderness and natural resources. In 1872, Congress created Yellowstone National Park in Wyoming and in the 1890s added Sequoia and Yosemite national parks in California. During the next 30 years, the federal government created numerous other parks around the country, thereby preserving millions of acres of wilderness and breathtaking scenery.

In 1891, Congress passed the Forest Reserve Act, empowering the President to create "forest reserves" by withdrawing land from the public domain. Forest reserves were not solely for wilderness preservation, however. Instead, they were open to planned use, subject to leasing under federal control to ranchers, timber and mining industries, and hunters. Conserving forests would also help the government to manage water resources in the arid West and Southwest, where it was especially

On a 1902 outing in California's Sequoia National Park, a group of Sierra Club members relaxes at the foot of one of the giant Sequoia trees. The Sierra Club was one of several organizations whose campaigns led to the establishment of a national park system.

important to preserve the trees near streams and rivers. The roots of riverside trees helped to sustain riverbanks and the leafy canopy slowed down evaporation. In 1905 the "forest reserves" became "national forests" and the National Forest Service moved from the Department of the Interior to the Department of Agriculture.

In response to the creation of the National Forest Service, preservationists such as John Muir began to distance themselves from conservationists, splitting the movement between those who wanted to protect wilderness areas completely and those who wanted to see the controlled use of natural resources. On the conservationist side, Gifford Pinchot, director of the Forest Service, whom Roosevelt had appointed, advocated the "wise use" of natural resources. He felt that proper government control could make forest and grasslands useful to the people and to future generations. Pinchot's efforts to save forests from unplanned and rapacious exploitation for profit made him many enemies among western mining and ranching interests. His 1906 plan to place the national parks under the Forest Service so that they, too, could be opened to resource development failed to pass Congress. Strict preservationists, fearing that the parks would be destroyed,

campaigned vigorously against Pinchot and his plans. In 1916, Congress finally established the National Park Service, a permanent separate bureau to administer and protect the national parks.

Pinchot continued in the Forest Service during President William Howard Taft's administration, but, in 1910, after he publicly criticized Secretary of the Interior Richard Ballinger's management of coal lands in Alaska, Taft fired him. Pinchot went on to create the National Conservation Association and to found the Yale University School of Forestry. His dismissal damaged the relationship between Taft and former President Theodore Roosevelt and contributed to the split in the Republican party in 1912.

John Muir and the Sierra Club campaigned from 1901 to 1913 to prevent the damming of the Tuolumne River in California's Hetch Hetchy Valley, which would flood the lower half of Yosemite National Park in order to create a water supply for the city of San Francisco. The state won that battle, allowing San Francisco to grow but in the process destroying an exceptionally beautiful natural resource.

Disputes between those who favor preservation of pristine wilderness and those who prefer the "wise" use of government-owned natural resources continue in the conservation movement to this day.

SEE ALSO
Environment; Mining; Muir, John; Pinchot, Gifford; Progressive movement; Ranching; Reform movements; Roosevelt, Theodore; Taft, William Howard; Women's voluntary associations

FURTHER READING
Nash, Roderick. *Wilderness and the American Mind.* 4th ed. New Haven: Yale University Press, 2001.
Righter, Robert W. *The Battle Over Hetch Hetchy: America's Most Controversial Dam and the Birth of Modern*

Environmentalism. New York: Oxford University Press, 2005.

Wyant, William K. *Westward in Eden: The Public Lands and the Conservation Movement.* Berkeley: University of California Press, 1982.

Constitution, amendments to

AMENDING THE U.S. Constitution is a demanding process. It requires passage by a vote of two-thirds of both houses of Congress and then ratification by three-quarters of all the states. Thus, in order for an amendment to become part of the Constitution, there must be wide popular support for the change.

Four amendments received ratification during the Gilded Age and Progressive Era. In 1913, the 16th Amendment legalized the income tax, and the 17th authorized the direct election of U.S. senators. Before then, most state legislatures elected their state's two Senators indirectly. In 1919, the 18th Amendment, often called the Prohibition Amendment, outlawed the manufacture, sale, or transportation of intoxicating liquors within the United States, as well as their importation or exportation. It was repealed by the 21st Amendment in 1933. The 19th Amendment, or Woman Suffrage Amendment, gave women the right to vote in 1920.

SEE ALSO

18th Amendment; 19th Amendment; 17th Amendment; 16th Amendment

FURTHER READING

Bernstein, Richard B., and Jerome Agel. *Amending America: If We Love the Constitution So Much, Why Do We Keep Trying to Change It?* New York: Times Books, 1993.

Kyvig, David E. *Explicit and Authentic Acts: Amending the U.S. Constitution, 1776–1995.* Lawrence: University Press of Kansas, 1996.

Consumer culture

TO SAY THAT we live in a consumer culture means that our lives are organized around buying things we think will make us happy. Consumer goods can include anything from prepared foods to clothing and home furnishings to the latest technological invention, such as electronic equipment or automobiles. The 19th-century Industrial Revolution gave rise to a consumer culture by producing a wide array of relatively cheap, standardized consumer goods. The Gilded Age and Progressive Era saw the first flowering of the new culture of consumption.

Advertising, which creates a desire in consumers for certain goods, was a prominent feature of the consumer culture. In the past, most markets were local and few products carried brand names. Soap was just soap, nails were just nails, and consumers often knew who had made them. The Industrial Revolution changed all this. Consumers now bought products manufactured by strangers in far-off factories. Moreover, products bore brand names so that consumers could identify the maker and buy the same brand again. By the end of the 1800s, an entire advertising industry had developed to create consumer loyalty to brand names.

Advertising was not new. It had existed primarily as announcements in newspapers and magazines or on posted broadsides. But in the Gilded Age, instead of just announcing a product's availability, advertisements tried to persuade people to buy it.

Makers of cheap household goods were early advertisers. A Fort Wayne, Indiana, druggist named Joseph C. Hoagland mixed up Royal Baking Powder in his store, and acting as his own agent placed ads in religious and women's magazines. Soap ads did particularly well. In 1882, a family in Cincinnati, Ohio, mixed one batch of soap for so long that it filled with air as it hardened and could float on water. Harley T. Proctor named it Ivory. "It floats," ads proclaimed, and it's "99 and 44/100 percent pure!" According to its ads, Ivory was not supposed to injure fine fabric or delicate skin. True or not, the slogan for the soap caught on and is still in use today.

By 1900, no business could hope to sell a product without advertising. Advertising experts developed brand names, jingles, and slogans to make products recognizable. Ivory soap, Welch's grape juice, Lea & Perrin's steak sauce, Johnson's wax, Coca-Cola beverages, Quaker oats, Heinz soups, and National biscuits became household words. Some brand names were so popular that they came to stand for their products: Kodak meant "camera"; Kleenex meant "paper handkerchief."

New forms of marketing were a second prominent feature of the consumer culture. Before industries expanded in the late 1800s, producers distributed goods primarily through wholesalers. These, in turn, sold the goods to retailers, or individual shopkeepers. As the size of some industrial outputs soared, manufacturers sought to bypass wholesalers by selling products through the mail or employing traveling salesmen, called "drummers," to sell to consumers directly. Yet others established their own retail operations. By the early 1920s, the Singer Sewing Machine Company was running 8,000 stores and employing

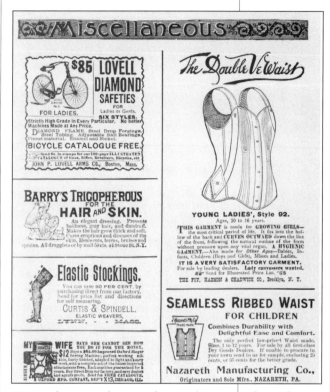

40,000 house-to-house salespeople; Heinz Foods had 58 branch offices and warehouses and 70 agencies in other countries to sell its products.

Retailers responded to the explosion in consumer goods by founding department and chain stores and mail-order houses. These retailers bought directly from manufacturers and turned their stock over rapidly. Some retailers also bought goods without brand names, put their own labels on them, and sold them at a discount, a practice that continues today.

The department store predated the Gilded Age. It came from the vision of Irish-born Alexander T. Stewart, who before the Civil War had built an eight-story, block-long shopping "palace" in New York City. Stewart's store featured set prices (no haggling, something middle-class women did not like to do) and periodic clearance sales. But the department store really took off during the Gilded Age. In the 1870s John Wanamaker

These advertisements from an 1893 issue of Godey's Lady's Book and Magazine *urge women to spend their money on such items as bicycles, undergarments, and cosmetics.*

built a store in Philadelphia that featured a liberal returns policy and fancily dressed windows. A larger store, which opened in 1911, featured the world's second-largest organ in its Grand Court.

By 1877, R. H. Macy's store in New York City had 24 departments. During the 1880s and 1890s, similar retail giants—New York's Lord & Taylor, Chicago's Marshall Field, Columbus's F. and R. Lazarus, and Milwaukee's Gimbel Brothers—added soda fountains, tearooms, telegraph and post offices, beauty parlors, child care, charge accounts, and banking services. Some offered live music, lectures and plays, meeting rooms, and branch libraries. In short, department stores helped make shopping an end in itself.

Chain stores also met with success in this era. The Great Atlantic and Pacific Tea Company (A & P) began in the 1860s as a tea-and-coffee firm. By 1900, it was operating nearly 200 grocery stores. Cincinnati's Great Western Tea Company (later Kroger's) had 36 stores by 1902. Frank W. Woolworth opened his 5-and-10-cent stores in Utica, New York, and Lancaster, Pennsylvania, in 1879; he had 7 by 1886, 25 by 1895, and 59 by 1900. Chain stores attracted customers with promises of low prices for standardized and durable goods.

Finally, the mail-order or catalogue store helped rural dwellers keep up with their city cousins. In 1872, Aaron Montgomery Ward of Chicago printed the first catalogue. Consisting of only one sheet, it described 163 hardware items for sale and offered "satisfaction guaranteed or your money back." It was an immediate success. Ward's business grew so rapidly that in 1884 he issued a catalog consisting of 240 pages and describing nearly 10,000 items. By the

early 1890s his "Great Wish Book" listed 24,000 items, ranging from pocket watches, underwear, and sewing machines to bathtubs, pianos, and windmills. Competitors to Ward's—the Spiegel, May, Stern Company, founded in 1882, and Sears, Roebuck, founded in 1893—were also well received, except by small-town merchants who could not compete with the variety or price of mail-order goods. These merchants lobbied unsuccessfully against Rural Free Delivery, the system established by the U.S. Post Office in 1897 to deliver mail to isolated farms. The merchants also spread racist rumors that Ward and Sears were African American or Jewish, hiding behind catalogues because they were afraid to show their faces.

The era's culture of consumption not only escalated demand for certain products but also changed the way Americans thought about themselves and how they lived. During a bicycle craze in the late-19th century, for example, ads showing women on bikes helped prepare society for the "new" woman, free to ride a bicycle, unescorted, through a city's streets. Similarly, a rising demand for soap changed American social habits. Ads convinced Americans, especially city dwellers, that a dirty face and hair and body odor were socially unacceptable. Ads taught women to use household cleansers to combat germs and protect their families. In 1879, the value of drug, toilet, and other household products sold exceeded $40 million; by 1920, it had soared to more than $765 million.

At first, advertising for products such as furniture, appliances, vehicles, jewelry, clocks and watches, silverware, musical instruments, and cameras stressed the product's reliability. Later, ads appealed to the buyer's desire for the higher social status that owning the product might bring. As the United States became more of a mixed community, with millions of people pouring in who might not look or talk or act like native-born Americans, owning certain products, such as grandfather clocks and grand pianos, came to mean "being American." Before immigrants even arrived, they recognized and yearned to own the brand-name items they had seen in American mail-order catalogs. Later, they might even sacrifice family necessities in order to keep up monthly payments on luxury items.

Not everyone benefited equally from the era's consumer culture. The poorest, who could not afford the carfare to get to department stores, much less the goods on display there, continued to buy from street peddlers and local shop owners. Often they went from one to another to get the best price. Nor did all immigrants rely on consumer goods to win social acceptance. Access to such goods eventually made the middle class more homogeneous, but it never fully erased the complexity of cultural and ethnic differences embedded in the American population.

SEE ALSO

Bicycle; Consumer movement; Immigration; Industry; Journalism; National Consumers' League

FURTHER READING

Benson, Susan Porter. *Counter Cultures: Saleswomen, Managers, and Customers in American Department Stores, 1890–1940*. Urbana: University of Illinois Press, 1986.

Ewen, Stuart, and Elizabeth Ewen. *Channels of Desire: Mass Images and the Shaping of American Consciousness*. Minneapolis: University of Minnesota Press, 1992.

Fox, Stephen R. *The Mirror Makers: A History of American Advertising and its Creators*. New York: William Morrow, 1984.

Leach, William R. *Land of Desire: Merchants, Power, and the Rise of a New American Culture*. New York: Pantheon, 1993.

Norris, James D. *Advertising and the Transformation of American Society*. New York: Greenwood, 1990.

Strasser, Susan. *Satisfaction Guaranteed: The Making of the American Mass Market*. New York: Pantheon, 1989.

Consumer movement

IN PREINDUSTRIAL TIMES, individuals usually made the goods they consumed or knew who had grown or made the products they bought. Thus they could hold that person accountable for a product's reliability. In the industrial era of the late 1800s, however, consumers were buying mass-produced goods made far from their homes and marketed across long distances. They usually had no recourse when products were defective or made them sick.

Beginning in the 1890s, middle-class women concerned about this issue began a consumer protest movement. They targeted both defective or harmful goods as well as the often unfair, unhealthy, and abusive conditions under which goods were made and sold. Late-19th-century consumers found models for their activism among earlier protests, such as boycotts of English tea in the American Revolutionary era and of products made by slave labor before the Civil War. The Progressive Era consumer movement began in 1888 when Leonora O'Reilly, a New York garment worker and labor organizer, invited prominent women to a meeting of the New York Working Women's Society and appealed to them for help. The women set up a committee to urge shoppers to give their business only to those employers who treated their workers fairly. In 1891, the women created a Consumers' League under the leadership of

Josephine Shaw Lowell. Other leagues formed in Massachusetts, Pennsylvania, and Illinois. In 1899, these state and local groups united into the National Consumers' League (NCL). The chief goals of the NCL were to outlaw child labor and pass a minimum wage and other protective labor laws.

The NCL was not the only consumer group active in this era. A Housewives League and professionals associated with the emerging field of home economics agitated for product testing and consumer education. Other groups questioned the rates charged by insurance companies and the levels at which government set taxes and tariffs. Working-class women mounted protests against exorbitant meat prices and high rents, sometimes engaging in vociferous urban demonstrations. Members of women's clubs and groups such as the Woman's Christian Temperance Union and the National Council of Jewish Women were active in campaigns to ensure pure food, meat, and drugs, and they pursued such reforms as workers' compensation laws, unemployment insurance, and the introduction of a social security system. Even suffrage organizations used consumer pressure tactics against manufacturers and department stores in order to get the business community to support the woman's vote.

Women were the chief leaders of the consumer movement, but many men supported its goals and worked hard in its campaigns. Business leaders generally resisted making the changes that consumer groups requested, but some cooperated in order to stabilize their industries and increase confidence in their products. Today consumer movements pay their greatest attention to product testing and safety issues. They have also mounted worldwide campaigns to curb abusive condi-

tions in sweatshops involved in the global economy.

SEE ALSO

Child labor; Consumer culture; National Consumers' League; Pure Food and Drugs Act (1906); Taxes and tariffs

FURTHER READING

Finnegan, Margaret. *Selling Suffrage: Consumer Culture and Votes for Women.* New York: Columbia University Press, 1999.
Mayer, Robert N. *The Consumer Movement: Guardians of the Marketplace.* Boston: Twayne, 1989.

Coxey's Army

COXEY'S ARMY was a movement of unemployed workers organized in 1894 in response to a severe nationwide economic depression. Their leader was Jacob Coxey, an Ohio businessman sympathetic to working people. Earlier in his life Coxey had run for political office under the banner of the Greenback Labor Party, founded in 1876 to promote the increased supply of cheap paper money, a step that would have helped poor people pay off their debts more easily. In 1892 Coxey proposed that the federal government issue "legal tender" bonds to raise funds for public projects such as road building, thereby providing work for the unemployed.

Members of Coxey's Army navigate their barge through a canal on their way to Washington, D.C., to demand government-funded public works projects.

When the government had refused to act on his proposal by mid-1894, Coxey and his followers decided to march from Massillon, Ohio, to Washington, D.C. "We will send a petition to Washington with boots on," Coxey announced, just before they set out on the march.

Word of the protest spread. Additional contingents of the "industrial army" set out from all over the country, walking, stowing away on freight cars, and sometimes hijacking whole trains bound eastward. Although the men found support in industrial towns, authorities fearing an outbreak of civil disruption arrested many and turned others back. Eventually, on May 1, 1894, a group of about 500 arrived in the nation's capital. They demonstrated until dispersed by a force of 1,500 federal troops. Police jailed Jacob Coxey and other leaders for trespassing and carrying banners on the Capitol grounds.

Coxey's Army was one of several protest "armies" of the era. Its actions inaugurated the great American tradition of marching on Washington to demand social justice. The appeal to the federal government for help was an early assertion that the government was responsible for the welfare of the people. Although this idea was unpopular in 1894, it became a basic foundation of progressive thought in the early 1900s.

Jacob Coxey remained politically active until the 1930s. He named his first-born son Legal Tender Coxey.

SEE ALSO

Labor; Populism; Strikes

FURTHER READING

Barber, Lucy G. *Marching on Washington: The Forging of an American Political Tradition.* Berkeley: University of California Press, 2002.

Schwantes, Carlos A. *Coxey's Army: An American Odyssey.* 1985. Reprint, Moscow, Idaho: University of Idaho Press, 1997.

Crazy Horse

- *Born: around 1840, Dakota Territory*
- *Accomplishments: Lakota Sioux warrior who led attack against U.S. forces at the Battle of Little Bighorn (1876)*
- *Died: Sept. 5, 1877, Fort Robinson, Nebr.*

DURING THE 1860s and 1870s, Crazy Horse was one of the most successful leaders among the Plains Indians in their wars with the United States. Born near what is now Rapid City, South Dakota, Crazy Horse was a member of the Oglala band within the Lakota or Teton tribe, one of several tribes comprising the Sioux nation. Oral histories of Crazy Horse describe him as a mystic who, in an adolescent vision quest, foresaw his future career as a warrior leading his people into battle.

As a young man, Crazy Horse fought under the command of the Oglala chief Red Cloud. Later, he led combined Cheyenne and Sioux forces against some of the U.S. Army's most renowned Indian fighters. In Montana in 1876, he defeated General George Crook at the Rosebud River, then joined with fellow Sioux war chiefs Gall and Sitting Bull for a decisive victory over Lieutenant Colonel George Armstrong Custer at the Little Bighorn River. Recent research at the Little Bighorn battle site has revealed that the total annihilation of Custer's force was not the tragic accident historians had once believed. Custer had seriously underestimated the strength of the Sioux forces. He had split his troops and was numerically overwhelmed. In addition to their numbers, the Sioux possessed rifles superior to those Custer's men had. The Sioux never permitted Custer's men to regroup. They surrounded and slaughtered each group they encountered, and eventually drove the remnant onto "Last Stand" hill, where they killed every man.

For a year after Little Bighorn, Crazy Horse continued to lead resistance against the U.S. Army, which was attempting to force the last of the Sioux onto reservations. In 1877, with his followers near starvation after many months on the run, Crazy Horse surrendered to General Nelson Miles at Fort Robinson, Nebraska. When rumors arose that he was plotting renewed warfare, a U.S. soldier who had been ordered to place Crazy Horse in the guard house instead bayoneted him to death.

In 1948, at the invitation of Lakota chief Henry Standing Bear, sculptor Korczak Ziolkowski began an enormous mountainside monument to Crazy Horse on Sioux lands near the town of Custer, South Dakota. Ziolkowski's descendents plan to complete the monument sometime in the 21st century.

SEE ALSO
Military; Native Americans; Sitting Bull; West, the

FURTHER READING
Freedman, Russell. *The Life and Death of Crazy Horse.* New York: Holiday House, 1996.
Marshall, Joseph M. *The Journey of Crazy Horse: A Lakota History.* New York: Viking, 2004.
Sandoz, Mari. *Crazy Horse: Strange Man of the Oglalas* 1942. Reprint, Lincoln: University of Nebraska Press, 1992.

Crime and corruption

LONG BEFORE the Gilded Age, American cities were notorious places for crime. As urban populations rose, crime levels increased. So did incidences of corruption. Government officials, dealing with the expansion of city services that accompanied population growth, found increasing opportunities to rake off profits from each contract they negotiated. Rising urban populations also led to the opening of more entertainment venues, such as saloons and houses for gambling and prostitution. Dishonest police officers took bribes from the managers of such places in return for turning a blind eye to illicit activities. They also exacted payoffs and kickbacks for "protecting" the businesses from raids and from gangsters running competing rackets.

Some crimes of the era, such as the assassinations of Presidents James Garfield in 1881 and William McKinley in 1901, were national news. The 1892 hatchet murders of Andrew and Abby Borden of Fall River, Massachusetts, brought notoriety to Andrew's daughter Lizzie. Although eventually acquitted, Lizzie Borden was widely blamed for the murder and became the subject of song and legend. Jesse W. James and his gang, who spent 16 years robbing trains and banks and shooting policemen in the West and Midwest, also entered national folklore. The highest proportion of crime per capita between the 1880s and the 1910s occurred in the West, although the crime of lynching, most often racially motivated, was most prevalent in the South.

The nation's first mass murderer appeared during this era. Herman Webster Mudgett, a former medical student who used the name Dr. H. H. Holmes, killed more than 20 women in Chicago. In 1893 he built a hotel to which he lured single women planning to attend the World's Columbian Exposition. After torturing and killing them, he either cremated them or dissolved their bodies in quicklime, after-

The body of Andrew Borden sprawls on the sofa where the Massachusetts businessman was hacked to death in 1892. His daughter, Lizzie Borden, stood trial for the murder of her father and stepmother and was found not guilty.

ward selling their skeletons to medical students. While investigating Holmes for the unrelated crime of insurance fraud, detectives uncovered his more lurid crimes. Holmes died on the gallows, with the total number of his victims remaining unknown.

Publishers of the nation's growing number of newspapers and magazines attracted readers by reporting the most grisly details of such crimes. Readers also responded eagerly to articles by investigative journalists, later called muckrakers, who specialized in vivid exposés of dishonest policemen and other corrupt officials. Crime stories often spurred citizens to mount campaigns to remove corrupt officials and reform the criminal justice system.

In 1894, the New York state legislature appointed a committee to investigate police corruption. Its revelations of police involvement in extortion, bribery, counterfeiting, voter intimidation, and election fraud led to the election of a reform mayor, Seth Low. In 1912, after gambler Herman ("Beansie") Rosenthal was gunned down just as he was about to reveal his connections with police lieutenant Charles Becker, investigations of the police found widespread incidences of graft and protection rackets. Becker himself

was eventually executed for having arranged the shooting.

Law enforcement personnel countered charges of corruption by increasing their efforts toward professionalization. In 1870 prison officials founded the National Prison Association (later, the American Correctional Association). A National Chiefs of Police Union (later, the International Association of Chiefs of Police) formed in 1871. The city of Cincinnati, Ohio, began the professional training of police officers in 1888. Between the 1890s and 1910s, the fields of criminology (the study of criminal behavior and psychology) and forensic science (the study of evidence discovered at a crime scene for use in a court of law) became established, and police departments began to apply new technologies—such as cameras, sound recordings, fingerprints, chemical analysis, and even lie detectors—to criminal investigations.

Crime rates began to drop as cities and states placed more legislative controls on activities that often led to criminal behavior, such as gambling, prostitution, and the liquor trade. The expansion of the public schools in the late 1800s helped as well, as they kept youth off the streets and emphasized habits of self-control and "good citizenship." To deal with idle youth outside of school hours or during vacations, social settlement workers convinced cities to fund parks, playgrounds, and supervised recreation.

Despite these efforts, the numbers of juvenile delinquents rose in this era, from 11,468 reported in 1880 to 25,038 in 1910. In 1899, in part in response to pressure from social workers, Illinois set up the nation's first juvenile courts. Courts gradually developed probation systems for both youth and adults, at first using volunteer probation officers as supervisors and eventually professionalizing them. States also appointed parole boards, which evaluated prisoners' rehabilitation and arranged for their supervised release. At the same time as these more humane approaches to criminal behavior developed, the number of executions rose, from 155 in the 1890s, to 289 in the 1900s, and 636 in the 1910s. The first execution by electric chair took place on August 6, 1890, at New York's Auburn Prison.

SEE ALSO

Cities; Gilded Age; Journalism; Lynching; Muckrakers; Prostitution; Reform movements; Settlement-house movement

FURTHER READING

Friedman, Lawrence M. *Crime and Punishment in American History.* New York: Basic Books, 1993.

Lane, Roger. *Murder in America: A History.* Columbus: Ohio State University Press, 1997.

Larson, Erik. *The Devil in the White City: Murder, Magic, and Madness at the Fair that Changed America.* New York: Crown, 2003.

Sloat, Warren. *A Battle for the Soul of New York: Tammany Hall, Police Corruption, Vice, and Reverend Charles Parkhurst's Crusade against Them, 1892–1895.* New York: Cooper Square, 2002.

Walker, Samuel. *A Critical History of Police Reform: The Emergence of Professionalism.* Lexington, Mass.: Lexington Books, 1977.

Cross of Gold speech (1896)

SEE Bryan, William Jennings

Dance

THE YEARS AROUND the turn of the 20th century marked a period of intense creativity in American recreational, stage,

and concert dancing. Recreational and stage dancing influenced one another. Minstrel shows, musical theater, and vaudeville dancers adapted contemporary forms of recreational dancing for use in their productions, and ordinary Americans then imitated what they saw on the stage for their own use at social gatherings and in dance halls. In this same period, a few innovative concert dancers abandoned classical ballet for more free and expressive styles of dancing. Their ideas laid the foundation for the interpretative or modern dance of today.

Late 19th-century recreational dancing drew heavily upon European dance forms, such as the waltz, polka, two-step, and "set" or "figure" group dances, including the quadrilles and cotillions from which today's square dances are descended. By 1900, these forms were losing their popularity to ragtime dances, which had evolved from dances performed by African American slaves in their festivities and cakewalks. Cakewalks were slow parades of slave couples dressed in their fancy clothing and doing high-stepping movements, for which the best performers won a cake. Minstrel shows of the latter 1800s popularized cakewalks and other black dances, such as the "buck-and-wing," a form of early tap dancing that combined clogs, jigs, and shuffles. Choreographers adapted these movements for the musical stage. Eventually, the new movements found their way into the public dance halls, where they evolved into dances set to ragtime or jazz, the syncopated music first developed in African American communities.

In the early 1900s, American youth went crazy for "ragged" or jazz dancing. One popular dance was the Turkey Trot, in which couples moved in fast one-step circles and flapped their arms like crazed turkeys. Others included the Grizzly Bear, Bunny Hug, and Kangaroo Dip. By 1910, the Argentine tango had arrived from South America, featuring dips, glides, and sways that evoked a drama of conquest and submission. For several years in this period, debates raged in the press and among women's groups and social workers over the effect of these dances on the morals of young adults. In 1912, for example, dance hall reformers in New York City charged that the new dances were "not dancing at all, but a series of indecent antics" that had originated in "houses of prostitution." Even when performed in modified form, the dance's pelvic motions encouraged the bodies to touch. Combined with the drinking of liquor, easily available even at the most select events, such as balls and cotillions, the dances could lead to "obscene" behavior.

In the early 1910s, Irene and Vernon Castle, who had danced in musical theater, developed more dignified versions of the new dances and began performing them in restaurant-cabaret exhibitions. A smash success, the Castles and their imitators perpetuated the dance craze throughout the 1910s, thereby preparing the way for the Charleston and dance marathon crazes of later decades. The craze also had an impact on fashion, as young women copied Irene Castle's bobbed hair and her skirts, which showed off her ankles and were slit up the side to allow for dips.

In the world of classical ballet, other changes were equally dramatic. By the late 1800s, some American dancers were breaking away from the French and Russian ballet traditions that dominated the era. Isadora Duncan studied ballet as a child but rejected its technique as ugly and unnatural. Taking inspiration from nature and

ancient Greek art, she danced barefoot in flowing tunics. She wrote in her journal in 1902, "As a child, I danced on the sea beach by the waves...the sun danced on the waves...the movement of the waves rocked with my soul...could I dance as they—their eternal message of rhythm and Harmony." She also took ideas from ancient Greek art, explaining in her 1927 autobiography, *My Life*, that she "naturally fell into Greek positions, for Greek positions are only earth positions." Some observers were scandalized by Duncan's bare arms and legs, but many found her expressive movements beautiful and liberating.

Another innovator, Loïe Fuller, began her career as an actress. In the 1890s she discovered that she could achieve dramatic stage effects by moving voluminous skirts as if they were extensions of her body. Using special lighting and flowing silks and gauzes, she created dances that made her appear as a flame, butterfly, or flower. These dances made La Loïe, as she was called, a star attraction throughout Europe and the United States. Ruth St. Denis trained in skirt dancing and other techniques, but abandoned these in the early 1900s when she developed intellectual interests in

Loïe Fuller created new dance styles to challenge the traditions of classical ballet. Fuller swirled voluminous silk costumes around her dancing body to create fluid images.

Egyptian, Indian, and other Eastern cultures. Her solo dances based on themes from these cultures became sensations. She was the first dancer to perform complete solo concerts. St. Denis, along with her husband and partner Ted Shawn, formed the Denishawn Dancers, a group that eventually spawned modern dance innovators such as Martha Graham.

SEE ALSO
Fashions; Music; Theater

FURTHER READING
Current, Richard Nelson. *Loïe Fuller, Goddess of Light.* Boston: Northeastern University Press, 1997.
Emery, Lynne Fauley. *Black Dance in the United States from 1619 to 1970.* 2nd rev. ed. Princeton, N.J.: Princeton Book Co., 1988.
Kurth, Peter. *Isadora: A Sensational Life.* Boston: Little, Brown, 2001.
Mazo, Joseph H. *Prime Movers: The Makers of Modern Dance in America.* Hightstown, N.J.: Princeton Book Co., 2000.
Stearns, Marshall Winslow, and Jean Stearns. *Jazz Dance: The Story of American Vernacular Dance.* New York: Da Capo, 1994.

Dawes Severalty Act (1887)

IN 1887, CONGRESS approved a landmark change in federal Indian policy by passing a law titled An Act to Provide for the Allotment of Lands in Severalty to Indians on the Various Reservations. Better known as the Dawes Act, after Henry Dawes, head of the Senate's Committee on Indian Affairs, the law eliminated what little cohesion remained in Native American culture by breaking up reservation land, the common property of an entire tribe, into parcels of private property held "in severalty" (that is, owned by separate individuals). The Dawes Act specified how much land each member of a tribe would receive—the maximum was 160 acres per head of household—and provided for non-Indian ownership of surplus reservation land not allotted under the new system. Individuals would have to register with the authorities to receive their allotments. In exchange for signing their names and agreeing to abide by the terms of the act, registrants gained full rights of U.S. citizenship.

Supporters of the Dawes Act argued that owning land in common was a vestige of an uncivilized past, and that individual real estate holdings would encourage Indians to give up their tribal identities and assimilate into American society. Lawmakers envisioned former hunters of the Plains embracing life as farmers and small capitalists. Opponents denounced the law as a tactic to take from Indians what little land they still controlled after decades of warfare with a rapidly expanding United States.

The law did not succeed in wiping out Indian culture, but severely weakened and impoverished many tribes. During cyclic economic depressions and hard times, Indians sometimes leased or sold their allotments when they were desperate for money. Their lack of education and intense poverty left them vulnerable to unscrupulous land speculators and even to fraud and misappropriation of their property by the government agents hired to administer the Dawes Act. During the nearly half century that the Dawes Act was in effect (Congress eventually replaced it with the Indian Reorganization Act of 1934), which restored some tribal land rights, tens of millions of acres of former reservation land passed into the hands of non-Indian owners.

SEE ALSO
Imperialism; Law; Native Americans

FURTHER READING

Carlson, Leonard A. *Indians, Bureaucrats, and Land: The Dawes Act and the Decline of Indian Farming*. Westport, Conn.: Greenwood, 1981.

Greenwald, Emily. *Reconfiguring the Reservation: The Nez Perces, Jicarilla Apaches, and the Dawes Act*. Albuquerque: University of New Mexico Press, 2002.

Washburn, Wilcomb E. *The Assault on Indian Tribalism: The General Allotment Law (Dawes Act of 1887)*. Melbourne, Fla.: Kreiger, 1986.

Debs, Eugene Victor

- *Born: Nov. 5, 1855, Terre Haute, Ind.*
- *Education: some high school*
- *Accomplishments: organizer, American Railway Union (1893); organizer, Pullman boycott and strike (1894); Socialist party candidate for President of the United States (1900, 1904, 1908, 1912, 1920); associate editor,* Appeal to Reason *(1907–12)*
- *Died: Oct. 20, 1926, Elmhurst, Ill.*

EUGENE V. DEBS was a labor leader, a peace activist, and a founding father of the Socialist Party of America. He ran for President as his party's candidate many times in the early years of the 20th century.

Debs dropped out of high school at age 14 in order to help support his mother. Attending night classes when he could, he joined the ranks of railroad firemen, whose work controlling steam pressure and stoking roaring boilers was the hardest in the industry, and some of the most dangerous. At the age of 15, Debs joined the Brotherhood of Locomotive Firemen. In 1880, uniquely articulate and self-educated, he became the editor of the brotherhood's national magazine and grand secretary of the organization.

Briefly serving as a Democratic state representative in Indiana, in 1893 Debs organized the first "industrial" union in the United States, the Ameri-

can Railway Union (ARU). Instead of organizing workers by specialty—engineer, fireman, or brakeman—the ARU made no distinctions. Whoever worked for the railroad industry could join. In 1894, Debs and the ARU helped organize workers striking against the Illinois company that made Pullman railroad cars. The workers went on strike because George Pullman, their employer, had cut their wages without lowering their rents or the prices of goods in company stores. Debs persuaded union members nationwide to refuse to operate trains carrying Pullman cars, thereby spreading the strike across the nation. Arrested for failing to obey a court order to stop from striking, Debs spent six months in jail.

Debs studied socialism in jail. He emerged convinced that the only help for laboring people was to replace capitalism with a new cooperative system in which goods would be produced for the needs of the people, rather than for profit, and class conflict and economic and social inequality would end. Determined to seek a political solution, Debs helped to found the Socialist Democratic party in 1897 and its successor, the Socialist Party of America. In 1905, he became one of the founders of the broad-based, militant international union, the Industrial Workers of the World, though he never shared its communist belief in the necessity of revolution.

Railroad worker, labor leader, and founder of the Socialist Party of America, Eugene V. Debs ran unsuccessfully five times for President on the Socialist party ticket.

Debs always identified with workers and never forgot his roots. "While there is a lower class," he once said, "I am in it. While there is a criminal element, I am of it. While there is a soul in prison, I am not free."

Debs ran for President on the Socialist party ticket five times, always losing but each time gaining more and more votes. Under his leadership, the Socialists presented American voters with a credible third-party alternative for several decades.

In 1918 the government imprisoned Debs under a wartime espionage act for giving a speech against the war in Europe and urging Americans not to participate. Debs's arrest clearly violated his right to free speech. Government authorities also disenfranchised Debs for life, effectively ending his U.S. citizenship by taking away his right to vote. He served 3 years of his 10-year sentence before President Warren Harding pardoned him and arranged for his release on Christmas Day 1921.

While in prison in Atlanta, Debs fought to obtain better conditions for his fellow inmates. He refused any special privileges for himself, even though he was running for President from his prison cell, gaining the largest Socialist party tally ever—915,000 votes, 6 percent of the total. On the day of Debs's release, the warden let 2,000 inmates out of their cells to say good-bye to him.

Prison conditions had weakened Debs. He remained politically active as long as he could but spent his last days in a sanatorium in Illinois, where he died in 1926.

History has tended to portray Eugene V. Debs as an idealistic failure, a man who simply did not understand economic and political realities or the selfishness of human nature. He is also seen as a representative victim of the Red Scare, the period of mass anti-

Communist hysteria after World War I. But historians also remember Debs as an extremely effective labor leader and a champion of important, though controversial, political ideas. Today the Labor Hall of Fame in Washington, D.C., honors his memory, as does the Eugene V. Debs Foundation of Terre Haute, Indiana.

SEE ALSO

Communism; Industrial Workers of the World; Labor; Labor unions; Pullman strike (1894); Railroads; Red Scare (1919–20); Socialism; Strikes

FURTHER READING

Currie, Harold W. *Eugene V. Debs.* Boston: Twayne, 1976.
Debs, Eugene V. *The Eugene V. Debs Reader: Socialism and the Class Struggle.* Edited by William A. Pelz. Chicago: Institute of Working Class History, 2000.
———. *Gentle Rebel: Letters of Eugene V. Debs.* Edited by J. Robert Constantine. Urbana: University of Illinois Press, 1995.
Ginger, Ray. *The Bending Cross: A Biography of Eugene Victor Debs.* Kirksville, Mo.: Thomas Jefferson University Press, 1992.
Salvatore, Nick. *Eugene V. Debs: Citizen and Socialist.* Urbana: University of Illinois Press, 1984.
Young, Marguerite. *Harp Song for a Radical: The Life and Times of Eugene Victor Debs.* New York: Knopf, 1999.

Decorative arts

THE DECORATIVE ARTS differ from the fine arts—painting, drawing, photography, and large-scale sculpture—in that they are primarily ornamental or functional. Decorative arts in the Gilded Age and Progressive Era included works in wood, glass, ceramics, metal, jewelry, and textiles. Decorative arts also included printing and illustration, domestic architecture, interior design, and hand-crafted furniture. Design inspirations came from

Using a textured surface and a design of stylized chrysanthemums, Ohio artist Laura Fry decorated this Rookwood Pottery jar from 1885.

Europe and Japan and, later in the period, from artwork of African or Oceanic (Pacific island) origin.

Influenced by English art critics John Ruskin and William Morris, many American decorative artists participated in an Arts and Crafts movement that was popular on both sides of the Atlantic. In promoting arts and crafts, Morris and Ruskin were reacting to what they saw as the ugliness and conformity of design in the mass-produced goods of the industrial era. They also disliked the ornate decorative styles associated with Victorianism. They urged a return to hand-crafted furniture, wallpaper, and ornaments, and to hand-made furnishings that would be beautiful because they were functional. In *The Stones of Venice* (1851) Ruskin rejected "all cast and machine work" as "bad; as work…it is dishonest." In a lecture he gave in 1880, Morris, famous for his fabric and book designs, explained, "simplicity of life, even the barest, is not a misery, but the very foundation of refinement."

The Arts and Crafts movement inspired architects Frank Lloyd Wright, Louis Sullivan, and Charles and Henry Greene. Wright's Prairie School of architecture, which aspired to achieve buildings in harmony with nature, grew out of the Arts and Crafts movement. The Greene brothers, who worked in Pasadena, California, transformed the humble bungalow style of house into a series of hand-crafted homes with mellow oak interiors, stained glass, and Japanese design elements. A furniture maker working

in the Arts and Crafts tradition, Gustav Stickley hand-crafted designs in oak that reflected the influence of styles found in the old Spanish missions of the southwestern United States and Mexico.

Furniture makers, illustrators, and other decorative artists of the late 19th century also worked in a style called Art Nouveau, a popular style that featured flowing, sinuous lines and stylized designs of flowers and foliage. Louis Comfort Tiffany, son of a prominent New York jeweler, opened his own glass studio in 1885. Tiffany captured the essence of Art Nouveau in his iridescent or opalescent stained glass windows and lamps, which featured designs of trees, grasses, flowers and butterflies.

Ceramics, particularly art pottery, also became an important decorative art of the period. The Rookwood Pottery, established in Cincinnati by Maria Longworth Nichols in 1880, and Newcomb Pottery, established in 1894 at the Sophie Newcomb Women's College in New Orleans, produced prime examples of Arts and Crafts and Art Nouveau vases, small sculpture, and decorative tile. These potteries specialized in hand-thrown pots glazed in either glossy or matte yellows, blues, and greens. Their vases and tiles featured smooth lines and hand-decorated designs drawn from nature.

Pottery, china painting, and textile design attracted women artists in particular. In an era when the fine art world took very few women painters and sculptors seriously, ceramicists such as Rookwood's Mary Louise McLaughlin and textile artists such as Candace Wheeler, who decorated the women's pavilion at the 1893 World's Columbian Exposition, found outlets for their talents in the decorative arts.

In 1895 Elbert Hubbard, a former soap salesman, established Roycroft, an Arts and Crafts printing press in Aurora, New York, where he set type by hand and printed hand-illustrated books. The print shop led to the establishment of a book bindery, and later to leather, copper, glass, and furniture workshops. Roycroft became a community of artisans dedicated to fine craftsmanship, and it attracted some of the foremost decorative artists of the period. One Roycroft artist, William Wallace Denslow, illustrated the first edition of *The Wizard of Oz* in 1900. Until 1938 Roycroft flourished as a community and a source of fine decorative works, although Hubbard himself died in the sinking of the *Lusitania* in 1915.

SEE ALSO

Architecture; Fine arts; Victorianism; World's fairs and exhibitions; Wright, Frank Lloyd

FURTHER READING

Bishop, Robert, and Patricia Coblenz. *American Decorative Arts: 360 Years of Creative Design*. New York: Abrams, 1982.
Kaplan, Wendy. *"The Art That Is Life": The Arts & Crafts Movement in America, 1875–1920*. Boston: Little, Brown, 1987.
Madsen, Stephan Tschudi. *The Art Nouveau Style: A Comprehensive Guide with 264 Illustrations*. Mineola, N.Y.: Dover, 2002.
Meikle, Jeffrey L. *Design in the U.S.A.* New York: Oxford University Press, 2005.

Democratic party

BEFORE THE CIVIL WAR, the Democratic party had achieved majority status and built a strong base made up of German and Irish immigrants, farmers, artisans and factory workers, and southern slaveholders. The party split over slavery and secession during the war, dropping into the minority and

remaining there until the end of Reconstruction. In the late 1800s it recovered with the two, nonconsecutive presidencies of Grover Cleveland and the election of powerful legislators, and in the 1910s with the two terms of Woodrow Wilson. The party lost its ascendancy in the 1920s.

Traditional Democratic party members believed in individual rights and enterprise and opposed interference by a strong central government. Southern whites flocked to the party after the Civil War, causing it to become identified with racial segregation and the disfranchisement of African Americans, an identity the party would keep long into the 20th century. In the 1890s, populist leader William Jennings Bryan brought more western and southern farmers into the party by calling for cheaper money, an income tax, and lower tariffs—all economic reforms designed to help the poor. Angered by the economic dominance of northeastern industrialists and bankers, farmers shifted the party away from its traditional resistance to strong government toward accepting the idea of more government control over big business. Democrats nominated Bryan for the presidency three times in the next two decades—in 1896, 1900, and 1908—but he was never able to capture the White House for his party.

Kentucky Senator Ollie Johnson urges the 1916 Democratic Convention to renominate President Woodrow Wilson, asking the delegates: "Who would say that we can afford to swap horses while crossing a bloody stream?"

In the early 20th century, the number of immigrants participating in the party grew, especially urban Catholics opposed to attempts by Republicans and Prohibitionists to control their consumption of alcoholic beverages. The party was dominated by the South, solidly Democratic and white, and by northern political bosses associated with urban party "machines," such as New York City's Tammany Hall. Woodrow Wilson's leadership in 1912 opened the party to support progressive reforms such as an income tax, lower tariffs, more federal controls over the currency and banks through a Federal Reserve Act, and better enforcement of the rules of competition in order to prevent abuses by business monopolies.

Wilson led the party to victory in the 1912 election in part because the Republican party had split between factions supporting Theodore Roosevelt and William Howard Taft. Wilson had also appealed to progressives by emphasizing principles of individualism along with a willingness to use government to curb powerful industrialists. His support for Great Britain during World War I cost him votes from ethnic Americans with Irish and German roots, who opposed Britain's war policies. Wilson's two terms in office included a triumphant participation in bringing the world war to an end and a failed attempt to convince the United States to join an international organization to prevent future wars, the League of Nations. The Democratic party was unable to win the White House throughout the 1920s, a period when Americans resisted foreign entanglements and reacted against progressive reforms at the national level. It recovered only after Republicans failed to provide sufficient relief to Americans suffering from the effects of the Great Depression of 1929.

SEE ALSO

Bryan, William Jennings; Cleveland, Grover; Federal Reserve Act (1913); Income tax; Machine politics; Republican Party; Tammany Hall; Wilson, Woodrow T.; World War I

FURTHER READING

Mink, Gwendolyn. *Old Labor and New Immigrants in American Political Development: Union, Party, and State, 1875–1920*. Ithaca, N.Y.: Cornell University Press, 1986.

Rutland, Robert Allen. *The Democrats: From Jefferson to Clinton*. Columbia: University of Missouri Press, 1995.

Sarasohn, David. *The Party of Reform: Democrats in the Progressive Era*. Jackson: University Press of Mississippi, 1989.

Dewey, John

- *Born: Oct. 20, 1859, Burlington, Vt.*
- *Education: University of Vermont, B.A., 1878; Johns Hopkins University, Ph.D., 1884*
- *Accomplishments: professor of philosophy, University of Michigan (1884–88, 1889–94), University of Minnesota (1888–89), University of Chicago (1894–1904), Columbia University (1904–30); president, American Psychological Association (1899–1900); president, American Philosophical Association (1905–6); author of more than 300 essays and books, including* Psychology *(1887),* The School and Society *(1899),* How We Think *(1910),* The Influence of Darwin on Philosophy *(1910), and* Democracy and Education *(1916)*
- *Died: June 1, 1952, New York, N.Y.*

EDUCATOR AND PHILOSOPHER

John Dewey was only 15 when he enrolled at the University of Vermont, where he studied philosophy and psychology. After graduating, he taught high school and continued to study on his own. An essay he published in the *Journal of Speculative Philosophy* persuaded the Johns Hopkins University philosophy department to accept him for doctoral work in 1882. It was there

John Dewey, philosopher, psychologist, and educational reformer, urged teachers to help children cultivate their imaginations, rather than force them to memorize and recite their lessons.

he earned his degree in only two years.

Dewey's book on psychology, entitled simply *Psychology,* which he published in 1887, established his reputation. After holding a series of academic posts, in 1894 he became head of Chicago University's department of philosophy, which then included psychology and pedagogy (the art of teaching). When he convinced the university to establish a separate department of education, he became its head as well. Increasingly drawn to progressive ideas about social and political reforms, he began to spend time at the Hull House settlement, where he met frequently with its head resident, social reformer Jane Addams, and her group of socially conscious reformers. In 1896 he founded a "Laboratory School" at the university where he and other educators could experiment with the best methods of teaching the young. His wife, Alice Chipman Dewey, served as principal.

Dewey saw education as critical to forming good citizens and preserving a democratic society. "Democracy has to be born anew every generation, and education is its midwife," Dewey wrote in one of his most influential books, *The School and Society.* Most primary school teaching methods of the day stressed rote learning and strict discipline. Dewey and his supporters wanted to expand children's abilities to solve problems, make judgments, and cooperate with others. "The imagination is the medium in which the child lives," he wrote, also in *The School and Society.* "Shall we ignore this native setting,…dealing, not with the living child at all, but

with the dead image we have erected, or shall we give it play and satisfaction?" Such questions, which furthered an already ongoing "progressive education movement," revolutionized American education.

After moving to Columbia University in New York City, Dewey continued to work on his pragmatic philosophical theory, which was known as instrumentalism. This approach judges the worth of ideas and theories not by how true or false they are, but by how well they actually work. Dewey saw ideas as "instruments" that human beings use to understand their environment, find guides to action, and ultimately improve their lives. He remained a social activist his entire life, helping to found teachers' unions and associations to protect academic freedom and civil liberties.

SEE ALSO

Addams, Jane; Hull House; Psychology; Education

FURTHER READING

Dewey, John. *The Essential Dewey.* Edited by Larry A. Hickman and Thomas M. Alexander. Bloomington: Indiana University Press, 1998.

Dykhuizen, George. *The Life and Mind of John Dewey.* Carbondale: Southern Illinois University Press, 1973.

Strathern, Paul. *Dewey in 90 Minutes.* Chicago: Ivan R. Dee, 2002.

Westbrook, Robert B. *John Dewey and American Democracy.* Ithaca, N.Y.: Cornell University Press, 1991.

Divorce

WHILE A CERTAIN number of American marriages have always broken down, before the late 19th century few couples could afford to get a divorce. Awarded through state legislatures, divorce was costly and time consuming.

Thus unhappily married couples had to use other means to end their unions. Some spouses won decrees of separate maintenance, called "separate bed and board," but these did not allow for remarriage. Other spouses simply deserted their marriages, the man more often than the woman. Since life expectancy was relatively short in pre-modern times, often one partner died prematurely, freeing the remaining partner to marry again. In extreme cases, spouses resorted to suicide or murder to end their unions.

Since none of these methods was especially desirable, Americans began to demand greater ease in getting a divorce. After the Civil War, as populations increased and the work of state legislatures became more complex, legislators turned such proceedings over to the courts. Most courts had the power to grant a divorce for any reason, as long as it was justified. Divorce became especially easy in the West. After 1850, Indiana became a divorce mill. Residency requirements were lenient, and the spouse being divorced did not even have to be present. The Dakotas and Oklahoma Territory became divorce mills during the 1880s and 1890s. By 1913, Nevada had joined them, combining lax divorce laws, leisure pursuits, and a six-month residency requirement (this became six weeks in 1931) with a long list of grounds for divorce.

Women's interest in divorce increased when courts began to display new attitudes toward the custody of children. At the turn of the 20th century, only nine states granted the sexes the same rights over their children in the case of death or divorce, and men still had greater custody rights over children than women. But judges were beginning to favor women's custody claims when the children were very young, as long as remaining with their mothers did not put the children in danger.

As divorce became more accessible, the divorce rate rose. In 1880, there was one divorce for every 21 marriages; by 1890, one for every 12; and by 1924, one for every 7. By the end of the 1920s, the United States had the highest divorce rate in the world, more than one in every six marriages. Women initiated two-thirds of the divorce proceedings, rejecting men who did not fulfill their financial or emotional needs. Their complaints centered on a husband's physical abuse, infidelity, or failure to support the family. Marital rape was not illegal at this time, but judges accepted sexual cruelty as valid grounds for divorce. Men's claims focused on their wives' excessive independence or "disregard" for wifely duties. Although men rarely accused women of physical abuse, they did charge women with cruelty.

As the divorce rate increased, a backlash arose against the trend toward making divorces easier. Easterners, appalled at the West's seeming moral laxity in the matter, dominated the anti-divorce movement. Between 1889 and 1906, eastern legislatures passed more than 100 laws to make divorce more difficult. Five states required the defense of an absent party. Fifteen forbade remarriage for one or two years after

DISAPPEARED.

FRANK LIMBACK of Owensboro, Ky.; gone since October 11, 1906. He is about 30 years of age; 5 feet 10 inches high; weighs about 175 pounds; smooth shaven; heavy cheek bones; gray eyes; Roman nose; rather sharp chin; heavy deep set jaws; powerful muscular build. Two years ago last September he received serious injury to his spine in a railroad wreck at Duncan, Indiana. Married, has wife and two children. By profession a blacksmith and a railroad man. He left Owensboro for Jasper, Indiana, Oct. 11th, never heard of since. Walks on crutches. Wife and children in destitute circumstances. Any information to the undersigned will be greatly appreciated.

MRS. FRANK LIMBACK,
OWENSBORO, KY.

A deserted wife describes her missing husband on this 1906 poster. In the late 19th century, divorce became an option, giving deserted wives the opportunity to remarry.

the award of a divorce. Eighteen increased residency requirements, and six restricted the grounds for divorce. Washington, D.C., and New York State permitted divorce only for adultery. In 1895, South Carolina banned divorce altogether.

A complementary movement arose to make divorce laws uniform throughout the United States. In 1903 an Inter-Church Conference on Marriage and Divorce brought together representatives from 25 religious denominations to bolster the ideal of lifetime marriage. Two years later, when representatives from this conference appealed to President Theodore Roosevelt for help, he deplored "the loosening of the marital tie among the old native American families" and remarked as well on their declining birth rate. "If the race commits suicide," he warned, referring to native-born white Americans, the nation will cease to make progress. In 1906 a National Divorce Congress proposed model uniform divorce laws, but few states adopted them.

The debates that raged over divorce in the early 1900s divided people into two factions. One argued that marriage was a sacrament that should last for life, with couples resorting to divorce only in extreme cases. Others, including feminists, insisted that an abused spouse had the right to be free and that divorce should become easier instead of harder to get. In addition, they argued that good divorce laws protected dependents. Today, one in every two American marriages ends in divorce. Americans still debate the meaning of divorce, especially for children, but they appear to have fully resigned themselves to the trend that began in the Progressive Era.

SEE ALSO

Family life; Law; Marriage

FURTHER READING

May, Elaine Tyler. *Great Expectations: Marriage and Divorce in Post-Victorian America.* Chicago: University of Chicago Press, 1980.
Riley, Glenda. *Divorce: An American Tradition.* New York: Oxford University Press, 1991.

DuBois, William Edward Burghardt (W. E. B.)

- *Born Feb. 23, 1868, Great Barrington, Mass.*
- *Education: attended Fisk College, 1885–88; Harvard University, A.B., 1890, M.A., 1891; doctoral studies, University of Berlin, 1890s; Harvard University, Ph.D., 1895*
- *Accomplishments: cofounder, Niagara Movement (1906) and National Association for the Advancement of Colored People (1909); convener, Pan African Congress (1921, 1923); editor in chief,* The Crisis *magazine (1910–34); author,* Suppression of the African Slave Trade *(1896),* The Philadelphia Negro: A Social Study *(1899),* The Souls of Black Folk *(1903),* Black Reconstruction *(1935),* Dusk of Dawn *(1940),* Autobiography of W. E. B. Du Bois *(1968), and others; awarded World Peace Council Prize (1952) and the Soviet Lenin Peace Prize (1959)*
- *Died: Aug. 27, 1963, Accra, Ghana*

W. E. B. DUBOIS, cofounder of the National Association for the Advancement of Colored People (NAACP), was the foremost black intellectual of his generation and a leader for many decades in the African American struggle for civil rights. In his landmark 1903 book *The Souls of Black Folk,* he wrote, "The problem of the twentieth century is the problem of the color line," a reference to political inequality based on race. DuBois devoted his long career to combating inequality through scholarship and political activism.

W.E.B. DuBois taught history and economics at Atlanta University between 1897 and 1910. Through his writing, DuBois hoped to dispel prejudices against African Americans.

DuBois distinguished himself as a student from an early age and worked in his teens as a correspondent for several newspapers. He studied at Fisk College (later Fisk University) in Nashville, Tennessee, and at the University of Berlin in Germany, and he became the first black scholar to earn a Ph.D. from Harvard, writing his dissertation on the history of the African slave trade. He taught Latin and Greek at Wilberforce University in Ohio, sociology at the University of Pennsylvania, and history and economics at Atlanta University.

DuBois also conducted extensive research on aspects of black life in the United States and published numerous social science studies on education, business, crime, and other subjects of importance to the black community. He hoped that careful scholarship—combining historical, economic, anthropological, and sociological analysis—would help to dispel racist stereotypes and move American society toward full inclusion of black citizens. But he grew increasingly frustrated with the white majority's stubborn determination to keep African Americans in a subordinate position. In time, he concluded that political action to demand civil rights would be more effective than scholarly attempts to reason racial prejudice out of existence.

DuBois militant stance put him at odds with Booker T. Washington, widely regarded as the most influential black leader of the early 20th century, who favored a less confrontational response to white racism. Washington urged African Americans not to antagonize the white establishment by agitating for equality but to tolerate segregation and to build an economically stable and socially respectable black community by pursuing vocational education in farming and other trades. DuBois rejected that approach, which he regarded as an acceptance of second-class citizenship. Instead, he urged black Americans to campaign actively to win the full range of political rights and social privileges enjoyed by their white fellow citizens. He advocated strongly for black access to higher education, believing that college could prepare the most gifted members of each generation—what he called the "Talented Tenth" of the black population—to provide leadership and uplift for the entire race.

In 1905, DuBois took a leading role in the foundation of the Niagara Movement, a civil rights organization committed to aggressive campaigning against lynching, segregation, and denial of black voting rights. The group survived for only a few years, but paved the way for the more successful NAACP, of which DuBois was also a founding member. He served for many years as director of research and publicity and was editor of the organization's monthly magazine, *The Crisis*. The NAACP succeeded in winning a number of court cases through the next two decades. These established the rights of African Americans to enter certain universities and receive commissions as U.S. army officers. They also won a Supreme Court ruling that prohibited states from segregating African Americans into residential districts. The NAACP failed to make significant headway against lynching and other aspects of racism in the South.

As his life progressed, DuBois grew increasingly disillusioned with his native country and came to see the civil rights movement in the United States as part of a larger international struggle against many varieties of social and economic oppression. In his 90s, he joined the Communist Party and renounced his American citizenship. He moved to the African nation of Ghana at the invitation of that country's president, Kwame Nkruma, who had asked him to direct the production of the *Encyclopedia Africana.* Dubois died in Ghana in 1963.

SEE ALSO

African Americans; Civil rights; Colleges and universities; National Association for the Advancement of Colored People; Race relations; Reform movements; Washington, Booker T.

FURTHER READING

DuBois, W. E. B. *The Selected Writings of W. E. B. DuBois.* Edited by Walter Wilson. New York: New American Library, 1970.
———. *The Souls of Black Folk.* New York: Penguin, 1989.
———. *W. E. B. DuBois: A Reader.* Edited by David Levering Lewis. New York: Henry Holt, 1995.
Lewis, David Levering. *W. E. B. Du Bois: Biography of a Race, 1868–1919.* New York: Henry Holt, 1993.
Marable, Manning. *W. E. B. DuBois: Black Radical Democrat.* Boston: Twayne, 1986.

Edison, Thomas Alva

- *Born: Feb. 11, 1847, Milan, Ohio*
- *Education: home tutoring, public schools*
- *Accomplishments: inventor of the phonograph, incandescent electric lightbulb, and motion picture projector; awarded 1,093 patents; awarded Congressional Medal of Honor (1928)*
- *Died: Oct. 18, 1931, Orange, N.J.*

AS A YOUNG MAN, Thomas Alva Edison showed an aptitude for business,

electricity, and the telegraph. These three fields would shape his life as an entrepreneurial inventor, that is, someone who focused on practical inventions that would make money. Edison spent his early career operating telegraphs in various midwestern cities. Despite partial deafness, he not only excelled in telegraphy but designed many technical advances for the field. He was one of several innovators who developed telegraphs that could receive and send multiple messages simultaneously. He also discovered a way to improve stock tickers, the machines that transmit gold and stock prices to brokers' offices. By 1869, he had become a full-time inventor. In 1870, he set up shop in Newark, New Jersey, and six years later moved to Menlo Park, some 15 miles south.

Working with a diverse team of physicists, chemists, and mechanics, Edison often focused on more than one project at a time, an approach that led to his 1877 invention of the phonograph, or record player. This invention emerged from his experiments with an "automatic telegraph," which used a stylus to transcribe the dots and dashes of an incoming message onto a rolled strip of paper, and a "carbon telephone," which exploited the special properties of compressed carbon to pick up sound waves from a vibrating diaphragm and convert them into electrical signals. By combining a diaphragm that transmitted

Thomas Edison, inventor of the electric light bulb, among other innovations, helped make the United States a technological leader. He once said, "I find out what the world needs, then I proceed to invent it."

sound waves and a stylus that inscribed vibrations on a moving surface, Edison created a machine that could record and play back the sound of his voice reciting "Mary had a little lamb." Early versions of the device used paraffin-coated paper and tin foil as recording surfaces. Edison eventually motorized the phonograph and developed wax cylinders on which to record sound.

Edison turned next to finding better methods of electric lighting. Street lamps and auditoriums already used electric arc lights, but these were too powerful and bright for use in homes or businesses. Starting around 1879, Edison tried heating various kinds of filaments. Most burned up too quickly. After countless experiments, he and his assistants found a workable carbon filament, placed it in a glass bulb, pumped out the air to make a vacuum, and applied an electric current. The "incandescent" bulb glowed, he said, with "the most beautiful light ever seen."

In the early 1880s, Edison developed central power stations to generate electric power on a large scale and distribute it over wires. To attract investors, in 1882 he built a power plant that lit 85 buildings in New York City's financial district. Investors, who included the financier J. P. Morgan, were impressed. Morgan helped Edison form the Edison General Electric Company (later, General Electric Company) to produce electric generating equipment, distribution supplies, and indoor electrical fixtures. By 1890, offices across the country were using electricity not just to light lamps but to power motors, fans, printing presses, and heating appliances.

By the late 1880s, Edison had built a huge new research laboratory in Orange, New Jersey. The following decade, writing that he planned to do for the eye what the phonograph had

done for the ear, he introduced the peephole kinetoscope, which allowed individuals to view a moving image. He followed this with machines—the ideas for which he borrowed from others—that projected images on a screen. He made a successful projector in 1896. He also continued to perfect the phonograph, finally abandoning wax cylinders for recording discs made of an early form of plastic.

Edison also developed a lucrative cement business, spurring advances in poured cement office buildings and factories. During World War I, he produced chemicals, such as carbolic acid and benzines (solvents), to replace those no longer available from Germany, and advised the navy on technological issues. With his friend the automaker Henry Ford, he took widely publicized motoring and camping trips. Ford helped finance Edison's last major inventive effort, which was to find a natural substitute for rubber. His work led to the discovery of latex.

Thomas Edison received more patents—1,093—than any other single American. His key inventions—the light bulb, the phonograph, the motion picture projector—changed the world and shaped much of the 20th century. His work both reflected and helped to strengthen the industrial and entrepreneurial spirit of his age.

SEE ALSO

Inventions; Motion pictures; Science and technology

FURTHER READING

Adair, Gene. *Thomas Alva Edison: Inventing the Electric Age.* New York: Oxford University Press, 1996.
Baldwin, Neil. *Edison: Inventing the Century.* New York: Hyperion, 1995.
Collins, Theresa M., and Lisa Gitelman. *Thomas Edison and Modern America: A Brief History With Documents.* Boston: Bedford/St. Martin's, 2002.
Israel, Paul. *Edison: A Life of Invention.* New York: John Wiley, 1998.

Education

FROM ITS EARLIEST DAYS as a democratic republic, the United States was committed to educating its citizenry. By the late 1800s, local and state governments had established public school systems throughout the Northeast and Midwest and in much of the Far West. In cities, school boards divided schools first into grades and later into elementary and secondary systems. In most rural areas, children still learned in one-room schoolhouses. Generally, public school teachers in the Gilded Age were women, many of whom had earned teacher certification at the nation's new teacher training schools, which were called Normal Schools. School principals and superintendents, who were more highly paid, were usually male.

The South before the Civil War had very few public schools, but following Reconstruction southern states gradually established public education systems. Southern districts provided two sets of schools, separate but supposedly equal, for the black and white races. Because municipalities allocated the lion's share of tax money to white schools, schools for black children always lacked funds.

The expansion of public high schools had lagged behind elementary schools, primarily because most people thought high schools were not necessary. Wealthy parents sent their children to private seminaries or academies, but the vast majority of American children older than 14 were already out of school and earning a living. In 1874, Michigan's Supreme Court ruled that the state's school districts had to have tax-supported public

high schools. As other states followed Michigan's example, secondary education became more widespread.

High school education also became more desirable because it was more necessary. The tremendous expansion of industry, the rise of big business, and the growth of retailing led American employers to demand an educated workforce. Firms sought employees with solid general skills: office and clerical staff who wrote and spoke good English and could use the latest office machinery, or workers who could read manuals and mechanical drawings and understand the fundamentals of chemistry. Employers discovered that schooling could make the ordinary office clerk, shop-floor worker, and even the farmer more productive. By 1915, young men had also discovered that an additional year of high school added more than 12 percent to their earnings.

Progressive reformers initiated a high school movement to make secondary education relevant for all American teenagers. They encouraged a varied curriculum that included academic, general, and vocational studies. Leaders of the National Education Association (NEA) hoped that high schools would not promote class distinctions between students going on to college and those stopping with a high school degree but would instead serve all classes with a rich and varied academic curriculum.

Other reformers felt that high school education should be more practical. In 1917, Congress passed the Smith-Hughes Act, which provided federal financing for courses in mechanical trades, home economics, and agriculture. In 1918, the NEA established the standards for a comprehensive high school, where students would follow different courses of

White children study geometry in Washington, D.C., in the late 1890s, a time when many schools, including those in the nation's capital, were racially segregated.

training in, for example, agriculture, business, clerical work, industrial labor, fine arts, and domestic science.

To develop responsible and well-informed young citizens, comprehensive high schools expanded their extracurricular activities. They invented systems for student government—class officers and student councils—not in order to give students real power but to teach American citizenship roles. They encouraged students to run their own yearbooks and newspapers, hoping thereby to foster school unity and loyalty and teach English and cooperative skills. Finally, they introduced organized athletics to encourage high standards of sportsmanship.

The high school movement was a resounding success. In the 1890s, a little more than 200,000 students were attending only about 2,500 high schools. By 1900, these figures had more than doubled, and a dozen years later more than a million students were attending high schools. By 1920, this figure, too, had doubled. By 1940, the number of 14- to 17-year-olds attending high school had increased to 70 percent of the entire age group, and

about one-half of those who entered high school received diplomas.

Several other educational innovations originated during the Gilded Age and Progressive Era. Taking inspiration from German educators, in the 1870s American educators began urging communities to establish kindergartens. One of the first appeared in St. Louis in 1873. Designed to protect preschool slum children from the streets, kindergartens taught children cleanliness, good moral habits, and self-control. Settlement-house leaders later persuaded school boards to provide kindergartners with free lunches and school nurses. By the mid-20th century, kindergartens were becoming available for middle-class children and public elementary schools began to offer a year of kindergarten before the first grade. Summer school was another innovation. In order to curtail juvenile crime when schools were closed, many districts started summer or "vacation" schools.

One group of progressive reformers who focused on schooling for young children wanted to alter the nature of education itself. These educators rejected the authoritarianism, rote learning (memorization), and dull curricula of most schools and sought new approaches to help young children become more interested in learning. To accomplish this goal, they adopted ideas from philosopher John Dewey, who stressed experimentation and practice in learning, and encouraged children to learn from their mistakes without fear of condemnation. Through the influence of Dewey and other progressives, the harsh environment of 19th-century schools gave way to the child-centered classrooms of the modern era.

To meet the needs of a growing and more varied population in an industrial age, American higher education expanded in the Gilded Age and Progressive Era. By the early 1870s, most publicly funded schools were coeducational, as were all schools for African Americans and most of the private, denominational schools founded in the Midwest to serve the children of farmers. By the early 1900s, many elite universities, such as Harvard, Brown, and Columbia, which at the time accepted only men, had founded sister (or "coordinate") colleges for women. Moreover, by then the elite all-female colleges, such as Vassar, Smith, Wellesley, and Bryn Mawr, were well established. Thanks to the free colleges set up in some of the nation's larger cities, such as City College and Hunter College in New York, the sons and daughters of factory workers and immigrants could also earn advanced degrees, many by attending class at night so that they could earn a living during the day.

SEE ALSO

Child Labor; Colleges and universities; Dewey, John; Progressive movement; Reform movements; Science and technology; Segregation; Settlement-house movement

FURTHER READING

Anderson, James D. *The Education of Blacks in the South, 1860–1935.* Chapel Hill: University of North Carolina Press, 1988.

Bever, Landon E., and Daniel P. Liston. *Curriculum in Conflict: Social Visions, Educational Agendas, and Progressive School Reform.* New York: Teachers College Press, 1996.

Cremin, Lawrence A. *The Transformation of the School: Progressivism in American Education, 1876–1957.* New York: Random House, 1961.

———. *American Education: The Metropolitan Experience, 1876–1980.* New York: Harper & Row, 1988.

Cuban, Larry. *How Teachers Taught: Constancy and Change in American Classrooms, 1890–1990.* 2nd ed. New York: Teachers College Press, 1993.

18th Amendment

PASSED BY CONGRESS on December 18, 1917, and ratified on January 29, 1919, the 18th Amendment outlawed the manufacture, distribution, and sale of alcoholic beverages in the United States. It also prohibited the importation and exportation of such beverages. On October 27, 1919, over President Woodrow Wilson's veto Congress passed the Volstead Act, which set up the enforcement mechanism for prohibition. Volstead went into effect on January 16, 1920.

Thus began what a later President, Herbert Hoover, would call "a noble experiment" in controlling human

An Oregon billboard shows the arguments of three Presidents against prohibition, the banning of the manufacture, importation, and sale of alcohol. Though many Americans supported prohibition, some argued that it would cause a loss of tax revenue and could not be enforced.

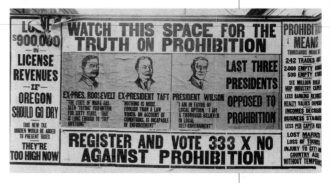

vices. Most Americans eventually concluded that it failed. Individuals at all levels of American society evaded the act, and criminals engaged in widespread bootlegging, or the illegal traffic in liquor. By the end of the 1920s, even prohibition's most ardent supporters agreed that it had given rise to more problems than it had solved. The 21st Amendment, adopted on December 21, 1933, repealed prohibition.

SEE ALSO

Reform movements; Temperance and prohibition movements

FURTHER READING

Hamm, Richard F. *Shaping the Eighteenth Amendment: Temperance Reform, Legal Culture, and the Polity, 1880–1920.* Chapel Hill: University of North Carolina Press, 1995.
Lucas, Eileen. *The Eighteenth and Twenty-first Amendments: Alcohol, Prohibition, and Repeal.* Springfield, N.J.: Enslow, 1998.

Electricity

ELECTRICITY IS a natural force that humans have recognized since ancient times in the form of static electricity, which produces sparks and causes objects to cling to one another when certain materials are rubbed together. The first devices to make practical use of electricity were primitive electric lights and motors that appeared in the early 1800s. By the 1840s, the telegraph was using electrical current (a moving charge flowing along a stream of particles) to send messages by wire across long distances. Only in the late 1800s did inventors finally harness electricity as an everyday energy source for homes, businesses, and industries.

Inventor Thomas Edison, who began his career by designing improve-

ments to the telegraph, played a key role in the electrification of American society. In 1879, he produced the first long-lasting, commercially useful electric lightbulb. To enable consumers to use lightbulbs and other electrical devices, he designed a system for power plants that could distribute electricity to nearby customers along a network of wires. In 1883, Edison's greatest business rival, George Westinghouse, introduced transformer that could receive a high-voltage current suitable for long-distance transmission, and convert it to a low-voltage current safe to distribute to individual electric company consumers.

Edison and Westinghouse favored two different forms of electricity, direct current (DC) and alternating current (AC). As a proponent of direct current, Edison sought to frighten the public by mounting demonstrations in which he used alternating current to give fatal electric shocks to animals. Westinghouse countered with an argument that appealed to consumers' economic interests. He constructed a plant that used the free power source of Niagara Falls to generate electricity, then used AC-based transformer technology to transmit the energy cheaply to customers in New York City. A Westinghouse exhibit at the World's Columbian Exposition in Chicago in 1893 dazzled spectators with the wonders of electricity. In the

Electric lighting, developed in the late 19th century, outlines some of the attractions in a nighttime view of Luna Park, an amusement park in Coney Island, New York.

long run, AC proved its commercial and technological superiority and established itself as the national standard.

By the 1910s the public had come to believe that electricity was a safer and more efficient lighting source than gas. Gas fixtures and gas-powered appliances lacked the portability of electric lamps and appliances, since they could not be moved away from gas lines in the walls. In addition, gas lighting produced an open flame and a risk of fatal fumes. Gradually, electric lights replaced kerosene lanterns and gas lighting fixtures on city streets and in public and private buildings. Gas and electricity remained rival power sources, however, for major appliances such as stoves, furnaces, and hot water heaters, which in some cases were less expensive to operate with gas than with electricity.

Many Gilded Age inventions popularized the use of electricity, including the electric stove (1891), the vacuum cleaner and washing machine (1903), the toaster (1910), the air conditioner (1911), and the refrigerator (1913). By 1920, homes and businesses throughout the United States were using electric light and power, although some poor rural areas did not become electrified until much later in the 20th century.

SEE ALSO

Cities; Edison, Thomas Alva; Inventions; Science and technology; Telephone and telegraph

FURTHER READING

Davis, L. J. *Fleet Fire: Thomas Edison and the Pioneers of the Electric Revolution.* New York: Arcade, 2003.
Jonnes, Jill. *Empires of Light: Edison, Tesla, Westinghouse, and the Race to Electrify the World.* New York: Random House, 2003.
Nye, David E. *Electrifying America: Social Meanings of a New Technology, 1880–1940.* Cambridge, Mass.: MIT Press, 1990.

Ellis Island

IMMIGRANTS FROM EUROPE in the late 19th century arrived at a variety of American ports from Boston to Baltimore, Savannah to New Orleans. By far the most popular destination, however, was New York City. By 1890, more than 8 million immigrants, mostly from northwestern Europe, had been processed at New York's Castle Garden, located at the southern tip of Manhattan.

Castle Garden proved to be too small to deal with the influx of immigrants from southern and eastern Europe who began arriving in the 1880s and 1890s. The U.S. government decided to build a new immigration reception center in New York Harbor. Officials chose Ellis Island, formerly one of a series of island forts protecting the city. The center eventually became a huge and imposing complex, which included the main reception and processing hall, kitchens, hospital buildings, dormitories, and contagious disease wards.

Ellis Island opened on January 1, 1892. The first immigrant processed there was Annie Moore, a 15-year-old girl from Ireland who was immigrating to the United States with her two little brothers. Millions more were to follow, hundreds of thousands a year until the outbreak of World War I cut the flow of passenger ships from Europe. In its peak year, 1907, Ellis Island processed 1.25 million immigrants.

The majority of immigrants who crossed the Atlantic hoping for new lives in America had traveled steerage, or third class. This meant they had spent two weeks or more in overcrowded and often unsanitary condi-

New arrivals from Europe line up for eye examinations at Ellis Island around 1913. Immigration officers rejected some immigrants for health reasons, and refused admission to others who they felt might become indigent.

tions in the lowest decks of steamships. Unlike the first- and second-class passengers, who disembarked at the dock in New York City, and cleared customs and immigration there, steerage passengers were off-loaded and taken by ferry to Ellis Island, where they waited in long lines in the Great Hall to have their documents, baggage, and physical condition examined. Looking for contagious diseases, doctors working for the U.S. Public Health Service were especially alert for tuberculosis and trachoma, a dangerous eye disease.

Officials of the U.S. Bureau of Immigration interviewed immigrants through translators to make sure they had enough money or job prospects or relatives already in America so as not to become a charge on public resources. They were also trying to exclude radical political agitators and prevent immigrants from entering as illegal contract laborers. Sometimes new arrivals were detained for a few days if they were sick but could recover, or if not all the paperwork was in order. For these detainees there were hospital rooms, dormitories, baths, dining rooms, and play facilities to entertain children.

In the long run, only 2 percent of immigrants were turned back at Ellis Island, but the prospect of being denied admission to the United States was enough to earn Ellis Island the nickname Island of Hope, Island of Tears. Exclusion could be especially sad when it broke up families, forcing one of the parents to return to Europe with a sick child, for example.

From Ellis Island, the newly admitted immigrants journeyed onward. Many stayed in New York City; others went by train to the South and West to begin their American lives. Traffic through Ellis Island diminished during World War I, when the center was used to intern suspected enemy aliens. In the mid-1920s, national anxieties about immigration caused the federal government to enact quota laws restricting the flow of newcomers. Ellis Island remained open for many years, processing immigrants and serving again as a detention center during World War II. It closed in 1954 and has subsequently been restored by the National Park Service as a museum of American immigration history.

SEE ALSO

Health, public; Immigration; World War I

FURTHER READING

Kotker, Norman, et al. *Ellis Island: Echoes from a Nation's Past*. Edited by Susan Jonas. New York: Aperture Foundation, 1989.
Moreno, Barry. *Encyclopedia of Ellis Island*. Westport, Conn.: Greenwood, 2004.
Pitkin, Thomas M. *Keepers of the Gate: A History of Ellis Island*. New York: New York University Press, 1976.
Reeves, Pamela. *Ellis Island: Gateway to the American Dream*. New York: Gramercy Press, 1991.
Yans McLaughlin, Virginia, and Marjorie Lightman. *Ellis Island and the Peopling of America: The Official Guide*. New York: New Press, 1997.

Environment

THE ENVIRONMENT is the complex of external factors and influences that affect an organism or a community and determine its form and survival. We tend to think of concern for the environment as a product of the late 20th century. Many late 19th-century Americans were aware, however, that human actions were causing harmful environmental changes.

By 1900, the thickly settled eastern half of the United States had lost almost all its old-growth forest, and secondary growth was beginning to overtake the farmlands cleared by the original colonists. Elsewhere in the country, farmers continued to clear land by burning trees, loading the air and landscape with ash. In the South, 150 years of cotton planting had exhausted much of the rich topsoil. In the Midwest, the tough, matted prairie sod had surrendered to the pioneering farmer's plow. On the Great Plains, buffalo were near extinction. In the Far West, lumber operations, practiced without any obligation to re-plant, had stripped thousands of acres of primitive forest. By the 1920s, plowing and cattle grazing had damaged enough western land to create massive areas of erosion. The loss of topsoil and the grass to hold it in place would lead to great dust storms in the 1930s. Throughout the country, formerly abundant animal species, such as the beaver and the wolf, had retreated to distant wilderness areas. By 1915, the passenger pigeon and the Carolina parakeet were extinct.

American cities had grown quickly and somewhat haphazardly, but even before the Civil War, local govern-ments had started to build sewers and water lines, these activities spurred by scientific discoveries linking polluted drinking water to urban outbreaks of the deadly diseases typhoid and cholera. But not until 1908 would the first effective filtration and chlorination systems begin to make drinking water safe for entire cities.

City dwellers everywhere suffered from air pollution. Furnaces and fireplaces and nearby coal-burning industries blackened the air and contributed to bronchitis, asthma, and emphysema. Cities at the turn of the century could spend many days a year blanketed in smog (a combination of the words *smoke* and *fog*) that made roads hazardous and leaked into homes, making people sick. In 1881, taking a lesson from London, where 700 people had died from smog the previous winter, American cities began to pass smoke abatement ordinances.

Industry had done much to enhance American life, but it brought new environmental hazards along with benefits. Coal mining and other mining operations polluted the air and poisoned the water and landscape. Some mining operations destroyed entire mountainsides, scooping away the earth to get at the valuable resources below. Copper smelting released sulfur dioxide, which killed trees and poisoned the air in neighboring communities. Other industrial wastes, as well as garbage and sewage, fouled the country's lakes and rivers, especially in the Northeast, where most industrial operations were located. Oil spills in the petroleum industry and leaks from chemical plants found their way into the water. Dams and drainage pipes made it impossible for some species of fish to swim upstream to spawn. There was no concept of hazardous waste disposal, and very little government oversight or regulation. Industries dumped poisonous waste products wherever they could.

Industrial processes could also poison industrial workers. Lead in paints and solder, lead dust, and arsenic, all used in many industrial processes, even the manufacture of wallpaper, could sicken both workers and consumers. Scientists in 1904 first linked childhood lead poisoning to lead in paint. The phosphorous in matches caused "phossy jaw," which involved swelling and abscesses and could lead to the loss of a matchmaker's jaw or an eye. In 1909, Dr. Alice Hamilton, an expert in industrial medicine, led a movement to substitute a different chemical for phosphorous, thereby saving workers in American match factories from the ravages of this disease.

Expansion, population growth, and above all, industrialization had caused environmental problems for the United States. The problems spurred responses from many citizens in all parts of the country. Some progressives were interested in urban environmental reforms and public health. They worked to eliminate pollution, create safe air and water, and protect citizens from contagious illness, dangerous working conditions, and industrial poisons. Other environmental reformers concerned themselves with the preservation of scenic areas, wilderness, and natural resources. Their work became known as conservation.

SEE ALSO

Agriculture; Buffalo; Cities; Conservation; Health, public; Industry; Labor; Mining; Progressive movement; Ranching; Science and technology

FURTHER READING

Andrews, Richard N. L. *Managing the Environment, Managing Ourselves: A History of American Environmental Policy.* New Haven: Yale University Press, 1999.
Carson, Rachel. *Silent Spring.* New York: Mariner Books, 2002.
McNeill, J. R., and Paul Kennedy. *Something New under the Sun: An Environmental History of the Twentieth-Century World.* New York: Norton, 2001.
Pringle, Laurence. *The Environmental Movement: From its Roots to the Challenges of a New Century.* New York: HarperCollins, 2000.
Smith, Duane A. *Mining America: The Industry and the Environment, 1800–1980.* Lawrence: University of Kansas Press, 1987.
Worster, Donald. *The Wealth of Nature: Environmental History and the Ecological Imagination.* New York: Oxford University Press, 1993.

Family life

BEFORE THE 20th century, hardly anyone lived alone. Instead, most people lived in a family of some kind. Either they were directly related to the family, or they lodged with one. Sometimes these lodgers were guests, at other times paying boarders or domestic servants. Thus, despite the migrations of the late 1800s, which tended to separate blood relations as individuals traveled to find better jobs or farmland, family households survived.

In addition to changes brought about by migration, other long-term trends affected the structure of families. Before industrialization, families generally made the goods they needed, selling or trading their surplus to others. Industrialization changed the way families made a living by moving much of their productive work out of their homes and into shops and factories. By the early 1900s, only farm families and first-generation immigrant families still produced goods at home, usually employing all family members, including children, in some part of the production process.

Three generations of a wealthy New York City family gather at home for this group portrait. The painting conveys a dual message of social status and family closeness.

By the 1920s, only the most isolated rural families were still making most of the goods they consumed.

The movement of productive work out of homes changed Americans' image of what a family was supposed to look like. Instead of all members of a family working together in the home or on a farm to earn their way, the ideal American family now consisted of a breadwinner, usually male, who went out of the house to work in a shop, factory, or office, and a woman who kept house and cared for her children at home. Families of all social classes aspired to this ideal, even though working-class and farm families could rarely make ends meet on a single wage. When immigrant families were able to move out of ghetto communities, they too adopted this ideal. If a woman family member was working outside the home, immigrant families believed this indicated that her father or husband was a poor provider. This middle-class family model remained in place until the modern feminist movement of the 1960s and 1970s encouraged women to work outside the home for their own economic and personal fulfillment.

Another major change in the family during the late 1800s and early 1900s was its diminishing size. By 1890, native-born, urban white parents on average had reduced the number of their offspring from seven to four. Perhaps because of access to new methods of birth control, by 1920 they were having three or fewer. Because the Roman Catholic church opposed birth control, Italian, French Canadian, and Polish families remained larger, normally with seven or more children each. Irish and German Catholic families were somewhat smaller, with about five children. African American families averaged only 2.9 children around the turn of the century, in part because poverty caused almost 20 percent of black infants to die before their first birthday in this era.

Families with fewer children became more child-centered. Parents focused more attention on the few children they had, and the children focused on play and education instead of on working for wages. Because farm and homesteading families still had relatively large families at this time, their children rarely had the luxury of not working. In such families, older children usually took responsibility for younger ones, and all children helped out with family chores. Usually, the women concentrated on dairy and kitchen garden work, preparing meals, preserving food, and doing laundry, cleaning, and repairs; men did the field work, but in planting and harvesting seasons or in times of crisis these strict divisions tended to blur. Also, just like men, many farm women participated in the cash economy by raising, growing, or making items to exchange for cash or other goods.

Family size also diminished during this time period because the number of family relations who lived together was decreasing. Again, this was a trend that had begun in earlier times, especially for the middle and upper classes living in urban settings. Younger members of such families set up their own households when they married, moving in with older generations only in times of personal or economic crisis. Working-class and farm families, however, took longer to make this change. Immigrant families often lived as extended families, merging several generations into one large family unit. Such families also took in boarders, some of whom might be relatives or friends, sometimes complete strangers, often single immigrant men of their own nationality. This kind of arrangement provided crucial income for widows or for older couples whose children had left home. In 1901, the U.S. commissioner of labor reported that 24 percent of working-class families across the country took in boarders. In 1912, 90 percent of immigrant families in Lawrence, Massachusetts, for example, took in boarders.

Urban working-class families in this period needed approximately $600 to $800 a year to live. But many wage earners' income fell below this, so survival was a cooperative family effort. Women took in laundry and sewed clothes. Elder daughters, who had gone out to work at ages 10 or 12, contributed their income to the family until they married. African American families relied heavily on extended families for financial support and for child care when one or both parents had to move

away to take a job in another location. Sometimes, when families had no other resources, they abandoned their children to orphanages or foster care.

Complex households—or households consisting of numerous unrelated or distantly related people—peaked between 1880 and 1900, especially in cities and among immigrant families. By 1920, complex households had decreased in number and the so-called nuclear family, consisting of only a married couple and their children, became the standard to which most Americans aspired.

SEE ALSO

Birth control movement; Childhood; Child labor; Consumer culture; Immigration; Marriage; Population and fertility

FURTHER READING

American Families: A Multicultural Reader. Edited by Stephanie Coontz with Maya Parson and Gabrielle Raley. New York: Routledge, 1999.
Coontz, Stephanie. *The Social Origins of Private Life: A History of American Families, 1600–1900.* New York: Verso, 1988.
Degler, Carl N. *At Odds: Women and the Family in America from the Revolution to the Present.* New York: Oxford University Press, 1980.
Scott, Donald M., and Bernard Wishy, eds. *America's Families: A Documentary History.* NewYork: Harper & Row, 1982.

Farmers' Alliances

ARISING IN RESPONSE to falling agricultural prices after the Civil War, Farmers' Alliances started out as cooperative networks designed to solve the common problems of farm communities. They first appeared in the mid-1870s in New York, Kansas, and Texas, but soon spread across the country. Some alliances developed marketing and purchasing cooperatives. They also agitated for federal loans to farmers and federal regulation of the railroads in order to ensure fair rates for shipping their produce to market.

By the 1880s, these organizations had become increasingly political. They endorsed the Greenback party, which was founded in 1876 and advocated an increased supply of cheap paper money. The party had 15 of its candidates elected to Congress in 1880. During the following decade, floods and droughts gave urgency to farmers' demands for federal loans and inspired alliances from different parts of the country to form large confederations. By 1889, the Texas Farmers' Alliance claimed 3 million members. Eventually, the alliances formed the backbone of the Populist, or People's, party, which was founded in 1891. The Populist Party called for government ownership of railroads and communication systems, an increased supply of paper money based on the value of silver, an income tax, direct election of U.S. senators, and a shorter workweek for industrial laborers.

Farmers' Alliances appealed especially to owners of mid-sized farms hurt by declining prices for their crops. In the South, however, several of the organization's chief leaders were able to rise to positions of prominence. Leonidas L. Polk of North Carolina became a successful farmer, town builder, and lecturer. Benjamin Tillman of South Carolina promoted state-funded agricultural education and won his state's governorship in 1890. Tom Watson of Georgia came from a landowning family that had fallen on hard times in his youth. A teacher and lawyer, Watson did well buying land and entering state politics, in which he championed southern independence from northern capitalists. Watson received a Vice Presidential nomination in 1896.

Farmers' Alliances not only admitted women as officers but endorsed women's political rights. In the days when women had few opportunities for public expression, women in the southern alliances became local organizers and leaders and many alliance publications were written and edited by women.

A separate but parallel Colored Farmers' Alliance, formed in Houston, Texas, in 1886, had more than a million members by 1891. Its existence marked a brief interlude of superficial biracial cooperation in the South.

SEE ALSO
Agriculture; Populism; Populist party

FURTHER READING
Barnes, Donna A. *Farmers in Rebellion: The Rise and Fall of the Southern Farmers Alliance and People's Party in Texas.* Austin: University of Texas Press, 1984.
Hicks, John Donald. *The Populist Revolt: A History of the Farmers' Alliance and the People's Party.* Lincoln: University of Nebraska Press, 1961.
Ostler, Jeffrey. *Prairie Populism: The Fate of Agrarian Radicalism in Kansas, Nebraska, and Iowa, 1880–1892.* Lawrence: University Press of Kansas, 1993.

Fashions

FASHIONS IN CLOTHING and hairstyles changed rapidly in the late 19th century. One of the chief reasons was the emerging field of advertising. Clothing designers (many of them based in Paris), manufacturers of ready-made clothing, and dress pattern makers advertised heavily in ladies' magazines and mail-order catalogs. Their advertisements convinced fashion-conscious women and men that they would be socially unacceptable if they failed to adopt the latest styles.

By the 1870s, the hoops and crinolines fashionable women used to

No. 917
Suit
$7.50

Sent to you with the full understanding and agreement that if not satisfactory to you upon examination you can return it

At Our Expense

and your money will be refunded.

No. 917
Blouse Tailored Suit

THE BIG STORE A CITY IN ITSELF
SIEGEL COOPER Co.
SIXTH AVE. 18 TH & 19 TH STS.
NEW YORK CITY. N.Y.

Send orders to New York only.

no branch houses, no agents.

Worn with an elaborate plumed hat, the dress in this 1905 advertisement features puffed-out leg-o'-mutton sleeves. The outfit sends a message of feminine modesty, but its narrow waist and prominent bust and posterior also emphasize female sexual allure.

puff out their skirts in the past had disappeared. Instead, designers were placing all of a skirt's fullness in the back. This design required a bustle, a large horsehair pad or whalebone structure draped with dress material, embellished by ribbons or ruffles, and placed over a woman's behind. Although bustles weighed less than hoops, they still limited women's freedom of movement, as did the bell-shaped skirts that arrived later. By the 1890s, designers were pushing leg-o'-mutton, or puffed-out, sleeves, along with trains for evening wear. Around 1908, designers began to narrow the bell-shaped skirts at the ankles, creating a hobbling effect on a woman's walk. All of these styles reinforced the Victorian trend of emphasizing the curves of a woman's body while preserving her modesty. Designers also enlarged women's hats and added plumage. Women generally still kept their hair long, wrapping it up into a chignon on the back of their heads.

Corsets remained fashionable for many women (and even some men) several decades into the 20th century. Because corsets restricted a woman's breathing and pushed her internal organs and breasts into unnatural positions, they had long been a target of "rational dress" reformers. Active since the 1850s, these reformers worked to convince women to dress more sensibly. Some reformers promoted bloomers, loose pantaloons inspired by Turkish trousers, over which women could wear tunics. Bloomers inspired so much mockery, however, that their advocates had to give them up. Some women made political statements with their clothing. Civil War physician Mary

Walker adopted men's dress in part for convenience as she worked but also as a protest against restrictions on women's public lives. Some college women shortened their hair and discarded their corsets. Working-class women rarely wore corsets, although some domestic servants insisted on wearing them, despite employers' concerns that corsets impeded physical labor.

By the turn of the 20th century, technological, social, and cultural changes were all influencing fashions. The introduction of automobiles, which were open to the elements in their early years, brought in dusters—long, loose coats for both men and women—and veiled hats for women. Sewing machines, which were electrified in the 1880s, expanded the machine-made clothing industry and fostered the appearance of simpler, more standardized clothing. As more women joined the workforce, they gravitated toward such styles, raising hems off the floor where they served only to collect dirt or cause accidents. Women moving into service and commercial industries or becoming professionals favored tailor-made suits, usually plain-fronted jackets over high-necked shirtwaists, or blouses. Instead of being puffed out, their skirts tended to be flat both in front and back.

The sports and bicycle crazes of the 1890s gave rise to greater informality of clothing for both women and men. Some men sported straw hats and handlebar mustaches, named for the bicycles' handlebars. To play golf and tennis or ride bicycles, some women wore culottes, or divided skirts, sometimes as short as mid-calf, over cotton stockings. Men, in turn, abandoned stiff collars for open-necked shirts and blazers. For women the dance craze of the 1910s brought in even shorter, lighter-weight skirts, sometimes slit up the sides to allow for dips. Women began bobbing their hair, in imitation of ballroom dancer Irene Castle's popular style. By World War I, when their work or leisure activities required, some women could even wear trousers without creating a scandal.

Other changes after 1900 included an increasingly clean-shaven look for men. The idea that facial hair harbored germs prompted this development. World War I introduced trench coats, leather coats (such as the ones pilots wore), and ever-rising skirt hems for women. By 1920, hems had reached mid-calf and dress material had become skimpier than ever. With her boyish, flat-chested silhouette, rolled stockings, and T-strap shoes, the "flapper" had arrived.

SEE ALSO

Bicycle; Consumer culture; Dance; Sports; Victorianism

FURTHER READING

Banner, Lois W. *American Beauty*. New York: Knopf, 1983.

Cunningham, Patricia A. *Reforming Women's Fashion, 1850–1920*. Kent, Ohio: Kent State University Press, 2003.

Hoobler, Dorothy, and Thomas Hoobler. *Vanity Rules: A History of American Fashion and Beauty*. Brookfield, Conn.: Millbrook, 2000.

Olian, JoAnne, ed. *Everyday Fashions, 1909–1920, as Pictured in Sears Catalogs*. New York: Dover, 1995.

Federal Reserve Act (1913)

BY THE LATE 1800s, the United States had some 7,000 nationally chartered banks and 20,000 state-chartered banks. Banks often failed, usually when a panic over a financial development convinced bank depositors to withdraw their savings all at once. Since banks make loans and investments with depositors' money, during such bank runs they usually have insufficient cash reserves to meet the demand to return this money and so are forced out of business. The frequency of bank collapses put pressure on national leaders to create a central agency not only to coordinate bank operations across the country but also to control the flow of currency both domestically and abroad.

In 1907, the collapse of several trust companies (banks or divisions of banks that hold money in trust or manage estates) led many depositors to withdraw their savings from banks. The banks, in turn, called in their loans, causing a general economic recession. Although financier James Pierpont Morgan and other New York bankers were able to save the country's finances by drawing on a special fund to prop up the failing banks, Congress resolved to take action. Many years of study, discussion, and compromise followed. Because Woodrow Wilson favored stronger government supervision of banks, his election to the presidency in 1912 increased support for the Federal Reserve Act, which finally passed on December 23, 1913.

The Act established a Federal Reserve Act of 12 districts, each with a Federal Reserve bank. All national banks had to join the system and contribute 6 percent of their capital to the Federal Reserve bank; state banks and trust companies could also join if they wished. A board of governors, consisting of presidential appointees who included the secretary of the treasury and the comptroller of the currency, oversaw the entire system. Although the act was imprecise about the relationship between the central board and the regional banks, a failing that would be corrected in the 1930s, it allowed the government to exercise much greater control over the nation's monetary policies.

SEE ALSO

Monetary policies; Morgan, John Pierpont; Wilson, Woodrow T.

FURTHER READING

Meltzer, Allan H. *A History of the Federal Reserve.* Chicago: University of Chicago Press, 2003.
Taylor, Gary. *The Federal Reserve System.* New York: Chelsea House, 1989.
Wells, Donald R. *The Federal Reserve System: A History.* Jefferson, N.C.: McFarland, 2004.

Federal Trade Commission

SEE Antitrust laws

Fine arts

LEWIS MUMFORD, a well-known critic of Gilded Age arts and architecture, called the years following the Civil War the Brown Decades. He used this term to describe the somber mood of American painters and other fine artists following the assassination of President Abraham Lincoln. He wrote that to these artists, the country "looked different—darker, sadder, soberer" in the wake of the massive losses of the war. As a consequence, they favored an artistic palette of the yellows, browns, and deep reds of autumn.

Although their mood was somber, in general fine artists avoided showing the darker side—the poverty and corruption—of Gilded Age life. Instead, painters and sculptors emphasized images of escape, such as exotic land-scapes, the jewels and rich drapery of middle- and upper-class homes, and heroic scenes derived from classical mythology. During the 1880s, American art reflected the influence of the European Renaissance. By the turn of the century the mood had lightened, and artists were also finding inspiration in the Japanese decorative arts and French Impressionism. American artists began to share the growing interest of artists everywhere in more abstract forms of expression.

Along with these important stylistic trends, the American art scene saw many institutional developments. Beginning in the 1870s, large cities such as Boston, New York, Providence, Philadelphia, St. Louis, and San Francisco founded the great museums and schools of fine arts that still exist today. By 1880, approximately 150 private art collectors had amassed significant collections, some of which became the basis of collections later opened to the public. Artists organized themselves into professional societies. In addition to founding the Society of American Artists in 1877, artists in the late 1800s specializing in particular media, such as watercolor, etching, sculpting, ceramics, and murals, all founded their own professional societies in order to advance their mutual interests and enhance their communication with one another.

After the Civil War, serious American artists studied abroad, primarily at the Ecole des Beaux-Arts in Paris. This school emphasized subjects derived from history, literature, and mythology and the importance of order and harmony in artistic production. These principles guided the American Renaissance, a period that lasted from the 1880s to the 1920s and drew inspiration from the Italian Renaissance, the period from the 14th century to the 17th, during

The Palace of Fine Arts at the World's Columbian Exposition in Chicago in 1893 displayed paintings and sculpture. The building was one of several dozen white, classical-style exhibit halls that made up the White City.

which the arts and sciences flourished in Europe. Wealthy patrons, who saw American Renaissance creations as art of high refinement, bought pieces to decorate their mansions, financial institutions, and churches. John La Farge, one of the period's most prominent muralists, designed the stained glass windows of Trinity Church in Boston, and John Singer Sargent, the era's most fashionable portraitist, painted a set of murals called *Triumph of Religion* for the third-floor gallery at the top of the main staircase of Boston's new public library. These artists made the church and the library into the first great monuments of the American Renaissance style. The harmoniously designed buildings of the White City, a model city built for the 1893 Chicago World's Columbian Exposition, which were all decorated according to Beaux-Arts ideals, illustrate the American Renaissance at its peak.

Other styles popular in the late 1800s include panoramic scenes of the West painted by such artists as Albert Bierstadt and Thomas Moran, who reaffirmed the beauty, uniqueness, and power of the disappearing frontier. Their work, along with the western photographs of Eadweard Muybridge, helped build public support for the conservation movement and ultimately the creation of the national park system. Bronze sculptures, paintings, and maga-

zine illustrations by Frederic Remington and Charles Russell immortalized the West of the cowboy and cattle drives, and the stern black-and-white photographs of Edward S. Curtis captured the faces and costumes of Native American tribes he thought were vanishing. Genre paintings—realistic depictions of local color—were often of rural scenes and expressed nostalgia for the simplicities of preindustrial life; this work also had appreciative audiences.

As the century drew to a close, the genre paintings of Winslow Homer, a former Civil War illustrator, became less benign. Instead of depicting subjects in harmony with nature, he showed them as troubled and struggling, especially with the forces of nature. Some critics interpret Homer's powerful seascapes and hunting scenes as pictorial equivalents of Charles Darwin's theory that only the fittest specimens survived in a natural process of selection, an idea that haunted late 19th-century American thought. Another genre painter, Thomas Eakins, rebelled against the romantic art of the previous century and became increasingly realistic in his work. *The Gross Clinic,* which depicts a surgical operation, was rejected for display at the Philadelphia Centennial Exposition of 1876 because of its gory subject matter. In his later work, Eakins emphasized the human body, drawing from nude models of both sexes rather than copying classical statues. In the mid-1880s, when objections arose to his use of nude male models, Eakins was forced to resign his teaching post at the Philadelphia Academy of Art.

The Aesthetic Movement was also significant in the late 1800s. Its ideals emphasized the design of the whole and harmony of color over the importance of conveying of any emotional or moral message. The Japanese decorative arts were a major influence here. James Abbott McNeill Whistler, an American-born painter and graphic artist who was active mainly in England, was one of the movement's greatest advocates. His mood paintings (which he called "night pieces in the Japanese manner") strove for harmony of form and color. Whistler is especially known for his 1871 *Arrangement in Gray and Black*. Subtitled "Portrait of the Painter's Mother," it de-emphasizes the human figure, instead focusing on a formal arrangement of tones. The British art critic John Ruskin derided another of Whistler's paintings, an impressionistic study of fireworks entitled *Nocturne in Black and Gold* (1875), as "a pot of paint" flung at the public. Whistler sued Ruskin for libel, and won, but as he received no money, he was forced into bankruptcy over court costs.

Even as new styles began to come to the fore, the older Renaissance and classical styles held on in architecture and the decorative arts. Sculptors created bronze memorials to the heroes of the Civil War, emphasizing the reunited nation and the valor of its soldier-citizens. Especially notable was the *Robert Gould Shaw Memorial* by Augustus Saint-Gaudens, a heroic bronze relief showing Shaw, erect in the saddle, leading the proud African American infantrymen of the Massachusetts 54th Regiment. The memorial is located off the Commons in Boston, Massachusetts. Another great sculptor of the period, Daniel Chester French, produced statues of the Revolutionary War's *Minute Man* for Concord, Massachusetts, and of Abraham Lincoln. French's huge statue of the seated Lincoln is the centerpiece of the Lincoln Memorial in Washington, D.C.

Established artists and critics were sure that neither women nor African Americans could produce memorable art. Giving the lie to such claims, a number of blacks and women made superb contributions to art in this period. Henry Ossawa Turner left the United States for Paris in order to practice his art. Before turning to biblical subjects, he painted scenes of African American life, such as *The Banjo Lesson* (1893). Painter Mary Cassatt also moved to France, where because of her sex she was not allowed to study at the Ecole des Beaux-Arts. She joined the Impressionists, who were seeking to record the effects of light on nature and modern life. Cassatt concentrated on pictures of women, especially of healthy mothers interacting with their golden-haired, pink-cheeked children.

At the same time as Aestheticism led to more appreciation of both Impressionism and abstract art, some early 20th-century artists were rejecting the emphasis on beauty. They wanted to make statements. In challenging conventional standards and ideals, some of their statements shocked the public. Followers of the Ashcan School were determined to present the social realities of urban working-class life. Living in New York after 1900, the movement's leader, Robert Henri, painted scenes of city life and portraits of the poor. Many painters soon gathered around him. When the National Academy of Design rejected their work

Marcel Duchamp's Nude Descending a Staircase *startled and outraged viewers at the 1913 Armory Show. The artist breaks the body's organic shape into jagged geometric fragments, using overlapping forms to represent movement.*

for an exhibition in 1908, Henri and his followers arranged their own gallery show and created a sensation. Some critics date the beginning of American modern art from this exhibition.

In February 1913, an even more stunning event took place in American art that changed its course. The International Exhibition of Modern Art opened at the 69th Regiment Armory on New York's Lexington Avenue. The exhibition, which lasted a month, signaled the widest public acceptance yet of more modern forms of art. It consisted of 1,250 paintings, sculptures, and decorative works by more than 300 European and American artists. Marcel Duchamp's painting, *Nude Descending a Staircase,* which depicted the nude not according to traditional ideals of female beauty but as a series of flat geometric shapes mechanistically connected to one another, scandalized some viewers, as did other works that emphasized themes of desire and sexuality. A reduced version of the Armory Show later traveled to Chicago and Boston, and a second Armory Show was mounted in New York in 1917.

SEE ALSO

Architecture; Cities; Decorative arts; hotography; West, the; World's fairs and exhibitions

FURTHER READING

Baigell, Matthew. *A Concise History of American Painting and Sculpture.* New York: Icon Editions, 1996.
Bjelajac, David. *American Art: A Cultural History.* New York: Abrams, 2001.
Brown, Milton. *The Story of the Armory Show.* New York: Abbeville Press, 1988.
Burns, Sarah. *Inventing the Modern Artist: Art and Culture in Gilded Age America.* New Haven, Conn.: Yale University Press, 1996.
Mumford, Lewis. *The Brown Decades; A Study of the Arts in America, 1865–1895.* 2nd ed., New York: Dover, 1955.
National Museum of American Art. *The Gilded Age: Treasures from the Smithsonian American Art Museum.* New York: Watson-Guptill Publications in association with the Smithsonian American Art Museum, 2000.
Van Hook, Bailey. *Angels of Art: Women and Art in American Society, 1876–1914.* University Park: Pennsylvania State University Press, 1996.

Ford, Henry

- *Born: July 30, 1863, Greenfield Township, Mich.*
- *Education: one-room schoolhouse through age 15*
- *Accomplishments: developed mass-production techniques for the automotive industry*
- *Died: Apr. 7, 1947, Dearborn, Mich.*

BORN ON A PROSPEROUS Michigan farm, Henry Ford found machines fascinating. In 1879 he left his family home to work as a machinist in Detroit. At his father's request, he returned briefly to farming but by 1891 had gone back to Detroit as an engineer for Thomas Edison's lighting company. In his spare time, he built an automobile. Weighing only 500 pounds, his 1896 gasoline-powered "quadricycle" was mounted on bicycle wheels and had no reverse gear. A few years later, Ford left the Edison Company to concentrate on manufacturing cars.

After gaining status in the industry by building racing cars, in 1903 Ford had won sufficient backing to found his own company. He and a team of talented engineers began to produce cars that he called Model A. In 1909 he settled on the Model T, or Tin Lizzie, as his most durable and economical design. Available only in black, it sold for $850. By 1913 Ford was producing 40,000 of these cars a year.

Ford wanted to democratize automobiles, that is, lower their costs so that ordinary people could buy them. To accomplish this goal, he had to make his production process more efficient. He applied two key ideas to this problem, product uniformity and the assembly line. Comparing automobiles to pins, one of which is like another, he said that all automobiles should look the same. He borrowed the assembly line idea from meatpacking plants, breaking the production process down into precise, uniform, and synchronized actions. He then assigned workers to each action, making them do the same task over and over. Fordism, as this segmented system was soon called, became a worldwide synonym for American business skill.

By 1914, the first year his assembly line was fully operational, Ford sold 248,000 cars at $490 each, almost half the cost of a "Ford" in 1910. The following year he dropped the price to $390. At the same time, he increased his workers' pay to $5 a day, an astounding salary for industrial workers in that era. Ford was a generous employer, but he also promoted a strong and somewhat coercive assimilation agenda for his immigrant workers. His goal in offering English classes, housing assistance, and other improvement programs was to create "new" Americans, who would abandon their Old World cultures.

Highly successful in business, Ford met with less personal success than he expected, given his enormous international reputation. In 1915, he launched a "peace ship" that carried delegates to Europe in an attempt to convince world leaders to end the current world war. In 1918 he ran for the U.S. Senate as a Democrat in the heavily Republican state of Michigan and lost, although fewer than 5,000 votes. In 1920, he allowed his newspaper, the *Dearborn Independent,* to blame the world's economic and moral problems on the Jews. After that, his public reputation sank. He suffered a stroke in 1938. After the death of his son Edsel in 1943, Ford left his company to his grandson, Henry Ford II. Four years later, Henry Ford died of a cerebral hemorrhage at his estate, Fair Lane.

SEE ALSO

Automobile; Edison, Thomas Alva; Inventions; Science and technology

FURTHER READING

Baldwin, Neil. *Henry Ford and the Jews: The Mass Production of Hate.* New York: Public Affairs, 2001.
Brinkley, Douglas. *Wheels for the World: Henry Ford, His Company, and a Century of Progress, 1903–2003.* New York: Viking, 2003.
Jardim, Anne. *The First Henry Ford: A Study in Personality and Business Leadership.* Cambridge, Mass.: MIT Press, 1970.
Lewis, David Lanier. *The Public Image of Henry Ford: An American Folk Hero and his Company.* Detroit: Wayne State University Press, 1976.
Rae, John B., ed. *Henry Ford.* Englewood Cliffs, N.J.: Prentice Hall, 1969.
Watts, Steven. *The People's Tycoon: Henry Ford and the American Century.* New York: Knopf, 2005.

Henry Ford demonstrates his first automobile, built in 1896. Called the quadricycle because it rolled on four bicycle tires, it was powered by a gasoline engine and weighed only 500 pounds.

Free silver

SEE Monetary policies

Fundamentalism

FUNDAMENTALISM IS the term
usually applied to any conservative
response to the challenge of modern
ideas. The term first surfaced in the
1920s to refer to the beliefs of Protestant
conservatives who opposed an approach
to the Scriptures that had emerged in
the late 19th century and that allowed
the Bible to be interpreted in its historical context rather than seen as a source
of literal truth. Many fundamentalists
also opposed the evolutionary theory of
scientist Charles Darwin, who held that
humans and apes share a common
ancestry. Still others opposed feminist
ideas that women should have the freedom to participate in the larger world
outside of the home. Religious conservatives included evangelical Protestants,
who believed that a personal conversion
experience was essential for salvation.
All of these conservatives held up the
Bible as an absolute authority on both
spiritual and secular (worldly) issues.

Between 1910 and 1912, leading
spokesmen for antimodernism published
a series of pamphlets called "The Fundamentals: A Testimony to the Truth."
These pamphlets reaffirmed a divine
creation, the imminent return of Jesus
Christ to earth, and women's traditional roles in church and home.
Throughout the West and South, some
fundamentalists worked to spread the
Gospel and encourage conversion.

In 1919 antimodernists formed the
World's Christian Fundamentals Association. This organization aimed to
keep the teaching of evolution out of
the schools and to purge Protestantism
of liberal theological ideas, such as the
belief that the Bible is not a source of
literal truth. In 1920, Curtis Lee Laws,
a journalist and a Baptist, applied the
term *fundamentalist* to those ready "to
do battle royal for the Fundamentals."
In 1925, in his last public act, politician and three-time Presidential candidate William Jennings Bryan defended
fundamentalism at the "monkey" trial
of John Scopes, a Tennessee teacher
accused of breaking the law by teaching evolution. After this trial, the fundamentalist movement declined in
force, but revived in the latter part of
the 20th century.

SEE ALSO

Bryan, William Jennings; Religion; Protestantism; Women's rights movement

FURTHER READING

Balmer, Randall Herbert. *Blessed Assur-
ance: A History of Evangelicalism in
America.* Boston: Beacon, 1999.
Marsden, George M. *Fundamentalism and
American Culture: The Shaping of Twen-
tieth Century Evangelicalism, 1870–1925.*
New York: Oxford University Press, 1980.

Galveston hurricane (1900)

ON SEPTEMBER 8, 1900, a hurricane
struck the coastal island city of Galveston, Texas, a major seaport with a
population of approximately 40,000.
The storm killed an estimated 8,000
people, more than the death toll from
any other natural disaster in American
history. Streets flooded and buildings
toppled as ocean waves in excess of 15
feet high crashed across a city that was
less than 10 feet above sea level at its

A team of stretcher bearers carries a dead body through the flooded streets of Galveston, Texas, in the aftermath of the 1900 hurricane that sent deadly ocean waves crashing across the low-lying coastal city.

highest point. Evacuation became impossible when a steamship broke from its moorings and destroyed the three bridges connecting the city to the mainland. Winds reached 100 miles per hour before destroying U.S. Weather Bureau instruments, thereby making it impossible to gauge the full force of the storm.

After the storm ended, survivors discovered that more than 2,500 homes had been destroyed and not a single building had escaped damage. Thousands of corpses lay decomposing in the Gulf Coast heat. To avoid a public health catastrophe, authorities incinerated bodies in mass funeral pyres.

In the aftermath of the hurricane, Galveston's citizens realized that their current government could not organize the rebuilding. A special five-member commission formed to run the city like a business, enacting ordinances, awarding building contracts, and making appropriations and appointments. The city's commission-style government inspired other progressive cities to develop similar approaches to local governance.

The federal government also intervened. The Army Corps of Engineers constructed a seawall 17 feet high to shield the city from future storms and raised the city further above sea level by jacking up buildings and filling in new land underneath. In 1915, the

rebuilt city weathered another massive hurricane with only eight fatalities.

FURTHER READING

Bixel, Patricia Bellis, and Elizabeth Hayes Turner. *Galveston and the 1900 Storm.* Austin: University of Texas Press, 2000.
Emanuel, Kerry. *Divine Wind: The History and Science of Hurricanes.* New York: Oxford University Press, 2005.
Green, Nathan C., ed. *Story of the 1900 Galveston Hurricane.* Gretna, La.: Pelican, 1999.
Larson, Erik. *Isaac's Storm: A Man, a Time, and the Deadliest Hurricane in History.* New York: Vintage, 2000.
Rogers, Lisa Waller. *The Great Storm: The Hurricane Diary of J. T. King, Galveston, Texas, 1900.* Lubbock: Texas Tech University Press, 2001.

Garfield, James A.

- *Born: Nov. 19, 1831, Orange, Ohio*
- *Education: Williams College, B.A., 1856*
- *Accomplishments: principal, Western Reserve Eclectic Institute (1856–61); Ohio Senate (1859–61); major general, Union army (1861–63); U.S. House of Representatives (Republican–Ohio, 1863–80); President of the United States (1881)*
- *Died: Sept. 19, 1881, Elberon, N.J.*

JAMES ABRAM GARFIELD, 20th President of the United States, served one of the shortest terms in American history. Shot by an assassin just four months after taking office, he died several weeks later. Garfield's Vice President, Chester A. Arthur, filled the remaining three and a half years of the Presidential term.

Having grown up in poverty, Garfield worked as a farmer, carpenter, canal boatman, janitor, and teacher and was able to put himself through Williams College in Massachusetts. He took a position teaching classics at Western Reserve Eclectic Institute (later, Hiram College), and became principal at the age of 26. He was also an attorney, an accomplished linguist who could write both Latin and Greek, and a lay preacher for his church, the Disciples of Christ. He served as a Republican member of the Ohio State Senate.

During the Civil War, Garfield fought in the Union army, reaching the rank of major general by 1862, the year he ran for Congress. When Garfield won, President Abraham Lincoln counseled him to resign from the army and take his seat in the House of Representatives. Reelected eight times, he became a leader among House Republicans. Along with President Ulysses Grant, Garfield was one of many public figures tarnished by the multimillion-dollar Crédit Mobilier scandal of the late 1860s, which involved corruption in construction contracts and stock sales related to the Union Pacific Railroad. Garfield also served as a member of the Republican majority on the controversial Electoral Commission that awarded the disputed Presidential election of 1876 to Rutherford B. Hayes.

Leading Republican contenders for the Presidency in 1880 included former President Grant, Speaker of the House James Blaine, and Treasury Secretary John Sherman. Garfield, a Sherman supporter, was a "dark horse"—a longshot—compromise candidate nominated on the 36th ballot after six days of convention deadlock.

The first Presidential candidate to campaign in two languages, Garfield gave speeches in both English and German. This strengthened his position among recent immigrants in the North and Midwest, who were honored that he communicated with them in their own language. He

narrowly defeated Democratic candidate Winfield Scott Hancock, another Civil War general.

As a Congressman, Garfield had followed Republican Party policy by opposing civil service reform, the effort to award government posts on the basis of merit instead of as patronage, that is, as a reward for political loyalty. He began his presidency, however, by refusing to nominate New York Senator Roscoe Conkling's choice for the position of collector of the port of New York, a post that controlled the distribution of some 1,500 jobs in the state. In the past, Conkling had used his control over the person who distributed the jobs to secure his own domination over the state party. Not surprisingly, then, he was furious that his candidate would not be appointed. Conkling became even more furious when Garfield nominated for the post one of his chief political enemies. In response, both Conkling and his younger colleague in the Senate, Thomas Platt, resigned. Since in the 1880s U.S. senators were still not directly elected by popular vote but were instead chosen by state legislatures, Conkling fully expected that the New York state legislature would immediately reappoint him and Platt. It did not, thereby sending a strong signal that President Garfield had won an important skirmish in the fight for civil service reform.

The demands of federal office seekers soon became more than merely a political issue for Garfield. On July 2, 1881, Charles Julius Guiteau, a lawyer, preacher, and petty criminal who had applied unsuccessfully for U.S. diplomatic positions in Vienna and Paris, stalked the President to a Washington train station and shot him twice with a pistol. One bullet inflicted a minor wound on Garfield's arm. The

James A. Garfield in his Civil War uniform. One of several veterans to run for the White House during the late 19th century, Garfield won election in 1880, but only a few months later became the second U.S. President to be assassinated.

other embedded itself near his spine and liver. Despite repeated probes with unwashed hands and unsterilized instruments—standard medical practice at the time—doctors were unable to recover the second bullet. Garfield lingered until mid-September, when he finally succumbed to infections and heart failure. Guiteau, who said that God had instructed him to carry out the assassination, was convicted and hanged in 1882.

After her husband's death, Lucretia Garfield inaugurated the tradition of Presidential libraries by establishing one at the Garfield home in Ohio.

SEE ALSO

Arthur, Chester A.; Compromise of 1877; Hayes, Rutherford B.; Presidency

FURTHER READING

Ackerman, Kenneth D. *The Dark Horse: The Surprise Election and Political Murder of President James A. Garfield.* New York: Carroll & Graf, 2003.
Doenecke, Justus D. *The Presidencies of James A. Garfield & Chester A. Arthur.* Lawrence: Regents Press of Kansas, 1981.
Peskin, Allan. *Garfield: A Biography.* Kent, Ohio: Kent State University Press, 1978.

Gentlemen's Agreement

THE GENTLEMEN'S Agreement refers to an informal, unofficial policy that governed relations between the United States and Japan regarding Japanese immigrants between 1908 and 1924. Although the United States restricted Chinese immigration in 1882 through an act of Congress, in 1894 it confirmed by treaty the right of Japanese laborers and their families to come into the country. Their increasing numbers on the West Coast, however,

aroused growing hostility among American workers and nativists. In 1906, the San Francisco school board voted to place the children of Japanese immigrants in segregated schools. This action deeply offended the Japanese government.

President Theodore Roosevelt, who had been involved in negotiating an end to the recent war between Japan and Russia, considered the Japanese a powerful and valuable ally in the Pacific. He persuaded the San Francisco school board to drop their policy of segregation. Then, in return for a U.S. promise to respect the rights of Japanese families already in the United States, the Japanese government promised to withhold passports from laborers, however skilled. A further provision of the agreement allowed the United States to exclude Japanese workers who attempted to evade the restriction by arriving in the United States from secondary destinations such as Mexico or Hawaii. The agreement allowed a reasonable number of "small farmer capitalists" to enter the United States as well as a few students, tourists, and family members of existing immigrants. These restrictions remained in place until the passage of the National Origins Immigration Act of 1924, which totally excluded Japanese and other Asians from immigration and naturalization.

Five Japanese railroad workers pose with tools of their trade. In response to hostility toward Japanese laborers, the U.S. and Japanese governments forged the Gentlemen's Agreement to prevent discrimination against Japanese already living on the West Coast in exchange for severely restricting new immigration.

SEE ALSO

Asian Americans; Chinese Exclusion Act (1882); Immigration; Imperialism; Nativism; Roosevelt, Theodore

FURTHER READING

Daniels, Roger. *Guarding the Golden Door: American Immigrants and Immigration Policy Since 1882.* New York: Hill & Wang, 2004.
Takaki, Ronald. *Strangers from a Different Shore: A History of Asian Americans.* Boston: Little, Brown, 1989.

George, Henry

- *Born: Sept. 2, 1839, Philadelphia, Pa.*
- *Education: Episcopal Academy, Philadelphia, Pa., private tutor*
- *Accomplishments: journalist, newspaper publisher, economic theorist; author,* Progress and Poverty *(1879)*
- *Died: Oct. 29, 1897, New York, N.Y.*

THE SON OF A BOOK publisher, Henry George worked as a store clerk and a typesetter, and then as a steward on a ship that took him from his home in Philadelphia to San Francisco, California. There, he became a printer and writer for various newspapers, but without meeting much success until the late 1860s. In 1868, he visited New York on newspaper business. The stark contrast he saw between the wealthy lifestyles of the city's elites and the grinding poverty of its masses prompted him to ask how such inequality could exist. The question became the basis of his emerging ideas about tax policies.

George summarized these ideas in *Progress and Poverty*, a book that brought him world fame. In it, he argued that the cause of economic inequality lay in treating land, along with its natural resources, as private property. When wealthy people buy up land and hold onto it until its price goes up, they not only make a profit on its eventual sale that they have not "earned" but also keep others from gaining benefit from the land. To break the stranglehold of monopoly, George proposed to end all taxes on improvements on land, such as housing and cultivation, and to fund government with a single tax on the rising value of land.

Land increases in value in several ways. Population growth makes land more valuable by increasing the demand for it in order to build housing. Road construction and other public improvements also raise the value of land. George proposed that people who own land, regardless of what they do with it, pay annual taxes on the land itself. Their taxes would increase as the land became more desirable and valuable. A single tax on land, George maintained, would help to eliminate poverty and social inequality by enabling all of society, not just a small wealthy elite, to benefit from rising land values.

Progress and Poverty sold millions of copies, inspiring "single tax," or "Georgist," movements in many countries. In an era without an income tax, when state and local governments financed themselves solely from property taxes, Henry George was an economic theorist who wanted to change property taxation to make it more fair or beneficial to more people. On the strength of this idea, George traveled the world as a lecturer and ran twice, unsuccessfully, for mayor of New York City. His tax proposals were influential in some other countries and in a few small communities. In 1894, between 40 and 50 converts to George's ideas established a single-tax colony in Fairhope, Alabama. Most policy makers, however, considered his ideas impractical.

SEE ALSO

Reform movements; Taxes and tariffs

FURTHER READING

Alyea, Paul E., and Blanche R. Alyea. *Fairhope, 1894–1954: The Story of a Single Tax Colony.* Tuscaloosa: University of Alabama Press, 1956.

George, Henry. *Progress and Poverty: An Inquiry into the Cause of Industrial Depressions and of Increase of Want with Increase of Wealth; the Remedy.* New York: Modern Library, 1938.

Rose, Edward J. *Henry George.* New York: Twayne, 1968.

Geronimo

- *Born: around 1823, Mexico*
- *Accomplishments: Apache military and spiritual leader*
- *Died: Feb. 17, 1909, Fort Sill, Okla.*

THE APACHE LEADER Geronimo was the last major Indian warrior in the American West to give up fighting against U.S. control of his ancestral homeland. During decades of raids and guerrilla warfare, he achieved legendary status among his own people and also in the American press.

Originally named Goyathlay—"one who yawns"—Geronimo was born on the upper Gila River in territory that was then part of Mexico and is now in Arizona or New Mexico. A member of the Bedonkohe Apache band, he was affiliated for most of his adult life with a larger group, the Chiricahua Apaches. He grew up to be both a fierce fighter and a medicine man, a spiritual leader who advised the chiefs and conducted healing ceremonies for the sick. Some of his fellow Apaches believed that he was invulnerable to bullets and credited him with other supernatural powers, such as the ability to see into the future and to walk without leaving footprints. His Mexican adversaries named him Geronimo (Spanish for *Jerome*). The U.S. media portrayed him as the most implacable of all the country's Indian foes, a ruthless killer of soldiers and civilians alike.

The 1858 slaughter of Geronimo's wife, mother, and children inflamed his hostility toward both Mexicans and white Americans in the Southwest. He took his revenge in a series of bloody raids. The details of his career during the 1860s are not clear, but it is probable that he also fought U.S. troops in military engagements under the leadership of such Apache chiefs as Mangas Coloradas, Cochise, and Victorio.

During the 1870s and 1880s, Geronimo and his followers clashed repeatedly with the U.S. Army as soldiers tried to confine the Apaches to reservations and make the rest of the Southwest safe for white American settlement. Geronimo led numerous escapes from the Chiricahua reservation and lived for various periods as a fugitive in the United States and Mexico. In 1886, he surrendered for the final time after a U.S. force of more than 5,000 tracked down and captured his small band, which consisted of some women and children and fewer than 20 warriors. His captors shipped Geronimo east, where he spent several years in military prisons. He never returned to his native Southwest, although the government moved him in 1894 to Oklahoma, where he lived as a prisoner of war for the rest of his life.

The terms of his confinement allowed him to appear at public events, however, which made him a celebrity in his old age. At the 1904 World's Fair in St. Louis, he sold autographs, photographs of himself, and other souvenirs. The following year, he

A fierce fighter against U.S. westward expansion and federal reservation policies, Apache warrior Geronimo surrendered to Army troops in 1886 and spent the rest of his life as a prisoner of war.

was a guest at President Theodore Roosevelt's inauguration. His autobiography, which he dictated to S. M. Barrett, an Oklahoma school superintendent, appeared in 1907, two years before his death.

SEE ALSO
Native Americans

FURTHER READING
Debo, Angie. *Geronimo: The Man, His Time, His Place.* Norman: University of Oklahoma Press, 1976.
Geronimo, *Geronimo: His Own Story.* Edited by S. M. Barrett. Introduction by Frederick W. Turner. 1907. Rev ed., New York: Plume, 1996.
Roberts, David. *Once They Moved Like The Wind: Cochise, Geronimo, and the Apache Wars.* New York: Simon & Schuster, 1993.

Gilded Age

HISTORIANS OFTEN use the term the *Gilded Age* to refer to the period from approximately 1877, which marked the end of the post–Civil War era known as Reconstruction, to approximately 1900. They adopted the name from *The Gilded Age* (1873), a novel by Mark Twain and Charles Dudley Warner. This novel satirized the politics of the era and the fantasies of get-rich-quick dreamers.

The first historians to use the term felt that the term fit the period 1877 to 1900 for several reasons. First, the term *gilded* implies a false glitter over a cheap base. By using this word instead of *golden*, historians called attention to the materialism of the age, corruption in business and politics, and the great disparity between the splendor in which the nation's wealthiest lived and the grinding poverty experienced by many Americans. They were suggesting that the prosperity

brought by industrial expansion did not touch most of the nation's working masses. Furthermore, although the Industrial Revolution had raised factory and farm productivity, business cycles of boom-and-bust, low wages, and rising farmer debt were causing deep discontent. To historians looking back, the government response to social problems seemed not only inadequate but compared unfavorably to the Progressive Era, when increasing numbers of individuals began to support a more active role for government in achieving public welfare.

Most historians today resist making too sharp a contrast between the Gilded Age and the Progressive Era. They recognize that many individuals during the Gilded Age sought ways to improve social and economic conditions and that some politicians took steps to address reform issues. Still, historians continue to use the term *Gilded Age* to indicate the period when reform was a smaller priority than it became after 1900.

FURTHER READING
French, Bryant Morey. *Mark Twain and the Gilded Age, the Book That Named an Era.* Dallas, Tex.: Southern Methodist University Press, 1965.
Greenwood, Janette. *The Gilded Age: A History in Documents.* New York: Oxford University Press, 2000.
Morgan, H. Wayne. *The Gilded Age: A Reappraisal.* Syracuse, N.Y.: Syracuse University Press, 1963.
Twain, Mark. *The Gilded Age.* 1873. Reprint. New York: Oxford University Press, 1996.

Gilman, Charlotte Perkins

- *Born: July 3, 1860, Hartford, Conn.*
- *Education: school to age 15, art studies at Rhode Island School of Design*
- *Accomplishments: author, "The Yellow Wallpaper" (1892), Women and*

Economics *(1898); The Home: Its Work and Influence (1900),* Herland *(1915), and many other books; editor,* The Forerunner *(1909–16)*
• Died: Aug. 17, 1935, Pasadena, Calif.

CHARLOTTE PERKINS GILMAN, a lecturer and writer on women's issues, grew up in poverty and without the benefit of much formal education. After studying art, in 1884 she married Charles Walter Stetson, a local artist, with whom she had a daughter. Suffering from depression, she consulted S. Weir Mitchell, a well-known physician who specialized in women's mental ailments and who prescribed a rest cure that forbade intellectual work of any kind. Following Mitchell's regimen, she became even more depressed and fled to California, where she eventually divorced her husband. Her experience with the rest cure inspired her most famous work of fiction, "The Yellow Wallpaper," a story in which a woman restricted to extreme rest becomes insane.

In the early 1890s, Charlotte Stetson recovered her strength and began to support herself by lecturing. She addressed progressive groups on subjects that included women, labor, and social organization. She also spent some time at the Hull House settlement in Chicago and campaigned for woman suffrage. In 1900, she married George Houghton Gilman, with whom she lived happily for more than 30 years.

Influenced by the ideas of sociologist Lester Frank Ward, Gilman began to imagine a world in which women could choose their own social roles and develop lives as autonomous human beings. In her most important theoretical work, *Women and Economics: A Study of the Economic Relation between Men and Women as a Factor in Social Relations,* she critiqued the economic dependence of women in marriage, which she called a "sexuo-economic" relationship. Her book, which was translated into seven languages and read all over the world, systematically demonstrated how women would contribute more to society if allowed to carve out their own life paths. To illustrate her vision of female autonomy, in 1915 she published a feminist novel, *Herland,* which tells the story of what happens when three men accidentally stumble upon a highly civilized, all-female world. Convinced that only men could have developed such a complex society, the travelers are soon shocked to find a land without traditional gender roles. Their situation gives Gilman the opportunity to develop her ideas about women's capacity for independent accomplishment.

After the death of her husband in 1934, Gilman moved to Pasadena, California, to be near her daughter and grandchildren. The following year, aware that she herself was dying of breast cancer, Gilman took her own life. Historians today regard Gilman as the foremost feminist intellectual of her time, and later feminists consider her a "founding mother" of their movement.

Author, feminist, and social theorist, Charlotte Perkins Gilman once said, "Woman should stand beside man as the comrade of his soul, not the servant of his body."

SEE ALSO
Literature; Sociology; Woman suffrage movement; Women's rights movement

FURTHER READING
Gilman, Charlotte Perkins. *Charlotte Perkins Gilman: A Nonfiction Reader.* Edited by Larry Ceplair. New York: Columbia University Press, 1991.
———. *The Charlotte Perkins Gilman Reader.* Edited and introduced by Ann J. Lane. Charlottesville: University Press of Virginia, 1999.
———. *The Living of Charlotte Perkins Gilman; An Autobiography.* 1935. Madison: University of Wisconsin Press, 1991.

Hill, Mary Armfield. *Charlotte Perkins Gilman: The Making of a Radical Feminist, 1860–1896.* Philadelphia: Temple University Press, 1980.

Lane, Ann J. *To "Herland" and Beyond: The Life and Work of Charlotte Perkins Gilman.* New York: Pantheon, 1990.

Girl Scouts

SEE Boy and Girl Scouts

Goldman, Emma

- *Born: June 27, 1869, Kovno, Russia*
- *Education: Some secondary education*
- *Accomplishments: founder and publisher,* Mother Earth *magazine (1906–17); author,* Anarchism and Other Essays *(1910),* The Social Significance of the Modern Drama *(1914),* My Disillusionment in Russia *(1925), and* Living My Life *(1931)*
- *Died: May 14, 1940, Toronto, Canada*

EMMA GOLDMAN was a radical writer, lecturer, and political activist whose anarchist and feminist thinking made her one of the most controversial public figures of her time.

Born in the Jewish ghetto in a part of czarist Russia that is now Lithuania, Goldman immigrated to the United States as a teenager. In 1887, while working in a clothing factory in Rochester, New York, she married, briefly and unhappily. She divorced her husband the following year and moved to New York City. In 1886, during a workers' protest held in Chicago's Haymarket Square, someone threw a bomb that killed policemen, and later several labor leaders were hanged for the crime, even though their connection to the bomb throwing had never been proved. The fate of the so-called Haymarket martyrs inspired Goldman to join the anti-government anarchist movement.

Anarchists regarded all governments as enemies of the working class. They believed that voluntary, cooperative associations were sufficient to maintain social order. Some anarchists favored the assassination of public officials and wealthy business leaders in order to bring attention to their cause. In 1892, Goldman helped fellow anarchist Alexander Berkman plan an attempt on the life of steel industry executive Henry Clay Frick. Berkman succeeded only in wounding Frick but then received a 22-year prison sentence.

Although Goldman avoided prison for the Frick attack, and later rejected her early embrace of political violence, she spent time behind bars for her political activities on more than 15 other occasions. In 1893–94 she spent 10 months in a New York prison for a speech in which she had urged the poor to steal bread if they could not afford to buy it. Since the authorities considered this speech as inciting the crowd to riot, the judge sentenced her to prison. In September 1901, police accused her of inspiring Leon Czolgosz to murder President William McKinley. Goldman quickly proved the charges were untrue, and she was released. In later years Goldman found herself in jail for violating obscenity laws by handing out birth control information, and for speaking against the government.

Goldman was a founder and editor of the anarchist magazine *Mother Earth*, and traveled the country lecturing in Yiddish, German, and English on such political and social topics as socialism, free speech, woman suffrage, religion, and political violence. Her lectures attracted large and enthusiastic audiences, as well as occasional hostility. Believing that a woman's personal, economic, and political liberation was an important cause, she

Emma Goldman's book Anarchism and Other Essays *expressed her belief that all governments were the enemies of working people, while anarchism stood for the absence of central government and a social order based on the "free grouping of individuals."*

called for an even broader emancipation than advocated by her contemporaries in the woman suffrage movement. In a lecture she published in 1906, "The Tragedy of Woman's Emancipation," she called for an emancipation that would allow everything in a woman "that craves assertion and activity" to "reach its fullest expression." She demanded that "all artificial barriers" against woman's achieving her highest goals be broken, and "the road towards greater freedom cleared of every trace of centuries of submission and slavery." Her advocacy of sexual freedom and birth control and her repudiation of the institution of marriage angered conservatives and some of her fellow radicals alike.

Goldman spent two years in prison for opposing the draft during World War I. In 1919, during the "Red Scare," a period of public hysteria about the actions of radicals, federal officials began deportation proceedings against Goldman and other radical activists for advocating anarchism. They managed to strip her of her U.S. citizenship and deport her to Russia, then in the throes of a civil war following the communist revolution. Initially sympathetic to the revolution, Goldman soon became disillusioned by the lack of freedom in the new Union of Soviet Socialist Republics. She lived the rest of her life in Europe and Canada, returning once to the United States for a 1935 lecture tour. When Goldman died in 1940, the United States honored her final wish, allowing her to be buried near the Haymarket martyrs in a suburban Chicago cemetery.

Because of her insistence that women's sexual and reproductive freedom should be an important part of the radical reform agenda, Goldman became after her death an icon for radical members of the late 20th-century feminist movement.

SEE ALSO

Anarchism; Birth control movement; Haymarket Square riot (1886); Red Scare (1919–20)

FURTHER READING

Falk, Candace. *Love, Anarchy, and Emma Goldman.* New York: Holt, Rinehart & Winston, 1984.
Goldman, Emma. *Anarchism and Other Essays.* 1917. Reprint, New York: Dover, 1969.
———. *Living My Life.* 1931. Reprint, New York: Dover, 1970.
———. *Red Emma Speaks: An Emma Goldman Reader.* Compiled and edited by Alix Kates Shulman. 3rd ed. Amherst, N.Y. : Humanity Books, 1998.
Waldstreicher, David. *Emma Goldman.* New York: Chelsea House, 1989.
Wexler, Alice. *Emma Goldman: An Intimate Life.* New York: Pantheon, 1984.
———. *Emma Goldman in Exile: From the Russian Revolution to the Spanish Civil War.* Boston: Beacon, 1989.

Gompers, Samuel

- *Born: Jan. 26, 1850, London, England*
- *Accomplishments: president, American Federation of Labor (1886–1924); vice president, Cigar Makers International Union (1886–1924)*
- *Died: Dec. 13, 1924, El Paso, Tex.*

SAMUEL GOMPERS came to the United States from England as a teenager, settling with his parents and brothers in New York City. He had little formal education but, like his father, a Jewish artisan originally from the Netherlands, he was a skilled cigar maker. For most of his life he earned

Samuel Gompers, president of the American Federation of Labor, prepares to cast his vote at a New York polling place. Gompers was a professional cigar roller who championed the rights of skilled workers.

his living rolling cigars; at 14 he joined the Cigar Makers International Union.

The London-born Gompers had a command of English not shared by many European immigrants in this period. With his fluency and intelligence, he became a spokesman for the cause of working men, rising quickly into leadership roles in the union movement. He proved himself an able administrator and, in 1886, helped to found and became president of the American Federation of Labor (AFL).

Gompers called his approach to labor organizing a "pure and simple" trade unionism. "Our mission," he explained, "has been the protection of the wage-worker...; to increase his wages; to cut hours off the long work-day, which was killing him; to improve the safety and the sanitary conditions of the workshop; to free him from the tyrannies, petty or otherwise, which served to make his existence a slavery." To Gompers, strong, well-financed trade unions were the key to the humane conduct of industry and the foundation of a society in which all classes could lead satisfying lives. He also believed that an educated working class, whose members enjoyed a comfortable standard of living, was the basis for a fair and democratic society.

Outside of the labor movement, conservative Americans viewed Gompers as a dangerous foreign-born radical and an enemy of private property. Gompers also had opponents inside the labor movement. Some of these

thought the AFL should not have limited its membership to skilled workers, thereby leaving the great mass of workers without union organization or protection. They rightly accused Gompers of elitism, saying he cared only for the skilled male workers who occupied the top levels of the working class. More radical labor organizers promoted the Industrial Workers of the World (IWW), an organization that differed from the AFL in that it promised membership to all workers in all industries, regardless of race, gender, or level of skill.

Nevertheless, many American political and social leaders respected Gompers's courage and integrity. Throughout his long career, he gave a voice and dignity to struggling members of America's working class.

SEE ALSO

American Federation of Labor; Industrial Workers of the World; Labor; Labor union movement

FURTHER READING

Gompers, Samuel. *Seventy Years of Life and Labor.* 1925. Edited by Nick Salvatore. Reprint, Ithaca, N.Y.: ILR Press, 1984.
Kaufman, Stuart Bruce. *Samuel Gompers and the Origins of the American Federation of Labor, 1848–1896.* Westport, Conn.: Greenwood, 1973.
Livesay, Harold C. *Samuel Gompers and Organized Labor in America.* 1978. Reprint, Prospect Heights, Ill.: Waveland Press, 1993.

Government reform

MANY PROGRESSIVES pursued government reform because they hoped it would curb the power of political party bosses. Presiding over political party "machines," unofficial organizations designed to keep political parties in

This cartoon from the mid-1880s uses Greek mythology to criticize the civil service program. Cerberus, the three-headed dog who guarded the gates to the underworld, represents the three members of the first Civil Service Commission, who now guard access to public service jobs. The powerful hero, Hercules, represents the old spoils system, in which politicians rewarded political supporters with government jobs.

power, these bosses were primarily interested in winning the next election. To achieve that end, they rewarded loyal voters with government jobs, many of which offered good salaries and pensions as well as access to payoffs and other kinds of graft. Progressives objected to this spoils system, so called from the saying of an early 19th-century New York politician, Senator William Learned Marcy, "To the victor belong the spoils." They believed that the spoils system entrusted government to individuals who had no interest in making government either efficient or responsible. Critics of government reformers referred to them derisively as "goo-goos," a term that stood for "good government" men. Convinced they could make government honest, government reformers remained undeterred.

Government reformers aimed first at setting up a merit-based civil service to regularize the hiring of government employees who were neither elected officials nor members of the military. Administered by an impartial civil service commission, the system would require a prospective employee to take a competitive examination before being hired for a government job, such as building inspector or tax collector. In 1883, Congress passed the Pendleton Civil Service Reform Act, which estab-

lished a bipartisan Civil Service Commission to oversee a merit system for federal offices with more than 50 employees. The system expanded during the following decades, so that by the 1920s, 80 percent of federal employment (560,000 employees in 1922) operated under a merit system. Moreover, most states and cities also set up civil service commissions. The movement for civil service reform transformed government bureaucracies across the country.

Government reformers also pursued electoral reforms. For some reformers, the goal was more "direct democracy," that is, more opportunities for ordinary citizens to play a direct role in electing their representatives and influencing political decisions. For others, the goal was a smaller, better informed electorate. Convinced that political machines manipulated poorly educated minority and foreign-born voters, these reformers wanted to restrict the electorate to only "qualified" voters. Thus electoral reform had as much potential for limiting democracy as for expanding it.

The movement for voters to elect all U.S. senators directly, instead of state legislatures choosing their senators, held a central place in electoral reform. Some states had adopted this change as early as 1828, but the U.S. Senate did not act until 1911 when it approved the 17th Amendment to the Constitution, calling for direct election of senators in all states. At the same time, other reformers pursued direct primary elections. Pioneered in Wisconsin by Governor Robert M. La Follette, the direct primary allowed voters, rather than party officials, to choose nominees for office. By 1916, all but three states had a direct primary.

Other electoral reforms included the introduction of the Australian bal-

lot, developed in Australia in the 1850s and adopted in Great Britain and Canada. This government-printed ballot replaced the old system, in which political parties printed their own ballots. In addition, voters marked Australian ballots secretly in a private voting booth. The Australian ballot eliminated illiterate voters, however, for it listed candidates by name instead of party symbol. Ninety percent of the states adopted the Australian ballot by 1896.

Progressives in states and municipalities also pursued four other electoral reforms: initiative, referendum, recall, and proportional representation. An initiative permits a percentage of voters to propose a law and send it directly to the people for ratification. A referendum allows voters to accept or reject laws approved by the legislature. A recall allows a percentage of registered voters to demand a special election to remove an official. And proportional representation awards legislative seats to political parties in proportion to the size of the vote they received. South Dakota's 1898 constitution was the first to authorize initiative; 20 other states followed. After Los Angeles adopted recall in 1903, almost a dozen states and more than a thousand municipalities followed. Starting in 1915, 22 cities adopted proportional representation, but most later repealed it. Although popular in European countries, proportional representation never took root in the United States, primarily because it occasionally resulted in the election of radicals and members of racial or ethnic minorities with whom mainstream politicians felt they could not work.

The impact of electoral reforms varied according to locale. A sweeping reform passed in 1911 in New Jersey, designed to reduce corruption and the influence of political machines, limited voter registration times and removed party identifications from ballots. The reform ended up reducing voter participation, especially in city wards where many foreign-born lived. In Jersey City, for example, turnout dropped from 69 percent in 1906 to 42 percent in 1913.

Government reformers explained reduced turnouts by claiming that they had rooted out fraudulent registrations. Although this was probably true, it is also true that their reforms disfranchised some voters. The reforms also reduced the power of parties along with the voter enthusiasm that accompanied party loyalty. Voter participation declined from 79 percent in 1896 to 49 percent in 1920. Eventually, voters were drawn to participate more in organized interest groups than in political parties.

SEE ALSO

La Follette, Robert Marion, Sr.; Machine politics; Progressive movement; Reform movements; 17th Amendment; Suffrage; Voting

FURTHER READING

Hoogenboom, Ari. *Outlawing the Spoils: A History of the Civil Service Reform Movement, 1865–1883.* Urbana: University of Illinois Press, 1961.
McCormick, Richard L. *The Party Period and Public Policy: American Politics from the Age of Jackson to the Progressive Era.* New York: Oxford University Press, 1986.
McGerr, Michael E. *The Decline of Popular Politics: The American North 1865–1928.* New York: Oxford University Press, 1986.

Grange

SEE Populism

Greenback Labor party

SEE Monetary policies; Politics

Greenwich Village

BEGINNING IN THE 1890s, Greenwich Village, an area on the lower West Side of Manhattan in New York City, developed into a colorful residential area and meeting place for Bohemians. This term originally referred to people from Bohemia, a region in central Europe where Gypsies supposedly came from. By the mid-19th century, people used the name *Bohemian* to imply a "vagabond," someone whose life was unsettled and on the outer edges of society.

New York's Bohemians consisted of a mixed group of artists and writers who liked the cheap housing they found on the lower West Side and the intellectual and artistic vitality of their fellow residents. Ivy League college students gravitated toward Greenwich Village to experience the unconventional lifestyles of the artists they met there. The era's "new women," mostly college-educated women eager to lead independent lives, went to the Village to escape traditional relationships. Finally, the Village attracted some of the city's immigrant intellectuals, looking to escape their ethnic ghettos.

Night life in the Village was very lively. Both sexes patronized cafés and restaurants, drinking and dancing to ragtime tunes and talking about contemporary topics, from politics to labor issues, woman suffrage, birth control, and alternative marital arrangements. Writer Max Eastman published the radical political and literary journal *The Masses* in the Village, and political journalist John Reed made his base there. Reed became famous for his dispatches on the Mexican Revolution and his later book about the Russian Revolution, *Ten*

Days That Shook the World (1919). In 1912 Village feminists founded Heterodoxy, a monthly discussion club for women only. Birth control campaigner Margaret Sanger, anarchist lecturer Emma Goldman, innovative dancer Isadora Duncan, and Catholic worker leader Dorothy Day all found the Village's social atmosphere congenial to their way of life. Among other well-known artists and writers who lived in Greenwich Village were painter Diego Rivera, playwright Eugene O'Neill, and poet Edna St. Vincent Millay.

Other American cities, such as Boston, Chicago, San Francisco, and New Orleans, also developed Bohemian quarters, but none as notoriously as New York. In her 1917 guidebook to Greenwich Village, Anna Alice Chapin wrote, "The village is not only a locality…it is a point of view. It reaches out imperiously and fastens on what it will." When people spoke of the "Village," they meant only one thing: Greenwich Village, where rebellion against convention was a way of life.

FURTHER READING

Barnet, Andrea. *All-night Party: The Women of Bohemian Greenwich Village and Harlem, 1913–1930*. Chapel Hill, N.C.: Algonquin, 2004.

Harris, Luther S. *Around Washington Square: An Illustrated History of Greenwich Village*. Baltimore: Johns Hopkins University Press, 2003.

McFarland, Gerald W. *Inside Greenwich Village: A New York City Neighborhood,*

A dance at the Purple Pup, a club in Greenwich Village, in the 1910s. Some contemporaries would have found the women's mid-calf skirt lengths and the cheek-to-cheek dancing rather scandalous.

1898–1918. Amherst: University of
Massachusetts Press, 2001.
Stansell, Christine. *American Moderns:
Bohemian New York and the Creation of
a New Century.* New York: Henry Holt,
2000.

Harrison, Benjamin

- *Born: Aug. 20, 1833, North Bend,
  Ohio*
- *Education: Miami University (Oxford,
  Ohio), B.A., 1852; legal apprenticeship*
- *Accomplishments: brigadier general,
  Union army 1865; U.S. Senate
  (Republican–Ind., 1881–87); President
  of the United States (1889–93)*
- *Died: Mar. 13, 1901, Indianapolis, Ind.*

BENJAMIN HARRISON, 23rd President of the United States and the last
Civil War general to serve in the office,
came from a long political dynasty. His
father was an Ohio congressman; his
grandfather, William Henry Harrison,
was the ninth President; and his great-
grandfather had signed the Declaration
of Independence. As President, Harrison's ambitious foreign policies laid the
groundwork for the expansionism of
two of his successors, William McKinley
and Theodore Roosevelt. Thus Harrison
linked the smaller, more inward-looking
United States of the mid-19th century
with the new imperial power that
emerged on the world scene in the 20th.

A lawyer in Indianapolis, Harrison
launched his political career when he
joined the new antislavery Republican
party in the 1850s. He held minor
local and state offices before the Civil
War, left Indiana to fight for the
Union, and came home a brigadier
general. In 1876, he lost a campaign
for governor, but in 1880, Indiana
elected him to the U.S. Senate. In
1888, his Senate experience, combined
with his military record, made him an
especially attractive Presidential nominee. His prospective
opponent, President
Grover Cleveland,
was a Democrat
who had avoided
military service and
angered veterans by
vetoing Civil War
pension bills.

Instead of trav-
eling, Harrison con-
ducted a "front
porch campaign." He stayed in Ohio
and delivered speeches to crowds that
gathered at his home. Both Harrison
and Cleveland were honest men, but
supporters in both parties practiced
bribery and other underhand tactics.
One supporter quipped that Harrison
would never know how many men had
risked felony convictions to put him in
the White House. In the end, Cleveland tallied more popular votes, but
Harrison won in the Electoral College.

Working with Republican majorities in Congress, Harrison signed laws
to raise tariffs, increase government
spending on veterans' benefits, and
add more silver currency to the
nation's money supply. Higher tariffs
on imports such as sugar, woolen
clothing, and tin-plated goods, shield-
ed some American businesses from
foreign competition and gave the federal government more money to spend
on popular programs, but they also
drove up prices. Harrison's silver policy attempted to steer a middle course
between "free silver" advocates, who
wanted to swell the money supply
with unlimited silver coinage, and supporters of the gold standard, who
opposed all silver currency.

Harrison signed the Sherman
Antitrust Act of 1890, which for the
first time gave the federal government
power to combat large corporations
that abused their enormous economic

*A handkerchief
advertises Ben-
jamin Harri-
son's 1888
campaign for
President. Both
Harrison and
his Democratic
opponent,
Grover Cleve-
land, were
backed by dis-
honest party
operatives who
made the cam-
paign the most
corrupt in U.S.
history up to
that time.*

power. During his Presidency, six western states joined the Union and the era of the Indian wars came to an end with the 1890 massacre of Sioux Indians at Wounded Knee, South Dakota. In 1892, Ellis Island in New York became the nation's chief port of entry for new arrivals from Europe. Harrison pushed unsuccessfully for voting rights legislation to protect former slaves and their freeborn descendants, and he appointed Frederick Douglass, a former slave and one of the country's most respected black leaders, as ambassador to Haiti. He proposed making Hawaii a U.S. territory and lived to see the United States annex those Pacific islands during the McKinley administration. The canal he envisioned across Nicaragua never materialized, but his vision was a step toward the Panama Canal.

In 1892 Harrison lost his reelection bid to Grover Cleveland by substantial popular and electoral vote margins. A surprisingly strong third-party candidate, former congressman James Weaver, captured more than a million popular votes for the People's party (also known as the Populists), and won the electoral votes of four states. Widowed and out of office, Harrison retired to Indianapolis, becoming a respected elder statesman. He married again and fathered a daughter less than four years before his death in 1901.

SEE ALSO

Antitrust laws; Cleveland, Grover; Ellis Island; Imperialism, McKinley, William; Monetary policies; Populist party; Presidency, Roosevelt, Theodore; Taxes and tariffs; Wounded Knee massacre (1890)

FURTHER READING

Calhoun, Charles W. *Benjamin Harrison.* New York: Times Books, 2005.
Socolofsky, Homer E., and Allan B. Spetter. *The Presidency of Benjamin Harrison.* Lawrence: University Press of Kansas, 1987.

Hayes, Rutherford B.

- *Born: Oct. 4, 1822, Delaware, Ohio*
- *Education: Kenyon College, B.A., 1842; Harvard Law School, LL.B., 1845*
- *Accomplishments: major general, Union army 1865; U.S. House of Representatives (Republican–Ohio, 1865–68); governor of Ohio (1868–70, 1870–72, 1876–77); President of the United States (1877–81)*
- *Died: Jan. 17, 1893, Fremont, Ohio*

REPUBLICAN RUTHERFORD B. Hayes became the 19th President of the United States after the disputed election of 1876, in which his opponent, New York governor Samuel Tilden, won the popular vote. But the Republican majority on a special commission created to decide the election chose Hayes. Despite Hayes's personal reputation for honesty, his questionable victory cast a shadow over his single term in office.

Hayes began his career as a lawyer practicing in Cincinnati in the 1850s, sometimes defending runaway slaves. He became a strong supporter of Abraham Lincoln and the new Republican party. At the outbreak of the Civil War, he volunteered for the Union army. Wounded in battle on four occasions, he rose to the rank of major general. When Ohio Republicans nominated him for a seat in Congress in 1864, Hayes won the election even though he remained on active duty, refusing to go home to campaign. Twice elected to Congress from Ohio, and three times elected governor of that state, Hayes secured Ohio's ratification of the 15th Amendment, granting black men the right to vote. In 1876, he won the Republican party's nomination for President. He was not a brilliant candidate, but, as writer Henry Adams put it, "He was obnoxious to no one."

Chief Justice Morrison R. Waite administers the oath of office at the 1877 inauguration of President Rutherford B. Hayes. After a controversial election in which he lost the popular vote and was accused of winning his Electoral College victory by fraudulent means, Hayes took office and served his single term with dignity and dedication.

By 1876, the public had become outraged over corruption in the administration of Republican President Ulysses Grant. Moreover, in the former Confederate states, now restored to full participation in national politics, many white southerners remained hostile to Grant's party. Samuel Tilden, the Democratic Presidential nominee that year and a crusader against political and business corruption, was expected to win.

It appeared at first that Tilden had indeed triumphed. He won the popular vote by more than 250,000 out of approximately 8.4 million ballots cast. But in the electoral votes of Florida, Louisiana, and South Carolina—southern states still occupied by federal troops—Democrats and Republicans both claimed victory. In Oregon, the two parties clashed over one of the state's three electoral votes.

To decide the winner, Congress established a 15-member Electoral Commission consisting of five senators, five congressmen, and five Supreme Court justices. Eight commissioners were Republicans, and seven were Democrats. On a series of 8-to-7 votes, the Republican majority awarded all disputed electoral votes to Hayes, giving him a one-vote edge, 185 to 184, in the electoral college. The Senate, with a Republican majority, was willing to accept this, but the Democratic majority in the House of Representatives balked. To win their agreement, Hayes promised to pull out the last federal troops still occupying southern states, to support federal aid to southern railroad and economic development, and to leave the South to sort out race relations on their own. This Compromise of 1877 marked the end of Reconstruction, leaving many black citizens without federal protection for their hard-won civil rights.

Widely ridiculed as "Rutherfraud" because of his irregular election victory, Hayes faced strong opposition from Democrats throughout his four-year Presidency. Even his own party gave him only halfhearted backing. He alienated the powerful Republican senator Roscoe Conkling of New York, whose associate, future President Chester A. Arthur, was serving as federal collector for the port of New York. From this position, Arthur oversaw hundreds of government jobs that Conkling could use to reward political supporters. Hayes struck a blow for civil service reform by removing Arthur from his post. This action caused a rift within the Republican party.

Hayes supported the Republican position in favor of the gold standard and against the "free silver" movement, which sought to base the value of paper money in part on silver. Over Hayes's veto, however, Congress passed the Bland-Allison Act, which required the federal government to buy silver bullion and issue silver coins. Hayes's appointments to the Supreme Court included John Harlan, who would become the dissenter in *Plessy v. Ferguson* (1896), the case that legalized "separate but equal" treatment of African Americans. On the contentious issue of Chinese exclusion, Hayes vetoed an anti-immigration law that violated treaty agreements with China.

During the national railroad strike of 1877, he called out federal troops to break up picket lines against striking railway workers, thereby becoming the first President to use federal troops in this manner.

As temperance supporters, Hayes and his wife, Lucy, banned alcohol and tobacco from the White House. The First Lady became known by the derisive nickname Lemonade Lucy.

SEE ALSO

Arthur, Chester A.; Chinese Exclusion Act (1882); Compromise of 1877; Government reform; Immigration; Monetary policies; *Plessy* v. *Ferguson*; Presidency; Race relations; Railroad strike (1877); Strikes

FURTHER READING

Hoogenboom, Ari. *Rutherford B. Hayes: Warrior and President.* Lawrence: University Press of Kansas, 1995.
Trefousse, Hans L. *Rutherford B. Hayes.* New York: Times Books, 2002.
Woodward, C. Vann. *Reunion and Reaction: The Compromise of 1877 and the End of Reconstruction.* 1951. Reprint, New York: Oxford University Press, 1991.

Haymarket Square riot (1886)

ON MAY 4, 1886, a group of German-American labor activists, members of an anarchist group known as the International Working People's Association, organized a huge protest meeting in Haymarket Square in the heart of Chicago. They were part of a nation-wide movement to gain the eight-hour workday for laborers and were protesting a recent police attack on striking demonstrators. While some 3,000 people gathered to listen to speeches, 180 Chicago police marched in to break up the meeting. Someone detonated a bomb, killing a policeman. In the shooting that followed, 7 more policemen died, as did a number of people in the crowd. More than 200 people were wounded. The bomb thrower was never found.

Authorities blamed eight protest organizers for the bomb, rounded them up, and brought them to trial. Prosecutors found no evidence that the eight men had engaged in the violence, but the jury heard plenty of evidence that each man had, at one time or another, publicly advocated violence against the government. The defense argued that his clients had a right to freedom of speech, but the chief prosecutor, voicing the powerful fears of many middle-class Americans, said to the jury, "Convict these men, make examples of them, hang them, and you save our institutions, our society!"

Condemned to death, three of the accused were ultimately pardoned, but five died. Albert Parsons, August Spies, Adolph Fischer, and George Engel were hanged; Louis Lingg committed suicide in his cell. On the scaffold, Spies defiantly declared: "There will be a time when our silence will be more powerful than the voices you strangle today!"

In the aftermath of the Haymarket riot, the labor movement experienced a setback. Many Americans thought that organized labor would bring in social revolution. They fastened blame

Samuel Fielden of the International Working People's Association shouts to be heard over the pandemonium at a Chicago labor protest as police and demonstrators exchange gunfire during the 1886 Haymarket Square riot.

on the eight-hour movement and on the Knights of Labor, the massive national union that had supported the anarchist defendants. The Knights' policies had never included violence, but they never recovered from their association with Haymarket. They lost most of their membership over the next decade.

Among the working classes, the Haymarket protestors became the Haymarket martyrs, symbols of the many individuals who made sacrifices in order to win fair treatment for America's working people. During the years that followed, the eight-hour day and many other labor demands became an accepted part of American working life.

SEE ALSO

Anarchism; Knights of Labor; Labor unions

FURTHER READING

Avrich, Paul. *The Haymarket Tragedy.* Princeton, N.J.: Princeton University Press, 1984.
Green, James. *Death in the Haymarket: A Story of Chicago, the First Labor Movement, and the Bombing That Divided Gilded Age America.* New York: Pantheon, 2006.
Smith, Carl. *Urban Disorder and the Shape of Belief: The Great Chicago Fire, the Haymarket Bomb, and the Model Town of Pullman.* Chicago: University of Chicago Press, 1995.

Health, public

PROFESSIONALIZATION AND expertise—two major emphases of Progressive Era thinking—helped improve American public health during the latter 1800s and early 1900s. Municipal, county, state, and federal governments had long recognized the need to take responsibility for public health. Rising populations, increasingly concentrated in congested towns and cities, required government agencies to take more concerted action to control the spread of disease. By the end of the century, the federal government had taken over the supervision of health issues that smaller agencies could no longer handle.

Setting up the U.S. Public Health Service is one example of such federal action. The service grew out of the Marine Hospital Service, originally founded in the late 18th century to care for sick and injured merchant seamen. In 1870, John Maynard Woodworth became the first supervising surgeon (later, surgeon general) of the Marine Service. In 1889, Woodworth's staff of uniformed physicians began to take responsibility for the control of contagious diseases, and by 1891 they were in charge of inspecting immigrants arriving at American ports for signs of disease. The service took the name U.S. Public Health Service in 1912.

The passage of the Pure Food and Drugs Act in 1906 is another example of federal action. In order to preserve food or make spoiled food look appetizing, commercial processors often adulterated foods with poisonous substances, such as boric acid and even formaldehyde. Drug manufacturers put harmful or addictive ingredients, such as alcohol and opium, into concoctions sold over-the-counter as "cures" for many ailments. Long advocated by consumers as well as by Dr. Harvey W. Wiley, chief chemist of the Department of Agriculture, the 1906 act set up inspections to ensure that the food and drugs Americans consumed would not harm them.

Medical discoveries about contagious illnesses also improved public health in this era. Most people had thought that tuberculosis, or the "white plague," an infectious disease primarily of the lungs, was hereditary.

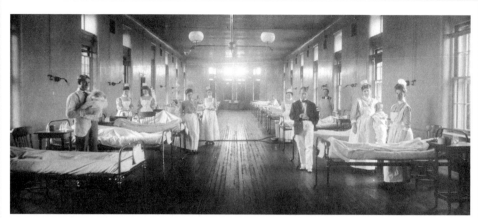

Nurses and doctors attend patients in the children's ward of a Colorado hospital in 1907. Because of public health improvements during the Progressive Era, nurses received better training and child mortality declined.

Dr. Robert Koch, a German researcher, discovered the bacterium that causes the disease in 1882, but campaigns to educate the public about proper treatment and prevention did not begin in earnest until the early 1900s. The National Association for the Study and Prevention of Tuberculosis, established in 1904, lobbied for local ordinances against public spitting, the most common way the germs were spread. In 15 years, the death rate from tuberculosis, a major killer in the tenements, dropped by 30 percent.

Public health officials also made concerted efforts to control typhoid fever. Spread by fecal contamination of food or water, the disease is characterized by a high, constant fever, stomach and intestinal distress, and headache, and kills 10 percent of its victims. During the Spanish-American War, it killed more soldiers than died on the battlefields. Incidences of the disease began to decline when cities built water filtration systems. Almost all American cities had such systems by 1920. Still, individuals could spread the disease, even those harboring the bacteria in their digestive tracts but otherwise showing no symptoms. Such was the case of Mary Mallon, a cook for a family in New York City. Public health authorities became convinced that she had infected the family, and others through cooking jobs she held

later, and they forced Mallon to spend the rest of her life in an isolated hospital cottage on an island in the East River. The press called her Typhoid Mary, a term she rejected, as she never felt ill herself.

Public health scientists also turned their attention to insect-borne diseases in this period. In 1900, Dr. Walter Reed, of the U.S. Army Yellow Fever Commission, confirmed that a certain type of mosquito, *Aedes aegypti*, spread the tropical disease. Though not always fatal, the disease caused high fevers, jaundice, or a yellowing of the whites of the eyes, and sometimes kidney and liver failure. Eliminating the places where mosquitoes bred, such as stagnant water and swamps, helped protect workers constructing the Panama Canal.

The rising number of diseases caused by exposure to chemicals and other harmful substances involved in the industrial process led to a new field, industrial or occupational medicine. Its founder was Dr. Alice Hamilton, named in 1910 by the Illinois Commission on Occupational Diseases to lead a nine-month survey of industrial diseases. Hamilton found high incidences of steel workers gassed by carbon monoxide and painters disabled by a palsy from lead poisoning. Two years later she became a special investigator of industrial diseases for the U.S. Bureau of Labor Statistics. Her studies of 23 factories that manufactured lead uncovered 358 cases of lead poisoning over a 15-month period. Sixteen of the cases had been fatal. Hamilton later studied lead poisoning in potteries, tile works, and the trade of painters and printers, and discovered the presence of other poisons in the making of rubber, explosives, dyes, and airplanes. Although manufacturers often accused Hamilton of exaggerating her findings, she always backed up her work with careful records of her on-site observations and her interviews with both workers and their physicians. As a result of Hamilton's work, a number of states and later the federal government passed laws requiring manufacturers to maintain better controls over the use of toxic chemicals. Other new laws made it possible for workers to receive compensation if they suffered from industrial diseases. Hamilton later published textbooks in industrial toxicology and became the first woman professor at Harvard University Medical School.

In the early years of the 20th century, infant mortality began to decline. The U.S. Children's Bureau, founded in 1912, conducted systematic surveys of child and maternal death rates. These surveys found a direct correlation between infant death and poverty. The bureau published highly popular reports and pamphlets on prenatal and child care, and its officials corresponded with mothers who needed advice and help. It also lobbied for the Sheppard-Towner Maternity and Infancy Act of 1921, the first federal legislation to concern itself with maternal and child health. Although criticized by conservatives as a government intrusion in private affairs, the act, which gave the states money to set up programs for maternal health education and infant nutrition, survived until 1929 and set a precedent for similar legislative programs in later decades.

Another positive step of the era was the elevation of nursing to professional status. Before the Progressive Era, nursing had been taught in hospitals and consisted largely of supervised work experience. Cincinnati-born Lillian Wald—who had founded a visiting nurse service and a settlement house deep in the heart of New York City's poorest Lower East Side district—persuaded Columbia University to appoint the first professor of nursing at a U.S. college or university. Nursing education today takes place in universities, augmented by practical experience in a teaching hospital.

By the turn of the 20th century, most medical practitioners accepted the germ theory of disease. They not only instituted better antiseptic procedures themselves but worked to convince the public of the benefits of personal cleanliness and better municipal sanitation such as sewer systems, garbage disposal, and water filtration plants. As a result, death rates from cholera, malaria, tuberculosis, typhoid fever, pneumonia, and diphtheria declined in the early 1900s. Still, epidemics could rage unchecked. Yellow fever swept through New Orleans in the early 1900s, poliomyelitis (infantile paralysis) affected thousands of New Yorkers in 1916, and the great influenza epidemic of 1918–19 killed more than half a million Americans.

SEE ALSO
Children's Bureau, U.S.; Pure Food and Drugs Act (1906); Influenza epidemic (1918); Medicine; Population and fertility; Spanish-American War; Settlement-house movement; Wald, Lillian

FURTHER READING
Duffy, John. *The Sanitarians: A History of American Public Health*. Urbana: University of Illinois Press, 1990.

Hamilton, Alice. *Exploring the Dangerous Trades: The Autobiography of Alice Hamilton, M.D.* 1943. Reprint. Boston: Northeastern University Press, 1985.

Leavitt, Judith Walzer. *Typhoid Mary: Captive to the Public's Health.* Boston: Beacon, 1996.

Mullan, Fitzhugh. *Plagues and Politics: The Story of the United States Public Health Service.* New York: Basic Books, 1989.

Hearst, William Randolph

- *Born: Apr. 29, 1863, San Francisco, Calif.*
- *Education: attended Harvard College, 1882–85*
- *Accomplishments: publisher,* San Francisco Examiner, New York Morning Journal, *and many other newspapers and magazines; U.S. House of Representatives (Democrat–N.Y., 1903–7)*
- *Died: Aug. 14, 1951, Beverly Hills, Calif.*

A NEWSPAPER AND magazine publisher, William Randolph Hearst grew up in a prominent California family. His father, George Hearst, was a mine developer, newspaper owner, and U.S. senator. His mother, Phoebe Apperson Hearst, endowed buildings and scholarships at the University of California, founded the National Congress of Mothers (a forerunner of the National Council of Parents and Teachers, or PTA), and after 1897 served as the first woman regent of the University of California.

In 1887, young Hearst took over the *San Francisco Examiner,* his father's newspaper. After turning it around and making the paper a success, in 1895 he bought a New York City paper, the *Morning Journal,* a direct challenge to Joseph Pulitzer's *New York World.* The secret of Hearst's success as a newspaper publisher lay in his family's willingness to sink a fortune into hiring journalists.

He lured away Pulitzer's staff by doubling their pay. At mid-career, Hearst owned seven daily newspapers, five magazines, two news services, and a film company.

Hearst's newspapers appealed to readers from many social classes and cultural backgrounds. He boosted circulation with what critics called "yellow journalism," a style of sensationalistic reporting named for the Yellow Kid cartoon figure used in both Hearst and Pulitzer publications that printed lurid stories. While opposing Asian American immigration to California, Hearst's papers favored many progressive causes, including labor unions, progressive taxation, public ownership of utilities, and antitrust legislation. He received criticism, however, for sensationalizing the news and arousing popular fears, especially in his coverage of Spain's actions in Cuba in the late 1890s. He highlighted the harsh treatment of Cuban rebels by Spain's general, Valeriano Weyler, and stirred up a women's campaign to save Evangelina Cisneros, the daughter of a Cuban rebel, who had been condemned to a penal colony in Africa. Before she could be sent to Africa, one of Hearst's reporters liberated Cisneros from prison and smuggled her out of Cuba disguised as a boy. Hearst organized an open-air meeting in New York City to let Congress know the depth of popular feeling in favor of a free Cuba. In this way he helped bring on the Spanish-American War.

When Hearst was supporting William Jennings Bryan's three

Newspaper publisher William Randolph Hearst, captured in a candid moment during a 1914 visit to Chicago. Hearst's many papers were notorious for sensationalized reporting. Hearst believed, "News is something somebody doesn't want printed; all else is advertising."

attempts to win the Presidency, he enjoyed wide political influence. He served two terms in the U.S. House of Representatives, and though rarely present for a vote came in second for a presidential nomination himself at the Democratic National Convention in 1904. He ran unsuccessfully for mayor, lieutenant governor, and governor of New York. In later years, as his influence declined, most of the political candidates he promoted failed to win election.

An avid art collector, Hearst spent lavishly on paintings, ceramics, and textiles. Although financial need forced him to sell much of his collection, the works that remained found a home in Hearst's "castle," built in San Simeon, California, on coastal land Hearst inherited from his mother. The mansion, designed by Julia Morgan, his mother's architect, was never finished but is now open to the public as a state historical monument. In 1941, Orson Welles directed and starred in *Citizen Kane,* a movie based loosely on Hearst's colorful life.

SEE ALSO
Journalism; Pulitzer, Joseph; Spanish-American War

FURTHER READING
Nasaw, David. *The Chief: The Life of William Randolph Hearst.* Boston: Houghton Mifflin, 2000.
Robinson, Judith. *The Hearsts: An American Dynasty.* Newark: University of Delaware Press, 1991.

Hispanic Americans

HISPANIC AMERICANS are of Spanish-speaking descent. They come from a variety of ethnic backgrounds, including European, African, Native American, and Asian. Many have ancient roots in the Americas and in the United States. Cubans, Puerto Ricans, Mexican Americans and Hispanic Americans from Central and South America and the Caribbean are also known as Latin Americans, or Latinos.

In the Gilded Age and Progressive Era, many Hispanic Americans were the descendents of Mexicans who had been living in the northern half of Mexico when the United States annexed that territory after the Mexican War of 1848. Those Mexican Americans lived in Texas and southern Colorado and in the territory that would become the states of New Mexico and Arizona in 1912. Mexican Americans gradually lost their land to white settlers who overwhelmed them in numbers and used lawsuits in state and federal courts to dispossess them of their land. By the 1880s, 80 percent were working as low-status wage laborers. Women performed domestic service in white homes, and men laid track for the railroads and worked as farm laborers, miners, and cowboys. Racism and anti-Catholicism in the dominant white population prevented most Hispanic Americans from succeeding economically or socially. Like many African Americans and poor whites in the deep South, Mexican Americans sometimes worked as sharecroppers, paying for the use of someone else's land with a half share of the produce they grew.

Southern California had been home to the *Californios,* descendants of the original Spanish colonial settlers. As white, or Anglo, Americans settled the state after 1848, the Californios also lost property. Their descendents retreated into segregated urban neighborhoods (barrios), where they lacked basic city services like running water and trash collection.

Members of a girls' drill team flourish their batons for this school photograph taken in Los Angeles, California. Although Los Angeles had integrated schools in the early 20th century, after 1920 white and Mexican American children attended segregated schools.

In 1902, Congress passed the Newlands Reclamation Act, which brought water through a massive system of dams and irrigation canals to the arid Southwest and California. Within a few years, vast farms emerged, and with them came a need for farmworkers. Encouraged by white landowners, Mexicans by the thousands crossed the border in order to take farm jobs. A revolution in Mexico in 1909 pushed more workers across the border. In those years, the United States imposed no restrictions on immigration from anywhere in Latin America. The Mexican newcomers performed hard, poorly paid labor that most white, native-born Americans disliked, so they were welcomed.

Many Mexicans made the United States their home and became permanent residents. With a few exceptions, they remained in the working class, and many never learned English. This was especially true of women, who spent their days as farm laborers and their nights looking after families at home. Children received little education, as they left school at young ages to work in the fields.

The Spanish-American War of 1898 and the Philippines War that followed it brought other Spanish-speaking people to the United States. The Spanish-American War, which took place between April and August 1898, left the United States in control of several former Spanish colonies, including Cuba, Puerto Rico, and the Philippines. Both Cuba and Puerto Rico had been part of Spain's empire. After the war, Puerto Rico became a U.S. territory, which meant that Puerto Ricans were U.S. citizens and could travel freely between the United States and their island home. Cuba became a U.S. protectorate, a status that involved mutual trade agreements and strategic alliances. A number of Cubans immigrated to the United States during those years, eventually establishing a prosperous community in south Florida.

The Philippines, a Pacific island nation, had also once been part of the Spanish empire. In 1900, its citizens were Asians who spoke indigenous languages and Spanish. As a result of four centuries of Spanish rule, almost all Filipinos were Catholic, and most had some fraction of Spanish ancestry. After U.S. soldiers completed their conquest of the Philippines by eliminating an independence movement, the Philippines became a U.S. territory. This meant that Filipinos were U.S. nationals, though not citizens. As nationals they could freely enter the United States, which many did, primarily through West Coast ports.

Many Filipinos settled in Hawaii, where they worked on sugar and fruit plantations. Those who came to the U.S. mainland held mostly low-wage service and manual labor jobs. They established Filipino-American communities called Little Manilas—after their country's capital—in a number of American cities. After the Philippines became an independent nation in 1946, Filipinos continued to immigrate to the United States, where they could now apply for U.S. citizenship.

Today's Filipino Americans and new immigrants from the Philippines consider themselves Asian Americans. They speak English and Tagalog, an indigenous language, rather than Spanish, although most have Spanish surnames, a legacy of the past. Hispano-Filipinos represent a small group within the American Filipino community who are interested in preserving some aspects of their Spanish heritage, such as language, religion, traditional foods, and festivals.

Over the years, Hispanic Americans have become the largest minority in the United States. Today, they are also the fastest-growing minority, as a result of a high birth rate and continuing immigration.

SEE ALSO

Agriculture; Asian Americans; Immigration; Imperialism; Race relations; Spanish-American War; West, the; Work

FURTHER READING

Anton, Alex, and Roger E. Hernandez. *Cubans in America: A Vibrant History of a People in Exile.* New York: Kensington, 2002.
Del Castillo, Richard Griswold, and Arnoldo De Leon. *North to Aztlan: A History of Mexican Americans in the United States.* Boston: Twayne, 1997.
Gonzalez, Juan. *Harvest of Empire: A History of Latinos in America.* New York: Viking, 2000.
Hoobler, Dorothy, and Thomas Hoobler. *The Mexican American Family Album.* New York: Oxford University Press, 1994.
Korrol, Virginia Sanchez. *From Colonia to Community: The History of Puerto Ricans in New York City.* Westport, Conn.: Greenwood, 1983.

History

HISTORY IS THE reconstruction of the past. In nonliterate societies, history takes the form of stories passed down through the generations. In literate societies, historians collect personal memories and documents about particular events or developments and then place the information they find into a coherent, written form. In the early 1800s, American historians saw their field as a branch of literature and wrote sweeping narratives that exalted the nation's democratic and moral virtues. By the end of the century, younger historians, many of whom had received formal training in German universities, advocated scientific methodologies in research, strict rules of evidence, adherence to objectivity in interpretations, and specialization in subject matter.

Historical study first appeared as an academic discipline in American universities in the 1870s. The field became officially professionalized with the 1884 founding of the American Historical Association (AHA). Herbert Baxter Adams, director of historical studies at Johns Hopkins University during the late 1800s, served as the AHA's executive secretary for its first 16 years. At first, Baxter wanted to include amateur historians, that is, writers who emphasized the "art" more than the "science" of historical writing. Eventually, however, academics came to dominate the association.

Despite their emphasis on scientific methods, American historians remained interested in making sweeping generalizations about the nation's past. Two American presidents, Theodore Roosevelt and Woodrow Wilson, were both AHA members who wrote broad works of history. The writings of both of these historians on the importance of the West influenced historian Frederick Jackson Turner. In his 1893 essay, "The Significance of the Frontier in American History," Turner asserted that he could explain all of American development up to the 1890s by the "existence of an area of free land, its continuous recession, and the advance of American settlement westward." He claimed that the frontier had shaped key features of the American character, such as "that coarseness and strength combined with acuteness and inquisitiveness; that practical, inventive turn of mind...; that masterful grasp of material things...; that restless, nervous energy; that dominant individualism,...and withal that buoyancy and exuberance which comes with freedom." These are "traits of the frontier, or traits called out elsewhere because of the existence of the frontier," he said. Although historians today criticize Turner's views as being too focused on male white settlers and not enough on women and indigenous populations, his idea that the frontier produced the highly individualistic, restless, and socially mobile American committed to democracy continues to influence the popular imagination.

SEE ALSO

Colleges and universities; Education; Social sciences; West, the

FURTHER READING

Higham, John. *History: Professional Scholarship in America.* Baltimore: Johns Hopkins University Press, 1983.

Holmes, Oliver Wendell, Jr.

- *Born: Mar. 8, 1841, Boston, Mass.*
- *Education: Harvard College, A.B., 1861; Harvard Law School, LL.B., 1866*
- *Accomplishments: coeditor,* American Law Review *(1870–73); professor, Harvard Law School, (1880–82); author,* The Common Law *(1881); associate justice (1883–99) and chief justice (1899–1902), Massachusetts Supreme Court; associate justice, U.S. Supreme Court (1902–32)*
- *Died: Mar. 6, 1935, Washington, D.C.*

CONSIDERED ONE OF the nation's most distinguished jurists, Oliver Wendell Holmes, Jr., served for 30 years on the U.S. Supreme Court. He was the son of a prominent physician, after whom he was named. Dr. Holmes educated his son at home and then sent him to Harvard College. Young Holmes's service during the Civil War fighting for the Union meant a great deal to him. He received three major wounds before being retired in 1864 with the rank of captain. In a speech he delivered to the graduating class at Harvard 31 years later entitled "The Soldier's Faith," he maintained the importance of devoting oneself to a cause, even if the cause was not completely understandable. To the end of his long life he preserved two blood-stained uniforms in his closet.

The Common Law, a compilation of lectures he published in 1881, made him famous among legal scholars and intellectuals. In it, he said, "The life of the law has not been logic; it has been experience." What he meant was that the law comes less from rules of logic than from the "necessities" of the times, current moral and political theories, institutions of public policy, and even the prejudices that all judges share. In short, "The law embodies the story of a nation's development through many centuries, and it cannot be dealt with as if it contained only the axioms and corollaries of a book of mathematics." With such views, Holmes contributed to the early 20th-century debate on the meaning of the law in a rapidly changing social, economic, and political climate.

Holmes briefly taught law at Harvard University but left to accept an appointment to the Massachusetts Supreme Court. He eventually became chief justice on this court. Attracted by Holmes's opinions upholding the right of the state to regulate the economy, President Theodore Roosevelt tapped him for the U.S. Supreme Court in

A staunch advocate of free speech, Oliver Wendell Holmes Jr., once wrote, "If there is any principle of the Constitution that more imperatively calls for attachment than any other it is the principle of free thought— not free thought for those who agree with us but freedom for the thought that we hate."

1902. Holmes won immediate and unanimous confirmation by the U.S. Senate.

On the Supreme Court, Holmes continued to defend the right of state legislatures to regulate the economy. In 1905, he argued against the Court's majority when it struck down a state law limiting work hours in bakeries (*Lochner* v. *New York*).

While refusing to say whether he agreed with a law that limited the working hours of bakers, Holmes asserted that his "agreement or disagreement has nothing to do with the right of a majority [of the legislature of the state of New York] to embody their opinions in law," and that "State constitutions and state laws may regulate life in many ways," even if Supreme Court justices think such laws are "injudicious."

In cases heard during 1919, when the nation was experiencing a period of mass fear about the presence of radicals in their midst (the Red Scare), Holmes took influential positions on the right of free speech. The first case, *Schenck* v. *United States*, concerned a man convicted under the Espionage Act for advocating draft resistance. Holmes upheld the man's conviction, not because he wanted to suppress the man's right to speak but because "The question in every case is whether the words used are used in such circumstances and are of such a nature as to create a clear and present danger that they will bring about the substantive

evils that Congress has a right to prevent." When his colleagues on the Court later appealed to the "clear and present danger" doctrine as a basis for upholding convictions for speech, Holmes became more cautious in his own use of it. Thus, in *Abrams* v. *United States*, which concerned a man convicted for distributing pamphlets criticizing Wilson for intervening militarily in the Russian revolution, Holmes dissented from the Court's majority, which sustained the man's conviction. In a careful reading of the defendant's pamphlets Holmes said he could find no material with the intent "to cripple or hinder the United States in the prosecution of the war." Hence he could not accept the idea of restricting free speech on "clear and present danger" grounds.

For his many dissents from the Supreme Court's majority opinions, Holmes became known as the Great Dissenter. Retired from the court in 1932, Holmes died just two days short of his 94th birthday, widely admired for his intellectual powers as a thinker about the law.

SEE ALSO

Law; Red Scare (1919–20); Supreme Court, U.S.

FURTHER READING

Baker, Liva. *The Justice from Beacon Hill: The Life and Times of Oliver Wendell Holmes.* New York: HarperCollins, 1991.

Holmes, Oliver Wendell. *The Essential Holmes: Selections from the Letters, Speeches, Judicial Opinions, and Other Writings of Oliver Wendell Holmes, Jr.* Edited by Richard A. Posner. Chicago: University of Chicago Press, 1992.

Menand, Louis. *The Metaphysical Club: A Story of Ideas in America.* New York: Farrar, Straus & Giroux, 2001.

White, G. Edward. *Justice Oliver Wendell Holmes: Law and the Inner Self.* New York: Oxford University Press, 1993.

———. *Oliver Wendell Holmes Jr.* New York: Oxford University Press, 2006.

Homestead strike (1892)

THE 1892 STRIKE AT Carnegie Steel Company in Homestead, Pennsylvania, was one of several violent industrial upheavals of the late 19th century. The strike began when the company locked its workers out of the steel mills just as it was due to start contract renewal negotiations with the workers' union, the Amalgamated Association of Iron and Steel Workers. During the lockout, the union's contract expired. Since the company wanted to get rid of the union, it refused to renew the contract. As a result, some 3,800 men were thrown out of work.

Perhaps because he knew trouble was coming, the company's owner, Andrew Carnegie, went on vacation in Scotland. His deputy, Henry Clay Frick, a fierce antiunionist, was in charge. Refusing to re-negotiate the union's contract, Frick brought in replacement workers, or scabs, and in order to protect them from irate employees who had lost their jobs in the lockout, he hired 300 men from New York's Pinkerton Detective Agency. These detectives were little more than thugs. As the Pinkertons approached the mills on barges along the Monongahela River, shooting broke out. When the day was done, three Pinkertons and seven of the locked out workers lay dead. Scores of others were wounded.

The Pinkertons withdrew from the fray, but six days later the governor of Pennsylvania sent in the National Guard to restore order. The presence of the National Guard allowed Carnegie Steel to treat the striking workers harshly, without fear that they would return to violence. The company had strike leaders arrested. It also evicted striking workers and their families from company-owned housing. In five months, the union was completely broken. Workers who were not blacklisted by the management went back to their jobs. The defeat was a blow for union organizing in the steel industry; it would not recover until the 1930s. The Homestead strike demonstrated that big business, when allied with state government, could defeat the growing influence of the labor movement.

Troops march into action against striking Carnegie Steel Company workers in Homestead, Pennsylvania, in 1892. A fatal gun battle led to the eventual crushing of the union.

SEE ALSO

Carnegie, Andrew; Labor unions; Strikes

FURTHER READING

Demarest, David P., ed. *"The River Ran Red": Homestead 1892.* Pittsburgh, Pa.: University of Pittsburgh Press, 1992.
Krause, Paul. *The Battle for Homestead, 1880–1892: Politics, Culture, and Steel.* Pittsburgh, Pa.: University of Pittsburgh Press, 1992.
Serrin, William. *Homestead: The Glory and Tragedy of an American Steel Town.* New York: Vintage, 1993.

Hull House

IN 1889, TWO YOUNG middle-class, college-educated women, Jane Addams and Ellen Gates Starr, rented a dilapidated mansion on Chicago's Near West Side. The mansion, which had once belonged to real estate developer Charles J. Hull, had been built in 1856 in the middle of open fields. By the time Addams and Starr moved into it, it was surrounded by factories and slums crowded around an open market on South Halstead Street. The people living in the area were ethnically diverse, consisting of Irish and Germans, Greeks and Italians, Eastern European Jews, and African Americans. Addams and Starr planned to live among them, hoping to learn from their neighbors how they might be helpful to them in some practical ways. Over time, the help that they offered became known as social work, and the place where they offered it Hull House.

Friends of Addams and Starr soon heard about Hull House and came to participate in the experiment. Among them were women who would later achieve national reputations in social reform—Julia Lathrop, first head of the U.S. Children's Bureau; Florence Kelley, later head of the National Consumers' League; and Alice Hamilton, founder of the field of industrial medicine, to name but a few. Other residents later applied to live at Hull House, defraying their own expenses (some received fellowships supplied by wealthy benefactors). Volunteers could stay from six weeks to six months, depending on the services they could offer. During Hull House's first three years, all of its residents were women, but nonresident men also volunteered

in its programs, which included nurseries and kindergartens, soup kitchens, clubs for all ages, and classes in art, crafts, drama, cooking, and the English language.

Impressed with this practical approach to social welfare, many wealthy benefactors supported Hull House programs. Intellectuals, reformers, and political figures came to speak to Hull House residents and neighbors, as well as to learn from their experiences. Hull House soon became a lively center for the exchange of ideas about modern city problems. One of its earliest achievements was the 1895 publication of *Hull-House Maps and Papers: A Presentation of Nationalities and Wages in a Congested District of Chicago*, the first systematic investigation of a working-class neighborhood in an American city. Commissioned by the U.S. Department of Labor, the book argued that poverty is not the result of an individual's laziness or failure to save money but the result of circumstances that have overwhelmed human powers of self-help. This became a founding idea of Progressive Era reform.

Eventually, Jane Addams and her associates bought or built additional structures. Only a year and a half after the founding of Hull House, they built

The children of immigrant families stand with their smiling teacher at Hull House, the pioneering settlement house established in Chicago. Hull House provided nursery schools, art and music classes, and gymnasiums for neighborhood residents.

Butler Gallery, a cheap two-story building that offered a supplementary living room, lecture room, branch library, and rooms for male residents. In 1895, they built a Children's House for clubs, a nursery, kindergarten, and music classes. A brick building known as the Jane Club provided housing for working women. Ultimately, Hull House encompassed 13 buildings, each offering a different aspect of the settlement's programs. The original Hull mansion and the settlement's dining hall are now Registered National Historic Landmarks.

SEE ALSO

Addams, Jane; Kelley, Florence; Settlement-house movement; Social work

FURTHER READING

Addams, Jane. *Twenty Years at Hull House.* Reprint, edited by Victoria Bissel Brown. Boston: Bedford/St. Martin's, 1999.

Polacheck, Hilda Satt. *I Came A Stranger: The Story of a Hull-House Girl.* Edited by Dena J. Polacheck Epstein. Urbana: University of Illinois Press, 1989.

Stebner, Eleanor J. *The Women of Hull House: A Study in Spirituality, Vocation, and Friendship.* Albany, N.Y.: State University of New York Press, 1997.

Immigration

THE UNITED STATES has always been a nation of immigrants and descendants of immigrants. In every census taken throughout the country's history, the foreign-born have accounted for at least 6 to 14 percent of the population. During the late 19th century, the nature of immigration to the United States began to change. Formerly a destination for people from northern and western Europe—British, Irish, Germans, and Scandinavians—the United States became host to an increasing number of immigrants from southern and eastern Europe—Italians, Greeks, Slavs, Poles, eastern European and Russian Jews, and Armenians.

Despite legal restraints on their immigration, newcomers also entered from a variety of Asian countries. Mexicans and Central Americans freely crossed the southern border, not even tallied as immigrants until 1907 and without being stopped by border patrols until 1924. French Canadians from rural Quebec abandoned their marginal farms and moved into New England, supplying much of the labor for factories and textile mills.

Between 1870 and 1920, nearly 29 million immigrants came to the United States. The peak decade was from 1900 to 1910, when the census recorded 8,795,386 new immigrants. This wave of immigration slowed with the advent of World War I and ended with the restrictive Immigration Act of 1924, which established quotas on the immigration of certain nationalities. But generally speaking, the "golden door," as Emma Lazarus called the entryway to America, stood wide open for white people. During the Gilded Age and Progressive Era, there were almost no limits on the number of people who could try to make new lives for themselves in the United States.

Immigrants left their native lands for a variety of reasons—lack of work, scarcity of land, evictions, political turmoil, revolutionary violence, even famine. On the Italian peninsula, most young men could not acquire either farmland or industrial jobs. Some immigrants, despised minorities in their homelands, suffered physical and social persecution. Jews, for example, met anti-Semitism everywhere, but they encountered particularly severe persecution in Russia and other central European countries, where soldiers and government authorities drove them from their ancestral villages. Other minorities, such as the pacifist Mennonites, left Europe when governments drafted their young men into the army. Many Europeans emigrated simply for greater opportunities. Industries seeking labor recruited some immigrants, as did companies such as the Santa Fe Railroad, eager to import farmers to fill up the Plains states where their new railroad lines ran.

Changes in sea travel made immigration easier than ever before. By 1900, the newest steamships crossed the ocean in a week. Transatlantic passage could cost as little as $15 if one traveled in steerage class, crowded deep into the lowest decks of the ship in relatively unsanitary conditions, without much food or privacy. Nearly 80 percent of immigrants went to New York City, where officials processed them at Castle Garden and, after 1892, at Ellis Island. New immigrants from Europe also entered the United States at Boston, Baltimore, Philadelphia, and New Orleans.

Ashore in the New World, many newcomers had little money and few contacts. Some headed for relatives already living in the city; others looked for what Yiddish-speaking immigrants called *landsmen*, acquaintances from their villages in the old world. Family and friends could help immigrants find housing and jobs, and their presence eased loneliness. Without the protection of family and friends, "greenhorns" could fall victim to hucksters and con artists, who took what money they had in exchange for empty promises of work or lodging.

Most European immigrants in this period stayed in the cities where they had first arrived or moved to other cities. Industrial Buffalo, Cleveland, Detroit, and Chicago were popular destinations because of the factory jobs available. Even though a majority of these immigrants had come from rural areas in their home countries, only a fraction were able to buy farmland in the United States. By 1920, three-quarters of all foreign-born inhabitants were living in cities.

Immigrants usually resided in city neighborhoods with people from their own country; these enclaves became known as *ghettos* or, in Spanish, *barrios*. New arrivals often shared scarce accommodations with other families or squeezed into small tenement apartments as boarders. One or more single men often lived with a family, each man paying rent for meals and lodging and saving money to bring members of his own family to the United States.

Not all immigrants stayed in the United States, however. About 10 percent each year returned to their native countries, usually after a period of employment which enabled them to go home with enough money to purchase land or other goods, marry, or reconnect with families and villages. Many single male immigrants, known as "birds of passage," made the round-trip journey numerous times.

The influx of immigrants and the growth of industrial America fed on each other. Every year more jobs became available and more people wanted them. Jewish and Italian men and women workers dominated the New York and Chicago garment industries; Catholic immigrants from central Europe, Poles, Czechs, Slavs, and others found work in the great steel mills of Pennsylvania and Ohio and later in the oil industry and automobile manufacturing. In the upper Midwest, on the Great Plains, and in the West and Southwest, immigrants from Scandinavia, central Europe, Mexico, Latin America, and Asia worked as miners, farm laborers, fishermen, railroad workers, and cannery operatives. Only a few industries recruited women. Most women immigrants went into domestic service, garment making, or light manufacturing. Men who brought skills from the old country—crafts such as carpentry, metalsmithing, and printing—earned much higher pay.

Immigrants encountered numerous obstacles. Most new arrivals experienced poverty and overcrowding, homesickness and disorientation. Many encountered hatred from old-stock Americans, whose distrust and suspicion of newcomers and their customs was a form of ethnic prejudice called nativism. Some minorities—Jews, Poles, Mexicans, and Asians—found work only among members of their own ethnic groups; their inability to speak English kept them out of other jobs. Even previous generations of immigrants could be unwelcoming. Some German Jews, for example, whose families had been in New York for several generations, looked down on Russian Jewish newcomers. They feared that the peasant manners and radical political ideas of some of the newcomers would give rise to renewed outbreaks of anti-Semitism.

Nearly all the immigrants who came to the United States were ambitious and eager to succeed, ready to work hard to meet their goals. They brought America their skills, customs, language, foods, music, arts, and literature. Words of Yiddish, Italian, Spanish, and other languages became part of common English usage. In addition to their impact on industry, technology, and urban growth, immigrants published newspapers in their own languages, opened restaurants and saloons, founded parochial and foreign language schools, and entered and soon controlled the police and fire

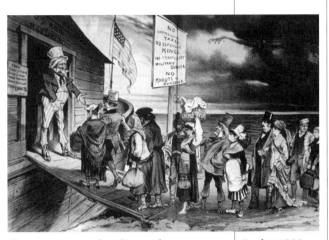

departments and politics of many American cities. Immigrants who had to work full-time during the day studied at night schools and colleges, founded particularly for them. Immigrants, many of them Jewish, started the film industry in the first years of the 20th century, first in New York and later in Hollywood, California.

The children of this immigrant generation went to school and learned English, though many also left school early to work. Better assimilated into American life than their parents, many sought higher education, became wealthy retailers and manufacturers, or found jobs in the professions of law, medicine, architecture, and education. They moved out of the ghettos where their parents had settled and contributed to the growth of suburbia.

Despite the contributions that the immigrants of the 1880 to 1920 era made to American culture and prosperity, many Americans still feared the impact of foreigners on their lives. This fear affected public policy. In the 1920s, the government began to limit immigration by applying quotas to different ethnic groups. Using a complicated formula based on the census, the immigration bureaucracy cut back severely on the number of southern and eastern Europeans who could apply for admission to the United

In this 1880 cartoon from the satirical magazine Puck, *immigrants wearing the traditional garb of many European countries stream toward Uncle Sam and an ark that represents safe haven in the United States.*

States. At the same time, these officials began serious efforts to police the border with Mexico. Laws dating back to the 1880s continued to exclude Asian immigrants, and the Alien Land Law of 1913 prohibited Asians from owning land. These policies were a triumph of prejudice and nativism.

SEE ALSO

Asian Americans; Chinese Exclusion Act (1882); Cities; Education; Ellis Island; Family life; Hispanic Americans; Labor; Motion pictures; Nativism; Railroads; Work; World War I

FURTHER READING

Bodnar, John. *The Transplanted: A History of Immigrants in Urban America*. Bloomington: Indiana University Press, 1985.
Daniels, Roger. *American Immigration: A Student Companion*. New York: Oxford University Press, 2001.
————. *Not Like Us: Immigrants and Minorities in America, 1890–1924*. Chicago: Ivan R. Dee, 1997.
Gabaccia, Donna. *Immigration and American Diversity: A Social and Cultural History*. Malden, Mass.: Blackwell, 2002.
Handlin, Oscar. *The Uprooted*. 2nd ed. Boston: Little, Brown, 1990.
Takaki, Ronald. *A Different Mirror: A History of Multi-Cultural America*. Boston: Little, Brown, 1993.

Imperialism

IMPERIALISM IS the policy of extending a nation's power and authority over a group of less powerful people. Sometimes nations simply buy or conquer territory belonging to others. Alternatively, they establish economic ties with weaker nations and over time secure those ties with political and military power.

The United States was always an imperialist nation, taking over lands held or owned by others, including Native Americans. U.S. citizens justi-fied this action with the argument that Indians were culturally inferior and uneducated, and therefore ignorant about proper land use and incapable of self-government. By the end of the Mexican War in 1848, many white Americans had come to believe in what politicians were calling Manifest Destiny. They assumed that God had ordained their settlement of all the land between the Atlantic and the Pacific and the Canadian and Mexican borders.

As it turned out, Manifest Destiny did not end with the settlement of the West. In 1856, the United States began reaching beyond its "natural" geographic borders when Congress authorized the U.S. annexation of any small island unclaimed by other governments. Within the next few years, Americans had annexed four Pacific Islands to provide way stations for shipping and acquired a naval base in Pago Pago, Samoa. In 1867, Secretary of State William Seward, a man firmly committed to American expansion, arranged the purchase of Alaska from Russia, which had held it since 1741. The area, twice as large as Texas, was sparsely settled, but had a population of Native Americans (the Inuits) and a substantial supply of natural resources, including gold and other minerals.

In the latter 1800s, the U.S. government stepped up the pace of territorial acquisitions. The motivations were complex. In part, the government wanted markets for the country's manufactured products and access to natural resources or agricultural products not available at home. Officials also hoped to compete on the world stage with major European nations, such as Britain, France, and Germany, who had been acquiring markets and imperial possessions around the world throughout the 19th century. Protection of shipping lanes, considerations of

BILL OF FARE

CUBA STEAK

PORTO RICO PIG

PHILIPPINE FLOATING ISLANDS

SANDWICH ISLANDS

WELL, I HARDLY KNOW WHICH TO TAKE FIRST!

An anti-imperi-alist cartoon criticizes Presi-dent McKinley's foreign policy by depicting him as a waiter tempting Uncle Sam with a menu of foreign territories: "Cuba Steak" is a pun on cube steak; the Philippine Islands are "floating islands," a custard-and-meringue dessert; Hawaii was once called "Sandwich Islands."

global military strategy, and attitudes of racial superiority also motivated all Western imperialist nations. Like Europeans, Americans assumed that their culture was superior to those of Asians, Africans, Pacific Islanders, and Latin Americans, and that this superiority justified the conquests of less advanced peoples. They convinced themselves that these people would welcome the Christianity, technology, and other elements of Western "civilization" that an American presence would bring to them.

In 1893, American sugar planters overthrew the Hawaiian monarchy and appealed to the United States for annexation. Strategically located in the mid-Pacific, the Hawaiian island of Oahu had a splendid harbor of great potential value to the U.S. Navy. While Congress and three successive Presidential administrations debated the unprecedented annexation of a sovereign nation, the Spanish-American War broke out. In this war, the United States went to the aid of Cubans rebelling against Spanish control. At the war's conclusion in 1898, having lost very little militarily, the United States acquired several important pieces of the former Spanish empire: Puerto Rico in the Caribbean

and, in the Pacific, the strategically located island of Guam and the island nation of the Philippines, considered by many a doorway to Asian trade. That same year, Congress finalized the annexation of Hawaii.

Because Philippine nationals wanted to rule their own country, the United States had to fight a drawn-out war there to retain imperial control over the islands. The United States was ultimately successful but only after a great cost in lives on both sides. During the next two decades, the American empire expanded farther with the addition of American Samoa and Wake Island in the Pacific (1899), the Canal Zone (1903, leased from Panama until the end of the 20th century), and the Virgin Islands, purchased from Denmark in 1917.

Many Americans were enthusiastic about imperialism: businessmen, industrialists, congressmen such as Senator Albert Beveridge from Indiana, and, most notably, President Theodore Roosevelt. Some saw imperial ventures as a way to reinvigorate American men, who had grown "soft" during the Victorian age, and as a chance to explore strange new lands and to conquer, control, and later uplift "inferior" peoples. As Senator Beveridge said in an 1889 speech, Americans had planted themselves across the New World, and "American law, American order, American civilization, and the American flag will plant themselves on shores hitherto bloody and benighted, but by those agencies of God henceforth to be made beautiful and bright."

Other Americans opposed U.S. expansion. They felt that the United States, a republic, should never take over other countries and subjugate their people. Nor did they want the responsibilities or the military expense that would inevitably accompany imperial ventures. They also deplored the racism implicit in imperialism as well as the competition that imperialism had created among Western nations, with each one scrambling for superiority, territory, and the chance to maintain economic spheres of influence.

Among the most noted anti-imperialists were author Samuel Clemens (Mark Twain), settlement-house leader Jane Addams, and four-time Presidential candidate William Jennings Bryan. In 1898, Twain and others formed the Anti-Imperialist League, inspiring the founding of state branches, women's auxiliaries, and conferences, such as the National Liberty Congress of Anti-Imperialists, held in August 1900. Another anti-imperialist was steel tycoon Andrew Carnegie. "Congratulations," Carnegie wrote with sarcasm to a friend who favored U.S. possession of the Philippines, "You seem to have about finished your work of civilizing the Filipinos. It is thought that about eight thousand of them have been completely civilized and sent to heaven. I hope you like it."

In the end, imperial rivalries among powerful nations became a precipitating cause of World War I, and a major factor in reshaping the global map after the war was over. The United States granted Philippine independence in 1945 and turned the Panama Canal over to Panama in 1999. Hawaii became a state, and islands in the Pacific and the Caribbean became U.S. or United Nations territories. Unlike states, which form parts of a federated country, territories are legally administered geographic areas that have lost or relinquished sovereignty and function under the authority of another country or international body. Other European nations dismantled their empires one country at a time over the last half of the 20th century. By the year 2000, most former imperial possessions had become independent, self-governing nations.

SEE ALSO

International relations; Panama Canal; Roosevelt, Theodore; Spanish-American War; West, the; World War I

FURTHER READING

Ninkovich, Frank. *The United States and Imperialism.* Malden, Mass.: Blackwell, 2000.
Rabe, Stephen G., and Thomas Patterson, eds. *Imperial Surge: The United States Abroad, the 1890s–Early 1900s.* Lexington, Mass.: D. C. Heath, 1992.
Smith, Bonnie G. *Imperialism: A History in Documents.* New York: Oxford University Press, 2000.
Stephanson, Anders. *Manifest Destiny: American Expansion and the Empire of Right.* New York: Hill & Wang, 1996.

Industrial Workers of the World

IN 1905, REPRESENTATIVES from a variety of American labor and political organizations established the Industrial Workers of the World (IWW). The IWW, whose members were nicknamed the Wobblies, would be open to all workers regardless of race, gender, or occupation. Moreover, the workers would be organized not by skill or craft, as in the American Federation of Labor (AFL), but by industry. All workers in any given industry, from clerks to machine operators to janitors, would be members of the same union. Soon there were IWW union locals for dockworkers, textile mill hands, and lumberjacks as well as miners, factory workers, and seasonal agricultural laborers. By 1917, the IWW had more than 100,000 members.

A number of Americans, including some progressive reformers, appreciated the Wobblies for their defense of free speech and the rights of common

A crowd gathers in New York City for a 1914 labor demonstration sponsored by the Industrial Workers of the World (IWW). IWW strikes sometimes led to violence, whereupon police blamed the strikers and often jailed them.

working people. In 1912 the IWW led a strike against a wage cut in the Lawrence, Massachusetts, textile industry and won a small pay raise. The following year, however, it failed to win a strike against silk manufacturers in Paterson, New Jersey, who had doubled the number of looms tended by a single worker. In the West, violent confrontations frequently erupted during IWW strikes. These episodes made many Americans distrust the Wobblies. During World War I, the U.S. government attacked the IWW for its sympathies with socialism and international communism. Claiming that strikes during wartime were unpatriotic and a danger to the country, government authorities began to seize IWW records. They also arrested IWW leaders, deporting a number of them after the war. Western miner "Big Bill" Haywood, the IWW's exuberant chief, sought voluntary exile in Russia.

Other leaders associated with the IWW included Elizabeth Gurley Flynn, a fiery orator, and Joe Hill, framed for a murder and executed in Utah. Stories of Wobbly exploits and songs such as "I Dreamed I Saw Joe Hill Last Night" and "Solidarity Forever" enhanced the powerful mystique of the IWW and its martyrs. The organization's own decentralization weakened it, however, and national suspicion, arrests, and trials almost destroyed it. The IWW, once regarded as the most egalitarian labor organization in American history, still exists and has union locals around the world.

SEE ALSO

American Federation of Labor; Labor unions; Strikes

FURTHER READING

Bird, Stewart, Dan Georgakas, and Deborah Shaffer. *Solidarity Forever: An Oral History of the IWW.* Chicago: Lake View Press, 1985.

Dubofsky, Melvyn A. *We Shall Be All: A History of the Industrial Workers of the World.* 2nd ed. Urbana: University of Illinois Press, 1988.

Kimeldorf, Howard. *Battling for American Labor: Wobblies, Craft Workers, and the Making of the Union Movement.* Berkeley: University of California Press, 1999.

Kornbluh, Joyce L., ed. *Rebel Voices, an I.W.W. Anthology.* Ann Arbor: University of Michigan Press, 1964.

Industry

THE FIRST Industrial Revolution—the economic transformation that resulted from the discovery of new technologies for production—took place in Great Britain in the 1750s. The United States began to industrialize at the beginning of the 1800s with the introduction of large-scale textile manufacturing machinery. Early textile factories used water power to drive their machinery. By the Civil War, many manufacturers had installed coal-fired steam engines. Coal also fueled the railroads and fired the blast furnaces and rolling mills that turned iron ore into iron and steel. After the Civil War, new technologies developed even more rapidly, bringing on what historians have called a second Industrial Revolution. By 1900, the United States, once a nation of farmers and merchants, had become an industrial giant.

The emergence of new industries depended on technological advances. The completion of the nation's modern transportation and communication networks—the railroad, telegraph, steamship, and trans-Atlantic cable, which made possible telegraphic communication between Europe and the United States—facilitated manufacturers' access to raw materials and markets for their finished goods. The advent of electricity in the 1880s provided a more flexible source of power than steam for industrial machinery. The telephone, which rapidly superceded the telegraph, made instantaneous business transactions possible.

Certain inventions helped expand particular industries. Refrigerated railroad cars, which kept meat fresh over long hauls, turned meatpacking into a national rather than a local industry.

Workers build cars on an assembly line in Detroit in 1913. New manufacturing technologies produced standardized goods rapidly and efficiently, lowering costs and increasing product availability.

The garment industry, which manufactured ready-made clothing, benefited from industrial sewing machines and electric lighting. The invention of typewriters led to the appearance of whole industries to manufacture them and other office machinery.

Some Gilded Age companies not only developed worldwide markets for their products but remain global enterprises to this day. Remington, for example, originally a gun maker, began making typewriters. National Cash Register and International Harvester got their start in the Gilded Age. In food processing, Borden made canned milk, and Heinz and Campbell produced canned vegetables and soups. The American Tobacco Company dominated the manufacture of cigarettes. During the 1890s, General Electric and Westinghouse took the lead in manufacturing electrical equipment, and massive chemical companies such as Dow and DuPont got their start.

As businesses expanded, they became corporations. *Incorporation* meant selling shares in a company to individual stockholders. By 1916, more than 340,000 businesses had incorporated, and more than 80,000 of these were in manufacturing, the rest in trade and services. The early entrepreneurs, such as John D. Rockefeller and Andrew Carnegie, who invested in marketing and management as well as in manufacturing, quickly dominated their industries—oil in the case of Rockefeller and steel for Carnegie. Retaining majority shares in their businesses, most entrepreneurs also arranged mergers with other businesses, a process that allowed them to control access to raw materials and standardize their manufacturing procedures. These changes permitted economies of scale, that is, they saved money by increasing the number of products they manufactured without significantly raising costs.

Mergers took two forms, vertical and horizontal. A vertical merger organized one industry from bottom to top, from raw material to finished product to its delivery to customers. Gustavus Swift, for example, started out as a butcher and then became a broker between western cattle ranches and eastern meat markets. Soon he owned stockyards, slaughterhouses, meatpacking establishments, and plants that used animal by-products. He also owned railroad cars for shipping meat to eastern markets, where Swift Company salesmen sold it. By the end of the 1890s, Swift controlled an empire run from a central office in Chicago. John D. Rockefeller organized Standard Oil in a similar fashion so that it owned everything from oil fields to refineries, from railcars for transport to oil distribution centers.

In a horizontal merger, business competitors joined each other in some form of association. Initially informal, these associations—sometimes called pools, combinations, or syndicates— allowed competitors to control both production and sales prices to mutual advantage. Horizontal mergers could help businesses cope with economic downturns, depressions, and failures by keeping up prices, but they never worked perfectly. In times of crisis, firms within the combination might fail to honor their agreements to maintain a certain price. Moreover, because such price-controlling agreements were generally illegal, they were unenforceable.

The trust—initially a legal device for managing property in the interest of someone else (such as a widow, child, or charitable institution)—also emerged as a way to control an entire industry. In a corporate trust, stockholders in a large number of related companies transfer their shares to a few trustees in exchange for trust certificates. They receive dividends but give up any say in decision making. After Rockefeller and his lawyers set up the Standard Oil Trust, which they kept secret, they controlled more than 90 percent of U.S. oil-refining capacity. Standard Oil proved so effective in controlling an entire industry that other industries (including tobacco, sugar, whiskey, leather, chemicals, and explosives) imitated them. When courts and legislatures later found secret trusts illegal, business lawyers developed other forms of stock "holding" companies to circumvent the rules.

A giant merger wave at the end of the 19th century produced the country's largest and most powerful corporations. Railroad mergers took place in this period, too. By the time the trend had peaked, large corporations had transformed the country's production, transportation, and exchange of goods. The trend also gave rise to much criticism. Observers of the process charged that huge corporations had too much power. They controlled pricing, got rebates from railroads, and kept patents from being released to competitors. They could, in short, restrain trade and keep rivals from entering their industries. By the end of the century, the clamor to curb big business forced government to respond. Congress passed a series of antitrust acts, starting in 1892 with the Sherman Act. This act declared that "Every contract, combination in the form of trust or otherwise, or conspiracy, in restraint of trade or commerce among the several States, or with foreign nations, is…illegal." Theodore Roosevelt was not antibusiness, but he made part of his presidential reputation as a "trust buster," or a fierce enemy of large trusts. In speeches he delivered in the early 1900s he said, "combination and concentration should be…supervised and within reasonable limits controlled," and since the "trusts are the creatures of the State," the State not only had the right to control them, but was "duty bound to control them wherever the need of such control is shown."

As corporations merged and expanded, the factories themselves also increased in size and complexity. Managers sought ways to make the flow of work more efficient. The most influential thinker in this area was Frederick Winslow Taylor, an engineer who analyzed work processes and created wage-incentive plans that encouraged workers to meet production goals. Planning offices directed a staff of coordinating supervisors who watched over the movement of materials, speed of work, quality control, repairs, and the behavior of workers on the shop floor. Scientific Management, or Taylorism, as this way of organizing factory work came to be known, spread slowly but gained wide acceptance in the 1920s.

American factories also adopted the "continuous process" method of putting products together, later known as the assembly line. Paced by the tempo of machines and the speed of the conveyor belt, workers performed one process over and over again, each person contributing only one element in the creation of the finished product. While workers found assembly lines monotonous and dehumanizing, they were undeniably efficient. In the early 20th century, Henry Ford perfected the assembly line for the manufacture of automobiles.

The results of this enormous industrial transformation continue to stir debate. Did industrialization improve American life? Without doubt, many American consumers benefited from the increased availability of inexpensive manufactured goods. Some individuals made fabulous fortunes for themselves and their families. Moreover, through the expanding influence of powerful corporations, the United States increasingly took a dominant role in world markets and politics.

Industrialization also had negative effects, however. Industry's constant quest for more efficient means of mass production reduced workers' control over their jobs. The reliance on fossil fuels for power led to pollution and other environmental damage. The rising global importance of American corporations led the U.S. government into imperialistic adventures beyond its own borders that brought hardship and suffering to groups of native peoples in other countries. Some Americans resisted these changes, but most adjusted to them. Today it is impossible even to imagine a world without industrialization.

SEE ALSO

Agriculture; Antitrust laws; Carnegie, Andrew; Consumer culture; Electricity; Ford, Henry; Inventions; Labor; Mining; Railroads; Regulation; Science and technology; Taylor, Frederick Winslow; Telephone and telegraph; Transportation, public; Rockefeller, John D.; Roosevelt, Theodore

FURTHER READING

Jacob, Margaret C. *Scientific Culture and the Making of the Industrial West.* New York: Oxford University Press, 1997.

Kanigel, Robert. *The One Best Way: Frederick Winslow Taylor and the Enigma of Efficiency.* New York: Viking, 1997.

Noble, David F. *America by Design: Science, Technology, and the Rise of Corporate Capitalism.* New York: Knopf, 1977.

Porter, Glenn. *The Rise of Big Business, 1860–1920.* Wheeling, Ill.: Harlan Davidson, 1992.

Influenza epidemic (1918)

MORE APPROPRIATELY called a pandemic, because it spread around the world, the influenza epidemic of 1918 killed more people than World War I. It also killed more people than the great bubonic plague (Black Death) that swept Europe in the 14th century. Infecting 28 percent of all Americans and most deadly for people ages 20 to 40, this flu killed an estimated 675,000 Americans, 10 times as many as died in the world war. Half of the American soldiers lost in Europe died from the influenza virus, not from battle wounds.

The first flu outbreak occurred in a military camp in Kansas. From there, troop shipments spread the flu to Europe and then back to the United States, where it hit the civilian population in the fall of 1918. The disease incubated rapidly, attacking the throat and lungs, and in its most virulent form killing within a day or two. Because neither antibiotics nor respirators were available in 1918, medical personnel were almost powerless to help stricken patients. Influenza swept through North America, Europe, Asia, Africa, Brazil, and the South Pacific. A particularly deadly outbreak in Spain

in May 1918 gave the disease its nickname, the Spanish flu.

Accustomed to wartime restrictions on their behavior and mobility, Americans cooperated with government orders banning public meetings and requiring health certificates for train journeys. Many stopped going to theaters and motion-picture shows.

By the end of 1919, the disease had run its course, leaving more than 20 million people dead around the world. Recent research suggests that the number may more accurately be around 40 million.

SEE ALSO

Health, public; Science and technology; World War I

FURTHER READING

Barry, John M. *The Great Influenza: The Epic Story of the Deadliest Plague in History.* New York: Viking, 2004.

Crosby, Alfred W. *America's Forgotten Pandemic: The Influenza of 1918.* New York: Cambridge University Press, 1989.

International Ladies' Garment Workers' Union

FOUNDED IN 1900, the International Ladies' Garment Workers' Union (ILGWU) organized the mostly Jewish

Masked workers at a California teachers' college attempt to protect themselves and their food preparations from possible contagion during the great influenza epidemic in 1918.

and Italian immigrant workers who made women's dresses, coats, shirts, and undergarments. In the ILGWU's early days, most of its members were men, but between 1909 and 1911, two spectacularly successful New York City strikes staged by women garment makers—the so-called uprising of the 20,000—convinced the union that women would make courageous members. Using women organizers, they enrolled women workers by the thousands. By 1916, ILGWU membership was 50 percent female.

The ILGWU survived economic downturns and a backlash movement by factory owners. It also survived political dissension among its own ranks, as anarchists, socialists, and communists struggled for years to control both the union's ideology and its tactics. In 1910, attorney Louis Brandeis, who later became a Supreme Court justice, acted as an arbitrator and engineered a court settlement between the ILGWU and several manufacturers. The settlement, called the Protocol of Peace, established grievance procedures for settling labor disputes and won national respect for the ILGWU. By the mid-1920s, the ILGWU had become one of the most powerful unions in all of organized labor, securing benefits for its members such as pension funds, health care, education, and cultural activities. By the early 1940s, it had more than 300,000 members. Today the ILGWU is a member of the Union of Needletrades, Industrial and Textile Employees (UNITE).

SEE ALSO

Labor union movement; Strikes

FURTHER READING

Dubinsky, David, and A. H. Raskin. *David Dubinsky: A Life With Labor.* New York: Simon & Schuster, 1977.
McCreesh, Carolyn Daniel. *Women in the Campaign to Organize Garment Workers, 1880–1917.* New York: Garland, 1985.

Tyler, Gus. *Look for the Union Label: A History of the International Ladies' Garment Workers' Union.* Armonk, N.Y.: M. E. Sharpe, 1995.

International relations

IN THE EARLY 19th century, the Monroe Doctrine served as the chief guiding principle of U.S. foreign policy. Proclaimed in 1823 by President James Monroe, the doctrine announced that the United States would resist any effort by a European power to impose its rule in the Western Hemisphere. As American power increased after the Civil War, Presidents and secretaries of state (the cabinet officer in charge of foreign policy) enlarged the scope of the doctrine. Increasingly, they used it to justify both the expansion of U.S. territory westward as well as strategic interventions into the affairs of other countries.

Various elements in American society combined to favor territorial expansion. Early in the 19th century, a strong belief in Manifest Destiny—or the God-given right to settle all the way to the Pacific Ocean—had propelled American expansion westward. By the late 1800s, some Americans were appealing to this same idea as a justification for moving beyond the nation's natural borders and across the globe. American business interests, increasingly competitive with advanced European countries for markets and investment opportunities abroad, supported this idea of a New Manifest Destiny. Advocates of a strong navy also pressed for expansion. After convincing Congress to fund a major modernization and growth program, navy officials argued that the United States now needed foreign outposts on which to build coaling, repair, and supply stations for the new fleet.

Strategic considerations lent further support to expansionism. As advanced European countries stepped up their economic, political, and military incursions into Africa and Asia, American policy makers felt that the United States should take similar steps in order to keep up. And finally, cultural assumptions about the superiority of U.S. civilization created a climate of opinion favorable to expansion. Some Americans believed that the next natural step after having conquered the western frontier was to extend American virtues and economic supremacy to less developed nations.

Victorian attitudes toward gender may also have influenced foreign policy. Worried that American men had grown "soft" after the closing of the frontier and the end of the Indian Wars, expansionists argued for an aggressive foreign policy that would bring glory to the nation's young manhood.

Expansionism as a key element in U.S. foreign policy arrived full-blown in the 1890s. During this decade the U.S. government used the navy to protect American shippers and sailors during rebellions in Brazil and Chile. In 1895, President Grover Cleveland invoked the Monroe Doctrine in warning Great Britain to cease disputing a boundary between Venezuela and the colony of British Guiana. The British backed down, in effect recognizing American dominance in the Western Hemisphere.

U.S. involvement in the Cuban rebellion for independence against Spain dominated international relations at the end of the 19th century. Aroused by journalistic exposés of Spain's mistreatment of Cuban citizens, Americans began to put pressure on their government to intervene.

Business owners also urged President William McKinley to protect their investments in Cuba. At first McKinley hesitated, unsure whether the United States could afford to go to war. A broad cross-section of Americans who supported Cuban freedom eventually convinced him to agree to a declaration of war.

The Spanish-American War lasted from April to August 1898. Congress declared that the United States had no desire for "sovereignty, jurisdiction, or control" over Cuba. Yet, at the end of the conflict, with Spain defeated, U.S. troops remained in Cuba as an army of occupation until 1902. Until 1934, the United States retained the right to intervene in Cuba's political and economic affairs. In the flush of victory from the Spanish-American War, President McKinley also approved the full annexation of Hawaii.

As a further consequence of the war, the United States took control of Guam, the Philippines, and Puerto Rico, all former Spanish colonies. Almost immediately, Americans assumed the role of the imperial power they had just defeated. Filipino rebels, who had been fighting against Spain, now turned to fighting Americans. From 1899 to 1902, the military campaign to put down the Filipino insurrection proved deadlier and more expensive than the brief combat in the Caribbean.

In the early 20th century, the U.S. government once again expanded the meaning of the Monroe Doctrine. President Theodore Roosevelt wanted to defend Latin and Central American nations against threats by European powers to collect debts or put down rebellions. In a message to Congress, later known as the Roosevelt Corollary to the Monroe Doctrine, Roosevelt denied any interest in acquiring more territory. But, he continued, if stronger nations intervene in the affairs of the Western Hemisphere, the United States would be forced to exercise "an international police power." In other words, the United States would intervene militarily to prevent intervention by others.

When Roosevelt later described the main ideas behind his foreign policy, he liked to quote the African proverb, "Speak softly and carry a big stick." For him, the "big stick" was the American navy. During his two terms in office he doubled the navy's size. He also vigorously pursued control over a canal linking the Atlantic to the Pacific. The building of this canal across the isthmus of Panama required not only great American expenditures in money and manpower but complex diplomatic negotiations in the region. The canal was not completed until 1914. By then, U.S. intervention in Latin America had become a routine occurrence. Americans would retain control of the Panama Canal until the year 2000, when it reverted to the Panamanian government.

In addition to acquiring new territories, the United States flexed international muscle in other parts of the world. During the 1890s, the world's great powers—Britain, France, Germany, Japan, and Russia—partitioned a weak China into "spheres of influence" which they dominated both economically and militarily. Anxious to have access to China's vast markets, in 1899 U.S. Secretary of State John Hay, an ardent expansionist, asked each nation to allow open international trade within its sphere of influence and to maintain China's territorial integrity and sovereignty.

In May 1900, before the powers could agree on such a policy, a popular uprising, the Boxer Rebellion, broke out in China. Hoping to rid China of all "foreign devils," the

insurgents killed hundreds of Europeans, including missionaries, and many Chinese Christians. Then they laid siege to Beijing's foreign legations. The United States transferred 5,000 troops from the Philippines to join a multinational force, which broke the siege in August. The rebellion ended shortly thereafter. Impressed with the recent display of American military might, the five powers agreed to Hays's Open Door policy, a concept that became a major new theme in U.S. foreign policy.

Roosevelt's successor, William Howard Taft, and his Secretary of State, Philander Knox, wanted to make the United States a commercial and financial world power. To this end, they sought to keep the open door in China and maintain stability in Latin America. They intended to use U.S. economic rather than military power to achieve these goals. Calling the new presidential policy "substituting dollars for bullets," Taft and Knox arranged for private bank loans to those countries that would accept American financial advisors and institute modern banking and tax systems and democratic governments. Taft's critics derisively called the policy "Dollar Diplomacy."

On coming to office in 1913, President Woodrow Wilson promised to remain as distant from foreign entanglements as possible but to intervene forcefully when U.S. interests were involved. Nonetheless, American interventionism in the Western Hemisphere continued. A cycle of revolution and dictatorship in Mexico that had begun in 1911 concerned U.S. investors, who held 43 percent of all Mexican property. They pressed Wilson to intervene militarily, and he did so, reluctantly. American troops then became caught up in several violent incidents that

accomplished little good and united warring Mexican factions against the United States. The leader of Mexican peasant rebels, Francisco "Pancho" Villa, began terrorizing Americans in Mexico and raiding border towns in the United States. On March 9, 1916, his men crossed the U.S. border into Columbus, New Mexico, burned the town, and killed more than 15 people. A military force under General John J. Pershing pursued Villa into Mexico but was never able to find him, as the local population refused to divulge his whereabouts. In the end, Wilson's interference in Mexican affairs soured relations between the two countries for years to come.

When war broke out in Europe in 1914, maintaining American security through ensuring stable governments in the Caribbean seemed increasingly important. To this end, American marines entered Haiti in 1915 and the Dominican Republic. By sending these troops, Wilson hoped to compel these nations' leaders to establish democratic governments and meet their financial obligations to other countries. Although American troops remained in the Dominican Republic until 1925 and in Haiti until 1934, Wilson's goal was never achieved.

After several years of insisting upon American neutrality in the Euro-

pean war, President Wilson finally decided that the United States had to intervene in order "to make the world safe for democracy." U.S. participation in World War I began in April 1917 and lasted until November 1918. Most Americans fought on the western front, but Wilson did send some troops into Russia in the middle of the Russian Civil War (1918–20), ostensibly to protect Allied soldiers and Western business interests, but also to thwart the Bolsheviks (communist revolutionaries), whose radical ideology and violent tactics Wilson opposed. As it turned out, there were never enough Allied troops in Russia to have any effect.

At the war's conclusion, Wilson played a central role in devising the terms of peace and charting a new course for both American and international diplomatic relations. His peace program of Fourteen Points called for an end to secret alliances, freedom of the seas, reductions in armaments, and attention to the rights of native populations. Wilson also demanded "self-determination" for nationalities previously under the control of a stronger country, although this demand seemed ironically at odds with Wilson's attempts to intervene in revolutionary Russia.

Finally, Wilson called for a League of Nations, an international body that would settle disputes among nations

Flanked by stone elephants, U.S. troops pause on the road to Beijing, China, in 1900. Their objective was to crush the Boxer Rebellion, an indigenous uprising aimed at ridding China of foreigners.

Delegates from all the countries involved in World War I, including the United States, England, France, Germany, and Italy, meet in the Palace of Versailles outside Paris to negotiate a peace treaty.

and thereby secure the peace for all time. Despite wide approval of Wilson's vision of a new kind of international relations, Congress refused to accept U.S. participation in the league or ratify the Treaty of Versailles, which officially ended the war. Instead, Congress made a separate peace with each enemy nation. In the war's aftermath, the world's major powers were all in debt to the United States for their war expenses. As the world's most important creditor, the United States played a dominant role in subsequent international affairs.

SEE ALSO

Cleveland, Grover; Imperialism; League of Nations; McKinley, William; Navy, U.S.; Panama Canal; Pershing, John J.; Roosevelt, Theodore; Spanish-American War; Taft, William Howard; Versailles, Treaty of (1919); Wilson, Woodrow T.; World War I

FURTHER READING

Hoganson, Kristin L. *Fighting for American Manhood: How Gender Politics Provoked the Spanish-American and Philippine-American Wars.* New Haven: Yale University Press, 1998.
LaFeber, Walter. *The New Empire: An Interpretation of American Expansion, 1860–1898.* Ithaca, N.Y.: Cornell University Press, 1963.
Levin, Norman Gordon. *Woodrow Wilson and World Politics: America's Response to War and Revolution.* New York: Oxford University Press, 1968.

Rosenberg, Emily S. *Financial Missionaries to the World: The Politics and Culture of Dollar Diplomacy, 1900–1930.* Cambridge, Mass.: Harvard University Press, 1999.

Inventions

"THE WHOLE modern system of existence," declared an 1890 article in *Scientific American* magazine, "depends on the inventors." During the Gilded Age, American inventors vaulted to international attention. They made a strong impression at the 1876 Centennial Exposition in Philadelphia, where they showcased such newfangled marvels as the typewriter, the telephone, and the largest steam engine ever built. The exposition helped the United States shed its unsophisticated frontier image and establish itself in the eyes of the world as a modern industrial power teeming with valuable new ideas. By the start of the next century, inventors such as Alexander Graham Bell, Thomas Edison, and the Wright brothers had become American heroes.

The United States patent system, created by Congress in 1790, played a key role in the success of American inventions. Patents protected an inventor's ability to profit from his work. Designed to strike a balance between the rights of the individual and the interests of society, the system granted inventors exclusive control of their inventions for a certain number of years. It required, however, that inventors disclose the workings of each invention so that others could manufacture competing products after the exclusive period had expired. In this way, the patent system guaranteed individuals a fair reward for their creative endeavors while preventing the rise of monopolies. By 1880, the U.S. Patent Office was issuing about 500 patents every week as inventors and their financial backers flocked to bring new ideas to market.

Not all of the period's pathbreaking inventions originated in the United States. The first automobiles and motion picture projectors came from Europe, and Guglielmo Marconi, an Italian, invented the first usable radio. By 1903, Marconi had set up a radio transmitter on Cape Cod in Massachusetts. The transmitter enabled President Theodore Roosevelt to radio his greetings to King Edward VII in England. The first U.S. radio station began operation in 1920. Nikola Tesla, an American scientist of Serbian descent, helped to spur the growth of the electrical power industry by inventing efficient systems for generating and transmitting electricity. Tesla also vied with Marconi for recognition as the inventor of the radio. The U.S. Patent Office recognized the claims of both men at different times, but Tesla was never as financially successful as his Italian rival.

In 1892 Herman Hollerith patented this keyboard punch for recording data. Entirely hand operated, this relatively simple device anticipated today's complex computers.

Gilded Age inventions brought dramatic changes. In the 1870s, people rode in horse-drawn vehicles and lit their homes with wax candles or oil lamps. Gaslights illuminated city streets at night and the only entertainment options involved personal attendance at live events. Long-distance communication relied on letters and telegrams, the railroads were the most advanced mode of transportation, and the only known way to fly was to use a balloon. By 1920, however, farmers worked their fields with gasoline-powered tractors, automobiles had dis-

placed horses on the nation's roads, airplanes were a familiar sight in the skies, and the glow of electric lightbulbs and the ring of telephones filled many homes. People were watching motion pictures, tuning in radio broadcasts, and listening to phonograph records. On a grimmer note, many states replaced their gallows with the electric chair, and advances in military technology, such as the machine gun and armored tank, had made World War I the greatest bloodbath in human history.

SEE ALSO

Airplane; Bell, Alexander Graham; Edison, Thomas Alva; Electricity; Motion pictures; Roosevelt, Theodore; Science and technology; Telephone and telegraph; Transportation, public; World's fairs and exhibitions; World War I; Wright, Wilbur and Orville

FURTHER READING

Cowan, Ruth Schwartz. *A Social History of American Technology.* New York: Oxford University Press, 1996.

Hughes, Thomas P. *American Genesis: A Century of Invention and Technological Enthusiasm, 1870–1970.* Chicago: University of Chicago Press, 2004.

Van Dulken, Stephen. *American Inventions: A History of Curious, Extraordinary, and Just Plain Useful Patents.* New York: New York University Press, 2004.

Ives, Charles Edward

- *Born: Oct. 20, 1874, Danbury, Conn.*
- *Education: Yale College, B.A., 1898*
- *Accomplishments: Pulitzer Prize for Third Symphony (1947)*
- *Died: May 19, 1954, New York, N.Y.*

A COMPOSER of modern concert music, Charles Ives grew up learning to play several instruments. The musical experiments of his father George Ives, a bandmaster, choir director, and music teacher, influenced Charles's musical development. In one experiment,

George had his children sing in one key while he accompanied them in another. In another, he marched two bands past one another playing different tunes.

Young Ives became a brilliant organist. At thirteen he began to compose short pieces and at fourteen he became the youngest paid church organist in Connecticut. As a student at Yale College, he studied organ and composition yet had energy left to hold a church organist position, play intramural sports, and write light pieces for college entertainments.

Warned by his father against a career in music in which it was hard to make a living, Ives went into the insurance business. He was successful in this field, ultimately establishing his own firm, but writing music remained a major activity. He also served as a church organist and choirmaster. In 1908, he married Harmony Twichell, a settlement-house nurse. They adopted a daughter 10 years later. As the years passed, Ives spent more time composing. In addition to using his father's experiments in his pieces, he also incorporated gospel, fiddle, and patriotic tunes, folk music, hymns, church bells, marches, and ragtime. Much of his musical output, which included symphonies, string quartets, sonatas, and songs, took its themes from everyday New England life and American history. One piece, the *Country Band March* (1903), playfully demonstrated the musical mistakes of small-town bandsmen. His most popular piece, *Three Places in New England* (1914), evoked scenes from the Civil War and the American Revolution, as well as the peaceful Massachusetts countryside.

Ives's special contribution to American music lay in his melding of traditional musical forms with sounds from everyday life— church bells, worshipers singing at outdoor camp meetings, bands marching at holiday time. Some of his music was too dissonant for audiences at the time. It combined different meters and keys played at the same time and used tone clusters, or masses of notes very close to one another.

Plagued by illness, Ives wrote his last new piece in 1926 and retired from business by 1930. He spent his final years revising earlier pieces and promoting the performance of modern music. As audiences grew more accustomed to the sounds of modern music, they became more accepting of his work. Even though his compositions received few performances during his lifetime, they are now heard often in concert halls.

SEE ALSO
Music

FURTHER READING
Perlis, Vivian. *Charles Ives Remembered: An Oral History.* New Haven: Yale University Press, 1974.
Swafford, Jan. *Charles Ives: A Life with Music.* New York: Norton, 1996.

Japanese Americans

SEE Asian Americans

Jim Crow

JIM CROW was originally the name of an African American character regularly featured in minstrel shows before the Civil War. White actors in blackface usually portrayed him as an irresponsible buffoon. The term *Jim Crow* became a racial slur associated with African Americans, and by 1900 it had come to apply to the southern laws that codified

This 1913 cartoon mocks the Jim Crow laws that enforced racial segregation in public spaces. White Southerners ride alongside an airplane pilot, while black passengers crowd into a separate compartment towed behind the plane.

and reinforced long-standing customs of racial segregation and disfranchisement. Interestingly, although Jim Crow laws are usually associated with the South, they actually began in the North in 1841, when Massachusetts allowed railroad companies to separate black and white passengers, a practice discontinued after the Civil War.

Throughout the South, where Jim Crow was firmly entrenched, the laws officially separated the races in public places and institutions, such as schools, parks, public transportation, and public restrooms. Waiting rooms, water fountains, and the entrances to public libraries, theaters, and courthouses all displayed "Whites Only" and "Colored" signs. Jim Crow laws not only enforced the subordinate position of black people in southern society, but they also facilitated the disfranchisement of African American males. By using such tactics as "white primaries," where only whites could vote in primary elections, southern white supremacists could make sure that the only candidates listed on the ballot on election day would be segregationists. Setting up polling places in venues designated as "white" was another way to keep black males from voting. The laws that kept segregation in place were not fully dismantled until the

Civil Rights Act of 1964, which forbade discrimination in employment, education, and public spaces on account of race or skin color, and the Voting Rights Act of 1965, which mandated a nationwide prohibition against denying or abridging the right to vote on the basis of literacy tests.

SEE ALSO

African Americans; Civil rights; Law; Race relations; Segregation; South, the; Transportation, public

FURTHER READING

DuBois, W. E. B. *Black Reconstruction.* 1935. Reprint, New York: Free Press, 1998.
Litwack, Leon. *Trouble in Mind: Black Southerners in the Age of Jim Crow.* New York: Knopf, 1998.
Packard, Jerrold M. *American Nightmare: The History of Jim Crow.* New York: St. Martin's, 2002.
Woodward, C. Vann. *The Strange Career of Jim Crow.* 3rd rev. ed. New York: Oxford University Press, 1974.

Jones, Mary Harris ("Mother")

• *Born: around 1837, Cork, Ireland*
• *Education: high school*
• *Accomplishments: cofounder, Social Democratic party (1898); cofounder, Industrial Workers of the World (1905); labor organizer, United Mine Workers (1900–1904, 1911–22); author,* Autobiography of Mother Jones *(1925)*
• *Died: Nov. 30, 1930, Silver Spring, Md.*

MARY HARRIS emigrated from Ireland to Canada with her family in the late 1830s and later moved to the United States. She worked as a seamstress and schoolteacher before marrying iron molder and union activist George E. Jones in 1861.

In 1867, Mary Jones lost her husband and all four of her children in a yellow fever epidemic. Attempting to recover from this tragedy, Jones eventually found her calling in the labor movement. She took a particular interest in miners, embracing their issues, which focused on a living wage and safer working conditions. She traveled the country to encourage their militancy, lived with them in shanty towns, and offered aid and comfort to their families. Everywhere she went, people knew her as the "Miners' Angel" and began to call her Mother Jones. Coal company owners found her unstoppable. Denounced on the floor of the U.S. Senate as the "grandmother of all agitators," she responded that she "hoped to live to become the great-grandmother of agitators."

Mother Jones led strikes in coalfields from West Virginia to Colorado; she also joined striking garment workers, steelworkers, and railroad workers in their labor actions. She worked many years as a paid organizer for the United Mine Workers Union, helped to found the Industrial Workers of the World (IWW), and was a lecturer for the Socialist Party of America. She led a group of women armed with mops and brooms to rout strikebreakers in the Pennsylvania coalfields. She also organized a group of children to march all the way from the textile mills of Kensington, Pennsylvania, to Theodore Roosevelt's home on Long Island to call attention to the problems of child labor.

Jones' biggest successes can be attributed to her skills as a strike organizer, her personal charisma, and her

This photograph of Mother Jones emphasizes the gentle, grandmotherly appearance of the fiery labor activist, who exhorted striking workers, "Pray for the dead, and fight like hell for the living."

grand sense of theater. Her women's and children's marches brought national attention to the plight of child laborers and the desperation of families who tried to make ends meet on inadequate wages. She was arrested and jailed on many occasions and once convicted of conspiracy in a murder case. Officials commuted her 20-year prison sentence after an investigation found that the charges against her were false.

Jones was a small woman whose speeches were known for their emotional appeal and their humor, but occasionally she astonished audiences with her towering rage against injustice. Asked once to describe herself, she said, "I am not a humanitarian. I am a hell-raiser!" Mother Jones always claimed she had been born on May 1, 1830, and that is the date she recorded in her 1922 autobiography. Historians believe she aged herself by more than half a decade, however, so that when she died in 1930, most people thought she was 100 years old. The assumption that she had lived a century raising hell in service to the cause of social justice became an aspect of the Mother Jones mystique.

SEE ALSO

Industrial Workers of the World; Mining; Labor unions; Strikes; United Mine Workers of America

FURTHER READING

Gorn, Elliot J. *Mother Jones: The Most Dangerous Woman in America.* New York: Hill & Wang, 2001.

Jones, Mother. *The Autobiography of Mother Jones.* 1922. Reprint edition by Mary Field Parton. Chicago: C. H. Kerr, 1990.

———. *The Correspondence of Mother Jones.* Edited by Edward M. Steel. Pittsburgh, Pa.: University of Pittsburgh Press, 1985.

———. *The Speeches and Writings of Mother Jones.* Edited by Edward M. Steel. Pittsburgh, Pa.: University of Pittsburgh Press, 1988.

Joplin, Scott

- Born: 1867 or 1868, East Texas (probably near Marshall)
- Education: high school; musical studies, George R. Smith College (Sedalia, Mo.), 1895–97
- Accomplishments: composer, "The Maple Leaf Rag" (1899), "The Entertainer" (1902), and Treemonisha, (1910), among many other works; awarded a special Pulitzer Prize (1976)
- Died: Apr. 1, 1917, New York, N.Y.

A COMPOSER of popular music, Scott Joplin was the son of a former slave and a free-born African American woman. At age seven, he began playing the piano in the house of a white family where his mother worked as a housemaid. He came to the attention of a German immigrant musician, who began to give him lessons. He soon developed into a talented singer and pianist. He also played the violin and cornet.

Although Joplin studied in the European classical musical tradition, when he began composing music, his inspiration came from ragtime. This music, which featured a syncopated rhythm set to a 4/4 march beat, was popular in the African American community. Joplin performed as a musician for 15 years—mainly in Sedalia, Missouri, where he had moved in 1880. He also toured, making a stop at the World's Columbian Exposition in Chicago in 1893, where his ragtime pieces drew favorable attention from white audiences. Beginning in 1895, some of his piano compositions were published. The piece that brought him fame, "The Maple Leaf Rag," was named for a black social club in Sedalia of which Joplin was a charter member. Over the next 10 years, he sold half a million copies of this piece,

The cover of "Searchlight Rag," a 1907 piano piece by Scott Joplin, mentions Joplin's "Maple Leaf Rag," published eight years earlier. "Maple Leaf Rag" was Joplin's most popular composition, remaining a favorite among piano students for many decades.

thereby earning a steady, although modest, royalty income.

Known as the King of Ragtime Writers, Joplin turned to compositions for the stage, including "The Ragtime Dance," "Swipesy Cakewalk," and "Sunflower Slow Drag." After moving in 1901 to St. Louis, a center for black ragtime, he began to write ragtime operas. A production of A Guest of Honor did not succeed, and its music has been lost. Treemonisha, a plea to the African American community to give up superstition and improve their lives through education, never received a full performance during his lifetime.

Joplin deserved much more success for his musicianship and creativity than he received. Sixty-four of his works had appeared before his death and he made some piano rolls of his music, but many of his other compositions and arrangements disappeared. By the 1910s, jazz was becoming more popular than ragtime. Interest in Joplin's work did not revive until the 1970s, when new recordings of his work came out and the producers of the film The Sting used his music in the film's score. The Pulitzer Prize

Board awarded him a special citation in 1976 "for his contributions to American music," and the U.S. Post Office issued a stamp in his honor in 1983.

SEE ALSO

Music

FURTHER READING

Berlin, Edward A. *King of Ragtime: Scott Joplin and His Era.* New York: Oxford University Press, 1994.

Haskins, James, and Kathleen Benson. *Scott Joplin.* New York: Stein & Day, 1978.

Preston, Katherine K. *Scott Joplin.* New York: Chelsea House, 1988.

Journalism

AMERICANS AT THE END of the 19th century got their information about current events from thousands of local newspapers and hundreds of nationally distributed magazines. Because radio broadcasts and newsreels shown in movie theaters would not become significant features of the nation's mass media until the 1920s, print journalism flourished unchallenged by other news sources. Readers in some major cities could choose from a dozen or more daily newspapers. Even small towns might have two or three daily or weekly papers.

Advances in technology helped bring about this media explosion. Linotype machines eliminated the slow chore of setting type by hand. Presses driven by steam engines and later by electricity could print thousands of pages in the time that it had once taken to produce a few dozen. A halftone printing process made it possible to reproduce photographs at low cost. A drop in postal rates and in the

NAVAL OFFICERS THINK THE MAINE WAS DESTROYED BY A SPANISH MINE.

price of paper further boosted production and distribution. Publishers could now mass-produce their papers, sell them cheaply to large numbers of readers, and use the circulation figures to attract advertising revenue.

The international telegraph network, which allowed news to travel quickly across great distances, shaped the style of journalistic writing. Correspondents saved on transmission costs by streamlining their reports and stating essential facts in opening sentences. This "pyramid" style of news writing—with the most important information at the top and supporting details underneath—is still in use today.

Many magazines aimed for special audiences. Women's magazines such as *Ladies' Home Journal, Good Housekeeping,* and *Woman's Home Companion* achieved national prominence

The February 17, 1898, front page of the New York Journal declares that Spain authorized the destruction of the U.S.S. Maine. Although that claim remained unproved, the hysteria it fueled helped to push the United States toward war.

during this time. These publications provided advertisements for products of interest to women; articles on fashion, beauty, health, housekeeping, and cooking; and fiction by well-known writers. *Harper's, McClure's, Collier's,* and *Cosmopolitan,* as well as *The Nation,* under its progressive editor E. L. Godkin, became known for their well-researched and well-written feature stories by top American writers. These magazines also published articles by muckrakers, journalists who exposed government and corporate corruption and specialized in analyzing social problems.

Smaller newspapers targeting ethnic audiences also expanded during this period. As millions of immigrants swelled the U.S. population, more than 1,300 newspapers in Yiddish, German, and other languages sprang up to serve them. Editors of African American newspapers, which multiplied in the years after Reconstruction, spoke out on the racial issues of their segregated era. For example, their *Colored Citizen,* a paper in Topeka, Kansas, editorialized against segregated schools as early as 1878, more than three-quarters of a century before the Supreme Court's landmark *Brown* v. *Board of Education* decision integrated Kansas schools. Journalist Ida B. Wells launched her 1890s crusade against lynching in the national black press.

Some newspaper publishers increased sales by filling their pages with sensationalism, such as stories of violent crime or sexual scandal. This type of reporting, designed not to inform readers but to arouse their passions, often diverted attention from the meaningful events of the day. Sometimes, however, it influenced national and international news. In the months leading up to the 1898 Spanish-American War, for example, two

major New York papers, William Randolph Hearst's *Journal* and Joseph Pulitzer's *World,* stirred up pro-war hysteria by publishing lurid accounts of Spanish atrocities against the people of Cuba, one of Spain's colonies, and unsubstantiated claims of Spain's involvement in the sinking of a U.S. ship, the *Maine*. At one point during the pre-war hysteria, the yellow press nicknamed General Valeriano Weyler, the Spanish governor of Cuba, "Butcher" Weyler. They never hesitated to attack him. One headline read, "WEYLER THROWS NUNS INTO PRISON. BUTCHER WAGES BRUTAL WARFARE ON HELPLESS WOMEN." Sensationalistic reporting came to be known as "yellow journalism," after the name of a comic strip character, the Yellow Kid, who appeared in both the *Journal* and the *World*.

Despite this trend toward yellow journalism, many journalists in this period strove to raise professional journalistic standards. The University of Missouri established the nation's first school of journalism in 1904. Reporters and editors increasingly embraced the goal of objective, unbiased reporting. Partisan journalism—newspapers linked to a particular political party—continued to thrive, but more and more newspapers worked hard at separating their editorial opinions from their factual reporting.

Investigative journalism got its start around the turn of the century, sometimes making heroes of reporters who risked their lives to get their stories. In 1887, Nellie Bly, who worked for the *New York World,* had herself committed to an asylum in order to write a story on the treatment of mental patients. A couple of years later, she took up a challenge to beat Jules

Verne's fictional globe traveler, Phileas Fogg, by traveling around the world in less than 80 days. Bly's breathtaking stories, telegraphed from distant ports, brought her international acclaim. She made the circuit in just 72 days.

The number of newspapers published in the United States peaked at about 2,600 dailies and 14,000 weeklies in the years just before World War I, then began a dramatic decline as many papers either merged with competitors or simply went out of business. Some newspaper owners, notably *Cleveland Press* publisher Edward Wyllis Scripps and *New York Journal* publisher William Randolph Hearst, bought large numbers of papers and created the first newspaper chains, which were media empires that owned publications in many different cities. With many independently owned papers disappearing from American cities, these chains would come to dominate the 20th-century newspaper business. A notable exception was the *Emporia Gazette* in Kansas, whose owner-editor, William Allen White, maintained his local newspaper's independence from chain ownership. Speaking through editorials in the *Gazette,* and through articles he contributed to popular national magazines, White himself became a spokesman for the virtues of life in small-town America.

SEE ALSO

Hearst, William Randolph; Muckrakers; Pulitzer, Joseph; Science and technology; Spanish-American War; Telephone and telegraph; Wells-Barnett, Ida B.

FURTHER READING

Campbell, W. Joseph. *Yellow Journalism: Puncturing the Myths, Defining the Legacies.* New York: Praeger, 2001.
Conolly-Smith, Peter. *Translating America: An Immigrant Press Visualizes American Popular Culture, 1890–1918.* Washington, D.C.: Smithsonian, 2004.
Emery, Michael, Edwin Emery, and Nancy L. Roberts. *The Press and America: An Interpretive History of the Mass Media.* 9th ed. Boston: Allyn & Bacon, 1999.
Kitch, Carolyn. *Pages from the Past: History and Memory in American Magazines.* Chapel Hill: University of North Carolina Press, 2005.
Pride, Armistead S., and Clint C. Wilson. *History of the Black Press.* Washington, D.C.: Howard University Press, 1997.
Smythe, Ted Curtis. *The Gilded Age Press, 1865–1900.* New York: Praeger, 2003.

Jubilee Singers

IN THE EARLY 1870s, Fisk University in Nashville, Tennessee—a school founded in 1865 to educate former slaves—was in financial trouble. In 1871, nine of its students formed a group they called the Jubilee Singers to raise money by touring churches and private homes. At first they sang only ballads and patriotic tunes. Soon, their director, George White, persuaded them to include slave songs (later called "Negro spirituals") in their programs. Performed in arrangements inspired by European musical traditions, these songs proved highly popular with white audiences.

The group not only preserved the memory of the spirituals but through the financial success of their tours

The Fisk Jubilee Singers, students at all-black Fisk University in Nashville, Tennessee, managed to raise enough funds with their concerts to save their financially endangered college.

funded the construction of Fisk University's first permanent building, Jubilee Hall, which still stands. It features a ceiling-to-floor portrait of the original Jubilee Singers. Queen Victoria of England commissioned this portrait and gave it to Fisk in memory of the group's command performance before her in 1873. A modern version of the Fisk Jubilee Singers is still active today.

SEE ALSO
African Americans; College and universities; Music

FURTHER READING
Cooper, Michael L. *Slave Spirituals and the Jubilee Singers.* New York: Clarion, 2001.
Ward, Andrew. *Dark Midnight When I Rise: The Story of the Jubilee Singers, Who Introduced the World to the Music of Black America.* New York: Farrar, Straus & Giroux, 2000.

Judaism

IN 1880, SOME 230,000 to 300,000 Jews lived in the United States. Over the next 40 years, as thousands of Jews fleeing religious persecution in central and eastern Europe and Russia arrived, these numbers grew dramatically. By 1920, approximately 3.5 million Jews lived in America, constituting slightly over 3 percent of the total population.

The American Jewish community was divided along ethnic and social class lines. The earliest American Jews were of Spanish or Portuguese ancestry. Sephardim, as they were known, considered themselves of higher social status than the Ashkenazim, or German and central European Jews, who began arriving in the early 1800s. Having started their lives in America as peddlers and merchants, by the late 1800s many German Jews had moved

into well-established positions in American banking, finance, and retail businesses. Even so, Sephardim still saw themselves as the "aristocrats" of American Jewry, and their religious rite dominated American Jewish practice.

At the end of the 19th century, increased immigration of Jews from rural villages (*shtetls*) in eastern Europe and Russia added new divisions to American Jewish life. Genuinely concerned to help their newly arrived co-religionists adjust to American life, German Jews gave them charity and provided them with jobs. They also financed settlement-house programs to teach English to the newcomers (often called "greenhorns") and help them learn skills for succeeding in America. At the same time, they worried that the old-fashioned dress, customs, and manners of the newcomers would increase anti-Jewish attitudes among native-born Americans. For their part, the new Jewish immigrants were ambivalent about the aid they received. While some newcomers rushed to become "Americanized," others accused their benefactors of trying to erase their original cultures and exploiting them as workers. Bitterness between older and newer Jewish immigrants troubled the American Jewish community for several generations.

Differences over religious practice further divided American Jewry. Laws regulating daily life and enforced by rabbis (the religious leaders of Jewish communities) formed a central part of Judaism. These laws covered such issues as the status of women, male circumcision, and banning work during the Sabbath. Dietary laws required Jews to keep kosher, that is, to eat only flesh slaughtered under rabbinical supervision, to keep dairy and meat products completely separate, and to abstain from "unclean" foods, such as

While the rabbi listens, a class in Scranton, Pennsylvania, in the 1880s studies for their confirmation. The boy in the center is reading from the Torah, part of Jewish holy scripture.

pork and shellfish, as called for in the Old Testament. In the United States, with the emphasis on secularism (separation of church and state) and individual freedom of choice, rabbis found enforcing these laws difficult.

As rabbinical authority declined in America, some Jews began to feel that much of Jewish law had become outmoded. Among these were women no longer willing to accept the traditional practice of being relegated to the balcony during religious services or excluded from the *minyan* (the minimum number of 10 necessary for a worship service). Some of these women even wanted rabbinical training.

In 1875 Reform Jews established Hebrew Union College (HUC) to train rabbis. In the 1880s, Reform Jews formed a Central Conference of American Rabbis under Rabbi Isaac Mayer Wise, their chief spiritual leader. By the 1890s, some Reform Jewish congregations had introduced mixed seating, mixed choirs, and confirmation ceremonies for girls. Further reforms brought about the relaxation of Jewish dietary laws and introduced services

conducted primarily in English instead of Hebrew. In 1890, in Spokane, Washington, Rachel ("Ray") Frank, a teacher in a Jewish Sabbath School and a well-known California journalist, became the first Jewish woman to preach sermons in a synagogue. She studied at HUC for a few months in 1893 but was never ordained.

Yet another group of Jews sought some accommodation to modern American life while preserving more of the past. Called Conservatives, this group developed an intermediary position between Reform and Orthodox (traditional) Judaism. Their movement took root in another rabbinical training institution, the Jewish Theological Seminary (JTS), founded in 1888. In 1913, Conservatives established an umbrella organization for their congregations, the United Synagogue, and in 1919, a professional organization for their rabbis, the Rabbinic Assembly. Conservative Judaism ultimately drew the allegiance of the largest number of American Jews.

Meanwhile, Orthodox Jews were far from idle. In 1897 they founded the Union of Orthodox Congregations, and in 1902 the Union of Orthodox Rabbis. Their *yeshivas,* or schools for the study of Judaic texts and laws, eventually led in 1928 to the founding of Yeshiva University in New York.

The last group of Jews to form was the smallest. Called Reconstructionist, this group took shape around the ideas of Rabbi Mordecai Kaplan, who in 1909 was the head of the JTS's Teacher's Institute. Kaplan hoped to unite Jews around an understanding of their common cultural legacy while incorporating American ideals of equality and democracy and adapting to changing social, political, and cultural conditions. Instead of seeing the heart of Judaism as obedience to God's commands, he taught that Judaism represented an entire civilization that its followers should feel free to study and interpret on their own. Kaplan saw the synagogue less as a place of worship than as a center, organized democratically with a voluntary membership and an elected leadership, in which the community of worshipers discovered their own religious authority. In 1922, he organized the Society for the Advancement of Judaism to promote his ideas. Reconstructionist Judaism did not have its own rabbinic college until 1968.

Anti-Semitism (prejudice against Jews), part of Western culture since the Middle Ages, plagued all Jews, no matter which branch claimed their allegiance. In the early 20th century, resort hotels and clubs excluded Jews, elite schools and colleges had quotas on the numbers of Jews they would accept, real estate agents conspired to keep them out of certain neighborhoods (a practice called "redlining"), and firms would not hire them. Hate groups such as the Ku Klux Klan were as virulently anti-Jewish as they were anti-black and anti-Catholic.

Despite such prejudice, many individuals of Jewish origin earned national reputations in the Gilded Age and Progressive Era. Poet Emma Lazarus, who wrote the "New Colossus" sonnet engraved onto the base of the Statue of Liberty, was descended from one of America's earliest Sephardic Jewish settlers. Lillian Wald, a descendant of Reform Jews from Cincinnati, Ohio, founded the Henry Street social settlement house on New York's Lower East Side. Rabbi Stephen Wise led movements to bring ideas of social reform into Judaism. Belle Moskowitz organized the campaign of the first Catholic to run for President, New York governor Alfred E. Smith.

An American Zionist movement promoting a Jewish state in the Holy Land began to take shape in the 1910s, as Jews uprooted by World War I sought a place of safety for themselves and future generations. After the war British leaders called for making Palestine, formerly part of the Ottoman Empire and home to some 20,000 to 25,000 Jews, into a national home for the Jewish people. In 1922, the League of Nations placed Palestine under a British mandate, or administration, that allowed more Jews to immigrate to the Holy Land. A tumultuous period followed, during which Muslims, Christian Arabs, and Jews in Palestine struggled to co-exist and Jews tried to prevent Palestine from becoming an Arab-majority state. The Holocaust, or the destruction of the European Jewish community during World War II, accelerated Jewish immigration to Palestine, which despite Arab opposition became the state of Israel in 1948. American Jews have been strong supporters of Israel's development ever since.

SEE ALSO
Immigration; Ku Klux Klan; Religion; Wald, Lillian

FURTHER READING

Diner, Hasia. *Jews in America.* New York: Oxford University Press, 1999.

Feingold, Henry. *Zion in America: The Jewish Experience from Colonial Times to the Present.* New York: Twayne, 1974.

Nadell, Pamela Susan. *Women Who Would Be Rabbis: A History of Women's Ordination, 1889–1985.* Boston: Beacon, 1998.

Sarna, Jonathan D. *American Judaism.* New Haven: Yale University Press, 2004.

Kelley, Florence

- *Born: Sept. 12, 1859, Philadelphia, Pa.*
- *Education: Cornell University, B.A., 1882; Northwestern University, LL.B., 1895*
- *Accomplishments: factory inspector, state of Illinois (1893–97); general secretary, National Consumers' League (1899–1932)*
- *Died: Feb. 17, 1932, Philadelphia, Pa.*

FLORENCE KELLEY was a national leader of the Progressive Era consumer movement. The daughter of a prominent Pennsylvania congressman, she was one of the first women to attend Cornell University. Failing to get into the University of Pennsylvania for graduate work because she was a woman, she eventually made her way to the University of Zurich in Switzerland. There she studied law and government, became a socialist, and married a medical student from Poland.

Upon her return to the United States with three children, her marriage fell apart. In 1891, Jane Addams accepted her as a resident of Hull House, a social settlement located in Chicago, and recommended her to the Illinois Bureau of Labor Statistics as an investigator of tenement sweatshops in the neighborhood. Kelley discovered children of all ages sewing garments in horrible conditions. The work rooms were so unsanitary that

an official brought in to witness them refused to enter, fearing he would get sick. In 1893, largely through Kelley's efforts, Illinois passed a law prohibiting child labor, limiting working hours for women, and controlling sweatshop conditions. Governor John Peter Altgeld put Kelley in charge of enforcing the law. Frustrated by the district attorney's refusal to prosecute cases against factory owners, Kelly earned a law degree in order to take legal action herself. Her successes were limited. In 1895 the Illinois Supreme Court struck down part of the factory inspection law, and when Governor Altgeld lost his bid for reelection in 1896 Kelley was not reappointed.

In 1899, the National Consumers' League, which investigated working conditions and worked for their improvement, invited Kelley to become its general secretary. In this role she spoke and published widely on the need to improve conditions for all wage-earners. She became a major force behind the passage of minimum wage legislation, which by 1913 had been adopted in nine states. In 1912, a federal Children's Bureau, designed in part by Kelley, became an agency in the Department of Commerce and Labor. The first federal agency to concern itself with children's welfare, the

Florence Kelley (third from left) and other women factory inspectors checked for safety violations in Illinois factories. Kelley inspired many women reformers to campaign for laws to protect women and children at work.

Bureau spearheaded the national campaign against child labor and for the improvement of maternal and child health. In 1918, when the Supreme Court struck down the nation's first prohibition against child labor (Keating-Owen Act), Kelley asked in despair, why are "seals, bears, reindeer, fish, wild game in the national parks, buffalo, [and] migratory birds all found suitable for federal protection, but not the children of our race and their mothers?" A powerful advocate for the just treatment of the weak and underprivileged, she persisted in her quest for a child labor amendment to the U.S. Constitution but was never able to achieve this goal.

SEE ALSO

Child labor; Children's Bureau, U.S.; Hull House; National Consumers' League

FURTHER READING

Goldmark, Josephine. *Impatient Crusader: Florence Kelley's Life Story.* Urbana: University of Illinois Press, 1953.
Sklar, Kathryn Kish. *Florence Kelley and the Nation's Work: The Rise of Women's Political Culture, 1830–1900.* New Haven: Yale University Press, 1995.

Knights of Labor

STARTED IN 1869 under the leadership of Uriah Stevens, the Knights of Labor was originally a brotherhood of workers united by secrecy and rituals. By the late 1870s, however, the Knights had abandoned secrecy and begun to organize both skilled and unskilled workers across entire industries. Idealistic and egalitarian in philosophy, the Knights stressed cooperation and inclusiveness. By the mid-1880s, they were welcoming women workers, African Americans, and even some employers to membership in their national organization. They excluded bankers, lawyers, and gamblers, however.

The Knights organized and facilitated a number of important boycotts and strikes, especially those involving the railroads. They sought equal pay for equal work, an eight-hour workday, and the abolition of child labor and convict labor. A primary goal was to educate both their own members and the American public about the dignity and worth of ordinary workers.

The organization reached its peak in the mid-1880s under the leadership of Terence Powderly, a master machinist and passionate labor organizer. In those years, it had more than 700,000 dues-paying members. The Knights' motto was "An injury to one is the concern of all."

The Knights of Labor foundered over internal disputes, mismanagement, and the loss of funds during unsuccessful strikes. Its reputation was severely damaged when the public blamed the Knights for the 1886 Chicago Haymarket riot, when policemen died in a bombing for which the Knights were not responsible. By 1900, membership had dropped to almost nothing, and the labor union movement had become closely identified with a powerful rival organization, the American Federation of Labor.

SEE ALSO

American Federation of Labor; Haymarket Square riot (1886); Labor; Labor unions; Railroads; Strikes

FURTHER READING

Fink, Leon. *Workingmen's Democracy: The Knights of Labor and American Politics.* Urbana: University of Illinois Press, 1983.
Foner, Philip S. *History of the Labor Movement in the United States.* Vol. 2. New York: International Publishers, 1955.
Weir, Robert E. *Beyond Labor's Veil: The Culture of the Knights of Labor.* University Park: Pennsylvania State University Press, 1996.

Ku Klux Klan

THE KU KLUX KLAN was the foremost of a number of white supremacist organizations that arose in the South after the Civil War in response to the upheaval in race relations. Members of the Klan hoped to turn back the clock, not to restore slavery but to prevent African Americans from achieving equality with whites.

Started in Tennessee in 1866 by a former Confederate general, Nathan Bedford Forrest, the Klan found its leaders among prominent southern citizens, professionals, merchants, and planters, as well as ex-army officers. *Ku-Klux* is a variation on the Greek *kuklos*, meaning circle. The term symbolized continuity and implied a secret circle or society.

The Klan rapidly moved from its social-club origins to activism and terror tactics. Wearing masks, robes, and cardboard hats, Klansmen rode out into the night, setting fires, destroying

Two armed Ku Klux Klan members wear robes and conceal their faces under masks. This picture was published in 1868, just two years after the Klan formed as a vigilante group dedicated to terrorizing black citizens and maintaining white supremacy.

property, and torturing and killing black Americans. They also attacked whites who were sympathetic to African Americans, especially Republicans from the North assisting with southern Reconstruction. At first, the Klan's objective was to stop African Americans from voting, a right guaranteed them in the 15th Amendment to the Constitution (1869). But the Klan and similar organizations also wanted to undermine any economic or social success African Americans might achieve. They targeted successful businessmen and black protection groups such as trade unions. By 1870, the Ku Klux Klan was playing a significant role in restoring white rule in several southern states.

In 1871, Representative Benjamin Butler of Massachusetts reported to Congress, "The Klan is inflicting summary vengeance on the colored citizens of these states by breaking into their houses at the dead of night, dragging them from their beds, torturing them in the most inhuman manner, and in many instances murdering." Congress responded with the Ku Klux Klan Act of 1871, which facilitated military suppression of Klan violence. But, by 1877, whites had regained control of the South, and the Klan subsided.

The Klan resurfaced and gained strength in 1915, following the success of Thomas Dixon's racist novel, *The Clansman* (1905), and the epic movie based on it, D. W. Griffith's *Birth of a Nation,* which celebrated white supremacy and the suppression and disfranchisement of African Americans. The National Association for the Advancement of Colored People dedicated itself to opposing Klan activities, but during the 1920s the Klan enrolled several million members, achieved political power nationwide, and expanded its campaign of hatred to include Jews, Roman Catholics, social-ists, and communists.

After almost disappearing during World War II, the Ku Klux Klan rose again to interfere with the civil rights movement of the 1960s. Ultimately unsuccessful, the Klan retreated once again, though it still has adherents and exists today in isolated pockets of the United States.

SEE ALSO

African Americans; National Association for the Advancement of Colored People; Race relations

FURTHER READING

Chalmers, David Mark. *Hooded Americanism: The History of the Ku Klux Klan.* New York: Franklin Watts, 1981.
MacLean, Nancy K. *Behind the Mask of Chivalry: The Making of the Second Ku Klux Klan.* New York: Oxford University Press, 1995.
Trelease, Allen W. *White Terror: The Ku Klux Klan Conspiracy and Southern Reconstruction.* Baton Rouge: Louisiana State University Press, 1971.
Wade, Wyn Craig. *The Fiery Cross: The Ku Klux Klan in America.* 1987. Reprint, New York: Oxford University Press, 1998.

Labor

THE WORD *labor* can be either a noun or a verb meaning "work." Used as a collective noun, *labor* also means the people who do the work. Groups of factory hands or farmworkers are sometimes referred to as labor. Collectively, the people who perform manual work for an industry, or even for a nation, make up the labor force.

By the late 1800s, industrialization had greatly expanded the need for workers in the United States. Between 1880 and 1910, while the U.S. population grew to more than 92 million, the nation's total labor force tripled,

reaching more than 35 million. The growth of industry and the growth of population were mutually dependent; both factors influenced the expansion of cities and the geographic mobility of working people. Many native-born Americans, for example, left their rural homes to find jobs in industrial cities. In Europe and in Latin America, people looked to the United States as a place where work was plentiful and immigrant labor would be welcome.

The situation for labor was far from straightforward, however. Because the supply of labor grew along with the population, the value of individual workers remained low. Most factory labor was unskilled, that is, workers could learn it on the job with little or no training. Employers could easily fire a worker and hire a replacement.

The growing labor force faced a number of issues. Work hours were long. Working conditions in factories, mines, and mills were often unsafe. The rate of industrial accidents was especially high in places where people worked close to huge machines, steam engines, open furnaces, explosives, or unstable mine shafts. By 1913, the industrial death rate stood at 61 per 100,000 workers. The areas with the worst records were the coal mines and the railroads. About 300 out of every 100,000 miners died in work accidents each year.

Even in safer occupations, work areas were often poorly lit, overcrowded, too cold or too hot. Workers were often poisoned by exposure to chemicals or toxic substances such as lead or phosphorus. In the relatively safe garment industry, the daily inhalation of airborne lint could damage the lungs. The incidence of contagious disease in garment workers was exceptionally high because they worked in cramped rooms with little ventilation.

In the early 1880s, there was no safety oversight in factories and no workers' compensation or accident insurance. Workers could sue employers if they were hurt, but such cases were difficult to win because employer negligence was hard to prove. The families of employees who died on the job had no guarantee of assistance; the average compensation for a fatal injury amounted to only about half a year's pay. Hours of work could be arbitrary, with seven-day weeks and 10- or 11-hour days common in some industries. There were no pension plans for retired workers. Finally, wages were too low to support most families, a situation that sometimes pushed young children into the industrial labor force to help supplement the family income.

Other aspects of industrial labor damaged the spirit even if they did not hurt the body. Large factories created an impersonal workplace; managers discouraged conversation or human interaction unrelated to the work at hand. Workers no longer paced their own work, as they had when they worked on farms or for themselves; instead, machines and conveyor belts set the pace of work. Performing one task over and over again, while an efficient mode of production, made work monotonous and meaningless. In the past, workers could make a pair of shoes or an armchair from start to finish and take pride in their finished product. Mechanization de-skilled the work, reducing it to labor performed for the sake of the wage and little else.

As the problems of industrial workers became more acute, in the late 1800s they also became more apparent to the public. Labor sought solutions in a number of ways. They organized unions to negotiate their

concerns with management. They used strikes and work stoppages to arouse public sympathy and get their points across when management refused to recognize their needs. Labor also turned to state and federal governments to pressure business owners to take more responsibility for their workers.

One subject of labor agitation was workplace safety. States initially responded to this concern by appointing factory inspectors, who had the authority to impose fines on factory owners who did not institute safety measures for their workers. In 1893, pressured by railroad regulators and workers, Congress passed the Safety Appliance Act, which mandated the development of better brakes and couplers for freight cars. These changes reduced the accident rate significantly.

After the turn of the century, labor's demands shifted from accident prevention in industry to accident compensation, mandated by law. Samuel Gompers, leader of the American Federation of Labor, and other labor advocates promoted "workmen's compensation" laws, a European idea. Instead of requiring injured workers to sue for damages in court, such laws would automatically compensate all

Young men and women make neckties in a tenement sweatshop in New York City. The photographer, Jacob Riis, helped expose the evils of sweatshop labor and the squalor of tenement life in the 1880s and 1890s.

injuries at a fixed rate, providing enough for medical care and lost wages. The federal government took the lead by establishing workmen's compensation for government employees involved in hazardous work. Congress passed the first federal Workmen's Compensation Act in 1916. States followed with their own policies, but workers' compensation laws did not appear in all states until after World War II.

In addition to pressuring the government for compensation and safety laws, labor leaders began demanding laws to regulate work hours and guarantee a minimum wage. The campaign for the eight-hour day, another idea that originated in Europe, began just after the Civil War. "Eight hours for work, eight hours for rest, eight hours for what we will," the slogan ran. The eight-hour day was a major focus of union agitation and strikes, including one that indirectly led to Chicago's Haymarket Square riot in 1886, when a bomb killed several policemen. When in 1916 Congress finally mandated an eight-hour day for railroad workers (the Adamson Act), other businesses and industries followed suit.

In 1912, under pressure from labor organizations and reformers, Massachusetts became the first state to institute a minimum hourly wage, initially applying it only to women and children. Employers had traditionally argued that minimum wages violated time-honored "freedom of contract" laws, which allowed workers and employers to set their own terms. The first minimum hourly wage was 14 cents an hour, an amount that seems small today but was an enormous boon to underpaid women workers, who had been making even less than that in many industries. Not until 1938 would Congress pass a federally mandated minimum wage law for all workers, setting the hourly wage at 25 cents.

Some reformers demanded that the government pass protective legislation specifically for women, including laws to prohibit night work. In *Muller* v. *Oregon* (1908), a case involving laundry workers, the Supreme Court ruled in favor of limiting women's work hours in order to protect their health and "maternal functions." Women labor leaders and reformers who had fought for such limits were pleased with the decision; others felt that protective legislation might end up limiting women's equal access to employment.

By 1900, Americans had begun to push for the regulation or elimination of child labor. Historians estimate that industrial labor in this period used 18 percent of the country's children aged 10 to 15. Children earned rock bottom wages and worked in terrible conditions that stunted their physical and mental growth and often left them injured. Most working-class families felt they had a right to send their children out to work and, in fact, depended on their children's wages. Nevertheless, a National Child Labor Committee, organized in 1904, kept up the pressure for reform. In response, some states did pass legislation, and Congress passed two laws in 1916 and 1918 limiting child labor. The Supreme Court declared both laws unconstitutional, however, and an attempt to end child labor through a constitutional amendment later failed. Changes to child labor came slowly and, in the end, came about more because of the diminishing need for child labor in industry than as a result of the earnest efforts to end it.

SEE ALSO
American Federation of Labor; Child labor; Haymarket Square riot (1886); Industry; Labor unions; Mining; Progressive movement; Railroads; Riis, Jacob; Work

FURTHER READING

Brody, David. *In Labor's Cause: Main Themes on the History of the American Worker.* New York: Oxford University Press, 1993.

Dubofsky, Melvyn, and Warren Van Tine, eds. *Labor Leaders in America.* Urbana: University of Illinois Press, 1987.

Freedman, Russell, and Lewis Hine, photographer. *Kids at Work: Lewis Hine and the Crusade against Child Labor.* New York: Clarion, 1994.

Le Blanc, Paul. *A Short History of the U.S. Working Class: From Colonial Times to the Twenty-First Century.* Amherst, N.Y.: Humanity Books, 1999.

Montgomery, David. *Worker's Control in America: Studies in the History of Work, Technology, and Labor Struggles.* New York: Cambridge University Press, 1979.

Weir, Robert E., ed. *Historical Encyclopedia of American Labor.* Westport, Conn.: Greenwood, 2004.

Labor unions

AMERICAN INDUSTRIAL workers began to form unions in the early 1800s. They believed they could win better wages and working conditions from business and factory owners if they made their demands as a group rather than confronting employers individually. They had a hard time establishing labor unions, however. Most Americans at the time valued individual enterprise. They also accepted an economic theory called laissez-faire (a French phrase that roughly translates as "let things happen"), which held that government should not interfere with the workings of business. Thus, when employers and workers clashed, government was usually unwilling to help workers fight for better conditions.

By the Gilded Age, two types of unions had emerged: craft (or trade) unions and industrial unions. Trade unions organized workers within specific lines of skilled labor, such as carpentry, iron molding, or shoemaking. Trade unions existed for specific industries and were linked through multiple "locals" around the country. In the 19th century, only white males could belong to trade unions. Industrial unions, on the other hand, offered membership to all workers, skilled or unskilled, within a particular industry. The American Railway Union, for example, was an industrial union open to every worker connected with the railroads, from track checkers to office staff to engine drivers.

Both trade unions and industrial unions belonged to national federations. In 1886, craft unions representing hundreds of different trades created the American Federation of Labor (AFL). Industrial unions were vast, and could themselves be affiliated with even larger umbrella-style confederations such as the Knights of Labor, founded in the 1870s, or the Industrial Workers of the World (IWW), founded in 1905. Both the Knights and the IWW welcomed women and African Americans as members. The AFL eventually encouraged women and minorities to form separate affiliated locals of their own. One such organization was the Women's Trade Union League, founded at an AFL meeting in 1903.

In this era, workers needed permission from their employers to organize a union. Most businesses and industries resisted unions, because unions forced them to share control with their workers. To prevent workers from forming unions, some managers fired union organizers. Other managers forced prospective employees to sign so-called "yellow dog" contracts in which they promised not to join a union. Yet other managers accepted unions, recognizing that doing so might prevent costly strikes. Once a business accepted a union, it agreed to let the union's elected leaders negotiate contracts on behalf of its members. This style of negotiation was known as collective bargaining.

Sometimes unions tried to institute "closed shops." In a closed shop, union members compelled the factory to hire only workers who would join the union. Court cases in the early 20th century overturned union rights to closed shops, however, arguing that such shops violated a worker's rights to contract freely with an employer. In this period, unions could be taken to court for "restraint of trade," and, just like giant corporations, could be indicted for operating "unlawful combinations" that restrained trade.

In the late 1800s and early 1900s, American labor unions used a number of tactics to win concessions from employers. Among these were strikes, boycotts, demonstrations, and lawsuits. They also formed alliances with political parties and social reformers. Through these strategies, they won the right to organize in many industries and to affiliate with other unions and federations. They founded a number of powerful unions, such as the United Mine Workers (UMW) and the International Ladies' Garment Workers' Union (ILGWU).

Using the courts, unions fought injunctions, or court orders, that prevented them from striking. Through legislation, they won maximum hours and minimum wages, workmen's compensation and workplace safety, and restrictions on child labor. Through strikes won and lost, including some in which striking workers died, labor unions pushed the government to mediate or arbitrate stalled disputes. Eventually, unions and their allies compelled the major political parties and prominent politicians, especially members of the Democratic party, to address labor concerns that minority parties from the Greenback Labor party to the Socialist party had been advocating since the 1870s.

Although many Americans sympathized with industrial workers, the union movement did not always enjoy widespread popular support. The public was especially suspicious of unions during national strikes and times of national crisis, such as wars and depressions, when some people feared that union agitation might lead to violent revolution. Nor did union appeals for government backing always succeed.

The government did respond positively to unions in several ways. First, it established a Bureau of Labor within the Department of the Interior and, in 1913, a full Department of Labor with a secretary in the President's cabinet. In 1914, Congress passed the Clayton Antitrust Act, which included a section declaring that unions could not be considered "unlawful combinations" operating in "restraint of trade" and that strikes, boycotting, and picketing did not violate federal law. By World War I, the U.S. government had abandoned laissez-faire policies and become more responsive to the issues that the union movement had brought to its attention.

SEE ALSO

American Federation of Labor; Child labor; Industrial Workers of the World; Industry; Knights of Labor; Labor; Laissez-faire;

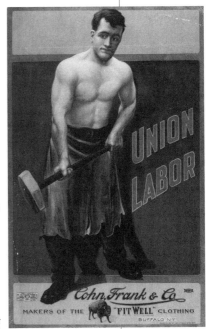

An advertising poster for a clothing manufacturer presents a heroic image of the working-class union movement and demonstrates that some employers supported unionism.

Reform movements; Regulation; Strikes; United Mine Workers of America; Women's Trade Union League; Work

FURTHER READING

Dubofsky, Melvyn. *Industrialism and the American Worker, 1865–1920.* New York: Crowell, 1975.
———. *We Shall Be All: A History of the Industrial Workers of the World.* Urbana: University of Illinois Press, 1988.
Milkman, Ruth, ed. *Women, Work and Protest: A Century of U.S. Women's Labor History.* New York: Routledge & Kegan Paul, 1985.
Montgomery, David. *The Fall of the House of Labor: The Workplace, the State, and American Labor Activism, 1865–1925.* New York: Cambridge University Press, 1987.

Labor, U.S. Department of

THE DEPARTMENT of Labor became an official part of the President's cabinet in 1913. Its establishment followed a half century of demands from organized labor and social reformers, who wanted the national government to collect information about laboring people and consider workers' concerns when formulating public policy. The stated purpose of the new department was "to foster, promote, and develop the welfare of working people, to improve their working conditions, and to enhance their opportunities for profitable employment."

The department took over a number of functions from the earlier Department of Commerce and Labor, absorbing the Bureaus of Labor Statistics, Immigration and Naturalization, and the Children's Bureau. The department also established funds and a conciliation program to mediate labor disputes. Another early function of the department was helping people find work through employment services set up in local immigration offices all around the country. The employment services became very popular, placing more than a quarter of a million workers in new jobs in 1917 alone.

With the U.S. entry into World War I, the Labor Department stepped up its efforts to ensure an adequate labor supply and peaceful relations between labor and management in industry. A War Labor Administration (WLA) initiated and supervised most of the government's wartime labor programs. The WLA set up a number of agencies, such as the Farm Service Division which provided underserved farming areas with labor, and the Working Conditions Service, which promoted workers' safety. The Women in Industry Service later became the Women's Bureau, a permanent division of the Department of Labor that promoted better jobs for women while safeguarding their health and welfare. Many war-era programs in the Department of Labor became models for programs in the New Deal, President Franklin Roosevelt's many-faceted attack on the Great Depression of the 1930s. The Department of Labor, for example, established an agricultural recovery program resembling the WLA's Farm Service Division, which was designed to help farmers with a set of problems that included labor shortages.

SEE ALSO

Children's Bureau, U.S.; Labor; Labor unions; Women's Bureau, U.S.; World War I

FURTHER READING

Breen, William J. *Labor Market Politics and the Great War: The Department of Labor, The States, and the First U.S. Employment Service 1907–1933.* Kent, Ohio: Kent State University Press, 1996.
Cutrona, Cheryl. *The Department of Labor.* New York: Chelsea House, 1988.
United States Department of Labor, The First Seventy-Five Years. Washington, D.C.: Government Printing Office, 1988.

La Follette, Robert Marion, Sr.

- *Born: June 14, 1855, Primrose, Wis.*
- *Education: University of Wisconsin, B.S., 1879*
- *Accomplishments: district attorney, Dane County, Wis. (1880–84); U.S. House of Representatives (Republican–Wis., 1885–91); governor of Wisconsin (1900–4); U.S. Senate (Republican–Wis., 1905–25); founder,* La Follette's Weekly Magazine, *later called* The Progressive *(1909); Progressive party candidate for President of the United States (1924)*
- *Died: June 18, 1925, Washington, D.C.*

KNOWN AS "Fighting Bob," Robert M. La Follette, Sr., was a fiercely independent progressive. Born and raised on a Wisconsin farm, he became a lawyer after studying at the University of Wisconsin. His wife, fellow student Belle Case, worked closely with him throughout his political career. He entered public life as a county district attorney, then served as a Republican congressman for six years. After a reelection defeat in 1890, he developed a lucrative law practice in Madison, Wisconsin.

Two events during the 1890s radicalized his politics. In the first case, he suspected a Wisconsin senator of attempting to bribe him in 1891 in order to win influence in a law case. This incident turned La Follette into a campaigner against corrupt party politics. The second event was the depression of 1893–97, which deepened his commitment to economic reforms for the benefit of farmers and workers. After twice failing to win the Republican nomination for governor, he finally won election in 1900.

As governor, La Follette initiated legislation for direct primary elections so that voters, instead of party leaders,

Robert "Fighting Bob" La Follette, senator from Wisconsin, addresses the microphone with clenched fists. La Follette was a vigorous and outspoken leader of the Republican party's progressive wing.

could choose party candidates directly. He also supported tax reform and industrial regulation, and used experts, such as university professors and legislative reference bureaus, in the drafting of laws. Called the "Wisconsin idea," his approach soon found imitators in other states. Despite opposition from his own party, La Follette won reelection in 1902 and 1904, each time increasing popular support for his reforms.

In January 1905, the Wisconsin state legislature elected La Follette to the U.S. Senate, but the governor delayed taking the post until he had made further progress with his reforms. Arriving in the Senate a year later, La Follette rose to greater national prominence by fighting for antitrust legislation and worker protection. By 1909, the year he and his wife founded *La Follette's Weekly Magazine* to promote his reform ideas, he was the acknowledged leader of the Republican insurgent legislators then in rebellion against the party's Old Guard. In 1912, La Follette opposed President William Howard Taft for reelection and then competed with Theodore Roosevelt for the Progressive party's Presidential nomination. After losing to Roosevelt, an embittered La Follette attacked Roosevelt as an "inconsequential play-boy." In dozens of speeches he charged that Roosevelt was not a "true pro-gressive" but a "switch engine," one that "first runs [on] one track, and then on another. Runs forward and then backs up. Makes a heap of noise and never gets anywhere."

Highlights from La Follette's remaining years in the Senate included his sponsorship of the La Follette Sea-men's Act (1915). A response to the sinking of the *Titanic* in 1912, this act gave seamen rights similar to those won by factory workers, such as a 56-hour week, minimum safety and clean-liness standards in their quarters, the right to sue for damages when ship owners were negligent, and the right to organize.

La Follette was one of only six Senators to oppose U.S. entry into World War I. He also opposed the draft and restrictions on free speech and the press. When the war ended, he joined other Republicans in opposing the Treaty of Versailles, on which his party had not been consulted, and the League of Nations, an international organization to prevent war, which he feared would drag the United States into more foreign entanglements.

La Follette's career ended with one final campaign. In 1924, he ran for President as an independent and a Progressive, campaigning for public ownership of water power and rail-roads, collective bargaining rights for labor, federal aid to farmers, and child labor laws. He won almost 5 million votes but carried only his home state of Wisconsin.

SEE ALSO

Progressive movement; Progressive party; Republican party; Roosevelt, Theodore

FURTHER READING

La Follette, Robert M. *La Follette's Auto-biography: A Personal Narrative of Polit-ical Experiences.* 1913. Reprint, Madison: University of Wisconsin Press, 1960.
Thelen, David P. *Robert M. La Follette and the Insurgent Spirit.* 1976. Reprint, Madison: University of Wisconsin Press, 1985.
Unger, Nancy C. *Fighting Bob La Follette: The Righteous Reformer.* Chapel Hill: University of North Carolina Press, 2000.

Laissez-faire

LAISSEZ-FAIRE—a French phrase meaning "let things happen"—was a popular political philosophy in the 19th century. It held that a nation's economy worked best when businesses and markets operated without any interference from government. The idea was a bulwark of the American capitalist system.

Proponents of laissez-faire believed that a country's government should conduct foreign policy, provide for the national defense, assist military veter-ans, collect taxes for essential projects, such as roads, canals, and bridges, and maintain civil order. Otherwise, they believed that government should leave its citizens alone, especially in their economic affairs.

In practice, however, U.S. Presi-dents, Congresses, courts, and other government authorities violated laissez-faire frequently by intervening in the economy on behalf of the busi-ness community. Claiming its actions were in the national interest, the U.S. government subsidized railroads, passed tariffs that protected domestic manufacturers, and sent troops to safeguard industrial property during labor disturbances.

Very late in the 19th century, some social activists began to suggest that government ought to intervene more, not less, in the economic and social affairs of the people. They argued that an industrial nation was far more complex than a nation of farmers and that ordinary people needed protection from exploitative employers and natural or economic disasters not of their making. Progressives began to talk about federal involvement in education and public welfare, government regulation of economic cycles, pensions or other provisions for the elderly and sick, federal arbitration committees for disputes between capital and labor, and a number of other policies antithetical to laissez-faire. Debate over these ideas escalated, and laissez-faire received serious challenges in the early 20th century when government enlarged its role in regulating the economy.

SEE ALSO

Labor; Labor unions; Progressive movement

FURTHER READING

Faulkner, Harold Underwood. *The Decline of Laissez Faire, 1897–1917: The Economic History of the United States.* 1951. Reprint, Armonk, N.Y.: M. E. Sharpe, 1989.

Fine, Sidney. *Laissez Faire and the General-Welfare State: A Study of Conflict in American Thought, 1865–1901.* Ann Arbor: University of Michigan Press, 1964.

Keynes, John Maynard. *The End of Laissez Faire.* 1926. Reprint, Amherst, N.Y.: Prometheus Books, 2004.

Law

CERTAIN THEMES dominated law-making throughout the Gilded Age and Progressive Era. At the state level, the regulation of various aspects of business was one of the most prominent. For example, western states, such as Washington and Utah, passed laws that restricted child labor in mines. Other

states set working hours and wages for certain groups of workers, regulated health and safety aspects of factory life, and set rates for railroads and grain elevators. New York's 1894 constitution required the preservation of forests against excessive commercial exploitation. On the federal level, Congress passed antitrust laws in an effort to combat anticompetitive practices by monopolies. The U.S. Supreme Court overturned or weakened some of these laws when business owners challenged them. The Court upheld regulatory laws, as it did in *Muller* v. *Oregon* (1908), only when the justices found that a larger public interest— in this case, the health of women workers, who were the nation's future mothers—overrode its reluctance to allow government to interfere in the economy.

In the South during the 1890s, states disfranchised African Americans by imposing literacy tests, poll taxes, and property requirements on voting. To ensure that poor and illiterate whites would not be disfranchised by these same requirements, southern states passed "grandfather clauses," exempting from tests and taxes anyone whose ancestors had voted before black suffrage. Although Jim Crow laws segregating blacks and whites in public accommodations pervaded the late 19th-century South, these laws actually began much earlier in the North. In 1841, Massachusetts allowed railroad companies to separate black and white passengers. Segregation laws were often challenged successfully in the North but remained intact in the South for decades. The Supreme Court legitimized "separate but equal" accommodations for black people in *Plessy* v. *Ferguson* (1896).

Other laws passed in the late 1800s created hardships for other

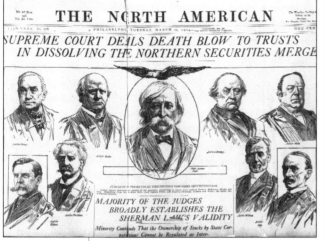

The nine Supreme Court justices who upheld the Sherman Antitrust Act receive prominent coverage on the front page of this 1904 newspaper. In the face of a challenge from a huge monopoly, the Court ruled that Standard Oil was operating "in unreasonable restraint of trade."

minority groups. The Dawes Severalty Act (1887) encouraged Native American assimilation by guaranteeing rights to Indians who agreed to give up their rights to tribal lands in return for ownership of individual plots. In hard times, many Indians leased or sold their plots to speculators, with the result that over time they lost even more of their ancestral lands. In 1880, San Francisco passed an ordinance that discriminated against the operation of laundries in wooden buildings, where most Chinese immigrants ran their businesses. Although the Supreme Court struck this ordinance down (in the 1886 case of *Yick Wo* v. *Hopkins*), Congress had already passed a Chinese Exclusion Act that effectively ended Chinese immigration. In addition, the Scott Act of 1888 prevented nearly 20,000 Chinese laborers who had temporarily left the United States from returning.

As the government assumed an increasingly active role in regard to citizens' welfare, new kinds of laws began to appear, such as those to protect consumers against shoddy products and medical malpractice. Some states modernized aspects of criminal law. A number of them abolished capital punishment. Wisconsin entered statehood without the death penalty, Michigan

abolished it in 1882 (except for the crime of treason), and Maine eliminated it in 1887. Some states initiated probation systems, following Massachusetts, which hired its first probation officer in 1878. By the end of the 19th century, states were providing probation for juveniles and separate trials in cases involving children. Urged by social settlement workers, and Judges Benjamin Lindsey of Denver and Julian Mack of Chicago, many local governments established juvenile justice systems.

Divorce laws underwent major changes in this period. By 1880 all states but Delaware had abolished divorces by legislative decree. Divorces awarded by state legislatures were time-consuming to obtain, as legislatures had to vote on each divorce case individually. After Delaware followed suit in 1897, all divorces were argued in the courts as legal cases. As divorces became easier to get, especially in the West where states required the shortest residencies, moral objections arose in the East against "easy divorce." Between 1889 and 1906, eastern legislatures raised residency requirements, restricted the grounds for divorce, and in the case of South Carolina banned divorce altogether.

Women made some advances in terms of equality before the law. Before the mid-1800s, under a legal concept called coverture, a married woman's property belonged to her husband. Starting in 1839 in Mississippi, states passed Married Women's Property Acts, which allowed wives to preserve property in their own names. In the latter 1800s, woman's movement activists pressed for more ambitious legislation that awarded wives the right to buy and sell property, keep their own wages, and be joint guardians of their children. By the late 1890s, all states had passed such acts, although they varied in content from state to state. The laws of almost all states, however, excluded women from juries and from most public offices.

Lawyers were, of course, at the center of both lawmaking and arguing cases before the courts. In the late 1800s, their profession changed radically. In earlier years, young men clerked for established lawyers, copying documents and reading major commentaries on the law until they were ready to apply for a license. By the end of the century, most lawyers trained in law schools. Approximately 60,000 lawyers were in practice in 1880, and 114,000 by 1900. Only a few women were among them, most of them trained in a senior lawyer's office or at coeducational universities. In 1879, Belva Ann Lockwood, a lawyer from Washington, D.C., became the first woman to plead a case before the U.S. Supreme Court.

The United States had 51 law schools by 1880, and 102 by 1900. Night courses allowed individuals with daytime jobs to study law, thereby opening up the profession to more members of the working and middle classes. A student could earn a Bachelor of Laws (LL.B.) degree in three years. Following the initiative of Dean Christopher Columbus Langdell of Harvard Law School, law schools at this time began adopting the case-law method of teaching, instructing students through the study of actual legal cases rather than scholarly treatises and lectures.

SEE ALSO

African Americans; Antitrust laws; Asian Americans; Chinese Exclusion Act (1882); Consumer Movement; Dawes Severalty Act (1887); Divorce; Labor; *Muller* v. *Oregon* (1908); Native Americans; *Plessy* v. *Ferguson* (1896); Race relations; Regulation; Segregation; Supreme Court, U.S.; Women's rights movement

FURTHER READING

Dershowitz, Alan M. *America on Trial: Inside the Legal Battles that Transformed Our Nation.* New York: Warner, 2004.
Friedman, Lawrence M. *A History of American Law.* 3rd ed. New York: Simon & Schuster, 2005.
Hall, Kermit. *The Magic Mirror: Law in American History.* New York: Oxford University Press, 1989.
Rabkin, Peggy A. *Fathers to Daughters: The Legal Foundations of Female Emancipation.* Westport, Conn.: Greenwood, 1980.

League of Nations

THE LEAGUE OF NATIONS, founded in 1919, was designed to resolve international disputes before they erupted into war. President Woodrow Wilson won its inclusion in the Treaty of Versailles, the document signed by the major European powers to end World War I. The league would not only arbitrate international disputes but impose sanctions on any nation that took military action on its own against another.

This last provision aroused controversy in the United States. One group of congressmen, who became known as the Reservationists, feared that it would restrict the freedom of the United States to take military action when its interests were endangered. The leader of this group, Henry Cabot Lodge, Republican senator from Massachusetts, argued for significant "reservations" on U.S. participation in the league. For example, he insisted that the United States assume no military obligation to preserve the territorial integrity or political independence of any other country, or interfere in controversies between nations, without Congress's express approval. He also refused to permit the league to have a say over any aspect of American domestic affairs, including immigration, labor relations, commerce, or level of military

IF WE WERE IN THE LEAGUE OF NATIONS

Copyright, 1920, by Star Company.

HI— SAM!
SEND ME OVER
A NEW ARMY!

Uncle Sam watches a flag-draped coffin roll down one gangplank and wounded troops descend another while John Bull, a symbol of England, calls for fresh cannon fodder. The message of this 1920 cartoon was that membership in the League of Nations would embroil the United States in destructive foreign wars.

preparedness. In rejecting the league, another group of congressmen, called the Irreconcilables, argued that joining it would force the United States to support British and French imperialism.

Determined to win grassroots support for the league, Wilson barnstormed the country, delivering three dozen speeches in 21 days. In the midst of this tremendous effort, he suffered a massive stroke that paralyzed one side of his body. He remained an invalid for the rest of his term in office.

In November 1919, the Senate twice refused to ratify the Versailles treaty, voting down both the original treaty and a version with "reservations." In the face of popular dismay at this outcome, the Senate reconsidered ratification in March 1920, but anti-league forces again prevailed. When on May 20, Congress passed a joint resolution simply to declare the war over, Wilson vetoed it because it did not include joining the league. It finally passed during the Presidency of Warren G. Harding.

The United States would never join the League of Nations. As a conse-

quence, the league remained a virtually powerless organization, notwithstanding some early successes defusing European border disputes and preventing the outbreak of a war in the Balkans. The League of Nations had no real ability to enforce decisions that were controversial, and with the founding of the United Nations at the end of World War II, it formally came to an end.

SEE ALSO

Imperialism; Versailles, Treaty of (1919); Wilson, Woodrow T.; World War I

FURTHER READING

Cooper, John Milton. *Breaking the Heart of the World: Woodrow Wilson and the Fight for the League of Nations.* New York: Cambridge University Press, 2001.
Ostrower, Gary B. *The League of Nations, 1919–1929.* Garden City Park, N.Y.: Avery, 1996.
Bendiner, Elmer. *A Time for Angels: The Tragi-comic History of the League of Nations.* New York: Knopf, 1975.
Northedge, F. S. *The League of Nations: Its Life and Times, 1920–1946.* New York: Holmes & Meier, 1986.
Scott, George. *The Rise and Fall of the League of Nations.* New York: Macmillan, 1973.

Leisure

In the early 19th century, few Americans had much time to spare. Unless they were wealthy, they spent most of their waking hours producing food, shelter, and clothing. To them, recreation was frivolous. If they had leisure time at all, they spent it in prayer or in family or community gatherings. On trips to a market or fair, they might see a public performance of some kind, but such occasions were rare.

Industrialization changed this pattern. Factories and service industries drew millions into cities, many to work long hours at tedious jobs. Thanks in part to a movement for an eight-hour workday, by the end of the 1800s some industries had introduced shorter work weeks and half-holidays on Saturday. Increasingly, workers with spare time wanted to spend it having fun.

Some recreation was free. After work, people could go for strolls, window shop, and scan the crowds. In residential areas, neighbors sat on front stoops, chatting and watching children play. Ethnic groups formed social clubs for recreational purposes. German clubs called *Turnverein* specialized in gymnastics and political and social events, Italians played cards and bocce ball, and the Scottish formed competitive track-and-field clubs. Labor unions, volunteer firemen, or other affiliated groups started amateur musical organizations, bands, and barbershop quartets.

Other amusements cost money. For the most part, the middle and upper classes entertained themselves at home, but they also patronized restaurants, museums, theaters, music halls, opera houses, and ballrooms. Men favored sporting events, especially horse racing, boxing, and the nation's pastime, baseball. Women used department stores as entertainment, meeting friends there and attending cultural events such as art shows, lectures, and chamber music concerts. Commercial

venues, including concert saloons (barrooms featuring a simple stage), dance halls (also often just bars with a dance floor), dime museums (displaying freaks or women in various stages of undress), variety shows, circuses, and amusement parks, catered more to the working classes.

At some of these commercial venues, patrons might drink excessively, gamble, or engage in prostitution. Police took bribes in return for protecting these establishments. In many cities such conditions led to Progressive-era campaigns for strict licensing of commercial "resorts," as they were called. Reformers also advocated government funding for more wholesome alternatives, such as parks, municipal dance pavilions, and recreation grounds.

Working-class men patronized saloons more than any other resort. By 1900 Denver had nearly 500 saloons, New York City an estimated 10,000. In addition to consuming food and alcohol there, men used saloons as social clubs, where they exchanged gossip, talked politics, and picked up tips on jobs. When new styles of social dancing, such as polkas and ragtime, began attracting younger clientele, saloon owners turned their establishments into dance halls, a change that made them more attractive to women. Dance halls played an important role in dating for working-class youth.

Inexpensive theatrical performances attracted large white-collar crowds in this period. By the 1910s, weekly attendance at New York City theaters reached some 2,000,000, and in San Francisco over 500,000. During summers, city residents attended performances in outdoor amphitheaters in city parks. Small towns brought in traveling theater troupes. First appearing in the 1870s, vaudeville, a variety show uniting elements from minstrel,

Well-to-do gentlemen and ladies play lawn tennis, a new sport in the 1880s. The women players wear long dresses with bustles, which limited their mobility but preserved their modesty.

music hall, circus, and burlesque routines, was the nation's most popular theatrical attraction.

Millions of families organized their vacations around visits to the world's fairs and expositions mounted in major American cities at fairly regular intervals from the 1870s on into the twentieth century. Organized to commemorate important anniversaries, such as the nation's centennial, Columbus's voyage to the New World, or the Louisiana Purchase, these events combined exhibitions of high culture along with the carnival-like activities of amusement parks. In many cities, increasing numbers of amusement parks sprang up at the end of trolley lines. These provided family entertainment at relatively low cost. Coney Island, a section of New York's beachfront in Brooklyn, provided the prototype. Starting in the 1870s, the area evolved into three huge amusement parks, Luna Park, Steeplechase, and Dreamland, and offered such attractions as fun houses, carnival sideshows, games, roller coaster rides, and a dark "Tunnel of Love." In 1909 alone, over 20 million people visited Coney Island.

Moving pictures grew in popularity in this period. Most of the early ones were slapstick comedies or peep shows, so called because they allowed viewers to see a moving image through a small peep hole. People watched them in viewing machines set up in nickelodeons, converted stores or warehouses that showed films for a nickel. When films moved to larger screens, nickelodeons catering to families became neighborhood social centers. By 1908, American cities had about 8,000 nickelodeons. Like vaudeville, silent movies crossed regional boundaries and helped create an American national identity. Surmounting the language barrier, they also gave immigrants imaginative outlets for their desires and a release from their daily woes.

Sports, amateur and professional, drew ever-larger groups of both participants and audiences. Baseball was Americans' favorite sport. By the 1880s, amateurs still played the game, but it had become professionalized. College men played football, college women played baseball, and both sexes played basketball, a winter sport introduced to keep players fit off-season. Bicycling, a craze in the 1890s, gave way to taking a spin in an automobile in the early 1900s.

Gilded Age upper classes had always left the city during summers, enjoying trips to Europe, mountain resorts, or hot springs, or weeks at their cottages (which were often mansions) in Newport, Rhode Island, the most fashionable summer retreat of the era. By facilitating family travel, the cheaper automobiles introduced in the mid-1910s made the summer vacation more available to the middle and working classes. By the 1920s, bathing, boating, and fishing in a rural environment for at least a week a year had become a necessity of life, although the paid vacation was decades away. Almost all leisure activities in this era were racially segregated. Even in the North, where such segregation was illegal, proprietors sat people of color, no matter how well off, in the poorest seats, forced them to enter hotels by a back door, or excluded them altogether.

SEE ALSO

Bicycles; Cities; Consumer culture; Dance; Ethnicity; Immigration; Labor; Motion pictures; Parks and playgrounds; Sports; Theater; World's fairs and exhibitions

FURTHER READING

Aron, Cindy Sondik. *Working at Play: A History of Vacations in the United States.* New York: Oxford University Press, 1999.

Kasson, John. *Amusing the Million: Coney Island at the Turn of the Century.* New York: Hill & Wang, 1978.

Nasaw, David. *Going Out: The Rise and Fall of Public Amusements.* Cambridge: Harvard University Press, 1999.

Rosenzweig, Roy. *Eight Hours for What We Will: Workers and Leisure in an Industrial City, 1870–1920.* New York: Cambridge University Press, 1983.

Lili'uokalani, Queen Lydia Kamakaeha

- *Born: Sept. 2, 1838, Honolulu, Hawaii*
- *Accomplishments: regent of Hawaii (1880–81, 1890), queen of Hawaii (1891–93)*
- *Died: Nov. 11, 1917, Honolulu, Hawaii*

LYDIA KAMAKAEHA Lili'uokalani was Hawaii's last monarch and the first woman ever to rule the Hawaiian Islands, located in the Pacific Ocean. Educated by Christian missionaries, she grew up close to the royal court. In 1862 she married John Owen Dominis, the son of an American sea captain from Boston. Together they traveled around the islands "to meet the people, that all classes, rich and poor, planter or fisherman, might have an opportunity to become acquainted with the one who some day should be called upon to hold the highest executive office," she later wrote.

Lili'uokalani came to the throne upon the death of her brother, King David Kalakaua, in 1891. In 1887, a Hawaiian League had forced him to accept a constitution that weakened his own power while strengthening that of the American sugar planters who dominated the economy of the island nation. In 1893, Lili'uokalani tried to revoke this constitution and restore the power of the monarch. In addition, she opposed the planters' strategy of

EX-QUEEN LILIOUKALANI

having the United States annex Hawaii so as to win exemption from American tariffs for their sugar crop. Hawaii's Supreme Court supported Lili'uokalani's new constitution, but the planters, led by Sanford B. Dole, refused to sign it. When the Queen attempted to rule by edict, a committee of planters decided to depose her. Supported by the American minister in Hawaii, John L. Stevens, who permitted U.S. troops to come ashore, the planters took over government buildings and ended the monarchy. In 1894, the planters declared the islands a republic and later petitioned the United States for annexation.

Although President Grover Cleveland initially believed Lili'uokalani to have been wrongfully deposed, he eventually turned the issue over to Congress, which recognized the legitimacy of the republic. In 1895, Lili'uokalani was put under house arrest when some of her followers staged a brief, unsuccessful revolt. Released after eight months, she formally abdicated the throne but continued her pleas to Washington, D.C., for the removal of U.S. troops. She got some of her own property back but was

A portrait of Lili'uokalani, deposed Queen of Hawaii, accompanies an 1897 newspaper article about her official protest against U.S. annexation of Hawaii. Despite her objections, the annexation took place the following year.

helpless when the United States finally annexed the islands in 1898 after the Spanish-American War.

A skilled musician, Lili'uokalani wrote many songs, including "Aloha Oe," a farewell to her country. Widowed early, she died without offspring and without ever accomplishing her enduring vision, the independence of her island homeland.

FURTHER READING

Allen, Helena G. *The Betrayal of Queen Liliuokalani, Last Queen of Hawaii, 1838–1917.* Glendale, Calif.: Arthur H. Clark, 1982.
Lili'uokalani. *Hawai'i's Story by Hawai'i's Queen.* 1898. Reprint, Rutland, Vt.: C. E. Tuttle, 1964.

Literature

MANY IMPORTANT writers flourished during the Gilded Age and Progressive Era. Among them were humorist Mark Twain (the pseudonym of Samuel Clemens), poets Walt Whitman, Emily Dickinson, Ezra Pound, and T. S. Eliot, novelists Willa Cather, Henry James, and Edith Wharton, and playwright Eugene O'Neill. During this period, unrhymed, non-metrical forms of poetry emerged, and novelists experimented with a variety of realistic styles and subject matter, often critiquing the social problems of the period. Intense, serious new dramas began to lure audiences away from the vaudeville and melodramas that had been standard 19th-century theatrical fare.

Almost all American writers at this time rejected the exotic settings and swashbuckling adventure stories of earlier Romantic writers, instead favoring new literary styles known as realism, naturalism, imagism, and modernism. Realist writers focused on

ordinary people dealing with everyday stresses and conflicts. They also explored social class issues and human psychology. When realist fiction portrayed the impact of industrialization and urbanization, it entered the realm of muckraking, or investigative journalism. Frank Norris's populist novel *The Octopus* (1901) dealt with the struggles between wheat farmers and the railroads. His work influenced later muckraking journalists, such as Ida Tarbell and Upton Sinclair. Sinclair's *The Jungle,* the 1906 muckraking novel about meatpacking in Chicago, spurred the passage of laws regulating food and drug production.

Other realist authors, such as Henry James and Edith Wharton, wrote about the American upper class. Both were masters of psychological observation, rendering deep, subtle portraits of the inner lives of characters. Influential editor, novelist, and critic William Dean Howells, author of *The Rise of Silas Lapham* (1885) and *A Hazard of New Fortunes* (1890), concentrated on the newly rich urban middle classes.

Naturalism, which overlapped with realism, depicted characters in the grip of powerful, sometimes uncontrollable, forces ranging from sexual desire to social and economic pressures. Some critics complained that naturalism was sordid or immoral; others appreciated its honesty. Authors associated with both realism and naturalism included Stephen Crane, remembered today for *The Red Badge of Courage* (1895), which portrayed Civil War soldiers as frightened human beings rather than as heroes, and for *Maggie: A Girl of the Streets* (1893), a prostitute's story. In his most popular novel, *Sister Carrie* (1900), Theodore Dreiser presented an unhappy picture of a woman's life in a large American city. Jack London, best known for *Call of the Wild* (1903), returned to the exotic settings of some earlier Romantics, but explored realist themes, such as the conflict between civilization and nature.

Like the fiction writers of the period, poets also rejected past models. In the early 1900s, they rebelled against the sentimentality, patriotism, flowery language, and ecstatic responses to nature that they associated with Romantic poets. Ezra Pound was a leading figure among the imagists, who stressed the importance of sharp physical images and precise, straightforward language. Other poets associated with the imagist movement included H. D. (the pen name of Hilda Doolittle), Amy Lowell, Marianne Moore, and William Carlos Williams.

Some imagist poets later became identified with modernism, an artistic movement that encompassed music, painting, and architecture as well as literature. Modernism was a response to the rapidly changing world that had produced industrialization and World War I. Some modernist poets wrote free verse while others used rhyme and meter. T. S. Eliot, an American-born writer who would eventually become a British citizen, was the foremost modernist poet, frequently dealing with themes of alienation and spiritual longing. The experimental writer Gertrude Stein was more concerned with elaborate wordplay than conventional storytelling.

The most popular literature of the period did not always fit into these literary categories, however. Lew Wallace's Christian-themed historical novel *Ben Hur* (1880) became a bestseller and the basis of several motion picture treatments. For many years, American readers devoured Marietta Holley's gently humorous and feminist books, which used the fictional character of Samantha, the long-suffering

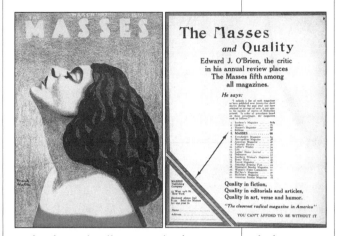

The literary magazine The Masses *published fiction and commentary by many prominent writers. It also showcased artists such as John Sloan and Frank Waits. Waits designed this cover for the March 1917 issue.*

wife of Josiah Allen, to poke fun at male pretensions to superiority. Americans also loved the *Personal Memoirs* of President Ulysses S. Grant, which appeared in two posthumous volumes in 1885 and 1886. *Looking Backward, 2000–1887,* a science fiction novel published in 1888 by Edward Bellamy, inspired a nationwide political movement with its imaginative depiction of a world free of war, class distinctions, and other negative consequences of capitalist competition. Horatio Alger wrote more than 100 books about virtuous poor boys rising from rags to respectability. The short stories of Ring Lardner, a cynical humorist, and O. Henry (the pseudonym of William Sydney Porter), known for his ingenious plot twists and surprise endings, were extremely popular. The Tarzan books of Edgar Rice Burroughs and Zane Grey's western adventure novels also had wide readership. Henry Adams, the descendant of two U.S. Presidents, wrote in many genres. Best known for his autobiography, *The Education of Henry Adams* (1907), Adams also used history and fiction to explore his country's political culture.

Regional writing—fiction and poetry associated with specific areas of the United States—helped bind the post–Civil War nation together by familiarizing readers with America's diversity. Bret Harte wrote humorous western stories. Owen Wister was an easterner whose 1902 novel *The Virginian* helped to build the legend of the American cowboy. Mary Austin set her best-known books in the desert country of southern California. Louisa May Alcott, author of *Little Women* (1868–69) and its many sequels, Sarah Orne Jewett, Mary E. Wilkins Freeman, and Dorothy Canfield Fisher were noted New England regionalists. Ellen Glasgow earned most praise for her portrayals of life in Virginia. Starting in 1913 with *O, Pioneers!*, Willa Cather wrote several acclaimed novels of frontier life on the Great Plains. Hamlin Garland applied stark realism to his treatments of life in the Midwest, with books such as *Main-Travelled Roads* (1891) and *Son of the Middle Border* (1917). Another midwesterner, James Whitcomb Riley, wrote folksy, humorous verse for children and adults. Booth Tarkington produced numerous novels evoking boyhood life in his native Indiana.

Not all regionalists wrote positive portrayals. Poet Edgar Lee Masters outraged some critics when his popular 1915 book *Spoon River Anthology* depicted the residents of a small midwestern town not just as embodiments of traditional American values but as human beings with a full range of vices and foibles. In his 1919 novel *Winesburg, Ohio,* Sherwood Anderson presented small-town life as narrow and inimical to individual fulfillment.

Southern regionalists were especially haunted by the legacy of slavery and the Civil War. George Washington Cable, a native southerner, wrote critically of white southern society and sympathetically about the lives of African Americans. Mary Johnston, Grace King, and Thomas Nelson Page idealized the Confederacy, the pre-war

South, and the culture of white supremacy. Joel Chandler Harris, who popularized the African American tales of Br'er Rabbit, was a white writer whose work dealt with black culture in a humorous but condescending manner. *The Clansman,* a 1905 novel by southern preacher and writer Thomas F. Dixon, Jr., glorified the Ku Klux Klan and opposed equal rights for black citizens. In 1915, filmmaker D. W. Griffith turned Dixon's novel into a three-hour silent film called *Birth of a Nation.* Historians believe the film provoked a resurgence of Klan activity in the United States.

Women writers broadened the scope of American literature. The Sioux author Zitkala-Sa, also known as Gertrude Simmons Bonnin, wrote for a general audience about Native American culture. White poet Helen Hunt Jackson denounced the mistreatment of American Indians in *A Century of Dishonor* (1881), following this nonfiction work with a highly popular novel on the same theme, *Ramona* (1884). In 1899, Kate Chopin published *The Awakening,* a controversial novel in which a New Orleans woman scandalizes her social set by repudiating her role as wife and mother and later committing suicide. Pioneering feminist writer Charlotte Perkins Gilman achieved fame for her 1892 short story "The Yellow Wallpaper," her treatise on gender and society entitled *Women and Economics* (1898), and her 1915 utopian novel *Herland.*

Ethnic and African American writers made notable contributions during this period. Foreign-born Jewish writers Mary Antin, Abraham Cahan, and Anzia Yezierska wrote about immigrant life in the United States. This topic also concerned American-born Jewish poet Emma Lazarus, whose sonnet "The New Colossus" appears on the base of the Statue of Liberty. African American scholar and political activist W. E. B. DuBois wrote the 1903 classic *The Souls of Black Folk,* combining an evocation of black life and culture with arguments for social justice. Charles Chesnutt, Paul Lawrence Dunbar, Alice Dunbar-Nelson, Frances E. W. Harper, Pauline Hopkins, and James Weldon Johnson were some of the leading black poets, essayists, and novelists who wrote at a time when slavery was still a recent national memory and racial segregation was at its height. Their work helped to set the stage for the 1920s upsurge in black literary creativity known as the Harlem Renaissance.

SEE ALSO

Alger, Horatio, Jr.; Bellamy, Edward; Cather, Willa Sibert; Clemens, Samuel Langhorne; DuBois, William Edward Burghardt (W. E. B.); Gilman, Charlotte Perkins; Muckrakers; Sinclair, Upton Beall; South, the; Statue of Liberty; West, the

FURTHER READING

Brown, Linda Joyce. *Literature of Immigration and Racial Formation: Becoming White, Becoming Other, Becoming American in the Late Progressive Era.* New York: Routledge, 2004.
Foote, Stephanie. *Regional Fictions: Culture and Identity in Nineteenth-Century American Literature.* Madison: University of Wisconsin Press, 2001.
Pizer, Donald, ed. *The Cambridge Companion to American Realism and Naturalism: From Howells to London.* New York: Cambridge University Press, 1995.
Richards, Philip. *African American Literature: An Introduction.* Malden, Mass.: Blackwell, 2005.

Low, Juliette ("Daisy") Magill Kinzie Gordon

- *Born: Oct. 31, 1860, Savannah, Ga.*
- *Education: boarding schools*
- *Accomplishments: founder, Girl Scouts of America. (1913); author, Scouting for Girls: Official Handbook of the Girl Scouts (1920)*
- *Died: Jan. 17, 1927, Savannah, Ga.*

IN 1911, Juliette Gordon Low, a wealthy widow from Savannah, Georgia, met Sir Robert Baden-Powell, the founder of British boy scouting, and became convinced that scouting would be superb character training for American girls. First, she organized a company of British Girl Guides, the female equivalent of Boy Scouts, in a village near her summer cottage in Scotland, and two companies in London. Upon returning to the United States in 1912, she organized the first American Girl Scout troops in her hometown of Savannah, Georgia. The following year she formed the Girl Scouts of America, serving as its president until 1920.

Low organized her program around complementary character-building elements, the first, moral, the second, practical, and the third, intellectual. On the moral side, each Girl Scout honored a promise to "do my duty to God and my country, to help other people at all times, and to obey the Girl Scout laws." On the practical side, girls learned skills useful in domestic life and emergencies and helpful

Girl Scout founder Juliette Gordon Low wanted American girls to learn wilderness skills. At one of the early Girl Scout camps, two scouts dressed as Indians practice lighting campfires.

in fulfilling their "promise." To encourage learning, Low adapted Baden-Powell's system of badges, pins, and ranks, all awarded for achievement. She then trained adult volunteers in how to organize activities that made the learning fun. Hearing impaired since early adulthood, Low formalized the inclusion of disabled girls in 1917, at a time when they were excluded from many other activities. In 1912 an African American troop was organized in Savannah, and by the early 1920s, African American troops existed in Boston, Indianapolis, Nashville, New Haven, New York, and Washington, D.C. The American Girl Scouts became increasingly inclusive, and its structures, activities, uniforms, and emphases became more modern over time.

After her resignation from the presidency, "Daisy," as Low was known among her friends and family, continued to participate actively with the organization. She developed its international component, organizing the world Girl Scout camp, which was held in the United States in 1926, and she inspired local Girl Scout leaders with her demonstrations of scouting techniques and principles. Even as she suffered from cancer, an illness she kept secret from most of her followers, she never lost her enthusiasm for scouting.

SEE ALSO

Boy and Girl Scouts

FURTHER READING

Howard, Jane. "For Juliette Gordon Low's Girls, a Sparkling Diamond Jubilee," *Smithsonian* 1987 18/(7): 46–55.

Saxton, Martha. "The Best Girl Scout of Them All," *American Heritage,* 1982, 38–47.

Shultz, Gladys Denny, and Daisy Gordon Lawrence. *Lady From Savannah: The Life of Juliette Low.* Philadelphia: Lippincott, 1958.

Lusitania

ON MAY 1, 1915, a year after World War I had begun in Europe, the British ocean liner *Lusitania* set sail from New York for Liverpool, England, carrying British, American, and Canadian passengers and food and medical supplies for England. On May 7, a German torpedo sank the ship off the south coast of Ireland. German submarines, or U-boats, had been sinking British shipping since early in the war in retaliation for the British blockade of German waters. As war conditions worsened, the Germans ignored warfare protocol and began attacking the ships of nonbelligerents and those carrying citizens of neutral countries. The *Lusitania* sank in 18 minutes, with a loss of nearly 1,200 lives, including 123 Americans. A fleet of small boats from the Irish port of Queenstown rescued some 750 survivors.

Suspicions that the *Lusitania* was actually carrying arms to Britain have persisted, reinforced by the discovery of documents to that effect years after

Two 1915 magazine illustrations depict the Lusitania: *the first shows the grandeur of the British liner; the second shows it sinking after being struck by a German torpedo off the coast of Ireland.*

Lusitania Sinking, the Greatest of Ocean Tragedies

THE LUSITANIA, WHICH SAILED FROM NEW YORK FOR LIVERPOOL MAY 1, 1915, WITH 1,959 SOULS ON BOARD, WAS SUNK BY A GERMAN SUBMARINE MAY 7, WITH A LOSS, INCLUDING WOMEN AND CHILDREN, OF 1,195.

THE SINKING OF THE LUSITANIA, THAT GREATEST OF OCEAN TRAGEDIES, IS HERE PORTRAYED BY A BRITISH ARTIST FROM DESCRIPTION AND WITH THE AID OF SURVIVORS. THE MARKINGS ON THE PICTURE GIVE THE MOST IMPORTANT DETAILS. THE MOMENT CHOSEN IS WHEN BOATS ARE PULLING AWAY WITH SURVIVORS the war. Divers searching the wreck, however, have found no trace of any weapons or ammunition being shipped.

Outraged by the attack on a passenger ship carrying innocent Americans, the United States added the sinking to a growing list of grievances against Germany. Historians consider the sinking a major motivation for the U.S. entry into the war in 1917.

SEE ALSO
World War I

FURTHER READING
Bailey, Thomas Andrew. *The* Lusitania *Disaster: An Episode in Modern Warfare and Diplomacy.* New York: Simon & Schuster, 1975.
Butler, Daniel Allen. *The* Lusitania: *The Life, Loss, and Legacy of an Ocean Legend.* Mechanicsburg, Pa.: Stackpole, 2000.
Preston, Diana. *Lusitania: An Epic Tragedy.* New York: Walker, 2002.

Lynching

THE TERM *lynching* derives from the name of a colonial landowner, Charles Lynch, who had the habit of taking the law into his own hands, staging impromptu trials, and inflicting punishment on those he felt had done him wrong. Lynching has come to mean killings committed outside the bounds of the law, usually by vigilantes bent on revenge for some offense, real or imagined. In a lynching, citizens assume the role of judge, jury, and executioner.

Lynchings were characteristic of the period between the end of the Civil War and about 1930. Most occurred in the Deep South, where most of the victims were black, but there were lynchings in 26 states, including North Dakota. Because of the secret and illegal nature of lynching, and because so few perpetrators were ever brought to trial, accurate data on lynching is hard to find.

Statistics compiled by the National Association for the Advancement of Colored People (NAACP) in 1921 indicate that between the years 1889 and 1918, at least 3,224 lynchings took place in the United States. Of that number, 2,522 were African Americans. The Tuskegee Institute in Alabama chronicled more than 4,000 lynchings during a similar period. In any account, though, roughly three-quarters of those killed by mob violence were African Americans. Hundreds of other ritual murders may have escaped detection. Lynching had wide popular support in the late 19th century, especially in the South, and became an important component of white supremacy. Between 1880 and 1905, it was almost impossible for the courts to convict someone of murder for taking part in such a killing, when southern juries were all white and vigilantism was part of local custom, few courts would convict a man of murder for taking part in a lynching.

Lynchings were the work of mobs, who tended to act spontaneously, or small groups of family members seeking to avenge a murdered or injured kin. Sometimes posses authorized by sheriffs killed the person they had been sent to apprehend. Organized terrorist groups like the Ku Klux Klan tended to use the lynching of black men as a form of economic and political repression or intimidation. Lynch mobs most commonly hanged or shot their victims, but they also mutilated them or burned them to death.

In the late 19th century, many people felt the justice system was inadequate, so the excuse for lynching was to see justice done swiftly. The perception was that the victims of lynching, most of them black, had murdered or attacked a white man or had sexually assaulted a white woman. As journalist Ida B. Wells established, and NAACP

The burned body of Jesse Washington, a black man lynched in 1916, hangs from a tree in Waco, Texas. Photographs of lynching victims surrounded by crowds of smiling white onlookers often appeared on souvenir postcards.

lawyers later confirmed, these were seldom the crimes actually committed, but the accusations created an excuse for the lynching of vagrants, people with mental problems, and socially or economically successful African American men or those who were having consensual relationships with white women. Lynch mobs accused their black victims of an astonishing array of "crimes." Many of their charges were ludicrous. Typical charges, in addition to the predominant murder and assault, included "hiding in a girl's bedroom," "insulting a white woman," "disorderly conduct," and even "race hatred."

Lynchings grew less frequent in the 20th century but continued into the 1960s. The Mississippi lynching of 13-year-old Emmett Till in 1955 was a catalyst for the modern civil rights movement. Although racially motivated killings still sometimes take place in the United States, they tend to be individual acts of violence; they are no longer mass public rituals regarded with approval (or at least indifference) by the courts, media, and public opinion.

Throughout the 20th century, southern senators managed to stop the U.S. Congress from passing a federal antilynching law. In 2005, the U.S. Senate finally issued a formal apology to lynching victims and their descendants for this failure.

SEE ALSO

African Americans; Civil rights; Ku Klux Klan; National Association for the Advancement of Colored People; Segregation; South, the; Wells-Barnett, Ida B.

FURTHER READING

Brundage, Fitzhugh. *Lynching in the New South: Georgia and Virginia, 1880–1930.* Urbana: University of Illinois Press, 1993.
Dray, Philip. *At the Hands of Persons Unknown: The Lynching of Black America.* New York: Modern Library, 2003.
Ginzburg, Ralph, ed. *100 Years of Lynchings.* Baltimore, Md.: Black Classic Press, 1988.
Wells, Ida B. *Southern Horrors and Other Writings; The Anti-Lynching Campaign of Ida B. Wells, 1892–1900.* Edited by Jacqueline Jones Royster. New York: Bedford/St. Martin's, 1996.
Zangrando, Robert L. *The NAACP Crusade Against Lynching, 1909–1950.* Philadelphia, Pa.: Temple University Press, 1980.

Machine politics

POLITICAL "MACHINES" arose out of the clashing political and economic interests that vied for control over the nation's growing Gilded Age cities. In any given city, the machine was an unofficial organization whose members wanted to concentrate that city's political power in the hands of one particular party or group. Most machines had a single, powerful boss, who might hold a political office himself. More commonly, the boss handpicked others to run for office, helped them win election by fair means or foul, and then controlled their activities while they were in office.

Ward leaders were men drawn from the ranks of saloon and hotel keepers and small business owners who ran things for the boss at the neighborhood level. They managed the machine patronage system, handing out city jobs and contracts as rewards for political support at election time. They did favors for residents, organized mutual benefit societies, paid for burials, and generally assisted families in their wards who needed help or were in trouble. Leaders knew everyone in their wards, and every family member by name. They might even know about the people left behind in the old country. If someone's nephew arrived on a ship one day, the ward leader would have a job for him the next. In return for such support, on election day, residents voted for the politicians who belonged to the machines.

Machines were usually corrupt and machine-organized voting was often fraudulent. But these organizations controlled most city jobs, including those in police and fire departments, schools, law courts, and hospitals, and on inspection, street, and sanitation crews. They made sure that city construction contracts were awarded to their own members. Urban government reformers, crusading for good government and an end to graft, often launched investigations of machines that exposed the corruption. Sometimes a machine boss had to spend time in jail, but his organization usually survived, primarily because urban working people relied on the machines for jobs and favors that "good government" politicians were slow to provide.

Boston ward leader Martin Lomasney explained how this worked in a statement he gave to the *Boston Globe* in 1923:

> Is somebody out of a job? We do our best to place him and not

This cartoon from the humor magazine Puck *demonstrates voters' power to end political corruption. A silo full of "public common sense" explodes through a globe filled with "freely cast ballots," which blow corrupt machine politicians sky high.*

necessarily on the public payroll. Does the family run in arrears with the landlord or the butcher? Then we lend a helping hand. Do the kids need shoes or clothing, or the mother a doctor? We do what we can, and...we keep old friends and make new ones.

Thus, machines made up for the lack of a welfare system.

Cincinnati's George B. Cox, a former saloon owner, was a fairly honest city boss. A Republican, in 1879 he won election to the City Council and worked with local reformers to improve the quality of police officers and city services. He remained in power for almost 20 years. William Marcy Tweed, boss of New York City's Democratic party club called Tammany Hall, amassed a huge fortune through graft and fraud. Convicted in 1873 of stealing millions of dollars from New York City, Tweed eventually died in jail. Tammany remained in power, however, dominating New York politics for another half century.

Machines held sway in dozens of cities, including Rochester, Jersey City, Philadelphia, Baltimore, Atlanta, Memphis, Kansas City, St. Louis, Omaha, Chicago, and San Francisco. Over the years, they produced some brilliant and popular politicians. In the end, however, the growth of a civil service and determined attacks from reformers brought the period of their greatest power to a close.

SEE ALSO

Cities; Government reform; Politics; Tammany Hall

FURTHER READING

Finegold, Kenneth. *Experts and Politicians: Reform Challenges to Machine Politics in New York, Cleveland, and Chicago.* Princeton, N.J.: Princeton University Press, 1995.
Zink, Harold. *City Bosses in the United States. A Study of Twenty Municipal Bosses.* 1930. Reprint, New York: AMS Press, 1968.

Marriage

AS THE 19TH CENTURY drew to a close, American attitudes toward marriage were changing. In one sense, young people of this period were just like their parents. They hoped to marry for love and believed that along with children, marriage would bring them closer to the goals that most human beings want, such as companionship, economic security, and the comforts of a home. By the late 1800s, however, they had more options outside of marriage for reaching at least some of these goals and therefore took more time selecting a mate.

In order to survive in earlier times, most women had to live within a household, either as wives, dependents in an extended family, or servants. By the late 1800s, this situation had changed. Women's opportunities for jobs and education were not anywhere near what they would be later on, but they were definitely improving. This meant that many women, especially urban women for whom jobs were most plentiful, felt less in a hurry to get married. In addition, as they established more independent lives, they freed themselves somewhat from parental controls. Arranged marriages, in which wealthy parents chose a daughter's husband and focused more on his social standing and income than on whether she loved him, became less frequent.

Changing urban conditions affected men in this period, but in a slightly different way. Securing the comforts of home was a prime reason why men married, but modern city life now provided men with comforts available in the past only through marriage.

Offered rich possibilities for housing, food, housekeeping, and entertainment in modern cities, men spent a longer time enjoying bachelorhood before marrying. Delaying marriage also gave them more time to get established financially or to locate wives whose financial resources and family connections would help their careers.

College-educated women began delaying marriage in this period, and when they did marry tended to have fewer children than their mothers. Sometimes they had none at all. Some professional women chose not to marry, instead establishing long-lasting and loving partnerships with other women with whom they shared property and living expenses. For such women, these partnerships were preferable to a marriage in which bearing children and maintaining a home would have limited their careers. Women of independent means, who had inherited property from family or a deceased husband, sometimes also entered such relationships. Some

A California bride and groom pose for a wedding photo around 1880. White gowns and veils would not become standard wedding attire until the 20th century.

observers called these same-sex female relationships "Boston marriages," after a Henry James novel, *The Bostonians* (1886), which depicted several such female couples. Although Boston marriages could be homosexual, they could also simply involve the mutual expression of romantic tenderness. There was little stigma attached to such relationships in this period.

In general, young people of this era had higher expectations of marriage than their parents. Their parents saw marriage as a duty and something they had to endure if they were unhappy. In contrast, young people of the late 1800s and early 1900s expected more personal satisfaction. They wanted expressions of romantic love, reciprocal respect, and a mutuality of desire and purpose. If this did not happen, they were increasingly prepared to seek a divorce.

As a result, the divorce rate went up in this era. In 1880, for every 21 marriages, 1 ended in divorce; by 1924, 1 in every 7 marriages ended in divorce. Alarmed at this trend, policy makers began to suggest steps to reverse it. Some argued that making marriage licenses more difficult to obtain would reduce the incidence of divorce. They pressed state governments to raise the age of consent for sexual intercourse and to require public notice and medical tests before marriage. Other reformers proposed alternatives to traditional marriage. Benjamin B. Lindsey, the first juvenile court judge in Denver, Colorado, advocated "trial marriage," a time when couples lived together openly on a trial basis in order to see if they were compatible. Anarchist Emma Goldman expressed even more radical ideas. She rejected marriage entirely, arguing that women and men should be able to love one another freely, without the approval of either state or religion.

Despite these challenges to traditional marriage, more people sought marriage than avoided it in this period, and most divorces ended in remarriage. Marriage remained especially important to sharecropping and homesteading families, for whom the division of labor on farms required that women, men, and children all shoulder household tasks. Homesteading men often placed notices in newspapers asking for women willing to come out West and be their wives, and some eastern women placed similar advertisements. Even if their marriages were not especially happy, farm, immigrant, and wage-earning couples often hung on to one another to get through hard times. For such couples, because income brought in by all family members was essential to survival, divorce was seldom an option, although desertions occurred frequently.

Marriages that blended couples of different racial, religious, and ethnic backgrounds were rare in this era. Some states outlawed interracial marriage. Even where it was legal—with the exception of marriages between male settlers in the West and Native American or Hispanic women—society frowned upon "mixed-blood" weddings. Most religious groups married within their own faiths or insisted that one spouse be converted to the religion of the other. First-generation ethnic groups watched carefully over the marital choices of their children to make sure they married within the group. But as second-generation children found increasing opportunities for independence in the modern city, such parental controls weakened.

In this era, some Native Americans and Mormons still practiced polygamy, the marriage of a man to more than one wife. By the late 19th century, however, state governments had declared such marriages illegal.

SEE ALSO
Divorce; Family life; Goldman, Emma

FURTHER READING
Chudacoff, Howard. *The Age of the Bachelor: Creating an American Subculture.* Princeton, N.J.: Princeton University Press, 1999.
Cott, Nancy. *Public Vows: A History of Marriage and the Nation.* Cambridge, Mass.: Harvard University Press, 2000.
May, Elaine Tyler. *Great Expectations: Marriage and Divorce in Post-Victorian America.* Chicago: University of Chicago Press, 1980.
Yalom, Marilyn. *A History of the Wife.* New York: HarperCollins, 2001.

McKinley, William

- *Born: Jan. 29, 1843, Niles, Ohio*
- *Education: Allegheny College (Pennsylvania), one term, 1860; Albany School of Law (New York), one term, 1865*
- *Accomplishments: major, Union army (1865); U.S. House of Representatives (Republican–Ohio, 1877–91); governor of Ohio (1892–97); President of the United States (1897–1901)*
- *Died: Sept. 14, 1901, Buffalo, N.Y.*

WILLIAM MCKINLEY, 25th President of the United States, was the last chief executive of the 19th century and the first of the 20th century, although his 1901 death from an assassin's bullet left the shaping of the new century's politics to other hands. McKinley was commander in chief during the Spanish-American War and started the United States on its career as an imperial power with overseas territorial interests.

The son of an Ohio iron manufacturer, McKinley attended Allegheny College in Pennsylvania for a short time and worked briefly as a teacher before the Civil War. He joined the Union army as a private, served under another future President, Rutherford B. Hayes, and rose to be a major. After the war, he practiced law in Canton, Ohio, and worked as a prosecutor. He married Ida Saxton in 1871. The couple had two daughters who died in early childhood. Ida McKinley suffered considerable trauma in delivering her second child and spent the rest of her adult life as an invalid, assiduously cared for by her spouse.

Ohio's Republican voters elected McKinley to Congress in 1876; he won reelection repeatedly through the 1870s and 1880s, making his reputation as a supporter of high tariffs. Tariffs (taxes on imported goods) raised the expenses of foreign companies, thereby giving certain American businesses a competitive edge. High tariff rates also expanded federal coffers, which let Congress fund popular social programs such as benefits for the families of Civil War veterans. McKinley's tariff policy did tend to stifle competition and inflate prices, however, which angered many voters.

McKinley lost his congressional seat in 1890 but went on to win two terms as governor of Ohio. In 1896, with the assistance of Marcus Hannah, a wealthy businessman with a powerful network of political connections, McKinley won the Republican nomination for President. He ran on a high-tariff, pro-business platform, also supporting pro-business currency policies associated with the gold standard, which favored a tight money supply based on the value of gold. His opponent, Democrat William Jennings Bryan, a former Nebraska congressman, made "free silver" the centerpiece of his campaign. Bryan's supporters demanded that both silver and gold become the basis of U.S. currency. Since silver was more abundant than gold, such a step would both

Republican President William McKinley (second from right on the platform) takes the oath of office at the start of his second term, March 4, 1901. Before the end of the year, McKinley would be killed by an assassin's bullet.

lower the value of money and increase its supply, and therefore ease the ability of indebted farmers to pay back loans. While Bryan campaigned across the country, McKinley waged a "front porch campaign," receiving visitors and delivering speeches at his home. His victory over Bryan was decisive.

Although his campaign stressed domestic economic policies, foreign affairs took center stage in McKinley's first term. He reversed the noninterventionist policies of his Democratic predecessor, Grover Cleveland, who had rejected annexation of Hawaii. McKinley and the Republican Congress made Hawaii a U.S. territory.

Cleveland had also opposed U.S. military involvement in the Spanish colony of Cuba, where rebel forces were fighting for independence. McKinley at first urged a negotiated settlement to the conflict. However, the destruction of the U.S. ship *Maine* in a Cuban harbor early in 1898 aroused such anti-Spanish sentiment in the United States that Congress soon declared war. The Spanish-American War lasted less than half a year and

ended with victory and new international status for the United States. Cuba won independence from Spain but accepted U.S. occupation troops.

As a result of the Spanish-American War, the United States took control over Spain's former colonies in the Pacific Ocean—Guam and the Philippines—though not without a prolonged struggle to subdue Filipino nationalists, who resented their new rulers as much as they had resented the Spanish. McKinley and his secretary of state, John Hay, secured U.S. trading rights in China by pressuring other powerful nations to adopt an Open Door policy, an agreement not to divide China into separate commercial "spheres of influence."

In 1900, the Republicans nominated McKinley for a second term. The convention chose New York governor and Spanish-American War veteran Theodore Roosevelt as his new running mate. William Jennings Bryan, renominated by the Democrats, campaigned against McKinley's imperialistic foreign policy. This policy remained popular, however, and the McKinley-Roosevelt ticket gave the Republicans an even more solid victory than in 1896.

In September 1901, McKinley visited the Pan-American Exposition, a fair being held in Buffalo, New York. He delivered a speech on international issues and then shook hands on the exposition grounds with a line of visitors. Leon Czolgosz, an unemployed and mentally unstable mill worker from Detroit, waited in the line with a concealed pistol. When Czolgosz, who considered McKinley an enemy of the working class, reached the President, he shot him twice in the chest. McKinley succumbed to his wounds a week later, and Roosevelt took office as the new President.

SEE ALSO
Bryan, William Jennings; Imperialism;
International relations; Monetary policies;
Presidency; Republican party; Roosevelt,
Theodore; Spanish-American War; Taxes
and tariffs

FURTHER READING
Morgan, H. Wayne. *William McKinley and
His America.* Kent, Ohio: Kent State Uni-
versity Press, 2003.
Phillips, Kevin. *William McKinley.* New
York: Times Books, 2003.

Medicine

BEGINNING IN the late 1800s, the
location, practice, and study of American
medicine went through a period of
extraordinary change. Researchers
gained new understanding of the bacte-
rial origin of many diseases. Prestigious
universities opened medical schools, some
of which admitted women. Physicians
began to earn more for their services,
and nursing became professionalized.
Standards of cleanliness and care rose
in hospitals and, as transportation facilities improved, so did access to that care,
especially for city dwellers. The combination of all of these changes led to a lower
rate of mortality for most Americans.

Scientists made great progress in
identifying the sources of specific diseases. By the early 1900s, European
researchers had isolated the germs that
caused typhoid fever, diphtheria,
cholera, pneumonia, tetanus, plague,
and dysentery, as well as those that
caused gonorrhea and syphilis, two
venereal, or sexually transmitted, diseases. American doctors who trained
in Europe brought this new knowledge
back to the United States and secured
funding for research programs of their
own. American companies manufactured antiseptics to control dangerous
microorganisms, and drug companies

arose to manufacture the chemical and
metallic compounds increasingly being
used in the field of pharmacology.

Other scientific advances, such as
X-rays, anesthesia, and blood transfu-
sions—all giant steps forward in
health care in this period—helped
improve the quality of hospitals. No
longer places where the poor went to
die, hospitals became centers for
advanced medical care. The number of
hospitals grew from barely a hundred
at the end of the Civil War to more
than 6,000 by 1920. The first sanato-
riums for the treatment of tuberculosis
appeared in the early 1900s. Although
institutions for the mentally ill multiplied in this era, their standards of
care did not rise. They remained essentially custodial, keeping patients relatively safe but doing little with psychotherapy, drug treatments, or other
means to help them get well.

The development of better antiseptic procedures and anesthesia increased
the number of successful hospital surg-
eries. It also led to the increasing med-
icalization of childbirth. Before 1900,
midwives attended most women in
childbirth and only the poorest of
women went to a hospital to give
birth. The lack of clean conditions in
hospitals led to high rates of childbed
fever, an infection of the uterus that
usually led to death for new mothers.
With the introduction of better anti-
sepsis in hospitals, physicians, who at
the time were overwhelming male,
campaigned against home births and
midwives, whom they accused of being
unprepared to deal with medical emergencies. The experience of childbirth
for middle- and upper-class women
moved increasingly to hospitals, where
various forms of anesthesia (ether or
chloroform) also became common.

Physician training became more
systematic and specialized. Before the

late 1800s, most doctors trained by apprenticing themselves to other physicians and seeking only one or two years of supplemental medical college training. Early in the 20th century, the American Medical Association (founded in 1847) changed this system. Between 1900 and 1910, its membership grew from 10,000 to 70,000. Its enlarged membership allowed it to fund a scientific journal, *The Journal of the American Medical Association,* to set up bureaus to study the effects of drugs, and to raise standards for medical training. In 1910 educator Abraham Flexner issued a scathing report on medical schools, entitled "Medical Education in the United States and Canada." His study of the schools' entrance requirements, quality of faculty and laboratories, and the availability of teaching hospitals for clinical work concluded that only a few schools could meet the highest standards of the profession. "We have indeed in America medical practitioners not inferior to the best elsewhere," he wrote in his report, "but there is probably no other country in the world in which there is so great a distance and so fatal a difference between the best, the average, and the worst." As a result of Flexner's report, many medical schools closed. By 1920, 85 schools remained, with the high scientific standards of The Johns Hopkins University School of Medicine, founded in 1893, serving as the prototype of excellence.

By the late 1800s, some medical schools, including Johns Hopkins and those at major state universities, were accepting women students. These women followed in the footsteps of earlier pioneers, such as Elizabeth Blackwell and her sister Emily, who ran the Infirmary for Women and Children in New York City and trained other women in maternal and pediatric medicine. By 1900, the United States had more than 7,000 women physicians, about 6 percent of the total profession. More than a hundred of these were African American. Most women physicians built practices around family care or worked as technical assistants in hospitals. The American Medical Association did not admit women until 1915.

The medical establishment excluded African Americans even more than it did women. Kept out of medical societies and off of hospital staffs, black physicians developed a completely

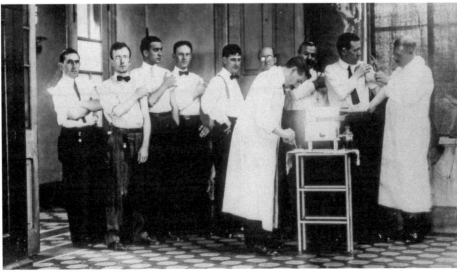

The first typhoid vaccine is administered at the Army Medical School in 1909. Typhoid is a potentially fatal disease of the intestinal tract caused by contaminated food or water.

separate medical care and training system. Howard University in Washington, D.C., opened its Medical Department in 1868, and the Methodist Church founded Meharry Medical College in Nashville, Tennessee, in 1876. Black physicians founded their own medical journals and, in 1895, their own medical society, the National Medical Association.

While many areas of medical science progressed rapidly during this era, the finding of cures for diseases moved more slowly. Poliomyelitis (infantile paralysis) and influenza caused epidemics that no known medication or vaccine could check. In 1894, an antitoxin was developed for diphtheria—an inflammation of the heart and nervous system caused by a toxin from bacteria—and the cure saved many lives. But the side effects of other "cures," including those for venereal diseases, were so harsh that physicians hesitated to use them. Mercury and the arsenic-based drug Salvarsan, for example, were used to treat syphilis, but both had toxic effects on the body. By 1914, medical records showed that Salvarsan had resulted in 109 deaths. Mercury led to the loss of teeth, tongue fissures, and hemorrhaging of the bowels.

In addition, many Americans continued to doctor themselves at home with "patent medicines," concoctions sold by quacks, or fake doctors. These brews, most of which contained alcohol, some as high as 44 percent, or addictive doses of opium or morphine, claimed to cure everything from baldness to menstrual "blockages." By 1900, the sales of patent medicines had grown from a pre–Civil War level of about $3.5 million to $75 million per year. In 1906, public indignation about the health effects of dangerous and addictive drugs led Congress to pass the Pure Food and Drugs Act, which created a system for testing foods and drugs destined for human consumption.

SEE ALSO

Collegs and universities; Health, public; Influenza epidemic (1918); Population and fertility; Psychology; Pure Food and Drugs Act (1906)

FURTHER READING

Duffy, John. From Humors to Medical Science: A History of American Medicine. Urbana: University of Illinois Press, 1993.
Leavitt, Judith Walzer. Brought to Bed: Childbearing in America, 1750 to 1950. New York: Oxford University Press, 1986.
Ludmerer, Kenneth. Learning to Heal: The Development of American Medical Education. New York: Basic Books, 1985.
Morantz-Sanchez, Regina Markell. Sympathy and Science: Women Physicians in American Medicine. Rev. ed. Chapel Hill: University of North Carolina Press, 2000.
Reverby, Susan M. Ordered to Care: The Dilemma of American Nursing, 1850–1945. New York: Cambridge University Press, 1987.

Mexicans

SEE Hispanic Americans

Military

IN THE DECADES that followed the Civil War, the United States reduced the strength of its army from 1,000,000 to 26,000 men. Stationed mostly in the West, these men engaged in a series of wars against Indians. Every western territory and state had an army fort, and usually more than one. Kansas alone had eight major forts. The forts served as supply stations, barracks, and staging areas for battles in the Indian wars. These wars, waged on behalf of white

An American military pilot poses with his single-engine airplane at a flight training facility in California. Although fragile in appearance, such planes fought aerial battles and dropped bombs and cargo during World War I.

settlers in the Great Plains and the Southwest, were attempts to clear Indians from desirable lands and control tribes that continued to resist being placed on reservations.

In the battles of the 19th century, cavalry (soldiers on horseback) and infantry (foot soldiers) had used both single shot and repeating rifles, reinforced from the rear by artillery such as small cannons and Gatling guns, early machine guns that could fire 300 rounds a minute. Cavalry played an important role in the Indian wars and also saw service in the Spanish-American War and World War I. Cavalry charges, however, were relics of an earlier age, when opposing armies faced each other on vast battlefields. By World War I, with the advent of trenches, barbed wire, and machine guns, cavalry charges were suicidal. Horses and mules remained useful as transport because the relatively new cars and trucks were often mechanically unreliable, but the days of the horse cavalry were over. After World War I, cavalry units began converting to units with tanks and armored cars.

Other changes in battlefield technology during the early 20th century altered the nature of warfare itself. These changes included, in addition to tanks, improvements to the repeating rifle and machine gun and the introduction of submarines, poison gas, and airplanes. Of all these new developments, the advent of air power did the most to change the course of military history. The use of airplanes in World War I demonstrated that aerial reconnaissance, bombing raids, and tactics for shooting down enemy aircraft would be crucial in the wars of the future.

Technology was only one aspect of the U.S. military that changed after the beginning of the 20th century. The army sought to improve leadership and tactical skills as well. In 1901, Secretary of War Elihu Root announced the founding in Washington, D.C., of the Army War College, where high-level officers could study national defense and military science. The army also reorganized its top offices and improved its cooperation with the National Guard and the navy. In 1916, President Woodrow Wilson sent 112,000 U.S. Army regulars and National Guardsmen to New Mexico to head off a threatened invasion by the Mexican General Pancho Villa. By the time of World War I, army strength was at about 225,000 men. New recruits of army regulars swelled the wartime ranks. National Guardsmen made up 40 percent of the soldiers who served in France.

In the late 1800s, African Americans found new career opportunities in the army. During the Indian wars, many soldiers served in all-black regiments. These troops, who came to be known as Buffalo Soldiers, usually served under the command of white officers. Black officers remained a rarity, although in 1877 West Point commissioned its first black graduate, Lieutenant Henry O. Flipper. African American soldiers also served in segregated units in the Spanish-American War and World War I.

Of the more than 350,000 African American soldiers who served in World War I, most never saw combat and only about 1,300 were officers. Even though the soldiers had been trained to fight, the army assigned them work as cooks and kitchen helpers, porters, manual laborers, and dockworkers. Disappointed, African American soldiers in the 369th Infantry Regiment appealed to the French to give them a chance to serve at the front. The French army, which did not discriminate against black soldiers, opened their ranks to include them. The members of the 369th, who became known as the Harlem Hell Fighters, fought with great bravery. At the end of the war, the French army awarded the entire regiment its most honored medal, the Croix de Guerre. In all, African Americans suffered just under 4,000 killed and wounded.

In the navy, historically more open to black enlistment than the army, African Americans actually lost status in the early 20th century. In the years leading up to World War I, the navy assigned black enlisted men to the Stewards' Branch, with duties including cleaning officers' quarters and preparing and serving food. The navy would not commission its first African American officers until the 1940s.

The Marine Corps remained quite small between the Civil War and World War I, usually numbering fewer than 10,000 men. Their ranks expanded gradually, and marines saw action in Cuba, Puerto Rico, Guam, and the Philippines during the Spanish-American War and in the Boxer Rebellion in China (1900). Between 1900 and 1916, Presidents Theodore Roosevelt, William H. Taft, and Woodrow Wilson chose the marines to lead "interventions" in

numerous Latin American countries, where civil disturbances threatened U.S. business or strategic interests. At the height of World War I, the Marines reached a strength of nearly 53,000 men and saw action in a variety of engagements in Europe. The 4th Marine Brigade earned the nickname of Devil Dogs for heroic action in several major battles. Pilots in the new aviation branch of the marines flew bomber missions over France and Belgium. More than 30,000 marines served in France during a period of six months, and more than a third of them were killed or wounded.

Many American women were eager to join the military for the war effort in 1917. The army was slow to include them, though it did establish a significant army nurse corps. Women in uniforms of the American Expeditionary Force, the name given to the armed forces in Europe during World War I, also worked as clerks and office staff. More than 300 women were members of the Army Signal Corps. Nicknamed the Hello Girls, these bilingual (French- and English-speaking) telephone operators performed crucial communications functions for troops in the field. The telephone operators, like the nurses, were actually enlisted in the army and held the rank of lieutenant. Officers addressed them as "Soldier." As many as 21,000 women served in the army during World War I, about half of them overseas.

The Marine Corps accepted only 300 women (marinettes), assigning them to clerical jobs in order to release men for combat, but the navy enrolled 11,275 yeomanettes, assigning them jobs as recruiters, general clerks, munitions makers, translators, radio operators, and designers of camouflage. Yeomanettes earned the same pay as navy yeomen, just under $1 a day. At the end of the war, the War Department thanked women for their service and mustered them out. Military careers for women lay in the future.

SEE ALSO

African Americans; Airplane; American Expeditionary Force; Automobile; Buffalo Soldiers; Native Americans; Navy, U.S.; Race relations; Roosevelt, Theodore; Science and technology; Segregation; Spanish-American War; Wilson, Woodrow; World War I

FURTHER READING

Gavin, Lettie. *American Women in World War I: They Also Served.* Boulder: University of Colorado Press, 1997.
Morris, James M. *America's Armed Forces: A History.* 2nd ed. Englewood Cliffs, N.J.: Prentice Hall, 1995.
Nalty, Bernard C. *Strength for the Fight: A History of Black Americans in the Military.* New York: Free Press, 1986.
Office of Military History, United States Army. *American Military History 1607–1958.* Honolulu, Hawaii: University Press of the Pacific, 2002.

Mining

MINING IS the extraction of mineral resources from beneath the ground. Some mining operations involve digging pits in the surface of the earth or stripping away surface layers of dirt and rocks to get at underlying mineral wealth. To extract more deeply buried minerals, miners construct shafts and tunnels that penetrate far below the surface. Products from mines include coal for fuel, salt for seasoning and preserving food, precious or semiprecious gems, and metals such as iron ore, copper, gold, and silver for manufacturing tools, weapons, coins, jewelry, machines, and other items. Stone quarrying is another form of mining.

Because the United States has extensive underground mineral supplies, mining has played a major role in American history. Coal mining was particularly important during the late 19th and early 20th centuries. Many of the period's technological advances relied on coal-burning power plants to boil the water for steam-driven electrical generators. Most buildings relied on coal-burning furnaces, fireplaces, or stoves for heating. Thirty-eight states hold coal deposits, with the largest in Montana, Illinois, Kentucky, West Virginia, and Pennsylvania.

Coal miners practiced one of the nation's most dangerous professions, and their union, the United Mine Workers of America (founded in 1890), figured prominently in the labor history of the period. The union was in the forefront of the fight for the eight-hour workday and other reforms. Striking coal miners sometimes suffered injury and death in their confrontations with mine owners and law enforcement officials.

The mineral wealth of the West was a driving force behind the nation's westward expansion throughout the 1800s. In some cases, a new discovery of valuable mineral deposits would spark a gold or silver "rush," attracting an influx of fortune hunters, provoking clashes with Indians, leading to federal troop deployments, and promoting the construction of new railroad and telegraph lines. A South Dakota gold rush in the mid-1870s

Miners and their mules work in a Gary, West Virginia, coal mine in 1908. The open-flame oil lamps on the miners' helmets were serious hazards in the presence of coal gas.

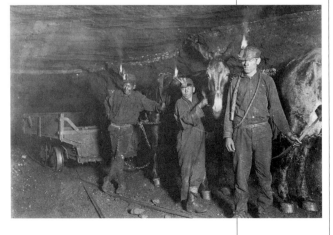

exacerbated conflict with the region's Indian tribes and helped set the stage for General George Armstrong Custer's 1876 defeat at the Battle of Little Bighorn. An 1882 gold rush in Idaho led to the discovery of silver mines far richer than the area's gold deposits. A gold rush in the western Canadian region known as the Klondike attracted thousands of treasure seekers in the late 1890s and touched off a secondary gold rush in nearby Alaska.

Communities that sprang up at gold or silver rush sites came to be known as boomtowns. Some flourished briefly but vanished as quickly as they had appeared, while others developed into stable, long-term settlements. A few people got rich mining gold, silver, and other metals, but often the chief beneficiaries of a boomtown economy were the entrepreneurs who supplied miners with housing, food, drink, equipment, laundry service, and other goods and services. In longer-term mining operations, the people who profited most were mine owners, corporate executives, and stockholders.

Western silver mining stimulated the free silver movement, which advocated an expanded national money supply based on silver as well as gold.

SEE ALSO

Industry; Labor unions; Monetary policies; Science and technology; Strikes; United Mine Workers of America; West, the

FURTHER READING

Freese, Barbara. *Coal: A Human History.* Cambridge, Mass.: Perseus, 2003.
Marks, Paula Mitchell. *Precious Dust: The American Gold Rush Era, 1848–1900.* New York: Morrow, 1994.
Miller, Donald L., and Richard E. Sharpless. *The Kingdom of Coal: Work, Enterprise, and Ethnic Communities in the Mine Fields.* Philadelphia: University of Pennsylvania Press, 1985.

Wallace, Robert, and the editors of Time-Life Books. *The Miners.* Alexandria, Va.: Time-Life Books, 1976.
Watkins, T. H. *Gold and Silver in the West: An Illustrated History.* Palo Alto, Calif.: American West Publishing, 1971.

Monetary policies

DURING THE second half of the 19th century, Americans held impassioned debates about the value of the country's paper currency. When governments issue paper money, they are essentially promising that citizens can redeem it at a bank or other financial institution for gold or silver. Traditionally, U.S. paper money relied on values assigned to both of these precious metals. This system was called bimetallism, a term that referred to the two metals being used as standards. In the mid-19th century, many other nations were eliminating silver as a standard and basing their money solely on gold in order to make it more valuable and prevent inflation. For this reason, American business and banking interests argued for an end to bimetallism and the adoption of a strict gold standard.

"Goldbugs," as the people who argued for this position were called, believed that a currency based on gold would be "tight," that is, issued in limited supply and thus worth more. Bankers and financiers, who lend money out, favored a tight money supply

In the 19th century, gold certificates like this one, worth five dollars, were pieces of paper that could be exchanged at a bank for their face value in gold coins. The U.S. Treasury discontinued gold certificates in 1933.

because it would prevent inflation. During inflation, two things happen: prices for essential commodities rise and a country's money declines in value. Bankers oppose inflation, because then the money they get back is worth less than the money they originally loaned out.

Arguments in favor of a strict gold standard began to heat up in the 1870s but were opposed by "Silverites" determined to retain bimetallism. Silverites received the backing of silver mine owners, who were selling their metal profitably to foreign markets as well as to the U.S. Mint. The mint would pay only a fixed price for silver, however, which meant that it was receiving less and less silver as mine owners sold their silver abroad. In 1873, when supplies of silver hit a temporary low and silver dollars were disappearing from the currency, Congress passed a Coinage Act demonetizing silver and eliminating the silver dollar as a U.S. coin. Almost simultaneously, mine companies discovered new silver sources and better extraction techniques. As a result, the supply of silver went up, forcing its price down. Now unable to sell their silver for a good price even to the U.S. Mint, the owners of silver mines protested, calling the Coinage Act of 1873 a "crime."

Desperate to restore silver as a basis for American coinage, Silverites won support from farmers and labor leaders, who argued that basing money on silver as well as gold would increase the money supply. They recognized that this would be an inflationary step, but they actually preferred inflation, for it meant that a farmer who had taken out a $1,000 mortgage in 1865 to buy more land would be able to pay it off in 1880 with cheaper currency. For them, silver came to symbolize economic justice for the mass of the American people, while gold symbolized the attempts of bankers to squeeze them dry. In response to protests against the demonetization of silver, in 1878 Congress passed the Bland-Allison Act, which restored the silver dollar as a legal coin.

The debates over silver had political consequences. In 1877, the Greenback Labor party formed, taking its name from the paper money printed during the Civil War. Greenbackers called for more paper money and the retention of bimetallism. Their platform also included calls for an eight-hour day for government employees and health and safety standards for workers. They were successful enough in the off-year elections of 1878 to win 1,060,000 votes and 14 seats in Congress. In the next election, they added calls for a graduated income tax, the regulation of interstate commerce, and woman suffrage to their platform, but after that their popular support declined.

During the 1880s, farmers continued to press for the unlimited or "free" coinage of silver. Congress responded by passing the Sherman Silver Purchase Act (1890), which increased government purchases of silver. This legislation lasted only a few years. Congress repealed it in the spring of 1893 when a panic arose over a sharp decline in the amount of federal gold reserves. Once again, farmers led the protests, charging that the eastern bankers who held their mortgages and other debts were sending them into ruin. They held on to "free silver" as their economic salvation, chanting,

> The dollar of our daddies,
> Of silver coinage free,
> Will make us rich and happy,
> Will bring prosperity.

"Free silver" became an important plank in the Populist party platform during the election of 1892 and the Populist and Democratic platforms of 1896. Both parties nominated Nebraska Congressman William Jennings Bryan, a highly popular and eloquent champion of free silver, as their candidate for President that year. Republican William McKinley won that election, however, and in 1900 a Republican majority in Congress enacted the Gold Standard Act, making gold the sole standard for all currency.

SEE ALSO

Bryan, William Jennings; Democratic party; McKinley, William; Mining; Politics; Populist party

FURTHER READING

Ritter, Gretchen. *Goldbugs and Greenbacks: The Antimonopoly Tradition and the Politics of Finance in America.* New York: Cambridge University Press, 1997.
Friedman, Milton, and Anna Jacobson Schwartz. *A Monetary History of the United States, 1867–1960.* Princeton, N.J.: Princeton University Press, 1963.

Morgan, John Pierpont

- *Born: Apr. 17, 1837, Hartford, Conn.*
- *Education: studied at the University of Göttingen (Germany), 1855–57*
- *Accomplishments: founder, J. P. Morgan and Company, 1861; founder, United States Steel Corporation, 1901*
- *Died: Mar. 31, 1913, Rome, Italy*

JOHN P. MORGAN built upon the fortune left to him by his father, merchant and banker Junius Spencer Morgan, to become one of the world's wealthiest financiers. During the decades following the Civil War, the young Morgan invested heavily in the railroad business, not building new lines but periodically refinancing bank-

rupt lines or consolidating them into larger systems. This process, which became known as Morganization, was always to his profit.

By 1890, Morgan had become enormously wealthy. His wide international connections and talent for business reorganization twice allowed him to rescue the nation's finances. The first rescue took place in 1895, after an economic downturn had depleted the U.S. Treasury's gold reserves. Acting as the nation's banker, Morgan replenished the reserves by selling government bonds for gold, much of it bought abroad through his foreign affiliates. The second rescue occurred in 1907, when the failure of several trust companies triggered a panic on the stock market. Turning to Morgan for help, the federal government entrusted its funds to him and his lieutenants, who then acted to save the most financially healthy of the New York banks. In performing this service, Morgan was, in essence, acting as the nation's central bank, an institution the United States lacked until Congress passed the Federal Reserve Act in 1913.

Two of Morgan's most highly publicized financial ventures occurred in 1901. In that year, he absorbed Andrew Carnegie's steel company into the United States Steel Corporation, the largest industrial concern of the nation. The second venture, the Northern Securities Company, was more con-

Financier J.P. Morgan, one of the wealthiest and most influential men in the United States, swings his cane angrily at the photographer who captured this image in 1910. Morgan was notoriously camera shy.

troversial. Morgan formed this trust as a way of resolving the competition between railroad barons James J. Hill and Edward H. Harriman, both of whom were trying to dominate the lines in the American Northwest. The trust's potential for reducing competition in this region aroused strong antitrust opposition. Encouraged by President Theodore Roosevelt, the government prosecuted Northern Securities under the Sherman Antitrust Act and in 1904 forced its dissolution.

Beyond steel and railroads, Morgan extended his financial empire over the insurance, urban transportation, electricity, and communications industries, in addition to shipping lines and many other banks and investment houses. He was a key figure in what progressive reformers of the time called the "Money Trust," a small group of exceedingly wealthy bankers who dominated the nation's finances. A congressional investigation in 1912, led by Arsène Pujo, a Democratic Congressman from Louisiana, sought to find ways to curb Morgan's huge financial power. It did not fully succeed. Pujo's committee attacked Morgan's use of "interlocking directorates," a system in which individuals close to him sat on the boards of hundreds of the nation's biggest companies. It also investigated Morgan's use of his vast financial resources to control money and credit. The committee made recommendations based on its findings, none of which became law, but the investigation did increase public pressure for the banking reforms embodied in the Federal Reserve Act, which in 1913 established greater governmental control over the nation's banks.

An avid collector of European paintings, sculptures, tapestries, rare books and manuscripts, and other artistic objects, Morgan donated many of his acquisitions to the Metropolitan Museum of Art in New York City. In 1902 he commissioned architect Charles F. McKim to design a building to house his huge collection of books, manuscripts, prints, and drawings. In 1924, Morgan's son, J. P. Morgan II, made this building a public institution, and it is now the Pierpont Morgan Library in New York City.

SEE ALSO

Antitrust laws; Carnegie, Andrew; Federal Reserve Act (1913); Monetary policies; Regulation

FURTHER READING

Carosso, Vincent P. *The Morgans: Private International Bankers, 1854–1913*. Cambridge, Mass.: Harvard University Press, 1987.
Chernow, Ron. *The House of Morgan: An American Banking Dynasty and the Rise of Modern Finance*. New York: Atlantic Monthly Press, 1990.
Strouse, Jean. *Morgan: American Financier*. New York: Random House, 1999.

Mormonism

MORMONISM IS a common term for the faith practiced by the members of the Church of Jesus Christ of Latter-day Saints. According to Mormons, their founder, a western New York farmer named Joseph Smith, received their beliefs from texts that he found inscribed on golden tablets buried in the ground. Smith said that he translated the tablets with divine help. In 1830, he published the texts as the Book of Mormon and began to gather adherents.

Believing that they had restored the church that Jesus originally established, Mormons kept themselves separate from both Catholic and Protestant denominations. Joseph Smith, who called himself the church's

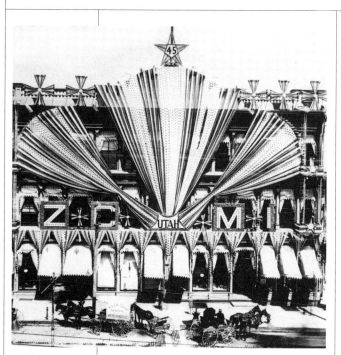

Early Mormon settlers in Salt Lake City founded ZCMI, Zion's Cooperative Mercantile Institution, the nation's first large department store. Decked out in bunting, ZCMI is celebrating Utah statehood in 1896.

first prophet and president, taught that Mormon priests have divine authority, and that the presidents of the church continue to receive divine revelation. Mormons maintain a strict morality, avoiding sex outside of marriage, tobacco, alcohol, caffeine, and other stimulants, such as drugs. Faithful Mormons tithe, or contribute one-tenth of their incomes to the church. They believe that their marriages continue after death, and they devote themselves to missionary activities, spreading the religion even to distant lands, as an article of their faith.

Mormons' isolation from other Christian sects made them vulnerable to persecution. More traditional Christians, as well as other Americans, were especially outraged by the Mormon practice of polygamy (the taking of more than one wife) and the Mormon claim that polygamy was divinely sanctioned. Arrested on a variety of charges, including treason, arson, and polygamy, in Nauvoo, Illinois, in 1844, Smith and his brother were dragged from jail by a mob and lynched. At this point, most Mormons followed an

early convert to Mormonism, Brigham Young, from Nauvoo to their "promised land" in the territory of Utah. In Utah, Young's followers established a strong religious community and for a time remained almost independent of federal control. Overcoming the hardships of the Utah climate, they irrigated dry lands and built Salt Lake City, a well-planned city with wide avenues and large yards and gardens. No longer living in the midst of enemies, they instituted a theocracy in which the church supervised all aspects of life.

Most of Utah's Mormons, including many Mormon women, supported polygamy, but because of the practice, the territory's repeated applications for statehood failed. In 1862, Congress passed a law banning polygamy but never enforced it. In the 1870s, after the Utah Territory gave women the right to vote, Congress stepped up its efforts to end polygamy. Mormons continued to defend it, finally arguing in the courts that a ban on polygamy interfered with their freedom of religion. This argument failed to convince the U.S. Supreme Court, which in 1879 formally declared polygamy illegal.

In 1887, Congress passed the Edmunds-Tucker Act, which not only reaffirmed a ban on polygamy but denied Utah's women the right to vote. Under pressure to obey federal law, in 1890 Mormon leaders agreed to end polygamy. This paved the way toward Utah's statehood. In November 1895, a state constitutional convention restored the vote to women, and early the next year the U.S. government allowed Utah into the Union. By then, there were almost 230,000 Mormons in the country, with settlements extending into Mexico and Canada. By 1920, Mormons numbered approximately half a million.

SEE ALSO

Religion; States and statehood; Woman suffrage movement

FURTHER READING

Arrington, Leonard J., and Davis Bitton. *The Mormon Experience: A History of the Latter-day Saints.* 2nd ed. Urbana: University of Illinois Press, 1992.

Bushman, Richard, and Claudia Bushman. *Mormons in America.* New York: Oxford University Press, 1998.

Shipps, Jan. *Mormonism: The Story of a New Religious Tradition.* Urbana: University of Illinois Press, 1985.

Motion pictures

THE DEVELOPMENT of motion pictures required two inventions, a camera that could take multiple photographs in a series and a projection system. Both of these appeared between 1870 and the early 1890s, thanks to the technical contributions of many photographers and inventors from Europe, Great Britain, and the United States.

In the early 19th century, the magic lantern was the most widespread projection system. It projected single images onto a wall or screen, much as slide projectors do today. Some inventors found ways to make these single images appear to move. One method involved mounting pictures of different stages of an activity, such as dancing or juggling, onto the inside of a circular, slotted drum. Watching through the slits as the drum was rotated gave viewers the illusion of movement. The invention of photography in 1839 by Louis Daguerre and then John Hyatt's use of celluloid as a base for photographic film in 1869 were important advances in image making. American inventor Thomas Edison's incandescent lightbulb, first demonstrated in 1879, contributed the bright light necessary for film projectors.

Meanwhile, British photographer Eadweard Muybridge, who was fascinated by human and animal movement, was taking consecutive pictures of a galloping horse. In 1879, by rotating the pictures in a projector, he made viewers think the horse was actually moving. The next advances came in the 1880s. French inventor Etienne-Jules Marey constructed a camera that could take 12 photographs per second, and American George Eastman invented perforated roll film. Now, one camera could take multiple photographs in a series.

Between 1890 and 1892, William Dickson, an assistant to Edison, synchronized a shutter with a sprocket system to move the film through a camera. The following year, he introduced the Kinetoscope, which allowed a single

Fred Ott, who worked for inventor Thomas Edison, sneezes for the camera in 1894. Edison's Kinetoscope took a sequence of still photographs and then displayed the pictures in rapid succession, which gave the illusion of a moving image.

viewer to see a moving image through a peephole. Next, both European and American inventors built projectors that enlarged images so that many people could see them at once. In 1895, the French brothers Louis and Auguste Lumière introduced the Cinématographe, a combination movie camera and projector that could be cranked by hand.

All of these advances led to the first exhibitions of motion pictures in the mid- to late 1890s. These films lasted from a few seconds to a few minutes and of course were silent and in black-and-white, although some were tinted by hand. Most films depicted actual events, such as the inauguration of a President, boxing matches, street scenes, or exotic locales. Others showed slapstick comedy and vaudeville routines, women in various stages of undress, or visual tricks (actions run backwards, and magical transformations or disappearances). Most Americans encountered the new medium in vaudeville houses or at special exhibitions.

The next development came from a French magician, Georges Méliès, who made films with narrative storylines, character development, and fantasy, all enhanced with trick photography. His science-fiction film, *A Trip to the Moon* (1902), was a great success. Building on what Méliès had done, Edwin S. Porter produced *The Great Train Robbery* (1903), America's first western. The film's fast-moving pace and shocking scenes, including the shooting of an innocent passenger and a bandit firing a gun straight at the camera, thrilled audiences. Western settings, crime, and romance became standard motion picture fare.

Nickelodeons—viewing areas set up in converted stores or warehouses and showing a continuous stream of films for a nickel—gave a boost to moviegoing. By 1908, the year of the first cartoon or animated films, the United States had about 8,000 nickelodeons. Given this kind of setting, going to the movies was a leisure activity that attracted chiefly working-class audiences. After entrepreneurs invested in cinema theaters and movie "palaces," movies began to bring in middle- and upper-class spectators.

American film companies competed heavily with one another during this period. Edison tried to dominate the field by buying out others' patents and harassing his competitors, but the industry grew too rapidly for him to monopolize. Before 1910, the industry was centered in New York City. Afterward, it began to move to Southern California, where entrepreneurs produced ever more ambitious films. After 1913, these had complex story lines based on the Bible, Shakespeare, or classic literature. Directors Cecil B. DeMille and D. W. Griffith specialized in spectacle films, featuring huge battle scenes, natural disasters, and wild festivities. Some movie stars, most notably Mary Pickford, Douglas Fairbanks, and Charlie Chaplin, became so successful that they were able to open their own filmmaking studios.

The content of motion pictures did not go unchallenged. Some Progressive Era reformers objected to film depictions of excessive violence and sexual content. Citizens in some cities formed local boards that previewed films and demanded cuts. Others objected to films that reinforced racial stereotypes. The best-known of these was *The Birth of a Nation,* Griffith's 1915 film of Thomas Dixon's novel *The Clansman* (1905). More than three hours long, the film painted African Americans as depraved and dangerous and glorified the white-robed night riders of the Ku Klux Klan.

During World War I, the government used motion pictures for propaganda. Movies with titles like *The Kaiser: The Beast of Berlin, To Hell With The Kaiser,* and *Pershing's Crusaders* (a reference to General John J. Pershing, head of the American forces in Europe) were shown in American movie theaters. After the war, the European film industry did not recover right away, thus enabling American films to dominate world markets. Hollywood produced some 86 percent of films shown worldwide.

SEE ALSO

Edison, Thomas Alva; Inventions; Leisure; Photography

FURTHER READING

Mast, Gerald. *A Short History of the Movies.* Indianapolis: Bobbs-Merrill, 1976.
Robinson, David. *From Peep Show to Palace: The Birth of American Film.* New York: Columbia University Press, 1996.
Sklar, Robert. *Movie-Made America: A Social History of American Movies.* New York: Random House, 1975.

Muckrakers

MUCKRAKERS WERE authors and investigative journalists who agitated for social change America by exposing the misconduct of the powerful and documenting the living and working conditions of the poor. Exercising their greatest influence in the years between 1890 and World War I, muckrakers campaigned for labor law reform, African American rights, nature conservation, the breakup of wealthy trusts and monopolies, and many other progressive causes. Muckraking exposés, published in such national periodicals as *American Magazine* and *McClure's,* helped spur public demands for reform.

Prominent muckrakers included Ida B. Wells, who crusaded against lynching; Upton Sinclair, whose 1906 novel *The Jungle* exposed unsafe conditions in the meat industry; Jacob Riis, whose late 19th-century writings and photographs chronicled the harsh reality of life in New York City's slums; and Ida Tarbell, author of *The History of the Standard Oil Company* (1904), which detailed corrupt practices in the petroleum business. Lincoln Steffens, an editor at both *McClure's* and *American Magazine,* wrote *The Shame of the Cities* (1904), an investigation of dishonest government officials. Ray Stannard Baker joined Steffens and Tarbell in founding *American Magazine* in 1906, and in 1908 he wrote *Following the Color Line,* the first book on American racial divisions by a prominent white journalist. In 1905, Baker's friend Samuel Hopkins Adams published a series of eleven articles in *Collier's Weekly* attacking the unregulated manufacture of patent medicines. The series, entitled "The Great American Fraud," helped secure the passage of the Pure Food and Drugs Act in 1906.

Lewis Hine photographed immigrants, sweatshop workers, and young children toiling in unregulated factories and mines. Nellie Bly, better known for her spectacular 72-day trip around the world, was an investigative reporter for the *New York World* who went

A 1905 cover illustration for Collier's, *an influential muckraking journal, uses a potent combination of images, dominated by a skull and bulging money sacks, to promote an article exposing abuses in the patent medicine industry.*

undercover to expose abuses in mental asylums. William T. Stead earned both admiration and resentment for *If Christ Came to Chicago* (1894), his exposé of Chicago's political corruption and its gambling and prostitution rackets. Stead died in the sinking of the *Titanic* after a colorful career as a muckraking journalist in the United States, Australia, and his native England.

Muckraking got its name following the publication of journalist David Graham Phillips's series, "The Treason of the Senate," which appeared in *Cosmopolitan* in 1906. Phillipss articles accused politicians in both parties of accepting bribes from lobbyists. President Theodore Roosevelt responded in a speech complaining that crusading journalists were overly obsessed with squalor and scandal. He compared them to an unappealing character in the 17th-century religious allegory, *Pilgrim's Progress*, "the man who could look no way but downward with the muck-rake in his hands." Although Roosevelt championed many of the reforms backed by the muckraking journals, he took offense at articles criticizing some of his political associates. The journalists themselves felt they were being maligned by Roosevelt's label, but the name *muckraker* stuck. The muckrakers' social reform successes included the passage of the Pure Food and Drugs Act and more than four dozen legislative curbs on big business combinations (trusts) during Roosevelt's administration alone. The writers of the muckraking era inspired later generations of investigative journalists.

SEE ALSO

Journalism; Literature; Photography; Pure Food and Drugs Act (1906); Regulation; Riis, Jacob; Roosevelt, Theodore; Sinclair, Upton Beall; Wells-Barnett, Ida B.

FURTHER READING

Filler, Louis. *The Muckrakers*. University Park: Pennsylvania State University Press, 1976.
Miraldi, Robert. *The Muckrakers: Evangelical Crusaders*. Westport, Conn.: Praeger, 2000.
Weinberg, Arthur, and Lila Shaffer Weinberg, eds. *The Muckrakers*. Urbana: University of Illinois Press, 2001.
Wilson, Harold S. McClure's *Magazine and the Muckrakers*. Princeton, N.J.: Princeton University Press, 1970.

Muir, John

- *Born: Apr. 21, 1838, Dunbar, Scotland*
- *Education: three years at the University of Wisconsin*
- *Accomplishments: founder, Sierra Club (1892); author,* Our National Parks *(1901), 12 other books, and more than 300 articles*
- *Died: Dec. 24, 1914, Los Angeles, Calif.*

JOHN MUIR was 11 when his family emigrated from Scotland to a farm near Portage, Wisconsin, where he and his younger brother roamed the countryside, reveling in the beauties of nature. Young Muir's inventions, including an alarm system that tipped him out of bed in the morning, won prizes at the Wisconsin State Fair. He spent three years at the University of Wisconsin before beginning a life of travel and odd jobs. Nearly blinded in an accident, Muir decided to cherish his eyesight and observe the natural world. His travels took him all over the United States and down into Central America. In California he explored the Sierra Nevada mountain range, making it his spiritual home, and lived in Yosemite as a shepherd.

In the 1870s Muir began to write. His travel books, nature studies, and lyrical articles about the Sierras and Yosemite gained him a national audi-

Naturalist John Muir wrote in 1901, "Keep close to Nature's heart...and break clear away, once in awhile, and climb a mountain or spend a week in the woods. Wash your spirit clean."

ence. His writings had a spiritual quality that was both compelling and energizing. He called on Americans to protect the country's natural beauty for their own enjoyment and to conserve it for future generations. "Only by going alone in silence, without baggage, can one truly get into the heart of the wilderness. All other travel is mere dust and hotels and baggage and chatter," he wrote in a letter to his wife in 1888. Luminaries such as poet Ralph Waldo Emerson and President Theodore Roosevelt came to consult with Muir. Government officials were impressed with his passionate love of nature. His influence led to the preservation of vast areas of natural beauty and the creation of Sequoia, Yosemite, Mt. Rainier, Petrified Forest, and Grand Canyon national parks.

In 1892, Muir and his supporters founded the Sierra Club, an organization dedicated to wilderness conservation and outdoor recreation. Muir served as the club's president for the rest of his life. The Sierra Club remains a large and active conservation group.

Muir's failure to save the Hetch Hetchy Valley near Yosemite was a devastating disappointment. In 1913, engineers dammed the Tuolumne River, completely flooding the valley, to create a water supply for the city of San Francisco. Still, John Muir saved hundreds of thousands of square miles of matchless terrain from development and exploitation.

SEE ALSO

Conservation; Environment; Parks and playgrounds; Roosevelt, Theodore

FURTHER READING

Ehrlich, Gretel. *John Muir: Nature's Visionary.* Washington, D.C.: National Geographic Society, 2000.
Marsh, Linnie Wolfe. *Son of the Wilderness: The Life of John Muir.* 1945. Reprint, Madison: University of Wisconsin Press, 2000.
Muir, John. *Nature Writings.* Edited by William Cronon. New York: Library of America, 1997.

Muller v. Oregon (1908)

MULLER V. OREGON was a U.S. Supreme Court case that played an important role in the development of protective labor legislation for women. It arose when laundry owner Curt Muller appealed his conviction for violating a 1903 Oregon law that limited women laundry workers to 10 hours of work per day. Courts had invalidated similar laws for men on the basis that they violated "freedom of contract," the right of individuals to sell their labor at any rate or under any conditions agreeable to them and their employers.

In arguing for limiting women's work hours, lawyer Louis D. Brandeis, representing the state, based his brief on sociological and medical data collected by Josephine Goldmark of the National Consumers' League. This data demonstrated that long work hours harmed women's health and reproductive capabilities in ways that were not harmful to men and that therefore the Court should set aside freedom of contract to protect women. The Court accepted this argument, upholding Oregon's law and thereby establishing a precedent for special protections for all women workers. Some labor advocates feared that basing workplace protections on differences between the sexes would lead to disadvantages for women in the workplace. Their opponents argued that it would eventually make protections for all workers possible.

SEE ALSO

Brandeis, Louis Dembitz; Labor; Law; National Consumers' League; Supreme Court, U.S.

FURTHER READING

Woloch, Nancy. Muller *v.* Oregon: *A Brief History with Documents.* Boston: Bedford/St. Martins, 1996.

Music

MUSIC WAS EVERYWHERE in the Gilded Age. Every midsized town had at least one brass band that would march in parades or perform at ceremonial events and on summer evenings in park band shells. Every church had its own choir, and many musicians made their living by holding choirmaster and organist jobs. Working-class and farm families entertained one another with folk music, transforming tunes that came from Europe or Africa into American versions. Most middle- and upper-class children received musical training, and many families owned pianos. Wealthy city dwellers of the Gilded Age funded many of the symphony orchestras, opera companies, choral societies, and music schools that still exist today.

The popular music played in homes, theaters, and cabarets between 1880 and 1920 ranged from love ballads and comedy songs to folk music, ragtime, the blues, and jazz. Long before the days of the electronic recording industry, people learned this music from one another. They also heard the music in vaudeville, minstrel, or theatrical shows and then bought printed copies to learn at home. Called sheet music, these copies consisted of arrangements for voice and piano placed between attractive covers, often decorated with pictures of the song's most well-known performers.

Beginning in the 1890s, sheet music publication became a thriving industry. Concentrated on West 28th Street in New York City in a district nicknamed Tin Pan Alley, the industry provided livelihoods to many composers and lyricists. Among the most popular songs of this period were "After the Ball" (1892), "The Sidewalks of New York" (1894), "The Maple Leaf Rag" (1899), "A Bird in a Gilded Cage" (1900), "Sweet Adeline" (1903), and "Meet Me in St. Louis, Louis" (1904). Ragtime composers Scott Joplin and Irving Berlin lived off of the sheet-music sales of their songs and later also wrote musical shows and operas. Berlin's "Alexander's Ragtime Band" of 1911 launched him into an international career in songwriting and musical theater.

The popularity of brass bands prompted the composition of many marches in this period. Beginning in the 1890s, bandleader and composer John Philip Sousa built a flourishing career composing marches and then later also wrote musical shows. Gilded Age audiences loved operettas, especially those written by the English duo W. S. Gilbert and Arthur Sullivan, Franz Lehar (who was based in Vienna), and

the Irish-born American, Victor Herbert. Occupying a place between the musical variety show and grand opera, operettas generally featured high-born characters in boy-gets-girl plots and classically trained singers who spoke lines as well as sang arias and duets. Herbert wrote 40 operettas, the most successful of which were *Babes in Toyland* (1903) and *Naughty Marietta* (1910).

The "Negro spiritual," or prayer song reflecting the African American experience in slavery, attracted increasing interest in this era. The first published collection of spirituals appeared in 1867. Beginning in the next decade, choirs from colleges established for African Americans, such as the Fisk Jubilee Singers and the Hampton Institute Choir, and individual performers such as African American baritone, composer, and arranger Harry T. Burleigh, performed spirituals to appreciative audiences in both the United States and abroad. Interest in the music increased when African American civil rights activist W. E. B. DuBois featured them in his 1903 book *The Souls of Black Folk*.

"Coon songs" were highlights of the era's minstrel and vaudeville shows. The songs usually depicted black males eating watermelon, chicken, and ham, drinking alcoholic beverages, and gambling—demeaning racial stereotypes that delighted many in the largely white audiences who patronized such shows. But even black performers sang them, as doing so was often the only way they could succeed on the vaudeville or musical theater stage.

A less demeaning form of music that emerged from the African American community evolved from the cakewalk. Cakewalks were dance or strutting contests held on slave plantations. Adapted for the minstrel-show stage, they inspired a syncopated, rhythmic music set to a 4/4 march beat that came to be known as ragtime. African Americans also developed the blues in this period, a form of singing that told of their hard times in the post-slavery period. Unlike the spirituals, which focused on the hereafter, blues topics were secular and dealt with the troubles of everyday life. Jazz, a form of music based on spontaneous improvisations and rooted in both the ragtime and blues traditions, was first heard in New Orleans around 1895. Its popularity grew over the following decades and became a national craze in the 1920s.

The nation's middle and upper classes enjoyed and sang popular music but also supported concert music and opera. Concert audiences in this era liked European Romantic composers best, flocking to concerts of the music of Franz Liszt, Johannes Brahms, and Richard Wagner. Antonín Dvořák, a Czech composer, who moved to the United States in 1891 to direct New York City's National Conservatory of Music, was also much admired. After spending a summer in rural Iowa, he wrote a symphony entitled *From the New World,* a string quartet called *The American,* and a cello concerto, all influenced by melodies and harmonies from both African American and Native-American musical traditions.

Charles Ives, a more modern American composer, also brought into his compositions musical sounds from American folk traditions and from daily life, such as hymns, church bells, and marching bands. Unlike Ives, who never received many performances of his work during his lifetime, other composers who stayed with more Romantic themes did better. These included Amy Beach, a concert pianist, who wrote more than 300 compositions. Beach became the nation's first notable female composer, writing music inspired by poetry and nature. Edward MacDowell, Columbia University's first professor of music, built a successful career writing songs and orchestral music, many inspired by scenes from nature and rural life.

American musical life between 1880 and 1920 was thus rich and varied. It contained both popular and high art elements. Long before the era when electronic recording and playing devices made the sounds of music easily accessible, music of all types pervaded the lives of all social classes, both inside and outside of their homes.

SEE ALSO

Dance; Ives, Charles Edward; Joplin, Scott; Jubilee Singers; Sousa, John Philip; Theater

FURTHER READING

Crawford, Richard. *America's Musical Life: A History.* New York: W. W. Norton, 2001.
Horowitz, Joseph. *Classical Music in America.* New York: W. W. Norton, 2005.
Kingman, Daniel. *American Music: A Panorama.* Belmont, Calif.: Schirmer, 2003.
Stewart, Earl L. *African American Music: An Introduction.* New York: Schirmer, 1998.

National American Woman Suffrage Association (NAWSA)

THE FORMATION of the National American Woman Suffrage Association (NAWSA) in 1890 merged two rival suffrage organizations, the National Woman Suffrage Association, led by Elizabeth Cady Stanton and Susan B. Anthony, and the American Woman Suffrage Association, led by Lucy Stone. Alice Stone Blackwell, Lucy Stone's daughter, worked for three years to bring the merger about. Stanton, and then Anthony, served as NAWSA's first two presidents.

The merger both strengthened the suffrage movement and made it more focused. Thousands of women in local and state branches all worked toward winning the vote. They hoped that, if they persuaded more state legislators to approve woman suffrage in their own states, Congress would feel compelled to pass a woman suffrage amendment to the U.S. Constitution.

The National American Woman Suffrage Association distributed this program at its 1913 parade in Washington, D.C. The woman on the cover resembles Joan of Arc, the French heroine many suffragists regarded as their movement's patron saint.

To this end, NAWSA held annual conventions to keep members energized, published a constant stream of pro-suffrage propaganda, and in the 1910s held a series of dramatic suffrage parades. In 1914, NAWSA expelled Alice Paul's Congressional Union, originally a NAWSA committee, on the grounds that its more militant methods of public demonstrations would alienate potential supporters for suffrage. The following year, NAWSA's president Carrie Chapman Catt announced a "Winning Plan" of unrelenting political work among state and federal legislators to win the vote.

After the 19th, or Woman Suffrage, Amendment was finally ratified in 1920, NAWSA reorganized itself into a nonpartisan group to educate voters called the League of Women Voters, an organization still in existence today.

SEE ALSO

Anthony, Susan Brownell; Catt, Carrie Chapman; National Woman's Party; Paul, Alice Stokes; Stanton, Elizabeth Cady; Woman suffrage movement; Women's rights movement

FURTHER READING

Graham, Sara H. *Woman Suffrage and the New Democracy.* New Haven, Conn.: Yale University Press, 1996.
Smith, Karen Manners. *New Paths to Power: American Women, 1890–1920.* New York: Oxford University Press, 1994.

National Association for the Advancement of Colored People (NAACP)

THE NATIONAL ASSOCIATION for the Advancement of Colored People (NAACP) was founded in 1909 to advocate legal resistance to segregation and fight for civil and political liberties for African Americans. It began as an interracial organization made up of professionals, intellectuals, and philanthropists. The founders intended the phrase *colored people* to mean persons of all shades other than white.

The association grew in part out of an earlier organization, the Niagara Movement (1905–10), which was made up of black intellectuals led by W. E. B. DuBois. The Niagara Movement's demands for full social and civic equality for black Americans stood in opposition to the philosophy of leading African American educator, Booker T. Washington, who believed blacks should not try to fight segregation, but rather accommodate themselves to it while improving their lives economically. Suffering from lack of funds and the absence of a permanent headquarters and staff, the Niagara Movement lost impetus in 1909 and disbanded in 1910. DuBois and several other members of the Niagara Movement then devoted their energies to establishing the NAACP.

The idea for the NAACP came from two white social researchers, William English Walling and Mary White Ovington. Their program immediately attracted a number of distinguished black and white Americans who served as officers, coordinators, and

From its founding, the NAACP was an integrated organization. African American and white members of the Washington, D.C., branch pose for this portrait during a 1917 meeting.

board members. Among these early members, in addition to Ovington, Walling, and DuBois, were the anti-lynching journalist Ida B. Wells, settlement leader Jane Addams, black activist and suffragist Mary Church Terrell, radical publisher Oswald Garrison Villard, and investigative journalists Lincoln Steffens and Ray Stannard Baker. Prominent Jewish Americans were also involved, including social settlement worker Henry Moskowitz and Columbia University Literature professor Joel E. Spingarn. Spingarn's brother, Arthur, established the NAACP's Spingarn Medal, still awarded today for outstanding achievement by a black American in any field.

The NAACP embarked on a series of court challenges to residential segregation, barriers to voting rights, exclusion of African Americans from juries, and restrictive real estate contracts. The latter prevented whites from selling houses to African Americans in order to keep white neighborhoods from being integrated. Case by case, NAACP lawyers established precedents that helped win rights for all minorities.

Starting with its nationwide protest of the racist film *The Birth of a Nation* (1915), which depicted Reconstruction-era African Americans as

irresponsible and dangerous and members of the white supremacist Ku Klux Klan as heroes, the NAACP began its long crusade against racial stereotyping and the violence that attended it. Its first major campaign concentrated on efforts to stem the epidemic of lynching that had plagued the United States since the 1880s. Risking personal safety, NAACP members conducted firsthand investigations of racial violence and published a review of 30 years of lynching records. They lobbied Congress year after year to pass a federal antilynching bill. Although the bill never passed, the exposure and political pressure generated by the crusade did help to reduce the incidences of lynching.

Active in pursuit of economic equality and employment opportunities for African Americans during the 1930s and 1940s, the NAACP went on to play a major role in the Civil Rights Movement of the 1950s and 1960s, initiating the Montgomery Bus Boycott in 1955 and joining with the Congress on Racial Equality and the Student Non-Violent Coordinating Committee in working for racial integration throughout the South. The NAACP continues today as the nation's largest advocacy group for the rights of minorities.

SEE ALSO

African Americans; DuBois, William Edward Burghardt (W. E. B.); Lynching; Race relations; Reform movements; Segregation; Washington, Booker T.; Wells-Barnett, Ida B.

FURTHER READING

Berg, Manfred. *The Ticket to Freedom: The NAACP and the Struggle for Black Political Integration.* Gainesville: University Press of Florida, 2005.

Fraser, Jane. *Walter White.* New York: Chelsea House, 1991.

Jonas, Gilbert. *Freedom's Sword: The NAACP and the Struggle against Racism in America, 1909–1969.* New York: Routledge, 2005.

Kellogg, Charles Flint. *NAACP: A History of the National Association for the Advancement of Colored People.* Baltimore, Md.: Johns Hopkins University Press, 1967.

Ovington, Mary White. *Black and White Sat Down Together: The Reminiscences of an NAACP Founder.* Edited by Ralph E. Luker. New York: Feminist Press of the City University of New York, 1995.

National Consumers' League

THE NATIONAL CONSUMERS' League (NCL) was one of the most prominent activist arms of the Progressive Era consumer movement. It was founded in 1899 to challenge employer abuses in industry and retailing. The NCL used both pressure tactics and legislative means to achieve this goal. To convince individual manufacturers and store owners to improve working conditions for employees, it adopted two labor union techniques, the "white list" and the "white label." The white list consisted of the names of factories and retail shops that obeyed state labor laws and did not employ children or require unpaid overtime. Garment workers would sew a white label into clothing made in approved shops. Leagues then urged consumers to patronize only approved establishments and buy only those clothes that displayed white labels.

When these methods proved insufficient to bring about widespread change, the organization turned to legislation. By the 1920s, it had won an impressive number of legal cases. The most important of these cases, the 1908 Supreme Court case of *Muller* v. *Oregon,* limited the hours of women laundry workers in Oregon to 10 hours a day. The Court's validation of limited hours laid the groundwork for protective labor legislation for all workers.

Under Florence Kelley's leadership, the NCL spearheaded national movements to outlaw child labor, establish a minimum wage, and create two federal agencies concerned with the welfare of women and children: the Children's Bureau, founded in 1912, and the Women's Bureau, founded in 1920. The federal government began to pass laws limiting child labor in 1916, and by 1920 most states had outlawed the employment of children under 14 and mandated compulsory education up to that age. Nine states adopted minimum wage laws by 1913, but a federal law establishing a minimum wage would not pass until 1938. In that year, the Fair Labor Standards Act, inspired in part by NCL agitation, banned the full-time employment of children under 16. Still in existence today, the NCL is one of the most enduring Progressive Era reform organizations.

SEE ALSO

Children's Bureau, U.S.; Consumer movement; Kelley, Florence; *Muller* v. *Oregon* (1908); Women's Bureau, U.S.

FURTHER READING

Storrs, Landon R. Y. *Civilizing Capitalism: The National Consumers' League, Women's Activism, and Labor Standards in the New Deal Era.* Chapel Hill: University of North Carolina Press, 2000.

National Urban League

THE NATIONAL URBAN LEAGUE developed in response to the large-scale migration of African Americans from the rural South to industrial cities in the North in the early 1900s. These newcomers found that although they had escaped institutionalized segregation, they still faced discrimination. Most well-paying jobs were closed to them, as were neighborhoods with good housing and good schools. To many, surviving in the city was an almost impossible challenge, offering nothing but poverty and poor social conditions.

Searching for ways to help these new urbanites adapt, an African American social worker, Dr. George Edmund Haynes, and a white woman philanthropist, Ruth Standish Baldwin, established the Committee on Urban Conditions Among Negroes (1910). The following year, this committee merged with the Committee for the Improvement of Industrial Conditions Among Negroes in New York and the National League for the Protection of Colored Women to form the National League on Urban Conditions, later shortened to the National Urban League. Progressive activist Dr. Edwin R.A. Seligman of Columbia University became the first chairman. Leadership in the league remained interracial, and women participated as staff members, volunteers, and local directors.

The league embarked on a national campaign to break down race barriers in employment, housing, and education. Using the scientific methodology of the new discipline of social work, they conducted research into urban problems, including housing, sanitation, and recreation. They trained black social workers to help find employment and educational opportunities for African Americans; they organized boycotts of businesses that discriminated against African Americans; and they pressured public school systems to add vocational training and other programs for black youth. They provided housing assistance and health and birth control clinics, kindergartens, and summer camps, as well as some general relief. By the 1920s, under the leadership of long-term president, Eugene Kinkle Jones, the league had chapters in 30 cities.

Today the National Urban League continues to work with young people, advocates affirmative action, fosters minority businesses, and develops programs for the economic empowerment of individuals and communities.

SEE ALSO

African Americans; Race relations; Segregation·

FURTHER READING

Guicard, Parris. *Blacks in the City: A History of the National Urban League.* Boston: Little, Brown, 1971.
Moore, Jesse Thomas. *A Search for Equality: The National Urban League, 1910–1961.* University Park: Pennsylvania State University Press, 1981.
Weiss, Nancy Joan. *The National Urban League, 1910–1940.* New York: Oxford University Press, 1974.

National Woman's Party

THE NATIONAL WOMAN'S Party (NWP) revitalized the campaign for a constitutional amendment for woman suffrage. Founded on March 2, 1917, the party merged two groups. One was the Congressional Union, previously a

committee of the National American Woman Suffrage Association (NAWSA), which had been set up to pursue passage of the amendment. The second was the Woman's Party, formed in the West to campaign against Woodrow Wilson and other Democratic party candidates because they had failed to support votes for women.

NWP methods for persuading Congress to pass the federal suffrage amendment drew mixed reactions. The members of NAWSA, a more moderate suffrage group, worried that the NWP's policy of holding the party in power responsible for the failure to pass the federal amendment would alienate potential supporters. When NWP members picketed the White House and burned copies of the President's speeches, NAWSA refused to support them, even though they were arrested and treated harshly in jail. The NWP also alienated members of the civil rights movement. As a Quaker, Alice Paul, the NWP's leader, denied she felt any racial prejudice. Out of a concern not to alienate southern white voters, however, she refused to let her organization take up the issue of voting rights for African American women.

The public demonstrations of the NWP may have been controversial, but they played a singular role in bringing greater publicity to the cause of the federal amendment. The NWP should receive credit, along with NAWSA, for the ultimate victory of winning, in 1920, the passage of the 19th Amendment, guaranteeing women the right to vote. After 1923, the NWP devoted itself solely to winning an Equal Rights Amendment to the U.S. Constitution. The party still exists, headquartered in a Washington, D.C., house donated in 1929 by a wealthy supporter, Alva Vanderbilt Belmont.

SEE ALSO

National American Woman Suffrage Association; 19th Amendment; Paul, Alice Stokes; Wilson, Woodrow T.; Woman suffrage movement

The National Woman's Party picketed the White House in 1917 to demand President Wilson's support for woman suffrage. One woman holds a sign with the message, "Mr. President how long must women wait for liberty?"

FURTHER READING

Ford, Linda G. *Iron-jawed Angels: The Suffrage Militancy of the National Woman's Party, 1912–1920.* Lanham, Md.: University Press of America, 1991.

Irwin, Inez Haynes. *The Story of the Woman's Party.* 1921. Reprint, New York: Kraus, 1971.

Nation, Carry A.

- *Born: Nov. 25, 1846, Gerrard County, Ky.*
- *Accomplishments: prohibition crusader in Kansas; national and international temperance lecturer*
- *Died: June 9, 1911, Leavenworth, Kans.*

BORN IN KENTUCKY, Carrie A. Moore was a lifelong resident of the Midwest. She left her alcoholic first husband, Charles Gloyd, whose death a year later left her a single mother. By the late 1890s, Carrie and her second husband, David Nation, were living in Kansas, where she became an active member of the Woman's Christian Temperance Union, an organization dedicated to convincing people to give up alcohol. In June 1900, frustrated with the proliferation of saloons in her state, she heeded an inner voice that directed her to smash saloons in the town of Kiowa with stones and brickbats. During the winter of 1901, wielding the hatchet for which she became famous, and accompanied by a band of women followers called the Home Defenders, the six-foot, 175-pound Nation moved on to destroy saloons and bars in Wichita and in the state capital, Topeka. Around this time, she changed the spelling of her name from Carrie, to Carry, so that her full name would embody her mission to "carry a nation."

Carry Nation and her supporters were attacked by mobs and repeatedly jailed. Nation herself petitioned the Kansas legislature to close saloons statewide, citing women's lack of political power as the reason for her violence: "You refused me the vote and I had to use a rock," she said.

Nation's prohibition campaigning was short-lived but had enduring effects. Many counties—and later states—voted themselves "dry" and banned alcohol sales in the months following her campaign. Nation spent several years on speaking tours, fund-raising and paying her expenses with the sale of miniature hatchet pins. She acted in a temperance play, and even appeared at Coney Island, New York City's amusement park, where her performance was treated as a vaudeville act.

Legend has painted Carry Nation as a crazed fanatic, but her cause was popular and she was generally well received. Temperance advocates throughout the country shared her passion, although they disapproved of her violence. Her activities were an extreme manifestation of a powerful national sentiment.

SEE ALSO

Temperance and prohibition movements; Woman's Christian Temperance Union

FURTHER READING

Grace, Fran. *Carry A. Nation: Retelling the Life.* Bloomington: Indiana University Press, 2001.

Harvey, Bonnie Carman. *Carry A. Nation: Saloon Smasher and Prohibitionist.* Berkeley Heights, N.J.: Enslow, 2002.

Madison, Arnold. *Carry Nation.* New York: Dutton, 1977.

Carry Nation strikes a pose holding two symbols of her crusade against alcoholic beverages, a Bible and a hatchet. Nation sold copies of her portrait to raise funds.

Native Americans

TOWARD THE END of the Civil War, the U.S. government began sending troops out to the Great Plains and the Southwest to subdue the Indian nations resisting invasion by white settlers and gold prospectors. An 1868 treaty signed at Fort Laramie in Wyoming assured the Sioux that they would have the "absolute and undisturbed use" of lands between the western Missouri River and the Rockies and that the government would provide them with schools and agricultural assistance. The treaty had a very short life span. The U.S. government soon found it was unable to protect the northern Plains tribes from encroaching whites.

In 1871 Congress approved the Indian Appropriations Act, which essentially ended tribal sovereignty by declaring that all Indians were wards of the nation and must be dealt with as individuals, not as members of tribes. The effect of the act was to remove power from tribal leaders and allow the U.S. government to claim that tribal chiefs no longer represented the members of Indian nations. After this point, the government could claim that all treaties made with chiefs were invalid.

In the mid-1870s, the government abrogated the Fort Laramie Treaty and other treaties with individual tribes. It also ordered the army to move all western Indians onto reservations. Resistance, especially among the Lakota Sioux, led to warfare. In the valley of the Little Bighorn River in Montana, on June 25, 1876, a well-equipped band of Lakotas, led by Sitting Bull and Crazy Horse, outmaneuvered and annihilated Lieutenant Colonel George Armstrong Custer's Seventh Cavalry.

Little Bighorn turned out to be the single victory in a long run of defeats for Native Americans. The following year, the Nez Percé, fleeing their Oregon reservation, traveled 1,500 miles before surrendering near the Canadian border. In New Mexico and Arizona, Apaches under Geronimo, Cochise, and Mangas Coloradas fought a guerilla war against the U.S. Army, harassing and killing soldiers whenever possible. They finally surrendered to the reservation system in 1886. The Kiowa and Comanches struggled to protect their hunting grounds until military authorities confined them to an Oklahoma reservation. After several attempts to return to the northern Plains, members of the Cheyenne and Arapahoe tribes also ended up in Oklahoma's "Indian territory."

By the end of the 1880s, despite pockets of resistance, all Native American tribes were living on government-designated reservation lands, many of them more than a thousand miles from their traditional homelands. A total of 67 tribes ended up in Oklahoma. The last armed resistance to the reservation system took place at Wounded Knee, South Dakota, in 1889, when government troops massacred more than 150 men, women, and children of a holdout band of Lakota Sioux under Chief Big Foot.

Land-hungry whites even took lands protected under the reservation system. In 1889 and again in 1893, government-sanctioned land rushes in Oklahoma permitted individuals to claim more than 2 million acres of land formerly given to Indian tribes. The General Allotment Act of 1887, also called the Dawes Severalty Act, divided up reservation land into individual family homesteads—part of a larger plan to turn reservation Indians into independent farmers. The govern-

In this formal portrait, taken in the last decades of the 19th century, members of the Ute tribe wear traditional garb, including breastplates and chokers, beaded belts, and medals.

ment sold non-allotted lands to outsiders. Over the years, individual Native Americans, pressed for cash to pay taxes and debts, also sold portions of their allotments. By the 1930s, reservation land had shrunk from a total of 138 million acres to fewer than 50 million acres, and many Native Americans were living off the reservation.

The Department of the Interior managed Indian reservations through a large bureaucracy called the Bureau of Indian Affairs (BIA). Also known as the Indian Agency, the BIA treated reservation Indians as dependents. Agents controlled the allotment scheme and doled out financial aid. They administered a "white man's" justice, assigning fines and jail sentences in ways that were alien to traditional tribal methods of problem solving, such as shaming or shunning the miscreant, or forcing him to compensate the injured party rather than incarcerating him. The BIA supported military suppression of Indian religions and customs and allowed missionaries to open churches and seek converts on reservation land. The agency's investment in Indian health care and education was inadequate, one of the many failures exposed in Helen Hunt Jack-

son's *A Century of Dishonor* (1881), a book about Indian rights that contained a sharp critique of the federal treatment of Indians.

Part of the BIA's long-range plan to bring Native Americans into the mainstream of American life involved sending reservation children to far-off boarding schools. The schools removed young Indians from tribal life, cut their hair, put them in uniforms, and trained them to behave as whites. By the end of the 19th century, there were 25 distant boarding schools and more than 80 boarding schools on reservation lands. Separation from parents and from all that was familiar in their lives was devastating for boarding-school students. In addition, the boarding schools were rife with contagious diseases, and students were often malnourished. Many endured brutal punishments for making mistakes or breaking rules. A number of young Indians did receive a good education, however, and some returned home to become tribal leaders.

In 1917 the government renounced its guardianship of non-reservation Indians. This step made them ineligible for federal services and any share of tribal property. As a result, Indians as a group became even more impoverished. In 1924, mostly as an extension of the government's assimilation policies, Congress officially conferred citizenship on all Native Americans, including those living on reservations.

Individual tribes would regain a measure of tribal sovereignty under the Indian Reorganization Act of 1934, which ended the allotment program, restored some tribal self-government, and gave reservation Indians the ability to manage their own land assets. However, the downward economic spiral begun in the allotment period continued, and reservations lost population and acreage through the sale of land. Today, there are 278 tribally distinct Indian reservations, and these areas occupy less than 2 percent of their original lands.

SEE ALSO

Civil rights; Crazy Horse; Dawes Severalty Act (1887); Education; Geronimo; Military; Race relations; Reform movements; Sitting Bull; West, the; Wounded Knee massacre (1890)

FURTHER READING

Adams, David Wallace. *Education for Extinction: American Indians and the Boarding School Experience, 1875–1928.* Lawrence: University Press of Kansas, 1995.

Brown, Dee Alexander. *Bury My Heart at Wounded Knee: An Indian History of the American West.* New York: Holt, Rinehart & Winston, 1971.

Hoxie, Frederick E., ed. *Indians in American History: An Introduction.* Arlington Heights, Ill.: Harlan Davidson, 1988.

Josephy, Alvin M., Jr. *500 Nations: An Illustrated History of North American Indians.* New York: Gramercy Books, 2002.

Nativism

NATIVISM IS an extreme expression of nationalism. Its central idea, which is fear and hatred of foreigners, has taken different forms in the United States, including anti-Catholicism, anti-Semitism, racism, and a belief in the supremacy of people from white Anglo-Saxon Protestant backgrounds. American nativists focused first on the Irish and German Catholic immigrants of the 1840s, whom they accused of being ignorant and dominated by priests. Nativists founded a secret society (the Know Nothings, so-called because when a member was asked about the society's doings, he was supposed to say, "I know nothing") and in the 1850s a political party, the American Party, which within a few years attracted more than a million members. The American Party ran a Presidential candidate in 1856. Nativists often found support among artisans and laborers, who feared that immigrants were lowering their wages and stealing their jobs.

During the Gilded Age, nativists focused on immigrants from southern and eastern Europe. Among other things, they feared these people would import radical political ideas into the United States. Misinterpreting the findings of geneticists, who were merely studying comparative skin color and bone structure of various ethnic and national groups, not assigning value to those findings, nativists were also convinced that many immigrants were of inferior racial stock and should be denied the opportunity to marry native-born white Americans.

Nativist fears influenced state and federal immigration legislation, starting with the Chinese Exclusion Act of 1882 and the exclusion of Japanese immigrants after 1906. In the 1920s, the U.S. government instituted a national origins quota system that severely restricted the flow of immigrants from eastern and southern Europe.

SEE ALSO

Asian Americans; Chinese Exclusion Act (1882); Immigration; Race relations

FURTHER READING

Billington, Ray Allen. *The Protestant Crusade, 1800–1860: A Study of the Origins of American Nativism.* New York: Peter Smith, 1938.

Higham, John. *Strangers in the Land: Patterns of American Nativism, 1860–1925.* New Brunswick, N.J.: Rutgers University Press, 1963.

Jacobson, Matthew Frye. *Barbarian Virtues: The United States Encounters Foreign Peoples at Home and Abroad, 1876–1917.* New York: Hill & Wang, 2001.

Navy, U.S.

IN THE LATE 1800s, the U.S. Navy emerged from a period of relative insignificance to assume world-class status. Prior to this time, the nation had focused on domestic matters, such as Reconstruction and Indian wars, and had not been overly concerned with naval power. But a new era began in the 1880s when the United States commissioned its first steel-hulled vessels and established the Naval War College, an advanced training and leadership school for naval officers. The pace of modernization accelerated after the 1890 publication of Alfred Thayer Mahan's *The Influence of Sea Power upon History, 1600–1783*. Mahan's ideas about the importance of naval strength appealed to industrialists, nationalists, and merchants; his book influenced leaders in favor of expanding American power beyond the nation's borders.

Between 1890 and 1910, the size of the navy went from just over 9,000 to more than 48,500 officers and enlisted men. Life on board ship improved as the navy grew. New ships brought better quarters for enlisted men, and faster sailing times meant more shore leave and better access to fresh foods. The tradition of flogging sailors for breaking the rules had ended some years earlier, making discipline more humane. In 1914, in order to avoid the dangers of drunkenness aboard ship, the secretary of the navy discontinued the sailors' daily rum or "grog" ration. By 1917, when the United States entered World War I, the officers' mess (dining hall) no longer offered wine.

American naval forces won national glory for their performance in

the 1898 Spanish-American War, particularly the decisive victory in the Battle of Manila Bay in the Philippines. In 1900, the U.S. Navy helped Japanese and European forces suppress China's Boxer Rebellion. In 1904, construction began on the Panama Canal, which finally opened in 1914, enabling navy ships to pass quickly between the Atlantic and Pacific. In 1907, President Theodore Roosevelt sent a group of 16 U.S. Navy battleships on a 14-month cruise around the world, visiting foreign ports to remind other nations of American military might.

Although World War I combatants fought mostly on land, the war was a turning point in naval history. Submarine and airplane combat signaled the end of an era in which navies could concern themselves exclusively with power on the surface of the ocean.

SEE ALSO

Military; Panama Canal; Spanish-American War; World War I

FURTHER READING

Hagan, Kenneth J. *This People's Navy: The Making of American Sea Power.* New York: Free Press, 1991.
Love, Robert W., Jr. *History of the U.S. Navy, 1775–1941.* Mechanicsburg, Pa.: Stackpole Books, 1992.
Miller, Nathan. *The U.S. Navy: A History.* Annapolis, Md.: Naval Institute Press, 1997.

Homeward bound, sailors mass on the deck of the Navy battleship USS Iowa *in New York Harbor in August, 1898, just after the end of the Spanish-American War.*

19th Amendment

THE 19TH AMENDMENT to the U.S. Constitution is sometimes called the Woman Suffrage amendment or the Susan B. Anthony amendment, after one of its most outspoken advocates. The amendment reads as follows: "The right of the citizens of the United States to vote shall not be denied or abridged by the United States or by any State on account of sex." Passed by Congress in June 1919, it was ratified in August 1920, after Tennessee became the last of the 36 states required for ratification to vote in its favor. Woman suffragists had campaigned 72 years to bring about this result.

SEE ALSO

Anthony, Susan Brownell; Woman suffrage movement

FURTHER READING

Flexner, Eleanor. *Century of Struggle: The Woman's Rights Movement in the United States.* Foreword by Ellen Fitzpatrick. Cambridge, Mass.: Belknap Press of Harvard University Press, 1996.
Scott, Anne Firor, and Andrew MacKay Scott. *One Half the People: The Fight for Woman Suffrage.* Urbana: University of Illinois Press, 1982.

Olmsted, Frederick Law

- *Born: Apr. 26, 1822, Hartford, Conn.*
- *Education: private tutors and academies*
- *Accomplishments: landscape architect, Central Park in New York City, among other parks, grounds, and campuses*
- *Died: Aug. 23, 1903, Waverly, Mass.*

MOST GILDED AGE city dwellers lacked easy contact with nature. As a result, many city leaders made the building of parks a priority. Frederick Law Olmsted had more influence over the design of such parks than any other landscape architect of his day. His many successes in parks brought him commissions to design other open spaces, such as public recreation grounds, academic campuses, and the grounds of private estates.

Destined for a life in business, the young Olmsted became interested in engineering, town planning, and travel writing. In 1848, he borrowed money from his father for a farm on Staten Island, New York, and became a scientific farmer, that is, he applied scientific principles to farming methods. After

Landscape designer Frederick Law Olmsted and his daughter explore the Biltmore Estate in Asheville, North Carolina. Commissioned by George Washington Vanderbilt II, Olmsted designed the estate's extensive gardens and parks.

traveling through England and the American South, he published several well-received travel books; those on the South criticized slavery for its stifling effect on American life. Olmsted seemed launched on a literary career, but in 1857, when the superintendency of Manhattan's Central Park became open, he applied and won the job.

The park's land, which was rocky, barren, and swampy, was hard to administer. Squatters built shacks on the park land, raising goats, slaughtering animals, and boiling bones. In addition, the park's design was unimaginative. When the park's commissioners announced a competition for a new design, Olmsted teamed up with Calvert Vaux, a young English landscape architect, and produced the winning plan. It was the only plan that included broad pedestrian walkways and roads and bridle paths that crossed the park only at over- and underpasses.

With its innovative design, emphasizing natural beauty rather than manicured perfection, Central Park won national admiration. Other landscaping commissions followed. Soon Olmsted was designing cemeteries and estates near San Francisco and consulting on the design of the area that would become Yosemite National Park. From 1865 to 1873, he worked on Brooklyn's Prospect Park. During the next 22 years, he designed, administered, or consulted on parks, parkway systems, college campuses (Stanford and Berkeley, California), private estates, and town plans in Chicago (including the grounds of the 1893 World's Fair), Buffalo, Niagara Falls, Boston, Montreal, Detroit, Rochester, Milwaukee, Louisville, Atlanta, and the grounds of the U.S. Capitol.

Olmsted also designed the suburban communities of Riverside, Illinois,

and Druid Hills in Atlanta. His plans envisioned livable and beautiful spaces, with roadways that followed the lay of the land. His ideas for parks allowed people to access nature easily and carry on multiple activities, such as walking, playing, hearing concerts, or picnicking, in serene surroundings. Parks designed or influenced by Olmsted and the two sons who carried on his work have given pleasure to countless urban residents.

SEE ALSO
Parks and playgrounds

FURTHER READING
Kalfus, Melvin. *Frederick Law Olmsted: The Passion of a Public Artist.* New York: New York University Press, 1991.
Roper, Laura Wood. *FLO: A Biography of Frederick Law Olmsted.* Baltimore, Md.: Johns Hopkins University Press, 1973.
Rosenzweig, Roy, and Elizabeth Blackmur. *The Park and the People: A History of Central Park.* Ithica, N.Y.: Cornell University Press, 1992.
Rybczynski, Witold. *A Clearing in the Distance: Frederick Law Olmsted and America in the Nineteenth Century.* New York: Scribners, 1999.

Panama Canal

THE PANAMA CANAL is a 50-mile-long system of locks, lakes, and waterways connecting the Atlantic and Pacific oceans. It passes through the narrowest stretch of land, the isthmus, in Central America. Currently owned and operated by the nation of Panama, the canal was completed in 1914 and belonged to the United States until the end of the 20th century.

In their competition for Central American products and markets, both the United States and Europe had long dreamed of an isthmian canal. For Americans, the canal would cut the sea

This view of the Panama Canal under construction reveals the engineering challenges involved in designing and building a system to move enormous ships through a narrow artificial channel.

journey between New York and San Francisco from 13,000 to 5,200 miles. In times of war, it would also enable the army and navy to move troops and military supplies between the oceans very quickly.

In 1870, France negotiated a contract with the South American nation of Colombia to dig a canal through Panama, then a Colombian province. Ferdinand de Lesseps, designer of the Suez Canal in Egypt, engineered the project. Beset by yellow fever, malaria, and mismanagement, however, the French abandoned the project in 1880, offering their remaining rights to the United States for $109 million. When the price fell to $40 million in 1902, Congress accepted, but Colombia held out for more money. Angered by Colombian resistance, President Theodore Roosevelt offered quiet support for a revolution against Colombia by Panamanian nationalists. When the revolt began in 1903, the United States stationed gunboats off the coast, preventing Colombia from landing troops. Panama quickly won its independence and recognition as a sovereign nation. The new government arranged to grant

the United States a 10-mile-wide strip of land for a canal zone, in exchange for $10 million and an annual rental of $250,000. Starting with a huge swamp-draining effort to control the mosquitoes that carried yellow fever, engineers and laborers started construction on the canal in 1906 and completed it eight years later.

Most Americans applauded Roosevelt's actions on the grounds that Central America clearly belonged within the protective sphere of the United States, and a canal was a key element in fulfilling U.S. strategic interests. Roosevelt's opponents argued that he had trampled on international law.

The Panama Canal left a long heritage of ill will. In 1921, after Roosevelt's death, Congress acknowledged the illegal means used to acquire the Canal Zone, and voted a "guilt" payment of $25 million to Colombia. The Panamanians themselves regretted having given the zone away, as it cut their country in two. After years of hard negotiation in the 1960s and 1970s, Panama won the right to control the zone after the year 2000.

SEE ALSO

Imperialism; International relations; Navy, U.S.; Roosevelt, Theodore

FURTHER READING

Lindsay-Poland, John. *Emperors in the Jungle: The Hidden History of the U.S. in Panama.* Durham, N.C.: Duke University Press, 2003.
McCullough, David. *Path Between The Seas: The Creation of the Panama Canal, 1870–1914.* New York: Simon & Schuster, 1978.

Parks and playgrounds

AS AMERICAN CITIES expanded in the early 1800s, residents rarely thought about the need to preserve natural scenery. Instead, they pushed city boundaries into the surrounding countryside, not realizing until later that the only places that offered peace, quiet, and natural beauty were city cemeteries. In the 1850s, a City Beautiful movement arose, promoting the deliberate preservation of green spaces within city limits as well as the beautification of streets. New York City's Central Park, designed by Frederick Law Olmsted and Calvert Vaux, represented one response to the movement's ideals.

Spurred by the tremendous growth of their populations in the late 1800s, other cities also began to invest in parks. Park advocates argued that beautifully landscaped open spaces would relieve the nervous strain of city life, provide a safety valve for youthful energies, and increase civic pride. The end result, they predicted, would be happier citizens, more productive workers, and less juvenile crime.

During the 1880s and 1890s, cities from Boston to San Francisco funded parks, "recreation grounds," and municipal boating and swimming facilities. The setting created for the enormously popular World's Columbian Exposition in Chicago in 1893—with its lagoons, waterways, and fine buildings—stimulated many cities to design similar environments for later celebratory events, and many of these sites remained as parks long after the event ended. A Tennessee Centennial Exposition held in Nashville in 1897, for example, became the nucleus of Centennial Park; St. Louis's Forest Park originally hosted the World's Fair of 1904. In the early 1900s, the park movement received yet another stimulus from Progressive Era city politics. City leaders knew they could win voter support by building playing fields, fountains, and wading pools for city residents.

Playgrounds took on increasing importance during this era. Playground advocates argued that children would be more likely to remain safe and out of trouble if they had decent, supervised places to play. Many settlement houses set up play gardens on their own roofs or unused city lots. Health reformers argued that physical exercise was critical to the well-being of growing children. Reform groups such as the Playground Association of America, cofounded in 1906 by health

Girls play dodgeball on a school playground about 1910. Progressive reformers pressured city officials to construct playgrounds in parks, schoolyards, and even vacant lots to encourage safe, healthful recreation.

reformer Luther Halsey Gulick, brought together recreation experts who pressured cities to build more playgrounds. Before 1900, only 10 cities had supervised playgrounds; by 1917, 414 cities had 3,270 play centers of various kinds.

As early as the 1830s, some states had begun to preserve their areas of natural beauty, mineral and hot springs, and historic places. The first true state park began with the federal transfer of Yosemite Valley and the Mariposa Big Tree Grove to California in 1864 for "public use, resort and recreation." Although the 20,000-acre area proved too expensive for California to administer and was later folded into Yosemite National Park, its creation spurred other states to venture into park construction. In 1883, New York rescued Niagara Falls from over-commercialization by creating the Niagara Reservation, which became a state park two years later. Other states created parks around famous battle sites, forests, mountaintops, and seashores, thereby preserving them from commercial exploitation. Today there are more than 5,600 state parks.

At the urging of explorers and nature writers, such as John Wesley Powell and John Muir, in 1872 Congress enacted legislation protecting the geysers of Yellowstone. In 1890, Yosemite became a national park. By taking these steps, Congress's first goal was to preserve the spectacular landscapes of the West, with their canyons, waterfalls, mountains, and forests. But legislators also saw the preserved areas—variously called parks, preserves, monuments, or memorials—as serving the "enjoyment of the people." Hence in some parks visitors could pursue recreational activities, such as swimming, hiking, and camping. Presidents Benjamin Harrison and Grover Cleveland preserved some 35 million acres of forest land by executive order. In 1907, however, partly in response to lobbying by the lumber industry, Congress denied the President the right to create national forests in six timber-rich western states. Naturalist and outdoor enthusiast Theodore Roosevelt managed to save 16 million additional acres before signing the bill. He also established 18 national monuments and 51 wildlife refuges.

By 1916 the U.S. Department of the Interior was administering 14 national parks and 21 national monuments. In that year, President Woodrow Wilson signed legislation creating the National Park Service, which administers the national park system to this day.

SEE ALSO

Cities; Conservation; Muir, John; Olmsted, Frederick Law; Powell, Joh Wesley; Roosevelt, Theodore; Settlement-house movement; West, the; World's fairs and exhibitions

FURTHER READING

Landrum, Ney C. *The State Park Movement in America: A Critical Review*. Columbia: University of Missouri Press, 2004.

Runte, Alfred. *National Parks: The American Experience*. 3rd ed. Lincoln: University of Nebraska Press, 1997.

Sellars, Richard West. *Preserving Nature in the National Parks: A History*. New Haven, Conn.: Yale University Press, 1997.

Wilson, William H. *The City Beautiful Movement*. Baltimore, Md.: Johns Hopkins University Press, 1989.

Paul, Alice Stokes

- *Born: Jan. 11, 1885, Moorestown, N.J.*
- *Education: Swarthmore College, B.A., 1905; University of Pennsylvania, M.A., 1907, Ph.D., 1912; Washington College of Law, LL.B., 1922; American University, LL.M., 1927, doctor of civil law, 1928*
- *Accomplishments: chairman, Congressional Committee, National American Woman Suffrage Association (1912); founder, Congressional Union for*

Woman Suffrage (1913), which became the National Woman's Party (1917); founder, World Party for Equal Rights for Women (1938)
• *Died: July 9, 1977, Moorestown, N.J.*

ALICE PAUL, a militant suffragist, grew up in a well-to-do Quaker family and went to college to become a social worker. Soon she turned to graduate work in sociology and economics, and after writing a master's thesis on equality for women received a scholarship to study in England. While there, she worked in a social settlement and became involved in the British woman suffrage movement. Far more militant than American suffragists, British suffragettes, as they were called, drew attention to their cause by marching in parades, disrupting public events, picketing, subjecting themselves to arrest, and engaging in prison hunger strikes.

Upon returning home, Paul wrote a doctoral thesis on women's equality and threw herself into the campaign for women's voting rights. In 1912, she and her friend Lucy Burns took charge of the National American Woman Suffrage Association's Congressional Committee. Set up to persuade Congress to pass the federal woman suffrage amendment, this committee had been inactive for years. Determined to revive it, Paul and Burns organized British-style parades and demonstrations in the nation's capital. These colorful activities brought tremendous publicity to the movement but clashed with the association's more ladylike approach to suffrage work and its agenda of winning individual states for suffrage. In 1914, the National American Woman Suffrage Association (NAWSA) expelled Paul's committee. Undeterred, Paul started a separate movement, transforming her committee into the Congressional Union for Woman Suffrage and, after 1917, the National Woman's Party.

Paul continued to publicize the need for a federal amendment with demonstrations, parades, and picketing. She also adopted the British technique of holding the political party in power responsible for Congress's failure to pass the amendment. As the Democratic party was then in the White House, her group campaigned against its candidates for office, especially in western states where women could already vote. Early in 1917, Paul and her colleagues began picketing the White House, calling attention to the United States' hypocrisy in "saving the world for democracy," President Woodrow Wilson's chief justification for entering the world war, while refusing the franchise to its own women citizens. Once Congress had declared war on Germany, the picketers appeared unpatriotic to the crowds of curious onlookers. Tussles broke out, and the picketers were arrested for "obstructing traffic." The abuse they suffered in jail drove them to mount hunger strikes. News of the conditions of their imprisonment, which included solitary confinement, force-feedings, and beatings, aroused tremendous public sympathy for their cause.

By committing acts of civil disobedience Paul showed the American public that she and her followers were

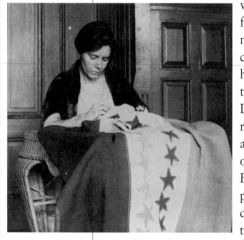

Alice Paul, leader of the National Woman's Party, sews stars on a suffrage flag. Each star represents a state where women had won the right to vote as they campaigned for a constitutional amendment for national woman suffrage.

deeply dedicated to their cause. Their actions certainly hastened the ratification of the 19th Amendment, which came in August 1920 and guaranteed women the right to vote. Three years later, Paul proposed that women begin working for complete equality with men before the law. This goal proved to be as controversial as her militant approach to winning the vote, as it raised questions about whether women should be treated exactly the same as men, or whether women and men were so different that equal treatment would actually do more harm to women than help them. For the rest of her life, Alice Paul would work, in vain, for an Equal Rights Amendment to the U.S. Constitution and for equality for all women worldwide. When asked the year before she died why she fought so hard for women's equality, she said: "It was a feeling of loyalty to our own sex and an enthusiasm to have every degradation that was put upon our sex removed. That's what I had anyway. It was just a principle that...if I belonged to any group and that group was regarded with contempt, given no power, and handicapped in every possible way it seemed to me,...I can't imagine not [helping out]."

SEE ALSO

National American Woman Suffrage Association; National Woman's Party; 19th Amendment; Wilson, Woodrow T.

FURTHER READING

Fry, Amelia R. "Conversations with Alice Paul: Woman Suffrage and the Equal Rights Amendment." Berkeley, Calif.: Bancroft Library, Regional Oral History Office, University of California, 1976. Available at: http://sunsite.berkeley.edu:2020/dynaweb/teiproj/oh/suffragists/paul/

Lunardini, Christine. *From Equal Suffrage to Equal Rights: Alice Paul and the National Woman's Party, 1910–1928.* New York: New York University Press, 1988.

Peace movement

PRESIDENT THEODORE Roosevelt had a poor opinion of pacifists. "No man who is not willing to bear arms and to fight for his rights," he said, "should be entitled to the privilege of living in a free community." But his critique did not deter pacifists from making their case for nonviolent responses to conflict. Protestant denominations took the lead here. The Quakers were the best known "peace church." Others included Mennonites from Germany and Russia, the Church of the Brethren (also called German Baptists or Dunkers), and the Disciples of Christ.

Except for the Quakers, however, members of these churches tended not to join in broader peace movements. These movements revived in the 1890s, as Americans appalled by imperialism sought more rational methods of resolving international conflicts. The intensification of the arms race and technological advances in weaponry convinced them that war was no longer constructive.

The work of Albert Keith Smiley, a Quaker schoolteacher who had built a resort at Lake Mohonk in the New York Catskills, gave impetus to the peace movement renewal of the 1890s. In 1895, Smiley hosted a meeting of 35 prominent supporters of international arbitration. Similar peace conferences, held at Lake Mohonk for 22 years, attracted prominent pacifists from all over the nation and popularized the appeal of nonmilitary solutions to international conflicts.

Pacifists were especially critical of jingoists, a term that came from a British music hall song of the late 1870s and that had come to mean

Peace activists gather for a conference at Mohonk Lake, New York, in 1915, after the outbreak of World War I. They hoped to help end the war in Europe and prevent U.S. participation.

"aggressive nationalists," ready to react militantly to any insult to national pride. Lucia Mead, a teacher and author who believed that expansion abroad prevented social reform at home, considered the Spanish-American War to be a "product of the jingo press" and saw American imperialism as renewing "race hatred." In a 1906 speech given at Stanford University on "The Moral Equivalent of War," psychologist William James admitted that war disciplined young citizens and committed them to work for unselfish social purposes. Rather than train young men to kill, however, he thought that three-year terms to work in fleets, factories, mines, and public works would accomplish the same results.

The American School Peace League, founded in 1908, took a different approach to youth, distributing reading materials and sponsoring essay contests in schools that promoted ideas of international justice and friendship. Within a few years the league's founder, Fannie Fern Phillips Andrews, was a special adviser to the U.S. commissioner of education. National teachers' associations endorsed the league, which eventually had branches in 40 states and inspired French, English, and Irish teachers

to launch school peace programs in their nations.

Even Theodore Roosevelt, for all his appreciation of war, advocated peace. When accepting the Nobel Peace Prize in 1906 for his role in settling the Russo-Japanese War, he called for an organization to arbitrate international disputes and prevent war. Under pressure from peace advocates, Roosevelt also called for a second international disarmament conference to meet at The Hague in 1907 (the first had been held in 1899). A ban on chemical weapons resulted.

During the following decade, the peace movement swelled. The publisher Edwin Ginn endowed the World Peace Foundation's research on ways to achieve and sustain peace. Steel magnate Andrew Carnegie gave $10 million to establish the Carnegie Endowment for International Peace, which worked to advance international cooperation. When war broke out in Europe in 1914, American women suffragists and social reformers organized an antiwar march, a national peace conference, and the Woman's Peace Party. In 1916, a group founded in New York the previous year as the Anti-militarism Committee evolved into the American Union Against Militarism. In addition to lobbying for peace, this group established a Civil Liberties Bureau that eventually became the American Civil Liberties Union, which is still in existence today, working to protect the rights of citizens to free speech, association, assembly, and other constitutional protections.

Peace advocates urged the founding of a world court to arbitrate disputes among nations. Some even suggested the establishment of a world parliament. The United States agreed to participate in the Permanent Court of International Arbitration, known as The Hague Tribunal, but the U.S. Senate reserved the right to protect the nation's interests in Asia and Latin America before any issue went to arbitration.

By 1917, the United States had entered World War I. Despite this defeat of their movement, pacifists never gave up hope that arms reductions and the arbitration of international disputes would lead to permanent peace. The Women's International League for Peace and Freedom, founded after the war in part by the Woman's Peace Party, is still pursuing this quest today.

SEE ALSO

Carnegie, Andrew; Imperialism; International relations; Roosevelt, Theodore; Spanish-American War; Woman's Peace Party; World War I

FURTHER READING

Craig, John M. *Lucia Ames Mead and the American Peace Movement.* Lewiston, N.Y.: E. Mellen Press, 1990.
De Benedetti, Charles. *The Peace Reform in American History.* Bloomington: Indiana University Press, 1980.
Johnson, Robert David. *The Peace Progressives and American Foreign Relations.* Cambridge, Mass.: Harvard University Press, 1995.
Lunardini, Christine A. *The ABC-CLIO Companion to the American Peace Movement in the Twentieth Century.* Santa Barbara, Calif.: ABC-CLIO, 1994.

Pershing, John Joseph

- *Born: Sept. 13, 1860, near Laclede, Mo.*
- *Education: Missouri State Normal School, A.B. 1880; U.S. Military Academy, 1886; University of Nebraska, LL.B., 1893*
- *Accomplishments: brigadier general (1906–16), major general (1916–17), and general (1917–20), U.S. Army; general of the Armies of the United States (1920); U.S. Army chief of staff (1921–24); awarded Pulitzer Prize for My Experiences in the War (1931)*
- *Died: July 15, 1948, Washington, D.C.*

JOHN PERSHING began his adult life as a teacher in a school for African Americans near his hometown in Missouri. After doing well on a competitive examination for admission to West Point Military Academy, he entered the academy in 1882 and graduated in 1886. As a Second Lieutenant in the cavalry, Pershing participated in the campaign against the Sioux Indians at Wounded Knee, South Dakota, and then taught military science for four years at the University of Nebraska in Lincoln, where he also earned a law degree.

Following his teaching assignment in Nebraska, Pershing led various cavalry expeditions, including one with the Buffalo Soldiers, the nickname of African American regiments that fought in the West. Fighting alongside Theodore Roosevelt in the assault on Cuba's San Juan Hill

General John J. Pershing, commander in chief of the American Expeditionary Force in France during World War I, strides down a gangplank in 1919, several months after the end of the war.

during the Spanish-American War, Pershing earned the reputation of being the coolest man under fire. He then sailed to the Philippines, where he helped put down the rebellion of Filipino tribesmen fighting against U.S. annexation after the war. He earned promotion to captain and later held administrative military posts in the Philippines.

In 1915 Pershing sustained a terrible tragedy. His wife and three daughters died in a fire at the Presidio, the military post in San Francisco, California. After attending their funeral, Pershing and his last surviving child, a son, moved to Fort Bliss in Texas, from where he led the unsuccessful military pursuit of the Mexican outlaw and revolutionary Pancho Villa. When the United States declared war against Germany in World War I, Pershing, now a major general, received appointment as commander of the American Expeditionary Force (AEF), the name given to the armed forces being sent to Europe.

In his new post, Pershing organized the supply, training, and growth of the AEF, which began as an inexperienced force of 27,000 and became a force of more than 2 million draftees and professional officers. Despite pressures on him to split up his soldiers among French and British troops, he insisted on keeping them together. He also scorned trench warfare, instead sending his troops on aggressive assaults against enemy positions. When the war ended, in gratitude for his service, the U.S. Congress named him General of the Armies of the United States, thereby awarding him the highest rank ever achieved by a military leader.

Although some Republicans urged Pershing to run for President in 1920, he declined to campaign actively and the nomination went to Warren G.

Harding. Pershing retired from active service in 1924, remaining a keen observer of the American military scene and writing a prize-winning memoir.

SEE ALSO

American Expeditionary Force; Buffalo Soldiers; Military; Roosevelt, Theodore; Spanish-American War; World War I; Wounded Knee massacre (1890)

FURTHER READING

Pershing, John J. *My Experiences in The World War.* 1931. Reprint, New York: Da Capo, 1995.

Smith, Gene. *Until The Last Trumpet Sounds: The Life of General of the Armies John J. Pershing.* New York: Wiley, 1998.

Vandiver, Frank E. *Black Jack: The Life and Times of John J. Pershing.* College Station: Texas A&M University Press, 1977.

Photography

INVENTED IN 1839, *photography* literally means "writing with light." Frenchman Louis-Jacques-Mandé Daguerre developed the first commercially viable daguerreotype—a method of making single photographs on copper plates. Two years later, Englishman William Henry Fox Talbot patented the calotype, a process for printing negative photographs on high-quality paper. By the time of the Civil War, the field had advanced far enough to permit American photographers to make an unprecedented photographic record of many aspects of the conflict.

A number of major developments took place in photography in the late 1800s. In 1878, in an experiment sponsored by the American railroad magnate Leland Stanford, Eadweard Muybridge took serial pictures of a trotting horse. These images, taken in

A photographer's customer, his head immobilized by a clamp to allow for a long exposure, sits for a portrait. The sign on the wall advertises ferrotypes, which were photographs on thin metal sheets.

half a second by 12 electrically controlled fast-shutter cameras, proved that when a horse runs, there is a moment when all four hooves are off the ground. Muybridge's technique later led to the development of motion pictures. It also advanced the use of photography as a scientific instrument.

George Eastman introduced flexible film in 1884 and the box camera in 1889. These innovations, which simplified photography, allowed anyone to take a picture of a scene in everyday life. When individuals used up a roll of film, they sent the camera with the film still in it to the factory for processing. After developing, the company returned the prints along with the camera, loaded with new film. Amateur photography became all the rage, a development enhanced by Eastman's introduction in 1900 of the one-dollar Brownie Camera, a simple device a child could use. By then, the name Eastman had devised as a brand name for his product, Kodak, which he chose because he liked the strong sound of its letters, was known worldwide almost as a synonym for a camera.

Alfred Stieglitz and Edward Steichen added great artistry to photography. Both took photos using a soft-focus, pictorialist style that moved photography beyond the documenting of reality and toward becoming a fine art. Muckraking documentary photographers Jacob Riis and Lewis Hine gave powerful impetus to Progressive Era social reform by using photographs. Their pictures exposed the slum life and factory conditions that industrial workers and their families endured.

Instead of publishing artist drawings, magazines and newspapers increasingly published photographs, which meant that the artists who had once drawn illustrations for newspapers lost their jobs. Women, however, found new employment in photography. Considered a socially acceptable field for women, photography studios at first employed women as photofinishers and retouchers, and then as camera operators. In 1890, Catharine Weed Barnes, a New York photographer, began writing a column on women's photography for the *American Amateur Photographer* and eventually became the journal's associate editor. Women photographers earned renown in this era, especially in the highly popular field of portraiture. One was Gertrude Käsebier, who produced portraits of individuals and families in imaginative domestic or natural settings. Photojournalist Frances Benjamin Johnston photographed the famous as well as the ordinary, including herself in 1896 in a provocative pose holding a cigarette and a beer stein and exposing a stockinged leg.

Small-format film (35 millimeters wide) producing high-quality negatives that could then be enlarged first appeared in Germany in 1914 but, because of World War I, was not widely available until the mid-1920s. Flashbulb photography arrived in the 1930s, and color film became commercially available in the 1940s.

SEE ALSO

Fine arts; Inventions; Motion pictures; Muckrakers

FURTHER READING

Davenport, Alma. *The History of Photography: An Overview.* Albuquerque: University of New Mexico Press, 1999.
Hirsch, Robert. *Seizing the Light: A History of Photography.* Boston: McGraw-Hill, 1999.
Marien, Mary Warner. *Photography: A Cultural History.* Upper Saddle River, N.J.: Prentice Hall, 2002.
Sandler, Martin W. *Against the Odds: Women Pioneers in the First Hundred Years of Photography.* New York: Rizzoli, 2002.
————. *Photography: An Illustrated History.* New York: Oxford University Press, 2002.

Pinchot, Gifford

- *Born: Aug. 11, 1865, Simsbury, Conn.*
- *Education: Yale College, B.A., 1889; graduate work at the French National Forestry School, 1890s*
- *Accomplishments: chief, Bureau of Forestry (later, Forest Service), U.S. Department of Agriculture (1898–1910); founder, Yale School of Forestry (1900); founder and president, National Conservation Association (1910–35); governor of Pennsylvania (1923–29, 1931–35); author,* Breaking New Ground *(1947)*
- *Died: Oct. 4, 1946, Milford, Pa.*

RAISED BY a wealthy family to dedicate his life to public service, Gifford Pinchot studied at Yale and learned about forestry in France. President Grover Cleveland appointed him to the Bureau of Forestry in the U.S. Department of Agriculture and in 1898 Pinchot became the bureau chief. By 1905, the bureau, renamed the Forest Service, controlled all national forest reserves in

the United States. Pinchot and fellow Republican Theodore Roosevelt coined the word *conservation* to describe a movement to protect natural resources and use them wisely.

Pinchot later wrote in his autobiography *Breaking New Ground*:

> When I came home [from France] not a single acre of Government, state, or private timberland was under systematic forest management anywhere on the most richly timbered of all continents. . . . The lumbermen . . . regarded forest devastation as normal and second growth as a delusion of fools. . . . And as for sustained yield, no such idea had ever entered their heads. The few friends the forest had were spoken of, when they were spoken of at all, as impractical theorists, fanatics, or "denudatics," more or less touched in the head. What talk there was about forest protection was no more to the average American than the buzzing of a mosquito, and just about as irritating.

During Roosevelt's Presidency, he and Pinchot worked together to add millions of acres to the national forests and to regulate their exploitation by the lumber business. Unlike naturalist John Muir and other strict preservationists, who wanted to protect

As chief forester of the United States, Gifford Pinchot was President Theodore Roosevelt's principal conservationist ally. While in office, Pinchot added more than 120 million acres to the nation's forest reserves.

national forests even from planned exploitation, Pinchot felt that private companies should be allowed to develop natural resources such as forests and grazing lands, provided they managed them with regard for the needs of future generations. Pinchot's policies included leasing federal conservation lands for fees so that their products could be used for "the service of man."

Under pressure from commercial interests to allow unrestricted exploitation of natural resources, Congress eventually undermined Pinchot by forbidding the executive branch to create any further forest preserves in the Far West. Pinchot also ran afoul of Roosevelt's successor, President William Howard Taft, who was not a strong conservationist. In 1910, Pinchot entered into a prolonged controversy with the Secretary of the Interior, Richard Ballinger. Long at odds over the use of natural resources, the two men clashed further over charges that Ballinger had misused coal lands in Alaska. President Taft cleared Ballinger of wrongdoing and fired Pinchot, an act that convinced the public that the President was anti-conservation. The Ballinger-Pinchot controversy was a factor in the split that took place in the Republican Party in 1912.

Pinchot went on to found the National Conservation Association, the goal of which was to lobby government for greater conservation efforts. It succeeded with the Weeks Act (1911), permitting more purchases of forest reserves, and the Water Power Act (1920), the beginning of federal regulation of water power. It failed to prevent the establishment of the National Park Service, which Pinchot saw as competitive with the Forest Service. He helped Roosevelt form the Progressive party in 1912, ran unsuccessfully for the Senate, and

served two terms as governor of Pennsylvania. His most notable accomplishments included government organizational reforms, increased regulation of public utilities, and, during the Great Depression of the 1930s, the paving of the state's many country roads. A giant redwood in Muir Woods, California, and a 1,312,000-acre section of national forest in southwest Washington State are named after Gifford Pinchot, considered the father of U.S. forestry. "Without natural resources life itself is impossible," he wrote. "From birth to death, natural resources, transformed for human use, feed, clothe, shelter, and transport us. Upon them we depend for every material necessity, comfort, convenience, and protection in our lives. Without abundant resources prosperity is out of reach."

SEE ALSO

Conservation; Muir, John; Parks and playgrounds; Progressive party; Republican party; Roosevelt, Theodore; Taft, William Howard

FURTHER READING

Hays, Samuel P. *Conservation and the Gospel of Efficiency: The Progressive Conservation Movement, 1890–1920.* 1959. Reprint, Pittsburgh, Pa.: University of Pittsburgh Press, 1999.
Miller, Char. *Gifford Pinchot and the Making of Modern Environmentalism.* Washington, D.C.: Island Press, 2004.
Pinchot, Gifford. *Breaking New Ground.* 1947. Commemorative ed. Washington, D.C.: Island Press, 1998.

Plessy v. *Ferguson* (1896)

IN THE DECADES following the end of Reconstruction, the period of rebuilding after the Civil War, southern states enacted laws and statutes to restore white supremacy and support the social, economic, and political segregation of African Americans. The U.S. Supreme Court developed a tradition of supporting decisions that enforced segregation in all southern public spaces and on common carriers, including trains and boats.

The most important of the early segregation cases is *Plessy v. Ferguson.* Homer Plessy was a 39-year-old black shoemaker. In a deliberate test of railroad segregation, he attempted to travel in the "whites only" car of the East Louisiana Railroad. After removing him from the train, the police arrested and fined him. Plessy and the groups supporting him protested the arrest and took their case to the local circuit court, where it was defeated under Judge Howard Ferguson. From there, they appealed the case, now known as *Plessy* v. *Ferguson,* to the Louisiana Supreme Court and finally to the U.S. Supreme Court, which on May 18, 1896 decided in favor of Judge Ferguson and the state of Louisiana.

Delivering the majority opinion, Associate Justice Henry Billings Brown asserted that distinctions based on race were constitutional and did not violate the 14th Amendment (1868), which was intended to secure the legal and civil rights of former slaves. "The object of the amendment," said Brown, "was undoubtedly to enforce the absolute equality of the two races before the law, but in the nature of things it could not have been intended to abolish distinctions based upon color, or to enforce social, as distinguished from political equality, or a commingling of the two races upon terms unsatisfactory to either." As far as Brown and seven other members of the Court were concerned, racial attitudes and customs could not be altered by recourse to the law.

The decision of the Court did not state that blacks and whites must have "separate but equal" facilities, although this is the phrase generally associated with the case. Nonetheless, the Court found segregated facilities legal and acceptable as long as those for blacks were not inferior in quality.

Only one member of the Supreme Court, Justice John Harlan, dissented from this decision. With great foresight he wrote: "Our Constitution is color-blind, and neither knows nor tolerates classes among citizens. In respect of civil rights, all citizens are equal before the law. . . . In my opinion, the judgment this day rendered will, in time, prove to be quite as pernicious as the decision made by this tribunal

Supreme Court of the United States,

No. 210, October Term, 1895.

Homer Adolph Plessy
Plaintiff in Error,

vs.

J. H. Ferguson, Judge of Section "A"
Criminal District Court for the Parish
of Orleans.

In Error to the Supreme Court of the State of
Louisiana

This cause came on to be heard on the transcript of the record from the Supreme Court of the State of Louisiana, and was argued by counsel.

On consideration whereof, It is now here ordered and adjudged by this Court that the judgment of the said Supreme Court, in this cause, be, and the same is hereby, affirmed with costs.

Per Mr. Justice Brown,
May 18, 1896.

Dissenting:
Mr. Justice Harlan

in the Dred Scott case." He was referring to the 1857 Supreme Court case that denied freedom and citizenship rights to a slave who had been taken to a free state.

Harlan was right. Americans would forever cite *Plessy* v. *Ferguson* as the case that gave legitimacy to a vicious system of segregation. The system would survive until 1954, when the Supreme Court officially overturned segregation in *Brown* v. *Board of Education of Topeka, Kansas*.

SEE ALSO

African Americans; Race relations; Segregation; Supreme Court, U.S.

FURTHER READING

Aaseng, Nathan. *Plessy v. Ferguson: Separate but Equal.* San Diego, Calif.: Lucent Books, 2003.
Fireside, Harvey. *Separate and Unequal: Homer Plessy and the Supreme Court Decision that Legalized Racism.* New York: Carroll & Graf, 2005.
Medley, Keith Weldon. *We as Freemen: Plessy v. Ferguson.* Gretna, La.: Pelican Publishing, 2003.
Thomas, Brook, ed. *Plessy v. Ferguson: A Brief History with Documents.* Boston: Bedford/St. Martin's, 1997.

Politics

THE TERM *politics* refers to the processes and institutions by which people negotiate their differences and govern themselves. In the United States, the term can encompass a wide range of subjects, such as elections, developments in political parties, changes in the suffrage (the right to vote), and the actions of interest groups that seek to influence public policy. Four issues dominated political discussions during the Gilded Age and Progressive Era: the link between politics and government jobs, the extent to which government

should curb the power of business and industry, government's role in providing social assistance to the needy, and citizenship rights for minorities and women.

Gilded Age politics began with a secret political agreement, the so-called Compromise of 1877, which resolved the disputed national election of 1876. A federal commission, organized to investigate claims by both Republican and Democratic parties that their candidate had won the presidential election, became dominated by Republicans. Announcing it had reached a compromise, the commission awarded the presidency to Republican candidate Rutherford B. Hayes. The Compromise marked the end of Reconstruction, or the period of rebuilding the nation after the Civil War, and signaled the end of efforts to secure the rights of former slaves. A contentious period in American politics followed. During this period, the two major political parties—the Democrats and the Republicans—remained fairly equal in strength. Between 1872 and 1896, no President won a majority of the popular vote. Only rarely did one of them command a party majority in Congress.

Democrats parade under a banner promoting Grover Cleveland for President and Adlai Stevenson for Vice President in the 1892 election. The frequency of such parades during this era indicates the popularity of political contests.

Republicans, who captured six of the eight Presidencies of the era, tended to be pro-business. They favored high protective tariffs, subsidies for railroad development, and aggressive foreign investments. They also sought to control immigrant and working-class behavior by regulating commercial amusements and the sale of liquor. In the late 1800s, disputes over the system of awarding government offices to party loyalists divided the party. In the early 1900s, disagreements over how far government should limit the power of the railroads, banks, and great industrialists divided the party even further. In the election of 1912, Republicans split between a progressive wing favoring a return of Theodore Roosevelt to the Presidency and a more conservative wing supporting a second term for William Howard Taft. The rift created the short-lived and unsuccessful Progressive, or Bull Moose, party and helped to propel Democrat Woodrow Wilson into the Presidency that year.

In the late 1800s, the Democratic party drew much of its strength from southern whites, thereby becoming identified with racial segregation and the disfranchisement of African Americans. In the 1890s, populist William Jennings Bryan brought western and southern farmers into the party, which also won adherents among northern factory workers and immigrants. These new followers shifted the party toward favoring a stronger government role in the economy. Woodrow Wilson's approval of such a role increased his appeal to progressives, who in 1916 helped him win a second term. Republicans recaptured the Presidency in the 1920s and held it until the election of Democrat Franklin Delano Roosevelt in 1932.

Of the four most important political issues of the era, the debate over the relationship between politics and government jobs surfaced first. In this era, the party in power could award government jobs as "patronage" to loyal followers. Government reformers

After a disputed 1893 election in Kansas, members of the new Populist party claimed victory and barricaded themselves in the statehouse. Armed Republicans drove them out and took control of the legislature.

opposed this arrangement, arguing that it could result in unqualified and dishonest people holding government posts. In 1883, as a first step toward weakening the link between politics and government jobs, reformers won passage of the Pendleton Civil Service Act, which established competitive examinations for some federal jobs and ended the practice of demanding political contributions from federal officeholders.

Eventually, many cities and states established similar civil service systems. This development, along with reforms that reduced party control over nominations and primary elections, weakened the power of political parties. Ironically, as the influence of parties declined, so did voter enthusiasm about elections. In the 1896 Presidential election, 70 percent of eligible northern voters turned out on election day; by 1920, less than 50 percent of such voters went to the polls.

Several new political parties emerged in this period, most of them anxious to curb the political influence of the nation's powerful industrial and financial elites and to expand the government's role in providing relief to the unemployed and the needy. The Greenback, Populist, Progressive, and Socialist parties all mounted campaigns to win elective posts from the Presidency on down. Only rarely were they victorious at the polls. Because election to the Presidency required an absolute majority in the Electoral College, minority candidates had almost no chance of winning. Nonetheless, over time, minority parties affected the platforms of the major parties. Populist calls in the 1890s for a graduated income tax and the direct election of U.S. senators, for example, became mainstream political goals in the 1910s. By the 1920s, Americans had

accepted the idea of government regulation of business practices, and in the 1930s, during the Great Depression, most Americans expected the government to take responsibility for the social welfare of its citizens.

Minority and women's voting rights were major political issues in this period. Southern states used fraud, intimidation, poll taxes, and literacy tests to prevent African Americans from voting. Convinced that immigrants were unduly influenced by political party machines, which were unofficial organizations designed to keep parties in power, progressives won laws that restricted immigrant voting rights. Awarded suffrage in a rising number of states during this era, women continued to campaign for full political citizenship. A National Woman's Party pursued a militant strategy to win woman suffrage, which included demonstrations in front of the White House during World War I. This strategy landed a number of its supporters in jail. Throughout the era, but especially during and immediately after World War I, political radicals—anarchists, socialists, and communists—also found themselves jailed and sometimes deported.

SEE ALSO

Bryan, William Jennings; Compromise of 1877; Democratic party; Government reform; Monetary policies; National Woman's Party; Political machines; Populist party; Presidency; Progressive movement; Progressive party; Republican party; Roosevelt, Theodore; Socialism; Suffrage; Taft, William Howard; Taxes and tariffs; Voting; Wilson, Woodrow T.

FURTHER READING

Gould, Lewis L. *Reform and Regulation: American Politics from Roosevelt to Wilson*. New York: Knopf, 1986.
McGerr, Michael. *The Decline of Popular Politics: the American North, 1865–1928*. New York: Oxford University Press, 1986.

Population and fertility

THE AMERICAN population grew rapidly during the Gilded Age and Progressive Era. Demographers, who study changes in population and fertility, are not sure exactly by how much. Even though the government conducted a national census every decade, the collection of information about births, deaths, immigration, and the movement of populations was spotty, and rarely systematic. Demographers believe that official censuses always undercounted or failed to apply consistent measurement standards. All of their figures are therefore approximations.

According to the official U.S. Census, the population was approximately 50 million in 1880 and 106 million in 1920. Demographers, however, think that a more accurate figure for 1920 is 114 million. A good part of the increase over this period came from immigration, but the population also grew because people were living longer.

Between 1900 and 1920, life expectancy for whites increased from 47 to almost 55 years and for people of color from 33 to 45 years. The percentage of people over the age of 65 nearly doubled. A rising standard of living, medical advances, and improvements in public health were the primary reasons that Americans were living longer.

At the same time as population rates were rising, birthrates were going down. In 1880, the U.S. census reported almost 40 births per 1,000 people, whereas in 1920 it reported only 28 births per 1,000. By 1890, native-born white women were having an average of four children (down from five in the previous generation), and by 1920, three or fewer. Fertility rates for African Americans were higher than for native-born whites, but the U.S. Children's Bureau estimated that almost 20 percent of black infants died before their first birthday, a rate almost certainly tied to the high rate of poverty among black Americans.

Immigrant families, many of whom were Roman Catholics and opposed to birth control, also showed higher birthrates. Italian, French Canadian,

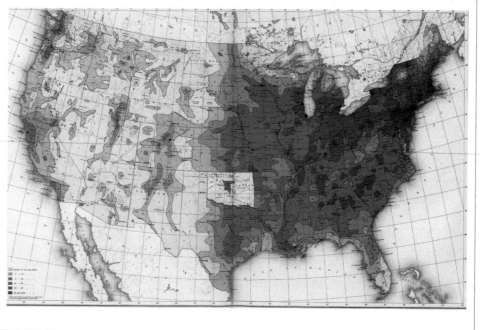

A map based on the 1890 census uses color shading to represent the number of people per square mile. The Northeast was the most densely populated region, while the West was still sparsely settled.

and Polish families were especially large, normally with seven or more children at the turn of the 20th century. Irish and German families were somewhat smaller, with about five children. Farmers and urban wage-earners had large families, with immigrant and farm families alike averaging six to eight children. The offspring of immigrants tended to have fewer children. Business owners and company managers typically limited their offspring to two or three. College-educated women tended to delay marriage, and when they did marry to bear fewer, if any, children. This trend prompted fears among some whites that the white, educated population was slowly committing "race suicide."

In a population shift almost as dramatic as changing family size, increasing numbers of people moved from the farm to the city in this era. In 1880, almost twice as many Americans lived in rural as in urban areas. By 1920, the number of people living in cities was now slightly more than those living in the country. The three largest cities in 1920 were New York, Chicago, and Philadelphia, with 5.6, 2.7, and 1.8 million people, respectively.

The heaviest concentrations of people were in the Northeast, Midwest, and South. While settlement in these areas doubled between 1880 and 1920, the population in the West, which included both the mountain and Pacific regions, grew at an even faster rate, climbing from slightly under 2 million to more than 9 million. In 1900, population density (numbers of people per square mile) was highest in the Northeast (with most people concentrated the Middle Atlantic states), followed by northern parts of the Midwest. People were the most spread out in the West and Southwest.

In 1920, almost 9 percent of the 106 million Americans were people of color. African Americans were a population on the move during this era. Between 1900 and 1920, the number of African Americans moving to the Northeast doubled (from 94,851 to 182,547), and the number moving to midwestern industrial states quadrupled (from 55,809 to 244,231). The migrants were moving north for several related reasons: they hoped to secure employment outside agriculture, raise their standard of living, and escape segregation in the southern states.

All of these changes—in birth and death rates, family fertility, and regional distribution—had significance for politics and public policies. As the American population aged, increasing focus came to bear on developing social and health insurance programs. Rising urban populations not only put pressure on city services but often led to new political alliances. The changing ethnic and racial composition of cities required attention to issues of discrimination in housing, education, and employment. Rising interest in family planning spurred the birth control movement, which sought to legalize the spread of information about contraception. In short, changes in population and fertility are more than mere numbers. They are major factors in shaping American history.

SEE ALSO

African Americans; Birth control movement; Cities; Family life; Health, public; Immigration; Marriage

FURTHER READING

Anderton, Douglas L., Richard E. Barrett, and Donald J. Bogue. *The Population of the United States.* 3rd ed. New York: Free Press, 1997.

Engerman, Stanley L., and Robert E. Gallman, eds. *The Cambridge Economic History of the United States.* Vol. 2, *The Long Nineteenth Century.* New York: Cambridge University Press, 2000.

Trotter, Joe William, ed. *The Great Migration in Historical Perspective: New Dimensions of Race, Class, and Gender.* Bloomington: Indiana University Press, 1991.

Populism

DURING THE LATTER decades of the 19th century, American farmers experienced a slow but steady decline in earnings. Although overproduction and greater international competition were largely responsible for this decline, farmers blamed market middlemen, railroad monopolies, and federal policies for many of their troubles. Building on an organization founded by Oliver H. Kelley in 1867, the Patrons of Husbandry, often called the Grange, farmers began to form political organizations that challenged the power of monopolies and laid the basis for many Progressive Era reforms.

The purpose of the Grange was to offer isolated farmers educational and social supports. To save farmers money, Grange members put together cooperatives that cut out middlemen, such as bankers and grain brokers. They also pressured legislators to regulate grain elevator operators and to prevent railroads from giving reduced rates to factory owners for long hauls while charging farmers more for short hauls.

Although the Grange proved popular, by the mid-1870s, the more political Farmers' Alliances began to win many members by launching strong attacks on monopolies. The Southern Farmers' Alliance, a grassroots organization founded in Texas to fight cattle thieving and fraudulent land claims, grew into a powerful group. By 1890, it claimed 3 million members. Forming large-scale cooperatives, this alliance called for the creation of state departments of agriculture, antitrust laws, and farm credit, as well as federal regulation of the railroads and a greater circulation of currency.

Farmers' Alliances held special importance for women. They not only admitted women as full members and officers but endorsed women's political rights. Fiery Kansas lawyer Mary Elizabeth Lease was one of their most popular speakers, calling on farmers "to raise less corn and more hell." African Americans worked through a separate but parallel Colored Farmers' Alliance. Founded in Houston, Texas, in 1886, this group had more than a million members by 1891.

The high tariff of 1890, which was designed to protect American manufactures, raised the prices of goods imported from Europe. Able to sell fewer goods to the United States, Europeans bought fewer farm products from Americans. Finding their overseas markets depressed, farmers increased their political agitation against high tariffs. Farmers' Alliance political candidates began to have success at the polls, especially in the South. In 1892, alliance members formed their own political party, the People's party. Its members, who called themselves Populists, demanded radical changes in American economic and social policies, including an increased circulation of money based on both gold and silver, a step that would make it easier for farmers to

Farmers Alliance members pose on the porch of the Texas cabin where the rural populist group held its first meeting in 1877. Exhibited at the 1893 Chicago World's Fair, the cabin was later chopped up and its pieces distributed to Populist partisans.

pay their debts; a graduated income tax; and the nationalization of the country's transportation and communication systems. They also supported the calls of industrial workers for an eight-hour workday and an end to the use of Pinkertons (private security forces) as strikebreakers. Finally, despite deeply rooted racial prejudices, they formed a united front between black and white farmers. The idea that the poor of different races shared a common cause in this era was unique to Populism, but one that lasted only a short time.

Although Populism generated tremendous excitement among farmers, the party's 1892 Presidential candidate, Iowa's James B. Weaver, won just over a million votes. In 1896, Populists supported William Jennings Bryan, a former congressman from Nebraska and a powerful orator who captured both Democratic and Populist party nominations for President. Bryan carried the Populist West and South but lost in the urban and industrial states of the Midwest and North. Despite Populism's broad appeal, it could not bridge the ever-widening gap between farm and city.

After 1900, crop prices began a slow rise that would last until 1920. The Populist movement died down. Some of its leaders became white supremacists; others, in expressing hostility to bankers, many of whom were Jewish, took up anti-Semitic views. Progressives, however, adopted many Populist ideas, such as the income tax and government control over transportation systems, and sought to apply Populist solutions to a number of urban and industrial problems.

SEE ALSO

Agriculture; Bryan, William Jennings; Farmers' Alliances; Monetary policies; Politics; Populist party; Taxes and tariffs

FURTHER READING

Goodwyn, Lawrence. *The Populist Moment: A Short History of the Agrarian Revolt in America.* New York: Oxford University Press, 1978.
McMath, Robert C., Jr. *American Populism: A Social History, 1877–1898.* New York: Hill & Wang, 1993.
Peffer, William Alfred. *Populism, Its Rise and Fall.* Edited by Peter H. Argersinger. Lawrence: University Press of Kansas, 1992.
Stiller, Richard. *Queen of Populists: The Story of Mary Elizabeth Lease.* New York: Crowell, 1970.

Populist party

THE POPULIST PARTY, or People's Party of America, was the political expression of the Farmers' Alliance, an organization built on farmers' discontent with their economic situation, which claimed several million members by 1891. The party was formed when the Republican and Democratic parties refused to endorse alliance proposals for reform.

Organized in Cincinnati, Ohio, in 1891, the Populist party held its founding meeting in Omaha, Nebraska, in 1892. It nominated former Civil War general and 1880 Greenback Labor party nominee James B. Weaver of Iowa for President. Its platform, which became known as the Omaha platform, attacked the dominance of corporate and financial interests and claimed to restore the "people's" interests to the highest priority of politics. Its planks included calls for "free silver," which meant changing the monetary system so that the value of paper money would not be based on gold alone, but on both silver and gold. Since silver is cheaper to mine than gold, this step would lower the value of money, increase its supply, and make it easier for farmers to pay off the debts they had incurred in buying land, seed, and farm machines. The Populists also called for the direct election of U.S. senators, that is, ending the election of senators by state legislatures and allowing voters to elect them directly. Finally, other party planks included calls for restrictions on further immigration (since the influx of many unskilled workers from abroad depressed wages for those already on the job), government ownership of railroads and communication systems, a graduated income tax, and a shorter workweek for industrial laborers. Weaver lost the election to Democrat Grover Cleveland, who was returned to the Presidency in 1892.

In 1896, the Populists nominated William Jennings Bryan, the former Nebraska congressman and avid proponent of free silver. Because the Democratic party had also nominated Bryan, the Populists tried to show their independence by nominating Tom Watson, a former Democratic congressman from Georgia, for Vice President. Republican William McKinley won that election. In 1900, the Populists nominated Wharton Barker for president, and in 1904 and 1908, Tom Watson, but none of these candidates ever won many votes. Between 1891 and 1903, 50 Populist candidates won election to Congress.

SEE ALSO

Agriculture; Bryan, William Jennings; Farmers' Alliances; Monetary policies; Populism

FURTHER READING

Clanton, Gene. *Populism: The Humane Preference in America, 1890–1900.* Boston: Twayne, 1991.
Woodward, C. Vann. *Tom Watson, Agrarian Rebel.* 1938. Reprint, Savannah, Ga.: Beehive Press, 1973.

Poverty

REAL WAGES—the amount people earn in relation to what they can buy—rose in the late 1800s, primarily as a result of industrialization. At the same time, however, during every decade of the latter 19th century, the American economy suffered setbacks. Depressions occurred in 1873, 1884, and 1893, with each one lasting from two to four years. During these events, which were followed by a "panic" in 1907, when many banks failed, as many as 40 percent of American wage earners lost their jobs. Despite the rise in real wages, then, many Americans experienced prolonged periods of poverty.

Certain groups of Americans most likely to be poor in this period included rural families, especially African Americans and Native Americans. Unskilled male and female immigrants, the elderly, the very young, and single-parent families were also likely to be poor. Denied funds after the Civil War to buy farmland, most southern blacks went to work for white landowners, signing labor contracts that kept them perpetually in debt. Job discrimination kept other African Americans in marginal occupations.

The government herded western Indians onto reservations and expected them to take up farming. As farming was an occupation with which most Indians had no experience, in the end they were forced to sell much of their remaining lands to white settlers. The increasing numbers of unskilled immigrants created a surplus of labor that allowed employers who hired them to cut wages to bare subsistence levels. Until the mid-1930s, the U.S. govern-

Children in a poor New York City neighborhood play next to a dead horse. Photographs depicting children amid urban squalor helped to spur social reform efforts in the early 20th century.

ment offered no Social Security to the elderly and little aid to young children without means of support, unless their fathers had served in the military.

At the turn of the 20th century, impoverished families inhabited housing without indoor plumbing, gas, or electricity. They owned so little clothing that they could not keep it clean or make it fit well. Children wore hand-me-downs or worn-out adult clothing bought second-hand and cut down to fit their small sizes. The diets of the poor lacked variety and were low in protein, fresh fruits, and vegetables. Often forced to go hungry, the poor frequently fell ill with infectious diseases. Few could afford to seek medical aid.

American attitudes toward poverty varied. Many blamed poverty on the poor themselves and accepted the arguments of Social Darwinists. These theorists applied the findings of the English evolutionary biologist Charles Darwin to human society, and argued against government aid to the poor as it might allow the unfit to survive. Most states limited their aid to the poor for fear of causing them to become dependent on aid and irresponsible. In this era, then, only private charities, usually organized along religious and ethnic lines, provided substantial aid to the poor. Social settlement houses set

up nurseries and kindergartens for working parents and medical clinics that helped the poor in particular neighborhoods. Founded in 1911, the National Urban League provided employment services to African Americans newly arrived in cities.

When all of these efforts proved inadequate, social reformers lobbied for new social policies to aid the poor. Investigative journalism and social science research provided convincing evidence of widespread poverty. Reporter and photographer Jacob Riis published several influential studies of slum life, including *How the Other Half Lives* (1890) and *Children of the Poor* (1902). In 1904, settlement worker Robert Hunter wrote a widely read book on the poor called *Poverty.* Hunter estimated that in 1900 about 12 percent of the American population was poor, a number that historians now think was closer to 40 percent.

American social investigators began to make systematic neighborhood surveys to establish how people were living on a daily basis and what they needed to make ends meet. Several important books resulted, including studies commissioned by the U.S. Department of Labor that surveyed the slums of major cities, including Baltimore, Chicago, New York, and Philadelphia. Investigators determined that at the turn of the 20th century, a family needed $800 a year to rise above poverty. Many American workers earned far below that. At the end of the 19th century, for example, 60 percent of eastern Pennsylvania's adult coal miners were earning less than $450 a year.

In the early 20th century, some states did implement new social policies to help alleviate poverty. In 1911, on the basis that it was better to aid poor mothers than to remove their children and put them in orphanages or foster homes, Illinois established the first mothers' pensions. The U.S. Children's Bureau was instrumental in spreading this idea to other states, so that by the end of World War I all industrialized states had adopted similar laws. In 1912, Massachusetts passed the first minimum wage law for women and children. Struck down by the U.S. Supreme Court in 1923, minimum wages for both sexes would have to wait until the Great Depression of the 1930s to receive wider acceptance.

SEE ALSO

African Americans; Children's Bureau, U.S.; Labor, U.S. Department of; National Urban League; Native Americans; Riis, Jacob; Settlement-house movement; Social Darwinism; Social sciences

FURTHER READING

Bremner, Robert H. *The Discovery of Poverty in the United States.* New Brunswick, N.J.: Transaction Books, 1992.

Gordon, Linda. *Pitied But Not Entitled: Single Mothers and the History of Welfare, 1890–1935.* New York: Free Press, 1994.

Patterson, James T. *America's Struggle against Poverty in the Twentieth Century.* Cambridge, Mass.: Harvard University Press, 2000.

Powell, John Wesley

- *Born: Mar. 24, 1834, Mount Morris, N.Y.*
- *Education: attended Wheaton College (Illinois) and Oberlin College (1855–57)*
- *Accomplishments: professor of natural science, Illinois Wesleyan College (1865–66); curator and lecturer, Natural History Museum at Illinois Normal University; special commissioner of Indian affairs (1872–73); director, Bureau of Ethnology, Smithsonian Institution (1879–94); director, U.S. Geological Survey (1881–94); president, American Association for the Advancement of Science (1888); author,* Explorations of the Colorado River *(1875),*

Contributions to North American Ethnology (1877), and Canyons of the Colorado *(1895)*
- *Died: Sept. 23, 1902, Haven, Maine*

AN EXPLORER, geologist, and anthropologist, John Wesley Powell grew up in the Midwest, worked on his family's farm, and taught school. At the same time, he collected objects from nature, gradually building a reputation as an expert in natural history. While fighting for the Union in the Civil War at the Battle of Shiloh, he lost the lower half of his right arm.

After the war, he took up teaching posts in Illinois. Soon, he was leading expeditions to explore the Rocky Mountains in Colorado. His anthropological studies of the Ute Indians and explorations of the Green and Colorado rivers earned him a national reputation. In 1869, the U.S. Congress awarded him funds to map and study large parts of the West. That same year, Powell and a party of explorers became the first white men to navigate the Colorado River through the Grand Canyon. His second Grand Canyon expedition produced hundreds of photos, bringing the wonder of the canyon to the attention of Americans everywhere.

Known among Native Americans in southern Utah as Kapurats ("Right-arm-off"), Powell received an appointment in 1872 as a special commissioner of Indian affairs. His assignment was to study the problems of Native Americans in Utah, Nevada, and northern Arizona. Thereafter he advised Congress and the Bureau of Indian Affairs (BIA) on policies concerning Indians, public land, federal science programs, and environmental issues. The authorities at first rejected his "Report on the Lands of the Arid

*John Wesley
Powell lost his
right arm in the
Civil War, but
in 1869 led a
team down the
Colorado River
to explore the
Grand Canyon.
"You cannot
see the Grand
Canyon in one
view," he
explained, "you
have to toil
from month to
month through
its labyrinths."*

Region of the United States" (1878),
which proposed government control of
southwestern water resources in order
to create the irrigation systems that
would ensure the land's fertility. After
1900, however, the document provided
the basis for land reclamation policies
in that dry region.

In the late 1870s, Powell pursued
his anthropological work on Indians,
contributing to dictionaries of Native
American languages and identifying
the Moundbuilders, prehistoric
builders of huge earthen structures
found in the Ohio and Mississippi
River valleys. In 1879, he played a
major role in the formation of the U.S.
Geological Survey, the federal agency
that provides scientific information
about the Earth and develops policies
for the management of natural
resources. He then became director of
the Bureau of Ethnology at the Smithsonian Institution, in 1881 taking over
the Geological Survey as well. He ran
both organizations until 1894, when
western developers who opposed his
approach to the development of public
land forced him out of the Geological
Survey. He retired to the Bureau of
Ethnology and continued to publish
on anthropological topics until his
death. Scholars still consult his works
on American Indian ethnography, linguistics, and archaeology.

SEE ALSO
Conservation; Native Americans; West, the

FURTHER READING
Bruns, Roger. *John Wesley Powell: Explorer
of the Grand Canyon.* Springfield, N.J.:
Enslow, 1997.
Cooley, John, ed. *Exploring the Colorado
River: Firsthand accounts by Powell and
His Crew.* Mineola, N.Y.: Dover, 2004.
Stegner, Wallace. *Beyond the Hundredth
Meridian: John Wesley Powell and the
Second Opening of the American West.*
2nd ed. Boston: Houghton Mifflin, 1962.
Worster, Donald. *A River Running West:
The Life of John Wesley Powell.* New
York: Oxford University Press, 2001.

Presidency

THE USUAL VIEW of Gilded Age
Presidents is that they were neither
strong nor memorable and merely
paved the way for the administrations
of the Progressive Era. Certainly, they
paled in comparison with some of their
predecessors, most notably Abraham
Lincoln. Nor could they match the
leadership reputations of some of their
successors, especially Theodore Roosevelt, the first Progressive Era president, and Woodrow Wilson, the
nation's leader during World War I.
And yet the Gilded Age administrations
were not insignificant. During Reconstruction, the period of rebuilding after
the Civil War, respect for the office of
the President had declined during the
impeachment trial of President Andrew
Johnson, Abraham Lincoln's successor.
The Gilded Age Presidents restored dignity to the office and strengthened it.
Without their efforts, the strong Presidencies of the 20th century would not
have been possible.

Like his immediate predecessor, the
last Reconstruction President, Ulysses
S. Grant, Republican Rutherford B.

Cast-iron novelties created for the 1908 presidential election display a portrait of William Jennings Bryan on the side of the Democratic donkey and a likeness of William Howard Taft on the Republican elephant.

Hayes singled out the civil service as most in need of reform. During this era, political parties distributed many government posts not on the basis of an applicant's abilities but on the extent of the person's political loyalty. In one of Hayes's earliest attempts to reform this system, he issued an executive order barring federal employees from participating in political campaigns and preventing political parties from requiring such employees to contribute to party coffers. Also like Grant, Hayes pressed southern states to guarantee the political rights of African Americans, and after Democrats won the midterm elections in Congress, he vetoed every effort to undo the laws passed during Reconstruction guaranteeing voting rights to black citizens. While his one term in office lacked drama, and his accomplishments fell short of his goals, Hayes nonetheless helped restore respect for Presidential authority.

James A. Garfield's term, although cut short by assassination, also contributed to an increase in Presidential authority. Garfield criticized Hayes for trying to reform the civil service by executive order instead of working through Congress, but he also asserted Presidential power by resisting pressure from members of his own party to make appointments he did not want. Hampered by a slim Republican majority in Congress during the first half of his term and a large Demo-

cratic majority in the second half, Garfield's successor, Chester A. Arthur, was unable to make much progress on the policy issues that interested him most. Nonetheless he, too, endorsed civil service reform, signing the 1883 Pendleton Act, which established the Civil Service Commission and launched the movement to modernize appointments to federal office.

Grover Cleveland, the first Democrat elected to the Presidency since the Civil War, also strengthened the office but in a way different from his predecessors. He used the veto more than 400 times, blocking twice as many bills from passage as all of his predecessors combined. Most of these bills were for individual pensions to Civil War veterans, but he also vetoed the more general Dependent Pension Bill, which would have provided aid to disabled veterans as well as to their families, and the Texas Seed Bill, which called for $10,000 to aid drought-stricken Texas farmers. In addition, in 1887 he won the repeal of the Tenure of Office Act, which for the previous 20 years had required Presidents to get Senate approval to remove appointed officials.

Republican Benjamin Harrison, who defeated Cleveland in 1888, introduced a new Presidential style, one that emphasized a strong relationship with newspaper reporters. Harrison thus anticipated Theodore Roosevelt's use of his office as a "bully pulpit" to win support for his ideas. Assisted by a Republican majority in Congress during the first half of his term, Harrison guided to passage not only the Dependent Pension Act, which his predecessor had vetoed, but also the McKinley Tariff, a high tax on imported goods that protected domestic manufactures from foreign competition; the Sherman Silver Purchase Act, which mandated government purchase of large amounts of silver and the issuance of Treasury notes redeemable in either gold or silver; the Sherman Anti-Trust Act, which banned business combinations that restrained trade; and a ban on lotteries. Harrison also set aside vast areas of forest land, thereby also anticipating the conservationist role of the President during the Progressive Era.

Democrats retook the office in 1892, bringing Grover Cleveland back into office. Cleveland did not believe in government aid either to business or laborers, but the depression of 1893 forced him to take a different tack. Hoping to restore business confidence, he pushed for the repeal of the Sherman Silver Purchase Act, which had lowered the value of the dollar, but succeeded only in dividing his own party into silver and gold factions. Without waiting for an invitation from the Illinois governor, he sent federal troops to quell the violence that had broken out during the strike of Pullman railroad car workers in 1894 and to bring the strike to an end. This blunt approach to the nation's problems alienated supporters, but his assertiveness impressed a later President, Woodrow Wilson, who praised him for having lodged national power firmly in his office.

Historians have called Republican William McKinley, Cleveland's successor, the first "modern" president. Having enjoyed a substantial congressional career, he came to the office with considerable knowledge about how to handle Congress. He used the press well, assigning staff to brief reporters twice a day and to "leak" information to test the waters on some of his policies. He raised the prestige of the Presidency with his conduct of the nation's foreign affairs. His administration successfully conducted the Spanish-American War, put down rebellion in the Philippines, opened China for trade, and began the negotiations that led to U.S. control of the Panama Canal. At the end of his administration, cut short by assassination at the start of his second term, the world looked increasingly to the White House instead of to Congress as the source of American policy and power.

Coming into office upon McKinley's assassination in 1901, his Vice President, Theodore Roosevelt, went even further in extending the Presidency's power. He vigorously pursued antitrust actions and insisted that industrialists submit to arbitration with striking workers. During his second term, he oversaw passage of major regulatory legislation in the railroad and food packaging industries. Despite opposition from private interests, he used the Presidency to preserve vast areas of the country's forest, mineral, and water power resources for public use. Roosevelt also expanded the President's power in foreign affairs, bypassing Congress through the use of executive agreements between himself and the heads of other governments. An eager imperialist, he increased the nation's role in global politics, announcing an aggressive U.S. policy toward European interference in the Caribbean and Central America. He acquired rights to land in Panama that permitted the United States to build the Panama Canal. Finally, after brokering a peace between Russia and Japan in 1905, he won a Nobel Peace

During his second inaugural address, Woodrow Wilson explained Americans' connection to the war in Europe: "We are provincials no longer. The tragic events of the 30 months of vital turmoil through which we have just passed have made us citizens of the world."

Prize, the first American President to do so.

Republican William Howard Taft did not pursue foreign policy as vigorously as Roosevelt had. To keep Asia open for trade and preserve stability in Latin America, Taft preferred "substituting dollars for bullets." That is, he hoped to create orderly societies abroad by increasing U.S. investment in their economies. This approach pleased public opinion and should have made money for American investors, but instead it created enemies, especially in the Caribbean and Central America, where local revolutionary movements arose to oppose (and expel) American influence. Taft had poor relations with the press. More significantly, he disappointed progressives in his own party, splitting it between conservative and progressive wings. The progressives' opposition to Taft brought Theodore Roosevelt out of retirement to run against him in 1912.

The victor in the 1912 four-way contest for the Presidency was Democrat Woodrow Wilson. He came into office committed to further progressive reforms. Economic reforms, including the federal income tax, the Federal Reserve Act (which established government controls over national banks), and the Federal Trade Commission Act (designed to limit unfair trade practices) were early triumphs. Wilson also oversaw the strengthening of antitrust legislation and protective labor legislation. Through his leadership during and immediately after World War I, the United States reached a new level of power and influence. His attempts to bring the United States into the League of Nations, an international body to prevent future wars, won him a Nobel Peace Prize. But he was never able to convince Congress that joining the league would still allow the United States to act independently in foreign affairs. After he suffered a stroke in 1919, his Presidency collapsed.

The Presidents of the second half of the 19th century made slow but steady progress toward strengthening the executive office. That the United States was generally evenly divided between the two major parties made this task difficult, as they rarely had the full backing of Congress. McKinley, Roosevelt, and Wilson were more successful, in part because the nation, facing unforeseen developments in foreign affairs, united behind their administrations and gave them the support they needed to enact landmark changes. But they were also able to draw upon a tradition of executive activism that they had inherited from their Gilded Age predecessors.

SEE ALSO

Arthur, Chester A.; Cleveland, Grover; Garfield, James A.; Harrison, Benjamin; Hayes, Rutherford B.; McKinley, William; Politics; Roosevelt, Theodore; Taft, William Howard; Wilson, Woodrow T.

FURTHER READING

Morgan, H. Wayne. *From Hayes to McKinley: National Party Politics, 1877–1896.* Syracuse, N.Y.: Syracuse University Press, 1969.
Pious, Richard M. *The U.S. Presidency: A Student Companion.* 2nd ed. New York: Oxford University Press, 2001.
Schlesinger, Arthur M., Jr. *The Imperial Presidency.* Boston: Houghton Mifflin, 1973.
Urofsky, Melvin I. *The American Presidents.* New York: Garland, 2000.

Progressive Era

THE PROGRESSIVE ERA was the time period around the turn of the 20th century when reformers sought to deal with massive social, economic, and political problems by involving government in their solution. The reformers came primarily from the urban middle classes and from groups associated with the populist and farm-labor movements of the West. They were most active from the 1880s onward, but the height of their political success came during the period from approximately 1890 through World War I. Thus most historians use the dates 1890 to 1920 as the period's chronological boundaries. But progressive ideas carried on long afterward, especially at local and state levels, where organized groups of new women voters were prominent in fostering them.

The idea that government should intervene in the economy and take responsibility for the care of the people was relatively new in the United States. Many Americans resisted it. Moreover, progressives themselves did not agree on all reform programs. They functioned primarily through coalitions, or temporary alliances of diverse interests pursuing different but related reform goals. Because of this diversity of opinion about reform, some historians dislike the term *Progressive Era,* for it implies that reformers pursued a unified program during a specific time period and that the vast majority of Americans supported their ideas. Most historians continue to use the term, however. They argue that many reformers identified themselves as progressives, and for a number of years supported a Progressive political party.

SEE ALSO

Progressive movement; Progressive party

FURTHER READING

Ekirch, Arthur A., Jr. *Progressivism in America: A Study of the Era from Theodore Roosevelt to Woodrow Wilson.* New York: New Viewpoints, 1974.
Link, Arthur, and Richard L. McCormick. *Progressivism.* Arlington Heights, Ill.: Harlan Davison, 1983.

Progressive movement

AROUND THE TURN of the 20th century, some Americans began to call themselves "progressives." These citizens came primarily from the business and professional worlds and included many college-educated women. Some farm-labor and populist groups who had been active in the West also thought of themselves as progressives. Beginning around the 1880s and 1890s, these diverse groups developed new ideas about how to solve the nation's economic, social, and political problems. These problems, which included great disparities of wealth created by an unchecked and unregulated industrialization, had become so massive that private efforts, such as charity or social settlement work, could not solve them. Government, progressives argued, needed to play a larger role in regulating the economy and taking responsibility for human welfare.

These reformers thought that their ideas would lead to "progress" for the entire American nation. Thus they contrasted themselves both with conservatives, who wanted government's role to remain minimal, and with radicals, such as socialists and communists, who wanted to abolish capitalism. Progressives believed that American capitalism had given them both a high standard of living and a high degree of personal liberty. They did not want to lose those benefits.

The most general progressive goals were to lessen the exploitation of industrial workers, preserve the nation's natural resources, and make its cities more livable. To accomplish these goals, progressives argued that government must regulate large businesses.

Sweatshop garment workers stagger under heavy loads of clothing. One of the chief goals of Progressive-era reformers was to secure better working conditions for garment and other industrial workers.

Although they opposed government *control* of all businesses, they hoped that government would take over and run the businesses that supplied essential services, such as gas, water, electricity, and transportation.

Progressives also believed that government should increase its responsibility for human welfare. At the time, workers had no guaranteed living wage or retirement fund, no protection from workplace hazards or unemployment during business downturns, and no reliable assistance in the event of accident or death. Progressives proposed that government pass laws to protect workers from unsafe and exploitative factory conditions. They also asked for social welfare programs, such as unemployment, accident and health insurance, and a social security system to cover disability and old age. Progressives presumed that government would use trained experts, not politicians, to formulate and administer these programs.

Since most progressives were based in cities, municipal reform became an important element in the progressive movement. Municipal reformers opposed the power of political machines (unofficial organizations designed to keep parties in power) and appointments to government posts on the basis of party loyalty instead of merit. They thought that a professional, nonpartisan civil service would make government more honest. They also favored saving taxpayer money with streamlined government structures, and they worked for "home rule," or the independence of cities from state governments, which were often dominated by people who had little knowledge or experience of urban problems.

In addition to business regulation, security for laboring people, and municipal reform, most progressives also wanted votes for women and an increased level of government control over housing, health, and even private morality. Convinced that drinking alcoholic beverages led to poverty and family violence, many progressives favored prohibition. They also supported the censoring of motion pictures and even of dancing styles and the playing of jazz music, which they believed led to premarital sex and family tragedy. To control the spread of sexually transmitted diseases, they sought to abolish prostitution by closing down brothels. These measures, intended to protect those in society least able to protect themselves, were humanitarian in motive but increased government control over individuals and were thus highly controversial.

Progressives worked systematically. First, they collected data on issues that concerned them, such as slum or sweatshop conditions. Next, they used scientists and other experts to interpret the data. Then they publicized the results and put pressure on legislators to pass reforms. Finally, they monitored the enforcement and amendment of the laws they won. Popular investigative writers, known as muckrakers, were critical in creating a groundswell of public opinion in favor of reform. Using the new mass-circulation media—daily newspapers and popular magazines—these writers alerted the public to corruption or wrongdoing, mostly on the part of political bosses or big businesses. Middle-class women's organizations, including clubs and charitable groups, were key means for publicizing, advocating, and monitoring legislation.

The progressive movement had broad impact. At the urban level, reform followed a variety of patterns, depending on local circumstances and leadership. In the summer of 1900, a hurricane and tidal wave killed one out of every six residents in Galveston, Texas. When the politicians on the city council botched the relief operation, city business leaders set up a nonpartisan commission to run the government. Other cities, such as Dayton, Ohio, used a "city manager" system. Under this arrangement, elected commissioners hired a professional manager to run city departments. By 1924, some 500 American cities had adopted government by commission; at least 167 had a city manager.

Many cities took over utilities. Reform mayors Hazen S. Pingree of Detroit, Samuel M. ("Golden Rule") Jones of Toledo, and Tom Johnson of Cleveland pioneered the city control or ownership of utilities. By 1915, nearly two out of three cities had some form of city-owned utilities. In some cities, machine politicians allied with reformers to develop voter registration projects and improve city services, including public health programs, tenement codes, and parks.

Progressive governors and legislators were also active at state levels. Governors Robert ("Fighting Bob") La Follette in Wisconsin, Hiram Johnson in California, and Woodrow Wilson in New Jersey introduced structural reforms to make government more efficient and responsive to the electorate. La Follette, a lawyer and former congressman who had won the governorship in 1900, brought about direct primary elections in his state. By 1916, all but three states had a direct primary, which permitted the voters, instead of party officers, to choose nominees for office.

Other reforms at the state level included the adoption of initiative, referendum, and recall. These measures allowed voters to propose and enact laws directly (initiative), vote on specific proposed legislation (referendum), and remove a person from office (recall). By 1912, a dozen states had initiative and referendum, and seven had recall. Political reforms peaked in 1912 with the passage of a significant progressive electoral reform, the 17th Amendment to the Constitution. Following this amendment, all U.S. senators would be elected directly by voters instead of indirectly by state legislatures.

State activists also targeted the workplace for reform. Applying the principle that employers and employees had to negotiate their differences, states established labor departments to provide information and services, including mediation, to both sides. By 1920, all but five states had established workers' accident insurance and compensation systems.

Making the workplace safer and less exploitative proved more difficult. Government efforts to control working conditions met legal opposition at every turn. In *Lochner* v. *New York* (1905), the Supreme Court invalidated a New York law setting maximum working hours for bakers. A few years later, in 1908, however, the Supreme Court in *Muller* v. *Oregon* upheld an Oregon law that limited women laundry workers to 10 hours a day. The Court came to this decision when convinced that women would be harmed by longer hours at laundry work. Other protectionist measures included the limitations on child labor in some 30 states by 1907. Minimum-wage legislation for women and children also made headway. Florence Kelley, head of the National Consumers' League, led the national campaign for state passage, and after Massachusetts adopted a minimum wage in 1912, eight other states followed.

Progressivism appeared at the national level in four areas: labor and industrial relations, the regulation of business and commerce, the preservation of the environment, and social welfare legislation. President Theodore Roosevelt used his powers vigorously in the area of labor and industrial relations. In May 1902, the United Mine Workers called a national strike. As winter approached and mine owners refused to talk to the union, a "coal famine" loomed. Roosevelt insisted that both sides submit to arbitration. In 1903, a commission granted the miners a 10 percent raise and reduced their workday from 10 to 9 hours. Roosevelt called this a "square deal" for both sides, a phrase that became his Presidency's slogan.

Although the Sherman Antitrust Act (1890) was supposed to prevent business combinations from restraining trade, previous Presidents had not enforced it vigorously. Calling for an end to special privileges for capitalists, Roosevelt instructed his attorney general to file suit against the Northern Securities Company—a huge holding company that had formed to control northwest railroading and drive out competitors. The suit forced the company to break up. Under Roosevelt, the government filed 43 antitrust actions against the beef, oil, tobacco, and railroad industries, thus earning Roosevelt his reputation as a trustbuster.

The environment also came in for further regulation. In the early 1900s, the government called in experts to develop a workable land and water use policy. In 1905, Roosevelt named Gifford Pinchot, a scientific forester, to head a new U.S. Forest Service. Pinchot supported conservation, but he also favored planned, regulated, and multiple uses for national land. At his recommendation, Roosevelt set aside more than 200 million acres of land for national forests, mineral reserves, and water projects. He also established 16 national monuments and 51 wildlife refuges. In 1916, a National Park Service was established to supervise them.

The federal government was active in social legislation as well. In response to pressure from social settlements and labor organizations, in 1912 the government established a Children's Bureau within the Department of Labor. A Women's Bureau was formed in 1920. These two bureaus provided information and support to advocates of legislation benefiting women and children.

Although not all progressives favored prohibition, many thought it would protect society from the poverty and violence associated with drinking. Urban reformers, social workers, and middle- and upper-class businesspeople regarded saloons as wasteful of workers' time and money. When prohibition legislation passed Congress in 1918, President Woodrow Wilson vetoed it, but Congress overrode him. The 18th Amendment became law in 1919. Until its repeal in 1933, Americans could not legally make, sell, or import liquor. They did not give up drinking it, however. A vast illegal trade in the manufacture and distribution of alcoholic beverages dominated the 1920s.

Photographer Lewis Hine filed this 1911 report of his investigation into child labor in Mississippi cotton mills. Hine, a leading Progressive Era photojournalist, often used his camera to depict the hard lives of working-class children.

Following up on measures taken under Roosevelt, in 1914 Wilson created a Federal Trade Commission to watch over business compliance with federal trade regulations. The Clayton Antitrust Act spelled out specific activities big businesses could not do in restraint of trade. Wilson also lowered many tariffs, thereby encouraging U.S. factories to operate more efficiently and stimulating international trade. He was less active in social justice legislation. He allowed his cabinet officers to extend racially discriminatory practices in federal offices that had begun in previous administrations. He also opposed a constitutional amendment guaranteeing women the right to vote because his party had not endorsed it.

Progressives left a mixed legacy. Some of them supported ideas that few today would call "progressive." For example, they favored immigration restriction, literacy tests for voters, and the forced sterilization of persons presumed "mentally deficient" or criminal. Instead of fulfilling the promise of a greater democracy, some Progressive Era electoral reforms, such as those designed to curb the power of political machines, actually reduced the involvement of voters in political life. Most of the Progressive Era efforts to reform human morality failed.

Moreover, despite their general concerns for human welfare, progressives ignored some elements of the population. Only the few settlement workers and intellectuals who helped found the National Association for the Advancement of Colored People felt obliged to do something about the worsening race relations of the era. Finally, many progressives uncritically supported imperialism. Just as they believed in the uplift of the slums and ghettos of American cities, they favored the "civilizing" of undeveloped nations.

The progressive movement laid the groundwork for President Franklin Roosevelt's response to the Great Depression of 1929. The Social Security system and boards of labor arbitration set up during the New Deal, which was Franklin Roosevelt's program for reforming the national economy, fulfilled progressives' ideas for an expanded governmental role in guaranteeing the welfare of its citizens.

SEE ALSO

Antitrust laws; Child labor; Children's Bureau, U.S.; Conservation; Education; Federal Reserve Act (1913); Government reform; Kelley, Florence; Muckrakers; *Muller* v. *Oregon* (1908); Politics; Progressive Era; Progressive party; Reform movements; Regulation; Roosevelt, Theodore; 17th Amendment; Temperance and prohibition movements; Women's Bureau, U.S.

CHILD LABOR IN THE COTTON MILLS OF MISSISSIPPI.

Photographic Investigation made by Lewis W. Hine in April and May, 1911. (Photographs and labels accompany this report.)

I.

From April 25th to May 16th 1911, I made quiet visits to every cotton mill in the state, with but one or two exceptions, and in all cases spending some time inside the mills during working hours, as well as other hours spent around the mills at noon-hours, and around the homes at various times. In some of the villages, I made a careful house-to-house canvass, locating the homes of the working children and getting data about them.

I found ten cotton mills and one knitting mill running. The four largest in the state have been closed down from one to two years. The State Textile School was well worth the visit.

II.   Meridian, Miss.

1. The Priscilla Knitting Mills, Meridian, Miss.

This mill, employing about 125 hands, is located out on the edge of town. Many of the workers came from the Meridian Cotton Mill, (a large mill, see Mr. Seddon's report, 1907), since it closed down. Photos #1349, 1449, 1489, 1967, #2006, 2011, #2030, #2031, show most of the youngest workers, and also the group of children under sixteen years who go home at 5:30 P.M., reducing their hours from 63 1/2 to 60. (See photo labels for names of children, etc.)

2. The Dependent Widower: (2069 to 2071.)

Mr. J. L. Mitchell, 1402 Eighth Ave., Meridian Miss, an able-bodied, Scotch-Irish farmer, after fifty years of farm life several miles from any railroad, came to Meridian two years ago in order to obtain better school advantages for the children (so he told me.) His wife and two children died a year ago and his oldest daughter keeps house for them, and this is the way the children take advantage of school opportunities:- - one child of eleven years and one of fifteen work in the knitting mill. Two smaller ones go to school very irregularly (the teacher told me,) and from close observation of Mr. Mitchell himself, for several days, I found his occupation consisted in loafing around the corner-grocery, toting dinner to the children, and lolling around the house and occasionally visiting the farm.

FURTHER READING
Chambers, John W. *The Tyranny of Change: America in the Progressive Era, 1890–1920.* 2nd ed. New Brunswick, N.J.: Rutgers University Press, 2000.
Diner, Steven J. *A Very Different Age: Americans of the Progressive Era.* New York: Hill & Wang, 1998.

Progressive party

THE PROGRESSIVE MOVEMENT came together into a formal political party in 1912. The party's original leadership consisted of Republican legislators, many from farm states, who had become disappointed with William Howard Taft's Presidency. Known as Insurgents, or dissenters, these politicians criticized Taft's failure to pass reform legislation and his continued support for high tariffs (taxes on foreign goods), which kept prices high at home.

In 1910, former President Theodore Roosevelt began speaking out for Insurgent candidates in the 1910 midterm congressional elections. Calling for more welfare legislation and federal regulation of business, he called his program a New Nationalism. The results were mixed: Democrats captured the House of Representatives, and a coalition of Democrats and Republican Insurgents dominated the Senate. By early 1912, despite a vow never to run again for President, Roosevelt had decided to oppose Taft for the Republican Presidential nomination.

Taft controlled the central party machinery, however, and prevented Roosevelt's delegates from taking seats at the national convention when it met in Chicago in June. Charging Taft's group with fraud, Roosevelt's support-ers marched out, vowing to form their own political party. They did this in a convention in August. In response to a question about his physical readiness for a campaign, Roosevelt said, "I feel fit as a bull moose!" The Bull Moose name stuck as the Progressive party's campaign nickname.

A progressive crusader from California, Hiram Johnson, served as Roosevelt's running mate. The Bull Moose platform included tariff reduction, woman suffrage, increased regulation of business, an end to child labor, an eight-hour workday, a federal workers' compensation system, and the direct election of senators (by voters, rather than by state legislatures). Many women joined the party, campaigned for Progressive candidates, and ran for state and local offices. Fearful of losing southern white support, however, party leaders kept African Americans out of party deliberations.

Four men sought the Presidency in 1912. Labor leader Eugene V. Debs ran on the Socialist ticket. Taft and Roosevelt split Republican voters. Woodrow Wilson, a political newcomer who was then governor of New Jersey, headed the Democratic ticket. Roosevelt trounced Taft, winning 4 million votes to Taft's 3.5 million, and 88 electoral votes to Taft's 8. But Wilson gathered in 6.3 million votes and 435 electoral votes. The Democratic party took both houses of Congress.

The Bull Moose party never recovered from its 1912 defeat. It ran candi-

This 1912 certificate of membership in the new Progressive (Bull Moose) Party features portraits of Theodore Roosevelt and his running mate, Hiram W. Johnson. Signed on the back by the candidates, such certificates were valued souvenirs.

dates in 1914 with little success, and in 1916—when Roosevelt refused its Presidential nomination—joined Democrats in endorsing Charles Evans Hughes, the Republican candidate, who subsequently lost to the incumbent Woodrow Wilson. The party revived briefly in 1924, running Wisconsin senator Robert M. La Follette for President. La Follette carried only his own state and North Dakota. After his death the following year, the party disappeared. It bears no relation to the Progressive party that formed in 1948.

SEE ALSO

La Follette, Robert Marion, Sr.; Politics; Roosevelt, Theodore; Taft, William Howard; Wilson, Woodrow T.

FURTHER READING

Chace, James. *1912: Wilson, Roosevelt, Taft & Debs—The Election That Changed The Country*. New York: Simon & Schuster, 2004.
Gable, John Allen. *The Bull Moose Years: Theodore Roosevelt and the Progressive Party*. Port Washington, N.Y.: Kennikat Press, 1978.
Pinchot, Amos. *History of the Progressive Party, 1912–1916*. 1958. Reprint, edited by Helene Maxwell Hooker. Westport, Conn.: Greenwood, 1978.

Prohibition

SEE Temperance and prohibition movements

Prostitution

PROSTITUTION IS the selling of sexual services. Although there have always been men and boys who sold sex, either to women or to other men, most prostitutes have been women, and most customers, men. In early 19th-century America, prostitution was officially illegal, but the authorities rarely prosecuted the participants as long as the practice remained out of sight. As the size of cities increased in the late 1800s, however, so did the visibility of prostitution, especially in red-light districts, so-called because of the red lights often put into the windows. With colorful names—such as Chicago's Levee, New York's Tenderloin, New Orleans's Storyville, and San Francisco's Barbary Coast—these districts were known far and wide for their brothels, the houses where prostitutes lived and worked. Some brothels were quite fancy and catered to high-class customers. Usually, madams, who both protected and exploited the prostitutes under their care, managed the establishments and arranged for protection from the local police force.

Movements to eradicate prostitution arose in the United States as early as the 1830s. At first, the concern of these movements was to "rescue" prostitutes from a life perceived as brutal and degraded and to raise the moral tone of city life. Antiprostitution forces exposed the names of prostitutes' customers and the owners of the buildings in which brothels conducted business. Later in the century, the campaign focused more on stopping the spread of venereal diseases, such as syphilis and gonorrhea, to the wives and offspring of prostitutes' customers. From 1870 to 1874, St. Louis

A 1914 newspaper article about antibrothel legislation in Washington, D.C., features a portrait of Dr. Kate Waller Barrett, a physician devoted to health care and social service programs for prostitutes and other women in need.

adopted the European approach to this problem, which was to legalize brothels, confine them to a specific part of the city, and conduct medical inspections of prostitutes. Church and women's groups opposed this system as an immoral use of state power to condone, instead of condemn, vice. Because no regulatory plan included inspections for prostitutes' customers, they also charged that this regulation discriminated against women.

During the Gilded Age and Progressive Era, social reformers continued to debate the issue of the social evil, as prostitution was then called. In the early 1900s, many cities set up vice commissions to make policy suggestions. Rejecting the European model of legalization and regulation, these commissions could only suggest that brothels be closed down. Sensational news stories about a so-called "white slave" traffic—a reference to the kidnapping of young, naive, and often immigrant women who were then forced into prostitution—resulted in more brothel closings. In 1910, Congress passed the Mann Act, which was designed to limit the traffic in women by preventing the transportation across state lines of underage women for "immoral purposes." Public concern about prostitution was so great in this period that in 1914 business tycoon and philanthropist John D. Rockefeller, Jr., funded the American Social Hygiene Association. This organization studied prostitution and promoted a sex education movement to teach young people about the dangers of venereal disease. During World War I, federal authorities closed red-light districts near military training camps and produced propaganda warning soldiers to avoid prostitutes at the risk of permanent danger to their health.

Although some cities managed to close brothels, this tactic did not stamp out prostitution. The closures merely sent prostitutes out onto the streets, where they became dependent on pimps for protection. One Progressive Era antiprostitution group in New York City, the Committee of Fourteen, tried to win passage of a law to prosecute the customers of prostitutes, but never succeeded.

SEE ALSO

Reform movements; Sex education movement; Sexuality

FURTHER READING

Brandt, Allan M. *No Magic Bullet: A Social History of Venereal Disease in the United States Since 1880.* New York: Oxford University Press, 1985.
Connelly, Mark Thomas. *The Response to Prostitution in the Progressive Era.* Chapel Hill: University of North Carolina Press, 1980.
Rosen, Ruth. *The Lost Sisterhood: Prostitution in America, 1900–1918.* Baltimore, Md.: Johns Hopkins University Press, 1982.

Protestantism

THE VAST MAJORITY of 19th-century American Christians were members of Protestant churches. Protestants accept the Bible as their religious authority and believe that laypeople, or those without formal theological training, should read and interpret the Bible on their own and participate in church governance. They disagree, however, on some key Christian doctrines, such as original sin, the divinity of Jesus, and the sacraments. As a result, Protestants have divided themselves into many denominations or sects, each interpreting doctrine and developing religious rites in their own ways.

In 1900, Methodism was the largest American Protestant denomination, with 53,908 churches. Founded by John Wesley in 18th-century England, Methodism incorporated a strict adherence to liturgy (the official rites and services of the church) with a belief in the power of divine grace to overcome the desire to sin. Its ministers preached abstention from all vices, such as drinking, gambling, and dancing. Methodists recruited converts through enthusiastic revivals or tent meetings and took highly moralistic positions on social and political issues. A number of Methodists, such as Frances Willard, longtime president of the Woman's Christian Temperance Union, were prominent in temperance and other social and moral reform movements.

Other American Protestant denominations were smaller: Presbyterians maintained 15,452 churches, Lutherans and Disciples of Christ each had about 10,000, and Episcopalians and Congregationalists had 6,264 and 5,604, respectively. The German Reformed (1,677), Quaker (1,031), Universalist (800), and Unitarian (455) denominations were among the smallest.

Racial and ethnic allegiances divided the larger Protestant denominations. Before the Civil War, Baptists had split into northern and southern branches over the issue of slavery. Further splits over theological issues, such as the nature of grace and free will, led to the formation of Primitive, Missionary, and Freewill Baptist sects. African Americans, who were overwhelmingly Baptist, maintained separate Baptist branches, as did ethnic German, Swedish, Danish, and Norwegian Baptists. Most black Baptists belonged to the National Baptist Convention, U.S.A., Inc., the first national organization of black churches. In 1915, a rival branch of black Baptists formed, the National Baptist Convention of America. Methodist African Americans were fairly evenly divided between the African Methodist Episcopal and the African Methodist Episcopal Zion churches.

Immigration of large numbers of Lutherans at the turn of the 20th century transformed American Lutheranism into the third largest Protestant denomination. Some 3 million Germans, 2.75 million Scandinavians, and others from the Austro-Hungarian Empire raised Lutheran numbers, which had stood at barely half a million in 1870, to 2.5 million by 1910. Although divided into various synods, loyal to divergent religious beliefs and ethnic customs, Lutherans ultimately formed a relatively united component of American Protestantism.

Some smaller Protestant denominations followed unique sets of beliefs. Seventh-Day Adventists adhered strictly to vegetarianism and drugless medicine and promoted Saturday as the true Sabbath. A small sect, they gained wide influence in the late 1800s through John Harvey Kellogg, the promoter of flaked breakfast cereals, who used his stature as the inventor of Kellogg's Corn Flakes and his reputation as an authority on health to bring converts into the church. In taking on this role, Kellogg insisted that he was "not after the business," a reference to his highly profitable sanitarium where he restored clients to health with a vegetable and grain diet; "I am after the reform; that is what I want to see."

The Shakers, or the United Society of Believers in Christ's Second Appearing, believed in God as both Father and Mother, practiced sexual abstinence, and owned all property in common. By the late 1800s, prosperous settlements from Maine to Indiana had lost many male community members

to other business opportunities and could not recruit new young members, who instead were turning to more liberal religions. The Church of Christ, Scientist, begun by Mary Baker Eddy in Boston in 1879, preached that illness was an illusion and that spiritual enlightenment could conquer it. By 1900, Christian Science, as it was called, had 504 churches. By 1908, it had 55,000 followers, the majority of whom were women, and a well-respected newspaper, the *Christian Science Monitor.*

Many Protestants responded to the changing economic and social conditions of the late 1800s by becoming involved in reform movements. Protestants were major leaders in the temperance and prohibition movements, which aimed to eliminate, or at least curtail, the manufacture, sale, and consumption of alcoholic beverages. Protestant ministers and academics also led the Social Gospel movement, which sought to focus churches less on issues of personal salvation and more on finding solutions to the day's social and economic problems. The Salvation Army evolved from Methodism and

used street revivalism and social programs—such as work relief, soup kitchens, and housing for the poor—to bring about religious conversions. The Young Men's and Young Women's Christian Associations (YMCA and YWCA) focused on helping urban youth retain their religious identities. The Y, whose origins went back to the 1840s and 1850s in England, came to the United States in the 1860s. From the 1870s onward, the Y expanded its services, offering Bible classes and low-cost, safe housing to urban youth.

Protestants responded in a variety of ways to the era's growing modernism, which included interest in more liberal interpretations of Scripture, Darwinian challenges to the biblical story of creation, and feminism. Congregationalists, Presbyterians, Episcopalians, and Methodists responded the most positively to modernism. Between 1910 and 1912, however, a group of conservative Protestants declared their opposition to these trends in pamphlets called "The Fundamentals: A Testimony to the Truth." These pamphlets reaffirmed a divine creation, the imminent return of Jesus

Christ to earth, and women's traditional roles in church and home. Revivalism and Pentecostalism were yet other responses to the challenges of modernism. In revivals, charismatic preachers convinced Protestants with weak ties to their faiths to recommit their souls to Jesus. As a result of their experiences in ecstatic prayer meetings, many believers felt that the Holy Spirit had healed their illness or disability.

Missionary work had long been integral to American Protestantism. Around the turn of the 20th century, the Social Gospel movement gave it a strong push forward. In 1895, Methodist John Mott created the World's Student Christian Federation, which in its first 20 years sent out 5,000 young missionaries on foreign assignments. As an official in the YMCA, Mott evangelized at college campuses and set up dozens of Y branches abroad. Missionaries sought to make converts but they also responded in practical ways to the desperate human needs they encountered in foreign lands. Missionary work appealed to many American women as a practical way to express their religious faith. By 1914, Baptist, Congregationalist, Methodist, and Presbyterian women had sent more than 3 million women into mission work. As doctors, nurses, teachers, or spouses of clergymen, they operated schools, hospitals, orphanages, leper colonies, and other charitable organizations around the world. By 1920, Protestant missionaries representing various denominations had planted outposts in China, India, Korea, Japan, Thailand, Burma, the South Pacific, and much of Africa.

Nineteenth-century American Protestants thought of themselves as the embodiment of the nation's moral force and democratic mission. The theme song of Theodore Roosevelt's Progressive party convention was the Protestant hymn "Onward Christian Soldiers." The wealthiest, most prominent Americans of the era were Protestant, and it was almost impossible to succeed in public life unless one was a Protestant. Many looked with suspicion upon the nation's newest non-Protestant immigrants. They worried that allegiance to the pope, a "foreign" power, would make Catholics incapable of being good American citizens. Having inherited centuries-old anti-Semitic prejudices, many Protestants also simply despised Jews. Protestants were at the forefront of both anti-Semitic and anti-Catholic campaigns of the era, including those waged by the Ku Klux Klan. Several decades would pass before such prejudices began to wane.

SEE ALSO

Fundamentalism; Ku Klux Klan; Religion; Revivalism and Pentecostalism; Salvation Army; Social Gospel; Temperance and prohibition movements; Willard, Frances; Women's rights movement

FURTHER READING

Balmer, Randall, and Lauren F. Winner. *Protestantism in America.* New York: Columbia University Press, 2002.
Handy, Robert T. *A Christian America: Protestant Hopes and Historical Realities.* 2nd ed. New York: Oxford University Press, 1984.
Noll, Mark A. *Protestants in America.* New York: Oxford University Press, 2000.

Psychology

PSYCHOLOGY IS a medical specialty that studies and seeks cures for mental illness. The field emerged in the late 1800s among philosophers interested in how the mind works. Two thinkers stand at the forefront of its earliest developments. William James was a trained in philosophy and then studied psychology in Germany and medicine at Harvard University in the late 1860s. Later, when he became a Harvard professor, he established the first psychological laboratory and published a major textbook in the field, *The Principles of Psychology* (1890). G. Stanley Hall, who studied with James and earned the first American doctorate in psychology in 1878, served as the nation's first professor of psychology (at Johns Hopkins University). He also founded the *American Journal of Psychology* in 1887, and in 1892, as president of Clark University, he established the first national professional association in the field. In 1904, Hall published a major work entitled *Adolescence*, which gathered together information on the psychology of teenagers.

By the early 1900s, psychologists had launched child-study and intelligence-testing programs that greatly influenced national trends in education. Schools became increasingly interested in quantifying students' intellectual levels and then using the results to track them into vocational or college-bound programs. In 1909, Dr. Sigmund Freud, famed Viennese psychoanalyst, visited the United States. Freud's ideas about the formation of the personality in childhood, the hidden workings of the unconscious, and the powerful force of the human sex drive increased interest in psychotherapy and psychoanalysis. A "behavioral" school of psychology emerged in 1913, which argued that, because psychologists could never be certain how the human unconscious actually works, they should focus instead on scientific observations of people's behavior and then develop ways to change it. During this era, the academic field of psychology remained primarily a topic for graduate study and research in departments of philosophy, education, and medicine.

SEE ALSO
Social sciences

FURTHER READING
Hale, Nathan G., Jr. *The Beginnings of Psychoanalysis in the United States, 1876–1917*. New York: Oxford University Press, 1971.
Ross, Dorothy. *G. Stanley Hall: The Psychologist as Prophet*. Chicago: University of Chicago Press, 1972.

Pulitzer, Joseph

- *Born: Apr. 10, 1847, Mako, Hungary*
- *Education: private tutors; studied law*
- *Accomplishments: Missouri House of Representatives (1869); police commissioner, St. Louis, Mo. (1872); delegate, Missouri constitutional convention (1875); publisher, St. Louis Post-Dispatch (1878–death) and New York World (1883–death); U.S. House of Representatives (Dem–N.Y., 1885); endowed the Pulitzer Prizes (1911)*
- *Died: Oct. 29, 1911, Charleston, S.C.*

BORN AND RAISED in Europe, Joseph Pulitzer immigrated to the United States in 1864 during the Civil War. When the war ended, he went to St. Louis, Missouri, where his fluency in German helped him find jobs with the city's German-speaking population. Eventually, he came to the attention of the owners of the city's German language daily newspaper, and in 1868 they offered him a job as a reporter.

As he pursued stories of wrongdoing in business and politics, he earned a reputation for fearless reporting. After a brief period as a state legislator (he won a special election) and as one of three of the city's appointed police commissioners, Pulitzer invested in local newspapers, studied law, and became more involved in politics. In 1872 he supported Republican Horace Greeley for President, but later became a lifelong Democrat.

Known for sensationalistic journalism, Joseph Pulitzer also believed that his newspapers should "undertake reforms, lead crusades, and thereby establish a name for individuality and active public service."

In 1878 Pulitzer bought the failed *St. Louis Evening Dispatch* for $2,500 and merged it with the *Evening Post.* The following year, he bought the *Post* from its owners and created the *St. Louis Post-Dispatch.*

The *Post* did well, attracting a wide readership of progressives interested in curbing the region's monied interests. In one early campaign, for example, the paper revealed how the city's wealthy residents evaded property taxes. Pulitzer explained his conception of what a newspaper should be by telling his son that it should do more than just print "every day first-rate news and first-rate editorials." It should also undertake reforms. Pulitzer married Kate Davis in 1878. He and his wife had seven children (five lived to adulthood), and in 1883 they moved to New York City.

The occasion for the move was Pulitzer's purchase of the then-failing *New York World* for $346,000. He made this newspaper a success as well. The *World* featured crowd-pleasing "sensational" stories about crimes, vice, and tragedies but also emphasized responsible coverage of public issues. It fostered the advance of investigative reporting (sometimes called "muckraking") and made strong editorial statements against business and political corruption. In 1885, the *World* raised $100,000 in small donations from readers for the pedestal of the Statue of Liberty and financed reporter Nellie Bly's 72-day around-the-world adventure. •

Had Pulitzer been born in the United States, he might have sought the Presidency. Instead, he used his power as a publisher to influence voters. He won election to Congress from New York in 1885 but, disillusioned by his lack of influence as a newly elected representative, resigned after only four months. Diabetes, encroaching blindness, and other illnesses slowed but did not stop him. In 1887, he established the *Evening World,* a more easygoing version of his morning paper.

In 1895, newspaper publisher William Randolph Hearst launched the *New York Journal,* luring away many of Pulitzer's staff members. Hearst and Pulitzer then vied with one another to see who could be more "sensational" in their approaches to the news and thereby win more readers. By publishing sensational stories of Spanish atrocities in Cuba, papers helped create the hysteria that made the 1898 Spanish-American War inevitable. After the war, the *World* downplayed sensationalism. It lost some readers but improved its reputation by attacking corruption in the insurance industry and taking up other progressive causes.

Near the end of his life, Pulitzer left $2 million to Columbia University for a graduate school of journalism. He also endowed the Pulitzer Prizes, which to this day recognize excellence in journalism, literature, and the arts.

SEE ALSO

Hearst, William Randolph; Journalism; Muckrakers; Spanish-American War; Statue of Liberty

FURTHER READING

Brian, Denis. *Pulitzer: A Life.* New York: Wiley, 2001.

Juergens, George. *Joseph Pulitzer and the New York World.* Princeton, N.J.: Princeton University Press, 1966.

Swanberg, W. A. *Pulitzer.* New York: Scribners, 1967.

Pullman strike (1894)

THE PULLMAN Palace Car Company manufactured sleeping cars for passenger trains. The manufacturing plant and company headquarters were located on the outskirts of Chicago in a company-built town named after its founder, George Pullman. Pullman provided housing, shops, and community services for the workers and their families but outlawed saloons, unions, and large public gatherings. The housing was comfortable, but rents were high and many workers felt constricted in the life that George Pullman had designed for them.

During the depression of 1893, Pullman laid off and fired many employees. He also cut wages by an average of 25 percent without lowering the rents or prices at company stores. In May 1894, the Pullman workers turned for help to the American Railroad Union (ARU) and its leader, Eugene V. Debs. Debs got union members nationwide to refuse to operate trains carrying Pullman cars, an action that crippled American rail service for weeks.

When workers in the American Railway Union went on strike at the Pullman Palace Car factory in 1894, members of the Illinois National Guard kept order outside the company town's Arcade building.

The strike action against the railroads also disrupted the transportation of the U.S. mail. Since interfering with the mail was a federal offense, President Grover Cleveland called in federal troops to end the strike. Trouble escalated when troops and strikers clashed in Chicago and angry workers burned freight cars and railroad equipment. Violence spread to other states. By mid-July, when the strike ended in defeat, 34 people had died and scores were wounded. Debs and other ARU leaders served prison sentences for civil contempt.

The widespread violence of the Pullman strike alerted Americans to the realities of class conflict in their own country. It motivated concerned citizens and progressive reformers to search for ways to resolve the deep conflicts between working people and business owners.

SEE ALSO

Cleveland, Grover; Company towns; Debs, Eugene Victor; Industry; Labor unions; Strikes

FURTHER READING

Carwardine, William Horace. *The Pullman Strike.* 1894. Reprint, Chicago: C. H. Kerr, 1973.
Lindsey, Almont. *The Pullman Strike: The Story of a Unique Experiment and of a Great Labor Upheaval.* Chicago: University of Chicago Press, 1994.
Stein, R. Conrad. *The Pullman Strike and the Labor Movement in American History.* Berkeley Heights, N.J.: Enslow, 2001.

Pure Food and Drugs Act (1906)

IN 1906, CONGRESS passed the Pure Food and Drugs Act, which established labeling requirements to inform consumers of product ingredients. The act

also instituted federal inspections to safeguard the public against adulterated foods and medicines. Together with the 1906 Meat Inspection Act, this law was a major victory for advocates of national consumer protection legislation. Foes of federal food and drug regulation ranged from wealthy meatpacking corporations to small manufacturers of "patent medicines," secret formulas that claimed a wide variety of curative powers but often contained harmful ingredients such as turpentine or mercury.

Pressure for Congressional action had been building for many years. Women's groups, in particular the Woman's Christian Temperance Union, which was concerned about products containing alcohol and opium, had long advocated food and drug legislation. During the Spanish-American War in 1898, the public had responded with outrage when tainted provisions (called "embalmed beef") caused sickness and death among American soldiers. Crusading journalists known as muckrakers stimulated demand for reform by publishing exposés about poisonous and addictive ingredients in the nation's food and drug supply.

One key figure in the reform movement was Harvey W. Wiley, chief chemist at the U.S. Department of Agriculture, who used his position to campaign for tough consumer protections. Another important influence was author Samuel Hopkins Adams, whose 1905 exposé in *Colliers Weekly,* "The Great American Fraud," alerted Congress to the dangers of patent medicines. In 1906, Upton Sinclair published his novel *The Jungle,* horrifying readers with his depiction of unsanitary conditions in the meatpacking industry. The book inspired a public outcry that motivated President Theodore Roosevelt to throw his support behind the Pure Food and Drugs Act.

In addition to being a landmark in the history of public health law, the legislation also served as a model for alcohol prohibition in the 1920s and the "war on drugs" at the end of the 20th century.

SEE ALSO

Health, public; Muckrakers; Reform movements; Roosevelt, Theodore; Sinclair, Upton Beall

FURTHER READING

Goodwin, Lorraine Swainston. *The Pure Food, Drink and Drug Crusaders, 1879–1914.* Jefferson, N.C.: McFarland, 1999.
Young, James Harvey. *Pure Food: Securing the Federal Food and Drugs Act of 1906.* Princeton, N.J.: Princeton University Press, 1989.

A federal inspector from the Department of Agriculture (at right, wearing a hat) enforces health and safety provisions of the 1906 Pure Food and Drugs Act by observing workers at a candy packaging plant.

Race relations

SCIENTISTS TODAY largely agree that all human beings on earth belong to a single biological species. Variations within that species have traditionally been called races. Thus the term "race" can be used to distinguish among human populations or geographic groups or physical types. Observed differences between humans include skin color, facial features, and ancestry, as

A white matron supervises Ojibwe girls in a Wisconsin sewing class in 1895. The teaching of "white" homemaking skills to Native Americans was intended to wean Indian children away from their tribal traditions.

well as traits that carry genetic markers, such as a predisposition to resist or succumb to certain diseases. While today's scientists do not rank differences between races in any particular order, late 19th-century Americans firmly believed in the reality of a racial hierarchy, or the superiority of one human group over another. Their attitudes about these differences shaped the period's race relations and influenced many aspects of social life and the law.

In the late 1800s, laypeople and scientists alike assumed that skin color, head or eye shape, and hair texture were indicators of racial superiority or inferiority. They also assumed that races coincided with places of national origin. White Americans, for example, thought that Anglo-Saxons (generally people from Germany and Great Britain) and people of Nordic origins were racially superior to other white-skinned peoples, including those of Celtic (the Irish) and Mediterranean origins (the Spanish, Greeks, and Portugese), as well as Poles, eastern Europeans, and Jews. According to 19th-century race theory in the United States, Native Americans were a distinct race, as were African Americans, the Chinese and Japanese, and Latin Americans. In addition, many Americans subscribed to a theory called Social Darwinism, a belief that differ-

ent races or societies of people evolved at different rates. According to this belief, white western societies—Northern European and North American—had evolved further than others and were therefore justified in treating other societies as inferior.

These almost universally held assumptions about racial hierarchies meant that race relations in the United States around the turn of the 20th century were far from harmonious. Americans treated some white-skinned Europeans as inferior but treated African Americans, Native Americans, and Asians much worse.

In the South, white supremacy was rampant. Between 1890 and 1920, legalized segregation became entrenched as every southern state passed Jim Crow laws that enforced separate accommodations in all public areas, including schools. Ku Klux Klan terrorism increased the incidence of lynching. Throughout the South, black voters found themselves thoroughly and systematically disfranchised.

Widespread intimidation and mistreatment of African Americans occurred in other parts of the country as well. Even in the North and West, which lacked Jim Crow laws, whites denied African Americans good jobs and decent housing, and kept them as much at a distance as possible. In those days, most white Americans opposed race mixing and interracial marriage. This opposition did not prevent white men, northern or southern, from routinely exploiting black women as prostitutes, however.

Not surprisingly, African Americans resisted categorization as inferior and the racist mistreatment that deprived them of civil rights and economic security. Educator Booker T. Washington urged African Americans to prove themselves equal to whites without challenging the segregated status quo. Other leaders, such as civil rights activists W. E. B. DuBois, and William Monroe Trotter, and Ida B. Wells, fought lynching and demanded the enforcement of equality under the law. They founded several organizations, including the National Association for the Advancement of Colored People (1909) and the National Urban League (1910), to combat discrimination and press for civil rights and economic opportunities for African Americans. Despite the best efforts of these groups, changes were slow in coming, and poverty, discrimination, and segregation remained a part of African American life.

Asian immigrants also suffered from discrimination. The Chinese had come to the United States during the gold rush of 1849 and stayed on to build railroads and run service businesses in western cities. Prejudices against the Chinese grew out of language and cultural differences and a fear that Chinese laborers were competing for scarce jobs. In 1882, Congress enacted the first of several Chinese Exclusion Acts, which effectively stopped Chinese immigration.

A less formal arrangement in 1907, the Gentlemen's Agreement between President Theodore Roosevelt and Japanese diplomats, brought an end to the immigration of Japanese laborers, though it did allow spouses to join those already in America. After the Spanish-American War and the annexation of the Philippines, Filipinos became U.S. nation-

A black nurse-maid poses with her employer's children. In an era when African American women had limited employment opportunities, many did housework and cared for the children of white families.

als, a status that enabled them to travel to the United States at will. They were hardly more welcome than the Chinese and Japanese, however.

Race relations with American Indians were never good. From colonial times, whites had broken treaties, stolen land, and fought wars against Native American tribes. By the end of the 19th century, following the last Indian resistance at Wounded Knee, South Dakota, in 1890, the U.S. government had pushed almost all Native Americans onto reservations. The Dawes Severalty Act (1887) sought to convert them into farmers, offering U.S. citizenship in return for abandoning tribal customs. Within their reserved lands, tribes retained some independence, but the U.S. Bureau of Indian Affairs interfered actively in reservation life and sought to make Indian children more like whites by educating them in boarding schools.

The fear and ignorance that governed white attitudes toward people of different skin colors and varied national origins produced a eugenics movement in the early 20th century. Eugenics is the science of controlled human breeding based on notions of desirable and undesirable traits. Fearing that "undesirable" people from the "inferior races" would reproduce at a high rate and overwhelm the desirable population, authorities, including President Theodore Roosevelt, encouraged people of white Anglo-Saxon descent to have many children. Although the American eugenics movement remained small, it nevertheless promoted the forced sterilization of the mentally disabled and laws against mixed marriages.

SEE ALSO
African Americans; Asian Americans; DuBois, William Edward Burghardt (W. E. B.); Chinese Exclusion Act (1882); Civil

rights; Dawes Severalty Act (1887); Gentlemen's Agreement; Immigration; Jim Crow; Judaism; Ku Klux Klan; National Association for the Advancement of Colored People; National Urban League; Native Americans; Race riots; Roosevelt, Theodore; Segregation; Social Darwinism

FURTHER READING

Bayor, Ronald H. *Race and Ethnicity in America: A Concise History.* New York: Columbia University Press, 2003.

Jacobson, Matthew Frye. *Whiteness of a Different Color: European Immigrants and the Alchemy of Race.* Cambridge, Mass.: Harvard University Press, 1998.

Kitano, Harry H., Pauline Agbayani, and Diane deAnda. *Race Relations.* 6th ed. Upper Saddle River, N.J.: Prentice Hall, 2005.

Takaki, Ronald T. *Iron Cages: Race and Culture in 19th-Century America.* Rev. ed. New York: Oxford University Press, 2000.

Race riots

BETWEEN THE 1890s and the mid-1920s, a pattern of mob violence known as the race riot emerged in the United States. They occurred in urban areas in both the North and the South, but more predominantly in the North, where the migration of thousands of southern African Americans to industrial cities before and during World War I exacerbated white fears about job loss and neighborhood integration.

Race riots in the North started with competition over jobs, disputes over segregated recreation areas, personal attacks, or even rumors of such attacks. In the South, riots broke out following accusations of rape of white women, or when long-smoldering resentment among black citizens about disfranchisement and segregation erupted into violence. Typically, during the riots, white mobs invaded black neighborhoods, beat and killed African

Americans, and destroyed their property. When African Americans fought to defend themselves, both sides experienced casualties, though the majority of those killed were black.

The six most serious race riots in this period occurred in Wilmington, North Carolina (1898); Atlanta (1906); Springfield, Illinois (1908); East St. Louis, Illinois (1917); Chicago (1919); and Tulsa, Oklahoma (1921). Most of the fighting took place in the hot summer months, when people were outside of their homes at all hours and often feeling frustrated from the heat. In the summer of 1919 alone, there were 26 race riots all over the country, including the Chicago riot, which was the largest and most damaging. Hundreds of African Americans died during these upheavals. Rampaging rioters injured hundreds more,

This Atlanta newspaper justified the antiblack violence of a 1906 race riot by citing recent episodes of "unbridled crime" allegedly committed by black men against white women.

burning shops and black neighbor-hoods and leaving thousands home-less. All-white police forces did little to quell the violence and frequently arrested the victims rather than the perpetrators. States sometimes called in militias or the National Guard to end the rioting.

SEE ALSO

African Americans; Chicago race riot (1919); Segregation; Race relations

FURTHER READING

Boskin, Joseph, ed. *Urban Racial Violence in the Twentieth Century*. 2nd ed. Beverly Hills, Calif.: Glencoe, 1976.
Mitchell, J. Paul. *Race Riots in Black and White*. Englewood. Cliffs N.J.: Prentice Hall, 1970.
Williams, Lee E. *Anatomy of Four Race Riots: Racial Conflict in Knoxville, Elaine (Arkansas), Tulsa, and Chicago, 1919–1921*. Hattiesburg: University and College Press of Mississippi, 1972.

Railroads

RAILROADS, POWERFUL symbols of the nation's technological progress and relentless westward expansion, were established features of the American landscape by the 1870s. After the 1869 completion of the first transcontinental railroad, the industry continued to grow, adding about 200,000 miles of track between 1870 and 1920. This brought the nation's total to approxi-mately a quarter of a million miles.

A typical railroad train consisted of a series of metal-wheeled cars riding on a pair of parallel metal rails. This metal-on-metal arrangement allowed a train to carry more weight and move at higher speed than a wheeled vehicle in contact with the ground. The power to move freight and passenger cars came from a steam engine in the loco-motive, the first car in the series. A locomotive engine burned coal to heat water in the boiler that produced the steam. Despite the invention of the diesel engine in the mid-1890s, the steam engine remained the industry standard for several more decades.

Coupling devices connected each car to the one in front of it. One of the most important railroad inventions of the late 19th century was the auto-matic coupler. It protected workers from being crushed between cars, a major cause of injury and death on the job. Other safety inventions included the compressed air brake, which could bring an entire train to a quick stop, and automatic electrical signals, which helped prevent collisions. In 1893, federal law made air brakes and auto-matic couplers mandatory equipment on all trains engaged in interstate transportation.

When U.S. railroad construction began in the 1830s, builders in differ-ent parts of the country used different track gauges (that is, different dis-tances between the rails). As railroads spread across the nation, trains designed for one rail system could not use another system's tracks. By the mid-1880s, the railroad industry had settled on a standard gauge of 4 feet 8 1/2 inches, a step that transformed an array of regional systems into a truly national network.

The industry also established new national time zones. In the 19th century, each community usually determined its own standard time, a situation that spawned hundreds of different time zones across the country and made accurate railroad scheduling virtually impossible. In 1883, the railroads divided the country into four zones and decreed that they would schedule their trains on the basis of uniform times within each zone and one-hour shifts between zones. Opponents complained that the new time zones trifled with nature for the sake of business convenience. The federal government did not officially adopt the four time zones until 1918.

As the country's first big business with coast-to-coast reach, the railroad industry played an important role in the history of labor-management relations. In 1877, conflict between railroad companies and their workers over reduced wages and layoffs escalated into the country's first nationwide strike. State and federal troops used armed force to get the trains moving again. Troopers forcefully dispersed picketers and kept them from blocking rail yard access for the replacement workers sent in to take their jobs. More than 100 people died in the violence. In 1894, the Pullman Palace Car Company responded to a national depression by cutting wages for its factory employees. The workers went on strike and sympathizers in the American Railway Union (ARU) refused to move any trains with Pullman cars. The federal government, declaring that the union was obstructing the movement of the U.S. mail, sent troops to break the strike.

Passengers on the Union Pacific Railroad in the mid-1890s enjoy a meal in the elegant dining car. Luxurious accommodations, combined with speed that devoured transcontinental miles, enticed many Americans to travel long distances by rail.

ARU president Eugene Debs criticized the government for siding with management against labor, but he also charged that white workers had weakened their cause by excluding black workers from the union. Many railroad jobs were not open to black workers at that time, though thousands of African American men did work as porters in the Pullman cars. Earning low wages and relying on tips for their livelihood, porters did not succeed in forming their own union until 1925.

The United States had encouraged the building of railroads by awarding companies more than 100 million acres of public land to promote new construction in the West. Nevertheless, railroad millionaires, such as Jay Gould, Leland Stanford, and Cornelius Vanderbilt, resisted federal regulation. By 1887, however, public discontent with corrupt financial dealings in the railroad industry pushed Congress to create the Interstate Commerce Commission (ICC), which was empowered to oversee shipping rates and require public disclosure of rates and practices. Additional legislation in the early 20th century gave the ICC even greater power to regulate the railroads.

The federal government took over control of the railroads during World War I in order to control troop movements and assure timely delivery of war materiel, but returned them to private ownership in 1920. By that time, the rise of the automobile and airplane industries had already begun to challenge the supremacy of the railroad train in the field of long-distance transportation.

SEE ALSO

Commerce; Debs, Eugene Victor; Inventions; Labor unions; Pullman strike (1894); Railroad strike (1877); Science and technology; West, the

FURTHER READING

Daniels, Rudolph. *Trains Across the Continent: North American Railroad History.* Bloomington: Indiana University Press, 1997.

Goddard, Stephen B. *Getting There: The Epic Struggle between Road and Rail in the American Century.* New York: Basic Books, 1994.

Gordon, Sarah. *Passage to Union: How the Railroads Transformed American Life, 1829–1929.* Chicago: Ivan R. Dee, 1996.

Josephson, Matthew. *The Robber Barons: The Great American Capitalists, 1861–1901.* 1934. Reprint, New York: Harcourt Brace, 1995.

Stover, John F. *American Railroads.* Chicago: University of Chicago Press, 2000.

Railroad strike (1877)

THE GREAT RAILROAD strike of 1877 was the first major strike in America's first major industry. It started in July in West Virginia, Pennsylvania, and Maryland when a number of rail companies, still feeling the effects of the depression of 1873, laid off workers and cut the wages of others. The companies also doubled the workload, thereby increasing the danger of accidents. The workers responded with a strike, which quickly spread to the Midwest, Texas, and California, disrupting rail service from Canada as far south as Virginia. Chicago and St. Louis sustained major disturbances. Soon, more than half the freight on the nation's 75,000 miles of track came to a complete stop. Unemployed workers in other industries joined the strikers and sympathy for the strike spread throughout the population, even among some city officials and merchants. In some places, farmers, who had suffered from high railroad rates, fed the strikers.

The strike turned violent when employers persuaded state governments to send in militia companies to break up the picket lines. Strikers retaliated by derailing trains and burning railroad property. The worst violence occurred in Pittsburgh on July 21, when state militiamen killed 10 rock throwers and wounded dozens more. The mob drove the soldiers into a roundhouse (a repair station for locomotives) and then set fire to nearly 40 buildings, more than 100 engines, and more than 1,000 freight and passenger cars. The soldiers shot their way out of the roundhouse, killing 20 more rioters.

President Rutherford B. Hayes sent in federal troops, which effectively ended the strike, though more people died before it was all over. The use of the U.S. military to break the strike set a precedent for the use of state and federal troops to repress labor disturbances.

The railroad strike of 1877 mobilized more than 100,000 workers. In its aftermath, more and more workers joined unions, significantly increasing membership in the Knights of Labor and later in the American Federation of Labor.

SEE ALSO

Labor unions; Railroads; Strikes

FURTHER READING

Bruce, Robert V. *1877: Year of Violence.* 1959. Reprint, Chicago: Ivan R Dee, 1989.

Foner, Philip S. *The Great Labor Uprising of 1877.* New York: Monad Press, 1977.

Stowell, David O. *Streets, Railroads, and the Great Strike of 1877.* Chicago: University of Chicago Press, 1999.

State troops in Maryland clash violently with striking railroad workers in 1877. After confrontations between workers and state militias escalated around the country, federal troops helped railroad companies restore order.

Ranching

RANCHING IS the business of raising animals, or livestock, either to train them for work or to sell their meat, hides, wool, and other products. American ranchers have raised many species of grazing animals, with horses, cattle, and sheep being the most significant.

After the United States acquired Texas and other territories in the 1848 Mexican War, ranching spread throughout the West. Mounted cowherds called cowboys were one of the most ethnically diverse workforces in any late 19th-century industry. An estimated one-fifth to one-third of all American cowboys were Mexican; another 15 to 25 percent were black. In addition, a number of Indian tribes operated ranches on their reservations, and many Indian cowboys worked for off-reservation ranchers.

Some cattle ranchers owned the grasslands that fed their herds, but many grazed their livestock on the millions of acres of public land still available in the sparsely populated West. Cattle belonging to many different owners roamed together on the open range, so ranchers identified their property with brands, distinctive marks burned into the animals' hides with hot irons. Conflicts about animal ownership and conflicts between different branches of the livestock industry over the use of grazing lands occasionally escalated into armed warfare. Cattle ranchers charged that sheep destroyed good grazing land by uprooting rather than cropping grass and damaged the soil with their sharp hooves. In a few cases, rival ranchers lost their lives in fighting over such issues.

From the end of the Civil War to the mid-1880s, Texas ranchers became known for their long-distance cattle drives. Because the nation's railroad system had not yet reached many parts of cattle country, there were no trains to carry livestock directly from ranches in the West to slaughterhouses and meatpacking plants in the East. To get the meat to market, teams of cowboys drove enormous herds of cattle on treks of a thousand miles or more from Texas northward through Oklahoma to railroad depots in Kansas. Other cattle-drive routes delivered livestock to far-flung locations throughout the West. Sheep ranching did not involve long-distance drives, because fleece shearing took place at the home ranch.

As the 19th century drew to a close, the growth of the nation's railroad system did away with the need for cattle drives. In the early 1900s, major meatpacking companies began to open plants in western cattle country. Additionally, ranchers had to adapt to new conditions as both population and land ownership in the West increased and barbed-wire fences began to mark property lines on the previously open range. Many ranchers began raising herds on fenced-in private land, growing alfalfa and other feed crops to substitute for open-range grass. The grazing of privately owned stock on public land

Cowboys herd livestock on a Texas ranch around 1901. By the 20th century, the Old West cattle drives were gone, but the ranching industry remained an economic powerhouse, and cowboys held on to their mythological status in popular culture.

continued in some parts of the West, however, and the multimillion-dollar ranching industry exerted a powerful influence on federal land-use policy.

Cowboys became heroes of American folklore. Real and fictional, they won a place in popular culture as rodeo stars and as the heroes of dime novels, Wild West shows, and silent movies.

SEE ALSO

Agriculture; Industry; Railroads; West, the

FURTHER READING

Graham, Don. *Kings of Texas: The 150-Year Saga of an American Ranching Empire.* Hoboken, N.J.: Wiley, 2003.

Iverson, Peter. *When Indians Became Cowboys: Native Peoples and Cattle Ranching in the American West.* Norman: University of Oklahoma Press, 1994.

Starrs, Paul F. *Let the Cowboy Ride: Cattle Ranching in the American West.* Baltimore, Md.: Johns Hopkins University Press, 1998.

Rankin, Jeannette Pickering

- *Born: June 11, 1880, Missoula, Mont.*
- *Education: University of Montana, B.A., 1902; attended New York School of Philanthropy (later Columbia School of Social Work), 1908–9*
- *Accomplishments: legislative secretary, National American Woman Suffrage Association (1914); first female member of the U.S. House of Representatives (Republican–Mont., 1917–19; 1941–43)*
- *Died: May 18, 1973, Carmel, Calif.*

JEANNETTE RANKIN had the distinction of being the first woman to serve in Congress. She also voted twice against her country's entry into a world war. A committed feminist and pacifist, Rankin grew up on a ranch in Montana. She worked first as a teacher and then as a social worker. After leaving these professions, she devoted herself to the

NATIONAL AMERICAN WOMAN SUFFRAGE ASS'N

woman suffrage movement, helping to achieve the vote for women in her home state of Montana in 1914. As a progressive Republican, she ran for Congress two years later. She campaigned for a federal woman suffrage amendment, child protection laws, and prohibition.

By the time Rankin arrived in Congress for her first term, war talk was in the air. Germany had been sinking U.S. ships and President Woodrow Wilson, who had previously insisted on American neutrality in the European war, now felt that the United States had to intervene. On April 6, 1917, Wilson asked Congress to pass a war resolution. Both houses of Congress agreed, but Rankin was one of 56 legislators to vote no. Because she was a woman, her negative vote received more public attention than anyone else's. It also lost her the support of most organized suffragists, who believed that Rankin's pacifism would hurt the woman suffrage cause.

Even though Rankin voted in favor of a military draft in 1917 and spent the duration of the war promoting the sale of war bonds, her political career floundered. In 1918, when a change in her election district prevented her from running for reelection, she tried to win her party's nomination for U.S. senator. When this failed, she ran as an independent, and lost.

Rankin spent the next 20 years working for peace and women's social

Montana native Jeannette Rankin greets a crowd of admirers from the balcony of the National American Woman Suffrage Association building. The first woman elected to Congress, Rankin was en route to her swearing in on April 2, 1917.

reform issues. In 1940, she again won a seat in the House of Representatives and, after Japan bombed Pearl Harbor on December 7, 1941, was the only member of Congress to vote against declaring war. Prominent in the anti-Vietnam war movement, at the age of 88 she led a group named in her honor, the Jeanette Rankin Brigade, in a protest march in Washington, D.C. In 1985, her state placed a bronze statue of her in the rotunda of the U.S. Capitol.

SEE ALSO

Peace movement; Woman suffrage movement

FURTHER READING

Davidson, Sue. *A Heart in Politics: Jeannette Rankin and Patsy T. Mink.* Seattle: Seal Press, 1994.

Josephson, Hannah. *Jeannette Rankin, First Lady in Congress: A Biography.* Indianapolis, Ind.: Bobbs-Merrill, 1974.

Lopach, James J. and Jean A. Luckowski. *Jeannette Rankin: A Political Woman.* Boulder: University Press of Colorado, 2005.

Smith, Norma. *Jeannette Rankin, America's Conscience.* Helena: Montana Historical Society Press, 2002.

Rauschenbusch, Walter

- *Born: Oct. 4, 1861, Rochester, N.Y.*
- *Education: University of Rochester, B.A., 1884; Rochester Theological Seminary, B.Div., 1886*
- *Accomplishments: professor, Rochester Theological Seminary (1897–1918); author,* Christianity and the Social Crisis *(1907),* Christianizing the Social Order *(1912),* The Social Principles of Jesus *(1916), and* A Theology for the Social Gospel *(1917)*
- *Died: July 25, 1918, Rochester, N.Y.*

A BAPTIST THEOLOGIAN and historian, Walter Rauschenbusch was the intellectual leader of the Social Gospel movement in American Protestantism.

The movement involved religious organizations in working toward the elimination of "vices," such as gambling, prostitution, and drinking, and in becoming more actively involved in missionary, moral, and social reform movements. Rauschenbusch was the son of a German immigrant who taught at the Rochester Theological Seminary. After extensive study in Germany, he earned a degree from the University of Rochester and was ordained for the ministry.

An 11-year pastorate near Hell's Kitchen, one of New York City's poorest neighborhoods, sealed his determination to work with the poor. He was especially distressed by the many children who died, essentially from poverty, at whose funerals he officiated. In a sermon he delivered in 1913, he remembered how the children's funerals "gripped my heart—that was one of the things I went away thinking about—why did the children have to die?" In 1891, he took a year's leave from his pastorate to study economics and theology at the University of Berlin. He also traveled to England, where he met British socialists and observed the mission work of the Salvation Army and the operations of purchasing cooperatives, which consumers had set up to counteract the profiteering of unscrupulous shopkeepers. He returned to New York determined to apply what he had learned from these organizations to helping the poor in the United States.

Rauschenbusch believed that the Kingdom of God was coming, but that Christians needed to play a part in bringing it about. In 1892, he joined with like-minded clergy to form the

Baptist minister Walter Rauschenbusch challenged Christians to embrace social reform: "Other organizations may conceivably be indifferent when confronted with the chronic or acute poverty of our cities. The Christian Church cannot... the Church has a tremendous stake in the social crisis."

Brotherhood of the Kingdom, a group committed to the practical application of Jesus' social teachings. He urged churches to focus less on personal salvation and more on solving the social problems created by the capitalist system. He promised an ethic of love and concern for community welfare. He refused, however, to identify the Kingdom of God with any one particular social program. "The Kingdom of God is always coming," he said, "but we can never say 'Lo here.'"

He also became involved in politics. In 1886, he participated in the New York mayoral campaign of reformer Henry George and labored with investigative photographer Jacob Riis on playground and housing reform. In his many writings he critiqued capitalism, argued that socialism and Christianity were compatible, and insisted that religion and ethics were inseparable. Translated into many languages, his books reached a wide readership.

In his later years, when increasing deafness hampered his ability to preach, Rauschenbusch accepted a professorship at Rochester Theological Seminary. He taught church history there, continuing to publish on contemporary social issues. World War I, with its horrible death toll and rabid anti-German attitudes, depressed him profoundly. By the time of his death, he had lost much of his optimism about the possibility of human redemption.

SEE ALSO
George, Henry; Poverty; Religion; Riis, Jacob; Social Gospel

FURTHER READING
Evans, Christopher Hodge. *The Kingdom Is Always But Coming: A Life of Walter Rauschenbusch*. Grand Rapids, Mich.: William B. Eerdmans, 2004.
Hunt, George Laird, ed. *Twelve Makers of Modern Protestant Thought*. New York: Association Press, 1971.
Minus, Paul M. *Walter Rauschenbusch, American Reformer*. New York: Macmillan, 1988.

Red Scare (1919–20)

DURING WORLD WAR I, many Americans feared that radicals—including peace activists, labor unions, socialists, and communists—threatened the American way of life. Three developments after the war heightened these fears. First, in 1919, the communists who had taken over the Russian government two years earlier organized a group dedicated to spreading revolution worldwide. Second, postwar strikes and race riots led many Americans to conclude that communists not only had started these disturbances but were plotting to take over their government. Finally, the explosion of terrorist bombs targeting the homes of prominent businessmen and government officials convinced many that a revolution was about to happen.

The result was a Red Scare, a time of national fear that Reds—a vague term referring to anyone suspected of being a socialist or communist that comes from the red flag of Russian revolutionaries—would soon take over the U.S. government. Given broad powers by the President and Congress to arrest and deport suspected Reds, Attorney General Alexander Mitchell Palmer and his lieutenant J. Edgar Hoover compiled a list of thousands of suspected subversives. Under the authority of the wartime Espionage and Sedition Acts, they launched unannounced searches, often without warrants, and rounded up thousands of residents, many of them aliens. These so-called Palmer Raids put

A 1919 cartoon expresses the fears behind the Red Scare, depicting the world hung over from years of war and menaced by figures that include striking workers, Bolsheviks (communists), and bomb-throwing terrorists.

Reform movements

many innocent people into jail without trial for weeks or months. About 600 were deported to the Soviet Union, including the feminist anarchist Emma Goldman.

By the spring of 1920, the Red Scare had died down. After prominent leaders denounced the violations of civil liberties, the government released some people from jail and canceled more than 1,500 deportations. Another significant Red Scare would not occur in the United States until the 1950s.

SEE ALSO

Anarchism; Communism; Goldman, Emma; Socialism; World War I

FURTHER READING

Coben, Stanley. *A. Mitchell Palmer: Politician.* 1963. Reprint, New York: Da Capo, 1972.
Feurlicht, Roberta Strauss. *America's Reign of Terror: World War I, the Red Scare, and the Palmer Raids.* New York: Random House, 1971.
Murray, Robert K. *Red Scare: A Study in National Hysteria, 1919–1920.* Minneapolis: University of Minnesota Press, 1955.
Preston, William, Jr., and Paul Buhle. *Aliens and Dissenters: Federal Suppression of Radicals, 1903–1933.* Urbana: University of Illinois Press, 1995.

TO REFORM A CUSTOM, an institution, or a political or economic system is to improve it by identifying its faults and pursuing ways to correct them. In many senses, the entire period from 1880 to 1920 was an age of reform. Faced with massive social and economic problems stemming from the second Industrial Revolution—rapid unplanned growth of cities and factories, an unprecedented influx of immigrants crowded into urban slums, political corruption, public health disasters, great disparities of wealth, and periodic economic slumps—many Americans wanted to "fix" what was wrong and set the nation on a new course. As a result, reformers and reform movements became a significant part of the Gilded Age and Progressive Era.

Reform had different meanings for different people. For some reformers, it meant more social control, meaning the use of government authority to control the behavior of individuals or groups. To others it meant ending injustice and poverty, or at the very least distributing the nation's wealth more fairly so as to close the gap between rich and poor. Still others envisioned a total transformation of social relations so that the United States would become a paradise on earth for all of its people.

Some movements focused on reforming the social "vices" of American life. The temperance movement to control the sale and consumption of alcoholic beverages was one such movement. Eventually, temperance advocates succeeded in passing the 18th, or Prohibition, Amendment to the U.S. Constitution, which effectively shut down the legal sale of alcohol until it was repealed in 1933. Other reformers attacked prostitution, working mostly on the local level, and sometimes as part of a broader campaign to "clean up" cities.

Urban reform was another major Progressive Era initiative. One branch of urban reformers attacked the corrupt political machines that ran city governments by handing out patronage jobs and contracts. Women's voluntary associations campaigned for a better quality of civic life, focusing on improvements to sanitation, stronger regulations for the building of tenement houses, and safer and more pleasant conditions for children. The City Beautiful movement to reroute thoroughfares, plant trees, and build fountains stemmed from the belief that America's haphazard cities had spawned crime and corruption, and that planned, attractive cities made better citizens.

Like urban reformers, education reformers had dual motives. In part, they wished to make schools happier places for children because they believed that students who enjoyed school were better learners. Some of these same reformers, however, also felt that schools should be used to assimilate the children of immigrants or Native Americans into white society and to create docile and cooperative citizens. Both urban and educational reforms had aspects of social control.

Men and women dedicated to improving life for city dwellers established residences, called settlement houses, in poor neighborhoods in order to learn how best to help the poor. They began the learning process with investigative research of neighborhood conditions, and then used their findings to lobby state legislatures to make changes in the laws governing labor and education. Settle-ment-house residents also ran programs to help immigrants and working people adjust to city life. Some became involved in the reform of garment-industry sweatshops, where low-wage workers toiled long hours in uncomfortable or even dangerous conditions.

Government reformers sought to end the distribution of government jobs as political rewards by instituting a civil service examination system at the federal level. They also promoted "good government" initiatives to make local, state, and federal governments more accountable to the electors, to free mayors and city councils from the control of corrupt party leaders, and to apply sound business methods in the running of government.

Many Americans were concerned about reforming labor conditions. Industrialization had provided wage work for millions of Americans, but it had also brought problems—dangerous work spaces in factories and mines, low wages, and discrimination against certain ethnic groups. Labor unions were the first to fight for industrial reform, using strikes, boycotts, and court action to push for the eight-hour day, workplace safety, and compensation for injuries incurred on the job. The labor union movement, with help from middle-class reformers, also fought to end child labor.

A number of individuals and organizations fought for the reform of race and ethnic relations in the United States and for improved civil rights for minorities. Black educators Booker T. Washington and W. E. B. DuBois dedicated their lives to ending second-class citizenship for African Americans. The National Association for the Advancement of Colored People (NAACP), founded in 1909, fought segregation and discrimination in the courts, in publications, and sometimes on the

A New York City exhibition displays a charitable society's model tenement apartment. The promoters claim that such apartments are well ventilated and provide basic amenities, such as bathrooms and wash tubs.

All rooms open on the street or on an interior Park 100 feet wide and 250 feet long.

Each apartment is self-contained, and provided with separate water closet, dust chute, wash tubs &.c. Buildings have paid 5% net profit.

Kitchen of Longshoreman's family. Rent $7.60 per month for 3 rooms. Model Tenements, Brooklyn, N.Y. Riverside Buildings of Mr. Alfred T. White.

picket line. A few lone voices spoke up for Native Americans, protesting the way whites stole their land and attacked their tribal traditions. Many more white Americans had a different view of reform for Native Americans, however, pushing them to adopt white farming methods, learn English, and abandon their traditions in favor of assimilation into the majority society.

Women's rights were a major reform initiative of the period. In particular, the Gilded Age and Progressive Era saw the final push for votes for women, which ended successfully with the passage of the 19th Amendment to the U.S. Constitution in 1920. Women also fought for access to information about birth control and to make college and professional careers more accessible to women. Labor activists working on behalf of women also pressed for changes in working conditions that would protect women's health and reproductive capacities from industrial accidents or toxins and hours of overwork.

Americans knew they had a beautiful country with an astonishing variety of mountains, forests, plains, deserts, and coastlines. Another type of reform, the conservation movement,

grew out of a desire to preserve these areas from development and exploitation. The conservation movement was a reform at odds with the American tradition of unfettered individual enterprise. Conservationists worked hard to persuade Congress and skeptical fellow citizens that saving wilderness through government action was better than limitless exploitation of the natural environment.

Many others in this era worked to roll back the evils of industrialization and bring about their dreams of a peaceful country where healthy lives and justice were available for all. Economic theorist Henry George wanted to make taxation fair for all Americans by instituting a single tax on the rising value of land. Socialist reformers wanted a new politics and a new social structure that would give economic power to the masses. Utopian reformers, such as author Edward Bellamy, created fictional societies where money had become obsolete and all Americans enjoyed a high standard of living in a world at peace. All of these visionaries had sizeable followings in the Gilded Age and Progressive Era, a period when people believed that major reform was possible.

FURTHER READING

Allen, Robert L, with Pamela P. Allen. *Reluctant Reformers: Racism and Social Reform Movements in the United States.* Washington, D.C.: Howard University Press, 1974.

Blocker, Jack S., Jr. *American Temperance Movements: Cycles of Reform.* Boston: Twayne, 1989.

Boyer, Paul. *Urban Masses and Moral Order in America, 1820–1920.* Cambridge, Mass.: Harvard University Press, 1978.

Crunden, Robert M. *Ministers of Reform: The Progressives' Achievement in American Civilization, 1889–1920.* New York: Basic Books, 1982.

Frankel, Noralee, and Nancy Schrom Dye, eds. *Gender, Class, Race, and Reform in the Progressive Era.* Lexington: University Press of Kentucky, 1991.

Hofstadter, Richard. *The Age of Reform.* 1955. Reprint, New York: Vintage Books, 1960.

Sanders, Elizabeth. *Roots of Reform: Farmers, Workers, and the American State, 1877–1917.* Chicago: University of Chicago Press, 1999.

Regulation

DURING THE Progressive Era, reformers demanded government regulation over the "monied interests," by which they meant big business—the entrepreneurs who provided city residents with services and utilities, the railroads, and the large corporations. Reformers charged these "interests" with many misdeeds. By driving smaller businesses into bankruptcy, large corporations stifled competition. Railroads gave cheap rates and rebates to big customers but charged more to small-scale shippers, many of them farmers. Monopolies that controlled public utilities overcharged for services people could not do without. Large companies not only underpaid their workers but refused to recognize the rights of labor unions to bargain collectively for their members. Makers of consumer goods sold shoddy products and foods and medicines that made people sick. If government could not break up these harmful businesses, reformers said, at least it should control them for the benefit of the public welfare.

The first big businesses to come under government control were the railroads. In 1887, in response to anger over inequities in railroad rates, Congress established the Interstate Commerce Commission (ICC). States had been regulating railroads within their own borders for decades, but the ICC was the first *national* regulatory commission. It forbade rebates on interstate commerce and directed railroads to eliminate some differential rates. The commission received no power, however, to set rates or punish companies for violations. Further legislation corrected these weaknesses. The Elkins Act (1903) prohibited rebates, and the Hepburn Act (1906) empowered the ICC to set rates. The Esch-Cummins Transportation Act of 1920 returned the railroads to private management but empowered the ICC to regulate railroad mergers. It also established a Railroad Labor Board to resolve labor disputes, especially those over wages.

States and cities set up commissions to regulate other businesses, such as banks, insurance companies, and public utilities. By 1896, slightly more than half of American cities had assumed ownership of their own waterworks. Although few commissions ever lowered rates, they made people feel that government was looking out for their interests. At least a public agency could hear complaints and require better management from privately owned utility and municipal transportation companies.

Federal regulation of monopolies also began in this period. To evade state laws prohibiting the fixing of prices and other anticompetitive measures, companies had increasingly merged into trusts and holding companies. Trusts were legal devices by which a few powerful companies controlled entire industries, such as oil refining and steel manufacturing. Large companies formed holding companies to "hold" the stocks of smaller ones and act in their behalf.

In an effort to stop such mergers, which were driving smaller companies out of business and keeping prices high for consumers, Congress almost unanimously passed the Sherman Antitrust Act in 1890. This act declared illegal "every contract, combination in the form of trust or otherwise, or conspiracy, in restraint of trade. "Its language was too vague to be easily enforceable. Moreover, corporation lawyers used the Sherman Act as a means to control labor unions. They convinced courts to rule that major strikes were "conspiracies" in "restraint of trade" and then to issue injunctions to bring such strikes to an end.

Despite its flaws, the Sherman Act showed that government was abandoning its traditional hands-off stance toward the economy. Over time, government used the act more effectively,

passing the Clayton Antitrust Act of 1914, which forbade the use of Sherman to control labor unions, and the same year setting up the Federal Trade Commission to enforce Clayton.

Other forms of regulation continued at state levels, where new laws restricted child labor, women's working hours, and unsafe working conditions. Many states also passed workers' compensation laws and even laws to provide unemployment insurance. Labor unions, however, had to wait until the Fair Labor Standards Act of 1938 to win permanent rights to bargain collectively.

A movement to manage the nation's vast natural resources was an important aspect of Progressive Era regulation. After the Civil War, many states passed laws to preserve their fish and game populations. They also established forestry agencies, park systems, geological surveys, and gas and oil regulations. Congress soon followed suit, empowering Presidents Benjamin Harrison, Grover Cleveland, and William McKinley to set aside

Railroad magnate Edward Harriman appears as a monstrous head swallowing up his company's competition in this 1907 cartoon. Public fear of the enormous power of large corporations created support for government regulation of trusts and monopolies.

millions of acres of forests. Theodore Roosevelt was especially active in conservation. He supported the 1902 Newlands Act, which financed irrigation projects in the West and Southwest and protected southern waterways from private development. He transferred additional forests into the national reserves and put coal and mineral deposits under public controls.

In the preindustrial era, when consumers bought shoddy or spoiled products, they could often complain directly to the person who made them. After industrialization, however, consumers were too distant from production to know whom to hold accountable for quality. Working through women's clubs and other groups, consumers turned first to state governments for action. During the 1880s, state legislatures began to require truthful labels and banned the use of cheap fillers such as sawdust and chalk in coffee, flour, and mustard. Cocaine (used in Coca-Cola until 1903), opium, and alcohol in patent medicines (trademarked remedies marketed without proof of their effectiveness) also came under regulation. Congress considered almost 200 pure-food bills before 1906, when it finally passed the Pure Food and Drugs Act to regulate the labeling of food and to establish government testing. A Meat Inspection Act the same year mandated federal inspection of slaughterhouses and meatpacking establishments, after journalist Upton Sinclair had exposed these companies' disregard of basic sanitation.

Regulation did not always work as its advocates hoped. Regulatory commissions to oversee the railroads and public utilities were supposed to reduce rates. But lacking enforcement power, they tended instead to work out compromises between government and the businesses they were supposed to regulate. Also, monopolies preferred regulation to being broken up or heavily taxed. Therefore they cooperated with commissions, later citing this cooperation as a stamp of official approval.

Regulation was, and still is, controversial. Opponents argued that government should stay as far out of economic affairs as possible (the theory known as laissez-faire, or "let things happen"). They insisted that the economy would do better if market forces were allowed free rein. Specific economic interests opposed regulation when it threatened to limit their profits. Western ranchers and lumber and electric power interests, for example, opposed some of President Theodore Roosevelt's conservation efforts. Industrialists fought laws that curbed their ability to contract with workers as they pleased. But regulation advocates insisted that without some government controls, the nation's economy would suffer from instability, workers would be unfairly exploited, and public health would be compromised. Today, the American public continues to debate how to maintain sufficient economic freedom for businesses so that they can thrive, while at the same time protecting society from the harm they can sometimes cause.

SEE ALSO
Antitrust laws; Child labor; Commerce; Conservation; Industry; Labor; Laissez-faire; Pure Food and Drugs Act (1906)

FURTHER READING
Gould, Lewis, L. *Reform and Regulation: American Politics from Roosevelt to Wilson*. 3rd ed. Prospect Heights, Ill.: Waveland Press, 1996.
Keller, Morton. *Regulating a New Economy: Public Policy and Economic Change in America, 1900–1933*. Cambridge, Mass.: Harvard University Press, 1990.

Religion

IN 1890, ABOUT 22 million Americans declared themselves members of religious institutions; by 1920, this number had reached 50 million, out of a total population of 106 million. Most of the Christian faithful adhered to some form of Protestantism. The size of the Roman Catholic population, which was at 8 million in 1890, had doubled by 1920, thanks to immigration from Ireland, Italy, Poland, central Europe, and Mexico. The number of Jews also grew in this period. About 230,000 to 300,000 Jews lived in the United States in 1880; by 1920, these numbers had swelled to 3.5 million, as a result of immigration from eastern Europe and Russia.

Certain religious populations were concentrated in particular areas of the country. Older Catholic groups, the descendants of French and German immigrants, had congregated in the Mississippi Valley. Southwestern communities contained Catholic Mexicans left behind after the 1848 Mexican war, when the victorious United States annexed Texas and Northern Mexico, as well as Mexicans who had immigrated later. Catholics and Jews arriving in the late 1800s settled in major cities across the continent but especially in the East. By the end of the 1800s, about 2 million Lutherans lived in ethnic enclaves from Ohio to the Dakotas. About 230,000 Mormons, members of the Church of Jesus Christ of Latter-day Saints, had established themselves in Utah. The Churches of Christ, which hoped to restore unity among Christians by accepting only the Bible as their source of religious truth, predominated in the South. Smaller sects, such as the Mennonites, Amish, and Shakers, lived in self-sufficient northern or midwestern communities.

Americans attended places of worship not only to seek aid and consolation from a higher power but also to connect with a larger community. Churches and synagogues organized social events, clubs, and other recreational activities. Some ran mutual benefit societies that provided life insurance and sick pay for members. In most religious institutions, men controlled the finances, holding the ministerial and administrative positions and representing their denominations at conferences. Women ran the Sunday schools and established voluntary associations that ran charities, funded missions, and launched social reforms.

Concerned about the mass suffering caused by economic downturns, many religious institutions became more socially conscious in this era. The leaders of a Social Gospel movement asked churches, synagogues, and voluntary organizations to help rid society of vice, such as gambling, prostitution, and drinking, and to become more actively involved in other missionary, moral, and social reform movements. The Salvation Army, founded in England by a Methodist minister in 1865 and brought to the United States in 1880, offered soup and sermons to the down-and-out, feeding their bodies while also trying to save their souls. Catholics became more involved in reform after Pope Leo XIII issued an encyclical, *Rerum Novarum,* in 1891, which sanctioned workers' rights and other social reforms.

Modern ideas, especially those of liberal theologians, scientists, and feminists, constituted the greatest challenge to traditional religion. Instead of regarding the Bible as literally true, liberals looked at Scriptures with a historical and critical approach supported by recent archaeological discoveries in the Holy Land and studies of a historical Jesus. Religious liberals drew upon Judeo-Christian traditions for moral and ethical truths but de-emphasized rituals, miracles, and issues of damnation or salvation. While insisting that science could be reconciled with religion, some religious liberals accepted Charles Darwin's theory of human evolution. In 1895, Elizabeth Cady Stanton, the nation's leading woman suffragist, published *The Woman's Bible,* which critiqued Scripture and the Church for limiting women's activities.

The call for a World Parliament of Religions was one response to the challenge of modernism. Held over seventeen days during the 1893 World's Columbian Exposition in Chicago, the parliament drew delegates primarily from Christianity and Judaism, but also some Buddhists, Hindus, Muslims, Zoroastrians, Shintoists, Confucians, and a Taoist and a Jain. For some participants, the parliament reaffirmed the importance of religion's continuing role in society. One of its most concrete results was the formation of the National Council of Jewish Women, the original purpose of which was to reaffirm Jewish women's religious identity. It also sparked an interest among Americans in Asian religions. A number of prominent religious conservatives had refused to attend, however. They feared that the parliament would make plural paths to religious truth more legitimate.

Fundamentalism was another response to modernism. By the 1920s, this was the term applied to the beliefs of Protestants who regarded the Bible as the absolute authority on such matters as divine creation, the role of women, and the second coming of Christ. In 1919, they formed the World's Christian Fundamentals Association,

which sought to ban the teaching of evolution in the schools, keep liberal theological ideas out of Protestant denominations, and lend support to the temperance and prohibition movements.

Some denominations, such as Christian Science, Mormonism, Greek and Russian Orthodoxy, and Asian religions, remained untouched by modernism. Northern Protestant denominations—such as the Congregationalist, Episcopalian, Unitarian, Quaker, Methodist, Presbyterian, northern Baptist, and Disciples of Christ—adopted more liberal creeds. In the mid-1800s, some Jews began to liberalize their religion, later founding Hebrew Union College in Cincinnati, Ohio, to train "reform" rabbis. Reform Jews relaxed traditional restrictions on women's participation in religious services and conducted these services primarily in English instead of Hebrew. Another modern offshoot of Judaism appeared in 1876

An 1879 cartoon mocks the competition for members among proponents of various religious denominations, including a shirtless Baptist, and a wealthy Catholic bishop.

when Felix Adler, a German-trained rabbi, founded the Society for Ethical Culture, a religion whose social activist motto was "Deed not Creed."

The late 1800s were a time of growth and expansion of social roles for African American churches. Freed slaves founded congregations uncontrolled by whites. By 1903, 3 million black Americans (out of a population of 8 million) were attending 26,000 churches, many of which published newspapers and sent out missionaries to foreign lands. Black churches were community centered, providing members with mutual-aid insurance, charity, and recreation. Church members visited the sick and imprisoned and ran kindergartens, dispensaries, and clubs. Black women found leadership opportunities in their churches otherwise denied to them in the larger society. They created their own departments within the church and engaged in missionary work, teaching, and social reform in their communities.

American religions responded to the challenges of modernism in different ways. Some either adapted to the calls for change, others reaffirmed their traditional religious practices. In response to the social and economic dislocations of the times, some religious institutions also used their faiths as springboards for the launching of reform movements. In choosing one or another of these paths, American churches and synagogues lost some adherents but gained others. In short, belonging to a church or synagogue continued to have great meaning for many Americans.

SEE ALSO

African Americans; Catholicism; Fundamentalism; Judaism; Mormonism; Protestantism; Salvation Army; Social Gospel; Stanton, Elizabeth Cady; Temperance and prohibition movements

FURTHER READING

Butler, Jon, Grant Wacker, Randall Balmer. *Religion in American Life: A Short History.* New York: Oxford University Press, 2003.

Carter, Paul. *The Spiritual Crisis of the Gilded Age.* De Kalb: Northern Illinois University Press, 1971.

Marsden, George M. *Religion and American Culture.* San Diego: Harcourt Brace Jovanovich, 1990.

Noll, Mark A. *A History of Christianity in the United States and Canada.* Grand Rapids, Mich.: William B. Eerdmans, 1992.

Republican party

THE REPUBLICAN PARTY originated in the 1850s during the furious debates over the expansion of slavery into the western territories. Its immediate impetus came from the passage of the Kansas-Nebraska Act (1854), which permitted settlers to decide for themselves if their state would allow slaves. Northern political leaders opposed to the extension of slavery formed the new party, giving it the name "Republican" in tribute to President Thomas Jefferson's Democratic Republican party. In addition to opponents of slavery, the party also attracted independent Democrats, proponents of federal support for economic development, and nativist "Know-Nothings," who opposed the influx of Irish Catholics fleeing the potato famine in Ireland.

Abraham Lincoln was the party's first elected President. After the Civil War, the party maintained its supremacy in part by "waving the bloody shirt," that is, constantly reminding the nation of the Democratic party's support for the rebellious Confederacy. Another Republican strategy was to run primarily Union army veterans for office. The Republican party also

The effects of a Tariff exclusively for Revenue as laid down in the Democratic Plat-form and which the Democratic Congressmen tried to enact last winter at Washington.

Democratic Free-Trade. Means low wages, children in rags and ignorance.
If you are satisfied with this picture vote for Cleveland and Hendricks.

The effects of Protection to American Industries as guaranteed by the Republican Party and Platform.

Republican Protection Means good wages, happy homes and education for your children.
If you prefer this picture vote for Blaine and Logan.

An 1884 Presidential campaign poster charges that Democrats hurt the U.S. economy by supporting free trade, while Republicans use high taxes on imports to protect American workers against foreign competition.

appealed to nativist sentiment by picturing the Democrats as the party of urban immigrants, whom they stigmatized as troublemakers. To control both immigrants and the laboring classes, Republicans promoted "blue laws," a term of unknown origins referring to attempts to control personal behavior, such as drinking, through Sunday closings for saloons and strict licensing of liquor suppliers. Finally, the Republican party fostered the nation's financial development through high tariffs and railroad subsidies and an aggressive pursuit of foreign investments.

During the Gilded Age, the party had three factions. "Stalwarts" followed New York senator Roscoe Conkling and defended the spoils system of awarding government offices to party loyalists. "Half-Breeds" followed Maine senator James G. Blaine and tried to balance the need for reform with loyalty to party. "Independents" opposed the spoils system. Educated women, like Josephine Shaw Lowell, a Bostonian active in social welfare

reform, allied themselves with the reformers. Opponents of reformers called them "goo-goos," a derisive term for people who favored "good government." Later, when Independents bolted the party to support Democrat Grover Cleveland, the term "Mugwump" became popular. An Algonquin word for "renegade chief," the term stuck when a newspaper editor joked that it really meant "unreliable Republicans," or voters whose "mugs" were on one side of the fence and "wumps" on the other.

By the turn of the 20th century, older party leaders (often called the Old Guard) were finding themselves challenged by insurgents wanting to curb the power of the great industrialists. Theodore Roosevelt, who became President upon the assassination of William McKinley, soon emerged as the chief insurgent standard-bearer. Soon called Progressives, these Republicans advocated government regulation of the railroads and factories. In 1912 the party split, with the more conservative wing supporting William

Howard Taft for President, and the Progressives supporting Roosevelt. The result of splitting the Republican vote was that the party lost to Democrat Woodrow Wilson. The Grand Old Party, as the Republican party was often called, returned to ascendancy in the 1920s, maintaining its dominance until the Great Depression of 1929.

SEE ALSO

Blaine, James Gillespie; Democratic party; McKinley, William; Nativism; Progressive party; Roosevelt, Theodore; Taft, William Howard; Taxes and tariffs

FURTHER READING

Casdorph, Paul D. *Republicans, Negroes, and Progressives in the South, 1912–1916*. Tuscaloosa: University of Alabama Press, 1981.
Gould, Lewis L. *Grand Old Party: A History of the Republicans*. New York: Random House, 2003.
Marcus, Robert D. *Grand Old Party: Political Structure in the Gilded Age, 1880–1896*. New York: Oxford University Press, 1971.

Revivalism and Pentecostalism

IN THE LATE 1800s, revivalism and Pentecostalism shifted the practice of American Protestantism toward a more emotional direction. Revivals, in which charismatic preachers sought to bring both believers and skeptics to a heart-felt religious commitment, were not new. There had been periodic outbreaks of revivals in American history—the largest were called Great Awakenings—since the colonial era.

After the Civil War, Chicago evangelist Dwight Moody, founder of the Moody Bible Institutes (training schools for evangelists), became a key figure in revivalism. Partnered with Ira David Sankey, a song leader who brought gospel singing to religious services, Moody preached to huge crowds. In his sermons, he stressed a simple theme: join any church; it did not matter which. His campaigns, which he held from New York to Saint Louis and on to the Pacific, resulted in thousands of converts.

Revivalism reached its peak in the 1910s. Between 1912 and 1918, 650 full-time and 1,200 part-time evangelists staged at least 35,000 revivals across the country. William ("Billy") Sunday, an outfielder for the Chicago White-Stockings, was perhaps the most famous. After taking Bible classes at the Chicago Young Men's Christian Association (YMCA), Sunday quit baseball and went to work for the Y. In 1895, he succeeded a revivalist he had been assisting. Accompanied by a trombone-playing song leader, Sunday used high dramatics, including contortions and the smashing of furniture, to hold his audiences. His sermons, which tore into the vicious habits of both high society and the "whisky-soaked, beer-guzzling, bull-necked" lower-class immigrants, were especially effective among middle-class whites. In 1917, a 10-week campaign in New York City netted an attendance of 1,443,000 people and 98,264 converts.

Pentecostalism was an early-20th-century religious movement that drew some of its features from revivals. The term comes from the Greek name for the Jewish Feast of Weeks, which begins on the 50th day after Passover. On this day the Holy Spirit descended upon the first Christians and they then "spoke in other tongues" (unintelligible speech known as glossolalia). Pentecostals insisted that Spirit baptism, or a sign that the Holy Spirit had descended upon a believer, should be a part of a believer's conversion to Christ. In ecstatic prayer meetings, believers showed that this baptism had occurred by glossolalia.

The movement began with an outbreak of glossolalia on New Year's Day, 1901, in a Bible school in Topeka, Kansas. Between 1906 and 1909, a three-year-long revival followed at the Azusa Street Mission in Los Angeles. Scores of Pentecostal sects then sprang up, many of them especially strong in the South and among working-class populations to whom they offered a message of hope and strong community support. Some Pentecostal sects ordained women and formed racially mixed congregations. Services were noted for ecstatic prayer, personal testimony, and healing of illness or disability. During World War I, African Americans flocked to Pentecostal churches, most of them in storefront locations in the urban North. Today Pentecostal churches and missions exist throughout the United States and abroad.

SEE ALSO

Protestantism; Religion

FURTHER READING

Balmer, Randall Herbert. *Blessed Assurance: A History of Evangelicalism in America.* Boston: Beacon Press, 1999.

McLoughlin, William G. *Revivals, Awakenings, and Reform: An Essay on Religion and Social Change in America, 1607–1977.* Chicago: University of Chicago Press, 1978.

Martin, Robert Francis. *Hero of the Heartland: Billy Sunday and the Transformation of American Society, 1862–1935.* Bloomington: Indiana University Press, 2002.

Noll, Mark A. *Protestants in America.* New York: Oxford University Press, 2000.

Riis, Jacob

- *Born: May 3, 1849, Ribe, Denmark*
- *Education: secondary school*
- *Accomplishments: author and photographer,* How the Other Half Lives *(1890),* Children of the Poor *(1892),* The Battle with the Slum *(1902),* Children of the Tenement *(1903); author,* The Making of An American *(1901)*
- *Died Mar. 26, 1914, Barre, Mass.*

DANISH IMMIGRANT Jacob Riis (pronounced "Reese") became a writer and photographer in New York City. He was an influential muckraker, or investigative journalist, who promoted social reform by calling public attention to the dismal living conditions of the poor.

Riis worked as a carpenter in his native Denmark before moving to the United States in 1870. He struggled initially with poverty and homelessness in his new country, but by 1873 he had found his first employment as a journalist. He worked for a number of newspapers in the following years and by 1888 was a reporter on the staff of the *New York Evening Sun.* In that position, he made it his mission to open the city's eyes to the desperate lives of the least fortunate. The poor, Riis said, were "the victims rather than the makers of their fate."

Prowling slum neighborhoods by night, he used the new technology of flash photography (employing quick-burning powder, not electric flashbulbs) to document the suffering and degradation he found in the dark streets and tenement buildings. He photographed large families crammed into small rooms, homeless boys sleeping on grates in the sidewalk, the grimy, dispirited residents of flophouses in skid row, and the facial expressions of weary prostitutes.

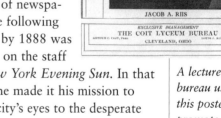

A lecture bureau used this poster to promote Jacob Riis's talks on the urban poor. Riis urged Americans to span the gap between wealth and poverty with "a bridge founded upon justice."

In the *Sun,* and later in *Scribner's Magazine,* Riis published accounts of slum life illustrated with his stark photographs (and sometimes, because of the limited photo reproduction techniques of the day, with drawings based on the photographs). Compiling his previous work, he brought out his book *How the Other Half Lives* in 1890. His work caught the attention of the president of New York City's police board, future President Theodore Roosevelt, who called Riis "the most useful citizen of New York" and began accompanying the pioneer photojournalist on some of his nighttime visits to the city's poorest neighborhoods.

Riis toured the country lecturing on urban poverty and displaying his photographs in magic-lantern presentations, an early type of slide show. Due in part to his efforts, New York began to enforce new sanitation and building codes that required landlords to improve living conditions for their impoverished tenants. One such code in 1901 forced owners and contractors to add airshafts and windows to the city's dark, claustrophobic tenement buildings.

SEE ALSO

Cities; Muckrakers; Photography; Reform movements; Roosevelt, Theodore

FURTHER READING

Alland, Alexander Sr. *Jacob A. Riis: Photographer & Citizen.* Millerton, N.Y.: Aperture, 1974.

Lane, James B. *Jacob A. Riis and the American City.* New York: Harper Collins, 1975.

Pascal, Janet B. *Jacob Riis: Reporter and Reformer.* New York: Oxford University Press, 2005.

Riis, Jacob A. *How the Other Half Lives: Studies Among the Tenements of New York.* 1890. Reprint, New York: Penguin, 1997.

Yochelson, Bonnie. *Jacob Riis.* New York: Phaidon, 2001.

Robber barons

IN 1934, AMERICAN historian Matthew Josephson chose *The Robber Barons* as the title for a book that looked critically at multimillionaire industrialists of the late 19th century. The term originated in medieval Europe, when "robber barons," or warlords, used their military might to prey upon merchants and travelers passing through their territories.

In the 19th century, journalists Henry Demarest Lloyd and E. L. Godkin resurrected the unflattering term to describe wealthy Gilded Age business leaders. According to Josephson and these journalist predecessors, America's richest industrialists relied on ruthless and even illegal methods to amass enormous fortunes, mistreating their workers, bribing corrupt politicians, and manipulating the stock market. Not all historians agree with this assessment. Some call these men "captains of industry" or "industrial statesmen," skillful entrepreneurs whose pursuit of personal wealth helped to fuel prosperity throughout the United States.

Among the prominent Gilded Age businessmen who became known as robber barons, two of the most brazen were Jay Gould and James Fisk. These men caused a national financial crisis in 1869 by conspiring to seize control of the country's gold industry and manipulate the price of gold for their own benefit. A few years after that scandal, Fisk's romantic involvement with a New York City actress led to his murder by a rival suitor. Gould lived on for another two decades, increasing his wealth with investments in railroads and earning a reputation as an enemy of ordinary Americans when he declared, "I can hire one half of the working class to kill the other half."

Other noted robber barons included bankers John Pierpont (J. P.) Morgan and Jay Cooke, steel industry pioneer Andrew Carnegie, oil millionaire John D. Rockefeller, and steamship and railroad magnate Cornelius Vanderbilt. During financial crises in 1893 and 1907, J. P. Morgan arranged complicated gold purchasing schemes with Presidents Grover Cleveland and Theodore Roosevelt to rescue the U.S. Treasury.

Critics have faulted these kingpins of the Gilded Age for living lavishly and making ostentatious displays of wealth while most Americans lived on incomes of about $500 a year. Supporters, on the other hand, have praised them for building the nation into an economic powerhouse by making American industry more efficient and productive. In addition, some industrialists, notably Carnegie and Rockefeller, devoted much of their vast wealth to philanthropic purposes. Some left huge estates filled with works of art, palatial mansions now open to visits from tourists of all classes and nationalities.

SEE ALSO

Carnegie, Andrew; Industry; Morgan, John Pierpont; Regulation; Rockefeller, John D.

FURTHER READING

Folsom, Burton W. *The Myth of the Robber Barons.* Herndon, Va.: Young America Press, 1991.
Josephson, Matthew. *The Robber Barons: The Great American Capitalists, 1861–1901.* 1934. Reprint, New York: Harcourt Brace, 1995.
Porter, Glenn. *The Rise of Big Business, 1860–1920.* Wheeling, Ill.: Harlan Davidson, 1992.

Rockefeller, John D.

- *Born: July 8, 1839, Richford, N. Y.*
- *Education: Central High School (Cleveland, Ohio); Folsom Mercantile College business course, 1855*
- *Accomplishments: president, Standard Oil Company (1892–1911); founder, Rockefeller Institute (1901); Rockefeller Foundation (1913)*
- *Died: May 23, 1937, Ormond Beach, Fla.*

JOHN D. ROCKEFELLER was one of America's most successful businessmen. As the founder of the modern oil industry, he amassed a fortune of hundreds of millions of dollars. The ruthless tactics he used to eliminate competitors and monopolize the petroleum products business in the United States gave rise to sharp criticism. Many institutions and individuals benefited, however, from his philanthropic work, which included contributing enormous sums to medical research.

Rockefeller was born in western New York and moved in his teens to northern Ohio. He went to work at 16 as a bookkeeper. At 19 he started his own business with a partner, selling agricultural products and other goods. The venture was a financial success, but Rockefeller soon saw bigger opportunities in what was then a relatively new business—refining petroleum to produce kerosene lamp fuel, lubricants, and other products. Rockefeller's Cleveland location put him close to the oil-rich region of northwestern Pennsylvania. After investing in oil refineries in the early 1860s, he spent the next three decades becoming the dominant figure in the oil industry.

As his wealth and power increased, Rockefeller began to practice what became known as a "horizontal" integration of the industry—acquiring or destroying competing businesses in order to dominate the industry. He bought out some of his competitors and schemed to drive others out of business. One strategy he used was to get railroad companies to lower his shipping

Oil baron John D. Rockefeller ruthlessly destroyed business competitors, but in his later years endowed universities and funded scientific research. He believed "that every right implies a responsibility; every opportunity, an obligation; every possession, a duty."

costs while raising those of rival companies. By 1880, his company, Standard Oil, had become Standard Oil Trust, a consortium of many companies, with stock held in common.

Standard Oil Trust controlled more than 75 percent of the U.S. oil industry and was the largest trust in the country. In 1892, anti-monopoly court action forced the trust's breakup. Rockefeller regrouped in New Jersey and formed the Standard Oil Company. In 1903, *McClure's Magazine* published "The History of Standard Oil," Ida Tarbell's muckraking exposé of Rockefeller's monopolistic practices.

To show how these practices caused "incessant discouragement and discrimination" for independent businessmen, Tarbell explained that shippers gave favorable rates to Standard Oil while multiplying switching and dock charges and demanding freight payment in advance from others. A "score of different ways are found to make hard the way of the outsider," she wrote in her exposé. "'If I get a barrel of oil out of Buffalo,' an independent dealer told the writer not long

ago, 'I have to sneak it out. There are no public docks; the railroads control most of them, and they won't let me out if they can help it. . . . They are all afraid of offending the Standard Oil Company.'" A U.S. Supreme Court ruling, invoking the Sherman Antitrust Act of 1890, dissolved the Standard Oil Company in 1911, separating it into 38 individual firms. Rockefeller retained a large portion of the shares in these firms, however, and his personal fortune continued to grow, peaking in 1913 at an estimated $900 million.

Rockefeller officially retired from running his oil business in 1911, by which time he had been a chief executive in name only for more than a decade, allowing others to manage the corporate empire. From the late 1890s until his death, he concentrated on philanthropic activities. A devout Baptist, he supported the church handsomely. He used his fortune to endow the University of Chicago and other colleges and universities. He also established several charitable foundations, notably the Rockefeller Foundation, which provided large grants for disease eradication and other projects in the physical sciences, social sciences, and humanities. The Rockefeller Foundation today funds a wide variety of programs to improve education, combat poverty and hunger, and contribute in other ways to its founder's stated goal of fostering "the well-being of mankind throughout the world."

SEE ALSO

Antitrust laws; Industry; Law; Muckrakers; Regulation; Supreme Court, U.S.

FURTHER READING

Chernow, Ron. *Titan: The Life of John D. Rockefeller, Sr.* New York: Random House, 1998.
Hawke, David Freeman. *John D.: The Founding Father of the Rockefellers.* New York: Harper & Row, 1980.

Nevins, Allan. *Study in Power: John D. Rockefeller, Industrialist and Philanthropist.* New York: Scribner, 1953.
Segall, Grant. *John D. Rockefeller: Anointed with Oil.* New York: Oxford University Press, 2001.

Roosevelt, Theodore

- *Born: Oct. 27, 1858, New York, N.Y.*
- *Education: Harvard College, A.B., 1880; Columbia University School of Law, 1880–81*
- *Accomplishments: New York State Assembly (1881–84); president, New York City Police Board (1895–97); assistant secretary of the U.S. Navy (1897–98); colonel, First Volunteer Cavalry (1898); governor of New York (1898–1900); Vice President of the United States (1900–1); President of the United States (1901–9); awarded Nobel Peace Prize (1905); posthumously awarded the Congressional Medal of Honor for heroism in the Spanish-American War (2001)*
- *Died: Jan. 6, 1919, Oyster Bay, N.Y.*

THEODORE ROOSEVELT, 26th President of the United States, was one of the most colorful and paradoxical personalities ever to hold the office. He was a war hero who won the Nobel Peace Prize, an heir to wealth and privilege who attacked corporate power and backed workers' rights, and a big game hunter who championed conservation. Roosevelt was an imperialist overseas and a reformer in domestic politics; he advocated increased U.S. power around the globe and greater federal authority to enforce social justice at home. An accomplished naturalist, historian, and biographer, Theodore Roosevelt was the author of more than two dozen books.

Roosevelt was born in New York City, son of an affluent family whose roots stretched back to the Dutch Colonial period. An asthmatic child plagued by weak vision and frail health, he practiced boxing, horseman-ship, and other vigorous physical exercises to toughen his body and remake himself closer to his ideal of manliness. After studying at home with private tutors, he later graduated from Harvard. He studied law a short time at Columbia, but gave it up to run for the New York State Assembly, where he served three terms, becoming known as an enemy of political corruption and a friend of social reform.

Roosevelt's wife and his mother died on the same day in 1884. Devastated, the young widower left his infant daughter in the care of his sister and sought the rugged life of a rancher and lawman on the western frontier. He spent two years in the Dakota Territory, then came home to run unsuccessfully for mayor of New York. In 1886, he married Edith Kermit Carow, with whom he had five more children. President Benjamin Harrison appointed him to a seat on the federal Civil Service Commission in 1889, of which he soon became chair. As a commissioner, he worked to eliminate corruption and build a system that hired government workers based on merit, not political connections. From that position, he went on to two years as president of New York City's police commission. An activist commissioner, he supported the work of Jacob Riis, investigative reporter and photographer, and other urban reformers to secure better housing for the poor and improve their working conditions.

In the late 1890s, as Spanish forces fought with rebels in Cuba and the United States moved closer to war with Spain, President William McKinley appointed Roosevelt assistant secretary of the U.S. Navy. A proponent of driving Europe's colonial empires out of the Caribbean, Roosevelt was eager for the coming conflict. He resigned his civilian job to recruit and lead a volunteer cavalry unit that went on to win battlefield fame in Cuba as the Rough Riders. By the end of the Spanish-American War, he was a nationally known war hero.

At that point, New York's Republican party asked him to run for governor. Although he won the election, his energetic anticorruption efforts soon led him to clash with his party's bosses. At the Republican national convention in 1900, the bosses arranged to remove Roosevelt from state office by having him nominated as McKinley's running mate. The Republican ticket that year won a resounding victory over Democrat William Jennings Bryan, the same candidate McKinley had defeated in 1896.

Six months after the inauguration, an assassin gunned McKinley down and Roosevelt became President. He soon established a reputation as a trustbuster, using federal legislation to rein in the power of giant corporations and protect the public from unethical business practices. His insistence that the coal industry accept federal arbitration of a labor strike marked the first time the government had intervened in labor relations without taking the side of management against the workers.

Roosevelt's popularity carried him to reelection victory in 1904. He now launched an ambitious reform program he termed the Square Deal. His own party in Congress resisted, but he was able to tighten regulation of the railroad industry and win federal authority to inspect food and drugs for safety. Calling the Presidency a "bully pulpit" (meaning "an excellent platform"), he used the office to preach to Congress and the American people about the evils of "predatory wealth" and the need to protect workers and consumers against the "criminal rich." During both of his terms in

the White House, Roosevelt used his executive power to protect tens of millions of acres of wilderness. He created the U.S. Forest Service, set aside land for national parks, wildlife refuges, and other federal sites, and vetoed legislation that would have opened up public land to private development.

Roosevelt was the first President to invite an African American—educator Booker T. Washington—to the White House, an action that caused great controversy. He brought a long-standing American dream to fruition by starting construction of the Panama Canal in 1904. In an address to Congress that year, Roosevelt issued a corollary to the 85-year-old Monroe Doctrine (which announced American resistance to European incursions into the Western Hemisphere), essentially justifying the use of U.S. police power to intervene in the affairs of Western Hemisphere nations. In 1905, Roosevelt negotiated a settlement that ended a war between Japan and Russia, an achievement for which he won the Nobel Peace Prize. In 1907, he sent the U.S. Navy's "great white fleet" on a trip around the world to demonstrate American naval power.

Roosevelt did not seek reelection in 1908 and supported the candidacy of his secretary of war, William Howard Taft. He then left for Africa on a prolonged safari to collect specimens for

This portrait of Theodore Roosevelt and his cow pony dates from the 1880s, when Roosevelt owned a ranch and punched cattle in the Dakota Territories. Roosevelt loved the West and relished opportunities to lead "the strenuous life."

the Smithsonian Institution. Four years later, disappointed with Taft's performance in office, Roosevelt campaigned against him. He ran as the candidate of the new Progressive party, popularly known as the Bull Moose party. Democrat Woodrow Wilson won the election, and Roosevelt finished second, far ahead of Taft. Later, during Wilson's second term, Roosevelt tried unsuccessfully to volunteer for combat in World War I. His four sons served in the war, and one died in battle. By the end of the war, Roosevelt looked like a strong candidate for the 1920 Republican Presidential nomination, but he died at home in 1919. "No man," he said, "has had a happier life than I have led."

SEE ALSO

Bryan, William Jennings; Conservation; Government reform; Imperialism; Industry; Labor unions; McKinley, William; Muckrakers; Navy, U.S.; Panama Canal; Presidency; Progressive party; Progressive movement; Riis, Jacob; Spanish-American War; Taft, William Howard; Wilson, Woodrow T.

FURTHER READING

Brands, H. W. *T. R.: The Last Romantic.* New York: Basic Books, 1997.
Dalton, Kathleen. *Theodore Roosevelt: A Strenuous Life.* New York: Knopf, 2002.
Gould, Lewis L. *The Presidency of Theodore Roosevelt.* Lawrence: University Press of Kansas, 1991.

Salvation Army

THE SALVATION ARMY began as the Christian Mission in 1865 in East London, England. Its founders, a Methodist preacher named William Booth and his wife, Catherine, based the mission on a simple idea. They would help sinners escape eternal damnation by leading them to accept Christ as their personal

savior. Renting nonreligious housing, such as tents, music halls, and theaters, for their meetings, the Booths recruited the "sinners" they saved to be workers in future missions. By the late 1870s they had added social programs, including soup kitchens and housing. They had also organized themselves along quasi-military lines, the better to wage "war" against sin. Local societies became "corps," and their evangelists were "field officers." General William Booth sat at the organization's head, and commissioners ran the program in the different territories, or nations, to which the movement soon spread.

Lieutenant Eliza Shirley, who had left England to join her parents in the United States, held the first American Salvation Army meeting in Philadelphia in 1879. In 1880, Commissioner George Railton and seven Hallelujah Lassies, as his women workers were called, arrived to establish a formal outpost. Three years later, despite ridicule and physical attacks, Railton and his workers had expanded their operation throughout the Northeast, Middle West, and in California. By 1910, they had established 871 corps and outposts in the United States and recruited 2,983 officers and cadets.

The army's military costumes, soup kitchens, work programs, and hymn-singing rallies on street corners distinguished them from other charities of

Uniformed members of the Salvation Army in frontier California. The Army used brass bands, hymn singing, and parades to attract converts and draw attention to its welfare work.

the era, many of which required the poor to demonstrate "worthiness" before receiving aid. In contrast, the army accepted all who pledged to give up sin, including the alcoholics, prostitutes, and drug addicts that most churches ignored.

SEE ALSO

Charity organization movement

FURTHER READING

McKinley, Edward H. *Marching to Glory: The History of the Salvation Army in the United States, 1880–1992.* 2nd ed., rev. and expanded. Grand Rapids, Mich.: W.B. Eerdmans, 1995.

Taiz, Lillian. *Hallelujah Lads & Lasses: Remaking the Salvation Army in America, 1880–1930.* Chapel Hill: University of North Carolina Press, 2001.

San Francisco earthquake (1906)

ON APRIL 18, 1906, a 290-mile section of California's San Andreas fault shifted violently, setting off a powerful earthquake. Studies of records would later estimate the quake's magnitude between 7.7 and 8.3 on the Richter scale. Communities all along the fault line suffered damage, but the devastation in San Francisco was especially intense owing to a three-day fire that raged through the city in the aftermath of the quake. The quake and fire destroyed 28,000 buildings, leaving approximately half the city's population homeless. Estimates of the death toll ranged as high as 3,000. Mayor Eugene Schmitz issued a shoot-to-kill order for anyone found looting. When federal troops arrived, General Frederick Funston divided the city into sectors and declared martial law. By dynamiting several blocks of buildings, he finally got the fire under control.

San Franciscans walk and drive on the streets of their devastated community in May 1906, a month after earthquake and fire had reduced much of the city to rubble.

After the quake and the rapid rebuilding of San Francisco, progressive reformers took control of the city government, ousting Mayor Schmitz and his corrupt administration. Fear of future earthquakes led citizens to demand stringent building codes during the city's reconstruction, although their actions did not prevent some rebuilding on dangerous sites during the early days of recovery. Earthquake refugees returned, some after many years' absence, and San Francisco regained its stature as a major western city.

As a further side effect of the disaster, some Chinese immigrants found a way to evade the Chinese Exclusion Act, which allowed Chinese immigrants to enter the United States only if they had family members already resident in the country. Because the great fire had destroyed many public records, young Chinese men, called "paper sons," produced documents that claimed their fathers were California residents. There was no way to check if the documents were valid, and many Chinese men were granted entry.

SEE ALSO
Chinese Exclusion Act (1882); Progressive movement

FURTHER READING
Fradkin, Philip L. *The Great Earthquake and Firestorms of 1906: How San Francisco Nearly Destroyed Itself.* Berkeley: University of California Press, 2005.

Jeffers, H. Paul. *Disaster by the Bay: The Great San Francisco Earthquake and Fire of 1906.* Guilford, Conn.: Lyons Press, 2003.

Kurzman, Dan. *Disaster! The Great San Francisco Earthquake and Fire of 1906.* New York: Morrow, 2001.

Winchester, Simon. *A Crack in the Edge of the World: America and the Great California Earthquake of 1906.* New York: HarperCollins, 2005.

Sanger, Margaret Higgins

- *Born: Sept. 14, 1879, Corning, N.Y.*
- *Education: Claverack College and Hudson River Institute, 1896; White Plains Hospital nursing program, 1900*
- *Accomplishments: publisher,* The Woman Rebel *newspaper (1914); founder, first birth control clinic (1916); publisher,* Birth Control Review *(1917); founder, American Birth Control League (1921)*
- *Died: Sept. 6, 1966, Tucson, Ariz.*

THE 6TH OF 11 CHILDREN, Margaret Sanger lost her mother at an early age. Later, after she became a nurse, Sanger came to believe that multiple pregnancies had caused her mother's premature death. She also became convinced that limiting family size was the key to improving her patients' lives. Marrying William Sanger in 1902, she bore three children, one of whom died young.

In 1912, Sanger began challenging the so-called Comstock Law. Passed by Congress in 1873, Comstock outlawed the sending of "obscene" material, including information about contraception, through the U.S. mails. First, she wrote newspaper columns on sex education ("What Every Girl Should Know"). She later collected these into a book that she published in 1920 and dedicated to the "working girls of the world." The book argued that "ignorance of the sex functions is one of the strongest forces that sends young girls into unclean living." It presented the "procreative act" as "natural, clean and healthful," one that beautifies nature and is consequently "devoid of offensiveness." Without taking a moral position on sexuality, Sanger tried just to "present the facts" about puberty, sexual impulses (including masturbation), reproduction, venereal (sexually transmitted) diseases, and menopause.

In 1914, she began to publish *The Woman Rebel,* a monthly newspaper that advocated the right to practice birth control. Threatened with prison, she fled to Europe, leaving behind instructions for the distribution of 100,000 copies of "Family Limitation," a 16-page pamphlet that explained the details of contraception, particularly the diaphragm. By the time she returned, the authorities had dropped the charges against her, and Sanger set out across the country to win more support for her cause.

In 1916, Sanger opened the nation's first birth control clinic in the Brownsville neighborhood of Brooklyn, New York. After allowing it to operate only a few days, the police closed it down and put Sanger in jail. Her 30 days in prison gained her a group of supporters who formed the base of a birth control movement. Sanger appealed her conviction, and although she lost, the court ruled that

Birth control advocate Margaret Sanger about 1920. "No woman," said Sanger, "can call herself free until she can choose consciously whether she will or will not be a mother."

physician prescriptions of contraception to women for medical reasons were exempt from the obscenity law.

Thereafter Sanger allied herself with the medical community. In 1921, she founded the American Birth Control League and in 1923 opened a legal, doctor-run birth control clinic. This clinic, which she called the Birth Control Clinical Research Bureau, served as a model for other clinics across the country. Later in her career, she renamed her movement "family planning." Because this term implied planning for a family instead of controlling births, an expression that seemed to focus on women's sexual and reproductive freedom, more people found it acceptable. Sanger spent her last years focusing on the international birth control movement and the development of a birth control pill.

SEE ALSO

Birth control movement; Comstock Law (1873)

FURTHER READING

Chesler, Ellen. *Woman of Valor: Margaret Sanger and the Birth Control Movement in America.* New York: Simon & Schuster, 1992.
Kennedy, David. *Birth Control in America: The Career of Margaret Sanger.* New Haven: Yale University Press, 1970.
Sanger, Margaret. *Margaret Sanger: An Autobiography.* 1938. Reprint, New York: Cooper Square Press, 1999.

Science and technology

BY THE LATE 19th century, the United States had become a world leader in technology, the practical application of scientific knowledge. Thomas Edison's lightbulb and Alexander Graham Bell's telephone were only two of the many American inventions from this period that helped to transform daily life. At the same time, the country was just starting to catch up with Europe in science education and in what was then called pure science, or basic science—research that adds to fundamental knowledge of the universe without necessarily producing new products for people to use. For example, it was primarily in European laboratories that scientists deciphered the underlying physics of electricity and expanded the frontiers of knowledge about atoms and electrons.

American respect for practicality led to a strong interest in technology. Their late-19th and early-20th-century technological innovations ranged from the invention of the zipper to refrigerated railroad cars to the first successful airplane flights; from the introduction of electric-powered washing machines, vacuum cleaners, and other household appliances to the mass production of affordable automobiles; from the birth of motion pictures to the invention of Bakelite, which launched the modern plastics industry.

Although achievements in technology took center stage throughout the Gilded Age and Progressive Era, U.S. scientists were also beginning to make discoveries destined to enhance the nation's reputation in the realm of pure science. Contributions included measurements of the speed of light, the discovery of moons orbiting Mars and Jupiter, the exploration of extensive dinosaur fossil fields in the western states, and the first studies linking chromosomes to specific inherited characteristics. In 1901, a leading German university tried to hire away a Harvard chemistry professor, an indication of increasing international respect for the quality of U.S. science.

In the field of physics, quantum mechanics opened new ways for American scientists to think about light waves, subatomic particles, and other features of the natural world. Physicist Albert A. Michelson, who first measured the speed of light in 1878, played a key role in laying the groundwork for Albert Einstein who, in 1905, published "The Special Theory of Relativity," an article introducing an entirely new concept of time and motion. As a mathematical addition to this theory, Einstein introduced the equation that has since become well known: E=mc2, or energy equals mass times the speed of light squared, which he called "energy-mass equivalence."

Michelson and his colleague, Edward W. Morley, developed sophisticated light-measuring equipment to try to detect the "ether," the substance scientists assumed enabled light from the sun, moon, and stars to reach the earth. Their finding that there was no "ether" inspired new thinking by Einstein and other theorists who would go on to revolutionize physics with new discoveries in quantum mechanics, particle theory, gravity, and electromagnetics. In 1907, Michelson became the first American scientist to win a Nobel Prize.

American scientists made great advances in genetics. Researchers in this field deepened their understanding of the biochemistry of living cells and the mechanisms by which genetic traits pass from parents to offspring. In the early 1900s, Clarence E. McClung, Nettie M. Stevens, and Edmund B. Wilson published the first studies on the role of the X and Y chromosomes in determining the sex of living organisms. A few years later, Thomas H. Morgan, who would win a Nobel Prize in 1933, began his landmark study of fruit fly genetics, producing the first maps showing the arrangement of genes along a chromosome.

Starting in 1877, the discovery of rich dinosaur fossil deposits in Colorado, Wyoming, and elsewhere in the West provided a treasure trove of data about extinct creatures that had roamed the planet for millions of years before the rise of the human species. On expeditions between 1900 and 1908, paleontologist Barnum Brown discovered the first *Tyrannosaurus rex* skeletons. Paleontological discoveries appeared to confirm Charles Darwin's theory of species evolution, a process Darwin called natural selection. Darwin had discovered that living species change and progress over thousands of years as a result of random mutations, which sometimes create improvements in individuals. Those individuals pass improved genetic traits for survival and reproduction on to succeeding generations, while those with less successful traits eventually die out.

Astronomers explored space with increasingly powerful equipment in this era. In 1887, the Lick Observatory near San Francisco installed the largest and most powerful telescope in the world. Ten years later, the Yerkes Observatory in Wisconsin dedicated an even larger instrument. The Mount Wilson Observatory in southern California surpassed both of those earlier telescopes in 1908 and surpassed itself in 1917 with a new telescope that remained the world's largest until 1948. American astronomers measured

Scientists assembled this 65-million-year-old Tyrannosaurus rex *from fossilized bones excavated in Montana between 1902 and 1908. Increased knowledge about the prehistoric Earth was one of the era's many important scientific advances.*

the sun's rotation, discovered the two moons of Mars, added three new Jupiter moons to the four that Galileo had discovered in 1610, predicted the existence of a ninth planet beyond the orbit of Neptune, and identified the magnetic properties of sunspots. In 1918, Harlow Shapley measured the Milky Way galaxy and mapped Earth's location near its outer edge.

Medical science progressed after the 1870s, when European scientists established that microorganisms, called germs, are what cause disease. The germ theory supplanted earlier ideas about the causes of illness and explained the sources of such ancient scourges as anthrax, diphtheria, plague, and tuberculosis. American physicians changed surgical practice, using sterilized instruments and techniques to avoid infecting patients. They adopted rubber gloves in 1890 and gauze masks in 1896. American physicians were also quick to use diagnostic X-rays, first discovered in 1895, and took advantage of new products to anesthetize patients, making surgery safer. Early in the 20th century, doctors and medical researchers began applying discoveries about germs and contagion to public health programs in order to prevent the spread of contagious diseases.

SEE ALSO

Bell, Alexander Graham; Edison, Thomas Alva; Electricity; Health, public; Inventions; Medicine; Motion pictures;

FURTHER READING

Brush, Stephen G. *History of Modern Science: A Guide to the Second Scientific Revolution, 1800–1950.* Ames: Iowa State University Press, 1988.
Duffy, John. *From Humors to Medical Science: A History of American Medicine.* Urbana: University of Illinois Press, 1993.
Heilbron, J. L., ed. *The Oxford Companion to the History of Modern Science.* New York: Oxford University Press, 2003.
Timmons, Todd. *Science and Technology in Nineteenth-Century America.* Westport, Conn.: Greenwood, 2005.
Spangenburg, Ray. *The History of Science in the Nineteenth Century.* New York: Facts on File, 1994.

Segregation

LESS THAN a generation after the Civil War and the end of slavery, racial segregation became a way of life in the South. Southern states enshrined in law a number of long-standing customs that kept blacks and whites separated in public places and institutions, such as schools, parks, public transportation, and all public buildings and places of amusement. The laws and customs also facilitated white supremacy and kept African Americans subordinate, disfranchised, and impoverished.

Acting outside the law, lynch mobs and white rioters gave additional support to the system of racial separation and inequality. Segregation also linked whites' personal and political control of black southerners with economic control by making professional positions and high-paying jobs in white-owned businesses unavailable to African Americans.

Segregated employment practices blocked the ladder to economic advancement for all but a few. On the very lowest rung were African Americans trapped year after year in a system known as debt peonage. Farming on white-owned land, they signed contracts they often could not even read, promising to repay advances to the white landowners, but never quite managing to work the debts off before they were due. This meant they had to borrow even more, in a cycle that kept them working the land for the owner's advantage.

A history class at Alabama's all-black Tuskegee Institute in 1902. Founded by Booker T. Washington in 1881, the Institute educated African Americans in an era when most other colleges refused them a place.

After 1883, when the Supreme Court declared unconstitutional the 1875 Civil Rights Act, which guaranteed equal access to all facilities and institutions, court challenges to segregation became increasingly difficult. Segregationists won a significant victory in *Plessy* v. *Ferguson,* the landmark 1896 Supreme Court case in which a black passenger sued a southern railroad for not allowing him to ride in the white section. The Court ruled that "separate but equal" public accommodations were legal and did not imply inferiority for the "colored race." In practice, separate accommodations for African Americans—especially public schools—were almost always inferior to those for whites.

By 1910, all the southern states had thoroughly undermined civil rights for African Americans. Most African American men could not even register to vote, because whites imposed expensive poll taxes, literacy tests, and other obstacles to ensure black disfranchisement. Poor whites escaped these restrictions through so-called "grandfather clauses," which gave them voting privileges if they had a grandfather who had voted before the Civil War. Without votes, African Americans had little hope of changing the system under which they lived.

Throughout the South, African Americans responded to segregation customs and laws—also called Jim Crow laws, after a minstrel show character—by establishing separate communities, businesses, institutions, churches, and clubs. Because whites often responded violently to any resistance to their supremacy, most black southerners tried to keep a low profile, appeasing rather than angering whites. Clergy and educational leaders felt powerless before the force and numbers of white officials, school boards, and businessmen determined to keep African Americans "in their place." Booker T. Washington, president of the all-black Tuskegee Institute in Alabama, urged African Americans to seek economic security and social respect before demanding equality with whites.

Many other African Americans left the South, hoping for better social and economic conditions in the North and West. Some became homesteaders; others sought factory work in industrial cities.

In the North, segregation of public facilities was not legal, but racially separate neighborhoods led to segregation in schools and commercial areas. Fed by entrenched prejudices, whites discriminated against blacks in hiring and in the workplace, which kept a majority of African Americans economically subordinate to and distant from whites in the North throughout much of the 20th century.

New organizations such as the National Association for the Advancement of Colored People (NAACP), founded in 1909, and the National Urban League (1911), began systematic court challenges to segregation during the 1920s, but segregation and "separate but equal" laws remained in force in the South until the Civil Rights Act and Voting Rights Act of the 1960s, which ended legal discrimination on the basis of race.

SEE ALSO

African Americans; Jim Crow; Lynching; Civil rights; National Association for the Advancement of Colored People; National Urban League; *Plessy* v. *Ferguson* (1896); Race relations; Supreme Court, U.S.; Washington, Booker T.

FURTHER READING

Hale, Grace Elizabeth. *Making Whiteness: The Culture of Segregation in the South, 1890–1940.* New York: Vintage, 1999.
Klarman, Michael J. *From Jim Crow to Civil Rights: The Supreme Court, Race, and the Constitution.* New York: Oxford University Press, 2003.
Massey, Douglas S., and Nancy A. Denton. *American Apartheid: Segregation and the Making of the Underclass.* Cambridge, Mass.: Harvard University Press, 1993.

Settlement-house movement

IN THE LATE 1800s, young, educated idealists developed a new approach toward improving the lives of the urban poor. Recognizing that charity met only the immediate needs of the poor, these young people wanted to provide something more constructive and long-lasting. They were not sure what this might be. To find out, they left their comfort-

able, middle-class homes and "settled" in urban slum districts. There, they hoped to learn firsthand exactly what they might do to help.

Thus was launched the movement that came to be known variously as the settlement-house, social settlement, or neighborhood movement. Its immediate inspiration was the English Social Gospel movement, which sought to apply Christian ethics to social problems. This movement had inspired privileged young men from Oxford University to move into the London slums and work with the poor. Stanton Coit, a young American college graduate, spent several months in one London settlement and, upon his return to New York in 1884, helped found the Neighborhood Guild on Manhattan's Lower East Side. In 1891, the guild became the University Settlement Society, a major leader in the settlement-house movement.

Meanwhile, college-educated women were also founding settlements. In 1887, Vida Scudder, a Smith College graduate and Wellesley College professor, founded the College Settlements Association in Boston. Jane Addams and Ellen Gates Starr founded Hull House in Chicago two years later, and Lillian Wald, a nurse, founded the Nurses' Settlement (later called the Henry Street Settlement) in New York in 1893.

In 1907, Mary Simkhovitch, founder of Greenwich House in New York City, wrote that the "settlement is not a mission, not a school, not a charity, but a group of persons living a common life, learning the meaning of life by which they are surrounded, interpreting this life to others and acting on what they have learned." This description fits perfectly with what many settlements tried to do. Their residents first asked their new neighbors what they needed and then developed ideas about what to offer them. Their initiatives ranged across a wide variety of programs and services. They included day nurseries for the children of working mothers, supervised playgrounds, kindergartens, English language and American citizenship classes, lending libraries and reading rooms, cafeterias that provided cheap dinners for working families, health clinics, visiting nurses, bathing facilities, boardinghouses and cooperative apartments for single working women, lectures and discussion groups, penny-savings banks (where one could deposit as little as a penny at a time), clubs for all ages and interests, exhibits, concerts, and theatrical productions.

Settlement workers went beyond just providing services and activities, however. They also became involved in political and social reform movements. They believed that the chief causes of poverty lay in environmental conditions beyond the control of the poor. Because poor people lacked the resources to cope with those conditions, settlements tried to provide them with some, such as public baths to help maintain basic sanitary standards or roof gardens where neighborhood children could play in safety. Because they could not change the environment without the help of the government, settlement workers asked city officials to reform the way tenements were built, construct public

Singing together, Hull House staff members, immigrant mothers, and children of all ages demonstrate the settlement movement's commitment to building community in diverse neighborhoods.

parks and playgrounds, and maintain decent sewage and waste systems in poor neighborhoods. In addition, they often were able to convince the government to take over some of the services the settlements themselves were providing, such as health clinics and kindergartens. Finally, many settlement residents became leaders in national political movements, such as campaigns for woman suffrage, the recognition of labor unions, sweatshop reform, and an end to child labor.

Settlements varied in origin and scope. Most were nondenominational, but some were based in religious denominations or served particular ethnic or racial groups. New York's Educational Alliance was founded to help eastern European and Russian Jewish immigrants adjust to American life; the founders of Christamore House in Indianapolis hoped to use their settlement to reinvigorate the Christian faith; and Lugenia Burns Hope helped found the Neighborhood Union to serve the African American residents living near Morehouse College in Atlanta, Georgia.

By 1897, the number of settlements had grown to 74; by 1910, there were 400. Both men and women went into settlement work, but the first generation of college-educated women, for whom other professional outlets had not yet fully developed, predominated in the field. Most residents lived only a short time in settlements before moving on to important careers in reform movements, the professions, and government. A few, such as Addams and Wald, remained there all their lives.

American settlements can take credit for many concrete accomplishments, including the creation of the field of social work and the establishment of two federal agencies, the U.S. Children's Bureau (1912) and the U.S.

Women's Bureau (1920), which concerned themselves with women's and children's welfare. Settlement workers also played major roles in the Progressive party's Presidential campaign of 1912 and were responsible for advocating much of the Progressive Era's labor and social welfare legislation. Many settlements still exist today, assisting new immigrant groups as they try to adjust to American life, but most of their workers are now professional social workers who do not necessarily live in the same neighborhoods they serve.

SEE ALSO
Addams, Jane; Cities; Hull House; Progressive party; Reform movements; Social Gospel; Wald, Lillian

FURTHER READING
Carson, Mina. *Settlement Folk: Social Thought and the American Settlement Movement.* Chicago: University of Chicago Press, 1990.
Crocker, Ruth. *Social Work and Social Order: The Settlement Movement in Two Industrial Cities, 1889–1930.* Urbana: University of Illinois Press, 1992.
Davis, Allen F. *Spearheads of Reform: The Social Settlements and the Progressive Movement.* New Brunswick, N.J.: Rutgers University Press, 1984.
Lasch-Quinn, Elisabeth. *Black Neighbors: Race and the Limits of Reform in the American Settlement House Movement, 1890-1945.* Chapel Hill: University of North Carolina Press, 1993.
Rouse, Jacqueline Anne. *Lugenia Burns Hope: Black Southern Reformer.* Athens: University of Georgia Press, 1989.
Wald, Lillian D. *The House on Henry Street.* 1915. Reprint, New Brunswick, N.J.: Transaction, 1991.

17th Amendment

BEFORE THE ratification of the 17th Amendment in 1913, state legislatures, rather than voters, elected each state's two U.S. senators. Progressives urged that a system of "direct" election by the people replace this system. They charged that the "indirect" method resulted in the election of senators who represented special interest groups instead of the larger political desires of a state's voters. Moreover, legislatures would often deadlock over choosing their senators. This might mean that a state would have no senator at all for substantial periods of time.

Beginning in 1893, the U.S. House of Representatives voted five times in favor of the direct election of senators. Each time, the U.S. Senate either ignored or voted down the amendment. By 1912, conditions had changed. Twenty-nine states had adopted primary laws that allowed their voters to express preferences for senatorial candidates. Because state legislatures generally approved the candidate who had won the most votes, in essence these states were already holding a form of direct election for senators. In addition, revelations in 1910 that Illinois assemblymen had accepted bribes in return for electing William Lorimer to the Senate convinced some senators to change their view of direct elections. After 10 senators who had opposed the amendment retired, the Senate finally approved the amendment and it was ratified a year later.

SEE ALSO
Constitution, amendments to; Government reform; Progressive movement

FURTHER READING
Gould, Lewis L. *The Most Exclusive Club: A History of the Modern United States Senate.* New York: Basic Books, 2005.
Ritchie, Donald A. *The Senate.* New York: Chelsea House, 1988.

Sex education movement

IN THE LATE 1800s, the incidence of venereal (sexually transmitted) diseases,

A 1918 poster reminds World War I troops that anyone returning from Europe with a sexually transmitted disease would be quarantined. Medical science at the time had no reliable cures for these diseases.

such as syphilis and gonorrhea, was rising at alarming rates. Physicians and social reformers argued that young people would be less likely to contract these diseases if they had more scientific knowledge about human sexuality. In 1905, Dr. Prince Morrow founded a society to promote sex education among adolescents. Shortly after his death in 1913, his society joined with others to form the American Social Hygiene Association (ASHA), which became the leader in the movement to bring sex education into schools and colleges. The task was not easy, as most Americans were reluctant to talk publicly about sexual topics. Eventually, however, the ASHA won endorsements for sex education from prestigious organizations such as the National Education Association, the American Medical Association, and the Young Men's Christian Association.

The public became more open to the need for sex education during World War I. Medical personnel collecting health information during the recruitment of soldiers found high rates of venereal disease among the nation's youth. In response, Congress passed the Chamberlain-Kahn Act in 1918. This law created a Venereal Disease Division in the U.S. Public Health Service and earmarked at least half of its $4 million appropriation for sex education. The federal government promoted the use of motion pictures to convince soldiers to avoid prostitutes. The film *Damaged Goods* told the story of a soldier who gets syphilis from a prostitute, passes it on to his wife and newborn baby, and in his despair commits suicide.

The sex education movement thus emphasized the dangers of human sexual activity rather than its pleasures. Some sex educators took a different tack. In 1915, Mary Ware Dennett wrote a pamphlet called "The Sex Side of Life" to educate her two teenage sons about sex. Her pamphlet stressed not only the "facts of life" but also the joyful side of sexuality. Dennett distributed 25,000 copies of the pamphlet before being convicted of violating the Comstock Law, which Congress had passed in 1873 to prevent anyone from sending "obscene" materials through the U.S. mail. The reversal of Dennett's conviction in 1930 opened the way for greater acceptance of sex education in American society. Although now included in many school curricula, it remains controversial in communities, that prefer to emphasize abstention from sex rather than knowledge about it.

SEE ALSO
Birth control movement; Comstock Law (1873); Sexuality

FURTHER READING
Chen, Constance. *"The Sex Side of Life": Mary Ware Dennett's Pioneering Battle for Birth Control and Sex Education.* New York: New Press, 1996.
Moran, Jeffrey. *Teaching Sex: The Shaping of Adolescence in the Twentieth Century.* Cambridge, Mass.: Harvard University Press, 2000.

Sexuality

BETWEEN 1880 AND 1920, many Americans changed their ideas about human sexuality. Before that time, most religious Americans considered sex outside of marriage to be a sin. In addition, few individuals beyond medical personnel wrote or spoke openly about sexual topics. By 1920, ordinary people were writing and talking about sex, many of them saying that sex is a natural instinct and that both sexes should be free to fulfill their sexual desires. Young urban sophisticates were engaging in sexual experimentation, and reformers were campaigning vigorously for the legalization of information about birth control.

Historians have labeled 19th-century attitudes toward sex Victorian, a reference to socially accepted moral views current in both Britain and the United States during the reign of Victoria, Queen of Great Britain from 1837 to 1901. Chief among these views was opposition to all premarital, extramarital, and homosexual relations. For Victorians, sex was of course crucial to reproduction, but otherwise it was a waste of energies that should be directed toward the preservation and advancement of civilization. Most Victorians considered masturbation to be evil, believed men needed sexual release but women did not, and saw individuals who indulged themselves sexually as morally suspect.

One illustration of American Victorian attitudes toward sexuality was the passage of the Comstock Law in 1873. Named after its initiator, Anthony Comstock, founder of the New York Society for the Suppression of Vice, the law outlawed sending through the

THE TWO PATHS
WHAT WILL THE GIRL BECOME?

AT 13 BAD LITERATURE
AT 20 FLIRTING AND COQUETTERY
AT 26 FAST LIFE-DISSIPATION
AT 40 AN OUTCAST
Copyright, 1903, by J. A. Hertel.

AT 13 STUDY AND OBEDIENCE
AT 20 VIRTUE AND DEVOTION
AT 26 A LOVING MOTHER
AT 60 AN HONORED GRANDMOTHER

THE above cut represents a beautiful little girl at seven—as pure as a sunbeam—she comes from a fine Christian family. Going to the left you see her at thirteen reading "Sapho," a vile novel that was suppressed several years ago in New York—it had a bad effect on our model little girl; at nineteen *Flirting and Coquetry*; third stage, a step lower; at twenty-six, *Fast Life and Dissipation*—this tells the sad story; at forty she is *an outcast*—the miserable result of *Social Impurity*.

To the right we have a brighter picture—at thirteen, *Study and Obedience*; next a young lady in church—*Virtue and Devotion*; at twenty-six—*A Loving Mother*—a most inspiring and lovely scene; at sixty—*An Honored Grandmother*.

U.S. mail any "obscene" or "lewd" books and pamphlets. These categories included even medical information about contraception and abortion. Around the turn of the 20th century, citizens in many cities took a further step to assure social "purity" by launching anti-vice campaigns. Citizens' commissions studied the prevalence of houses of prostitution (brothels), published the results, and then worked to pass laws to shut them down. They also campaigned to close down other "indecent" places, such as saloons, dance halls, and gambling dens, where prostitutes tended to hang out. They claimed these places corrupted youth and spread venereal (sexually transmitted) diseases. To combat prostitution, in 1910 Congress passed the Mann Act (named after Illinois Con-

From a 1903 book on "social purity," this illustration depicts the two paths a young girl might take in life. It shows immoral books and sexually impure conduct leading to degradation, but religion and wholesome family life bringing respect and happiness.

gressman James R. Mann), which forbade the transportation across state lines of women under age eighteen for "immoral purposes."

Even while activities to suppress vice were in high gear, more liberal attitudes toward sexuality began to surface. The 1886 publication of Richard von Krafft-Ebing's *Psychopathia Sexualis,* a systematic survey of sexual deviance, opened up sexuality for greater scientific study. Other doctors interested in the relationship between the mind and body, such as Viennese physician Sigmund Freud, argued that the repression of sexual desire could lead to psychological problems. Another popular writer on sexual topics, Havelock Ellis, campaigned for the sexual liberation of women and greater tolerance of "sexual inversion," the term then used for homosexuality. Dr. Clelia Duel Mosher and Katharine Bement Davis both surveyed women to understand female sexual response. Even though a growing campaign for sex education in the schools emphasized abstinence in order to prevent venereal disease, it nonetheless resulted in young people learning more about their sexuality.

The causes of this gradual breakdown of Victorian sexual attitudes were complex. One factor was the impact of industrialization on city life. In the nation's growing cities of the late 1800s, millions of women traveled the city streets without chaperones, rode streetcars alone, and frequented places of public amusement, such as dance halls and amusement parks. By the early 20th century, most urban women had shed their corsets, shortened their skirts, and begun to bob their hair. The bicycle and later the automobile gave women both greater mobility and privacy in their dating activities. Places like Greenwich Village in New York City attracted young educated women who were proclaiming their right to sexual self-expression.

The mixing of immigrant and racial cultures in cities also contributed to a liberalization of sexual attitudes. While many immigrant groups from southern and eastern Europe were fiercely protective of the chastity of their daughters, they nevertheless brought with them a warmer, more open approach to sexual matters in general. African Americans were as insistent on marital fidelity as whites but traditionally had been more open about their sexuality. By the turn of the century, their music and dance styles had evolved into ragtime dancing, a leisure-time activity with sexual overtones that attracted people of all ages, races, and ethnicities in the early 1900s.

Even though new attitudes were beginning to prevail, however, old attitudes hung on. By 1920, an entire spectrum of views on sexuality existed across American society, from strict Victorian ideals of public morality to calls for "free love," which meant that people should be able to express their sexuality with whomever they wanted, whenever they wanted. Many Americans were still profoundly influenced by their religion's teachings on sexuality; others felt confused about what was "right" and "wrong" in sexual matters. A double sexual standard still prevailed: boys wanted access to sex, but planned to marry virgins; girls who engaged in premarital sex, especially with multiple partners, were considered wayward, even delinquent. Prostitution, while officially illegal, was often condoned or ignored, but when prosecuted, only the prostitute, never the customer, went to jail. Homosexuals were also liable to prosecution. The Comstock Law remained in force, sending birth control advocates to jail until it was finally amended in 1936.

SEE ALSO

Birth control movement; Comstock Law (1873); Prostitution; Victorianism; Women's rights movement

FURTHER READING

D'Emilio, John, and Estelle Freedman. *Intimate Matters: A History of Sexuality in America*. New York: Harper Collins, 1988.

Horowitz, Helen Lefkowitz. *Rereading Sex: Battles over Sexual Knowledge and Suppression in Nineteenth-Century America*. New York: Knopf, 2002.

Pivar, David J. *Purity Crusade: Sexual Morality and Social Control, 1868–1900*. Westport, Conn.: Greenwood, 1973.

Sinclair, Upton Beall

- *Born: Sept. 20, 1878, Baltimore, Md.*
- *Education: City College of New York, B.A., 1897; Columbia University, 1897–1900*
- *Accomplishments: author of numerous books, including* The Jungle *(1906),* The Profits of Religion *(1918),* Oil! *(1927), and* Dragon's Teeth *(1942), which won the Pulitzer Prize for fiction*
- *Died: Nov. 25, 1968, Bound Brook, N.J.*

UPTON SINCLAIR, muckraking (investigative) journalist and author, wrote the novel *The Jungle*, which exposed the unsanitary conditions in the meatpacking industry. Published in 1906, it stands second only to Harriet Beecher Stowe's *Uncle Tom's Cabin* (1852) among influential social protest novels in U.S. history. Sinclair was also a socialist and an aspiring politician. He never won elective office, despite a campaign for Congress from New Jersey and two runs for governor of California.

Sinclair moved to New York City as a young boy. His salesman father suffered from alcoholism and was often unable to provide for the family. The boy lived on occasion with his mother's well-to-do parents, and he would say later that he became a socialist through his firsthand experience of the gap between riches and poverty. He began writing jokes and short stories for pulp magazines in his teens and was soon turning out a dime novel every week. He earned enough to pay his way through college and help support his parents.

Sinclair's first few attempts at serious literature, novels published in the early years of the 20th century, did not sell well, but his fortunes changed when the Kansas-based socialist magazine *Appeal to Reason* hired him to investigate the lives of immigrant workers in Chicago's stockyards and meatpacking plants. That assignment led to *The Jungle*, which was serialized in the magazine in 1905. Published in book form the following year, it brought the author his first taste of fame and financial success.

In addition to portraying the brutal mistreatment suffered by meat industry workers, *The Jungle* provided lurid descriptions of unsanitary practices that threatened public health by putting tainted meat on the market. These passages affected readers profoundly. Commenting on his book's impact, Sinclair said, "I aimed at the public's heart, and by accident I hit it in the stomach." The novel prompted a storm of public outrage that led to the passage in 1906 of important new federal laws, the Meat Inspection Act and the Pure Food and Drugs Act. Sinclair even met with President Theodore Roosevelt, who disagreed with the author's socialist politics but told him that the government, even in a capitalist system, should take "radical action" against

A poster advertises The Jungle, *Upton Sinclair's 1906 novel about the meatpacking industry. The lion atop its prey and the smokestacks in the background suggest that industrial capitalism is a brutal system in which the rich destroy the poor.*

the "arrogant and selfish greed" of big-money special interests.

With the money he earned from *The Jungle,* Sinclair helped found a cooperative living community in New Jersey. That living experiment lasted only four months before fire destroyed the community's buildings. Sinclair broke with many fellow socialists by favoring U.S. participation in World War I but spoke out against the imprisonment of antiwar socialist leaders. Later, in the 1920s, Sinclair said that he had been wrong to support the war. Unsuccessful in several attempts to gain political office, he continued publishing politically motivated books throughout his long life, and he won a Pulitzer Prize for *The Dragon's Teeth,* his 1942 novel about the rise of the Nazi party in Germany.

SEE ALSO

Industry; Muckrakers; Literature; Pure Food and Drugs Act (1906); Regulation

FURTHER READING

Harris, Leon. *Upton Sinclair: American Rebel.* 1975. Reprint, New York: Thomas Y. Crowell, 1991.

Scott, Ivan. *Upton Sinclair, the Forgotten Socialist.* Lewiston, N.Y.: Edwin Mellen, 1997.

Sinclair, Upton. *The Jungle: The Uncensored Original Edition.* Edited by Kathleen de Grave. Tucson, Ariz.: See Sharp Press, 2003.

Sitting Bull

- *Born: around 1831, Grand River, Dakota Territory*
- *Accomplishments: Sioux chief and holy man*
- *Died: Dec. 15, 1890, Standing Rock, S. D.*

THE SIOUX CHIEF Sitting Bull (Tatanka-Iyotake in his native language) was among the foremost Indian leaders at the end of the 19th century, when U.S. troops were fighting the tribes of the Great Plains. Born to the Hunkpapa band, part of the Lakota (or Teton) branch of the Sioux, Sitting Bull earned a dual reputation as a warrior and a holy man. In the 1860s, he became chief of all the Lakota.

In 1868, the Sioux nation and the U.S. government signed the Fort Laramie Treaty, which guaranteed that the Black Hills region of South Dakota would remain forever in Indian possession. The United States honored the treaty for less than a decade. In 1875, pressured by white settlers and gold prospectors who wanted access to the area, the government ordered the Sioux to abandon most of the Black Hills and settle on designated reservations.

Sitting Bull, along with Crazy Horse and another chief named Gall, led the resistance to the reservation order. Assisted by Cheyenne and Arapahoe allies, the Sioux army enjoyed some initial success. Their greatest victory occurred in 1876 at the Little Bighorn River in Montana, where the combined Indian forces annihilated Lieutenant Colonel George Armstrong Custer and all his troops. In the months after that battle, however, Sitting Bull and his followers had to flee to Canada to avoid the thousands of U.S. troops bent on avenging Custer's death.

In 1881, with his people threatened with starvation, Sitting Bull returned

For this portrait of Sitting Bull, taken around 1888, the photographer shot the Indian leader from the side to capture the full length of his feathered war bonnet.

to the United States. The last of the Sioux chiefs to surrender, he spent nearly two years in a military prison and then went to live as a farmer on the Standing Rock reservation near his birthplace. In 1885, he toured for a few months with Buffalo Bill's Wild West Show. Legend has it that he would sometimes address the show's audience, cursing them in his native language while they, not understanding the words, cheered his performance.

In 1890, the Ghost Dance religion was gaining popularity among the Sioux, who believed that ritual dances and the wearing of special garments would help them regain their lands. The religion soon became militant. Suspecting that Sitting Bull might use his spiritual authority to encourage the Ghost Dancers in renewed warfare, Indian Agent James McLaughlin sent a contingent of tribal police to his home at Standing Rock to arrest him. A fight broke out as a group of his supporters tried to prevent the arrest, and Sitting Bull died in the exchange of gunfire. Two weeks later, U.S. troops crushed the Sioux Ghost Dancers in the massacre at Wounded Knee, South Dakota.

SEE ALSO

Crazy Horse; Military; Native Americans; West, the; Wounded Knee massacre (1890)

FURTHER READING

Marrin, Albert. *Sitting Bull and His World.* New York: Dutton, 2000.
Utley, Robert. *The Lance and the Shield: The Life and Times of Sitting Bull.* New York: Henry Holt, 1993.

16th Amendment

THE 16TH AMENDMENT, proposed in September 1909 and ratified in Feb-

ruary 1913, says that "Congress shall have power to lay and collect taxes on incomes, from whatever source derived, without apportionment among the several States, and without regard to any census or enumeration." The amendment was worded in this way so as to avoid calling the income tax a "direct tax." According to the U.S. Constitution, Congress could assess a direct tax only if it took apportionment and population into account.

Before the 16th Amendment, the government had earned the bulk of its funding through tariffs, which are taxes imposed on imported goods. Although high tariffs protected American industries, they also raised the price of consumer goods. Westerners, southerners, social reformers, labor groups, populists, and many economists therefore opposed high tariffs and argued for a taxation system based on an "ability to pay." These groups created the national consensus that led to a constitutional amendment allowing the government to tax incomes.

The income tax remains controversial to this day. Opponents argue that lower rates will stimulate economic growth, but advocates say that any other form of taxation, such as a national sales tax, would place the largest tax burden on those least able to pay.

SEE ALSO

Taxes and tariffs

FURTHER READING

Buenker, John D. *The Income Tax and the Progressive Era.* New York: Garland, 1985.
Weisman, Steven R. *The Great Tax Wars: Lincoln to Wilson: The Fierce Battles over Money and Power that Transformed the Nation.* New York: Simon & Schuster, 2002.
Witte, John F. *The Politics and Development of the Federal Income Tax.* Madison: University of Wisconsin Press, 1985.

Social Darwinism

SOCIAL DARWINISM arose in the mid-19th century as a theory that attempted to explain racial differences and social inequalities. The theory came from a misapplication of the findings of English biologist Charles Darwin. Having observed that species of plants and animals evolved over many thousands of years, Darwin theorized that those species that adapted best to their surroundings survived, while those that did not adapt became extinct. Darwin called this process natural selection. Some people simplified the idea to the phrase "survival of the fittest."

Conservative thinkers in England and the United States converted Darwin's observations into a theory of human society, something Darwin himself never attempted. Following the lead of popular British social theorist Herbert Spencer, they ranked various societies on a scale of human progress and claimed that white Europeans and Americans had evolved further and

faster than the other peoples of the earth. They then used this belief to justify their imperialistic rule over "less evolved" societies. They assumed these societies would need to remain under European or American control until they evolved enough to be capable of self-government.

Social Darwinists also applied their "science" to their own societies, arguing that the Caucasian, European-derived male industrialist was at the apex of evolution and was therefore destined to dominate. To these thinkers, the poor were merely victims of their own genetic bad luck, laziness, or even immorality, and were destined to remain subordinate to their "betters." True, the theorists admitted, some employers exploited workers and some businessmen used corrupt means to crush competitors, but the ability of businessmen to contribute to the nation's progress, according to Social Darwinists, depended on their liberty to pursue their own ends. Thus, Social Darwinists favored a laissez-faire style of government, one that did not interfere with the workings of business or attempt to address issues associated with economic and social inequality. Social Darwinists reasoned that because no external authority could reverse the workings of natural selection in the life and death of animal species, no government or regulatory institution should interfere in the struggles of economic competition.

Social Darwinists also believed that any attempt to provide welfare for the poor was tragically misguided. They thought that feeding or housing the poor simply allowed them to survive and transmit their unfitness to their children, who in turn would pass it on to their children. Even if private charity could temporarily alleviate suffering, they believed that no govern-

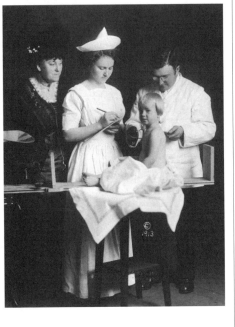

Medical professionals examine a six-year-old in a "Better Babies" competition at the 1913 Louisiana state fair. Baby contests stemmed from an outgrowth of Social Darwinist beliefs called eugenics, which sought ways to breed better human beings.

ment programs ought to interfere in the natural demise of the unfit. For Social Darwinists, industrial society's general prosperity proved the correctness of their views. Some suffering would naturally accompany progress, they thought, but the rewards reaped by the successful would raise the general standard of living and eventually restore society's balance. Government interference could not guarantee this restoration, they claimed, and might even make things worse.

In its most extreme form, Social Darwinism embraced the concept of eugenics, the scientific breeding of human beings to produce better stock and weed out undesirable characteristics. Eugenics never became social policy, but President Theodore Roosevelt encouraged the educated middle classes to have many children so that the American gene pool would not become dominated by the offspring of the poor and immigrants.

Eventually, Progressive Era critics of Social Darwinism learned to use the language of evolution for their own purposes. Because human society was continuing to evolve, they asked, who was to say that helping people was not part of that evolutionary process? Human communities had to adapt to change. In times of transition, they argued, it was in society's larger interest to take some positive action and utilize the regulatory capabilities of the state and federal government for the good of the poor and needy.

SEE ALSO

Imperialism; Laissez-faire; Progressive movement; Race relations; Regulation

FURTHER READING

Bannister, Robert C. *Social Darwinism: Science and Myth in Anglo-American Social Thought.* Philadelphia, Pa.: Temple University Press, 1988.
Degler, Carl N. *In Search of Human Nature: The Decline and Revival of Darwinism in American Social Thought.* New York: Oxford University Press, 1991.
Hofstadter, Richard. *Social Darwinism in American Thought.* 1983. Reprint, Boston: Beacon, 1992.

Social Gospel

THE SOCIAL GOSPEL is the name given to a religious movement that sought to apply Christian ethics to social problems. It arose in the 1880s among American Protestant ministers who felt that their churches should address more directly the economic suffering caused by industrialization. The movement's name came from the idea of sending out a new gospel (literally, "good news") with a strong, and essentially optimistic social message. This message announced that Christians could achieve a better society by using the power of their churches to control the social and economic forces of their times.

Among Social Gospel leaders, Baptist theologian Walter Rauschenbusch from Rochester, New York, was perhaps the most passionate. In his 1907 book, *Christianity and the Social Crisis,* he called on churches to focus

This illustration from an 1893 edition of the Christian magazine Ram's Horn *criticizes businessmen who are preoccupied with the pursuit of wealth and too busy to heed Jesus' humanitarian message.*

less on issues of personal salvation and more on finding solutions to social problems. In *For God and the People* (1910), he asserted that a "new social purpose"... "is enlarging and transforming our whole conception of the meaning of Christianity." Washington Gladden, a Congregationalist minister in Columbus, Ohio, wrote stringent critiques of the free-enterprise system in which he called for public ownership of utilities and cooperative management of many industries. Josiah Strong, minister of a Congregationalist church in Cincinnati, Ohio, convened interdenominational congresses and used surveys and statistics to present his diagnoses of social problems.

Academics were also involved in the Social Gospel movement. Francis Greenwood Peabody, a Unitarian at the Harvard Divinity School, instituted the first systematic course on social ethics. The only Social Gospeler to address issues of race, Peabody stressed the necessity of cooperatives and a social security system as ways to assist poor minorities. Richard T. Ely, an Episcopalian economist at the Johns Hopkins University, expressed his opposition to laissez-faire economic theory in *Social Aspects of Christianity,* a collection of essays published in 1889. Ely advocated improvements in workers' lives and working conditions, reductions in inequalities of wealth and opportunity, and government ownership of monopolies operated in the public interest, such as transportation and power facilities. Albion W. Small, a Baptist who organized the first sociology department at the University of Chicago, taught that sociology should be based in strong ethical foundations and be used to improve the human condition.

All of these individuals spoke out on public issues, but the ministers among them sought first and foremost to reform the churches themselves. In sermons, they led their congregations to deeper commitments to social responsibility. Some congregations built new facilities and social settlement houses to serve immigrants in their neighborhoods, and seminaries added social work courses to ministers' training.

The movement drew some of its leaders into politics. Social Gospelers supported Progressive Era causes, such as temperance, public control over utilities, and an end to prostitution and corrupt political practices. They also campaigned for child labor reform, workers' rights, factory safety, low-income housing, public health programs, and conservation. The movement culminated in the formation in 1908 of the Federal (later, National) Council of Churches, which formulated a "Social Creed of the Churches."

SEE ALSO

Progressive movement; Protestantism; Rauschenbusch, Walter; Reform movement; Religion; Settlement-house movement

FURTHER READING

Curtis, Susan. *A Consuming Faith: the Social Gospel and Modern American Culture*. 1991. Reprint, Columbia: University of Missouri Press, 2001.
Gorrell, Donald K. *The Age of Social Responsibility: The Social Gospel in the Progressive Era, 1900–1920*. Macon, Ga.: Mercer University Press, 1988.
Handy, Robert T., ed. *The Social Gospel in America, 1870–1920*. New York: Oxford University Press, 1966.

Socialism

SOCIALISM IS a group of theories that try to address the problem of economic inequality in human society. Socialists seek to organize society so that the masses of ordinary people, rather than

In 1879, The Socialist, *a political newspaper, promoted labor union efforts to win shorter working hours. Socialist candidates had limited success at the polls, but Republicans and Democrats later adopted many of their issues and ideas.*

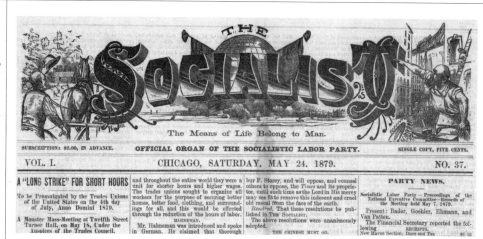

the wealthy elites, own and manage their economic resources. In contrast to capitalism, which stresses competition and individual ownership, socialism stresses cooperation and the welfare of the larger society over that of only a few.

In the late 1800s, the socialist theories of German historian Karl Marx and his colleague Friedrich Engels became the most influential among America's new immigrant, working-class populations. Marx and Engels argued that the struggle between social classes was not only inevitable but would also eventually lead to a violent revolution. During this revolution, workers (the proletariat) would seize control of the state from the capitalists who dominated it, establish a "dictatorship of the proletariat," and nationalize all industries and utilities. A "Central Directing Authority" would control all aspects of society and ensure that a "classless" society evolved over time.

American followers of Marx often joined the labor movement in order to influence working-class politics with their ideas about the need for social transformation. Enthusiastic socialist spokesmen inspired workers to stage the national railroad strike of 1877, and over the course of many years contributed to successful agitation for the eight-hour day. Government

authorities routinely singled out socialists for repression. They blamed them, for example, for the deaths in 1886 of several policemen and civilians from a bomb thrown during a strike meeting in Chicago's Haymarket Square. The authorities sentenced eight socialist and anarchist leaders to death, even though there was no evidence of their connection to the bombing.

Despite the hostility against them, by the late 1880s immigrant socialists had created the Socialist Labor party. In 1890, they chose Daniel DeLeon as spokesman and editor of the party journal *The People.* Because DeLeon was a revolutionary and scornful of the existing trade union movement, which accepted only skilled workers as members, the Socialist Labor party tended to alienate rather than attract skilled workers.

In general, revolutionary socialists had a difficult time attracting much of a following. The socialist message that workers could never gain decent wages until they seized control of the state from capitalists was too pessimistic for American conditions. Talk of reorganizing society under a "Central Directing Authority" jarred with the tradition of American individualism. Even those socialists who favored peaceful progress through unions or the ballot box insisted on an idea of class consciousness and class antagonism that attracted few American workers. Most workers wanted to believe that, in a modern democratic society, the middle class was growing and that, through perseverance and hard work, they could become part of it. In short, they could not reconcile socialism with their American dream of upward social mobility.

By the 1890s, some American socialists were trying to fashion a version of socialism more appropriate for the United States. They gave up belief in working-class revolution and instead pressed for laws that would improve the working and living conditions of laborers, immigrants, and the poor. Practical socialists began to work for public sanitation systems, safety in the workplace, factory inspections, improved education, and other progressive (but not radical) reforms.

Socialism adapted further to American circumstances by reconciling itself with Christianity. Advocates of Christian socialism stressed the golden rule and self-sacrifice. They sought to bring people of different social classes closer together, particularly emphasizing the connections intellectuals could establish with working-class families in industrial cities. They believed that the United States should set an example to the world by de-emphasizing individual rights and opportunities and emphasizing shared citizenship.

Christian socialism also received a boost from Edward Bellamy's 1888 utopian novel, *Looking Backward,* which imagined a peaceful classless future, and from the formation of hundreds of Bellamy, or Nationalist, clubs around the country. Both Utopian socialism and Christian socialism lacked practicality, and their goals were difficult to achieve. The idealism of these systems seemed to appeal to middle-class, rather than working-class people.

Political socialism was reborn at the turn of the century with the merger of the old Socialist Labor party with a newer Socialist Democratic party under the leadership of Eugene V. Debs, former head of the American Railway Union. At its peak, the Socialist party, as it was now called, had 100,000 members. Especially popular in the Southwest and among tenant farmers, miners, and railroad workers, it offered a vision of production-for-use instead of for profit, economic and social equality, and global solidarity with other workers. People everywhere freely discussed socialism, and millions of people read socialist newspapers.

During the 1910s, Socialist party goals became increasingly appealing to many Americans. In the years before World War I, voters elected two Socialist congressmen, more than 70 mayors, and scores of state legislators and city councilors. Even though he did not win, Eugene V. Debs ran a strong third-party campaign in the Presidential races of 1912 and 1920, receiving close to a million votes each time. Socialist party members opposed U.S. participation in World War I, and many, including Debs, were imprisoned for war resistance. After the war, the party split between more moderate American socialists and those who supported the communist revolution in Russia.

Unlike its European counterparts of the same period, the American socialist movement never fully managed to create worker solidarity across the country's ethnic and racial lines. Nor did it bridge the gap between skilled and unskilled workers. It did, however, have a lasting impact in the United States. While Karl Marx's brand of revolutionary socialism eventually evolved into communism, some proposals of American socialists from the years 1900 to 1920 found their way into mainstream American life, among them the graduated income tax, the eight-hour workday, the abolition of child labor, equal suffrage for men and women, and the creation of a cabinet-level Department of Labor to oversee issues important to workers.

SEE ALSO

Bellamy, Edward; Communism; Debs, Eugene Victor; Haymarket Square riot (1886); Labor; Politics; Railroad strike (1877); Reform movements; World War I

FURTHER READING

Buhle, Mari Jo. *Women and American Socialism, 1870–1920*. Urbana: University of Illinois Press, 1981.
Buhle, Paul. *Marxism in the United States: Remapping the History of the American Left*. New York: Verso, 1991.
Lipset, Seymour Martin, and Gary Marks. *It Didn't Happen Here: Why Socialism Failed in the United States*. New York: Norton, 2001.
Morgan, H. Wayne. *American Socialism, 1900–1960*. Englewood Cliffs, N.J.: Prentice Hall, 1964.

Social sciences

CERTAIN FIELDS of study that analyze human beings and their social issues—such as anthropology, sociology, psychology, political science, and economics—use scientific methods in their research. These disciplines belong to the social sciences. Social scientists generally begin their studies by asking a series of questions, defining their terms, and suggesting possible answers, called hypotheses. They then test their answers against empirical data, that is, information derived from controlled experiments, systematic observation, or the collection of statistics.

American interest in the social sciences accelerated after the Civil War. In those years, social reformers came to believe that applying scientific methods

to contemporary social problems would help government make better public policies. In 1865, a group of these reformers created the American Social Science Association. This organization eventually inspired the founding of professional associations in more specific fields. It also promoted the adoption of codes of ethics and standards of research in individual disciplines.

In 1885, Richard T. Ely, an influential economic theorist at the Johns Hopkins University who advocated the reform of American capitalism to make it more socially responsible, founded the American Economic Association. Columbia University's John William Burgess, a political theorist, organized the Academy of Political Science to establish links between academics and the larger world of practical politics and government. Twenty-two scholars interested in promoting the social sciences in general founded the American Academy of Political and Social Science in 1889. A year later, they launched a bimonthly publication, *The Annals*, which became the premier journal for the scholarly discussion of contemporary political, economic, and social issues.

In 1892, G. Stanley Hall, a psychologist and president of Clark University, helped found the American Psychological Association. The American Political Science Association formed in 1903, and the American Sociological Association, in 1905. The purposes of all of these organizations were to facilitate communication among scholars and between scholars and the wider community, including government leaders and ordinary citizens.

Influential publications of the era that used social science research techniques included *Hull-House Maps and Papers* (1895), a systematic social survey of the ethnic and racial groups living in and around the Hull House social settlement in Chicago. Social science methods informed W. E. B. DuBois's 1899 survey of the Philadelphia Negro, which over a 15-month house-to-house survey gathered information from 40,000 black residents of Philadelphia on their daily lives, homes, organizations, and relation to the white majority.

Other significant social science studies of the era include the 1907–8 survey of the living and working conditions of industrial workers in Pittsburgh, and the 1911 report of the U.S. Congress's Joint Commission on Immigration, which documented immigration. In the case of *Muller* v. *Oregon*, lawyer Louis D. Brandeis used social science research to convince the U.S. Supreme Court to sustain the right of the state to regulate women's working conditions.

SEE ALSO

Brandeis, Louis Dembitz; DuBois, William Edward Burghardt (W. E. B.); Hull House; Psychology; Sociology

FURTHER READING

Haskell, Thomas L. *The Emergence of Professional Social Science: The American Social Science Association and the Nineteenth-Century Crisis of Authority.* Urbana: University of Illinois Press, 1977. Ross, Dorothy. *The Origins of American Social Science.* New York: Cambridge University Press, 1991.

Social work

SOCIAL WORK—providing aid to the poor and underprivileged—emerged as a profession in the late 1800s. It arose from two chief sources. The first was the work of Charity Organization Societies (COS), founded in many cities beginning in the late 1870s to coordi-

nate and improve the delivery of aid to the poor. The COS trained "friendly visitors," volunteer women who visited the poor in their homes to assess the "worthiness" of their applications for aid, to instruct them in parenting and homemaking, and in general to help them become productive citizens. The detailed records that friendly visitors kept on their cases led to the casework methods of modern-day social workers.

The second source came from the settlement-house movement. This movement inspired young women and men to settle in city slums in order to learn directly from the poor how they could best help them. In the process of organizing activities and programs for their neighborhoods, settlement house residents developed skills that later formed part of social work training. Settlement house pioneers Sophonisba Breckinridge and Edith Abbott would go on to establish the School of Social Service Administration at the University of Chicago.

Organized in 1874, the National Conference on Charities and Corrections (later, National Conference of Social Work) provided a professional forum for social workers. In 1898 the New York COS established the New York

Graduate students training to become professional social workers pose outside New York City's United Charities Building. Formal social work training began in 1898, when Columbia University joined forces with the New York Charity Organization.

School of Philanthropy to train social workers. The Russell Sage Foundation, a private philanthropic group, helped finance this school as well as similar schools in Boston, Chicago, and St. Louis. The foundation also financed the COS's journal, *The Survey*, the most important journal of the day to publish articles on social and political issues of interest to social workers.

SEE ALSO

Charity organization movement; Poverty; Settlement-house movement; Sociology

FURTHER READING

Fitzpatrick, Ellen F. *Endless Crusade: Women Social Scientists and Progressive Reform.* New York: Oxford University Press, 1990.
Kunzel, Regina G. *Fallen Women, Problem Girls: Unmarried Mothers and the Professionalization of Social Work, 1890–1945.* New Haven: Yale University Press, 1993.
Lubove, Roy. *The Professional Altruist: The Emergence of Social Work as a Career, 1880–1930.* Cambridge, Mass.: Harvard University Press, 1965.

Sociology

SOCIOLOGY IS the study of human social interactions. Sociologists seek to discover the scientific laws that guide these interactions and to find solutions for contemporary social problems. The field first emerged in Europe and the United States in response to the social problems caused by industrialization, mass immigration, labor strife, and the rapid growth of cities.

The French philosopher Auguste Comte coined the term *sociology* in 1832, when he was looking for a term to replace "social physics," the term social scientists were then using to discuss the scientific laws of social interaction. In the early 19th century, the goal of these scientists was to seek solutions to the social disorder created by the political and economic revolutions of the time. Comte saw sociology as a science that would integrate the findings of all other sciences into one cohesive body of knowledge. The English social theorist Herbert Spencer wrote the first books in the field, entitled *The Principles of Sociology*, which were published between 1876 and 1896. Yale professor William Graham Sumner used them when he began teaching the first college course entitled "sociology."

In their quest to understand human society, Spencer and Sumner adapted some of Charles Darwin's theories. Darwin, an evolutionary biologist, had described a process he called natural selection, in which living species change and progress over thousands of years, the "fittest" individuals passing improved genetic traits for survival and reproduction on to succeeding generations and the less fit falling by the wayside. Applying evolutionary theory to their understanding of human society, Spencer and Sumner argued that society would be wise not to interfere in the competition among human beings to survive, an approach to social problems that came to be known as "Social Darwinism." Sociologist Lester Ward opposed this view, arguing that society should take positive advantage of scientific knowledge to improve itself. During the 1890s, social worker Jane Addams and social scientist W. E. B. DuBois applied Ward's ideas in their studies of particular social communities in Chicago and Philadelphia, suggesting concrete steps both individuals and governments could take in order to achieve a more just society.

Albion W. Small established the first university department of sociology at the University of Chicago in 1892. In 1895, Small founded the *American Journal of Sociology,* which later became the official publication of the American Sociological Association, founded in 1905. Beginning with 115 members, by 1920, this association, which united the interests of both theoretical sociologists and practical social workers, had grown to more than a thousand.

SEE ALSO

Addams, Jane; DuBois, William Edward Burghardt (W. E. B.); Social Darwinism; Social sciences; Social work; Sumner, William Graham

FURTHER READING

Turner, Stephen Park, and Jonathan H. Turner. *The Impossible Science: An Institutional Analysis of American Sociology.* Newbury Park, Calif.: Sage Publications, 1990.

Sousa, John Philip

- *Born: Nov. 6, 1854, Washington, D.C.*
- *Education: Music conservatory (Washington, D.C.), 1861–67*
- *Accomplishments: conductor, U.S. Marine Band (1880–92); organizer and leader, Sousa Band (1892); composer, "Semper Fidelis" (1888), "The Stars and Stripes Forever" (1896), among others*
- *Died: Mar. 6, 1932, Reading, Pa.*

JOHN PHILIP SOUSA was America's "March King." His marches, written over a hundred years ago, remain extremely popular. They can be counted on to arouse an American audience to foot tapping, rhythmic clapping, and even cheers. For that reason, hardly a ceremonial occasion, sporting event, or holiday parade is complete without a band playing a Sousa march.

Sousa, whose father was a trombonist in the U.S. Marine Band, began musical studies at age six. He learned to play several band instruments—flute, cornet, trombone, and alto horn—and also studied voice and violin. Not long after young Sousa attempted to join a circus band at age 13, his father enlisted him as an apprentice in the U.S. Marine Corps, where he played in the Marine Band. He soon began writing music, publishing his first composition, "Moonlight on the Potomac Waltzes," in 1872. Discharged from the Marines in 1875, he began to play the violin in theater orchestras. Occasionally, he conducted such orchestras and arranged music for them. He also composed songs, instrumental works, and the music for variety shows.

In 1880, the Marine Band invited Sousa to return as its conductor. Sousa led the band for twelve years, in 1888 composing the Marine Corps's signature march, "Semper Fidelis." "The Washington Post March," commissioned by the capital's newspaper in 1889, proved so popular that ballroom dance teachers created the two-step to accompany it. In later years, dancers would often ask bands to play a "Washington Post" when they wanted to perform the two-step.

In 1892, a band promoter and businessman, David Blakely, persuaded Sousa to organize a civilian concert band. The success of Sousa's band was so great that he was able to take it on several international tours before

John Philip Sousa, composer of "Stars and Stripes Forever" and other rousing military marches, carries a ceremonial sword as he parades at the head of a military band during World War I.

World War I. He also toured the United States, bringing exciting musical entertainments to almost every American town. To honor Blakely's memory, Sousa later wrote "The Stars and Stripes Forever," a march that some have called America's national march.

Even though the popularity of concert band music declined during Sousa's last years, he continued to tour. He received several honorary degrees and testified twice before Congress on behalf of composers' copyrights. Sousa, who always seemed to know how to put audiences in a good mood, made an enduring contribution to American musical culture.

SEE ALSO
Dance; Music

FURTHER READING
Bierley, Paul E. *John Philip Sousa, American Phenomenon.* Rev. ed. Westerville, Ohio: Integrity Press, 1993.
Newsom, John, ed. *Perspectives on John Philip Sousa.* Washington, D.C.: Music Division, Library of Congress, 1983.
Sousa, John Philip. *Marching Along: Recollections of Men, Women, and Music.* 1928. Edited by Paul E. Bierley. Westerville, Ohio: Integrity Press, 1994.

South, the

FOR MOST WHITE southerners, the period of the Civil War and Reconstruction was one of deep disappointment. Their attempt to preserve their accustomed way of life, based on slavery, through the formation of a separate nation, the Confederate States of America, had failed. Reconstruction, the period of rebuilding after the Civil War, had been painfully humiliating. Southerners felt that only after the Compromise of 1877 had resolved the disputed Presidential election of the previous year and U.S. troops had been withdrawn could the building of a "new" South truly begin.

The first task was to restore the region to economic prosperity. Boosters—people who promote an area's future prospects—played an important role in this process. One of the most successful was Henry Grady, managing editor of the *Atlanta Constitution* and a talented orator, who traveled to the North to encourage financiers to invest in the South. Grady described a South ready to be reconciled to the nation and blessed with natural resources and a large labor supply. He downplayed racial difficulties at home, claiming that nowhere in the country "is there kindlier feeling, closer sympathy, or less friction…than between the whites and the blacks of the South to-day." At the same time, he was sure that southern whites would find ways to maintain their supremacy over black citizens.

Impressed by southern boosters, northerners soon began pouring money into southern transportation and industrial enterprises. They invested heavily in the processing of southern raw materials, mining, and manufacturing, especially of textiles. They also invested in the expansion of southern railroads. Eventually, southerners hoped to free themselves from dependence on northern money, but in the meantime such investment was crucial to the South's rebirth.

The manufacture of tobacco products flourished in the South. In the 1880s, James Buchanan Duke took over his father's Durham, North Carolina, tobacco firm and began to mass-produce cigarettes. In 1889, Duke organized five U.S. tobacco firms into the American Tobacco Company, which by 1907 was producing a huge percentage of the world's tobacco products. Duke's company made tobacco farming increasingly important in the South, although growers were never happy with the prices Duke paid them.

Despite some forays into industry, most of the South remained agricultural. Cotton dominated as the region's premier cash crop. After the Civil War, southern farmers increased their cotton output, producing more than 10 million bales by 1900, twice the amount grown in 1860. Only the largest cotton plantations prospered, however.

Owners of small farms, and those who farmed as tenants or sharecroppers, never had enough land to make much profit. In addition, as cotton production outside the United States increased in the late 1800s, the price for American cotton fell. Worse, in the 1890s, the South experienced invasions of boll weevils and boring beetles, which ruined many cotton harvests. Not surprisingly, Populism, a political movement of the 1880s and 1890s that drew together many discontented farmers to press for more government regulation of transportation facilities as well as direct relief, found eager recruits among struggling southerners.

Hemmed in by racial segregation and economic discrimination, the region's African Americans received little from the New South's prosperity. The few who became economically successful risked harassment and lynching by white supremacists. The rest, primarily tenants and sharecroppers on land owned by whites, had to accept the region's least desirable jobs. Black men found work as porters in southern cities and on railroads, and in the timber, mining, and shellfish processing industries; black women went into domestic service, serving as cooks, laundresses, and nannies. Those dissatisfied with such work slowly

began to leave the South. Some, such as the Exodusters in the late 1870s, sought open land and less discrimination in the Midwest; others ventured farther afield into northern cities and western mining camps in their quest for economic opportunity.

In the early 20th century, while farmers in the Midwest achieved greater prosperity, southern farmers remained economically depressed, primarily because they were reluctant to diversify their crops. Progressives formed a Country Life movement to promote more efficient farming practices, better roads and schools, and improved communications systems as a way of increasing prosperity. They also hoped to keep the region's young people from moving away to take up industrial or service jobs elsewhere. Despite their efforts, most rural areas of the New South had stalled by 1915, stagnating in poverty, racial divisions, and outmoded farming practices.

Southern cities, such as Atlanta, Birmingham, Nashville, and New Orleans, grew rapidly in the Gilded Age. Atlanta boosters hosted international expositions in 1881, 1887, and 1895 to attract new businesses. It was at the exposition of 1895 that African American educator Booker T. Washington made a speech, later called the Atlanta Compromise, indicating his willingness to accept social inequality for black Americans while they worked toward economic success in farming and the trades. In this speech, which he delivered to a racially mixed audience, he raised his hand and said, "In all things that are purely social, we can be as separate as the fingers, yet one as the hand in all things essential to mutual progress."

Southern blacks and women saw some positive developments in this period. Higher educational opportunities

A white land-owner in his Mississippi cotton field is surrounded by black workers. Although slavery was abolished in 1865, many African Americans in the South continued to work in poorly paid agricultural jobs.

increased for southern African Americans, thereby allowing many to launch teaching careers that helped improve conditions in black communities. One of many southern institutions at which black men and women could earn college degrees, the Tuskegee Institute—founded in Alabama by Booker T. Washington in 1881—grew and prospered because of the reputation of its founder and his faculty. The African American scientist George Washington Carver did most of his research on agriculture, especially peanuts, at Tuskegee. In another development, the ragtime music and blues played by blacks in New Orleans, Memphis, and other southern cities gradually evolved into jazz, a musical style that influenced American musical and theatrical styles.

An energetic women's movement got underway in the South in the late 1880s. Pursuing the vote for women, temperance (control of the drinking of alcoholic beverages), and improved property rights for married women, southern women activists achieved many victories at the state and local level. Primarily white, these activists tried to persuade white men to vote for woman suffrage by arguing that doubling the white vote would help ensure the continuation of white supremacy in the South. Their argument convinced many Southern men to accept the woman's vote.

By the 1890s, southerners worried that the passage of time would dim memories of their valiant actions during the Civil War. They began to speak nostalgically of the Old South and to describe the war as a "lost cause." Associations of veterans and of "sons" and "daughters" of the Confederacy had already cropped up to see to the needs of veterans and their families and the proper burial of Confederate dead. Organized in 1894, the United Daughters of the Confederacy (UDC) brought together the different southern women's memorial and soldiers' aid societies into one federation. In 1914, in an act symbolizing reconciliation with the Union, the U.S. government permitted the UDC to build a Confederate War Memorial at Arlington National Cemetery.

In 1890, in another act of memorialization, Richmond, Virginia, began erecting monumental statues of Confederate generals. An equestrian statue of Robert E. Lee was the first of five heroic sculptures to adorn Monument Avenue, which has become a major tourist attraction. A hundred years later, protests against the city's continued support for the Confederate statues led to the erection in 1995 of a monument to the city's African American tennis star, Arthur Ashe.

SEE ALSO

African Americans; Agriculture; Carver, George Washington; Colleges and universities; Compromise of 1877; Lynching; Populism; Race relations; Railroads; Segregation; Temperance and prohibition movements; Washington, Booker T.; Woman suffrage movement; Women's rights movement; Work

FURTHER READING

Ayers, Edward L. *The Promise of the New South: Life after Reconstruction.* New York: Oxford University Press, 1992.
Blight, David W. *Race and Reunion: The Civil War in American Memory.* Cambridge, Mass.: Harvard University Press, 2001.
Link, William A. *The Paradox of Southern Progressivism, 1880–1930.* Chapel Hill: University of North Carolina Press, 1992.
Spruill, Marjorie Julian. *New Women of the New South: the Leaders of the Woman Suffrage Movement in the Southern States.* New York: Oxford University Press, 1993.
Woodward, C. Vann. *Origins of the New South, 1877–1913.* 1951. Reprint, Baton Rouge: Louisiana State University Press, 1971.

Spanish-American War

THE SPANISH-AMERICAN War lasted barely more than 100 days, from late April through mid-August 1898. But this brief conflict—one American diplomat would later call it a "splendid little war"—dramatically altered the role of the United States on the world stage. Its outcome, which left the United States in control of several former Spanish colonies, was a clear victory for expansionists, who had been arguing for some time that the United States needed to acquire territory beyond its continental borders.

The conflict originated in the Spanish colony of Cuba, just 90 miles south of Florida. Cuban revolutionaries had long been fighting for independence from Spain, and many Americans were outraged by the brutal tactics, such as incarcerating rebels in concentration camps, that Spanish authorities used against the rebels. Two New York City newspapers, the *Journal* and the *World,* adopted aggressive anti-Spain editorial stances and stirred up American support for the Cuban rebels by publishing lurid accounts of Spanish cruelty. After a failed rebel uprising in 1895, the Spanish military confined 300,000 people in concentration camps. Reports of sickness, starvation, and abuse in the camps led to increased pro-Cuban, anti-Spanish sympathies in the United States. At the same time, American commercial interests, with extensive investments on the island, worried about the economic impact of the fighting. Officials in Washington also saw the island's unstable military and political situation as a threat to U.S. interests in Central America.

For all these reasons, President William McKinley, elected in 1896, was eager to see an end to unrest in Cuba. During his first year in office, he prodded the Spanish government through diplomatic channels to change its Cuba policies. By late 1897, these efforts achieved some concessions, including an end to the concentration camps and an offer of partial autonomy for Cuba. The rebels rejected this offer from Spain, however, preferring to fight for complete independence. In January 1898, rioting broke out in Havana, Cuba's capital city.

Soldiers of Company F, United States 21st Infantry, bivouac outside Santiago, Cuba. The 21st were among the troops of the Fifth Army Corps, who captured San Juan Hill on July 1, 1898.

McKinley responded by dispatching a battleship, the *Maine,* to Havana Harbor, a show of force intended to protect Americans living in Cuba and to safeguard American property on the island. In February, an explosion of unknown origin sank the *Maine,* with the loss of more than 250 U.S. sailors. Many historians now believe a fuel accident inside the ship destroyed it, but at the time, most Americans were convinced that a Spanish mine in the harbor was responsible for the sinking. "Remember the *Maine!* To hell with Spain!" became a rallying cry for pro-war forces. Spanish-American relations deteriorated rapidly over the next two months. In April, both countries issued declarations of war.

The first major battle took place in May, not in Cuba but in the waters off Manila, the capital city of the Philippines, another Spanish colony halfway around the world. Spain had a substantial military presence in the Philippines, a nation occupying an archipelago, or group of islands. Throughout the islands, local rebels, like those in Cuba, were waging a revolution against Spanish imperial power. In fighting that lasted just a few hours, U.S. forces under Commodore George Dewey sank or captured all the Spanish ships in Manila Bay. Two months later, on July 3, U.S. ships inflicted a similarly catastrophic defeat on a Spanish fleet in Cuban waters. With these decisive victories in the Pacific and the Atlantic, the United States gained an insurmountable advantage by crippling Spain's ability to reinforce or resupply its fighters.

The United States also benefited from the military efforts of Cuban and Filipino revolutionaries who continued battling their colonial masters throughout the war, thereby making it impossible for the Spanish military to focus all its energies on fighting the Americans. In the Philippines, Americans were able to take control of Manila. In Cuba and on the nearby island of Puerto Rico, another Spanish colony, U.S. land forces won relatively easy victories. Leading a group of his own recruits in a bold uphill charge in the San Juan Range above Havana, Colonel Theodore Roosevelt made himself a hero of the brief war and the most famous man in America. His reputation for bravery would become a key factor in his later electoral victories.

Spain asked for peace terms in August and the fighting came to a halt. U.S. troops, hastily recruited and trained, and badly supplied, sometimes with items left over from the Civil War, lost only 460 men on the field of battle, but more than 2,500 to infections, contagious illnesses, and tropical diseases.

In a treaty signed in December and ratified by the U.S. Senate the following February, Spain withdrew all claims to Cuba and turned over the Philippines, Puerto Rico, and the small Pacific island colony of Guam to the United States in return for a payment of $20 million. Although Cuba received its independence, the Platt Amendment, passed by the U.S. Congress in 1901, severely limited its sovereignty. Cuba had to agree to give the United States the right to intervene in any future attempt of another nation to control its affairs, and to accept a perpetual lease on the naval station at Guantánamo Bay.

Except for the lease of the naval station, which persists to this day, the rest of the agreement ended in 1934. Puerto Rico came under U.S. control as a territory and is now a Commonwealth, though not a state. Guam became an unincorporated, organized U.S. territory, and is today the site of many U.S. naval and air force bases. The people of Puerto Rico and Guam are U.S. citizens, but do not vote in Presidential elections.

As soon as the war was over, the United States found itself embroiled in a new conflict. Filipino rebels, angry that the war had brought them not independence but a new colonial ruler, turned from fighting the Spanish to fighting the Americans. A protracted war followed, characterized by atrocities on both sides. U.S. interrogators used unscrupulous methods, such as water torture, to question captured insurgents, justifying their behavior in the name of white racial superiority.

U.S. forces captured the most important rebel leader, Emilio Aguinaldo, in 1901 and declared the islands "pacified" in 1902. Guerrilla warfare in the archipelago continued sporadically over the next decade, killing far more U.S. troops than the Spanish-American War. Total casualties from the Philippines War included more than 4,200 Americans and more than 200,000 Filipinos, mostly civilians. The Philippines became an unincorporated U.S. territory and the site of a number of U.S. military bases. Its people were U.S. nationals, but not U.S. citizens. The Philippines finally became an independent nation in 1946.

SEE ALSO

Imperialism; International relations; Journalism; McKinley, William; Military; Navy, U.S.; Roosevelt, Theodore

FURTHER READING

Musicant, Ivan. *Empire by Default: The Spanish-American War and the Dawn of the American Century.* New York: Henry Holt, 1998.

Schoonover, Thomas David. *Uncle Sam's War of 1898 and the Origins of Globalization.* Lexington: University Press of Kentucky, 2003.

Smith, Joseph. *The Spanish-American War: Conflict in the Caribbean and the Pacific, 1895–1902.* New York: Longman, 1994.

Trask, David F. *The War with Spain in 1898.* New York: Macmillan, 1981.

Sports

BEFORE THE MIDDLE of the 19th century, sports were rough, unorganized, and amateur activities. Men dominated them, both as participants and spectators. With the increase in leisure time created by shorter work hours in the late 1800s, more Americans became interested in sports. By 1900, sports had become organized and in some cases professionalized. The creation of sports teams and the manufacture of sporting goods turned into large commercial enterprises. Moreover, many sports became so respectable that middle-class women could engage in them and even compete in tournaments.

The growth in city populations in the late 1800s made these developments possible. Social reformers began to promote sports as a release from urban tensions and as a means for improving residents' health. Even as sports became permanent features of school curricula, organized sports outside of schools became less accessible to wage earners. Some immigrants who came from countries with sports traditions were able to form ethnic sports clubs. But most workers, including African Americans, were excluded from many organized sports.

The most popular sport was baseball. The sport evolved from rounders, an English game played by gentleman's clubs. As the pressure to field winning teams mounted, American baseball clubs brought in skilled athletes regardless of their social class. Cities began to form clubs, clubs became teams, and club presidents became managers. Audiences grew, prompting entrepreneurs to enclose fields and charge admission. In the 1870s, teams formed regional leagues, began to play championships, and standardized the rules. Baseball journalism increased the sport's popularity. By the 1880s, baseball players were earning salaries.

At first, most spectators were middle-class businessmen and white-collar workers. In the 1870s, tickets cost 50 cents, plus 25 cents for a seat in the stands or 10 cents for one in the bleachers; by 1910, fans were paying a dollar to a dollar and a half for a box seat. This was not cheap (in comparison, admission to an amusement park cost a dime), but Americans loved the speed and split-second timing of the game and were willing to pay. Padded gloves, which appeared in the early 1880s, made players less hesitant to catch balls and the plays more spectacular. When some cities began to allow Sunday games after the turn of the century, and workers got Saturday afternoons off, blue-collar worker attendance rose. In an effort to attract families, entrepreneurs banned liquor and introduced Ladies' Days, hoping that women's presence would have a calming effect on male spectators. In 1910, President William Howard Taft inaugurated the tradition of throwing out the first ball of the season.

Although professional baseball remained a sport identified primarily with male players and spectators, college women also played baseball and

Denton T. "Cy" Young winds up for a pitch in 1908. Young was the first Major League pitcher to throw a perfect game, retiring 27 consecutive batters.

"bloomer girls" teams played exhibition games against men's teams. In 1911, Helene Hathaway Robison Britton inherited the St. Louis Cardinals from her uncle and ran the team for eight years. Although Native Americans and immigrant groups produced big league baseball heroes, the 1867 rules of the National Association of Base Ball Players barred black players and clubs from league membership. A segregated but highly popular Negro League, with its own share of legendary players, lasted until professional baseball was integrated in the late 1940s.

Other popular sports of the period included football, which evolved in 1869 from the English game of rugby. Originally a club sport, football moved into colleges in the 1890s. College administrators hired professional coaches and used the game to increase alumni loyalty. It was a violent game, played without pads or helmets. In one year, 18 students died of injuries. Still, the sport's popularity kept growing, and by the 1890s, it was attracting crowds as large as 30,000 to 40,000. Industrial cities across the Midwest from Ohio to Iowa hired college stars to play in professional leagues. The Intercollegiate Athletic Association of the United States formed in December 1905 to regulate the conduct of college sports and to eliminate brutality and unsportsmanlike behavior. This group later became the National Collegiate Athletic Association.

Many women were avid sports enthusiasts. Women ice skated, sailed and rowed, went horseback riding, climbed mountains, and took part in archery competitions. In the 1890s, they were swept up into the national bicycling craze. Women played croquet, bowls, badminton, lawn tennis, and golf, competing in tournaments in all of those sports. They practiced calisthenics, gymnastics, and swimming, but modesty required them to wear black cotton stockings under short dresses or bloomers.

Women students also played softball, which, like basketball, was a game played by both sexes to remain active during the winter. Women basketball players participated in their first intercollegiate competition in 1896. On the assumption that stiff competition and hard physical exertion harmed women's reproductive organs, recreation experts devised special rules for women's games. Although American men began Olympic participation in the First Olympiad in Athens in 1896, American women participated only unofficially in the Second Olympiad, held in Paris in 1900. Even when official participation of women was finally allowed in 1908, the American Olympic Committee denied women permission to enter unless they wore long skirts.

SEE ALSO
Bicycle; Parks and playgrounds

FURTHER READING

Cahn, Susan K. *Coming on Strong: Gender and Sexuality in Twentieth-Century Women's Sport*. New York: Free Press, 1994.
Riess, Steven A. *Sport in Industrial America, 1850–1920*. Wheeling, Ill.: Harlan Davidson, 1995.
Seymour, Harold. *Baseball: The Early Years*. New York: Oxford University Press, 1960.
Sparkhawk, Ruth M., et al., eds. *American Women in Sport, 1887–1987: A 100-Year Chronology*. Metuchen, N.J.: Scarecrow Press, 1989.

Stanton, Elizabeth Cady

- *Born: Nov. 12, 1815, Johnstown, N.Y.*
- *Education: Troy Female Seminary, graduated 1832*
- *Accomplishments: author, "Declaration of Sentiments," delivered at Seneca Falls Woman's Rights Convention (1848); co-organizer, Women's National Loyal League (1863); president, National Woman Suffrage Association (1869–92); cofounder, International Council of Women (1888); president, National American Woman Suffrage Association (1890–92) author,* The Woman's Bible *(1895)*
- *Died: Oct. 26, 1902, New York, N.Y.*

WHEN WOMAN SUFFRAGE leader Elizabeth Cady Stanton was growing up, two key experiences influenced her. First, she heard stories in her father's law office about how the law discriminated against married women, sometimes depriving them of their property and even custody of their own children. Second, when her only brother died, her grief-stricken father moaned that he wished Elizabeth had been born a boy. Determined to make her father proud, she studied Greek, Latin, and mathematics, subjects usually taught only to boys. Then she insisted on an advanced education at the Female Seminary in Troy, New York.

In 1840, Elizabeth married Henry Brewster Stanton, a journalist and abolitionist. While attending the World's Anti-Slavery Convention with him in London, she was shocked to find that women delegates were excluded from the convention floor. Consulting with Lucretia Mott, a Quaker delegate from Philadelphia, Stanton vowed to respond to the many humiliations that women suffered. In 1848, Mott and Stanton organized the world's first women's rights convention, held in Stanton's home town of Seneca Falls, New York.

At this meeting, Stanton read her "Declaration of Sentiments," which set forth her views on women's subordinate status in American society and called for major reforms, including the right to vote. "We hold these truths to be self-evident," the Declaration began, imitating the opening of the American Declaration of Independence, "that all men and women are created equal; that they are endowed by their Creator with certain inalienable rights." The Declaration then explained precisely how government and society oppressed women, preventing them from exercising their "inalienable rights" and excluding them from the benefits of citizenship.

Stanton devoted the rest of her life to the women's rights cause. The mother of seven children, she did much of the writing, lecturing, and other intellectual work of the campaign, while her lifelong collaborator, Susan B. Anthony, did most of the organizational work. In agitating for women's rights, Stanton called for more liberal divorce laws, professional and educational opportunities for women, independent property rights for married women, dress reform, and, of course, the vote. She testified before

congressional committees on behalf of a constitutional amendment that would guarantee women the right to vote. A short, portly woman with white curls, she charmed audiences with her wit and motherly warmth, but was never able to persuade Congress to pass a resolution in favor of woman suffrage.

In her later years, she worked with Anthony and other suffragists on a multivolume *History of Woman Suffrage,* still the basic source for the history of the movement. One of her last publications, *The Woman's Bible,* estranged her from many of her suffragist colleagues. This book was a scathingly critical commentary on the Bible, which Stanton saw as filled with stories and interpretations that justified woman's subordinate status. She found particularly offensive the treatment in Genesis of woman's creation as a divine afterthought merely to assuage Adam's loneliness. "It is on this allegory that all the enemies of women rest their battering rams, to prove her inferiority," Stanton wrote in the book's opening passages. "Accepting the view that man was prior in the creation," she continued, "some Scriptural writers say that as the woman was of the man, therefore, her position should be one of subjection. Grant it, then as the historical fact is reversed in our day, and the man is now of the woman, shall his place be one of subjection?" Fearing that this book would alienate potential supporters of votes for women, in 1896 the National American Woman Suffrage Association, an organization that Stanton had helped found, adopted a resolution disassociating the organization from it.

When Stanton died at age 86, Anthony grieved deeply. Writing to a colleague, she said, "It seems impossible—that the voice is hushed—that I

Elizabeth Cady Stanton (right) maintained a lifelong friendship with fellow suffrage campaigner Susan B. Anthony. Stanton predicted that equality for woman would bring with it "an entire revolution in all existing institutions."

have longed to hear for 50 years—longed to get her opinion of things—before I knew exactly where I stood." Indeed, while Anthony had been the movement's organizational genius, it was Stanton's voice that had provided its intellectual force.

SEE ALSO

Anthony, Susan Brownell; National American Woman Suffrage Association; Woman suffrage movement; Women's rights movement

FURTHER READING

Banner, Lois. *Elizabeth Cady Stanton, a Radical for Woman's Rights.* Boston: Little, Brown, 1980.
Griffith, Elisabeth. *In Her Own Right: The Life of Elizabeth Cady Stanton.* New York: Oxford University Press, 1984.
Sigerman, Harriet. *Elizabeth Cady Stanton: The Right Is Ours.* New York: Oxford University Press, 2001.

States and statehood

ACCORDING TO the U.S. Constitution, only Congress can admit territories to statehood. Typically, a territory wanting to become a state proposes a constitution, shows that a majority of its voters want statehood, and then proves that it has enough population and resources to support a state government and its share of the federal government. The process begins when a territory petitions Congress for permission to draw up a constitution. Territorial residents must then ratify this constitution and submit it to Congress, which, if it approves, passes a joint resolution declaring the territory a state. The final step is the President's signature.

Between 1889 and 1912, 10 territories became states. North and South Dakota (both formerly part of the Dakota Territory), Montana, and

WANTS TO BE A STATE.

Washington entered the union in 1889. Idaho and Wyoming followed in 1890. These last two states used unconventional means to become states, as they both called constitutional conventions without federal authority. A unique provision of Wyoming's constitution gave women the right to vote, thereby earning Wyoming the nickname "Equality State."

Utah's admission was so controversial that almost 47 years passed between the territory's petition for statehood and its admission. Congress would not approve the petition until the leaders of the territory's majority religion, Mormonism, renounced polygamy, or plural marriage. This renunciation occurred in 1890. After a state constitutional convention in 1895, Congress awarded Utah statehood the following year.

The last admissions to statehood in this period took place in 1907, when lands carved out of Oklahoma and Indian territories formed Oklahoma, and in 1912, with the admissions of New Mexico and Arizona. Controversies surrounded the admission of these last two southwestern states. New Mexico first petitioned for entry in 1850, but southern congressmen blocked the request because the territory's proposed constitution prohibited slavery. Other issues delaying

An 1888 cartoon ridicules frontier aspirations to statehood by depicting a farmer in the Dakota Territory cutting notches in a stick to tally the local population, which consists mostly of animals.

its admission included range wars, Indian uprisings, and disputes over Spanish and Mexican land titles.

In 1912, the United States consisted of 48 contiguous states and would remain in this configuration for more than four decades. Hawaii first petitioned for statehood in 1903 but did not become a state until 1959. Alaska, annexed as a territory in 1867, also earned statehood in 1959.

FURTHER READING

Laney, Garrine P. *Statehood Process of the Fifty States.* New York: Novinka Books, 2002.

Smith, Duane A. *Rocky Mountain West: Colorado, Wyoming, and Montana, 1859–1915.* Albuquerque: University of New Mexico Press, 1992.

Statue of Liberty

DESIGNED BY the sculptor Frédéric Auguste Bartholdi, the Statue of Liberty was a gift from the people of France to the United States in celebration of their shared dedication to the ideals of freedom and democracy. The bronze female figure, dressed in classical robes, was cast in France. Bartholdi shipped it across the ocean in pieces and had it reassembled on Bedloe's Island in New York Harbor. Standing 305 feet above sea level on a granite pedestal constructed by American workmen, the Statue of Liberty was unveiled on October 28, 1886. She raises a flaming torch with her right arm and in her left carries a keystone-shaped tablet with the date of the Declaration of Independence, July 4, 1776, inscribed in Roman numerals. At her feet are broken chains, symbolizing the defeat of slavery.

A plaque on the pedestal displays poet Emma Lazarus's sonnet "The New Colossus." Lazarus, a descendant

In an 1886 drawing, workers clamber up the nearly complete Statue of Liberty. Only the torch and crowned head remain to be installed before the monument's dedication.

of Jewish immigrants, had written the poem to help raise money for the construction of the pedestal. The last five lines of the poem have become a familiar part of the romanticized story of America's immigrant past.

> Give me your tired, your poor,
> Your huddled masses yearning to breathe free,
> The wretched refuse of your teeming shore.
> Send these, the homeless, tempest-tossed to me,
> I lift my lamp beside the golden door!

The statue, facing the entrance of the harbor, became the symbol of freedom and opportunity for millions of immigrants entering the United States, who sailed by her on their way to the immigrant processing station at Ellis Island. Today, the statue is a national monument in the care of the National Park Service and a popular tourist attraction.

SEE ALSO

Ellis Island; Immigration

FURTHER READING

Dillon, Wilton S., and Neil G. Kotler, eds. *The Statue of Liberty Revisited: Making a Universal Symbol.* Washington, D.C.: Smithsonian Institution Press, 1994.

Moreno, Barry. *The Statue of Liberty Encyclopedia.* New York: Simon & Schuster, 2000.

The New York Public Library and the Comité officiel franco-américain pour la célèbration du centenaire de la Statue de la Liberté, with Pierre Provoyeur and June Hargrove. *Liberty: The French-American Statue in Art and History.* New York: Perennial Library, 1986.

Strikes

STRIKES, OR WORK stoppages designed to compel an employer to meet workers' demands, occur for many reasons. The most common cause is a dispute over wages. Workers also sometimes walk off the job and picket factories in order to defend their control over a work process, or to oppose contract terms, such as 12-hour shifts. They also strike to protest unsatisfactory workplace conditions or to demand that the employer recognize a union. In the past, workers sometimes called strikes to exclude minorities or women from the workplace.

During the Gilded Age and Progressive Era, as the labor movement grew rapidly, so did the frequency, size, and intensity of strikes. Workers found little sympathy in the population at large, however. In addition, the government for many years regarded unions as "conspiracies," which made them illegal under U.S. law. This view enabled officials to ask courts, in many disputes, to issue injunctions to stop union activity. The penalties for continuing strikes in defiance of a court order were lengthy jail sentences and heavy fines.

Most employers wanted to run their businesses traditionally, making all the decisions about hiring and firing, hours, wages, and conditions, without any bargaining with unions over workers' rights. What was more, an abundance of immigrant labor allowed employers to ignore their workers' demands. They could easily recruit replacement workers (scabs, or strikebreakers) if their employees complained.

As workers grew more frustrated, both union-organized and spontaneous strikes became more widespread, with a strike in one industry infecting others through sympathy strikes. Some strikes led to nationwide work stoppages, serious violence, and even deaths.

Starting in the 1870s, a series of long and bitter strikes on the railroads, in the New England textile industry, and in the anthracite coal mines drew national attention to the disputes between business owners and their workers. As the industrial crisis deepened between 1880 and 1900, 24,000 strikes took place. In 1886 alone, there were 1,500 strikes, involving more than a million workers.

The rising violence of strikes terrified many Americans, who feared that strikes were the forerunner of social revolution. Because such fears were widespread, state and federal governments became increasingly involved in the struggle between employers and unions. Between 1875 and 1910, government officials called out state troops nearly 500 times to deal with labor unrest. Government intervention in strikes during this period was almost all on the side of the employer, though usually undertaken in the name of keeping public order. Increasingly, factory owners asked for, and won, state and federal court injunctions against strikers.

Two strikers walk a New York City picket line during a massive garment workers' protest that brought more than 20,000 women wage earners into the streets in 1909 and 1910.

Government intervention to restore order and enforce employers' control was a key factor in the Homestead and Pullman strikes, two of the most notorious strikes of the 1890s. The strike at Homestead, Pennsylvania, pitted steel workers against the Carnegie Steel Company in 1892, and the 1894 strike in Pullman, Illinois, starting with workers employed by the Pullman Railroad Car factory, spread to railroad workers all over the country. Both strikes led to disorder, violence, and deaths.

A series of metal mining strikes in the Rocky Mountains climaxed with the involvement of the U.S. Army. Most notorious of these was the strike at the Colorado Fuel and Iron Company in Ludlow, Colorado, in 1914. When the company refused to recognize the miners' union, an affiliate of the United Mine Workers, the strikers moved out of the company town into a tent city in the foothills, where they were eventually routed by Colorado state troops.

The soldiers set fire to the tents and machine-gunned people trying to escape. Twenty-one people died, including 11 children. Further violence induced President Woodrow Wilson to send in the U.S. Army, which crushed the strike. A congressional inquiry and

public revulsion at the violence helped pass laws favorable to labor in the following years, such as the Clayton Antitrust Act of 1914. Declaring that "The labor of a human being is not a commodity or article of commerce," the act gave legal sanction to labor, agricultural, and other groups organized "for mutual benefit."

Well into the first decade of the 20th century, unions continued to resist organizing women and minorities and often tried to have them excluded from the workplace. Even when unions ignored or excluded them, however, women and immigrant ethnic minorities struck to demand their rights. Their presence was especially notable in strikes in the textile, garment, and transportation industries. During the bitter winter of 1909–10, women shirtmakers on strike in New York finally gained recognition and assistance from the International Ladies' Garment Workers' Union, whose members made women's clothes. The union soon began enrolling women in large numbers.

Women, immigrants, and families also struck to protest pay cuts in the textile industries of the Northeast. In Lawrence, Massachusetts, in 1912, where state laws had cut workers' hours, the textile companies cut pay and sped up the machines to compensate for lost time. Twenty thousand workers of 40 nationalities turned out on strike, half of them young women aged 14 to 18. "We want bread and roses, too," they cried—meaning they wanted a life of beauty and dignity as well as mere survival. The Industrial Workers of the World (IWW) organized the strike and sent a number of young children into temporary foster care in New York City to protect them from violence and the threat of starvation. When police attacked and brutalized one group of departing children, public opinion turned against the mill owners. The workers actually went back to work with pay raises and overtime pay.

A prolonged 1913 strike in Paterson, New Jersey, among immigrant silk workers—men, women, and children—was a defeat for labor and for the IWW, which organized the strike to protest a doubling of the number of looms each worker had to tend. The employers exploited the ethnic divisions among the workers, turning them against each other, and the strike fell apart.

Labor unions were not eager to encourage strikes, which could be costly and ineffective and generate bad publicity. Moreover, the courts and government troops frequently defeated striking workers. Trying to avoid strikes, unions increasingly looked to arbitration or collective bargaining—negotiating with employers about wages, work rules, and grievances—to settle differences. By the second decade of the 20th century, many unions were avoiding strikes through mediation, or turning their problems over to the Federal Mediation and Conciliation Service, established in 1914.

During World War I, leaders of the American Federation of Labor promised to refrain from strikes, but many unions found it hard to resist the opportunity to press their claims in a time of labor shortage. Labor agitation peaked in 1919, when 4 million workers went on strike. Ultimately, the surge in militancy was checked by the Red Scare of 1919, a period of mass hysteria over suspected revolutionaries, when union activity was equated with the influence of foreign radicalism. When strikes resumed during the Depression of the 1930s, working people found government more inclined to

sympathize with them than at any previous time in U.S. history. By 1938, the federal government had implemented the Fair Labor Standards Act, which provided minimum standards for both wages and overtime hours, regulated child labor, and promoted equal pay for equal work.

SEE ALSO

American Federation of Labor; Homestead strike (1892); Industrial Workers of the World; International Ladies' Garment Workers' Union; Labor unions; Pullman strike (1894); Red Scare (1919–20); United Mine Workers of America; Wilson, Woodrow T.; World War I

FURTHER READING

Babson, Steven. *The Unfinished Struggle.* Lanham, Md.: Rowman & Littlefield, 1999.
Brecher, Jeremy, and Manning Marable. *Strike.* Rev. ed. Boston: South End Press, 1997.
Dubofsky, Melvin, and Foster R. Dulles. *Labor in America: A History.* 6th ed. Wheeling, Ill.: Harlan Davidson, 1999.
Zinn, Howard. *Three Strikes: Miners, Musicians, Salesgirls, and the Fighting Spirit of Labor's Last Century.* Boston: Beacon, 2002.

Suffrage

SUFFRAGE AND *franchise* both mean the "right to vote." During the Gilded Age and Progressive Era, American women made progress toward winning the right to vote but did not secure a constitutional amendment guaranteeing it until 1920. At the same time, many African American males in the South found their right to vote increasingly curtailed and eventually eliminated. Similarly, male immigrants, who in previous years could vote just by declaring their intention to become citizens, also experienced growing suffrage restrictions.

Only the story of women's growing access to the franchise shows an expansion in democracy during the latter 1800s. By 1890, 19 states allowed women to vote on school issues, and 3 also permitted them to vote on tax and bond issues. The territory of Wyoming awarded full suffrage to women in 1869, and when the territory became a state in 1890, women retained that right. Women had achieved full suffrage in only 19 of the 48 states by 1920, however. That year saw the ratification of the 19th Amendment, granting the vote to all women citizens over the age of 21.

The situation for African Americans was quite different. In 1870, the 15th Amendment made discrimination against voters on the basis of race or "previous condition of servitude" illegal. As increasing numbers of black freedmen voted, however, white southerners did all that they could to disfranchise them. At first, they used fraud and intimidation, throwing out ballots cast by black men or threatening violence if they voted. Another technique was the "all-white" primary. Declaring itself a private club, the Democratic party—the chief, and sometimes the only, political party in the South—required that all of its members be white. This provision eliminated any black person who sought to vote in the party's primary elections. Yet other techniques to disfranchise black voters included a two-year residency requirement, which kept sharecroppers and tenants from registering, as they tended to move frequently. Some districts levied poll taxes of one to two dollars a year per voter, payable months in advance along with any other missed taxes; others instituted literacy tests, with local white registrars deciding who could understand certain passages in the U.S. Constitution.

During the Gilded Age, nativists advanced legislation to restrict the immigration of certain foreign groups,

In this 1884 cartoon, Irish American and African American men, who are allowed to vote, deny admission to the polls to a Chinese American man and suffragist Susan B. Anthony.

especially Asians. At the same time, some progressives advocated increasing restrictions on immigrants' right to vote. Such restrictions, electoral reformers thought, would protect American democracy from uninformed, and possibly illiterate, voters who could be easily manipulated by corrupt politicians. Among electoral reforms was the secret ballot, which replaced voice voting. Although paper ballots and private voting booths made fraud more difficult, the secret ballot also kept individuals who could not read English away from the polls.

Other suffrage reforms included stricter registration procedures and, in some states, literacy tests. After 1874, states began to repeal legislation that awarded the suffrage to immigrants who declared an intention to become citizens. Other states challenged immigrant claims of citizenship, requiring them to show their naturalization papers or wait 90 days after naturalization before they could vote.

In short, while access to the suffrage expanded for white women during this period, southern black men and immigrants experienced increasing difficulties in voting. Mechanisms for curtailing voting rights would remain in the code books of many states until after World War II, when both the U.S. Supreme Court and, finally, the U.S. Congress would declare them illegal.

SEE ALSO

African Americans; Immigration; Nativism; 19th Amendment; Political machines; Voting; Woman suffrage movement

FURTHER READING

Keyssar, Alexander. *The Right to Vote: The Contested History of Democracy in the United States.* New York: Basic Books, 2000.

Sumner, William Graham

- *Born: Oct. 30, 1840, Paterson, N.J.*
- *Education: Yale College, B.A., 1863; studied at the University of Göttingen (Germany) and Oxford University (England), 1863–66*
- *Accomplishments: ordained Episcopal priest (1867); professor of political and social science, Yale University (1872–1909); author,* Folkways *(1907) and* Science of Society *(1927)*
- *Died: Apr. 12, 1910, Englewood, N.J.*

IN AN AGE marked by numerous social reform movements, sociologist and political scientist William Graham Sumner was a major dissenting voice. He believed in individual liberty and innate inequalities among men. He was a supporter of laissez-faire capitalism, opposing government intervention in business and the economy and arguing that public money should not be used to provide a safety net of assistance programs for the poor.

Sumner grew up in a working-class family, graduated from Yale in 1863, then studied at two European universities and returned to teach classics at Yale. He became an Episcopal priest in 1867 and served briefly in that capacity, but he resumed his academic career when Yale hired him in 1872 as a professor of political and social science.

Maintaining that society was best served by a market economy that operated without government interference, Sumner opposed protective tariffs, or taxes on foreign goods, and public programs to relieve the suffering of the unemployed, even during times of nationwide depressions. He saw wealth and power as indications of virtue and believed that the misery of the poor resulted from individual or racial inferiority, not social injustice.

In holding such views he allied himself with Social Darwinists, thinkers who explained racial differences and social inequalities by applying the findings of English evolutionary biologist Charles Darwin to human society. Adapting Darwin's ideas about natural selection, or the competitive process by which plant and animal species evolve, Sumner argued that the poor were inferior creatures whom government should not help to pass on their "unfitness" to their offspring, and that government attempts to ease social inequality would only penalize society's most productive members—the middle classes and the wealthy—while elevating the "undeserving" poor at their expense. As he wrote in an essay published in 1911, "if we should try by any measures of arbitrary interference and assistance to relieve the victims of social pressure from the calamity of their position we should only offer premiums to folly and vice and extend them further."

Sumner's books and essays were influential among many American champions of laissez-faire, Social Darwinism, and eugenics, or the use of selective breeding to improve the human race. He also originated the concept of ethnocentrism, a term we now use to describe attitudes of superiority about one's own racial or ethnic group in comparison with others.

SEE ALSO

Laissez-faire; Social Darwinism; Sociology

FURTHER READING

Curtis, Bruce. *William Graham Sumner.* Boston: Twayne, 1981.
Hofstadter, Richard. *Social Darwinism in American Thought.* 1955. Reprint, Boston: Beacon, 1983.
Sumner, William Graham. *On Liberty, Society, and Politics: The Essential Essays of William Graham Sumner.* Edited by Robert C. Bannister. Indianapolis, Ind.: Liberty Fund, 1992.

Supreme Court, U.S.

BETWEEN 1880 AND 1920, American presidents appointed 24 justices to the Supreme Court. President William Howard Taft named 6 of these, more than any of his predecessors. The three chief justices of the period were Morrison Waite, who served from 1874 to 1888; his successor, Melvin Fuller, who served until 1910; and Edward White, who held the position from 1910 to 1921. Oliver Wendell Holmes, Jr., who was appointed by Theodore Roosevelt in 1902, and Louis D. Brandeis—the Court's first Jewish justice, appointed by Woodrow Wilson in 1916—were among the Court's most distinguished members, noted for the brilliance of their opinions. All of the justices were male and white; most had been lawyers or statesmen. During this period, the justices began hiring law school graduates as clerks, although few other aspects of the Court changed from previous decades.

In general, the Court's decisions during this period were pro-business, unsympathetic to labor, and restrictive of civil rights. In almost all cases dealing with the regulation of business, the Court took a laissez-faire (French for "let things happen") approach, declaring unconstitutional most of the government's attempts to regulate business. In 1877, the Court allowed the state of Illinois to fix rates for operators of grain elevators (*Munn* v. *Illinois*), arguing that states may regulate grain operators "when such regulation becomes necessary for the public good." In *Wabash, St. Louis & Pacific Railway Company* v. *Illinois* (1886), however, the Court ruled that states cannot regulate interstate railroads. This decision prompted Congress to pass the Interstate Commerce Act of 1887, which subjected the railroads to federal regulation, but then the Court denied jurisdiction over railroad rates to the Interstate Commerce Commission.

With another pro-business decision in 1886 (*Santa Clara County* v. *Southern Pacific Railroad Company*), the Court declared corporations to be "persons" who cannot be deprived of liberty or property (including their profits) without due process of law. This decision opened the door to a host of corporate abuses. In 1890, in order to stop price fixing and other anticompetitive measures in interstate commerce, Congress passed the Sherman Antitrust Act, which declared illegal every trust (business combination), contract, or conspiracy that restrained interstate or foreign trade.

The Court responded in 1895 with three important decisions favorable to business. The first, *United States* v. *E. C. Knight Company,* prevented the government from breaking up the sugar monopoly. The second, *In re Debs,* permitted employers to get a

The U.S. Supreme Court in 1916. This court, which remained unchanged until 1922, included two of the most distinguished jurists in Supreme Court history: Oliver Wendell Holmes, second from right, bottom row, and Louis Dembitz Brandeis, top left.

court injunction against strikers when a strike interfered with federal commerce or the delivery of the mail. The third, *Pollock* v. *Farmers' Loan and Trust Company,* declared the federal income tax unconstitutional. Congress had to pass a constitutional amendment, the 16th, in 1913, in order to make such a tax legal.

In the early 1900s, most notably in *Northern Securities Company* v. *United States* (1904) and two cases from 1911 (*Standard Oil Company* v. *United States* and *United States* v. *American Tobacco Company*), the Court did uphold government efforts to break up monopolies that restrained commerce. Later decisions concerning relations between workers and employers, however, continued the Court's pro-business rulings. In *Lochner* v. *New York* (1905), the Court protected bakery owners by preventing New York State from controlling their employees' hours. In his dissent, Oliver Wendell Holmes argued strongly for the right of legislative bodies to pass laws that reflect the people's will.

Then, in 1908, thanks to a vigorous presentation of facts by lawyer Louis Brandeis and the National Consumers' League that long hours of work in laundries injured women's health, the Court allowed a state to regulate working hours for women only (*Muller* v. *Oregon*). This decision eventually opened the way for protective labor legislation for both sexes. Other decisions of the era were less clearly pro-labor. In *Adair* v. *United States,* also in 1908, the Court prevented Congress from outlawing so-called "yellow-dog" contracts, or contracts forbidding union membership, which employers used to fire labor activists. And in 1918, the Court declared the 1916 federal Child Labor Act unconstitutional.

The act (named Keating-Owen, after its sponsors) had prohibited the interstate shipment of goods produced by child labor. The act was actually a clever strategy to discourage manufacturers from hiring children, since they would lose profits if they could not ship child-made goods out of the state in which they were produced. The Court ruled that, since "production" was not "commerce," Congress had no power under the Interstate Commerce Act to regulate such goods. Justice Holmes dissented. Referring to federal laws prohibiting the sale of "strong drink," he failed to see why Congress was powerless to regulate "against the product of ruined lives," that is, against "the evil of premature and excessive child labor."

While the Supreme Court occasionally moved beyond laissez-faire economics to allow federal regulation of the economy, on race and civil rights it remained consistently conservative. In 1883, it declared unconstitutional the Civil Rights Act of 1875, which forbade racial discrimination in public accommodations. In *Plessy* v. *Ferguson* (1896), the Court affirmed that "separate but equal" facilities for blacks and whites were legal, a decision deplored by African Americans and others seeking racial equality at the time. The lone dissenter in *Plessy,* Justice John M. Harlan, appointed by

Rutherford B. Hayes in 1877, protested that distinctions made on the basis of race were unconstitutional.

During World War I, civil liberties issues took more of the Court's attention. In 1917, Congress passed the Espionage Act, outlawing "reports" beneficial to the enemy, acts that might cause mutiny among the armed forces, and any obstruction to the recruitment of enlisted men. Three decisions in 1919 upheld this act. In *Schenck* v. *United States*, which concerned the arrest of a socialist who opposed the draft, Holmes affirmed an individual's right of free speech but restricted it in cases where the speech poses a "clear and present danger" to the nation.

In *Frohwerk* v. *United States*, the Court ruled against a pro-German newspaper editor who published articles against the war. And finally, in *Debs* v. *United States*, the Court allowed the imprisonment of labor leader Eugene V. Debs for advocating opposition to the war. Even though the wording of the law was vague, the Court upheld the 1918 Sedition Act, which made "disloyal" speech or writing a crime. Both Brandeis and Holmes dissented in *Abrams* v. *United States* (1919), saying that since the defendant's distribution of pamphlets critical of U.S. policy toward the communist revolution in Russia posed no "clear and present danger," he was not guilty of sedition.

SEE ALSO

African Americans; Brandeis, Louis Dembitz; Commerce; Debs, Eugene Victor; Holmes, Oliver Wendell, Jr.; Labor unions; Laissez-faire; *Muller* v. *Oregon* (1908); National Consumers' League; *Plessy* v. *Ferguson* (1896); Regulation; 16th Amendment; Taft, William Howard; World War I

FURTHER READING

Bailey, Mark Warren. *Guardians of the Moral Order: The Legal Philosophy of the Supreme Court, 1860–1910.* Dekalb: Northern Illinois University Press, 2004.
Hall, Kermit L., ed. *The Oxford Companion to the Supreme Court.* 2nd ed. New York: Oxford University Press, 2005.
Irons, Peter H. *A People's History of the Supreme Court.* New York: Viking, 1999.
Patrick, John J. *The Supreme Court of the United States: A Student Companion.* 3rd ed. New York: Oxford University Press, 2006.
Semonche, John E. *Charting the Future: The Supreme Court Responds to a Changing Society, 1890–1920.* Westport, Conn.: Greenwood, 1978.

Taft, William Howard

- *Born: Sept. 15, 1857, Cincinnati, Ohio*
- *Education: Yale College, B.A., 1878; Cincinnati School of Law, LL.B., 1880*
- *Accomplishments: U.S. solicitor general (1890–92); chair, Philippines Commission (1900); governor of the Philippines (1901–4); U.S. secretary of war (1904–8); President of the United States (1909–13); chief justice of the United States (1921–30)*
- *Died: Mar. 8, 1930, Washington, D.C.*

WILLIAM HOWARD TAFT, 27th President of the United States, did not aspire to be President. His goal was to be chief justice, an ambition he finally realized eight years after leaving the White House, when President Warren Harding appointed him to the Supreme Court. As the only American who was both a President and a chief justice, Taft was the only former President to administer the oath of office to future Presidents.

Taft grew up in Cincinnati, son of a financially comfortable and politically prominent family. He graduated from Yale and from law school in Cincinnati and worked in Ohio as a journalist, prosecutor, tax collector, and judge. A man of huge girth, Taft had to have chairs and bathtubs made to accommodate his size. In 1886 he married an Ohio socialite named Helen Herron. They had three children. Taft's sons, grandsons, and grandsons, and great grandsons would all follow him into politics and public service.

In 1890, President Benjamin Harrison appointed Taft solicitor general, a high-ranking position in the Justice Department. Taft moved from that position to a seat on a federal circuit court. In 1900, after the Spanish-American War, President William McKinley appointed Taft to head a commission on the Philippines, a former Spanish colony that had come under U.S. protection as part of the post-war settlement. U.S. troops were fighting a guerrilla war against Filipino rebels, and Taft's job was to engineer a peaceful transition from military to civilian government. Although the Philippines did not achieve full independence until after World War II, Taft's work as civil governor helped to improve relations between the United States and the former colony. After McKinley's assassination, President Theodore Roosevelt offered Taft a seat on the Supreme Court, but he declined in order to keep working on his task in the Philippines. In 1904, he agreed to return to Washington to become secretary of war in Roosevelt's cabinet.

In 1908, with Roosevelt's backing, Taft won the Republican Presidential nomination. He defeated Democrat William Jennings Bryan, who had lost two previous Presidential races to William McKinley. Progressives who

had favored Taft's election said, "Roosevelt has cut enough hay. Taft is the man to put it into the barn." They meant that Roosevelt had initiated a number of new programs and changes to the country's laws and it was time for Taft to make sure they were all put into action.

As President, Taft had pledged to carry on Roosevelt's program of progressive legislation. He fulfilled that promise, pursuing some 90 antitrust cases to break up big corporations that were unfairly squeezing out small businesses. He supported the 16th Amendment, which allowed the federal government to collect income taxes. He was less enthusiastic about the 17th Amendment, which provided for the election of U.S. Senators by popular vote, rather than selection by state legislatures, but it passed during his administration. He was not able to fulfill promises of tariff reform, which would have reduced the import taxes on certain foreign goods so as to make those goods cheaper for American consumers. Farmers demanded tariff reform and big businesses always fought it. Taft had to bow to pressure from business interests connected with his own Republican Party.

Taft became entangled in a party crisis over conservation involving his Secretary of the Interior, Richard Ballinger. Ballinger had opened some public lands in the Alaskan wilderness to private coal mining interests. Forest Service Director, Gifford Pinchot, a Roosevelt appointee, was outraged at Ballinger's disposal of lands that were supposed to be protected under U.S. conservation laws. When Pinchot publicly denounced Ballinger, Taft fired Pinchot for insubordination. The firing placed Taft at odds with the "Insurgents," Republican members of Congress who wanted more progressive legislation and were disappointed at Taft's failure to reform tar-

William Howard Taft attends a 1910 baseball game in Washington, D.C. Taft was the first President to mark the start of the baseball season by throwing a ceremonial first pitch.

iffs. The Insurgents took control of the House Rules Committee and managed to block many of Taft's initiatives. In four years in office, however, Taft was able to reserve more public lands and bring more antitrust suits than Roosevelt had done in eight. He also supported the founding of the Children's Bureau, a federal agency concerned with the welfare of children, and the passage of the Mann-Elkins Act (1910), which brought telephone and telegraph rates under the control of the Interstate Commerce Commission.

In conducting foreign policy, however, Taft lacked his predecessor's assertiveness. He wanted only to maintain trading relationships with Asia through the open-door policy and to assure peace and stability in Latin America. As for international relations in general, Taft preferred "substituting dollars for bullets." By this he meant creating orderly societies abroad by increasing U.S. investment in foreign economies rather than trying to subdue unruly countries through military action. Such an approach, Taft said, "appeals alike to idealistic humanitarian sentiments, to the dictates of sound policy and strategy, and to legitimate commercial aims." In other words, it pleased public opinion and made money for U.S. investors.

"Dollar diplomacy" did not succeed as well as Taft had hoped. It increased the level of U.S. financial involvement abroad but not always with profitable results. It created enemies, both in Asia and in Latin America, but especially in the Caribbean and Central America, where local revolutionary movements arose to oppose (and expel) American business entrepreneurs and the paramilitary soldiers they hired to defend their operations.

By 1912, Taft had become less popular than Roosevelt, and he had lost the former president's friendship. Even without Roosevelt's support, Taft's followers were able to control the Republican convention and win him re-nomination for President. Roosevelt supporters responded by running their candidate under the banner of the Progressive party (nicknamed the Bull Moose party). Roosevelt and Taft split the Republican vote, allowing New Jersey governor Woodrow Wilson to win a lopsided electoral vote victory. Later, during his years on the Supreme Court (1921–30), Taft served with dignity and distinction. One of his most significant accomplishments was his advocacy of the Judges Act (1925), which empowered the Court to give precedence to cases of national importance. Taft's role on the Supreme Court was so important to him that he claimed he did not even remember his time as President. He died just five weeks after his retirement from the Court.

SEE ALSO

Bryan, William Jennings; Conservation; Imperialism; International affairs; Harrison, Benjamin; McKinley, William; Pinchot, Gifford; Presidency; Progressive Party; Roosevelt, Theodore; Seventeenth Amendment; Sixteenth Amendment; Spanish American War; Wilson, Woodrow T.

FURTHER READING

Anderson, Judith Icke. *William Howard Taft: An Intimate History*. New York: Norton, 1981.
Benson, Michael. *William H. Taft*. Minneapolis: Lerner, 2005.

Tammany Hall

TAMMANY HALL was the name of New York City's Democratic political machine, an informal organization designed to keep parties in power. Incorporated in 1789 as a social club

On this 1889 cover of the humor magazine Puck, the Tammany Tiger, symbol of New York City's powerful Democratic political machine, tries to hide his illegal patronage schemes under a cloak of virtue, pictured as a monk's cowl.

called the Society of St. Tammany, or Columbian Order, it became the focus of local Democratic party activity during the early 19th century. After the Civil War, Democrats used the club's networks to dominate city politics while raking in bribes and kickbacks on local building contracts. William Marcy Tweed, Tammany's "boss" between 1867 and 1871, amassed a huge fortune through his Tammany connections until he was brought down, in part, by Thomas Nast's cartoon depictions of the greed and corruption of the "Tammany Tiger."

Even after Tweed's fall, Tammany remained powerful through its deep roots in the city's working-class community, especially among the city's Irish. Through a system of "contracts," the club's ward leaders—who were usually local saloon or hotel keepers loyal to the current boss—handed out food baskets, fuel, jobs, and other favors to the needy. If someone got in trouble with the law, ward leaders put in a good word at the local police station or courthouse, where they always had powerful friends. On holidays, they organized neighborhood picnics, boat excursions, and parades. They also boosted neighborhood recreational life by sponsoring saloons, dance halls, gambling houses, and even brothels.

Upset by many of these activities, middle-class New Yorkers mounted repeated efforts to undercut or destroy the club's influence. Occasionally, they defeated Tammany-sponsored political candidates. In 1901, reformers elected former Columbia University president Seth Low as mayor, thereby causing the fall of Tweed's successor, Tammany boss Richard Croker. In 1913, Tammany's opponents put progressive lawyer John Purroy Mitchel in the mayor's office. Neither Low nor Mitchel served more than one term. Tammany reached the height of its powers under boss Charles F. Murphy, who in 1918 saw one of his loyal followers, Alfred E. Smith, elected governor of New York State. Despite intermittent later defeats at the polls, Tammany continued to dominate New York Democratic party politics until the 1960s.

SEE ALSO

Democratic party; Government reform; Machine politics; Politics

FURTHER READING

Allen, Oliver E. *The Tiger: the Rise and Fall of Tammany Hall.* Reading, Mass.: Addison-Wesley, 1993.
Riordon, William L. *Plunkitt of Tammany Hall: A Series of Very Plain Talks on Very Practical Politics.* Edited by Terrence J. McDonald. Boston: Bedford/St. Martin's, 1994.

Taxes and tariffs

IN THE EARLY 20th century, the source of government taxes shifted. In earlier decades, the federal government earned most of its income from sales of land and from tariffs, or taxes on imported goods and products. The 16th Amendment, ratified in 1913, legalized a federal income tax. From then on, taxes on personal incomes and corporate profits provided an increasing amount of the government's financial base.

In the previous century, to meet the expenses of the Civil War, the federal government not only raised tariffs but passed special excise taxes on consumer goods, licenses, corporations, legal documents, inheritances, and even incomes. After the war, most of these taxes expired or were phased out, but Republicans continued to support high tariffs. Tobacco and alcohol taxes were popular among moralists because such taxes seemed to punish people who used "sinful" products. But as the size and cost of government increased, a coalition of Democrats, populists, and progressives put pressure on the government to lower tariffs and assess a tax on incomes.

The movement away from a reliance on tariffs and toward an income tax aroused intense political debate. Americans were deeply divided over the benefits and disadvantages of tariffs. These special duties on imports brought in considerable income and also protected domestic industries from foreign competition. At the same time, however, they raised the price of imported goods and thus put a burden on some consumers. Southern planters and western farmers, in particular, often protested high tariffs because they raised the price of manufactured goods imported from abroad. At the same time high tariffs depressed the agricultural export market, since foreign manufacturers were selling fewer finished goods to the United States and thus had less ready cash to buy American produce. In 1890, Congress passed a high tariff named for William McKinley, then a powerful Republican congressmen and later President. Hurtful to farmers, the McKinley tariff gave impetus to the Populist movement.

A progressive income tax—that is, a tax with rates that rise along with income—passed Congress in 1894, but the following year the Supreme Court ruled that the Constitution forbids all "direct taxes" unless assessed in proportion to the population. Over the next decade, the Court stepped back from this view, but in the meantime, Congress got around constitutional objections by redefining the income tax as an "indirect" instead of a "direct" tax. After the ratification of the 16th Amendment in 1913, which gave the federal government the power to collect an income tax, a Democratic majority in Congress passed the Underwood-Simmons Tariff, which both restored pre–Civil War tariff levels and instituted the nation's first income tax. Income tax rates were at first so low that 95 percent of Americans did not earn enough to be required to pay. But, supplemented by taxes on corporate profits above a "normal" rate of return, income taxes provided President Woodrow Wilson with sufficient revenues to fund U.S. participation in World War I.

At the same time as the federal government was moving toward an income tax, state governments were also changing their methods of raising revenue. In the past, state and local governments taxed personal property and real estate. The value of personal property was hard to assess, however. Over time, local governments moved away from personal property taxes and toward a greater reliance on real estate, which was easier to assess. They also adopted special taxes, such as those on sales and licenses. In 1911, Wisconsin adopted the first state income tax.

SEE ALSO
Commerce; 16th Amendment

FURTHER READING
Brownlee, W. Elliot. *Federal Taxation in America: A Short History.* New York: Cambridge University Press, 1996.

Reitano, Joanne. *The Tariff Question in the Gilded Age: The Great Debate of 1888.* University Park: Pennsylvania State University Press, 1994.

Weisman, Steven R. *The Great Tax Wars: Lincoln to Wilson: The Fierce Battles over Money and Power that Transformed the Nation.* New York: Simon & Schuster, 2002.

Taylor, Frederick Winslow

- *Born: Mar. 20, 1856, Philadelphia, Pa.*
- *Education: Stevens Institute of Technology, engineering degree, B.S., 1883*
- *Accomplishments: author,* Principles of Scientific Management *(1911) and* Shop Management *(1911)*
- *Died: Mar. 21, 1915, Philadelphia, Pa.*

IN THE EARLY 20th century, Frederick Winslow Taylor emerged as the world's most influential thinker on the subject of worker efficiency. He began his career as a machinist and toolmaker. Working for the Midvale Steel Company, he rose from the position of shop clerk to positions of ever greater responsibility, including research director and chief engineer.

At Midvale, Taylor began to study the relationship between the time workers spent on certain tasks and their productivity. Using a stopwatch, he timed every aspect of workers' movements as they performed certain tasks. He also experimented with the weights and sizes of tools in order to find the most effective combinations. After determining the best way of performing tasks, he offered workers higher wages if they followed his plan and met his production goals. Eventually, Taylor added planning offices to his management program. In these offices, coordinating supervisors watched over all aspects of the production process, including the move-ment of materials, the speed of work, control of product quality, repairs, and shop floor discipline, such as the prevention of loafing or talking on the job. Taylor called his ideas "scientific management." Later his system would become known as Taylorism.

Not everyone appreciated the benefits of Taylorism. Workers despised the efficiency experts who timed their motions and told them how to do their jobs. Moreover, because the efficient use of workers could enable factories to achieve greater productivity with fewer employees, workers feared that Taylor's ideas could result in layoffs. Some managers and industrialists also resented Taylor for his criticisms of their traditional business methods.

In 1910, Taylor became famous when lawyer and future Supreme Court justice Louis Brandeis used his ideas to argue against a rise in railroad rates. As a result of the Mann-Elkins Act of 1910, railroads had to prove to the Interstate Commerce Commission (ICC) that they needed higher rates. Brandeis convinced the ICC that the railroads could actually lower their rates if they used their workers more efficiently. To the fury of railroad entrepreneurs, the ICC turned down the rate increase.

Widely sought out as a lecturer after this landmark case, Taylor won international renown for technical inventions and consulting work. Despite accusations that Taylor dehumanized work by making it mechanical, Taylorism gained wide acceptance in many industries during the 1920s.

Frederick Winslow Taylor promoted time-management studies to increase industrial efficiency. "A big day's work for a big day's pay" became a slogan in scientific management, a field he created.

SEE ALSO

Brandeis, Louis Dembitz; Industry; Labor

FURTHER READING

Gabor, Andrea. *The Capitalist Philosophers: The Geniuses of Modern Business—Their Lives, Times, and Ideas.* New York: Times Books, 2000.

Haber, Samuel. *Efficiency and Uplift: Scientific Management in the Progressive Era, 1890–1920.* Chicago: University of Chicago Press, 1964.

Kanigel, Robert. *The One Best Way: Frederick Winslow Taylor and the Enigma of Efficiency.* New York: Viking, 1997.

Nelson, Daniel. *Frederick W. Taylor and the Rise of Scientific Management.* Madison: University of Wisconsin Press, 1980.

Telephone and telegraph

MODERN COMMUNICATIONS began in the 1840s with Samuel F. B. Morse's invention of the telegraph, which carried messages along electrical wires. The telegraph worked by spelling out messages in a coded alphabet that represented each letter as a combination of dashes and dots (long and short electrical impulses). The pulses, tapped in by hand, traveled through wires; telegraphers on the receiving end translated them back into words, printed them on paper, and then sent them out for delivery. Telegraphy was most closely associated with railroad scheduling, but business, industry, the military, and newspapers increasingly came to rely on it. Early in the 20th century, inventors developed wireless telegraphy, which used radio waves rather than wires to transmit messages to ships at sea. Modern communications have abandoned, most forms of telegraphy.

While telegraphy was in use, many 19th-century inventors were also experimenting with improved methods of wire communication, including systems for transmitting speech. In 1876 and 1877, Alexander Graham Bell received patents for the telephone, which transformed voice vibrations into electrical signals. These signals traveled along a wire to a receiving device that turned the signals back into speech sounds.

Beginning to market his invention in 1877, Bell had 3,000 telephones in service by the end of the year and nearly 50,000 by 1880. By the turn of the century, Americans were using more than a million telephones, and by 1910, there were 10 million telephones in service around the world, with 7 million of them in the United States. Bell's company grew so large and wealthy that by 1909 it was able to purchase a controlling interest in Western Union, the country's major telegraph company.

Bell's company (which would eventually become the American Telephone and Telegraph Company, or AT&T) started by leasing its phones in pairs. Customers had to string their own wires to connect the two instruments. As the new invention grew in popularity, the company developed central exchanges. Customers telephoned the exchange to request a connection to some other customer in the local system. The development of

In a 1903 telegram from Kitty Hawk, North Carolina, Orville Wright informs his father in Dayton, Ohio, of successful airplane flights. Transmission errors misspelled the pioneer aviator's name and shortened his 59-second flight.

long-distance service had to await improvements in voice transmission technology. AT&T began offering New York–Philadelphia connections in 1885 and New York–Chicago service in 1892. By 1915, telephone customers on the East or West Coast could call across the country.

The first employees to staff a telephone exchange were teenage boys, but after customers complained that the boys were discourteous, the exchanges began hiring women. Telephone operator soon became an exclusively female occupation, though hiring was restricted to women high-school graduates who spoke unaccented English. By the time the United States entered World War I, nobody could imagine a telephone operator who was not female. The U.S. Army hired a cadre of women operators, the Hello Girls, to run telephone field communications in France.

After Bell's patents expired in 1893 and 1894, thousands of competitors began offering telephone service in small towns and rural areas. Because AT&T dominated the industry nationally and would not allow its smaller rivals access to its lines, customers of smaller companies could not call other companies' customers. In 1913, the federal government challenged AT&T's monopolistic practices, forcing it to give up control of the Western Union Telegraph Company and to open its lines to other phone companies. Even so, AT&T retained the lion's share of the telephone business for many years until the early 1980s. In response to increasing competition from electronic mail and cell phones, Western Union retired its telegram delivery service in January 2006.

SEE ALSO
Bell, Alexander Graham; Inventions; Science and technology; World War I

FURTHER READING
Fischer, Claude S. *America Calling: A Social History of the Telephone to 1940.* Berkeley: University of California Press, 1992.
McCormick, Anita Louise. *The Invention of the Telegraph and Telephone in American History.* Berkeley Heights, N.J.: Enslow, 2004.

Temperance and prohibition movements

THE TEMPERANCE and prohibition movements are closely related. Temperance advocates tried to persuade individuals to reduce their consumption of alcoholic beverages, or better yet, to stop consuming them altogether. Advocates of prohibition wanted to outlaw the manufacture, distribution, and sale of intoxicating beverages entirely. The two movements have not always agreed on tactics but over the years have generally cooperated with one another.

Native Americans anxious to keep liquor away from their tribes were the first temperance reformers. In the early 1800s, other reformers besides Native Americans began to voice concerns about the medical consequences of alcohol consumption, which had become startlingly high in this period. These critics of liquor soon joined with religiously motivated groups to organize temperance societies. By the 1830s, thousands of such societies were active in the United States. The temperance cause won its first legislative victory when Maine passed a prohibition law in 1851. Even though the law was never well enforced, it provided a model for the growing movement.

Among the national organizations that formed after the Civil War were

Titled "A Bad Example," this 1909 illustration depicts an athletic boy equipped for healthful exercise, but in danger of being led astray by a father who drinks alcohol.

the Prohibition party (1869), the Woman's Christian Temperance Union, or WCTU (1874), and the nonpartisan Anti-Saloon League (1893). Although the WCTU devoted most of its efforts to persuasion rather than political action, together these groups helped shift the movement's focus toward passing more "Maine" laws and electing "dry" congressmen. By 1916, 23 states were legally dry, meaning no alcohol could be sold, manufactured, or consumed. At the end of 1917, in part motivated by a spirit of patriotic self-sacrifice during World War I, Congress passed the 18th, or Prohibition, Amendment to the U.S. Constitution. The amendment forbade the manufacture, distribution, sale, importation, and exportation of alcoholic beverages in the United States. It was ratified in 1919 and, with the passage of the Volstead Act, which set up an enforcement mechanism, put into effect in 1920.

People supported prohibition for different reasons. Some saw the saloons, which sold alcoholic drinks, as the tools of political machines, the often corrupt organizations that ran local politics. Many city bosses used saloon keepers as ward leaders. If saloons could be abolished, temperance workers reasoned, American political life would be less corrupt. Employers and industrialists also favored prohibition, as closing off access to alcohol would mean a more disciplined, hardworking labor force. Yet others linked excessive drinking to the lifestyles of recent immigrants. The fact that many of the nation's brewers and distillers were of foreign origin seemed to confirm such nativist prejudices. During World War I, when the United States was at war with Germany, heightened biases against the nation's numerous brewers of German origin helped create a national consensus for prohibition. Making a reference to the German kaiser, Wayne Wheeler of the Anti-Saloon League used the motto, "Kaiserism abroad and booze at home must go."

Temperance attracted both men and women but held special appeal for women. Many women had direct experience of husbands and fathers who had drunk up their paychecks at saloons, turned abusive or violent when they were drinking, or died from alcohol poisoning, leaving their families destitute. Such was the experience of Carry Nation, who actually wielded her hatchet against saloons and crusaded against the evils of drink. In the belief that strict controls over alcohol would improve family lives, thousands of women of all classes and races joined temperance crusades and organizations. Temperance was so popular among women that by the early 1890s the WCTU had some 150,000 members, many more than had allied with the woman suffrage cause by that point. Only when WCTU leader Frances Willard realized that securing the vote for women would strengthen her organization's cause did significant numbers of temperance workers join the suffrage movement.

The nation's experiment with prohibition did not last long. The Association Against the Prohibition Amendment developed as early as 1918 to protest the increase in federal power the amendment had brought. That power was widely evaded, however, by both ordinary individuals and criminals, who built a lucrative trade in bootleg (illegal) liquor, a phrase that comes from smuggling small items in a boot to get them past the authorities. By the late 1920s, even women's groups that had once supported prohibition had turned against it, arguing that parents who drank were teaching their children not to respect the law and that prohibition had enriched the nation's criminal element. Prohibition actually succeeded in reducing alcohol consumption, especially among the working classes who could least afford to buy bootleg liquor. But after the Great Depression began in 1929, most Americans agreed that prohibition had not worked and, more important, that holding on to it impeded economic recovery. The 21st Amendment, which was ratified on December 21, 1933, repealed the 18th Amendment and brought the nation's effort to ban alcoholic beverages to an end.

SEE ALSO

Anti-Saloon League; 18th Amendment; Nation, Carry A.; Reform movements; Willard, Frances; Woman's Christian Temperance Union

FURTHER READING

Blocker, Jack S., Jr. *American Temperance Movements: Cycles of Reform.* Boston: Twayne, 1989.
Bordin, Ruth. *Woman and Temperance: The Quest for Power and Liberty, 1873–1900.* Philadelphia, Pa.: Temple University Press, 1981.
Rorabaugh, W. J. *The Alcoholic Republic: An American Tradition.* New York: Oxford University Press, 1992.
Timberlake, James H. *Prohibition and the Progressive Movement, 1900–1920.* Cambridge, Mass.: Harvard University Press, 1963.

Theater

THE AMERICAN THEATER thrived during the late 1800s. Middle-class audiences, who were enjoying more spending money and greater leisure in this period than ever before, were especially avid patrons of vaudeville and minstrel shows, melodramas, Wild West shows, and plays based on Harriet Beecher Stowe's popular novel *Uncle Tom's Cabin* (called "Tom shows"). More select audiences attended operettas, operas, and serious dramas written predominantly by Shakespeare and other European authors. Beginning in the 1910s, realistic American dramatists began to attract greater attention.

Vaudeville evolved from circuses and traveling variety shows. Designed for middle-class family audiences, it featured comic sketches (often based on ethnic or racial humor), song-and-dance routines, ventriloquists, jugglers, and trapeze artists. In the hope of attracting entire families, vaudeville owners kept ticket prices low and their shows as "wholesome" as possible. As one poster bragged, they banned everything considered "unfit for the ears of ladies and children." Some owners even regulated audiences, handing out notices forbidding cigars or cigarettes or any demonstration other than polite clapping. Many offered only ice water to drink.

Vaudeville often included acts from minstrel shows. Performed mostly by whites using burnt cork to blacken their faces, minstrel shows originally consisted of exaggerated imitations of slave life. Two male characters predominated: Jim Crow, an ignorant plantation slave, and Zip Coon, an urban slave who brags about women.

Minstrel productions usually opened with comic banter between a master of ceremonies (the "interlocutor") and Mr. Tambo and Brother Bones (the "end-men"). Sentimental songs, a promenade (cakewalk), and an olio, a combination of singing, dancing, and verses, came next, followed by a grand finale with the whole cast. Even though black entertainers considered minstrelsy demeaning, they too "corked up" to perform in minstrel shows, as they had few other possibilities for stage work.

William F. ("Buffalo Bill") Cody, a former army scout, buffalo hunter, and after 1883, a showman, developed the highly popular Wild West shows in 1883. Thousands of paying spectators watched his steer-roping contests, rodeos, and staged battles between "civilized" cavalry men and "savage" Indians. Even the great Sioux chief Sitting Bull appeared as an attraction. In addition to cowboys, women, and children, Cody employed hundreds of Mexican and Native American performers to take roles in historic reenactments such as the "Bison Hunt," "Train Robbery," and "Custer's Last

Ironically, this poster advertising the Hurly-Burly Extravaganza and Refined Vaudeville Show features bare-legged dancers. Most Victorian Americans would have considered neither the costumes nor the entertainment refined.

Stand." He made a star out of Annie Oakley, a sharpshooter.

Other forms of show business also produced stars. Lillian Russell, who grew up in Chicago, arrived in New York City in 1877, where she got a part in the chorus of *H.M.S. Pinafore* by the English team of Gilbert and Sullivan. Later billed as "Lillian Russell, the English Ballad Singer, a Vision of Loveliness and a Voice of Gold," she rose to stardom on the musical theater and cabaret stage. "King of Handcuffs" Harry Houdini also achieved international stardom. In the early 1900s he made a fortune on the stage and in outdoor publicity stunts demonstrating incredibly fast escapes from handcuffs, straitjackets, tanks of water, and jail cells.

Theatrical producer Florenz ("Flo") Ziegfeld got his start in show business booking acts for variety shows. In 1907, he began mounting the Follies, a revue consisting of comic acts followed by large musical production numbers that featured beautiful women in luxurious, sometimes scanty, costumes. Huge successes, the Follies launched the careers of many comedians, including Will Rogers, Eddie Cantor, W. C. Fields, and Fanny Brice, all of whom went on to star in film and radio productions. Many other film stars, such as Irene Dunne, Barbara Stanwyck, and Paulette Goddard, began in Ziegfeld's Follies, as did singers Maurice Chevalier and Sophie Tucker, dancers Fred and Adele Astaire, and composers Sigmund Romberg, George Gershwin, and Richard Rodgers.

By the turn of the 20th century, American theater had become a big business. Syndicates of investors and theater entrepreneurs based in New York City organized bookings for cross-country theatrical tours. By 1904, these syndicates had put more than

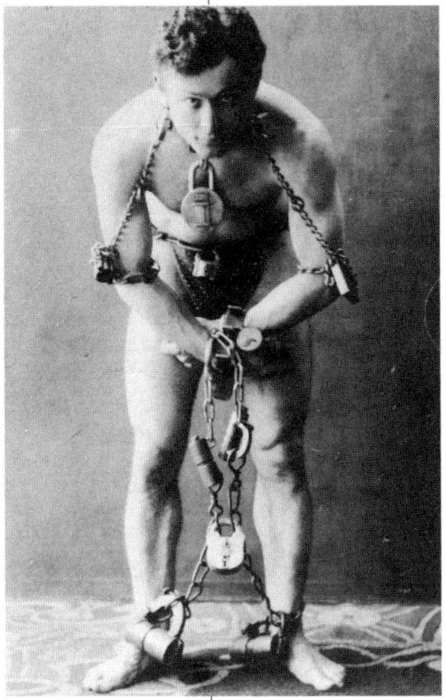

In this 1899 publicity photo, magician Harry Houdini prepares to perform one of the seemingly miraculous escapes that earned him a place among the era's most popular entertainers.

400 touring companies on the road. They promoted the national reputations of stage actors such as Maude Adams, who made a name for herself in plays by J. M. Barrie, the author of *Peter Pan,* and of Lionel, Ethel, and John Barrymore, siblings who all enjoyed triumphant careers on the stage. In 1899, actor William Gillette dramatized the character of the fictional detective Sherlock Holmes, portraying him more than a thousand times for the next 30 years.

Melodramas remained the most popular form of American stage play long into the 20th century. *Hazel Kirke,* for example, a play by actor and director Steele MacKaye, told the story of the struggle between a father and daughter over whom she should marry. The play not only ran longer (nearly 500 performances) than any other nonmusical to that date (1880), but was then taken across the country by 14 touring companies. Playwright and director David Belasco also produced successful melodramas, including *Madame Butterfly* and *The Girl of the Golden West,* both were transformed into operas by the Italian composer Giacomo Puccini and are still performed today.

Actors in this period became increasingly interested in performing in plays of greater psychological realism, however, and thus promoted the dramas of European writers such as Bernard Shaw, Henrik Ibsen, and August Strindberg. Modern American writers found welcome in two experimental theatrical movements fostered by the Washington Square Players and the Provincetown Players. These companies signaled a new era in American theater by producing serious dramas by writers such as newcomer Eugene O'Neill, who became the nation's most celebrated playwright. By 1920, however, the growing popularity of motion pictures, cut into popular interest in the theater.

SEE ALSO

Dance; Music

FURTHER READING

Bordman, Gerald M. *American Theatre: A Chronicle of Comedy and Drama, 1869–1914.* New York: Oxford University Press, 1994.

Henderson, Mary C. *Theater in America: 250 Years of Plays, Players, and Productions.* New York: Abrams, 1996.

McArthur, Benjamin. *Actors and American Culture, 1880–1920.* Philadelphia, Pa.: Temple University Press, 1984.

Wilmeth, Don B., and Christopher Bigsby, eds. *The Cambridge History of American Theatre.* Vol. 2, *1870–1945.* New York: Cambridge University Press, 1998.

Titanic

THE RMS *TITANIC* was a luxury ocean liner built by the British steamship company Cunard. It was the largest man-made moving object in the world. On the night of April 14, 1912, in the middle of its maiden voyage from Southampton, England, to New York City, the *Titanic* struck an iceberg off the coast of Newfoundland and sank in about three hours. There had been 2,227 passengers and crew aboard. With the ship's 20 lifeboats launched less than half full, and many passengers trapped below decks, only 705 people survived. The *Titanic*'s five-piece orchestra played on deck until the moment the ship sank. Those who were

The New York World *devoted its entire April 16, 1912 front page to the sinking of the ocean liner* RMS Titanic. *More than 1,500 people died in the accident, making it one of the worst maritime disasters in history.*

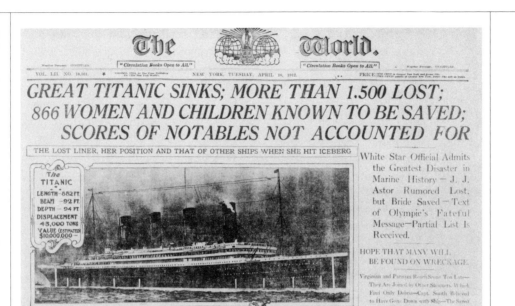

not pulled under with the ship died in the freezing water. The *Carpathia*, another Cunard liner, rescued the survivors early the next morning.

The *Titanic* sinking remains a subject of intense inquiry and interest. Who was to blame for such a disaster? The Cunard company, in its belief that the ship was unsinkable, had not bothered to supply enough lifeboats for all passengers and crew. Apparently, the captain had ignored radioed iceberg warnings. Although the ship was evacuated with women and children first, the survival rate of first- and second-class passengers was twice as high as that of steerage passengers. Historians, filmmakers, and deep-sea researchers have viewed the sinking of the *Titanic* as a tragic commentary on the pride and class snobbery of the Gilded Age, a dramatic prelude to the world war that would end the era forever.

Among those who died in the sinking of the Titanic were millionaire merchant John Jacob Astor; Macy's department store founder Isidor Strauss and his wife Ida (who refused to get on a lifeboat without him); and the English investigative journalist William T. Stead. Harry Elkins Widen-

er, a 1907 Harvard graduate, also died. His mother, who survived the disaster, gave Harvard University several million dollars to build its magnificent library and name it after her son. When newspaper reporters asked Molly Brown, a wealthy socialite from Denver, Colorado, how she had survived, they reported her as saying that she was unsinkable, the very adjective originally ascribed to the Titanic itself.

FURTHER READING

Butler, Daniel Allen. *Unsinkable: The Full Story of RMS Titanic.* Mechanicsburg, Pa.: Stackpole Books, 1998.

Eaton, John, and Charles A. Haas. *Titanic: Triumph and Tragedy.* 2nd ed. New York: Norton, 1995.

Lord, Walter. *A Night to Remember.* New York: Henry Holt, 1955.

Transportation, public

THE TERM *public transportation* can refer to any mode of travel that carries passengers. Examples during the Gilded Age and Progressive Era included stagecoaches, trains, boats, and ships for long-distance travel, and streetcar systems that served individual cities. All forms of mass transportation, they carried numerous fare-paying passengers at a time and traveled on scheduled routes. Typically, cities financed mass transport systems with tax revenues and either built and ran the systems themselves or hired the work out to private contractors. In many cities, taxicabs that followed no fixed route were also available for hire by individual passengers. Air travel became possible in the early 20th century, but the United States did not begin developing a significant airline industry until after World War I.

By the 1870s, horse-drawn stagecoach travel had largely disappeared east of the Mississippi River but still served some areas of the West until the early 20th century. Moreover, Americans could travel from coast to coast by train. Railroad expansion continued during the next several decades, with tracks reaching out to more destinations in the western states and territories. Horses remained important to public transportation in many major cities, where they pulled metal-wheeled passenger cars along metal tracks. The animals remained in service even as other streetcar power sources, such as steam engines and electricity, began to gain popularity. New York City, for example, did not retire its last horse-drawn streetcars until 1914. Horse-drawn taxicabs also endured into the 20th century, surviving a short-lived challenge from battery-powered electric cabs in the late 1890s. Just as streetcars gave way to gasoline-powered buses in the 20th century, horse-drawn taxicabs finally gave way to gasoline-powered automobiles with meters that calculated the fare.

San Francisco introduced cable cars in the 1870s, replacing the muscle power of horses with the mechanical power of underground cables. Motors kept the cables in constant motion, and a car started or stopped by using a gripping device to grasp or release a moving cable. Electric-powered streetcars began appearing in the late 1880s, first in Richmond, Virginia, and Cleveland, Ohio, then in many other cities. Most streetcars drew their power from overhead wires strung above the tracks, though some used underground power conduits. The device that connected the car to the electrical source was called a trolley, and people soon applied that term to the car itself. To avoid traffic congestion, some cities removed their streetcar tracks from street level, either excavating tunnels for subway systems or constructing elevated railways that let trolleys run high above the street. New York had elevated rail service as early as 1868. Boston opened the nation's first subway system in 1897.

Because streetcars made living several miles from city centers convenient, they contributed to the growth of metropolitan areas. "Streetcar suburbs" flourished on the outskirts of some major cities around the turn of the century, harbingers of the nationwide suburban boom that would accompany the rise of the automobile industry.

Bridge construction and railroad expansion during the Gilded Age and

Boston city officials and uniformed conductors mark the opening of the nation's first subway system in 1897. Their vehicle resembles the electric trolley cars in use above ground.

Progressive Era diminished the demand for boat travel but did not eliminate it. Many people relied on ferries for short trips across rivers where no bridges were available, and steam-powered vessels continued to carry passengers on the Great Lakes, the Mississippi River, and other inland water routes. In the years before airplane service, international travel required oceangoing ships. Wealthy Americans traveled to and from Europe in ocean liners that resembled floating luxury hotels. Millions of immigrants arrived in the United States by ship, traveling in steerage, the cheapest accommodations on board.

Most ships burned coal to boil the water that ran their steam engines, although riverboats sometimes used wood, readily available along the riverbanks. Even after the invention of the diesel engine in the 1890s, passenger vessels continued to use steam engines. Steamships used two kinds of propulsion devices, paddle wheels and propellers. Paddle wheelers, which could operate in relatively shallow water, were popular on some river routes. The faster propeller ships dominated on the seas. The practice of carrying sails as a backup propulsion system faded away in the late 1800s as advances in technology made steam engines more reliable. In time, gasoline and diesel engines replaced almost all other power sources for public transportation.

SEE ALSO
Airplane; Automobile; Cities; Electricity; Inventions; Railroads; Science and technology

FURTHER READING

Cudahy, Brian J. *Cash, Tokens and Transfers: A History of Urban Mass Transit in North America.* New York: Fordham University Press, 1990.
Davidson, Janet. *On the Move: Transportation and the American Story.* Washington, D.C.: National Geographic, 2003.
Miller, William H. *Famous Ocean Liners: The Story of Passenger Shipping, from the Turn of the Century to the Present Day.* New York: Harper Collins, 1987.
New York Transit Museum with Vivian Heller. *The City Beneath Us: Building the New York Subway.* New York: Norton, 2004.
Richter, William Lee. *The ABC-CLIO Companion to Transportation in America.* Santa Barbara, Calif.: ABC-CLIO, 1995.
Warner, Sam Bass. *Streetcar Suburbs: the Process of Growth in Boston, 1870–1900.* Cambridge, Mass.: Harvard University Press, 1962.

Treaty of Versailles (1919)

THE TREATY OF VERSAILLES ended World War I. It was the result of a peace conference held in Paris in 1919 between the defeated Germany and the victorious Allies: the United States, France, Great Britain, and Italy. President Woodrow Wilson, who led the U.S. delegation to the conference, tried to get all participants to agree to his program of Fourteen Points, which in part called for the right of subject nationalities—colonies and imperial possessions—to determine their own futures, a principle called self-determination. He also called for the establishment of a League of Nations to secure the peace by mediating disputes.

Wilson's European allies were more interested in humiliating and weakening Germany. Although Wilson eventually won their participation in a future League of Nations, he had to agree to their takeover of Germany's colonies under a shared "mandate." This was only the first of several concessions Wilson would be forced to make that further undermined the principle of self-determination. Later, France took advantage of Wilson's embarrassment over American opposition to joining the League of Nations to press harsh financial conditions upon Germany. These included control over the mineral resources of Alsace-Lorraine, the coal- and iron-rich region between Germany and France, and demands for billions of dollars in reparations (payments for the costs of war) from the defeated nation.

On May 7, 1919, the Allies presented the treaty to the Germans, who at first refused to sign until France threatened an invasion. On June 28, the powers signed the treaty at the palace at Versailles, the former home of the French kings some 13 miles southwest of Paris. The severity of Germany's punishment under the treaty would contribute to the country's economic collapse in the 1920s and the subsequent rise of a dictator, Adolf Hitler, to power.

President Wilson was never able to convince the U.S. Congress to ratify the Versailles treaty or accept the idea of joining the League of Nations.

SEE ALSO

League of Nations; Wilson, Woodrow T.; World War I

FURTHER READING

Macmillan, Margaret Olwen. *Paris 1919: Six Months that Changed the World.* New York: Random House, 2002.

Marks, Sally. *The Illusion of Peace: International Relations in Europe, 1918–1933.* New York: Palgrave Macmillan, 2003.

Triangle Shirtwaist Factory fire (1911)

NEAR CLOSING TIME on Saturday, March 25, 1911, a fire broke out in the Triangle Shirtwaist Factory, situated on

the 9th and 10th floors of a multifactory building on Washington Square, in New York City. Trying to escape the rapid combustion, the workers, most of them young Jewish and Italian immigrant women, found locked exit doors and no working elevators. As they tried to flee, rusted fire escapes collapsed under their weight. Fire department hoses and ladder trucks could not reach the 9th floor. Trapped in the flames, women leaped from the building, some of them with their hair on fire; firemen's nets could not break their falls. Other women tried unsuccessfully to slide down the elevator cables. The final death toll was 146.

Triangle, one of many garment-manufacturing sweatshops in New York City, was a place where women sewed piecework for very low wages. They specialized in assembling women's blouses, or shirtwaists, as they were called. Just two years earlier, thousands of New York women shirtmakers and their supporters had struck for better wages, hours, and working conditions. Triangle was one of the factories that promised reform and did not follow through. The managers had locked exit doors to prevent workers from taking unauthorized breaks or stealing material; they had failed to provide adequate fire escapes; and they had not installed sprinkler systems, although the technology was available at the time.

The bodies of fire victims are laid out in a long line of coffins, as family members and New York police try to identify the garment workers who died in the 1911 fire at the Triangle Shirtwaist Company.

Nobody knew the exact cause of the blaze, though it was probably a spark from machinery, but the negligence of the factory owners seemed clear. When a jury acquitted them of homicide, an outraged International Ladies' Garment Workers' Union joined with labor and reform organizations to lobby for a thorough investigation of the tragedy and the creation of safety regulations for manufacturing. Responding to the outcry, state legislators Robert F. Wagner and Alfred E. Smith cochaired a commission that resulted in stringent building codes and regular factory inspections across the state. Other states followed their example. Many advances in workplace safety date from the Triangle fire, one of the worst fire disasters in U.S. history.

SEE ALSO
International Ladies' Garment Workers' Union; Strikes

FURTHER READING
Stein, Leon. *The Triangle Fire.* 1962. Reprint. Ithaca, N.Y.: Cornell University Press, 2001.
Von Drehle, David. *Triangle: The Fire That Changed America.* Boston: Atlantic Monthly Press, 2003.

Twain, Mark

SEE Clemens, Samuel Langhorne

United Fruit Company

IN 1871, MINOR C. KEITH, a 23-year-old man from Brooklyn, New York, arrived in Costa Rica to help his uncle build a railroad. When the uncle died, Keith took over the operation. In the meantime, he had planted banana trees

to help feed his railroad workers, and when in the 1890s it became clear that Costa Rica could not supply enough passengers to keep the railroad going, he began using his trains to transport bananas to seaports. From there, the fruit went by steamship to the United States, where a growing urban American population was eager to get it. The banana trade became highly profitable.

In 1899, Keith brought about a merger of some 20 fruit and steamship companies into the United Fruit Company. United Fruit eventually became the largest banana company in the world, with plantations across the Caribbean, Central America, and down into Colombia in South America. By 1913, United Fruit was exporting 50 million bunches of bananas to American ports. In addition, through a series of political and financial maneuvers, it was dominating the government, finances, communications networks, and commerce of Costa Rica, Guatemala, and Honduras. For this reason, the press often referred to these countries as "banana republics."

SEE ALSO
Commerce; Imperialism

FURTHER READING
Langley, Lester, and Thomas Schoonover. *The Banana Men: American Mercenaries and Entrepreneurs in Central America, 1880–1930.* Lexington: University Press of Kentucky, 1995.

Watched over by a federal inspector, African American dock workers in Baltimore in 1915 unload bananas imported from Central America by the United Fruit Company.

United Mine Workers of America

IN 1890, COAL MINERS affiliated with the Knights of Labor and the National Progressive Union of Miners and Mine Laborers joined together to form the United Mine Workers of America (UMW). Coal mining was one of the nation's most dangerous occupations. The union fought long hours, low wages, and unsafe working conditions as well as the high cost of living in mining towns. High rents and inflated prices in company-owned housing and stores sometimes exceeded a family's earnings, thereby keeping miners perpetually in debt to their bosses.

The UMW attracted tens of thousands of new members. Its successful strikes in several states helped to win such landmark reforms as the eight-hour workday. Sometimes unionization drives met violent opposition. While marching in support of an 1897 coal strike, 19 unarmed workers were shot and killed, and dozens more wounded, by deputy sheriffs in Lattimer, Pennsylvania. During a 1914 strike at a coal mine in Ludlow, Colorado, antiunion forces not only gunned down strikers, but also massacred women and children by setting fire to a tent encampment of mining families who had been evicted from company houses. The slaughter generated national outrage and increased sympathy for the miners.

The UMW enjoyed some significant victories. President Theodore Roosevelt intervened in a 1902 strike on the side of the miners, threatening to nationalize coal mines unless the owners came to an agreement with the union. In time, the union's influence extended beyond the coal industry and helped strengthen organized labor in general. One early UMW official, William B. Wilson, a founder and secretary-treasurer of the union, later became a congressman. He chaired the House Labor Committee, helped draft legislation that created the Department of Labor, and then served in the cabinet of President Woodrow Wilson (no relation) as the nation's first secretary of labor. John L. Lewis, elected UMW president in 1920, would go on to lead the union for 40 years, establishing himself as one of the giants of the 20th-century labor movement. A powerful and charismatic presence, Lewis commanded enough respect to persuade Presidents and congresses to support labor legislation.

SEE ALSO

Company towns; Knights of Labor; Labor unions; Labor, U.S. Department of; Mining; Roosevelt, Theodore; Strikes

FURTHER READING

Aurand, Harold W. *From the Molly Maguires to the United Mine Workers: The Social Ecology of an Industrial Union.* Philadelphia, Pa.: Temple University Press, 1971.

During the bloody Colorado coal strike of 1913–14, miners in the town of Ludlow listen to strike organizers from the United Mine Workers of America.

Victorianism

HISTORIANS USE THE TERM *Victorianism* to refer to the moral values of the middle classes who lived in the United States and Great Britain during the reign of Queen Victoria, from 1837 to 1901. The core of Victorianism was a faith in the advancement of civilization through industrialization and science. At the same time as Victorians valued change, they also stressed the importance of maintaining public and social order. To accomplish this blend of progress and order, they adopted specific ideas about the proper behavior of individuals and certain social classes.

First and foremost, they believed in personal self-control, especially over the human sexual passions. Victorians reined in their passions so as to conserve their energies for advancing and preserving Western civilization. They therefore opposed premarital, extramarital, and homosexual relations, which they called vices, although many people indulged in these practices in private. Although many Victorians opposed prostitution and fought to end it, others accepted it as an inevitable aspect of human society. Some assumed that the availability of prostitutes saved middle-class women from having to endure their husbands' excessive sexual demands.

The second most prominent belief among Victorians was that all members of families—men, women, and children—should not deviate from their assigned social roles. Women should occupy themselves primarily with the private sphere, maintaining an orderly home and raising well-behaved children, while men engaged with the public sphere, earning a living and dealing with politics. Victorians expected children to defer to parental, and especially paternal, control and in general to be seen and not heard.

Third, Victorians believed that white, western forms of civilization were superior to the "primitive" cultures of nonindustrialized regions. They also believed that the white middle classes were foreordained to be civilization's chief guardians. These beliefs allowed them to justify their imperial conquests of nonwhite populations, such as the Indian tribes of the American West and the indigenous peoples of the Pacific islands and the African subcontinent, on the basis that they were bringing them the benefits of a more "advanced" civilization.

Victorian values predominated in mid- to late 19th-century America to such an extent that nonwhites and immigrants often adopted these values as they became more prosperous and moved into heavily settled urban areas. Some artists and writers, such as poet Walt Whitman, rebelled against Victorianism, as did feminists and "new women" active in the women's rights movement, who wanted opportunities for more varied social roles than Victorians were willing to give them. The arguments of early 20th-century psychologists that human sexual desire was natural eventually led to

A husband and wife sit proudly in their Portsmouth, New Hampshire, parlor around 1890. Their ornate furniture and elaborate knick-knacks reflect Victorian ideals of elegance.

a loosening of Victorian values concerning sexuality. Even so, Victorian sexual values held on far into the 20th century, after other aspects of Victorianism had faded. During the later 20th century, many people associated the term "Victorianism" with sexual prudery and emotional repression, losing sight of the original power and social complexity of its ideas.

SEE ALSO

Family life; Imperialism; Prostitution; Sexuality; Women's rights movement

FURTHER READING

Howe, Daniel Walker, ed. *Victorian America*. Philadelphia: University of Pennsylvania Press, 1976.
Schlereth, Thomas J. *Victorian America: Transformations in Everyday Life, 1876–1915*. New York: HarperCollins, 1991.

Voting patterns

THE NUMBERS of Americans going to the polls peaked during the Gilded Age but then declined during the Progressive Era. In the 1896 Presidential election, more eligible voters—70 percent of them—turned out than ever before in American history. By 1920, however, less than 50 percent were voting. Despite a slight rise in 1928 and during the 1930s, by the 1960s, rates of voter participation had dropped to the levels of the 1920s.

Scholars have essentially three theories to explain why this happened. First, they argue, the decline in the power of the political parties reduced voter enthusiasm for elections. Earlier in the 19th century, the parties got out the vote. Using precinct captains to get voters to the polls, the parties then rewarded loyal voters with government jobs (called patronage) and other favors.

Around 1900, however, Progressives began to win reforms that reclassified many patronage jobs as civil service, that is, as jobs available only to applicants passing examinations that showed they were qualified to hold them. Civil service reform resulted in more expert government administrators, but in undercutting the power of political parties, it also contributed to the decline of voter interest in the outcome of elections.

The second reason for the decline in voting was, ironically, the 1920 passage of the 19th Amendment, which gave women the right to vote. Overnight, the size of the electorate doubled, but in the following years, women's turnout at the polls lagged 20 to 30 percentage points behind men's, thereby pushing down overall figures for voter participation. Several generations would have to pass before women became accustomed to voting at the same rates as men.

Third, governments made exercising the right to vote increasingly difficult during the Progressive Era. While Jim Crow laws systematically disfranchised black voters in the rural South, progressive efforts to ensure proper voter registration in the cities ended up disfranchising less well-educated voters. Many states across the nation not only extended their residency requirements but also imposed literacy and other tests for voting. Earlier, in the 19th century, many voters, including resident aliens, had been able simply to show up on election day and cast their ballots. By the end of the 1920s, 46 states required some sort of formal registration and restricted voting to

Designed to guard against election fraud, this late-19th-century ballot box features a counting mechanism and a hand-operated crank that advances the count by one as it draws in each voter's ballot.

citizens, changes that many Americans wanted but which further reduced the number of voters.

Progressive Era government reforms made voting more orderly and government bureaucracies more honest and qualified. But the loss of the parties' grip on the election process meant that fewer Americans cared enough about the process to make the effort to vote.

SEE ALSO

Civil rights; Government reform; Jim Crow; Politics; Suffrage; Woman suffrage movement

FURTHER READING

Kleppner, Paul. *Continuity and Change in Electoral Politics, 1893–1928.* Westport, Conn.: Greenwood, 1987.

Kornbluh, Mark Lawrence. *Why America Stopped Voting: The Decline of Participatory Democracy and the Emergence of Modern American Politics.* New York: New York University Press, 2000.

McGerr, Michael. *The Decline of Popular Politics: The American North, 1865–1929.* New York: Oxford University Press, 1986.

Wald, Lillian

- *Born: Mar. 10, 1867, Cincinnati, Ohio*
- *Education: New York Hospital Training School for Nurses, graduated 1891*
- *Accomplishments: founder, Visiting Nurse Service of New York (1893); cofounder, Women's Trade Union League of New York (1903) and National Child Labor Committee (1904); co-organizer and first president, National Organization of Public Health Nurses (1912); author, The House on Henry Street (1915) and Windows on Henry Street (1934)*
- *Died: Sept. 1, 1940, Westport, Conn.*

A SETTLEMENT-HOUSE leader and social reformer born in Cincinnati, Ohio, Lillian Wald studied nursing in New York City. After graduation, she entered Women's Medical College, intending to become a physician. While

teaching home nursing and hygiene to immigrant women on the city's Lower East Side, she answered a young girl's call to help her sick mother. "Over broken asphalt, over dirty mattresses and heaps of refuse we went," she wrote in her memoir. Finding a family of seven living in only two rooms that they shared with boarders, Wald felt "ashamed of being a part of society that permitted such conditions to exist." This experience made her determined to leave her medical studies and organize a visiting nurse service. The program she created with her friend Mary Brewster became the model for public health nursing throughout the United States.

In 1895, Wald raised money to buy a house on Henry Street on the Lower East Side so that she and other nurses could live in the neighborhood they served. Originally called the Nurses' Settlement, Wald's house evolved into the Henry Street Settlement, which played a leading role in many Progressive Era reform movements, for better housing and against child labor. Wald not only expanded her visiting nurse services but also helped neighbors with housing and employment needs and worked to provide educational and recreational resources for the community. She also became an advocate for social and political reforms, persuading city officials to fund local parks and provide nurses, free school lunches, and special education classes for students at city schools.

During the following decades, Wald helped build movements to improve race and labor relations, abolish child labor, reform factory work

Visiting nurse and pioneer social worker, Lillian Wald founded New York's Henry Street Settlement House in 1893. "Ever since I have been conscious of my part in life," said Wald, "I have felt consecrated to the saving of human life."

conditions, preserve international peace, protect civil liberties during World War I, and win woman suffrage. Along with Florence Kelley, general secretary of the National Consumers' League, she helped persuade the federal government to establish the U.S. Children's Bureau in 1912 to report on all matters concerning the welfare of children. She was widely revered for her humanitarianism and lifelong work for social improvement. Both of her creations, the Visiting Nurse Service of New York and the Henry Street Settlement, still exist today.

SEE ALSO

Children's Bureau, U.S.; Health, public; Kelley, Florence; Settlement-house movement

FURTHER READING

Coss, Clare, ed. *Lillian D. Wald: Progressive Activist.* New York: Feminist Press, 1989.
Daniels, Doris G. *Always a Sister: The Feminism of Lillian Wald.* New York: Feminist Press, 1989.
Siegel, Beatrice. *Lillian Wald of Henry Street.* New York: Macmillan, 1983.

Walker, Madam C. J.

- *Born: Dec. 23, 1867, Delta, La.*
- *Accomplishments: founder, Walker College of Hair Culture and Walker Manufacturing Company in Indianapolis, Ind. (1910)*
- *Died: May 25, 1919, Irvington-on-Hudson, N.Y.*

FOUNDER OF a cosmetics company catering to black customers, Madam C. J. Walker (born Sarah Breedlove) was one of the first American women to become a self-made millionaire. Born in 1867 to sharecroppers who had spent most of their lives in slavery, she rose to national prominence as a businesswoman, philanthropist, and social activist who used her wealth and influence to improve the lives of black Americans.

Growing up on a Louisiana cotton plantation, Sarah Breedlove was orphaned at age seven, married for the first time at 14, and widowed at 20. She worked from childhood into her 30s as a field hand, domestic servant, and washerwoman. When she discovered she was losing her hair, she became interested in hair and scalp treatments and went to work as a sales agent for Annie Turnbo Malone, another African American entrepreneur who made a fortune in the hair care business.

In 1905, she began manufacturing and selling her own line of hair preparations. Madam C. J. Walker adopted her professional name after marrying her third husband, journalist Charles Joseph Walker, who helped her set up a mail-order business. She continued to use his name even after that marriage ended in divorce.

Walker traveled widely, popularizing her wares with visits to private homes and demonstrations at churches and other black community institutions. In 1910, basing her operations in Indianapolis, Indiana, she established a training institute for a door-to-door sales force of female employees she called "hair culturists," along with a factory to manufacture and package her popular cosmetics. Contrary to legend, she did not invent the hot comb or straightening comb, although the Walker Hair Care System did use that device in conjunction with shampoo, ointment, and other Madam C. J. Walker Manufacturing Company products.

Walker gave extensive charity to schools, nursing homes, antilynching campaigns, and the National Association for the Advancement of Colored People (NAACP). She was also the

A badge worn at one of the Walker Company's annual conventions, where sales agents received awards for community service, features an image of clasped hands and a portrait of company founder Madam C. J. Walker.

major contributor to a successful African American women's campaign to purchase and preserve the home of abolitionist leader Frederick Douglass.

FURTHER READING

Bundles, A'Lelia. *Madam C.J. Walker, Entrepreneur.* New York: Chelsea House, 1991.

Bundles, A'Lelia. *On Her Own Ground: The Life and Times of Madam C. J. Walker.* New York: Scribner, 2002.

Lowry, Beverly. *Her Dream of Dreams: The Rise and Triumph of Madam C. J. Walker.* New York: Knopf, 2003.

Washington, Booker T.

- *Born: Apr. 5, probably 1856, Hale's Ford, Va.*
- *Education: Hampton Normal and Agricultural Institute (Hampton, Va.), 1872–75*
- *Accomplishments: president, Tuskegee Normal and Industrial Institute, Tuskegee, Ala. (1881); founder, National Negro Business League (1900); author,* The Future of the American Negro *(1899),* Up from Slavery *(1901), and other books*
- *Died: Nov. 14, 1915, Tuskegee, Ala.*

BORN THE SON of a white man and a slave woman, Booker Taliaferro Washington spent his childhood in slavery and his adolescence working in salt and coal mines in West Virginia. At 16, he walked some 500 miles to the all-black Hampton Institute in Virginia, seeking an education. He paid his tuition by working as a janitor. At Hampton, Washington learned both academic and practical subjects, including brick masonry, and absorbed the school's philosophy of utilitarian education and character building. After graduation, he became a teacher himself, returning to teach at Hampton.

In 1881, philanthropic white southerners who hoped to found an institute resembling Hampton in Alabama offered Washington the presidency of a school he would have to create from the ground up. He started building with student labor and local donations, but swiftly became adept at fund-raising on the national lecture circuit. Washington's program at Tuskegee, which stressed the Protestant work ethic, high moral standards, and the development of industrial skills such as carpentry, farming, and domestic arts, attracted funding from such notable benefactors as industrialist Andrew Carnegie and John D. Rockefeller. In less than three decades, the school grew to 100 buildings on 2,000 acres of land. It also had an endowment of nearly 2 million dollars and an all-black faculty of 200, including eminent botanist George Washington Carver and sociologist Monroe Nathan Work.

In 1895, Washington's reputation as a speaker and a representative of black America earned him an invitation to address the Atlanta Cotton States Exposition. In his speech, he expressed the belief that African Americans should be educated to work for economic success in farming and the trades and would settle for respectability without agitating for social equality. "Our greatest danger," Washington said in the speech, "is that in the great leap from slavery to freedom we may overlook the fact that the masses of us are to live by the productions of our hands....No race can prosper till it learns that there is as much dignity in tilling a field as in writing a poem. It is at the bottom of life we must begin, and not at the top. Nor should we permit our grievances to overshadow our opportunities." Washington's speech pleased southern whites, whose support Washington needed to keep Tuskegee running, but

Booker T. Washington was an effective public speaker. Here he addresses a racially mixed audience in Mississippi, in 1912. "My friends," he once said, "there is no mistake; you must help us to raise the character of our civilization or yours will be lowered."

angered militant black leaders like W. E. B. DuBois and William Monroe Trotter, who felt he had promised whites that African Americans would advance through "property, industry, skill, intelligence, and character" but would also continue to cooperate in their own disfranchisement and social segregation. They derided the speech by calling it the Atlanta Compromise.

After Atlanta and the publication of his popular autobiography, *Up from Slavery,* in 1901, Washington became the unofficial black affairs adviser to white politicians and government officials. Presidents Theodore Roosevelt and William Howard Taft consulted with Washington in all matters concerning African Americans, including appointments. Roosevelt even invited Washington to dine at the White House in 1901, though he later regretted the action because of the public indignation it aroused among whites.

Black and white supporters of the early 20th-century civil rights organizations, the Niagara Movement and the National Association for the Advancement of Colored People (NAACP), increasingly opposed Washington, whose philosophy undercut their own calls for civil rights. Instead of preaching

Washington's ideas of "accommodation," these groups urged people to protest segregation and violence against blacks. They called Washington's political influence the "Tuskegee Machine."

Washington fought his critics, sometimes even planting spies in their organizations. But he was not blind to the real problems African Americans faced in his day. He worked behind the scenes, secretly sponsoring civil rights and antiviolence lawsuits and funneling support to black colleges. Privately, he supported many of the NAACP's goals while publicly urging black Americans to work hard and exercise good citizenship, patience, and Christ-like love to overcome the hatred of white Americans.

Complex, manipulative, and shrewd, Washington chose not to challenge the racial hostility of his time, but did what he felt was necessary to ensure the future of African Americans in the segregated South.

SEE ALSO

African Americans; Carver, George Washington; Civil rights; DuBois, William Edward Burghardt (W. E. B.); Colleges and universities; National Association for the Advancement of Colored People; Race relations; Roosevelt, Theodore; Segregation; South, the; World's fairs and exhibitions

FURTHER READING

Harlan, Louis F. *Booker T. Washington: The Making of a Black Leader, 1856–1901.* New York: Oxford University Press, 1972.
———. *Booker T. Washington: The Wizard of Tuskegee, 1901–1915.* New York: Oxford University Press, 1983.
Moore, Jacqueline M. *Booker T. Washington, W. E .B. Du Bois, and the Struggle for Racial Uplift.* Wilmington, Del.: Scholarly Resources, 2003.
Verney, Kevern. *The Art of the Possible: Booker T. Washington and Black Leadership in the United States, 1881–1925.* New York: Routledge, 2001.
Washington, Booker T. *Up from Slavery.* 1901. Edited by William L. Andrews. New York: Oxford University Press, 2000.

Wells-Barnett, Ida B.

- *Born: July 16, 1862, Holly Springs, Miss.*
- *Education: teacher training, Rust College, Holly Springs, Miss., 1878*
- *Accomplishments: editor and co-owner,* Memphis Free Speech and Headlight *(1889–92); secretary, National Press Association (1887); founding member, National Association of Colored Women's Clubs (1896), National Afro-American Council (1898; secretary 1899–1902), National Association for the Advancement of Colored People (1910); founder, Chicago Woman's Era Club, later called the Ida B. Wells Club (1893), Negro Fellowship League (1910), Alpha Suffrage Club (1913); author, "Southern Horrors: Lynch Law in all its Phases" (1892), "The Reason Why the Colored American is Not at the World's Columbian Exposition" (1893), "A Red Record" (1895), "Lynch Laws in Georgia" (1899), and* Crusade for Justice: The Autobiography of Ida B. Wells *(published posthumously, 1970)*
- *Died: Mar. 25, 1931, Chicago, Ill.*

BORN TO SLAVE parents in the middle of the Civil War, Ida B. Wells was studying to be a teacher in 1878 when her mother and father died in a yellow fever epidemic. Only 16, she kept her young brothers and sisters together and supported the family by teaching school in and around Memphis, Tennessee. When she was traveling by train one day, a conductor forcibly ejected her from a segregated passenger car reserved for white women. Wells sued the railroad and published her story in a local black newspaper. Although a lower court ruled in her favor, the state Supreme Court reversed the decision and she lost her case.

In the meantime, Wells had begun a career as a journalist. Using the pen name Iola, she wrote for black newspapers all around the country, earning a reputation as an uncompromising idealist and a critic of folly and injustice. She became a powerful foe of all forms of racism. In 1889, she bought a part ownership in the *Memphis Free Speech and Headlight* and became its editor. In 1892, when envious whites murdered three successful black Memphis grocers, Wells launched the antilynching crusade for which she became famous.

In a series of articles and pamphlets, Wells attacked the common justification for lynching—that it protected white women from black rapists. With meticulous research, Wells repeatedly demonstrated that only a tiny number of lynchings were actually about charges of rape. Many lynchings, in fact, were acts of revenge against African Americans for becoming educated and economically successful. "This," wrote Wells, in an autobiography published after her death, "is what opened my eyes to what lynching really was. An excuse to get rid of Negroes who were acquiring wealth and property and thus keep the race terrorized and 'keep the nigger down.'"

She advised her black readers to protect themselves from white violence by whatever means necessary and to leave Memphis and the South if they could. Wells's *Free Speech* editorials earned her the undying enmity of white Memphis. While she was attending a convention out of town, angry whites destroyed her newspaper offices. The death threats that followed kept Wells from ever returning to the South.

Wells moved to New York City, where she wrote for the *New York Age,* and later to Chicago. Her lectures on lynching throughout the northern United States and in Great Britain earned her so much acclaim that her message became impossible to ignore.

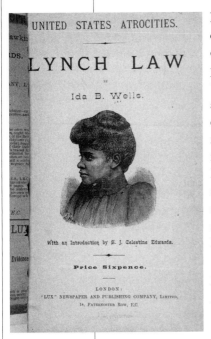

UNITED STATES ATROCITIES.

LYNCH LAW

by

Ida B. Wells.

With an Introduction by S. J. Celestine Edwards.

Price Sixpence.

LONDON:
"LUX" NEWSPAPER AND PUBLISHING COMPANY, LIMITED,
1s, PATERNOSTER ROW, E.C.

Anti-lynching crusader Ida B. Wells wrote this 1892 pamphlet, which debunks the claim that white mobs murdered black men in order to protect white women's sexual purity.

In the North, her crusade provoked outrage at the prevalence of the "southern horror" and aroused a new comprehension that rape was a manufactured pretext for lynching, not a persistent factor of southern life. As she later said in her autobiography, "Having lost my paper, had a price put on my life, and been made an exile from home for hinting at the truth, I felt that I owed it to myself and to my race to tell the whole truth now that I was where I could do so freely."

Allied with the venerable abolitionist Frederick Douglass, in the summer of 1893, Wells publicized the exclusion of African Americans from the Chicago World's Columbian Exposition in a pamphlet entitled "The Reason Why the Colored American is Not at the World's Columbian Exposition." They arranged to have the pamphlet distributed to crowds of visitors outside the gates, because black Americans, other than laborers, were not allowed elsewhere on the fairgrounds.

In 1895, Wells married Ferdinand Barnett, a Chicago attorney. Together they had four children. In addition to continuing her writing, she became a civic activist and woman suffrage leader in Chicago. Although critical of the racism in the movement to secure the vote for women, she allied with suffragist Susan B. Anthony. Wells also helped organize the National Association for the Advancement of Colored People in 1909–10. She served as a

probation officer in Chicago, helped to defeat a move to segregate Chicago's public schools, and ran unsuccessfully for the state senate in the late 1920s. Her work on behalf of racial justice was a lifelong crusade.

SEE ALSO

Lynching; National Association for the Advancement of Colored People; Race relations; Woman suffrage movement

FURTHER READING

McMurry, Linda O. *To Keep the Waters Troubled: The Life of Ida B. Wells.* New York: Oxford University Press, 1998.
Schechter, Patricia Ann. *Ida B. Wells-Barnett and American Reform, 1880–1930.* Chapel Hill: University of North Carolina Press, 2001.
Wells-Barnett, Ida B. *Crusade for Justice: The Autobiography of Ida B. Wells.* Edited by Alfreda M. Duster. Chicago: University of Chicago Press, 1970.

West, the

AFTER THE CIVIL WAR, the United States accelerated its settlement of lands west of the Mississippi River. These lands included the Great Plains (the Dakotas, Nebraska, and Kansas), the Great Basin (Nevada and Utah), the Rocky Mountains (Montana, Wyoming, and Colorado), the Pacific Northwest (Oregon, Washington, and Idaho), and the Southwest (Oklahoma, Texas, Arizona, and New Mexico). California was also a part of the West, but because of the gold rush in late 1840s, it was already a state by 1850. During the Gilded Age and Progressive Era, 10 other western territories won statehood.

The late 19th-century West contained a mixture of cultures and ethnic groups. Native Americans, white native-born Americans, freed African American slaves, and immigrants from Europe, Asia, and Mexico all encountered one another there. Some, like the African American "Exodusters," southern blacks who fled discrimination and settled Kansas in the late 1870s, were escaping racism. European immigrants, many of them experienced farmers, went to homestead on land the U.S. government offered for a mere $10 registration fee. Asians—from China, Japan, Korea, and eventually the Philippines—also came to the West for economic reasons. These groups found work building railroads, providing services to the growing urban communities of the West, and in agriculture.

Sometimes these diverse groups got along; often they clashed. Asian populations faced stinging prejudice and sometimes mob violence in the urban environments where they settled. In the Southwest, Catholic Mexican Americans also faced prejudice from the white Protestant Anglos. These white settlers overwhelmed the Mexican Americans in numbers and used lawsuits in state and federal courts to dispossess them of their land. Forced into segregated neighborhoods (*barrios*), most of these Spanish-speaking residents ended up in low-status jobs as manual and domestic workers or sharecroppers. The federal government used black soldiers (called Buffalo Soldiers) to suppress rebellious Native American tribes and Mexican raiders in the Southwest.

Life in the remote parts of the West was far from easy. In the late 1800s, settlers fought severe droughts and periodic infestations of devastating insects. While waiting for land to yield a crop, men traveled far afield to earn cash in nearby towns and cities, or they did railroad, timber, and mining work. Even as more manufactured goods were becoming available to city folk, women on remote homesteads still had to produce much of what

their families needed, such as clothing, soap, candles, dairy products, and preserved foods. The arrival around the turn of the century of Rural Free Delivery, the delivery of mail to rural areas, meant that they could receive mail-ordered goods from catalog sales companies such as Sears Roebuck and Montgomery Ward, provided they had the cash to pay for them.

Women often led efforts to bring standards of decency, civility, and culture to frontier communities. They opposed gambling, prostitution, and liquor, and established schools, benevolent societies, hospitals, and cultural institutions. They also campaigned to improve women's business and professional opportunities and to ease restrictions on divorce. By 1887, the West had the nation's highest divorce rates, thanks to generally liberal grounds. In Colorado, for example, grounds for divorce included impotence, bigamy, adultery, desertion, mental or physical cruelty, failure to provide financial support, drunkenness or drug addiction, or conviction of a felony. Western women launched the first successful municipal and state campaigns for the vote. By 1914, women were voting in 11 states, all but one (Illinois) west of the Mississippi.

In settling the West, Americans took land from Native Americans and eventually forced them to live within the boundaries of special reservations. The Dawes Severalty Act of 1887 divided up tribal lands within the last major tract of western Indian land, which was located in present-day Oklahoma. The act required tribes to register for individual plots of 160 acres per head of household. Two years later, Congress opened up to non-Indian homesteaders nearly 2 million acres of "unassigned" Indian land. White settlers, known as "Boomers" (or

"Sooners," if they came in to claim land before it became officially available on April 22, 1889) took over the remainder of Indian territory. Oklahoma became a state in 1907.

By the end of the 19th century, land for homesteading had become hard to find and the frontier seemed to have "closed." In 1893, historian Frederick Jackson Turner gave a speech in which he claimed the frontier was critical in forming the American character. It had forced Anglo-American and European settlers to shed their old ways and adapt, innovate, and invent. The result, he concluded, was a highly individualistic, restless, and socially mobile American—an American ready for adventure, bent on self-improvement, and committed to democracy.

Historians have since modified the Turner thesis, as his view came to be called. They point out that his characterizations of settlers as Anglo-Americans and other white Europeans was too narrow and that women's experience on the frontier was not the same as men's. Moreover, he failed to acknowledge the impact of settlement on the Native American and Spanish-speaking inhabitants who were already there.

An increasingly complex view of the West now prevails. Life in the West certainly appealed to the restless, adventurous man, but it also appealed to adventurous women, although many women went west reluctantly. Wrenched from family and friends, women often felt dislocated and lonely in the West. Nor was it a land of unlimited opportunity. "Booms" inevitably led to "busts," especially when prices fell for the commodities settlers worked so hard to produce. Moreover, the development of the West depended on more than just the grit and hard work of individual pioneers. The federal government played a major role, starting with land grants to railroads, which in turn sold their surplus acreage to settlers. Later the government leased federal lands to ranchers and lumber and mining companies at low rates. The success of western "private" enterprise was heavily dependent on government help.

The frontier did seem to nurture democratic values, as Turner claimed. Western communities built strong legislatures and insisted that officials stay in office for only short terms. During the Progressive Era, western states and cities pioneered government reforms that emphasized popular control, such as initiative, which allows voters to propose laws, and recall, which allows voters to remove an official. South Dakota was the first state to authorize initiative (1898), and Los Angeles, California, was the first city to adopt recall (1903). On the other hand, some settlers and their descendants rode roughshod over the rights of minority populations. On the West Coast white laborers, fearing competition for jobs, mistreated Asian immigrants and Mexicans. In the 1870s in Los Angeles, for example, a mob lynched more than a dozen Chinese. In 1885, white residents in Tacoma, Washington, forcibly expelled 700 Chinese, burning down their homes and businesses; the next year, Seattle residents hauled their Chinese neighbors to the port by wagon and loaded them on ships waiting to take them away.

Settlement of the West was not kind to the land. The vast natural resources may have seemed limitless, but they were not. Railroad tunnels destroyed whole mountains. The construction of huge mines scarred the land, and timber harvesting depleted forests. Overcultivation eroded fields. The bison disappeared. To preserve the region's many natural beauties, Congress protected the geysers of Yellow-

Based on "American Progress," an 1872 painting, this illustration represents the nation's spirit as a symbolic female figure stringing telegraph wire westward, across the frontier.

stone and in 1890 made Yosemite a national park. Years later, however, other areas were sacrificed when dam builders needed to secure water for arid western settlements.

Myths about the frontier have lingered on. In the popular imagination, it remains a place of endless open spaces where fearless, hard-working Americans reaped the fruits of their labor. Literature fostered these myths long before the frontier had begun to close. As early as the 1870s, popular writers of dime novels (cheap paperbacks that actually cost only five cents) seized on the cowboy as the essential American hero who dealt out righteous justice. Beginning in the 1880s, Wild West theatrical productions contributed to these myths with staged battles between "good" cavalry regiments and "bad" Indians. In the early 20th century, the motion picture industry, which moved to California after 1910, carried on these traditions with their early westerns.

Most stereotypes from the West were male. The West was where a young man could find freedom and opportunity and toughen his body and soul. President Theodore Roosevelt, who wrote histories of the West, urged American men to experience the

"strenuous life" before modern civilization made them too weak. Some of these themes also appealed to women. In 1912 Juliette Low founded the American Girl Scouts, in part because she feared that civilization had made girls too "soft." Using hardy women homesteaders as her heroines, she built her program around tracking, woodcraft, and wilderness survival. In the end, images of the West influenced many kinds of Americans, and continue to do so to this day.

SEE ALSO

African Americans; Agriculture; Asian Americans; Buffalo Soldiers; Conservation; Dawes Severalty Act (1887); Government reform; Hispanic Americans; Immigration; Literature; Low, Juliette ("Daisy") Magill Kinzie Gordon; Mining; Native Americans; Populism; Railroads; Ranching; Roosevelt, Theodore; States and statehood; Woman suffrage movement

FURTHER READING

Hine, Robert, and John Mack Faragher. *The American West: A New Interpretive History.* New Haven: Yale University Press, 2000.
Lamar, Howard R. ed. *The New Encyclopedia of the American West.* New Haven: Yale University Press, 1998.
Nugent, Walter. *Into the West: The Story of its People.* New York: Knopf, 1999.
White, Richard. *"It's Your Misfortune and None of My Own": A New History of the American West.* Norman: University of Oklahoma Press, 1991.

Willard, Frances

- *Born: Sept. 28, 1839, Churchville, N.Y.*

- *Education: North Western Female College (Evanston, Ill.), Laureate of Science, 1859*

- *Accomplishments: president, Evanston College for Ladies (1871); dean, Woman's College of Northwestern University (1873–74); president, Chicago Woman's Christian Temperance Union (WCTU, 1874); president, Illinois WCTU (1878); president, National WCTU (1879–98); president, Woman's National Council of the United States*

(1888–90); organizer and president, World's WCTU (1891)
• *Died: Feb. 17, 1898, New York, N.Y.*

FRANCES WILLARD was a world leader of the temperance movement, the movement to reduce or eliminate the drinking of alcoholic beverages. She was born in New York, grew up in Ohio, and then moved to rural Wisconsin. After graduating from college in Illinois, Willard toured Europe with a wealthy woman friend and then began teaching English and aesthetics at her alma mater. She spent some time as a college administrator before becoming involved in the temperance movement, then a highly popular cause among her fellow Methodists. It was in that movement that she found her true vocation.

During her 20-year term as president of the national Woman's Christian Temperance Union (WCTU), Willard drew the organization into a wider world of reform and propelled it into the national limelight. Basing temperance in the need to protect the home, she argued that to accomplish this goal the campaign had to move beyond persuading individuals not to drink or sell intoxicating beverages. It had to attack the root causes of drinking, such as poverty, the lack of workers' rights to organize into labor unions, and women's subordination in the economy and politics. She became especially vigorous in speaking out on this latter point, arguing for women's right to have access to all professions and for equal participation in all councils of government and institutions of learning.

Among Willard's other, related concerns were dress reform, the movement that opposed the wearing of tightly laced corsets and promoted more sensible clothing for women. She also

argued for the reform of penal institutions, for the replacement of drinking, gambling and bawdy entertainment with wholesome amusements, and for all American children to have access to kindergartens. In pursuit of her goals, she engaged in party politics, at one point trying to bring together the Populist party, the Knights of Labor, and the WCTU. This effort did not succeed. Although she served as the vice-chair of the Populist party convention in 1892, she was unable to get either a woman suffrage or temperance plank into its platform. She was, however, able to influence local and state legislatures to establish temperance education programs in schools. The children exposed to these programs were the ones who, as adults, supported national prohibition when it was passed in 1918.

Willard called her wide-ranging social reform approach a "Do Everything" policy. "Everything is not in the Temperance Reform, but the Temperance Reform should be in everything," she said. A woman of tremendous energy, she devoted herself unstintingly to her cause, traveling extensively and delivering long, forceful speeches. Speaking in 1891 to the Woman's National Council of the United States, she announced, "I would have woman

Temperance reformer Frances Willard said she "always felt a strong attraction toward the bicycle...the skill in handling it obliges those who mount to keep clear heads and steady hands."

everywhere treated as an individual and not as belonging to a tribe. I would have her portion under the sun assigned to her in severalty, and would teach her as rapidly as possible to become a citizen of the world on equal terms with every other citizen." These and other visions of a future in which women and men worked side-by-side for a better world inspired thousands of followers worldwide.

Near the end of her life, Willard spent much time in England, where she announced she had become a socialist. For her, socialism was "applied" Christianity and the only way to bring about a just society. After her death, her admirers raised money for a statue to be sculpted and then placed in the Capitol Building in Washington, D.C. For many years, she was the only woman to be so honored.

SEE ALSO

Temperance and prohibition movements; Woman's Christian Temperance Union; Women's rights movement

FURTHER READING

Bordin, Ruth. *Frances Willard: A Biography.* Chapel Hill: University of North Carolina Press, 1986.
Leeman, Richard W. *"Do Everything" Reform: The Oratory of Frances E. Willard.* Westport, Conn.: Greenwood, 1992.
Willard, Frances Elizabeth. *A Wheel Within a Wheel: How I Learned to Ride the Bicycle with Some Reflections by the Way.* 1895. Reprint. Bedford, Mass.: Applewood Books, 1997.

Wilson, Woodrow T.

- *Born: Dec. 28 (some sources say Dec. 29), 1856, Staunton, Va.*
- *Education: College of New Jersey (later Princeton), B.A., 1879, University of Virginia, LL.B., 1883, Johns Hopkins University, Ph.D., 1886*
- *Accomplishments: professor, Bryn Mawr College (1885–88), Wesleyan University (1888–90), Princeton University (1890–1902); president,*

Princeton University (1902–11); governor of New Jersey (1911–13), President of the United States (1913–21)
- *Died: Feb. 3, 1924, Washington, D.C.*

WOODROW WILSON, 28th President of the United States, was the first Democrat to occupy the White House in the 20th century and the first southerner elected since the Civil War. He was the last President chosen before the 19th Amendment extended the vote to women. Wilson came to the Presidency as some of the great powers in Europe, Asia, and the Middle East were on the brink of World War I. He brought the United States into the conflict, hoping to lead the way in building a new international order in the postwar world, but he left office without achieving Senate support for his vision of a League of Nations dedicated to international peace. Puerto Rico became a territory and its residents gained U.S. citizenship in the Wilson years. The United States ratified four constitutional amendments during his administration. World events during his Presidency included the overthrow of the Russian czar by a communist revolution.

The son of a Presbyterian minister, Thomas Woodrow Wilson (he changed the order of his name when he entered public life) spent his youth in Virginia, Georgia, South Carolina, and North Carolina, and graduated from the New Jersey college that later became Princeton. He briefly practiced law in Atlanta, then changed direction to find success in an academic career. He earned a Ph.D. in history from Johns Hopkins in Maryland, wrote books of biography, history, and political science, taught college in Pennsylvania and Connecticut, and became a Princeton professor. In 1902, Princeton

In September 1919, Woodrow Wilson traveled 8,000 miles, giving 40 speeches in 22 days during his unsuccessful campaign to muster support for the League of Nations. Weeks later, exhausted and discouraged, Wilson suffered a debilitating stroke.

trustees elevated him to president of the university. Wilson married twice (his first wife died in 1914) and had three children.

In 1910, Wilson ran for governor of New Jersey as a Democrat, won decisively, and embarked on a vigorous reform program that included new state election laws, public utility regulations, and worker compensation rules. In 1912, with the support of three-time nominee William Jennings Bryan, Wilson won the Democratic nomination for President.

Wilson's two main competitors in the 1912 race were William Howard Taft, the Republican incumbent, and former President Theodore Roosevelt, who had abandoned the Republicans to lead the Progressive ("Bull Moose") party. By splitting the Republican vote, Taft and Roosevelt enabled Wilson to win an electoral vote landslide, even though he captured less than 42 percent of the popular vote. Socialist party candidate Eugene Debs took 6 percent of the popular vote.

During his first term, Wilson proved to be a progressive, prodding Congress to lower tariff rates, levy income and estate taxes, pass new laws to benefit workers, and clamp down on corporate abuses. He championed the Federal Reserve System to stabilize the nation's economy, and the Federal Trade Commission to increase government oversight of business activity. The first President to have a secretary of labor in his cabinet, Wilson appointed a former coal miner and union official to the post. His other Presidential appointments included Louis Brandeis, the first Jew to serve on the Supreme Court. Wilson

brought the country to the brink of war with Mexico, with U.S. and Mexican troops actually invading one another's countries, but was able to avoid an all-out conflict.

When war broke out in Europe in 1914, Wilson strove at first to preserve U.S. neutrality. The United States was a nation of immigrants; its citizens had ties to every country involved in the conflict. German Americans did not want their adopted country to go to war with their ancestral homeland. Irish Americans opposed joining the war on the side of England. Isolationist Republicans insisted that the United States should keep its distance while the great powers across the ocean fought out their ancient rivalries among themselves. Socialists opposed a war in which millions of working-class soldiers on both sides would be slaughtering each other while a few industrialists got rich selling supplies to the warring nations.

War fever flared in the United States in 1915, however, when a German submarine sank the British passenger ship *Lusitania,* killing more than 1,000 people, including 100 Americans. But Wilson chose to deal with that incident and others like it through diplomatic channels. Running for reelection in 1916 as the President who had kept the nation out of war, he won by a slim margin over the Republican nominee, Supreme Court justice Charles Evans Hughes. The Socialists still commanded enough votes to keep the Democratic and Republican totals under 50 percent. Wilson became the first President to win two terms without a popular vote majority either time.

It did not take long for the antiwar candidate to transform into a pro-war President. In 1917, Germany adopted a policy of unrestricted submarine attacks not just on enemy ships, but on the vessels of neutral nations as well.

Telling Congress that U.S. participation in the overseas conflict could help make the world "safe for democracy," Wilson asked for and received a declaration of war. Congress went on to authorize a draft and to outlaw criticism of the government's war effort, legislation the Wilson administration used to imprison hundreds of opponents, including Socialist leader and former Presidential candidate Eugene Debs.

Never a supporter of women's political equality, Wilson also allowed the incarceration of a number of suffragists who were embarrassing him by picketing the White House. The women pointed out that the President who wanted to make the world safe for democracy should practice full democracy at home. After the war, Wilson became more sympathetic to the suffragist cause and helped secure passage of the 19th Amendment in 1920, which gave women the vote.

When the war ended in 1918, Wilson wanted a treaty settlement that would set the stage for a new era of international peace. He became the first President to travel to Europe while in office, attending the treaty conference in Versailles, France, and pushing for a League of Nations to settle future differences without recourse to war. Some of the victors insisted on punishing Germany more severely than Wilson recommended, and historians would later suggest that the harshness of the Versailles treaty gave rise to World War II by fostering the German resentment that exploded in the Nazi period.

Wilson was not entirely happy with the treaty, but it did include provisions for establishing a League of Nations, and he urged Congress to approve it. To gather public support for the treaty, he embarked on an arduous cross-country speaking tour that left him physically shattered. He suffered a

stroke in the fall of 1919 and spent the remainder of his term in virtual seclusion, communicating only through his wife and a few other intimate associates. He won the Nobel Peace Prize in 1919, but the Senate refused to ratify the World War I treaty, the Democrats lost the White House in 1920, and Wilson left office without achieving support for the League of Nations, the goal he cared about most. He died in 1924. It was more than two decades after his death, in the aftermath of the century's second world war, that the United Nations finally gave substance to Wilson's vision of U.S. participation in an international agency committed to keeping the peace.

SEE ALSO

Federal Reserve Act (1913); Imperialism; International Relations; League of Nations; *Lusitania;* Presidency; Progressive movement; Versailles, Treaty of (1919); Woman suffrage movement; World War I

FURTHER READING

Auchincloss, Louis. *Woodrow Wilson.* New York: Viking Penguin, 2000.
Brands, H. W. *Woodrow Wilson.* New York: Times Books, 2003.
Clements, Kendrick A. *The Presidency of Woodrow Wilson.* Lawrence: University Press of Kansas, 1992.

Wizard of Oz

SEE *Wonderful Wizard of Oz*

Woman's Christian Temperance Union

IN DECEMBER 1873, a spontaneous women's crusade against liquor arose in the Midwest. Groups of women marched

In this photograph from about 1900, a sign on the Denver, Colorado, branch of the Woman's Christian Temperance Union offers free medical services. In most American cities the WCTU's social programs went beyond temperance and prohibition.

on saloons and other businesses that sold liquor in order to convince owners and patrons to sign temperance pledges. When rebuffed, the marchers knelt down, sometimes on a drugstore's sawdust floor or out in the snow, to pray and sing hymns. In many cases, the sheer moral force of this spectacle moved men to renounce alcohol and sign pledges.

Word of the crusades spread across the country, like "a prairie on fire," according to temperance leader Frances Willard. By the following summer, the crusade had touched many hundreds of communities across 31 states and territories. To consolidate their success, Ohio temperance advocates called for delegates from local temperance organizations to form a national union. The result was the founding in Cleveland, Ohio, in November 1874 of the Woman's Christian Temperance Union (WCTU). The union would grow to become the largest woman's organization of the 19th century, claiming 200,000 members by 1900.

Annie Wittenmyer was the union's first president. Frances Willard, who succeeded her in 1879, held the position for 20 years. Under Willard's presidency, the WCTU expanded its work for prohibition laws and temperance education to include anything that might foster

the security of home and family. The union therefore campaigned for many causes besides temperance, including woman suffrage, protective labor legislation, the eight-hour workday, equal pay for equal work, labor unions, legislation to ensure pure food and drugs, kindergartens, dress reform, prison reform, higher penalties for the seduction and rape of women and girls, and an end to prostitution. Women did all the organization's work and held all of its executive positions.

The WCTU reached the peak of its influence between 1900 and the passage of the Prohibition Amendment in 1918. Out of its multistory office building in Chicago (called the Woman's Temple), it ran a publishing company, a medical center, and international missions that claimed millions of participants worldwide by 1900. The union's membership came predominately from white, lower- and middle-class evangelical Protestants. Almost anyone could join the movement, however, as dues were minimal. The WCTU badge, a rosette of white ribbon symbolizing the purity of the home, could be made for less than a nickel.

African American women, especially from among the professional classes, were deeply involved in temperance work but through separate branches. Journalist and novelist Frances E. W. Harper served as superintendent of the Colored Section of both the Philadelphia and Pennsylvania WCTUs in the 1870s and 1880s. African American temperance unions played an important role in racial uplift among black women in the South by providing them with an organization through which they could work for social and economic improvements in their local communities.

The WCTU declined after prohibition's repeal in 1933. Although its membership is small today, the organization continues to work in the interests of reducing the consumption of both alcohol and illicit drugs.

SEE ALSO

18th Amendment; Protestantism; Reform movements; Temperance and prohibition movements; Willard, Frances

FURTHER READING

Blocker, Jack S., Jr. *American Temperance Movements: Cycles of Reform.* Boston: Twayne, 1989.
Bordin, Ruth. *Woman and Temperance: The Quest for Power and Liberty, 1873–1900.* New Brunswick, N.J.: Rutgers University Press, 1990.
Clark, Norman. *Deliver Us from Evil: An Interpretation of American Prohibition.* New York: Norton, 1976.

Woman's Peace Party

MANY AMERICAN women were deeply distressed when World War I broke out in Europe in August 1914. Carrie Chapman Catt and Jane Addams, prominent leaders of the woman suffrage and social reform movements, decided to take action. First they organized an antiwar march. On August 29, 1,500 women dressed in black carried peace banners down New York City's Fifth Avenue to protest the war. Then they organized a follow-up women's peace conference. Taking place in Washington, D.C., in January 1915, this conference gave birth to the Woman's Peace Party (WPP).

The WPP called for international laws to prevent war, limitations on the manufacture of armaments, compulsory mediation of all international conflicts, an international police force instead of national armies and navies, and attention from policy makers to the economic causes of war. The WPP also called for votes for women, along with the appointment by the U.S. government of a commission of men and women to promote international peace. In April 1915, WPP members joined European women at an international meeting in the Netherlands to protest the war's continuation.

By February 1916, the WPP was 40,000 members strong. As a result of the United States entering the European war in April 1917, its membership split and declined. Some branches threw themselves into patriotic war work. Others, such as the militant New York City branch led by Crystal Eastman, continued to protest government war policies. Their radicalism later made them targets of harassment during the postwar Red Scare, when government officials who feared communists slandered and even jailed some peace activists whom they considered dangerous to American security.

When the war ended, male leaders of the warring nations met in Versailles, France, to work out the terms of peace. In May 1919, the WPP and other international women's organizations met in Zurich, Switzerland. They protested the harsh provisions of the Versailles Treaty, which included high reparation payments from Germany, but approved of the League of Nations as an international body to ensure peace in the future. In addition, they formed the Women's International League for Peace and Freedom (WILPF),

This photo of a Woman's Peace Party demonstration appeared in the 1916 exhibition "War Against War." The WPP promoted the importance of cooperative international efforts to prevent war and resolve disputes.

an organization that still works to achieve world disarmament, women's rights, racial and economic justice, and an end to all forms of violence.

SEE ALSO

Addams, Jane; Catt, Carrie Chapman; Peace movement; Red Scare (1919–20); Versailles, Treaty of (1919); World War I

FURTHER READING

Addams, Jane. *Peace and Bread in Time of War.* 1922. Urbana: University of Illinois Press, 2002.
Alonso, Harriet Hyman. *Peace as a Woman's Issue: A History of the U.S. Movement for World Peace and Women's Rights.* Syracuse, N.Y.: Syracuse University Press, 1993.
DeBenedetti, Charles. *The Peace Reform in American History.* Bloomington: Indiana University Press, 1980.

Woman suffrage movement

"[W]OMEN HAIN'T no business a votin'," proclaimed Josiah Allen, a fictional character created by Marietta Holley, a writer of popular humor, in 1891. He went on to say that "they had better let the laws alone, and tend to thier [sic] housework. The law loves wimmin and protects 'em." Josiah's long-suffering wife Samantha retorted: "If the law loves wimmin so well, why don't he give her as much wages as men get for doin' the same work? Why don't he give her half as much, Josiah Allen?" Holley's character put the issue well. Only if women could vote would they be assured of living under laws concerned about their welfare.

By the late 1800s, thousands of women and many male supporters had joined the suffrage movement, which had split into two factions in 1869. The National Woman Suffrage Association (NWSA) represented the more radical side. Led by Elizabeth Cady Stanton and Susan B. Anthony, this group accepted only women members, published a newspaper called *The Revolution,* and called for an end to all forms of oppression of women. In 1878, the NWSA got a woman suffrage amendment introduced into Congress, but nine years passed before the body would even debate it. The Senate then voted it down, with senators from the South forming a solid block against it. A more moderate suffrage faction functioned as the American Woman Suffrage Association (AWSA). Led by Lucy Stone and her husband, Henry Blackwell, it published *The Woman's Journal,* avoided inflammatory issues (including a constitutional amendment), and pursued the woman's vote at state levels only. By century's end, the AWSA had won woman suffrage in only two western territories (Wyoming in 1869 and Utah in 1870) and two western states (Colorado in 1893 and Idaho in 1896).

In 1890, a younger generation of suffragists brought the movement back into one organization, forming the National American Woman Suffrage Association (NAWSA). New leaders emerged. Carrie Chapman Catt, a former superintendent of schools in Mason City, Iowa, headed NAWSA from 1900 to 1904, and then again after 1915. She systematized the organization's political techniques, insisting on precinct-by-precinct canvassing of legislators in its state suffrage campaigns. Harriot Stanton Blatch (Elizabeth Cady Stanton's daughter) brought working women and later trade unions into the movement through the Women's Political Union. Blatch also began suffrage parades. At first, it seemed unladylike to march, and crowds lining the streets were unruly, hurling insults at the marchers. Soon,

A suffrage parade in New York City in 1912. Carrying American flags and accompanied by their small children, these white-clad women demonstrate their commitment to patriotism and maternity, even while they are demanding "Votes for Women."

however, suffrage parades became completely acceptable.

Other new activists included journalist Ida B. Wells-Barnett, who organized African American women for the vote and insisted on marching in whites-only suffrage parades. Alice Paul and Lucy Burns took over the NAWSA's Congressional Committee, which was supposed to be working on getting the federal woman suffrage amendment passed in Congress. But NAWSA soon expelled Paul's group, then renamed the Congressional Union, for advocating militant activities inspired by British suffragists, such as holding the party in power responsible for the failure of suffrage at the polls and mounting public demonstrations in front of the White House. When Paul and her followers demonstrated in front of the White House and were later jailed for disturbing the peace, NAWSA refused to support them.

By 1913, suffragists had won the vote in 10 states. In 1915, however, campaigns in New York, Pennsylvania, Massachusetts, and New Jersey failed. At that point, NAWSA reinstated Catt in the presidency and gave her free rein to bring about victory. Paul's group stepped up its actions, going on hunger strikes in jail and enduring force-feedings that resulted in increased publicity and wide sympathy. Other events also helped the cause. In 1917, the nation entered World War I. Women volunteered for ambulance and medical work and took up jobs at home left vacant by men. Attitudes about women being suited only for domestic life seemed like ridiculous stereotypes. Later that year, New York State, which controlled 45 electoral votes, approved woman suffrage. And in 1918, after Congress adopted the Prohibition Amendment, the liquor interests, which had always assumed that women voters would favor prohibition, stopped their active opposition to woman suffrage. In 1919, Congress finally approved the 19th Amendment, which declared that "the right of citizens of the United States to vote shall not be denied or abridged...on account of sex."

The amendment still had to be ratified by the states. The 36th and last state needed was Tennessee. After days of deadlock, Harry Burn, the

Tennessee legislature's youngest member, who had originally lined up with suffrage opponents, received a letter from his widowed mother. "Hurrah and vote for suffrage," she wrote. "Don't forget to be a good boy and help Mrs. Catt put the 'rat' in ratification." In deciding to vote "yes" for his mother, Burn broke the tie in the legislature. On August 26, 1920, the 19th Amendment was declared officially ratified.

Women had fought for suffrage, long and hard, for 72 years. Their victory changed everyone's lives, men and women alike. After suffrage, women may not have voted in the numbers hoped for, and they won few political offices until many decades later, but they now had the dignity of individual citizenship. Woman suffrage is an important part of the larger story of the gradual expansion of America's democratic promise, and it proved in the end to be a landmark step toward women's eventual political equality with men.

SEE ALSO

Anthony, Susan Brownell; Catt, Carrie Chapman; National American Woman Suffrage Association; Paul, Alice Stokes; Reform movements; Stanton, Elizabeth Cady; Women's rights movement

FURTHER READING

DuBois, Ellen Carol. *Woman Suffrage and Women's Rights*. New York: New York University Press, 1998.
——— and Karen Kearns. *Votes for Women: A 75th Anniversary Album*. San Marino, Calif.: Huntington Library, 1995.
Flexner, Eleanor, and Ellen Fitzpatrick. *Century of Struggle: The Woman's Rights Movement in the United States*. Cambridge, Mass.: Harvard University Press, 1996.
Scott, Anne Firor, and Andrew MacKay Scott. *One Half the People: The Fight for Woman Suffrage*. Urbana: University of Illinois Press, 1982.
Smith, Karen Manners. *New Paths to Power: American Women 1890–1920*. New York: Oxford University Press, 1994.

Women's Bureau, U.S.

THE WOMEN'S BUREAU began as an agency in the U.S. Department of Labor during World War I. Originally called the Women in Industry Service, the agency developed standardized wages, hours, and working conditions for women wage earners. After the war, women's organizations and progressive reformers successfully lobbied Congress to make the bureau permanent. Mary Anderson, a former labor organizer and founder of the Chicago branch of the Women's Trade Union League (WTUL), became its director. Working closely with white middle-class reformers such as Florence Kelley and leaders in the National Consumers' League and the Women's Educational and Industrial Union, Anderson and the Women's Bureau pursued the minimum wage and protective labor legislation for women workers.

Women's Bureau officials assumed that a woman's primary role is motherhood, and that therefore government should regulate working conditions for women to protect the health of mothers and potential mothers. Consequently, the Bureau did not support the Equal Rights Amendment, which feminists proposed in the 1920s. This amendment stated, "Equality of rights under the law shall not be denied or abridged by the United States or by any state on account of sex." Anderson and others opposed to the amendment assumed that it would backfire on women, and actually remove the special protections, such as shorter hours and safer working conditions, that they had won over the years for women in industry. The amendment itself never became a law.

Relatively small and powerless in its early years, the Women's Bureau made slow progress in labor legislation. It did, however, collect abundant data on working women. During the New Deal and World War II, this data helped determine women's availability for industrial work and set standards for that work. For example, in the early 1940s, information collected by the Women's Bureau helped government and industry recruit women workers of appropriate age and skill levels from all over the country and relocate them to work in shipyards and air craft assembly plants on the West Coast.

SEE ALSO

Kelley, Florence; Labor; National Consumers' League; Women's Trade Union League; Women's voluntary associations; World War I

FURTHER READING

Anderson, Mary. *Woman at Work: The Autobiography of Mary Anderson as Told to Mary N. Winslow.* 1951. Reprint, Westport, Conn.: Greenwood, 1973.
Kessler-Harris, Alice. *In Pursuit of Equity: Women, Men, and the Quest for Economic Citizenship in 20th Century America.* New York: Oxford University Press, 2001.
Laughlin, Kathleen A. *Women's Work and Public Policy: A History of the Women's Bureau, U.S. Department of Labor, 1945–1970.* Boston: Northeastern University Press, 2000.

Women's rights movement

A WIDESPREAD movement for women's rights arose in the mid-1800s. In that era, its followers called it the woman's rights movement, because they thought of all women as having the same or similar needs and desires. Today we use "women's rights," a term that gives greater recognition to women's diversity.

The immediate impetus to the 19th-century women's rights movement came from the involvement of middle-class northern white women in the movement to abolish slavery. As these women campaigned to free the slaves, they found themselves increasingly handicapped by society's limits on their ability to play leadership roles. They were also angered by legal limits on their ability to manage their own property, gain an education, achieve professional fulfillment, and exercise political power. From the late 1840s on, these women came together in meetings across the East and Midwest to protest these handicaps and petition government to remove them and to grant women the right to vote.

Advocates for women's rights suspended much of their activity during the Civil War. Afterward, they took up their cause with renewed vigor. By then, industrialization had drawn increasing numbers of women into paid work outside the home and into movements to improve labor conditions and expand workers' rights. In addition, educational opportunities for middle-class women had provided growing access to the professions, especially in teaching, journalism, medicine, and the law. Finally, thousands of women formed temperance movements, which opposed the use of alcoholic beverages, and many others organized clubs or other types of voluntary associations that undertook cultural and reform projects.

By the late 1800s, women's roles in culture and society had changed and expanded. Yet society was slow to accept the idea that women should have greater economic and political rights. Despite their growing accomplishments outside the home, most women were still expected to give priority to home and family. Women

Marjory Stinson takes the air-mail pilot's oath in 1915. Stinson's opportunity to fill two traditionally male roles— pilot and mail carrier—owed a debt to decades of pressure from women's rights advocates for equal opportunities.

wage earners at all levels of the economy—from factory workers to teachers to medical doctors—received lower pay than men. Educated women could pursue professional training, but only in fields considered appropriate for women, such as teaching and social work, and usually only if they remained single. Finally, by century's end, the campaign for the right to vote had yielded positive results in only four western territories or states: Wyoming, Utah, Colorado, and Idaho.

The contradiction between society's expectations of women and their own hopes and ambitions became known as the "woman question." Debated widely—at family meals, in the press, and among legislators—the question came to focus around certain demands. Women should be able to vote. They should be paid the same as men for doing the same work. They should have equal access to higher education and the professions, be able to control their own property, and not have to turn their wages over to their husbands. They should not have to tolerate abuse and violence in their family lives, and they should have the same access to divorce and the custody of children as men had. In this period, people did not call these demands feminist. Instead, they spoke of working for women's rights.

Achieving these rights was not easy. Traditionalists insisted that making women equal to men would upset the social order. Some even argued that women's public roles unsexed them, or destroyed their femininity. But most women's rights activists saw no contradiction between their desire for more fulfilling, independent lives and their identities as women. They reminded their critics that society saw women as more nurturing and morally pure than most men. Thus women were "naturally" suited to reforming social ills and should be given tools such as professional training and access to the vote in order to accomplish their goals.

By the 1890s, the women's rights movement had expanded to include middle-class African American women. These women had not only organized their own voluntary associations but pledged them to work actively for women's rights. In addition, younger women of all races were not waiting for the arrival of new rights to reject some features of traditional lifestyles. By the 1890s, they had simplified the fashions they wore, loosening or abandoning corsets, raising their hemlines, and wearing simple shirtwaists (blouses) and skirts. These outfits made their work lives more convenient and also eased their participation in sports, such as bicycling, golf, and tennis. By the 1910s, following a fashion set by Irene Castle, a popular cabaret dancer, they began to bob, or shorten, their hair.

Many "new women" (as these younger women were sometimes called) also changed their courting customs. Instead of receiving a caller at home, working-class women went out on dates. When middle-class women married, they often sought greater control over their reproductive lives. Their insistence that motherhood be voluntary helped build support for Margaret Sanger's campaign to legalize the spread of information about birth control. New women still hoped to marry, but their expectations for the quality of their marriages were now higher. They expected marriage to bring them more personal satisfaction, including mutual respect and companionship with a loving, responsible spouse. The divorce rate reached 1 in 12 marriages by 1900, and 1 in 9 by 1916. People with more traditional views thought that this trend justified their warnings that equal rights for women would destroy the family.

Some feminist activists held radical views. The widely read writings of feminist and suffragist Charlotte Perkins Gilman, for example, questioned a social system in which men earn a living, retain control over property, and make women dependent on them. Confining women to domestic roles stifles their creativity and makes them less than fully human, Gilman argued. To free women for more creative lives, she pressed for apartment complexes with central kitchens and suggested hiring professionals to cook for families and take care of children.

At the turn of the 20th century, however, the majority of women resisted such radical ideas. They wanted their rights but still saw a happy marriage, children, and a comfortable home as their chief goals in life. Working-class women rarely enjoyed the leisure to debate feminist issues. Still, even they got caught up in the woman suffrage movement. Achieving the vote became the one concrete issue on which women from many walks of life could agree.

SEE ALSO

Birth control movement; Colleges and universities; Divorce; Fashions; Gilman, Charlotte Perkins; Marriage; Woman suffrage movement; Women's voluntary associations

FURTHER READING

Cott, Nancy F., ed. *No Small Courage: A History of Women in the United States.* New York: Oxford University Press, 2000.
Evans, Sara. *Born for Liberty: A History of Women in America.* New York: Free Press, 1989.
Flexner, Eleanor, and Ellen Fitzpatrick. *Century of Struggle: The Woman's Rights Movement in the United States.* Cambridge, Mass.: Harvard University Press, 1996.

Women's Trade Union League

IN 1903, MIDDLE-CLASS reformers concerned about working conditions for women became impatient with the American Federation of Labor, the union of skilled workers formed in 1886 that had refused to include women members. They joined forces with female union activists to found the Women's Trade Union League (WTUL). With branches in New York, Chicago, and Boston, the league became the first national organization for working women. It sought to help these women organize trade unions and also to connect them to the woman suffrage movement, which at that time had a mostly middle-class membership. Among the founders of the WTUL were labor leaders Leonora O'Reilly and Mary Kenney O'Sullivan and settlement leaders Jane Addams and Lillian Wald.

Between 1907 and 1922, under the leadership of Margaret Dreier Robins, the organization fought for improvements in women's education and for federal and state

The official seal of the National Women's Trade Union League conveys the idea that fair treatment for women industrial workers improves the quality of life for all American families.

protective legislation for women and children. Their goals included an eight-hour workday, a minimum wage, and the abolition of child labor. The WTUL also helped women financially during strikes, most notably the great New York City garment workers' strikes from 1909 to 1911. League members organized boycotts of antiunion clothing manufacturers. They also marched alongside striking workers and provided bail for those who were arrested.

By the 1920s, leadership of the WTUL had passed from middle-class reformers to working-class women. One notably successful leader was Rose Schneiderman, a Jewish immigrant cap maker who spearheaded the WTUL's four-year investigation of factory conditions following a disastrous fire at the Triangle Shirtwaist Factory in New York City in 1911. Schneiderman campaigned vigorously for woman suffrage and helped to establish the International Ladies' Garment Workers' Union. She was president of the WTUL from 1926 to 1949. By the late 1940s, most labor unions enrolled women members. Lacking funds and facing declining membership, the WTUL had become increasingly irrelevant. It closed its doors in 1950.

SEE ALSO

Addams, Jane; American Federation of Labor; International Ladies' Garment Workers' Union; Labor unions; Strikes; Triangle Shirtwaist Factory fire (1911); Wald, Lillian; Woman suffrage movement

FURTHER READING

Dye, Nancy Schrom. *As Equals and as Sisters: Feminism, the Labor Movement, and the Women's Trade Union League of New York.* Columbia: University of Missouri Press, 1980.
Foner, Philip S. *Women and the American Labor Movement: From the First Trade Unions to the Present.* New York: Free Press, 1982.
Payne, Elizabeth Anne. *Reform, Labor, and Feminism: Margaret Dreier Robins and the Women's Trade Union League.* Urbana: University of Illinois Press, 1988.
Tax, Meredith. *The Rising of the Women: Feminist Solidarity and Class Conflict, 1880–1917.* New York: Monthly Review Press, 1980.

Women's voluntary associations

VOLUNTARY ASSOCIATIONS are groups of people who come together as volunteers to achieve particular goals, such as to set up a charity or bring about a reform. In the 1800s, many voluntary associations formed by men either excluded women or refused them the right to hold office within the organization or speak out in public. For this reason, activist women formed their own groups, primarily to pursue moral reforms, such as temperance, the abolition of slavery, or the eradication of prostitution. Other women's groups worked on charitable projects, such as the founding of hospitals and raising money for widows and orphans.

After the Civil War, women's interest in associations soared. Thousands of middle-class women, looking for intellectual stimulation and sociability, formed clubs. Meeting on a regular basis, club members studied cultural topics, gave talks to one another, and heard lectures by distinguished guests. Most clubs pursued purely cultural interests. African American club women in Atlanta, for example, followed a curriculum provided by a national adult education program. The Chicago Woman's Club read Karl Marx's writings on capitalism.

By the end of the century, many clubs had added civic betterment to their programs. Members of the New England Women's Club, founded in

Members of the San Antonio, Texas, Women's Progressive Club in 1906. The club, dedicated to civic activism on behalf of African Americans, was part of the National Federation of Colored Women's Clubs.

1868, pursued temperance, girls' education (they helped launch the Girls' Latin School in Boston), and dress reform (they opened a store where women could buy "sensible" clothing, which did not cinch the waist or drag on the ground). Other clubs founded town libraries, public playgrounds, and housing and recreation rooms for young working women.

Around 1900, the number of women's reform organizations mushroomed. Often founded at a local level first, some groups spread to other towns and then formed into statewide and even national organizations. The Woman's Christian Temperance Union, an Ohio organization founded in 1874, grew into the largest women's voluntary association in the country. The National American Woman Suffrage Association (1890) reunited the suffrage movement, which had split in 1869 over the issue of voting rights for black men. The Women's Trade Union League, founded in 1903, worked to encourage women to join labor unions and support woman suffrage.

African American women such as Anna Julia Cooper and Ida B. Wells-Barnett spurred educated black women to form groups that fostered work and educational opportunities for black girls and women in the South and helped southern migrants adjust to life in the North. When in 1890, more than 200

local clubs of white middle-class women formed the General Federation of Women's Clubs, African American women united their own clubs into leagues and then formed the National Association of Colored Women's Clubs in 1896. The association's motto, "Lifting As We Climb"—meaning that members were dedicated to uplifting the downtrodden even as they pursued their own personal progress—inspired thousands of black women and girls for many generations.

Women's voluntary associations were important for two reasons. First, they trained women in organizational skills. Members learned how to run large meetings, speak in public, carry on wide correspondence, maintain financial records, and work with government officials. Thus, even if a particular group did not join the campaign for women's rights, it nonetheless encouraged independence and self-confidence. Indeed, club work was often a woman's first step toward public life.

Second, women's associations accomplished many significant reforms, including votes for women, controls on the liquor trade, and the correction of many social and political abuses. They also improved the educational lives of children, beautified cities, and insisted that municipal governments develop modern sanitation systems, pure water, and controls on air pollution. By joining such organizations, women learned that even without the vote or access to public office, they could use the power of collective action to bring about change.

After 1900, more professions opened up to women, bringing with them new opportunities for public activity. Moreover, by the 1910s, women could vote in many states. National woman suffrage passed in

1920. Afterward, women continued to unite in single-sex groups designed to support their lives at home and at work and to pursue many political and social goals. Increasingly, however, they also joined mixed-sex groups, such as local and national reform associations and political parties. After the 1920s, women-only clubs and associations continued to exist but in competition with many other kinds of organizations of interest to women.

SEE ALSO

Labor unions; Reform movements; Temperance and prohibition movements; Wells-Barnett, Ida B.; Woman's Christian Temperance Union; Woman suffrage movement; Women's rights movement; Women's Trade Union League

FURTHER READING

Blair, Karen J. *The Clubwoman as Feminist: True Womanhood Redefined, 1868–1914.* New York: Holmes & Meier, 1980.
Martin, Theodora Penny. *The Sound of our Own Voices: Women's Study Clubs 1860–1910.* Boston: Beacon, 1987.
Scott, Anne Firor. *Natural Allies: Women's Associations in American History.* Urbana: University of Illinois Press, 1991.
Sigerman, Harriet. *Laborers for Liberty: American Women, 1865–1890.* New York: Oxford University Press, 1994.

Wonderful Wizard of Oz

THE WONDERFUL Wizard of Oz, published in 1900, was the first of a series of successful children's books by L. Frank Baum. It tells the story of Dorothy, a young girl who lives on a bleak Kansas farm with her Aunt Em and Uncle Henry and her best friend, a dog named Toto. A tornado carries her house to Oz, where it lands on (and kills) the Wicked Witch of the East, freeing the Munchkins from her rule. The

Good Witch of the North puts the dead witch's silver shoes on Dorothy and sends her along the yellow brick road to the Emerald City to consult the wizard about how to get back home. The Scarecrow, Tin Woodman, and Cowardly Lion accompany her on her route.

Some historians have thought that Baum's book is a commentary on the heated economic and political debates of the late 19th century. During the 1890s, the country was in a severe depression. Unemployment was high and crop prices were down. Dorothy, some historians argue, represented the ordinary midwesterner, and the Wicked Witch of the East stood for the eastern banker who favored a tight currency based solely on a gold standard. The Emerald City was Washington, D.C., where politicians were supposed to have the answers to America's monetary crisis. The Scarecrow represented the farmer who only thought he had no brains; the Tin Woodman, once an artisan, stood for the rusted-out, unemployed industrial worker; and the Cowardly Lion was the silver-tongued Nebraska congressmen William Jennings Bryan.

Other historians, however, dispute this interpretation, saying that the book has nothing to do with these issues at all but is, instead, an American fairy tale inspired by Baum's fascination with the mechanized Christmas window displays of Chicago department stores. Thus, instead of criticizing industrial society, the *Wizard of Oz* reinforced its values.

SEE ALSO

Bryan, William Jennings; Literature; Monetary policies; Populism

A woodcut illustration for the first edition of The Wonderful Wizard of Oz *shows Dorothy scolding the Cowardly Lion for frightening her dog and upsetting the Tin Woodman and the Scarecrow.*

FURTHER READING
Leach, William. *Land of Desire: Merchants, Power, and the Rise of a New American Culture.* New York: Vintage, 1993.
Rogers, Katharine M. *L. Frank Baum, Creator of Oz.* New York: St. Martin's, 2002.

Work

DURING THE LATE 19th century, industrialization and new technologies transformed the nature of work. Millions of immigrants and native-born Americans traveled to the growing cities in search of work. By the end of World War I, the country was no longer predominantly a nation of farmers. It was, instead, an increasingly urban nation with a labor force engaged in industry, professional occupations, and service work connected with urban life. By 1910, the labor force had grown to 37.5 million, with agriculture's share of total employment dropping to 31 percent. Industry employed from 20 to 25 percent of all workers.

In the earlier, preindustrial nation, the rhythms of work depended on the seasons, harvests, hours of daylight, the length of the task to be done, and the needs of animals. In the new world of industry and commerce, people worked by the clock. They went home when the bell rang or their shift was over. They resumed the same repetitive, assembly-line work the next day, under the eye of a foreman who maintained strict factory discipline. Instead of living off the land, as their ancestors had done, industrial workers earned an hourly wage. For the most part, their work did not require any special training, and they had no connection to the management of the factory or to the distribution and sale of the products they made.

Industrialization both altered the nature of work and expanded the number and types of jobs people performed. Companies required foremen in the factories, office and sales staff, and people to transport finished goods to sales outlets. In turn, the proprietors of these stores needed their own clerical staff, accountants, and maintenance workers. A whole new world of white-collar office and sales work grew out of the expansion of industry and commerce. White-collar jobs required at least a high-school education and polite conventions of behavior and dress. Office staff received salaries rather than wages, a further indication of status. As office work expanded, a class of professional managers emerged, and by 1920, high schools and colleges were offering courses in business management.

The growth of office work created new job options for women, especially white native-born women with some education. The increased availability of consumer items stimulated the construction of elegant new department stores. These stores hired female salesclerks to serve their customers, who were also, increasingly, women. The advent of the telephone brought a need for switchboard operators. Occupations such as typing, telephone switchboard operating, sales clerking and, later, secretarial work became "feminized." This meant that men would not enter them any more and that they would remain relatively poorly paid. Women, however, felt such jobs were respectable and considered them a step up from factory work or domestic service.

Immigrant women's factory work tended to be concentrated in the textile, garment, and food-processing industries. The majority of immigrant women, however, especially the Irish,

Germans, and Scandinavians, entered domestic service—that is, they worked as maids, cooks, or nannies. In domestic service, they received room and board but their lives lacked privacy and workdays could last 12 hours or more.

Regardless of the type of employment, most white women who worked for wages or salaries were single. Married women in this period were solely responsible for homes and children; some earned money by taking in boarders or performing piecework (making individual items and being paid by the piece) or laundry service in their homes.

For southern African American women, even factory work was closed. Typically, they worked on farms and plantations as wage laborers or sharecroppers, or they worked in white women's homes as domestic servants. Some operated independent small businesses as laundresses or beauticians. Not until World War I did African American women, making their way to northern cities, find factories that would employ them and pay a reasonable wage. By the 1920s, black women dominated domestic service in northern cities, though they altered the nature of this work by refusing to live in the homes of their employers. Whether in the North or South, these women typically continued to work for wages even after starting families, managing both child care responsibilities and paid work in order to keep their families afloat and make sure the children went to school.

Other changes in the nature of work affected men as well as women. African American men in the South had struggled since Reconstruction to find well-paying work. For much of the period from 1880 to 1920 they could work only as farm laborers, sharecroppers, timber cutters, day

laborers on construction crews, and in male domestic service (waiting tables or serving as hotel and railroad porters, coachmen, and chauffeurs). They gained industrial work during the Great Migration, the mass movement of southern blacks to northern cities during World War I.

The children of European immigrants took advantage of American educational opportunities to move into higher-status work. Within a generation, many had entered public service occupations, such as police work and firefighting. Others became doctors, lawyers, and teachers; some owned businesses or entered politics. Women in this second generation became secretaries, nurses, librarians, teachers, and social workers. Asian immigrants, most of whom lived in western states, were less fortunate; racial discrimination limited their work opportunities as well as their access to property ownership for farming and, after 1882, even their right to immigrate to the United States.

Technology brought significant changes to the nature of work and to the workplace itself. After 1900, electric- and petroleum-powered engines replaced the steam engines that drove industrial machinery. Electric lighting illuminated work spaces, making work safer and enabling manufacturers to institute night shifts. Typewriters and, later, telephones speeded the pace of office work. Power drills and jackhammers accelerated the work of miners; harvesters powered by steam, and later gasoline, allowed 2 farmworkers to do work that formerly took 20. Housework changed with the advent of washing machines, refrigerators, and vacuum cleaners, though efficient household appliances were not available to most families until the 1930s and 1940s. Gasoline engines led to the production of automobiles and trucks, profoundly altering all aspects of transportation connected with work as well as transportation work itself.

By 1920, the world of work in the United States had left the farm and moved to the city. The majority of American wage earners were now skilled and unskilled workers who lived in urban areas and employed technologies unimaginable before industrial expansion began in the 1870s.

SEE ALSO

African Americans; Agriculture; Asian Americans; Cities; Commerce; Industry; Immigration; Inventions; Labor; Mining; Science and technology; Telephone and telegraph; Transportation, public

FURTHER READING

Davies, Margery W. *Woman's Place Is at the Typewriter: Office Work and Office Workers, 1870–1930*. Philadelphia, Pa.: Temple University Press, 1982.

Dubofsky, Melvyn, and Foster Rhea Dulles. *Labor in America: A History*. Wheeling, Ill.: Harlan Davidson, 2004.

Gutman, Herbert George. *Work, Culture, and Society in Industrializing America: Essays in American Working-Class and Social History*. New York: Vintage, 1976.

Jones, Jacqueline. *A Social History of the Laboring Classes: From Colonial Times to the Present*. Malden, Mass.: Blackwell, 1999.

Katzman, David M. *Seven Days a Week: Women and Domestic Service in Industrializing America*. New York: Oxford University Press, 1981.

Kessler-Harris, Alice. *Out to Work: A History of Wage-Earning Women in the United States*. New York: Oxford University Press, 1982.

World's fairs and exhibitions

AT LEAST A DOZEN major American cities hosted world's fairs and expositions during the Gilded Age and Progressive Era. Attracting tens of millions of visitors, these enormous public spectacles provided opportunities to show-case the nation's achievements and define its public image. Each of them built on the tremendous success of the country's first world's fair, the 1876 Centennial Exhibition. The centennial celebrated the nation's 100th anniversary in Philadelphia, where the country's first leaders signed the Declaration of Independence in 1776.

Among the most significant fairs of the Gilded Age were the 1893 World's Columbian Exposition in Chicago, the 1895 Cotton States and International Exposition in Atlanta, the 1901 Pan-American Exposition in Buffalo, and the 1904 Louisiana Purchase Exposition in St. Louis.

Organizers of the World's Columbian Exposition conceived the event as a 400th anniversary celebration of Christopher Columbus and his 1492 voyage of discovery. Sprawling over more than 600 acres on Chicago's South Side, the fair featured two main attractions, the White City and the Midway. The White City dominated most of the fairground. It consisted of an idealized urban environment of fountains, outdoor sculptures, open spaces, and monumental buildings full of historic, artistic, scientific, and technological exhibits. Individual states and other countries erected pavilions to promote their own agricultural, cultural, and industrial products.

The mile-long Midway offered a carnival of popular culture amusements, such as belly dancers, a wax museum, and the world's first Ferris wheel. The Midway included live exhibits of American Indians, Polynesian villagers, and other nonwhite peoples, all presented as entertaining examples of primitive human existence. The White City's grandeur and the Midway's condescending ethnic exhibits conveyed a message that white Americans were more civilized than

A Ferris wheel, first introduced at Chicago's World Columbian Exposition in 1893, looms above the 1904 St. Louis World's Fair. The giant wheel carried 36 enormous wooden cars, each holding 60 people.

other peoples and therefore justified in their feelings of racial superiority.

Except for one day in the fair's six-month run, African Americans could not gain entrance to the fairgrounds unless they were waiters and porters. Journalist Ida B. Wells and former abolitionist Frederick Douglass exposed this racist policy in a pamphlet entitled "The Reason Why the Colored American is Not in the World's Columbian Exposition." They distributed it to fair-goers from foreign countries.

After some debate about how best to include women's achievements in the fair, organizers working through the Board of Lady Managers agreed to exhibit women's cultural productions from everywhere in the world in a single pavilion, the Woman's Building. They reasoned that women's creations, unless collected together, might be ignored amid larger exhibits in the huge buildings. The board hired a woman architect to design the building and other women to design and decorate the interior. One vast mural was the work of an American Impressionist painter, Mary Cassatt. Women appreciated their building, but some would have preferred exhibit space shared with

men. To them, the separate space symbolized women's limited social status.

Investors in the Columbian Exposition earned a million-dollar profit. Their success encouraged promoters of subsequent world's fairs. In addition, the classical-style White City influenced architecture and city planning well into the 20th century, particularly affecting the City Beautiful movement. This movement preached that parks, monuments, and attractive streets and buildings could help deter crime and other social ills. The City Beautiful legacy is visible in many American cities today, particularly in the section of Washington, D.C., devoted to government buildings and historical monuments.

Organizers of Atlanta's 1895 Cotton States and International Exposition saw their fair as a way to promote southern economic development and to show the world a "New South." The white leaders of the Atlanta fair established the Negro Department to involve selected African Americans in the event. At the fair's opening ceremonies, black educator Booker T. Washington delivered his "Atlanta Compromise" speech, in which he promised that African Americans would not seek social and political equality with whites but would focus instead on contributing to the national economy as agricultural and industrial workers. Although this speech angered many blacks, many whites found it comforting.

The Pan-American Exposition of 1901 emphasized outreach to Latin American countries, which had become important export markets. Having won the Spanish-American War in 1898 and taken over some of Spain's former colonies, the United States was eager to reassure Latin America of its neighborly good intentions. Like the Columbian Exposition, the 1901 fair featured U.S. civilization as the pinnacle of human evolution. But the Spanish architectural style of the fair's buildings communicated a symbolic welcome to nations with Spanish heritage. The Pan-American Exposition gained an unwanted place in history when it became the site of President William McKinley's assassination.

The 1904 Louisiana Purchase Exposition commemorated a landmark event in the history of westward expansion, the 1803 acquisition that had doubled the nation's territory. As at earlier expositions, the fair's exhibits and promotional materials linked the ideals of growth and progress with the concept of white racial superiority. That attitude would persist for several more decades. Not until after the civil rights movement of the 1950s and 1960s would the United States begin to see its national identity in more inclusive terms.

SEE ALSO

Architecture; Cities; McKinley, William; Washington, Booker T.; Wells-Barnett, Ida B.

FURTHER READING

Rydell, Robert. *All the World's a Fair: Visions of Empire at American International Expositions, 1876-1916.* Chicago: University of Chicago Press, 1984.
———, John E. Findling, and Kimberly D. Pelle. *Fair America: World's Fairs in the United States.* Washington, D.C.: Smithsonian, 2000.
Weimann, Jeanne Madeline. *The Fair Women.* Chicago: Academy Press, 1981.

World War I

IN AUGUST 1914, all of the major European powers went to war. Many Americans hesitated to become involved. Some argued that the war was not the business of the United States. Others took a pacifist position, saying that resorting to arms would not solve international conflicts. Two factors eventually pushed the United States into the war: Germany's disregard for the American claim of neutral status and the country's need to defend its financial interests abroad.

How the "Great War" began

The immediate cause of the "Great War," as it was called, lay in a complex system of secret treaties that bound each European power to come to the aid of another in the event of attack. For a while, the system served as a deterrent to war, as it created a fragile balance of power that no nation dared disrupt. In 1914, however, this system failed.

The war began with an assassination in Bosnia, a small enclave of Slavic people within the Austro-Hungarian Empire. Bosnians wanted to leave Austrian control and unite with Serbia, their Slavic neighbor to the southeast. On June 28, 1914, when the heir to the Austro-Hungarian throne and his wife were in Sarajevo, Bosnia's capital, a terrorist shot and killed them.

Austria was convinced that Serbia was behind the assassination. On July 23, the empire demanded that Serbia make a full apology, ban all anti-Austrian propaganda, and allow Austrian participation in the Serbian investigation of the crime. When Serbia refused, Austria-Hungary declared war. Russia, bound by the alliance system to protect Serbia, began to amass its troops. Two days later, Germany, Austria-Hungary's chief ally, demanded that Russia stop this mobilization. Russia refused. Russia's ally, France, then began to mobilize. Realizing that soon it would be trapped between France attacking from the west and Russia from the east, Germany too readied its troops.

Several African American soldiers of the 369th (15th New York) Infantry Regiment, an outfit that spent 191 days under fire. In 1918 the French government awarded the regiment the Croix de Guerre for gallantry in action.

In 1914, mobilizing for war took immense organization and money. During the previous 40 years, France and Germany had doubled the size of their standing armies. Russia had a huge western frontier to cross. To call up their forces, equip, supply, and then deploy them strategically took time. Once the process began, it could be stopped only at the risk of losing crucial strategic advantage.

On August 1, Germany declared war on Russia. To deter a French invasion, Germany decided to strike France first, but to get to France, its troops had to invade Luxembourg and Belgium. This invasion brought Great Britain, Belgium's protector, into the war. All of Europe was now ablaze, with Germany and Austria-Hungary making up the Central Powers; Russia, France, and Great Britain were the Allies.

In earlier wars, a forceful offensive could bring victory. All of the belligerents thought this was still true and that the war would be over in six weeks. But defensive forces now had modern firepower. In September, a combined French and British force stopped the German advance 30 miles from Paris. Both sides dug in. Facing each other from a line of muddy, lice- and rat-infested trenches, for months they tried—in vain—to overwhelm enemy lines. At the end of 1914, Turkey entered the war for the Central Powers; in spring 1915, Italy came in for the Allies. The two sides fought many more battles, using the new killing machines of modern warfare—airplanes, machine guns, hand grenades, and poison gases. Despite huge losses, no side made significant gains.

The American response

Americans followed the news from Europe with mounting alarm. Some, especially immigrants who still felt close to the old countries, were personally involved. Most Americans saw Germany and Austria-Hungary as cruel autocracies and therefore favored the Allies. Others were more neutral but worried about their commercial interests abroad. Between 1897 and 1914, U.S. overseas investments had increased from $700 million to $3.5 billion. Now German submarines were sinking U.S. ships and a British naval blockade of the North Sea was not only bringing famine to Germany but also harming American trade.

Declaring the country officially neutral, the U.S. government tried to act as a peacemaker. Citizens' peace movements suggested the founding of a world court to arbitrate and settle disputes, or a world federation to guarantee collective security. At the same time, others were urging war preparedness. By late summer 1915, demands from the preparedness movement for a stronger army and navy and more military training had won over President Woodrow Wilson.

During the next two years, pressure for war mounted. When on May 7, 1915, a German submarine (U-boat) sank the British ocean liner *Lusitania,* drowning almost 1,200

American, Canadian, and British civilians, many Americans believed that Germany should be crushed. While authorizing New York bankers to make a huge loan to the Allies, Wilson counseled patience but no longer claimed neutrality. In 1916, he ran for reelection under the banner "He Kept Us Out of War," and he won, but American participation in the war seemed closer than ever.

In February 1917, Germany resumed unrestricted submarine attacks. Wilson broke off diplomatic relations with Germany and armed U.S. merchant ships. Then, the British revealed the contents of an intercepted German telegram to Mexico. In it, Arthur Zimmerman, Germany's foreign secretary, proposed an alliance with Mexico against the United States. In return, he promised to restore to Mexico all territories they had lost to the Americans. The Zimmerman telegram raised war cries to fever pitch.

On March 20, after Germany had sunk two more U.S. ships, Wilson's cabinet voted unanimously for war. Casting the issue in idealistic terms, on April 2, Wilson told Congress, "The world must be made safe for democracy." Congress passed a war resolution by a vote of 82 to 6 in the Senate and 373 to 50 in the House of Representatives, where its only female member, Jeannette Rankin, cast one of the negative votes. On April 6, the President declared war.

At first, the War Department sent General John J. Pershing over to Europe with only 14,500 men. Soon, Pershing was asking for more troops. Congress complied and in May passed a Selective Service Act, or draft. A lottery picked 3 million conscripts from those who had been required to sign up. Volunteers and National Guardsmen made up the rest of the American

Expeditionary Force (AEF). Eleven thousand uniformed women would eventually serve in the AEF as nurses, drivers, clerks, and telephone operators. By the end of the conflict, some 25,000 women had served abroad, in uniform or as civilians working for government or private agencies.

Pershing did not integrate his "doughboys," as his men were called, with the Allied defensive troops. He wanted to keep them fresh for offensives. He also kept his 300,000 African American troops separate from whites. The marines refused to accept blacks altogether and the navy used them for menial labor only.

The war at home

Going to war had a huge impact on American society and government. To pay for it, the federal government had to raise taxes. It also issued Liberty Bonds, sending out 75,000 "Four Minute Men" to give four-minute speeches before motion picture shows, plays, and school or union meetings to get people to buy these bonds.

The government also set up new agencies to regulate the economy. The War Industries Board controlled industry, doling out raw materials, telling manufacturers what to produce, and even fixing prices. The Fuel Administration introduced gas-less days and daylight saving time to increase daylight hours and lower fuel consumption. The War Trade Board licensed foreign trade and blacklisted firms suspected of dealing with the enemy. The National War Labor Board mediated labor disputes, and the War Labor Policies Board standardized wages, hours, and working conditions in war industries. Using the slogan "food will win the war," the government set up the Food Administration to increase

Little AMERICANS Do your bit

Eat Oatmeal-Corn meal mush-
Hominy - other corn cereals -
and Rice with milk.
Save the wheat for our soldiers.

Leave nothing on your plate

UNITED STATES FOOD ADMINISTRATION

A World War I government poster shows an American child saluting a bowl of cereal. The United States Food Administration urged civilians to save wheat for the military by eating other grains.

agricultural output and reduce waste in food consumption.

Government also regulated news and propaganda, establishing the Committee on Public Information, the country's first propaganda machine, which worked to increase public support for American war aims. In addition, vigilance against sabotage increased. In June 1917, Congress passed the Espionage Act, making it a crime to aid the enemy. The following year, it passed the Sedition Act, which outlawed antigovernment speech. Socialist Eugene V. Debs received a 10-year jail sentence under this act for urging Americans to oppose the war. He remained in jail until Congress repealed both acts in 1921.

Nativism revived. In 1917, Congress approved literacy tests for immigrants before they could enter the country, even over President Wilson's veto. Hostility toward German culture permeated American society. Symphonies excluded German composers and German-born musicians from their concerts. German measles became "liberty measles," and a hamburger was a "liberty sandwich." The California Board of Education condemned German as a language that spreads "the ideals of autocracy, brutality and hatred." In April 1918, Robert Prager, a young German-born citizen, tried to enlist in the navy but

failed for medical reasons. A mob of 500 people near St. Louis lynched him.

Woodrow Wilson had claimed that the U.S. entry into the war was a fight for liberty and democracy. Many, including women who were still denied the vote, found the claim ironic. It was particularly galling to those who suffered from wartime restrictions on their civil liberties. This included school personnel, who had to sign loyalty oaths. The government imposed censorship on the radical press and banned some publications from the mails.

American economic life was now more regulated than most Progressive Era social reformers had ever dreamed possible. When regulation spilled over into more private areas of life, however, some progressives wondered if public power had become excessive. In addition, regulation did not reduce corporate power. Indeed, during the war, the government relaxed its antitrust efforts, the influence of business leaders grew, and corporate profits tripled.

The war comes to an end

In November 1917, communist revolutionaries overthrew the Russian monarchy. In March 1918, faced with civil war, the new Russian government made a separate peace with Germany and withdrew from the war. This freed the Germans from fighting on an eastern front and allowed them to pound more heavily at French and British lines in the west.

In June, a combined force of U.S. Marines and doughboys saved Paris, blunted the edge of the German advance, and began to turn the tide of the war. Using British tanks, a new tool that gave troops protection along with mobility, the Allies began to break the German lines. On August 8, at the Battle of Amiens in northern France, the Allies stopped the German advance once and for all. On August 11, the German general in charge advised his government to seek terms for ending the war.

The Allies were not interested in offering terms; they wanted total surrender. In September, some 500,000 U.S. troops, assisted by 100,000 French, began to hit the final German strongholds. Soon the Germans were in full retreat. The Allies also began to use airplanes to drop bombs. Although Colonel Billy Mitchell's fleet of more than 1,400 bomb-carrying planes was not especially efficient, it signaled the start of a new era in military tactics.

The final assault came on September 26. More than a million AEF troops began to expel the Germans from France and cut their supply lines. There were many individual acts of heroism. Sergeant Alvin York of Tennessee saved an entire platoon by picking off machine gunners with his rifle and then capturing a number of prisoners. The French awarded the entire 369th Infantry Regiment, a troop of African Americans known as the Harlem Hell Fighters, their highest medal, the Croix de Guerre.

The Central Powers were soon eager for the war to end. Troops were in mutiny, some flying the red flag of the communist revolution. The German commanders begged for peace but still hoped to dictate some terms. The Allies refused. On November 11, armistice was declared and the guns fell silent.

More than 50,000 American soldiers died in battle, and many thousands more died of war-related injuries and disease. This toll seems minute in comparison with the estimated 8 million European war dead. France alone suffered more than a million deaths and the destruction of 4,000 towns. Great Britain lost 900,000 troops and suffered 2 million wounded. Across Europe, the war killed 20 million civilians during and immediately after the conflict. They died of starvation, disease, and war-related injuries.

Ending the war, failing with the peace

At the conference held in Paris to conclude the war, President Wilson's peace program of Fourteen Points was a major force. This program called for an end to secret alliances, the restoration of freedom of the seas, a reduction in armaments, and attention to the rights of native populations in adjusting imperialist claims to colonies. Wilson also demanded that subject nationalities determine their own futures, a principle called self-determination. Finally, he called for an association of nations—a League of Nations—to secure the peace by mediating future disputes.

When Wilson arrived in Europe for the conference, Parisians greeted him as a conquering hero. All would not go his way, however. The Allies were more interested in the spoils of war than in a permanent resolution of issues. Some of them wanted to divide up Germany's colonies. France, determined never to endure another German invasion, wanted Germany humiliated, if not destroyed. Although Russia was absent from the conference, everyone wondered if its new communist government would press war claims of its own.

Wilson had to agree that the great powers could take over Germany's colonies under a shared "mandate," a decision that negated his idea of self-determination. He did get the other powers to postpone further discussions of Germany's fate, however, and to move directly to his ideas for collective security. After ten days of hard work, Wilson produced a plan for the League of Nations. He then left for home, hoping to persuade Congress and the nation to accept his ideas.

For Wilson, the heart of his proposal was Article 10. This provision pledged league members to "respect and preserve as against external aggression the territorial integrity and existing political independence of all Members of the League." Because the league would not have any military power, the force of the article was moral only. Nevertheless, 39 Republican senators or senators-elect, led by Henry Cabot Lodge, rejected it because they feared it would drag the United States into foreign disputes. Wilson had to promise this group a guarantee of American diplomatic independence.

When Wilson returned to the peace conference, France's premier, Georges Clemenceau, used Wilson's embarrassment over American opposition to the League of Nations to press harsh conditions upon Germany. These included a 15-year period of French control over the mineral resources of Alsace-Lorraine, the coal- and iron-rich region between Germany and France. Wilson feared that this decision would lead to future wars, but he could not get Clemenceau to budge.

Wilson had to compromise elsewhere. Self-determination proved hard to apply in central Europe, an area of monumental ethnic complexity. The treaty created the new nations of Czechoslovakia and Yugoslavia, more nearly following ethnic lines than before the war. But the arrangements did not last. Wilson met his greatest defeat when he gave in to Allied insistence on German war guilt and financial responsibility. The French wanted to cripple Germany's economy. The

British wanted reparations. In 1921, the Reparations Committee ruled that Germany owed the Allies $33 billion, an amount far beyond its ability to pay, especially with France controlling its coal fields. Germany never forgot or forgave this humiliation.

The Allies presented the treaty to the Germans on May 7, 1919. Pointing to its violations of Wilson's Fourteen Points, the Germans refused to sign. Threatened with a French invasion, they gave in. On June 28, the powers signed the treaty outside of Paris at Versailles, the former home of the French kings. On July 8, Wilson returned home to great acclaim, but powerful forces in the U.S. Congress refused to ratify the treaty or accept the idea of a League of Nations. After more than a year of conflict with Wilson and other league advocates, Congress opted instead merely to declare the war over, ratifying separate peace treaties with Germany, Austria, and Hungary that October.

The aftermath of the war at home

When men entered the armed services, about 400,000 women joined the industrial workforce for the first time. White working-class women moved into jobs previously closed to them, such as telegraph messenger, elevator operator, letter carrier, and transit worker. Middle-class white women moved into mid-rank executive positions. As the war cut off the flow of immigrants from Europe, factories that used to discriminate against African Americans and Mexican Americans began to recruit them. These changes accelerated the migration northward of southern blacks. Social mobility increased for most segments of the population.

The war brought a culmination to the temperance and prohibition movements, by then almost a century old. In 1918, Congress approved a constitutional amendment prohibiting the manufacture, sale, and importation of alcoholic beverages. That body's concern was less for the safety and health of families than to show patriotism. The fermented grain used to make alcohol was supposed to make bread to meet home and overseas needs.

The biggest winners from the war were American business and finance. After the war, Europe owed the United States $22 billion. New York City now surpassed London as the financial center of the world. The woman suffrage movement finally triumphed, in part because congressmen felt that women should be rewarded for the extraordinary service they had rendered during wartime.

There were negative effects of the war as well. Demobilization was hard on workers. The federal agencies controlling the economy during the war shut down, abruptly canceling war contracts and providing no plan for reintegrating returning troops into society. Many thought that if women withdrew from the jobs they had taken during the war, there would be plenty of jobs for veterans. Many women did withdraw voluntarily; others were simply fired.

Women's absence from the job market did not solve problems of postwar unemployment, however. Desperate American workers went out on strikes, some of them violent. Veterans marched on Washington, D.C., to demand bonuses promised to them but never paid. A rising interest in left-wing political ideologies prompted a government backlash against radicalism, especially communism, called the Red Scare. Several hundred prominent radicals of foreign birth were deported.

African American soldiers came home heroes. Marching triumphantly up New York's Fifth Avenue, they received the enthusiastic cheers of huge crowds of both whites and blacks. Similar crowds turned out in St. Louis and Chicago. But when the soldiers tried to find jobs, the reception changed. Unemployment, substandard housing, race riots, and lynching soon gave rise to a new period of black militancy.

And finally, disease took a huge toll. Erupting in the spring of 1918, the Spanish flu killed millions across the world. Returning soldiers brought the flu home to the United States, where it killed half a million people, 43,000 of whom were servicemen.

SEE ALSO

African Americans; Airplane; American Expeditionary Force; Committee on Public Information, U.S.; Debs, Eugene Victor; Industry; Influenza epidemic (1918); League of Nations; *Lusitania*; Military; Nativism; Navy, U.S.; Pershing, John Joseph; Race riots; Rankin, Jeannette Pickering; Red Scare (1919–20); Science and technology; Temperance and prohibition movements; Versailles, Treaty of (1919); Woman's Peace Party; Woman suffrage movement; Wilson, Woodrow T.

FURTHER READING

Brown, Carrie. *Rosie's Mom: Forgotten Women Workers of the First World War.* Boston: Northeastern University Press, 2002.

Coetzee, Frans, and Marilyn Shevin-Coetzee. *World War I: A History in Documents.* New York: Oxford University Press, 2002.

Harris, Stephen. *Harlem's Hell Fighters: The African American 369th Infantry in World War I.* Washington, D.C.: Brassey's, 2003.

Kennedy, David M. *Over Here. The First World War and American Society.* New York: Oxford University Press, 1980.

Strachan, Hew, ed. *The Oxford Illustrated History of the First World War.* New York: Oxford University Press, 1998.

Tuchman, Barbara. *The Guns of August.* New York: Macmillan, 1962.

Zieger, Robert H. *America's Great War: World War I and the American Experience.* Lanham, Md.: Rowman & Littlefield, 2000.

Wounded Knee, Battle of (1890)

AT WOUNDED KNEE Creek in South Dakota, on January 29, 1890, U.S. Army troops surrounded and killed a band of Lakota Sioux warriors, women, and children. This event marked the end of decades of Indian wars on the Great Plains.

During the 1880s, the government had forced the Sioux, like other Plains tribes, to move onto reservations. Toward the end of the decade, a Paiute shaman named Wavoka had a vision prophesying that Indian people could recapture their old way of life. In his vision, the dead would return, the prairies would be replenished with game, and the whites would disappear in a horrible catastrophe. To bring about this event, Indians were to dance the Ghost Dance, wearing colored shirts with images of eagles and buffaloes. They believed white soldiers' bullets could not penetrate the "Ghost Shirts."

Wavoka's prophecy spread rapidly through the Plains tribes. Ghost dancing revitalized the Sioux spirit of resistance but also alarmed the government's white reservation agents, who called in the military. In December 1889, officers killed Chief Sitting Bull while trying to arrest him. His immediate successor,

Big Foot, led a retreat southward toward the Pine Ridge Reservation. Soldiers intercepted and attacked them as they camped at Wounded Knee. The ensuing battle left 300 Sioux and about 25 U.S. soldiers dead.

The battle of Wounded Knee ended armed Indian resistance to white expansion and brought about the final surrender of Native Americans to the reservation system.

SEE ALSO

Native Americans; Sitting Bull; West, the

FURTHER READING

Brown, Dee. *Bury My Heart at Wounded Knee: An Indian History of the American West.* New York: Henry Holt, 1971.
Coleman, William S. E. *Voices of Wounded Knee.* Lincoln: University of Nebraska Press, 2000.
Viola, Herman J. *Trail to Wounded Knee: The Last Stand of the Plains Indians, 1860–1890.* Washington, D.C.: National Geographic, 2003.

Wright, Frank Lloyd

- *Born: June 8, 1867 (sometimes reported as 1869), Richland Center, Wis.*
- *Education: did not finish high school, studied briefly at the University of Wisconsin, 1885*
- *Accomplishments: architect of 1,141 buildings, 532 of which were built; author of 20 books, including* Autobiography *(1932);* The Disappearing City *(1932);* The Future of American Architecture *(1953);* The Natural House *(1954);* An American Architecture *(1955);* The Living City *(1958)*
- *Died: Apr. 9, 1959, Phoenix, Ariz.*

FRANK LLOYD WRIGHT, one of the founders of modern architecture, designed innovative houses. After growing up on a farm in Wisconsin, where he gained an appreciation for the American prairie landscape, he worked as a draftsman and took a few courses in civil engineering. He then joined the Chicago architectur-

The opening fight of the Battle of Wounded Knee from the U.S. soldiers' point of view. Wounded Knee was not much of a battle, however; U.S. troops massacred an entire Sioux band, including women and children.

AMERICAN·MODEL·J902·PATENTS·APPLIED·FOR
AMERICAN·SYSTEM·BUILT
HOUSES·DESIGNED·BY
FRANK·LLOYD·WRIGHT
THE·RICHARDS·COMPANY
PROPRIETORS·MILWAUKEE

An advertisement for a Milwaukee housing company promotes "system-built" (prefabricated) homes designed by architect Frank Lloyd Wright. Wright is better known for his designs of unique houses commissioned by wealthy individuals.

al firm of Louis Sullivan, designer of many of the period's new skyscrapers. In 1893, Sullivan found out that Wright was designing homes on the side and fired him. Wright then opened his own office.

Wright developed a distinctive approach to home design. Drawing inspiration from the interaction of Americans with their unique landscape, he designed homes that evoked the midwestern prairie. With their low-pitched, horizontal roofs and natural materials, such as wood and stone, these "prairie houses" seemed rooted in their natural environments. In addition, instead of adopting the boxed-off, dark rooms characteristic of 19th-century homes, Wright's designs featured rooms flowing into one another, filled with interior light coming from unexpected places.

His designs for commercial buildings featured skylit atriums and large plate-glass windows. As he wrote in *The Disappearing City* (1932), "Steel and glass will be called in to fulfill their own [comforts]—steel for strength, durability and lightness; translucent glass, enclosing interior space, would give privacy yet make of living in a house a delightful association with sun, with sky, with surrounding gardens. The home would be an indoor garden, the garden an outdoor House." Later in his career, Wright moved toward a greater use of circles, squares, and triangles, forms

found in abundance in early cultures, and designs built along diagonals.

Wright's designs sought to achieve an organic unity between a home's interior, its external setting, and its owners' lifestyle. He designed Taliesin, which he built for himself in Spring Green, Wisconsin, to look as though it grew organically out of a hill instead of being placed upon it. Fallingwater, completed in 1935, was a western Pennsylvania home consisting of a set of cantilevered concrete trays set atop waterfalls that cascade over ledges. In the late 1930s, he began to build a winter residence for himself outside of Phoenix, Arizona, which came to be known as Taliesin West. In both residences, Wright housed apprentices who, while learning drafting techniques, helped maintain the properties.

Rarely attracting commissions from large corporations or government institutions, Wright gained most of his clients from the world of midwestern business. Friends and supporters created the Frank Lloyd Wright Foundation to stabilize his finances. During the 1940s and 1950s, his fame grew. His international reputation led eventually to a commission for New York City's Solomon R. Guggenheim Museum (completed in 1959), the central feature of which was a spiral ramp. The Guggenheim remains one of Wright's most exciting and well-known creations.

SEE ALSO
Architecture

FURTHER READING
Boulton, Alexander O. *Frank Lloyd Wright, Architect: An Illustrated Biography.* New York: Rizzoli, 1993.
Huxtable, Ada Louise. *Frank Lloyd Wright.* New York: Lipper/Viking, 2004.
Secrest, Meryle. *Frank Lloyd Wright.* New York: Knopf, 1992.
Twombly, Robert. *Frank Lloyd Wright: His Life and His Architecture.* New York: Wiley, 1979.

Wright, Wilbur and Orville

- *Born: Wilbur, Apr. 16, 1867, Millville, Ind.; Orville, Aug. 19, 1871, Dayton, Ohio*
- *Education: Wilbur, high school, Richmond, Ohio; Orville, high school, Dayton, Ohio*
- *Accomplishments: inventors of the airplane*
- *Died: Wilbur, May 30, 1912, Dayton, Ohio; Orville, Jan. 30, 1948, Dayton, Ohio*

BORN INTO A LARGE midwestern family, the sons of a Protestant bishop, Wilbur and Orville Wright never finished high school. Instead, they went into business together. Using an old tombstone as a press-weight, they started a small printing business and later opened a bicycle repair shop, the Wright Cycle Company. Soon they were making their own bicycle models. Inventive geniuses by nature, intrigued by engineering and completely self-trained, the brothers were admirers of glider inventors Otto Lilienthal and Octave Chanute. They became fascinated with gliders and began experimentation. Building a series of kites, gliders, and, finally, machine-powered aircraft, they worked out all the problems that had baffled previous inventors and achieved successful piloted flight in 1903.

By 1905, the brothers had a craft capable of sustained flight, and by 1908, they had taken out a number of patents to protect their invention. They toured Europe demonstrating flight techniques and built planes under contract for the U.S. Army. In 1909, they founded the American Wright Company. Troubles over patent rights and the theft of designs by European manufacturers haunted the rest of Wilbur's short life—he died of typhoid fever in 1912. Orville then sold the business, worked as a consulting engineer, and lived until after the end of World War II. He witnessed the development of airplanes for both military and commercial purposes.

SEE ALSO

Airplane; Inventions; Science and technology

FURTHER READING

Crouch, Tom D. *The Bishop's Boys: A Life of Wilbur and Orville Wright*. New York: Norton, 1990.
——. *The Wright Brothers and the Invention of the Aerial Age*. Washington, D.C.: National Geographic, 2003.
Kelly, Fred C. *The Wright Brothers: A Biography*. 1943. Reprint, Mineola, N.Y.: Dover, 1989.
Wright, Orville. *How We Invented the Airplane: An Illustrated History*. 1953. Reprint, Mineola, N.Y.: Dover, 1989.

Orville and Wilbur Wright conduct one of their first successful airplane test flights on December 17, 1903. The brothers took turns piloting the plane that day; their best flight lasted 59 seconds.

IMPORTANT DATES DURING THE GILDED AGE AND PROGRESSIVE ERA

1865–70
14th and 15th Amendments make illegal the denial of political rights, including the right to vote, on grounds of color or creed

1869
Wyoming Territory becomes first jurisdiction to grant woman suffrage

The first transcontinental railroad is completed

Knights of Labor is founded; the union will eventually organize both skilled and unskilled workers

1870
John D. Rockefeller incorporates Standard Oil Company in Ohio

1871
Congress passes Ku Klux Klan Act in an attempt to end racist terrorism in southern states

Chicago fire starts on October 8

1873
Comstock Law outlaws distribution of information about contraception

Mark Twain (Samuel Clemens) coins the term *Gilded Age*

Economic depression begins, lasts several years

1874
Woman's Christian Temperance Union is founded

1876
Sioux Indians defeat Lieutenant Colonel George Armstrong Custer's Seventh Cavalry at the Battle of Little Bighorn on June 25

Alexander Graham Bell demonstrates first successful telephone

1877
Compromise of 1877 settles disputed election of 1876, and Republican Rutherford B. Hayes becomes President

Railroad strike nationwide

Thomas Edison invents the phonograph

1881
President James A. Garfield is assassinated, and Chester A. Arthur becomes President

1882
Congress passes first Chinese Exclusion Act

1883
Brooklyn Bridge opens

Congress passes Pendleton Civil Service Act to remove government jobs from the patronage system

1885
Grover Cleveland begins his first Presidential term

1886
Haymarket Square riot erupts on May 4

American Federation of Labor is formed

Statue of Liberty, gift from France, is dedicated in New York Harbor

Geronimo surrenders to U.S. troops on September 4

1887
Dawes Severalty Act breaks up Native American tribal lands

Congress passes Interstate Commerce Act to regulate the railroads and other industries

1888
Edward Bellamy's utopian novel *Looking Backward* is published

1889
Benjamin Harrison becomes President

Jane Addams and Ellen Gates Starr found Hull House social settlement in Chicago

1890
Congress passes Sherman Antitrust Act to break up monopolies

National American Woman Suffrage Association is founded

Jacob Riis's *How the Other Half Lives* is published

Battle of Wounded Knee, in South Dakota on December 29, marks the end of Sioux resistance to reservation policy

1892
Workers strike at the Carnegie Steel Company in Homestead, Pennsylvania

Populist party is founded

Ellis Island opens as a processing center for immigrants

Ida B. Wells begins antilynching crusade

1893
Grover Cleveland begins his second Presidential term

World's Columbian Exposition opens in Chicago

Major economic depression begins

Henry Ford manufactures first working automobile

1894
Workers strike against the Pullman railroad car company

Coxey's Army marches on Washington to demonstrate plight of the unemployed

1895
Booker T. Washington gives Atlanta Compromise speech, accepting segregation for African Americans in return for economic opportunity

1896
U.S. Supreme Court decision in *Plessy* v. *Ferguson* legalizes racial segregation

National Association of Colored Women's Clubs is formed

1897
William McKinley becomes President

1898
Spanish-American War; the United States annexes Guam, Philippines, and Puerto Rico in its aftermath

The United States annexes Hawaii

1899
National Consumers' League is founded, advocates labor-industrial reform

1900
Hurricane and flood hit Galveston, Texas; thousands perish

Secretary of State John Hay announces Open Door policy in China

Eugene V. Debs founds Socialist party

1901
J. P. Morgan buys out Carnegie Steel and creates U.S. Steel, the first billion-dollar corporation

President William McKinley is assassinated; Theodore Roosevelt becomes President

1902
United Mine Workers is founded

War ends between the United States and the Philippines

1903
The Wright brothers fly the first airplane at Kitty Hawk, North Carolina, on December 17

Women's Trade Union League is founded

The Souls of Black Folk by W. E. B. DuBois is published

1904
Upton Sinclair's *The Jungle,* a muckraking novel about the meatpacking industry, is published

1905
U.S. Supreme Court decision in *Lochner* v. *New York* invalidates maximum-hours law for bakers

"Big Bill" Haywood and others found the Industrial Workers of the World

1906
Congress passes the Pure Food and Drugs Act

San Francisco earthquake

1908
U.S. Supreme Court decision in *Muller* v. *Oregon* upholds a 10-hour workday for women

1909
William Howard Taft becomes President

National Association for the Advancement of Colored People (NAACP) is founded

Shirtwaist makers strike in New York City

1911
Triangle Shirtwaist Factory fire kills 146 workers, mostly young immigrant women

National Urban League is founded

1912
Titanic sinks on April 14

Progressive ("Bull Moose") party is founded

1913
Woodrow Wilson becomes President

16th Amendment introduces income taxes

17th Amendment authorizes direct election of U.S. senators

Congress passes Federal Reserve Act

1914
Panama Canal opens

Congress passes Clayton Antitrust and Federal Trade Commission acts

President Wilson sends troops to intervene in Mexican Revolution

1915
German submarine sinks British ocean liner *Lusitania* on May 1

1916
Margaret Sanger opens first birth control advice center in Brooklyn, New York

Alice Paul launches National Woman's party

1917
United States enters World War I

Bolshevik revolution in Russia

1918
World War I ends on November 11

1918–19
Worldwide influenza epidemic

1919
18th Amendment makes the manufacture, importation, and sale of alcoholic beverages illegal

Treaty of Versailles is signed on June 28

Red Scare pervades the United States

1920
19th Amendment gives women the vote

FURTHER READING

Each article in this book contains references to works dealing with the article's specific subject. The following are more general works that cover the broader period discussed in this Companion.

THE GILDED AGE AND PROGRESSIVE ERA

Ayers, Edward L. *The Promise of the New South: Life after Reconstruction.* New York: Oxford University Press, 1993.

Barney, William L., editor. *A Companion to 19th-Century America.* Malden, Mass.: Blackwell, 2001.

Hansen, Jonathan M. *The Lost Promise of Patriotism: Debating American Identity, 1890–1920.* Chicago: University of Chicago Press, 2003.

Jacobson, Matthew Frye. *Barbarian Virtues: The United States Encounters Foreign Peoples at Home and Abroad, 1876–1917.* New York: Hill & Wang, 2000.

Nugent, Walter. *Crossings: The Great Transatlantic Migrations, 1870–1914.* Bloomington: Indiana University Press, 1992.

Painter, Nell Irvin. *Standing at Armageddon: The United States 1877–1919.* New York: Norton, 1989.

Sanders, Elizabeth. *Roots of Reform: Farmers, Workers, and the American State, 1877–1917.* Chicago: University of Chicago Press, 1999.

THE GILDED AGE

Brands, H. W. *The Reckless Decade: America in the 1890s.* Chicago: University of Chicago Press, 2002.

Calhoun, Charles W., ed. *The Gilded Age: Essays on the Origins of Modern America.* Wilmington, Del.: Scholarly Resources, 1996.

Cashman, Sean Dennis. *America in the Gilded Age: From the Death of Lincoln to the Rise of Theodore Roosevelt.* 3rd ed. New York: New York University Press, 1993.

Cherny, Robert W. *American Politics in the Gilded Age, 1868–1900.* Wheeling, Ill.: Harlan Davidson, 1997.

Editors of Time Life Books. *Prelude to the Century, 1870–1900.* Alexandria, Va.: Time-Life Books, 1999.

Edwards, Rebecca. *New Spirits: Americans in the Gilded Age, 1865–1905.* New York: Oxford University Press, 2006.

Josephson, Matthew. *The Politicos, 1865–1896.* 1938. Reprint, New York: Harcourt, Brace & World, 1963.

Keller, Morton. *Affairs of State: Public Life in Late Nineteenth Century America.* Cambridge, Mass.: Harvard University Press, Belknap Press, 1977.

Morgan, H. Wayne. *From Hayes to McKinley: National Party Politics, 1877–1896.* Syracuse, N.Y.: Syracuse University Press, 1969.

Schlup, Leonard, and James G. Ryan. *Historical Dictionary of the Gilded Age.* Armonk, N.Y.: M.E. Sharpe, 2003.

Summers, Mark Wahlgren. *The Gilded Age, or, the Hazard of New Functions.* Upper Saddle River, N.J.: Prentice Hall, 1997.

Trachtenberg, Alan. *The Incorporation of America: Culture and Society in the Gilded Age.* New York: Hill & Wang, 1982.

THE PROGRESSIVE ERA

Buenker, John D., and Edward R. Kantowicz. *Historical Dictionary of the Progressive Era, 1890–1920.* Westport, Conn.: Greenwood, 1988.

Chambers, John Whiteclay, II. *The Tyranny of Change: America in the Progressive Era, 1890–1920.* New Brunswick, N.J.: Rutgers University Press, 2000.

Crunden, Robert M. *Ministers of Reform: The Progressives' Achievement in American Civilization, 1889–1920.* Urbana: University of Illinois Press, 1984.

Dawley, Alan. *Changing the World: American Progressives in War and Revolution.* Princeton, N.J.: Princeton University Press, 2005.

Diner, Steven J. *A Very Different Age: Americans of the Progressive Era.* New York: Hill & Wang, 1998.

Gould, Lewis L. *America in the Progressive Era, 1890–1914.* New York: Longman, 2001.

Hofstadter, Richard. *The Age of Reform: From Bryan to F.D.R.* New York: Knopf, 1955.

———. *The Progressive Movement, 1900–1915.*1963. Reprint, New York: Simon & Schuster, 1986.

Link, William A. *The Paradox of Southern Progressivism, 1880–1930.* Chapel Hill: University of North Carolina Press, 1992.

McGerr, Michael. *A Fierce Discontent: The Rise and Fall of the Progressive Movement, 1870–1920.* New York: Free Press, 2003.

Wiebe, Robert H. *The Search for Order, 1877–1920.* 1967. Reprint, New York: Hill & Wang, 1995.

ART AND ARCHITECTURE

Burns, Sarah. *Inventing the Modern Artist: Art and Culture in Gilded Age America.* New Haven, Conn.: Yale University Press, 1996.

Prelinger, Elizabeth. *The Gilded Age: Treasures from the Smithsonian American Art Museum.* New York : Watson-Guptill, 2000.

COLLECTIONS

Clark, Judith Freeman. *America's Gilded Age: An Eyewitness History.* New York: Facts on File, 1992.

Fink, Leon, ed. *Major Problems in the Gilded Age and the Progressive Era: Documents and Essays.* Lexington, Mass.: D.C. Heath, 1993.

Greenwood, Janette Thomas. *The Gilded Age: A History in Documents.* New York: Oxford University Press, 2000.

Gregory, Alexis. *Families of Fortune: Life in the Gilded Age.* New York: Rizzoli, 1993.

Rugoff, Milton. *America's Gilded Age: Intimate Portraits From an Era of Extravagance and Change, 1850–1890.* New York: Holt, 1989.

WEBSITES

GENERAL

The American 1890s: A Chronology
*www.bgsu.edu/departments/acs/1890s/
america.html*
Created by the American Culture Studies Program of Bowling Green State University, the site provides material on the personalities; social, political, literary, economic, and cultural events; and the art, music, and architecture of the 1890s.

American Experience
www.pbs.org/wgbh/amex/index.html
The program "American Experience," produced by WGBH, a Public Broadcasting System television station in Boston, has several websites related to Gilded Age and Progressive Era history, including features on Presidents Theodore Roosevelt and Woodrow Wilson, the cities of Chicago and New York, World War I, the influenza epidemic of 1918–19, Coney Island, the Fisk Jubilee Singers, Andrew Carnegie, Emma Goldman, Harry Houdini, Thomas Edison, and George Eastman.

Boondocksnet.com
www.boondocksnet.com
Jim Zwick, an American studies scholar whose specialties include Mark Twain, U.S. social and political history, and educational uses of the Internet, maintains this website. Among his topics are several relevant to the Gilded Age and Progressive Era, including Twain, anti-imperialism, the Philippine-American War, the American labor movement, the campaign to end child labor, the role of political cartoons, and world's fairs and exhibitions. Some good primary sources are available here.

Chicago Historical Society
www.chicagohs.org
Contains source materials for the World's Columbian Exposition, the Chicago fire of 1871, and other Gilded Age and Progressive Era events and personalities related to Chicago.

Famous Trials
*www.law.umkc.edu/faculty/projects/
FTrials/ftrials.htm*
The Law School at the University of Missouri at Kansas City provides historical background, documents, and analysis for a number of important and dramatic Gilded Age and Progressive Era court cases, including the trials of Susan B. Anthony (1873), "Big Bill" Haywood (1907), and the owners of the Triangle Shirtwaist Factory (1911).

The Library of Congress: American Memory
http://memory.loc.gov/ammem/index.html
This rich collection includes photos, films, documents, maps, sound recordings, and bibliographies relevant to the period covered by this *Companion*. Some topics include immigration, work life, vaudeville and popular entertainment, U.S. presidents and inaugurations, conservation, industrialization, African American history, women's history, the West, and much more. Consult the index before attempting to navigate.

National Park Service
www.cr.nps.gov/history/index.asp
This site contains extensive information on U.S. history connected with the parks founded between 1880 and 1920. Material includes National Park Service history, individual park histories, oral histories, and historical themes, such as immigration and ethnicity.

Native American History and Studies
www.tntech.edu/history/nativam.html
The Department of History at Tennessee Technological University lists links to dozens of sites on Native American history.

PRIMARY SOURCES

National Center Blog
*www.nationalcenter.org/Historical
Documents.html*
This project of the National Center for Public Policy Research is a source for historical primary documents.

Society for Historians of the Gilded Age and Progressive Era
www.h-net.msu.edu/~shgape/internet/
An organization for historians interested in this period, the society maintains this website, which contains links to many other resources. It also provides full texts of some speeches and editorials from the period, such as William Jennings Bryan's "Cross of Gold" speech and Kansas journalist William Allen White's "What's the Matter with Kansas?"

ADVERTISING

Emergence of Advertising in America: 1850–1920

http://scriptorium.lib.duke.edu/eaa/

Presents more than 9,000 images relating to the early history of advertising in the United States. The materials are drawn from the Rare Book, Manuscript, and Special Collections Library at Duke University.

ART AND ARCHITECTURE

Armory Show of 1913

http://xroads.virginia.edu/~MUSEUM/ Armory/armoryshow.html

Created by the American Studies Department of the University of Virginia, this site displays items exhibited during the Armory Show of 1913.

The Arts and Crafts Archives

www.arts-crafts.com/archive/archive.shtml

Maintained by the Arts & Crafts Society, this website offers historical material on the early 20th-century Arts and Crafts Movement.

Chicago Landmarks

www.ci.chi.il.us/Landmarks/Architects/ Architects.html

Maintained by the City of Chicago, this site has information on Chicago architects from the turn of the 20th century, including Daniel Burnham, Louis Sullivan, and Frank Lloyd Wright.

Digital Archive of American Architecture

www.bc.edu/bc_org/avp/cas/fnart/fa267/

Maintained by Boston College's Fine Arts Department, this site contains digitized images from the classical, or Beaux Arts, period of American architecture and of the work of specific architects, such as Henry Hobson Richardson, Louis Sullivan, and Frank Lloyd Wright.

BIOGRAPHICAL INFORMATION

William Jennings Bryan

www.mission.lib.tx.us/exhibits/bryan/ bryan.htm

The Speer Memorial Library of the Hidalgo County Historical Museum (Mission, Texas) maintains an exhibit and online information about populist leader William Jennings Bryan.

The Centennial of Flight

www.centennialofflight.gov

Essay on Orville and Wilbur Wright; includes extensive bibliography on flight history.

Eugene V. Debs

www.eugenevdebs.com

The official website of the Eugene V. Debs Foundation includes research materials on his life and social activism.

The Edison Papers

http://edison.rutgers.edu

The website of the Thomas A. Edison Papers at Rutgers, the State University of New Jersey, contains biographical and other information about the inventor.

Henry Ford

www.hfmgv.org

The website of the Henry Ford Museum at Greenfield, Michigan, contains information about Ford's life and work and describes the huge collection of artifacts on display at the museum.

The Emma Goldman Papers

http://sunsite.berkeley.edu/Goldman

The Emma Goldman Papers Project is a complete collection of her writings and correspondence at the University of California at Berkeley.

The Samuel Gompers Papers

www.history.umd.edu/Gompers/index.htm

Primary sources related to the history of American labor.

Frank Norris

www.wsu.edu/~campbelld/Howells/ norris.htm

A collection of research materials, including pictures and writings, associated with the Gilded Age writer.

John Wesley Powell Memorial Museum

www.powellmuseum.org

The website of a museum established in Powell's memory in Page, Arizona. It consists of biographical and pictorial material related to Powell's career.

Ida Tarbell

http://tarbell.alleg.edu

Staff at the Pelletier Library at Allegheny College have created this website of materials from the archives of the muckraking journalist.

Frank Lloyd Wright Foundation
www.franklloydwright.org/
Photographs and descriptions of the architect's work, as well as biographical information.

ELECTIONS

Atlas of U.S. Presidential Elections
www.uselectionatlas.org
Provides the results of all U.S. Presidential elections.

1912: Competing Visions of America
http://history.osu.edu/projects/1912/ default.htm
This Ohio State University site contains a detailed discussion of all events and personalities connected with the Presidential election of 1912 and links to further information.

The Presidential Campaign: Cartoons and Commentary
http://projects.vassar.edu/1896/1896home. html
Created by Professor Rebecca Edwards and students at Vassar College, this website provides access to political cartoons related to the election of 1896, election results by state, a bibliography, and material about contemporary newspapers.

The Presidential Elections: 1812–1912
http://elections.harpweek.com/
Political cartoons from the collections of *Harpers Weekly*.

IMMIGRATION AND RACE

The Buffalo Soldiers on the Western Frontier
http://www.imh.org/imh/buf/buftoc.html
An exhibit organized by the International Museum of the Horse.

Five Views: An Ethnic Historic Site Survey for California
http://www.cr.nps.gov/history/online_books /5views/5views.htm
This site, maintained by the National Park Service, provides information on California's five largest minorities present during the 50 years after 1848: American Indians, African Americans, Chinese Americans, Japanese Americans, and Mexican Americans.

The Japanese American Network
www.janet.org
Historical material provided by a partnership between the Japanese American organizations based in Los Angeles, California.

PRESIDENTS AND POLITICS

The Rutherford B. Hayes Presidential Center
www.rbhayes.org/hayes/
Maintained by the Rutherford B. Hayes Presidential Center in Fremont, Ohio, the site provides primary sources, biographical information, and pictures of the 19th President.

Red Scare
http://newman.baruch.cuny.edu/digital/ redscare/default.htm
Images and other historical material about the detention and deportation of political radicals after World War I.

Theodore Roosevelt: Icon of the American Century
www.npg.si.edu/exh/roosevelt/index.htm
Photographs of Roosevelt, his family, friends, and associates organized by the National Portrait Gallery, in conjunction with other government agencies.

The White House
http://www.whitehouse.gov/history/ presidents/
The official government site for information concerning American Presidents.

SEGREGATION

The History of Jim Crow
www.jimcrowhistory.org/home.htm
An award-winning site on the history of segregation from the 1870s to the 1950s.

Jump, Jim Crow: Or, What Difference Did Emancipation Make?
http://sunsite3.berkeley.edu/calheritage/ Jimcrow/
Created by Lynn Jones, a librarian at the Teaching Library, University of California at Berkeley, for the California Heritage Project, this site provides a great deal of material (texts, songs, stories, images) about Jim Crow, the system of laws that segregated whites and blacks.

Jim Crow Museum of Racist Memorabilia
www.ferris.edu/news/jimcrow/
A virtual tour of the museum, located on the campus of Ferris State University in Big Rapids, Michigan.

STRIKES AND LABOR

The Dramas of Haymarket
www.chicagohistory.org/dramas/index.htm
A project produced by the Chicago Historical Society and Northwestern University, this site provides illustrative materials on the riot and places them in their historical context.

Homestead and Pullman Strikes
http://projects.vassar.edu/1896/strikes.html
Maintained by Vassar College, this site provides primary sources and photographs on the strikes of 1892 and 1894.

The Illinois Labor History Society
www.kentlaw.edu/ilhs/
Provides links to many resources in labor history of the period.

Seattle General Strike Project
http://faculty.washington.edu/gregoryj/strike/
The University of Washington's Harry Bridges Center for Labor Studies provides primary sources on the strike of 1919.

The Triangle Factory Fire
www.ilr.cornell.edu/trianglefire/
Maintained by the Cornell University School of Industrial and Labor Relations, this site includes recently discovered photographs of the 1911 fire.

TENEMENTS AND SETTLEMENT HOUSES

Jane Addams Hull-House Museum
http://wall.aa.uic.edu:62730/artifact/ HullHouse.asp

Urban Experience in Chicago: Hull-House and Its Neighbors
www.uic.edu/jaddams/hull/urbanexp/ contents.htm
Two websites created at the University of Illinois at Chicago provide details about Jane Addams and Hull House.

Lower East Side Tenement Museum
www.tenement.org
This museum was created out of abandoned tenements on the Lower East Side of New York City. Research resources include images of artifacts, teaching materials, and song lyrics.

On the Lower East Side: Observations of Life in Lower Manhattan at the Turn of the Century
http://tenant.net/Community/LES/ contents.html
Essays and documentary sources on urban life between 1880 and 1920.

TRANSPORTATION

Philadelphia Trolleys
www.library.phila.gov/pix/trolleys/ trolleys.htm
Photographs of early trolleys, mounted by the Free Library of Philadelphia.

WOMEN

National Women's Hall of Fame
www.greatwomen.org/home.php
Features biographies of significant women in American history.

Women and Social Movements in the United States, 1600–2000
http://womhist.binghamton.edu/index.html
Developed by Professors Kathryn Kish Sklar and Thomas Dublin of the State University of New York at Binghamton, this website contains historical projects that, through an introductory historical essay and extensive primary documents, illustrate the roles of women in American social movements.

Woman's Christian Temperance Union
www.wctu.org
The site of the Woman's Christian Temperance Union includes historical information and a timeline.

The Coalition for Western Women's History
www.westernwomenshistory.org
This site provides many links to relevant sites.

Studies, Treatises, Union Publications, and Vocational Texts, 1845–1970s
www.nyu.edu/library/bobst/research/tam/ women/oldstuds.html
Tamiment Library at New York University provides an extensive bibliography of primary sources on women and labor.

WORLD'S FAIRS

1904 World's Fair: Louisiana Purchase Exposition
http://washingtonmo.com/1904
An illustrated history of the 1904 World's Fair.

The Panama Pacific International Exposition
www.sanfranciscomemories.com/ppie/ panamapacific.html
History and images from the 1915 World's Fair held in San Francisco, California.

The World's Columbian Exposition: Idea, Experience, Aftermath
http://xroads.virginia.edu/~MA96/WCE/ title.html
Contains photographs and an explanatory text about the World's Columbian Exposition of 1893.

WORLD WAR I

The Great War and the Shaping of the 20th Century
www.pbs.org/greatwar
The website for this TV series for PBS; the show is a KCET/BBC coproduction in association with the Imperial War Museum (London, England).

An Internet History of the War
www.worldwar1.com
Links to articles and photographs concerning the first World War.

INDEX

ACKNOWLEDGMENTS

We extend our deepest thanks to our spouses, Lewis Perry and Chris O'Carroll, for their abundant patience while we worked (it seems endlessly!) on this project. We would also like to thank Abe Smith for keeping us laughing when we were in the home stretch. We are very grateful for the kindness of colleagues who read and commented on drafts of some of our entries or responded to inquiries—in particular, Nancy Unger, T. Michael Ruddy, Melvyn P. Leffler, Fred Krome, Kathryn Kuhn, Sr. Angelyn Dries, Shawn Smith, Phillippa Strum, Kriste Lindenmeyer, and Robert Cherny. Thanks also to Elisabeth's research assistants Jennifer Ann Price and Joshua Sopiarz. Josh went the extra mile for us when we were under final deadlines, and for that help we are especially grateful. And a special thank you to Chris O'Carroll for the extended and invaluable research help he gave to Karen. Thanks also to Nancy Toff, Karen Fein, and Nancy Hirsch, our editors at Oxford University Press, for including us in the *Companion* series and for cheering us on to the finish line.

PICTURE CREDITS

Elisabeth Israels Perry earned her Ph.D. from the University of California at Los Angeles. She is the author of *Belle Moskowitz: Feminine Politics and the Exercise of Power in the Age of Alfred E. Smith* and co-editor of two anthologies, *The Challenge of Feminist Biography: Writing the Lives of Modern American Women* and *We Are Here to Stay: American Women and Political Parties, 1880–1960*. She also co-authored a high school textbook, *America: Pathways to the Present*, and co-edited an edition of an 1878 novel, *An American Girl, and Her Four Years in a Boys' College*. From 1998 to 2000 she served as president of the Society of Historians of the Gilded Age and Progressive Era. Since 1999 she has held the John Francis Bannon Chair in History at Saint Louis University, and she has been a Distinguished Lecturer for the Organization of American Historians since 2001.

Karen Manners Smith earned her Ph.D. in American history from the University of Massachusetts. She teaches U.S. history, women's studies, immigration history, and the history of the Gilded Age and Progressive Era at Emporia State University in Emporia, Kansas. She is the director of the university's ethnic and gender studies program. Dr. Smith is the author of *New Paths to Power: American Women 1890–1920*, and is a contributor to *No Small Courage: A History of Women in the United States*. She is currently co-editing a collection of first-person memoirs of the 1960s.